THE CENTRAL BANK AND THE FINANCIAL SYSTEM

The Central Bank and the Financial System

C. A. E. Goodhart

The MIT Press
Cambridge, Massachusetts

First MIT Press edition 1995

© 1995 C. A. E. Goodhart

Printed and bound in Great Britain

Library of Congress Cataloging-in-Publication Data

Goodhart, C. A. E. (Charles Albert Eric)
    The central bank and the financial system / C. A. E. Goodhart. —
1st ed.
        p. cm.
    Includes bibliographical references and index.
    ISBN 0–262–07167–3
    1. Banks and banking, Central. 2. Bank of England. 3. Banks and
banking, Central—Europe—State supervision. I. Title.
HG1811.G618 1995
332.1'1—dc20   94–37741
                                                          CIP

Contents

Acknowledgements

The author and publishers acknowledge with thanks permission from the following to reproduce previously published material:

Oxford University Press, for Chapter 1, 'Why do Banks Need a Central Bank?', *Oxford Economic Papers* (1987).

Elsevier Science Publishers B.V., for Chapter 2, 'Can we Improve the Structure of Financial Systems?', *European Economic Review* (1993).

Kluwer Academic Publishers, for Chapter 3, 'The Implications of Shifting Frontiers in Financial Markets for Monetary Control', in D.E. Fair (ed.), *Shifting Frontiers in Financial Markets* (1986).*

Physica-Verlag, for Chapter 4, 'Central Bank Independence', *Journal of International and Comparative Economics* (1994).

Macmillan Press Ltd, for Chapter 5, 'Alternative Monetary Standards' in K. Dowd and M.K. Lewis (eds), *Current Issues in Financial and Monetary Economics* (1992).

Blackwell Publishers, for Chapter 6, 'The Conduct of Monetary Policy', *The Economic Journal* (1989).

The Cyprus Journal of Economics, for Chapter 7, 'Banks and the Control of Corporations' (1993), and also *Note Economiche*, Riviste del Monte dei Paschi di Siena (1994).

Princeton University Press, for Chapter 8, 'The Political Economy of Monetary Union', in P. Kenen (ed.), *Understanding Interdependence: The Macroeconomics of the Open Economy* (1995).

The Reserve Bank of Australia, for Chapter 9, 'What do Central Banks Do?', from *Visiting Specialists Papers Presented to the 17th SEANZA Central Bank Course*, supplement to *Issues in Central Banking*, (1989); and for Chapter 10, 'The Objectives for, and Conduct of, Monetary Policy in the

---

* Kluwer Academic Publishers have asked us to repeat the original copyright notice verbatim, as follows:

1990s', in A Blundell-Wignall (ed.), *Inflation, Disinflation and Monetary Policy* (1992).

The London School of Economics and Political Science, for Chapter 11, 'Advising the Bank of England', in J. Mayall (ed.), *Annual Review* (1992).

Philip Allan Publishers, for Chapter 12, 'The Operational Role of the Bank of England', *The Economic Review* (1985).

Edward Elgar Publishing Ltd, for Chapter 13, 'Money Supply Control: Base or Interest Rates', in K. Hoover and S. Sheffrin (eds), *Monetarism and the Methodology of Economics* (1995).

Macmillan Press Ltd and the Bank of Japan, for Chapter 14, 'Price Stability and Financial Fragility', in *Financial Stability in a Changing Environment* (1995).

Blackwell Publishers, for Chapter 15, 'A European Central Bank', in A Mullineux (ed.), *European Banking* (1992).

Centro di Economia Monetaria e Finanziaria 'Paolo Baffi', Università Commerciale Luigi Bocconi, for Chapter 16, 'Institutional Separation between Supervisory and Monetary Agencies', jointly with D. Schoenmaker, in F. Bruni (ed.), *Prudential Regulation, Supervision and Monetary Policy* (1993).

Macmillan Press Ltd, for Chapter 17, 'Bank Insolvency and Deposit Insurance: A Proposal' in P. Arestis (ed.), *Money and Banking: Issues for the Twenty-First Century* (1993).

Institute for Economic Affairs, for Chapter 19, 'The Costs of Regulation', in A. Seldon (ed.), *Financial Regulation – or Over-Regulation* (1988); and for Chapter 20, 'Investor Protection and Unprincipled Intervention', *Economic Affairs* (1987).

National Westminster Bank, for Chapter 21, 'Financial Regulation and Supervision: A Review of Three Books', *National Westminster Bank Quarterly Review* (1987).

Introduction

Although the current day-to-day operations of Central Banks are subject to continuous comment and frequent criticism, their structural role within the economic system as a whole is generally accepted without much question; they are part of the existing institutional furniture, the status quo. It is one of the proper functions of academics regularly to reassess and to challenge the legitimacy and value of existing institutional arrangements; an intellectual exercise which inertia and lack of time prevents for most of the rest of us.

There have been several such challenges in recent decades. Some monetarists would have liked to see the functions of a Central Bank reduced to a simple automated exercise, expanding the monetary base by a given, constant, percentage each working day. More recently, there has been an even more radical attack from the new school of advocates of Free Banking, who would abolish all Central Banks, *sine die*. What, if anything, they ask is special about banking, that requires banks, unlike the providers of other services, e.g. insurance, law, accounting, or of goods, to have a public sector central controlling body that tries to manage their aggregate rate of growth and usually helps to regulate and to supervise their behaviour in some detail?

There is, undoubtedly, a critical case to answer, and most of the academic running has been made by the critics (the incentive structure of academia naturally tends to reward criticism rather than conformism to existing structures and thought). This has not, perhaps, impinged greatly as yet on the general public's perception of the structural role of Central Banks. Central Bankers could abide by Montagu Norman's dictum (see Clay, *Lord Norman*, p. 484), 'The dogs may bark, but the caravan moves on'. They would do so at their peril: there is nothing more powerful than an idea whose time has finally arrived.

I worked for seventeen years in the Bank of England (1968–85), as an economic adviser specialising in domestic monetary issues, and since then I have been the Norman Sosnow Professor of Banking and Finance at the London School of Economics. It has been part of my job, in both places, to assess the role and functions of the Bank of England in particular, and of Central Banks in general. I have been able to relate the, often critical, assessments of outside commentators to the actual working of Central Banks as I have perceived them from within. While inside, practical experience will be advantageous, it will, of course, also help to colour one's views and prejudices. If there is a critical case to answer, I believe that there is an even better defence for the maintenance of the main roles and functions of Central Banks. Moreover, since 1985, I too have become an academic, and my views and opinions are as personal and independent as that of any other author.

Part I of this collection of papers on Central Banking relates to the general purposes and functions of the Central Bank within the financial system. In Chapter 1, I jump right into the middle of the debate by asking 'Why do banks need a Central Bank?' This reproduces, and extends, the analytical sections of my more historically oriented monograph, *The Evolution of Central Banks* (1988). In part, the answer to this question lies in the particular structure of commercial banking with nominally-fixed-value deposits matched by fractional reserves and risky loans of uncertain 'true' value. So, in Chapter 2, we ask the hypothetical question, what would happen to the system in general, and to Central Bank control in particular, if certain possible structural changes (reforms) were introduced? The first of these would be to devise a means of paying specific interest on outstanding notes. The second is to require banks to adjust the value of their deposits to the ascertained market value of their assets, either by keeping deposits with fixed-nominal-value but restricting bank assets to safe securities (the narrow bank proposal), or by making the nominal value of deposits vary in line with the market value of assets (mutual fund banking). One of the reasons for exploring the first of these possible reforms, the payment of interest on notes, is that a number of economists have argued that both monetary definitions and demarcation lines, e.g. between monetary and non-monetary assets, *and* Central Bank control depends crucially on certain *legal restrictions*, notably the non-payment of interest on bank note issue. This question is explored in Chapter 3.

The most common academic criticism of Central Banks is that, by their very nature as monopolistic, public sector entities, they are prone to be manipulated by, and become subservient to, the Central Government. In turn, the government is perceived as likely to use the Central Bank as a source of revenue (seigniorage), and to be willing to subvert the condition of price stability that a free banking system committed to convertibility might otherwise attain. The current fashionable theory is that Governments are induced to create inflationary monetary surprises by the desire to win up-coming elections, (a combination of the Political Business Cycle and Time Inconsistency theories). So the latest idea is to grant the Central Bank statutory independence from government with a clear specific mandate to achieve price stability. While I support the concept of Central Bank independence in general, I give the supporting arguments a critical and sceptical examination in Chapter 4.

Central Bank independence (if, when, and how introduced), would represent a major regime change for the conduct and operation of monetary policy. There have been a number of such regime changes in recent decades e.g. the shift from pegged, but adjustable, exchange rates to free floating in the early 1970s; the period of monetary targetry from the mid-1970s to the mid-1980s; ERM and EMU. Such 'Alternative Monetary Standards' are assessed first in Chapter 5 and then at greater length and more depth in Chapter 6, an *Economic Journal* review article on 'The Conduct of Monetary Policy'.

The greatest regime change of the 1980s was, however, undoubtedly the collapse of communism. Under communism, corporate plans and activity were directly controlled and constrained by the Plan and by the Government. Within a capitalist market system, corporate management is subject, when things go wrong, to financial pressures, especially from banks who often are in a position to enforce a strategic decision between refinance and bankruptcy. Particularly in the light of the continuing nexus between the fragile commercial banks and the State Owned Enterprises in the ex-communist countries we examine, in Chapter 7 on 'Commercial Banking and Corporate Control', some of the problems besetting the transition to a Western-style banking system in these countries.

While various regions of the former USSR, and former Yugoslavia, are splitting into separate Republics with their own 'national' currencies and Central Banks, Western Europe has been trying, with difficulty, to move towards monetary union (EMU). In the final chapter of Part I (Chapter 8), the various forces and considerations, economic and political, that determine the boundaries of a currency area, and of its associated Central Bank, are assessed. I argue that political forces are more important than those economic issues normally analysed in the theory of optimal currency areas, but that the really crucial political issues are not purely monetary, but involve interactions between monetary and trade, and monetary and fiscal, policies.

In Part I of the book the main theme is the evolution over time in the structure of the financial system, the role of the Central Bank in such varying contexts, and the changing nature of the monetary regime. In Part II we look more closely at the conduct of Central Bank operations within the present structural setting.

We start, in Chapter 9, with a brief résumé of the historical development of the role and functions of Central Banks, concluding that 'currently the prime objective for which Central Banks adjust their discretionary instrument, notably their command over short-term interest rates, remains the control and limitation of inflation'. That same theme is then taken up, extended, and emphasised in Chapter 10, on 'The Objectives for, and Conduct of, Monetary Policy in the 1990s'.

I turn next from the general question, of the role of a Central Bank, to the particular worm's-eye view of my role as an (outside academic) economic advisor in the Bank of England. This is a more personal piece, presented here as Chapter 11, and taken from the LSE *Annual Review* (1992).

Whereas there is now a fairly wide consensus, perhaps only excluding some Keynesians on the left, that the overriding medium-term objective of the Central Bank ought to be the attainment of price stability, there is much less agreement on the operational process whereby the Central Bank might seek to attain that end. In particular, there has been a continuing debate between a large group of academics on the one hand, who propose that Central Banks should use their control over the *monetary base* directly to induce a chosen growth rate in the monetary aggregates and hence in inflation, and Central Banks on the other who claim that they can use their control over money market *interest rates* to control monetary growth and inflation, perhaps more indirectly but nevertheless more smoothly and satisfactorily (than through the exercise of monetary base control, mbc). Two studies that focus on this operational question come next, Chapters 12 and 13. The first is a more descriptive piece, written in 1985 just before my return to academic life. The second is a more recent essay which records and describes the course of the debate between advocates of mbc and their opponents, often in Central Banks, who prefer to stick with the discretionary adjustment of (short-term) interest rates as the key operational instrument.

As already noted, it has been widely agreed that the primary objective for Central Banks should be the achievement of price stability in the medium term, but what exactly do we mean by that? In the period 1988–93 the current rate of inflation, as measured by the Retail or Consumer Price Index, did not show much variation, e.g. in Japan, but asset prices, particularly of real estate, land, property, and buildings, followed a dramatic boom and bust. How, if at all, should fluctuations in asset prices be factored into Central Bank macro and micro monetary policy decisions. In Chapter 14 I argue that Central Bankers tended systematically to pay too little attention to such fluctuations in asset prices, with the consequence that monetary policy in many countries was too lax in the earlier years of this period, (1988–90), and held too tight thereafter (1991–93).

There would be a dramatic change to the role and conduct of the Bank of England should the UK become a full member of a European Monetary Union and the Bank, therefore, one of the national members of the European System of Central Banks (ESCB). In Chapter 15 the Statutes, governance, and functions of the prospective European Central Bank (ECB) and of the ESCB are outlined and discussed.

Most of Part II of this book relates to the chief function of the Central Bank, i.e. the maintenance of price stability, and to the debates about the best operational procedures (i.e. interest rate or monetary base control), for achieving that objective. Central Banks also, however, have a second major function and objective, that of maintaining the stability of (some parts of) the payments, monetary and financial systems. They carry out this role both directly, e.g. by their Lender of Last Resort operations, by acting as effective guarantor of (net) payments systems, and by taking prime responsibility for arranging the resolution (by rescue or otherwise) of potential banking failures and crises; and also indirectly by being a major participant and protagonist in the discussions on, and design of, financial structures and regulations with the aim of enhancing systemic stability. Given their direct provision of various types of safety-net arrangements for the banking system (plus their leading role in advising on bank regulation more widely), there is a natural case for the Central Bank also to act as a supervisor for the commercial banks which it helps to protect. Since such protection is difficult, probably impossible, to price correctly, its mispricing may lead to moral hazard, distortions to portfolios and potential losses to the Central Bank (and to the Government and taxpayer, perhaps, at one remove).

On the other hand there are a variety of arguments, which perhaps look increasingly cogent should Central Banks be made independent, for hiving much, or all, of the prudential function off to a different, but still associated, body, whose prime function would be that of bank regulation and supervision. These arguments for, and against, leaving the supervisory function with the Central Bank are discussed in Chapter 16 (written jointly with Dirk Schoenmaker).

As noted in Chapter 16, deposit insurance schemes have become applied in an increasing number of countries, especially in Europe, in recent years. It is sometimes unclear whether the main purpose of such schemes is, and should be, for consumer protection only, in which case limits to the proportion, and to the maximum loss, payable would seem appropriate; or whether the scheme is intended to prevent bank runs and panics, in which case 100 per cent insurance would seem to be required, but then with potentially severe adverse effects on moral hazard. In Chapter 17 I set out these issues and propose that deposit insurance should concentrate on consumer protection, leaving the achievement of systemic stability to the Central Bank through other routes.

In the discussion in Part II of this book on the conduct of Central Bank operations, I am clearly on the Central Bank side of the argument about operational procedures (i.e. between interest rate control and mbc). In the regulatory debate, positions, including my own, are somewhat more complicated. There are those who argue that bank regulation is unnecessary and undesirable, that banking systems would be stable without outside regulation (or Central Banks), and/or that the side-effects of regulation, involving moral hazard, portfolio distortion, etc., make the end result worse than *laissez-faire*. Moreover, even in so far as any such regulation might still be desirable, it could adversely deflect the aims and even the reputation of Central Banks to do the supervision themselves; it should be hived off.

On the other hand, there are those, particularly in the aftermath of some financial failure, some perceived lapse in the functioning of the existing regulatory system, who would make financial regulation more extensive, more comprehensive and, in the process, more costly (than it was before). This latter syndrome was clearly apparent in the UK in the 1980s in the run-up to the passage of the Financial Services Act (1986), which seemed to be trying to ensure legally that all financial intermediaries should follow 'best practice', a virtually impossible exercise.

As a result I have found myself on differing occasions arguing both against those who would strip the Central Bank of all regulatory functions, and against those who would impose an excessive blanket coverage of regulation and supervision. I tried to set out an overall position in the assessment of 'The Regulatory Debate in London', Chapter 18. Chapters 19 and 20 contain arguments that the regulatory regime established under the FSA and in the early days of the Securities and Investments Board (SIB) was excessively complex and costly. Part III, and the book, then concludes in Chapter 21 with a review of three major volumes on financial regulation in the UK and the USA, which allows me to compare and contrast the tone of the academic discussions in these two countries.

I have worked as a student, official advisor, and academic in the field of money and banking in general, and of Central Banking in particular, for some three decades. It has been a most eventful period. In certain particularly disturbed periods, notably 1971–5 and 1979–82, circumstances, economic conjunctures, structures and regimes changed so drastically and totally that many of us wanted the passage of events to slow down, so that our intellectual understanding would have a chance to catch up.

Yet at the same time one is aware of the permanence of many structures, such as Central Banks, and of many intellectual ideas and debates, such as rules versus discretion in the conduct of monetary policy. Again such ideas and structures can mutate, and come into prominence rather quickly (such as the current fashion for Central Bank independence), as circumstances and the context change. The old Chinese curse, 'May you live in interesting times', is likely to continue to hold true for Central Bankers.

Part I

Financial Systems

1 Why do Banks Need a Central Bank? (1987)*

1.1 INTRODUCTION

In *The Evolution of Central Banks* (1985), especially Chapter 3, I sought to examine the key features that distinguished banks from other financial intermediaries, and, in particular, necessitated the support of a Central Bank. This paper continues and extends that work.

Fama, in his paper on 'Banking in the Theory of Finance', (1980), describes banks as having two functions, the first being to provide transactions and accounting services, the second being portfolio management. Yet transactions services are carried out by other institutions, e.g. giro, Post Office, non-bank credit card companies, etc., without much need for special supervision, etc. by a Central Bank.[1] More important, I shall argue that it would be perfectly possible, generally safer, and a likely development, for transactions services to be provided by an altogether different set of financial intermediaries, i.e. intermediaries providing mutual collective investment in (primarily) marketable securities. If this was to occur, would it make such mutual investment intermediaries, e.g. unit trusts, open-end investment trusts, into banks? Would such intermediaries then become subject to the same risks as banks, and need to be subject to the same kind of supervision/regulation?

I shall argue, in section 1.2, that there is no necessary reason why banks alone among financial intermediaries should provide transactions services, and in their role as portfolio managers, banks have much in common with other intermediaries acting in this capacity (though, as I shall argue later, in section 1.3, certain crucial distinctions remain between the characteristic form of portfolios held by banks as compared with those held by non-bank financial intermediaries). Nevertheless, it is this *joint* role that is held to give a special character to banking, and to require special treatment for banks through the establishment of a Central Bank, e.g. to provide Lender of Last Resort (LOLR)

* *Oxford Economic Papers*, 39 (1987): 75–89. This paper was originally prepared for the Manhattan Institute Conference in New York, March 1986, and was also presented at seminars at Nottingham University and Brasenose College, Oxford. I have benefited greatly from comments made on those occasions, notably by Max Hall, Mervyn Lewis, Bennett McCallum and Lawrence White, and subsequently by Gavin Bingham and my referees, but they should not be blamed for my remaining idiosyncrasies.

and other support services for banks in difficulties, support which goes beyond the assistance envisaged for other financial intermediaries that get into trouble.

Thus Tobin (1985) states (p. 20) that

The basic dilemma is this: Our monetary and banking institutions have evolved in a way that entangles competition among financial intermediary firms with the provision of transactions media.

But what actually are the problems caused by this entanglement? The problem is often seen, and so appears to Tobin, as arising from the propensity of banks, acting as competing financial intermediaries, to run risks of default, which then, through a process aggravated by contagion, puts the monetary system, whose successful functioning is an essential public good, at risk.

I begin section 1.2 by recording that Tobin's suggestion, in accord also with Friedman's views, is that institutions (banks) seeking to offer deposits involving payments' services should be required to segregate these in special funds held against risk-free earmarked safe assets. As historical experience shows, however, such a restriction would reduce the profitability, and not just the riskiness, of banking. An alternative method of providing protection against runs, and systemic crises, could, however, be obtained by basing the payments' on the liabilities of mutual collective investment funds, the value of whose liabilities varies in line with the value of their marketable assets. Since the banking system developed first, the banks established a branch system, clearing houses, etc. which provided them with economies of scale and familiarity in running the payments' system, but technological change is eroding, and could even be reversing, banks' advantages in this respect.

Indeed, non-bank mutual investment funds are already beginning to provide payments' services and there is no (technical) reason why this development should not proceed much further. It is often claimed, however, that people would be unwilling to make payments against asset balances which fluctuate in value over time. In practice, however, payments already often incorporate a probabilistic element, in the sense that the payer may have some uncertainty whether the balance, or overdraft facility, available will be sufficient for the bank drawn on to honour the cheque. The additional uncertainty involved could possibly be reduced sufficiently to make people prepared to use payments' services offered by non-bank investment funds.

Since these latter financial intermediaries would be protected from illiquidity by their holding of marketable assets, and from insolvency by the fact that the value of their liabilities varies in line with their asset values, a Central Bank should welcome their entry into the provision of payments' services and need impose no further supervisory/regulatory constraints on them. This development would, however, raise further questions about the meaning of money, since the estimated nominal value of balances capable of being used in payments would vary automatically with the prices of the assets held by these intermediaries. Indeed, the central intuition of section 1.2 is that the monetisation of assets is *not* necessarily limited to a restricted set of financial intermediaries, i.e. banks.

So, I demonstrate in section 1.2 that the provision of payments' services jointly with portfolio management does *not*, *per se*, require the involvement of a Central Bank – if, for example, the joint function is undertaken by mutual collective investment funds. Clearly it is not so much the joint function, but rather the particular characteristics of banks' liabilities and asset portfolios that makes them especially vulnerable. Indeed I try to highlight this by enquiring, in section 1.3, whether the banking system would still require Central Bank support even if banks were to withdraw altogether from providing payments' services, i.e. funding their asset books only through time deposits and CDs.

The reason why the answer to this question is 'Yes' lies in the fundamental *raison d'être* of banking. Why do borrowers seek loans from banks and depositors place savings with banks rather than transact directly through the market place? In part the answer lies in the costs of obtaining and assessing information on the credit worthiness of (most) borrowers. Banks have a specialised advantage in this function, but, even so, the costs and limitations of such information induce banks to extend (non-marketable) loans on a *fixed nominal value basis*. With their assets largely on such a fixed nominal value basis, it is less risky for banks also to have their deposit liabilities on the same, fixed nominal value, terms: and the same concerns with only having access to limited information about their bank's 'true' position also makes the depositor prefer mixed nominal value banks deposits.

The resulting combination of uncertain 'true' bank asset valuation, and fixed nominal value deposits, leads to the possibility of bank runs: lengthening the maturity of bank deposits slows down the potential *speed* of such runs, but does not prevent them. What is, however, particularly interesting in recent analysis of banking is that it has been realised that much of the economic damage caused by bank crises and failures rebounds on bank *borrowers*. The loss of wealth to depositors, and the dislocation of the payments' system, have already been fully appreciated in the literature. What is new now is the view that the added pressures placed on bank borrowers by such crises, e.g. the removal of access to new loans, the need to obtain facilities elsewhere at an awkward time, and, in some cases, the demand by receivers for the repayment of their outstanding borrowing, can represent an additional deleterious effect.

1.2   THE PROVISION OF PAYMENTS' SERVICES BY BANKS AND BY OTHER FINANCIAL INTERMEDIARIES

Tobin (1985, p. 23) states:

> Even if bank managers act with normal perspicuity in the interests of the stockholders, even if all temptations of personal gain are resisted, sheer chance will bring some failures – insolvency because of borrowers' defaults or other capital losses on assets, or inability to meet withdrawals of deposits even though the bank would be solvent if assets' present values could be immediately realized. The probability is multiplied by the essential instability of depositor confidence. News of withdrawals triggers more withdrawals, sauve qui peut, at the same bank, or by contagion at others. For these reasons the banking business has not been left to free market competition but has been significantly regulated.

On p. 24 Tobin notes:

> Government deposit insurance in the U.S. protects not only means-of-payment deposits but all other deposits in eligible institutions, including non-checkable saving accounts and time deposits. Similar obligations of mutual funds and other debtors not covered by deposit insurance are not guaranteed. It is not clear why all kinds of liabilities of covered institutions should be insured, except that the assets are so commingled that withdrawals of non-insured deposit liabilities would imperil the insured deposits. That indeed is why the insurance guarantee was *de facto* extended beyond the statutory limit.

Tobin's suggestion is:

> This problem could be avoided by segregating and earmarking assets corresponding to particular classes of liabilities permitting a depositor in effect to purchase a fund which could not be impaired by difficulties elsewhere in the institution's balance sheet. In this way, a bank would become more like a company offering a variety of mutual funds, just as these companies – which are not insured – are becoming more like banks.

In particular, Tobin, following an earlier suggestion made by Friedman, advocated 100 per cent reserve-backed funds for checkable deposits, as has also Henry Wallich, in his paper, 'A Broad View of Deregulation', and several other US economists. Thus Tobin continues,

> The 100% – reserve deposit proposed, . . . ,would be one such [mutual] fund, but there could be others. For example, many households of modest

means and little financial sophistication want savings accounts that are safe stores of value in the unit of account. *They can be provided in various maturities without risk by a fund invested in Treasury securities. They can be provided as demand obligations either by letting their redemption value fluctuate with net asset value* or by crediting a floating interest rate to a fixed value (emphasis added).

With such illustrious, and wide, support from economists why has this idea not had more practical success? The concept of a 100 per cent segregated reserve against checkable deposits would, however, reverse the evolution of banking. Initially goldsmiths received deposits of gold coin from customers and acted purely as safety vaults. It was the realisation that it would be profitable, and under most circumstances relatively safe, to loan out some proportion of these reserves to prospective borrowers, in addition to the loans made on the basis of their own capital, that transformed such entrepreneurs into bankers. Naturally when such early bankers did run into difficulties, by over-trading, proposals were made to force such commercial bankers back to stricter segregation. Thus the fore-runner of the Swedish Riksbank, founded by John Palmstruch in 1656, was organised on the basis of two supposedly separate departments, the loan department financing loans on the basis of longer-term deposits and capital, and the issue department supplying credit notes on the receipt of gold and specie. But even when Palmstruch's Private bank had been taken over by Parliament,

> A secret instruction, however, authorized the advance by the exchange department to the lending department of the funds at its disposal, though on reasonably moderate terms.[2]

The reason why such segregation and hypothecation of certain safe assets to checkable deposits will not work in the case of commercial banks is that it largely removes the profitability of banking along with its risks. The regulatory constraint on the banks' preferred portfolio allocation, under such circumstances, would be seen – as historical experience indicates – as burdensome: attempts would be made to avoid, or to evade, such constraints, e.g. by the provision of substitute transactions' media at unconstrained intermediaries, which, being free of such constraints, could offer higher returns on such media. Only in the case of non-profit-maximising banks, such as the Bank of England, divided into two Departments on much the same theoretical basis by the 1844 Bank Charter Act, would such segregation be acceptable and not subject to avoidance and evasion. Of course, if the public sector were prepared to subsidise the provision of payments' services either by operating them directly itself, or by paying some interest on the 100% – reserves held by private sector intermediaries, then it could be done; but, in the light of Congress' recent response to suggestions for paying interest on required reserves in the USA, it seems difficult to envisage the public being prepared to vote tax funds for this purpose.

Anyhow, there is a simpler, and less expensive, alternative which Tobin almost reaches when he comments that the public's savings accounts could be

> provided as demand obligations, . . . , by letting their redemption value fluctuate with net asset value.

We are so used to having payments' services provided against checkable fixed nominal value liabilities, with 100 per cent convertibility of demand deposits, that we have not – mostly – realised that payments' services could be just as easily provided by a mutual collective investment financial intermediary, where the liabilities are units representing a proportional claim on a set of marketable assets. The value of the units fluctuates, of course, with the underlying value of the assets in the portfolio. Because the (close-of-day) market value of the portfolio is known, the value of the unit can be published each morning, and each depositor then knows how much his or her units are worth. Because there will be a period of float, during which underlying assest values will change, and because the attempt by the mutual funds to meet net outflows by net sales of assets could itself influence prices, one would expect a mutual fund to limit payments services and convertibility by requiring some minimum balance in units to be held normally, with a progressive penalty in terms of yield foregone for dropping below this balance, plus some emergency arrangements for occasional overdrafts, say from an associated bank. This concept of required minimum balance has been adopted often enough, by commercial banks, and the public is familiar with it. The cheques would, of course, have to be drawn in terms of the numéraire – otherwise they would not be useful in clearing debts. The value of the drawers' units would change between the date of writing the cheque and of its being presented,[3] and – in a period of falling asset prices – there would be a danger of the drawer being overdrawn at the latter date, while having had funds to spare at the earlier date; but this problem would seem also to be generally soluble by only providing guaranteed payments' services up to a minimum credit balance in units, (plus an emergency overdraft arrangement, perhaps with an associated bank).

I see no insuperable technical problem why payments' services could not be provided by mutual collective investment intermediaries in this manner. They would need to hold some liquid reserves, vault cash to pay depositors demanding currency, and liquid assets to meet net outflows at times when the fund manager judged that it would be inopportune to realise investments, (n.b. this latter need is *neither* for liquidity *nor* for solvency purposes. Liquidity is always available from the ability to sell marketable assets, and solvency is assured because the value of liabilities falls with the value of assets. Instead, the desire for liquid assets would arise from desire to maximise the net asset value of units under varying market conditions,[4] and thus improve reputation, service fees, and managerial earnings). Nevertheless the need to hold vault cash, at least, might lower the expected return on the intermediaries' assets, but the effect of this on the demand for units should be (more than) counterbalanced by the improved liquidity to the unit holder of his investments, and the associated advantages of being able to use them for transactions purposes.

Be that as it may, the current trend already is for (limited) transactions' services to be provided by investment-managing non-bank financial intermediaries on the basis of depositors' funds, the value of which varies with the market value of the underlying assets. Merrill Lynch cash management service is one example. Certain other unit trusts and mutual funds, such as money market mutual funds, are also providing (limited) payments' services. Similarly certain building societies and certain mortgage businesses in other countries are considering allowing borrowers to draw additional top-up mortgages up to a stated proportion of the market value of their house.[5]

A common response to this idea is that, whereas it would be perfectly possible, as a technical matter, to provide payments' services against liabilities with a varying market value, the public would not happily accept it, and it would not succeed in practice. It is argued, for example, that there is a large psychological gulf between being absolutely certain that one has the funds to meet a payment, and being 99 per cent certain of that. But is such 100 per cent certainty a general feature of our existing payments' system? Unless one monitors one's bank account, outstanding float, etc., continuously, and knows exactly what overdraft limits, if any, the bank manager may have set, the willingness of the bank to honour certain cheque payments will have a probabilistic element.

Lawrence White (1984, p. 707) put this general case, *against* basing payments' services on liabilities with a varying market value, most persuasively:

Demand deposits, being ready debt claims, are potentially superior to mutual fund shares, which are equity claims, in at least one respect. The value of a deposit may be contractually guaranteed to increase over time at a preannounced rate of interest. Its unit-of-account value at a future date is certain so long as the bank continues to honor its obligation to redeem its deposits on demand. No such contractual guarantee may be made with respect to an equity claim. A mutual fund is obligated to pay out after the fact its actual earnings, so that the yield on fund shares cannot be predetermined. In the absence of deposit rate ceiling regulation, the range of anticipated possible returns from holding fund shares need not lie entirely above the deposit interest rate. Risk-diversifying portfolio owners might therefore not divest themselves entirely of demand deposits even given a higher mean yield on mutual funds. It is true that the characteristic pledge of money market mutual funds to maintain a fixed share price, or rather the policy of investing exclusively in short-term highly reputable securities so that the pledge can be kept, makes fund shares akin to demand deposits in having near-zero risk of negative nominal yield over any period. The difference between predetermined and postdetermined yields – between debt and equity – nonetheless remains. The historical fact is that deposit banking did not naturally grow up on an equity basis.

Because the provision of payments' services by mutual funds, whose liabilities have a market-varying value, would not only be a somewhat novel concept, but would also worry those unused to any probabilistic element in payments, I would expect its introduction to be gradual, and probably to start with richer customers better able to cope with such probabilistic concerns. Moreover, such a limited introduction could prevent the mutual funds making use of economies of scale in the provision of payments' services. There are, therefore, some observers who believe that this possible development will fail the practical test of success in the free, open market.

On the other hand there seems no technical reason why the trend towards the provision of payments' services against the value of units in a collective investment fund (up to a minimum balance) should not proceed much further, especially now that technological innovations in the provision of such services, e.g. shared automated teller machines (ATMs), electronic fund transfer (EFT) and home-banking, are transforming the production function of payments' services, especially in reducing the economies of scale to a network of manned branch buildings. White's arguments (pp. 707–8) that the provision of payments' services by non-bank (mutual fund) intermediaries has been more expensive could be reduced in force, or even reversed, by the new technologies in this field.

Moreover, there would seem considerable cause to welcome such a development, not only for the extra competition that this would inject in this area, but also because the characteristics of mutual, collective investment funds should serve to make them naturally *more suitable* purveyors of payments' services than banks. In particular, both the likelihood of a run on an individual bank, and of systemic dangers to the monetary system arising from a contagion of fear, would be greatly reduced if payments' services were provided by mutual collective-investment intermediaries, rather than by banks. For example, the announcement of bad news reducing the market value of such an intermediary's assets, assuming an efficient market, would immediately reduce the value of depositors' units. There would be no risk of insolvency for the intermediary, and no advantage, again assuming an efficient market, for any depositor to withdraw his funds from that intermediary.[6] Again, since the asset portfolios of such intermediaries are publicly reported and their value at any time exactly ascertainable, there would seem little scope for rumour or fear to take hold. Certainly if a particular fund manager did significantly worse (better) than average, depositors would find it difficult to distinguish bad (good) luck from bad (good) management, and would probably switch funds in sizeable amounts to the ex post more successful, but such switching of funds between funds would hardly damage the payments' system, rather the reverse.

There would still be a possibility of a sharp general fall in market values leading depositors to shift en masse out of market valued unit holdings into the fixed nominal value numéraire, thereby forcing the collective investment funds to have to sell further assets, and thereby deepening the asset price depression. Unlike the case of a run on banks, which raises the subjective probability of failure elsewhere, and thus reduces the expected return on holding deposits, at least the fall in market values on the assets in the portfolio of the mutual fund should tend to increase the expected running yield on such units, and thus act as an offset to the inducement to hold cash. Moreover, it would still be possible for the authorities, perhaps the Central Bank, to undertake open market operations to offset the shift of unit holders into cash, possibly by buying the assets, say equities, that the funds were selling. There are precedents for such actions: at one time the Japanese intervened to support Stock Exchange values.

Thus a monetary system in which transactions' services were provided to unit holders of collective investment mutual funds would seem inherently safer and more stable than the present system, in which such services are provided to (a sub-set of) bank depositors. Indeed, the nature of bank portfolios, largely filled with nonmarketable assets of uncertain true value held on the basis of nominally fixed value liabilities, would seem remarkably unsuited to form the basis of our payments' systems. Why did it develop in this way? The answer is, I think, to be found in the accidents of historical evolution. Broad, well-functioning, efficient asset markets are a reasonably recent phenomenon. Because of people's need both to borrow and to find a secure home for savings, banks developed well before mutual collective investment funds. The historical form of bank development led them inevitably into the payments' business. Thereafter, the economies of scale involved in the existing structure of the payments' system, the clearing houses, branch networks and the intangibles of public familiarity and legal and institutional framework, left the banks largely – indeed in some Anglo Saxon countries absolutely – unrivalled in the provision of payments' services.

Owing to the various innovations noted earlier, such bank monopoly of the payments' system may now be coming to an end. The authorities should welcome the opportunity to encourage the development of a safer payments' system. They should certainly not put obstacles in the way of properly-run collective investment funds offering payments' services. Indeed there is a question exactly what concern the authorities (and/or the Central Bank) needs to feel about the amount of monetary units thereby created, and with the state of the intermediaries creating them.[7] So long as such intermediaries abided by their deeds of establishment and restricted their investments to marketable securities, of a certain class, with the value of the units adjusted continuously in line, solvency should never be in doubt, and would not be affected by the additional offer of payments' services. Similarly liquidity would be assured by marketability. So it is not clear why a Central Bank should need to impose *any* additional regulation/supervision over mutual funds offering payments' services.

Moreover, in a world where payments' services were predominantly provided by monetary units of collective investment funds rather than by banks,[8] why should the authorities pay any particular attention to the quantity of money itself, particularly since its nominal value would shift automatically with asset market prices? In such circumstances how would the quantity of money be measured? Indeed, the intuition of this Section is that the monetisation of assets is *not* necessarily limited to a restricted set of financial intermediaries, i.e. banks. A much wider range of financial intermediaries could, in principle, monetize a much wider set of assets than is currently done. Under these circumstances the definition of money would either have to contract, to become synonymous with the dominant, 'outside', base money, assuming that such still continues to exist,[9] or become an amorphous concept almost devoid of meaning.

1.3   BANK PORTFOLIOS AND CENTRAL BANK SUPPORT

It would appear, therefore, that the provision of payments' (monetary) services on units offered by collective investment intermediaries would *not, ipso facto*, require the involvement of the authorities (the Central Bank) to monitor and regulate the provision of such services. The next question is whether the withdrawal of commercial banks from the provision of payments' services, (so that demand deposits, NOW accounts, and the like were no longer offered), would absolve the Central Bank from its central concern with the well-being of the banking system. If banks offered only time deposits, CDs, etc., leaving payments' and transactions' services to others, would there be any need for special support for the banking system?

The answer to this, I believe, is that cessation of payments' services would make little difference to banks' riskiness or to the real basis of Central Bank concern with the banking system. There is little, or no, evidence that demand deposits provide a less stable source of funds than short-dated time deposits, CDs or borrowing in the inter-bank market; rather the reverse appears to be the case.[10] Recent occasions of runs on banks have *not* involved an attempt by the public to move out of bank deposits into cash, but merely a flight of depositors from banks seen as now excessively dangerous to some alternative placement (not cash). The Fringe Bank crisis in 1973–4 in the UK, and Continental-Illinois, are instances of this, and earlier U.S. historical experience examined by Aharony and Swary (1983) points in the same direction. Earlier, it was suggested that flows of funds from one collective investment fund to another would *not* have damaging repercussions for the payments' system, were such funds offering monetised units and providing the (bulk of) such services. Yet I shall argue that, even were banking to be entirely divorced from the provision of payments' services, such flows between banks would be extremely damaging for the economy, and would require a continuing support role for a Central Bank to prevent and, if necessary, to recycle such flows.

The reasons why this is so are to be found in the fundamental *raison d'être* of banking itself. In particular, consider why there is a need for banks to act as intermediaries in the first place? Why cannot people simply purchase the same diversified collection of assets that the bank does? There are, of course, advantages arising from economies of scale, and the provision of safe-keeping services, but these could be obtained by investing in a collective investment fund. The key difference between a collective investment fund and a bank is that the former invests entirely, or primarily, in marketable assets, while the latter invests quite largely in non-marketable (or, at least, non-marketed) assets.

Why do borrowers prefer to obtain loans from banks rather than issue marketable securities? The set-up costs required to allow a proper market to exist have represented, in practice, formidable obstacles to the establishment of markets in the debt and equity obligations of persons and small businesses. Underlying these are the costs of providing sufficient public information to enable an equilibrium fundamental value to be established (e.g. the costs of issuing a *credible* prospectus), and the size of the expected regular volume of transactions necessary to induce a market maker to establish a market in such an asset. In this sense, as Leland and Pyle (1977), Baron (1982) and Diamond (1984) have argued, the particular role of banks is to specialise[11] in choosing borrowers and monitoring their behaviour. Public information on the economic condition and prospects of such borrowers is so limited and expensive, that the alternative of issuing marketable securities is either non-existent or unattractive.

Even though banks have such an advantage (*vis-à-vis* ordinary savers) in choosing and monitoring prospective borrowers, they too will be at a comparative disadvantage, compared with the borrower, in assessing the latter's condition, intentions and prospects.[12] Even though there would be advantages in risk sharing resulting from extending loans whose return was conditional on the contingent outcome of the project for which the loan was raised, it would reduce the incentive on the borrower to succeed, and the bank would have difficulties in monitoring the ex post outcome. Businessmen, at least in some countries, are sometimes said to have three sets of books, one for the tax inspector, one for their shareholders, and one for themselves. Which of these would the banks see, or would there be yet another set of books.[13]

In order, therefore, to reduce information and monitoring costs, banks have been led to extend loans on a fixed nominal value basis, irrespective of contingent outcome (with the loan further supported in many cases by collateral and with a duration often less than the intended life of the project to enable periodic re-assessment). Even so, both the initial, and subsequent, valuation of the loan by a bank does depend on information that is generally private between the bank and its borrowers, or, perhaps, known only to the borrower.[14] Thus the true asset value of the bank's (non-marketed) loans is always subject to uncertainty, though their nominal value is fixed, subject to accounting rules about provisions, write-offs, etc. Under these conditions it will benefit both bank and depositor to denominate deposit liabilities also in fixed nominal terms. The banks will benefit because the common denomination will reduce the risk that would arise from reduced covariance between the value of its assets and of its liabilities (as would occur, for example, if its liabilities were indexed, say to the RPI, and its assets were fixed in nominal value, or, alternatively if its assets fluctuated in line with borrowers' profits while its liabilities were fixed in nominal value). The depositor would seek fixed nominal deposits from the bank for the same reason that the bank sought fixed nominal value terms from borrowers: depositors cannot easily monitor the actual condition, intentions and prospects of their bank, so that information and monitoring costs are lessened, and the incentives on the bank to perform satisfactorily are increased, by denominating deposits in fixed nominal terms.

The combination, however, of the nominal convertibility guarantee, together with the uncertainty about the true value of bank assets, leads to the possibility of runs on individual banks and systemic crises. Moreover, once the nominal convertibility guarantee is established, the effect of better public information on banks' true asset values is uncertain. For example, 'hidden reserves' were once justified by practical bankers as likely to reduce the likelihood of runs and to maintain confidence. Again, Central Bankers have been, at most, lukewarm about allowing a market to develop in large syndicated loans to sovereign countries, whose ability to service and repay on schedule was subject to doubt, because the concrete exhibition of the fall in the value of such loans could impair the banks' recorded capital value, and potentially cause failures. An economist might ask who was being fooled? Yet on a number of occasions financial institutions have been effectively insolvent, but, so long as everyone steadfastly averted their gaze, a way through and back to solvency was achieved.

Be that as it may, under these conditions of private and expensive information, and fixed nominal value loans, any major flow of funds between banks is liable to have deleterious effects on *borrowers*, as well as on those depositors who lose both wealth and liquidity by having been left too late in the queue to withdraw when the bank(s) suspended payment. Even if the prospects of the borrower of the failed bank are at least as good as on the occasion when the borrower first arranged to loan, the borrower will have to undergo expensive search costs to obtain replacement funds. Assuming the borrower searched beforehand, and found the 'best' deal, the likelihood is now that the borrower will obtain less beneficial arrangements.

Bank runs, however, tend to happen when conditions for many borrowers have turned adverse. The suspicion, or indeed the knowledge, of that is what prompted the run in the first place. Accordingly the expected value of the loans of many borrowers will have fallen. If they are forced to repay the failing bank, by the receiver to meet the creditors' demands,[15] they would not be able to replace the funds required on the same terms, if at all, from other banks. Thus bank failures will place the economic well-being, indeed survival, of many borrowers at risk, as well as impairing depositors' wealth.[16] Consequently flows of funds from suspect banks to supposedly stronger banks can have a severely adverse effect on the economy, even when there is no flight into cash at all. A Central Bank will aim to prevent, and, if that fails, to recycle such flows – subject to such safeguards as it can achieve to limit moral hazard and to penalise inadequate or improper managerial behaviour.[17]

1.4 CONCLUSION

To summarise and conclude, it is often claimed that banking is special and particular, requiring additional regulation and supervision by a Central Bank, *because* it is unique among financial intermediaries in combining payments' services and portfolio management. I hope to have demonstrated that this is false. Monetary payments' services not only could be provided, (and are increasingly being provided), by other collective-investment funds, but could also be provided more safely than by banks. Moreover, the characteristics of such funds are such that their entry into this field (the provision of monetary services) need not cause the authorities (the Central Bank) any extra concern; they could be left to operate under their current regulations. Similarly, if banks were to abandon the provision of payments' services, and restrict their deposit liabilities to non-checkable form, it would not much reduce bank riskiness. They would still require the assistance of a Central Bank.

All this follows because the really important distinction between banks and other financial intermediaries resides in the characteristics of their asset portfolio, which, in turn, largely determines what kind of liability they can offer: fixed value in the case of banks, market-value-related for collective investment funds. It is these latter differences, rather than the special monetary nature of certain bank deposits, that will maintain in future years the distinction between bank and non-bank financial intermediaries.

NOTES

1. Except insofar as the Central Bank has a direct concern for the smooth and trouble-free operation of the payments' system itself, e.g. the working of the clearing house(s) and the settlement system(s), as contrasted with the institutions providing the transactions services.
2. See Flux (1911, p. 17) and also Goodhart (1985, pp. 109–16 and 159–62).
3. It would, of course, be just as simple to keep the value of each unit constant, but alter the number of units owned by each depositor as asset values change. I cannot see why that shift in presentation should affect people's behaviour in any way.
4. The analysis, of course, stems from Tobin (1958).
5. Building societies, of course, will have been entering more actively into the provision of payments' services, once the Building Societies Bill (December 1985) passed into law. But payments will normally be on the basis of their nominally fixed-value convertible liabilities. The example above, however, envisages building societies, in certain circumstances, also being prepared to monetise assets with a varying market value.
6. Mutual funds seeking to attract depositors, in part on the grounds of an offer to provide payments' services, face a trade-off in this respect. Because of depositors' familiarity with fixed-nominal-value convertible deposits as a basis for the payments' system, some mutual funds, to attract such depositors, have given some commitments to hold the value of their liabilities (normally) at such a fixed nominal value. But this opens them up to runs as soon as the publicly observable value of their assets falls towards, or below, the (temporarily) fixed value of their liabilities. This happened with the UK Provident Institute in April 1986. White (1984, p. 707) and Lewis, in personal discussion, have reported such behaviour among mutual funds in the US and Australia respectively.
7. There would still have to be protection against fraud, but that is a common requirement, not particularly related to the provision of transactions' services.
8. Something of a half-way house between a monetary unit and a bank demand deposit would be an *indexed* demand deposit provided either by a bank or another intermediary. It might actually be slightly *more* difficult technically to organize payments services on the basis of these, than on mutual funds invested in marketable assets, since the latter are continuously revalued while the former have (partly unanticipated) jumps on discrete occasions with the publication of the (RPI/CPI) price index to which the deposit was related. Again payment might only be guaranteed up to some minimum real, or nominal, balance. Some way would also have to be found to allow continuous revaluing of the deposits through the month in line with the anticipated change in the forthcoming RPI. Still, these technical problems should be surmountable. Given that there are fiscal advantages to (most tax-brackets of) depositors in holding indexed rather than nominal deposits, (i.e. no Capital Gains Tax on the inflation element in the indexed deposit; whereas income tax on the whole nominal interest on ordinary deposits is charged less the allowance given against bank charges), and that, in the UK, riskless short-term assets for such an intermediary to hold exist in the form of Government indexed bonds, it is surprising that no intermediary has yet started to offer indexed banking, with both liabilities and assets in indexed form. Perhaps the most likely reason, besides inertia and set-up costs, is that intermediaries basically require a combination of riskier and higher yielding assets, together with safe assets, to hold against liabilities, all denominated in the same form. The disincentive for intermediaries in the

UK from setting up as indexed bankers is an apparent absence of borrowers prepared to take loans in indexed form: why that should be so is beyond the scope of this paper.

9. For surveys of this latter issue, see White (1984) and McCallum (1985).

10. Of course the risk of a run still depends, in part, on a maturity transformation by the bank, with the duration of liabilities being generally shorter than that of assets. But even if there was *no* maturity transformation, a fall of asset values relative to the nominally fixed value of liabilities would make depositors unwilling to roll-over, or extend, further funds to the bank [except on terms which made such depositors preferred, earlier creditors (than depositors with later maturities), a course which would be subject to legal constraint]. So, the absence of maturity transformation would delay, and slow, the development of a run, but would not stop depositors from running when, and as, they could.

11. An interesting question, suggested to me by Professor Mervyn Lewis, is to what extent banks obtain useful information about borrowers' conditions from their (complementary) function in operating the (present) payments system. In so far as banks do obtain information that is useful for credit assessment from the handling of payment flows, this would provide a stronger economic rationale for the present combination of banking functions. Research into, and analysis of, the customarily private and confidential question of (informational) relationships between banks and their borrowers needs to be developed further, and we cannot say with any confidence now how far banks benefit in seeking to assess credit worthiness from their provision of payments services.

12. At least this will be so until, and unless, a large borrower runs into prospective problems in meeting contractual repayment obligations. To a casual observer, banks seem to try to limit the informational costs of making the initial loans, e.g. by resorting to standardized grading procedures; but once a (sizeable) borrower runs into difficulties, the bank responds by greatly increasing its monitoring activities, becoming often very closely involved with that borrower's future actions.

13. This is not, as it happens, a purely hypothetical question. The Muslim prohibition on interest payments is causing certain Islamic countries to require their banks to issue Mushariqi loans, which do represent a form of equity share in the project being financed. Students of banking theory and practice might find it informative to give closer study to Islamic banking. See, for example, the article, 'Islam's Bad Debtors' in the *Financial Times* (8 April 1986).

14. Much recent literature on banking and credit has assumed that the borrower's selection and management of projects may not be observed by any outside party, even the banker himself: see, for example, Stiglitz and Weiss (1981, 1983).

15. Insofar as constraints, either external or self-imposed, exist which stop the receiver from calling in loans outstanding at failed banks, this source of potential loss to society would be lessened. Even so, at a minimum, the borrower would lose the ability to obtain *additional* loans from the failing bank, and that ability could be crucial to survival in a cyclical depression.

16. This feature of banking, whereby calling of loans by failed banks causes economic disruption, has been recently noted and modelled by Diamond and Dybvig (1983), and by Bernanke (1983).

17. Even in the absence of a Central Bank there will be some incentives for commercial banks to act, either independently or collusively, in the same way, i.e. to recycle deposit flows to banks facing liquidity problems and to support, or to take over, potentially insolvent banks. But the public good aspect of such actions will be less compelling to competing commercial banks, (e.g. why help a competitor that got into trouble through its own fault?), and the risk to their

own profit positions of such action more worrying to them than to a Central Bank. Moreover the usual circumstances of a rescue, at very short notice under conditions of severely limited information, makes it more difficult for commercial banks to act collusively, than for an independent Central Bank to act swiftly and decisively.

2 Can We Improve the Structure of Financial Systems? (1993)*

2.1 INTRODUCTION

The main theme of this paper is that several of the characteristics of our present Western monetary and banking systems have been crucially dependent on the particular temporal process of historical development, and are not an essential feature of more fundamental preferences or technological conditions. They exist in part because we take them for granted. It is the purpose of this paper to examine what might change, in both theory and practice, if some of these inessential characteristics were to be changed.

The first of these characteristics that I shall hold up for review is the proposition that money, or any sub-set of monetary assets, such as currency, need necessarily offer a zero nominal interest rate. I wish to examine a world in which all monetary assets, including currency, can offer a competitive market rate of interest. In such a world, for example, some of the arguments for concentrating the control of the note issue in the hands of a monopoly supplier, i.e. the Central Bank, lose their force. But if commercial banks are set free to provide competitive interest-bearing note issues, competitive with the note issue of the Central Bank, what then determines *the* short-run nominal rate of interest within the economic system?

Since commercial bank notes and deposits could not be 'legal tender', without causing a threat of monetary instability and hyperinflation, they have to be *convertible* into some object of value. This leads us to consider exactly how the determination of the short-term rate of interest may depend on the particular form of convertibility arrangements under consideration.

One possible basis for converting bank liabilities (notes and deposits) into objects of value is to make them translatable (on demand or after notice) into a pro rata share of the *value* of bank assets, what I have elsewhere described (Goodhart, 1987) as mutual fund banking (earlier seminal contributions on this concept include Black, 1970 and Fama, 1980, 1983). It is the fact, however, that a considerable proportion of present bank assets, notably

---

* *European Economic Review*, 37 (1993): 269–91.

My thanks are due to G. Bishop, K. Dowd, J. Galbraith, G. Getty, G. Kentfield, M. King, A. Pollock, L. Price, T.K. Rymes, N. Schnadt, X. Vives and J. Yam for mental stimulation, advice and useful comments on this paper. But the responsibility for all remaining errors is my own.

those which do not have full collateral or which cannot easily be securitised, are of *uncertain* value that serves as one cause of the preference for convertibility into some alternative known store-of-value, e.g. Central Bank money, gold, or a basket of goods/assets.[1] A common feature of many current proposals for banking reform, especially those emanating from the USA, is that those banks which operate the payments system, i.e. which issue checkable deposits (or bank notes), should be legally prevented from holding assets which do not have a continuously ascertainable market value. Once bank assets are limited to those whose value is precisely known at all times, it is possible to make a secondary decision whether to limit banks to holding virtually capital certain assets, or to allow them to hold assets with greater price volatility, thereby opening up the possibility of insolvency – assuming that deposits maintain a fixed nominal value – and requiring a procedure for seeking to close banks before their capital becomes exhausted.

One potential advantage of such 'narrow bank' proposals, which form my second major focus, is that, subject to appropriate checks and constraints on fraud, a bank that abided by such restraints on its asset portfolio would not seem to require the apparatus of official bank regulation and supervision, an apparatus that has appeared simultaneously costly and inefficient in numerous cases in recent years (BCCI and S&Ls, for example). Such expressions of relief would, in my view, be premature.

Much of the narrow bank, and also the mutual bank, discussion has focused on achieving absolute security and safety for transactions deposits, and the banks that provide them. But this is essentially a simple matter. Any fool can run an old-style Trustee Savings Bank. The essence of banking lies in the assessment, monitoring and risk-handling of loans in circumstances where information is partial and asymmetric.[2] Yet, the narrow bank proposals would, in effect, exclude the credit assessment/bank loans part of present banks from the prospective, safe narrow bank. Since I perceive that as the essence of banking, the main question to be answered is not what a prospective narrow bank might look like (a dull simulacrum of our old TSB), but rather how the (broader) loan intermediary would operate, without it is presumed any explicit or implicit deposit insurance. Properly designed narrow banks might be able to dispense with some, perhaps all, of the services of a Central Bank, probably depending on how the systemic risk in the operation of the payments' system was handled, but how would the residual, broad loan intermediary, in which all the credit and contagion risks would then be concentrated, manage without a Central Bank?

2.2   INTEREST BEARING MONEY

The standard macro-economic model involves two financial assets, non-interest bearing money and interest-bearing non-monetary assets. Thus, in Begg *et al.*

(1991, p. 423) we read that, 'People can hold their wealth in various forms – money, bills, bonds, equities and property. For simplicity we assume that there are only two assets: money, the medium of exchange that pays no interest, and bonds, which we use to stand for all other interest-bearing assets that are not directly a means of payment'. Given that initial taxonomy, we can then ask why people demand non-interest-bearing monetary assets when interest bearing assets are available as partial substitutes, how changes in the supply of money may affect the rate of interest on non-monetary financial assets, and, following Wallace (1983, also 1988), why bank intermediaries cannot arbitrage between the zero nominal rate of interest on money and the positive rate on riskless interest-bearing non-monetary financial assets.

My initial purpose is rather different, which is to query either the necessity, or the theoretical advantage, of basing monetary analysis on the assumption of money being non-interest-bearing. It is a matter of fact that all categories of bank deposit (checkable sight/demand deposits as well as time deposits) can in most countries, and now usually do, offer interest payments. By the same token commercial bank reserves in the form of deposits at the Central Bank could receive interest (see for example Galbraith and Rymes, 1992), and do so in some cases, as in the case for example of the Banca d'Italia and the Banco de España. In those cases where no such interest is paid by the Central Bank, or where the interest paid is below competitive market rates, the differential is now treated and analysed as a specific tax.

It is, of course, normally the case that the interest rate offered on sight deposits is well below the money market rate for overnight money. In part this is because banks generally cross-subsidise those who use the payments system (more than average) by not charging for the large real costs of making such payments, and instead recouping such costs by offering below market rates on (sight) deposits, and the current tax system further encourages such cross-subsidisation.[3] Nevertheless all deposits can in principle be interest bearing, and actually now mostly are so in practice. This means that the description of money as a non-interest-bearing asset is only applicable to a sub-set of monetary assets, notably currency. It is most certainly true that the notes in your wallet are non-interest bearing. But this is not technically inevitable.[4] Indeed there have been sporadic occasions in a number of countries, notably Sweden and the USA, when interest-bearing currency notes, usually with tear-off coupons, have circulated (see, for example, White, 1984a; Jonung, 1985 and Goodhart, 1988. Currently it would be quite feasible to implant some intelligent chip into (at least large value) notes, so that the nominal value of the note increases at some rate of interest, and if the chip could receive messages from outside that rate could be time varying (see White, 1987).

But both these options have flaws. The effective rate of interest on holding a coupon-bearing note will vary with the time till the coupon payment can be demanded. The implanted chip would lead to notes whose value would not be in round numbers, but expressed in terms of the smallest available monetary unit, e.g. the cent or penny, and continuously changing. Except, perhaps, for very large value notes, which are rarely wanted by persons because of the danger of loss or theft, the extra interest payment on a normal note, which would be tiny given the standard holding period, would not offset the additional transactions costs (of having to handle notes with non-round numbers). This point was nicely made by White (1987), who noted that 'a 20 dollar note held for one week at 5 percent interest would yield less than 2 cents'.

There is, however, a simple way around this problem, which was independently advocated by McCulloch (1986) and Goodhart (1986). It is not strictly necessary to offer everyone an actual, common rate of interest on each note, so long as one can equate the *expected* rate of interest on note holding to the appropriate external market rate. This can be done perfectly easily. Each note has a serial number, which, pace forgery, should be unique. The numbers on notes issued, and then subsequently cancelled, can be recorded, using optical scanners and computers at low cost. Thus the serial numbers of all outstanding notes should be ascertainable. Given the oustanding value of each currency denomination, it would be simplicity itself to work out the requisite total lottery pay-out in order ·to provide the appropriate expected rate of interest to note holders. This then would square the circle of minimising information and transactions costs by maintaining the general 'ability to calculate appropriate exchanges of currency of goods' (Fama, 1983, p. 14), while at the same time offering a competitive expected return on currency. In order to avoid any bias to the most transaction efficient distribution of note holdings by denomination, there should be a separate lottery for each denomination, e.g. 5 pounds, 10, 20, etc. This would still leave subsidiary coinage as non-interest bearing, but anyone wishing to base monetary theory on such de minimis coins is welcome to his predilections.

One could, therefore, combine a national lottery with the payment of interest on notes. Given that many people seem to appreciate opportunities to engage in gambles with positive skew (i.e. a tiny chance of a huge gain balanced by a huge probability of a tiny loss), this could make note holdings considerably more popular than now.

It would not be necessary for the Central Banks, the official note issuers, to initiate such a scheme. It could be done by private issuers of travellers cheques, which similarly have inscribed serial numbers. Indeed I once suggested just such a step to Richard O'Brien of American Express. As you already know, no private sector producer of travellers cheques has taken up this opportunity. This is not, I am sure, because it is technically infeasible. Rather it is, I believe, because the potential private sector issuers fear that, once they had met the set-up costs and were ready to roll, the respective governments would legislate to prevent this innovation from occurring. The legal restrictions here (see Wallace, 1983 and Galbraith and Rymes, 1992), may be implicit, but would appear to be no less effective for that.[5]

Governments would do so because the regular flow of seigniorage income, in the guise of the transfer of Central Bank seigniorage income to the Treasury, is a nice little fiscal earner: the Treasury would not like to see such seigniorage, the monopoly profits on note issue, competed away by the private sector. In this sense the continued non-interest-bearing condition of currency is a fiscal decision, a semi-conscious tax measure, and in no way represents a necessary, nor a competitive, equilibrium condition. While it is the case that this fiscal decision is the norm across all countries (indeed in some countries seigniorage represents a significant proportion of tax revenues, see Cukierman *et al.* 1992), it is *not* a necessary equilibrium condition.

It may well be the case that the fiscal decision, to impose (an implicit) tax by paying zero interest on Central Bank money, is correct on welfare and efficiency grounds. Currency provides an anonymous means of payment, which is therefore the preferred medium of exchange in the black economy. Such a seigniorage tax may be almost the only way to obtain some small fiscal revenue from illegal activities. It is not the purpose of this paper to argue that the fiscal decision to offer zero interest on Central Bank money is mistaken. Rather my purpose is to note that in theory the decision could go the other way, and to explore the implications of that alternative. It is my contention that it would be worthwhile, and interesting, to examine what theoretical and practical changes would follow, if the practicable alternative of paying an (expected) rate of interest of currency was to be adopted.

Let us, therefore, make, for the purposes of analytical exploration, the assumption that Central Banks abandon their present fiscally-driven decision to pay no interest on currency. Money, i.e. currency, is no longer non-interest-bearing. What then happens?

Besides the desire to protect their seigniorage earnings, another reason for the authorities to be concerned about competition from commercial banks in note issue, so long as the Central Bank's own legal tender notes have a zero nominal interest rate, is that such competition might tend to drive the nominal interest rate (on riskless government debt) down towards zero also. This might occur, as Wallace (1983) pointed out, as the banks arbitrage between the zero yield on notes and the positive yield on debt (also see Kareken, 1981 and Jao 1984; but see White, 1987, for counter-arguments). The expected result might then be feared to be hyperinflation and monetary instability. Once, however, *all* notes, *including* those of the Central Bank, bear a market rate of interest, such a result need not occur.

Consequently there would then seem no powerful macro-policy case for the Central Bank to prevent competition in note issue from commercial banks for this reason. One comment (which I owe to Joseph Yam) was that if competitive issue of interest-bearing notes was to be done by my preferred lottery route, there could then be an undesirable multiplicity of lotteries with some reduction in productivity as people spend time checking note serial numbers and discovering lottery results. My solution would be to synchronise lottery draws overnight with the results available for the morning Press and Radio.

Of course, if the Central Bank were to be still the sole issuer of (such interest-bearing) notes, and commercial banks held such notes and deposits at the Central Bank as their cash reserves, then the authorities' control over short-term interest rates would be even more immediate than at present. Rather than vary the quantity of zero-yielding base, they would simply make a direct adjustment to the time varying expected rate of return on Central Bank money. So we must ask whether competition from commercial banks in (interest-bearing) note issue would complicate the authorities' ability to control the general level of short-term interest rates, under conditions where commercial banks still promise ultimate convertibility of their notes and coins into the legal tender notes of the Central Bank.

So long as that convertibility condition was supported by some constraint on the limit to which the commercial banks could hold a net debt position against the Central Bank, or by a sufficient penalty rate of such an excess net debt position, then the Central Bank retains control over interest rates, despite note competition.[6] In these circumstances commercial bank notes and deposits will not be *perfect* substitutes for Central Bank notes and deposits, since commercial banks can use such Central Bank liabilities, but not, in aggregate, the liabilities of other commercial banks, to limit the probability of being forced up against an (expensive) reserve constraint at the Central Bank. Moreover, claims on other commercial banks involve some default risk. Commercial banks, and possibly other agents, will prefer to hold net claims on the Central Bank, than on other commercial banks.

By raising the interest rate that it offers on notes and deposits, the Central Bank can enforce a net credit position against the commercial banks at the clearing. So long as the commercial banks cannot go indefinitely into debt against the Central Bank (or it is too expensive for them to do so), they cannot allow such a deficit at the clearing to continue, and so must raise rates to match that posted by the Central Bank. Similarly, since their notes are legal tender, but no other bank's notes are, the Central Bank can always expand its book by buying assets, even when commercial banks' notes and deposits are offering more. The Central Bank can, therefore, always flood the system with liquidity to enforce a reduction in interest rates.

Given much greater substitution, though not, as noted, perfect substitution, between Central Bank and commercial bank money, the money multiplier might be considerably more volatile. Nevertheless, the combination of required convertibility, plus a limitation (or penalty rate) on commercial bank debt positions with the Central Bank, should suffice to retain control over short-term nominal interest rates. So long as such interest rates are varied in order to maintain the stability of the price level, or of nominal incomes, thus providing a nominal anchor (see for example McCallum, 1981, 1986; Barro, 1989; Fuhrer and Moore, 1992), then the price level will be determinate.

This conclusion differs from the price level indeterminacy results of Sargent and Wallace (1985) for two main reasons. First, while commercial bank note liabilities would become much closer substitutes for Central Bank liabilities than heretofore, in the assumed conditions that Central Bank notes were 'legal tender' and commercial bank notes were not, and that commercial banks would need, or be required, to maintain convertibility, such substitution would not be perfect. Second, Sargent and Wallace explicitly assume an exogenously fixed monetary base, whereas I assume that the Central Bank uses the fulcrum of the, possibly volatile but non-vanishing demand for its own liabilities to maintain an interest rate structure of its own choosing.

Such a system, with competitive interest-bearing currencies, would offer a number of advantages. The demand for liquidity would be (almost) satiated, and there would be no-one to question on theoretical grounds the optimality of a zero rate of inflation. Shifts in the demand for currency could be more easily met (see, for example, Selgin, 1988). Competition would extend further in the monetary field, and the present somewhat artificial distinction between the bearer liabilities of banks (i.e. bank notes) – currently under strict Central Bank monopoly control – and their inscribed liabilities (i.e. bank deposits), competitively provided, would terminate. We make no serious distinction between bearer and inscribed bonds. Why should there be such a distinction for bank liabilities? Competition in the provision of interest-bearing currency would end this artificial distinction in the banking field. It would eliminate present distortions in the distribution of money holdings between currency and deposits. Meanwhile, the ability of the Central Bank to control the general level of short-term interest rates, and hence (assuming appropriate policy decisions), the stability of the nominal price level would remain.

Critics of Central Banks' performance might contend that they have manifestly failed to use their powers to control short-term interest rates in such a way as to provide price stability in recent decades. It may be that this failure arose from incorrect analysis (i.e. seeking to achieve a trade-off on a supposedly downwards sloping Phillips curve), or a poor incentive structure, or political interference (driven by time inconsistency). Such shortcomings may be rectified by requiring the Central Bank to give overriding priority to the achievement of price stability, and independence to take whatever decision and actions are needed to achieve that end.

Be that as it may, there are a number of alternative candidates for providing the monetary base, into which competitive bank notes and deposits could be made convertible (see, for example, White 1989, and also the seminal papers by Hayek, 1976, 1984). Possibly the simplest such alternative would take the form of a single object of value, such as gold.[7] We might then ask whether, and how, a switch from non-interest-bearing to interest-bearing competitive currency issue might affect the working of a gold standard. One effect would be to reduce the substitution between bank notes and gold as currency, since the former, being interest bearing, would be preferred unless there was some real possibility of bank insolvency. This might seem to allow the banking system to construct an enormous super-structure of notes and deposits on a very small gold base: McCulloch (1986) claimed this as an advantage for the scheme in that it would reduce the resource cost of returning to a gold standard. So long, however, as other banks (domestic and foreign) or the government, strictly limited (or imposed a penalty rate on) the extent to which any bank could run a net debt position with themselves (with all debts beyond that limit having to be met by gold flows), there would remain a significant bank demand for gold, and the market rate of interest would respond to fluctuations in the availability of that base.

Indeed, the need to pay a competitive rate of interest on notes (by making the lottery prizes sufficiently attractive) could act as an enhanced market discipline on commercial banks, making them, perhaps, less likely to engage in undue asset expansion, than might have been the case in the early years of the Gold Standard before the consolidation of the bank note issue with the Central Bank. Critics of the system then, prior to the 1844 Bank Charter Act, pointed to the unbridled note issue of the country banks in the UK as perhaps the main deficiency of the system at that time, though the validity of this criticism remains a debatable issue. For a recent discussion of this subject, see Mourmouras and Russell (1992). The need to pay a competitive rate on note issue could serve to act as a constraint on over-issue. To that extent the payment of competitive interest rates on notes might serve to make a commodity standard, such as the Gold Standard, work rather better, and remove one of the causes that led to the establishment of Central Banks.

Nevertheless, other reasons for the evolution of a Central Bank remain. With gold being non-interest-bearing, there could be incentives for smaller, peripheral banks to keep their reserves in the form of interest-bearing claims on a larger central bank, leading to a concentration of gold, the responsibility for the maintenance of convertibility, and for decisions of whether to lend to peripheral banks in the hands of the Central Bank. Again asymmetric information prevents most small creditors of banks from knowing whether high interest rates (on notes as well as deposits) reflect greater efficiency or greater risk. Whether such tendencies would lead to a natural evolution towards a Central Bank, or whether the appropriate supervisory and Lender of Last Resort powers could be satisfactorily handled by a clearance house or oligopoly of large banks remains contentious (Selgin and White, 1987; Goodhart, 1988; Dowd, 1993).

2.3   ALTERNATIVE BANK STRUCTURES

These latter arguments for the establishment of some central body for the banking system, to supervise and to act as a Lender of Last Resort, depend in large part on the possibility of bank insolvency and failure, both in regards to systematic risk and externalities, and to client protection in the face of asymmetric information. One response to this is to try to restructure the banking system so that bank insolvency becomes virtually impossible, either for the commercial bank as a whole or for a subset of protected deposits. Since the risk of insolvency, other than from fraud, primarily arises from the uncertain and varying value of some classes of bank assets, this generally leads on to a proposal to restrict the assets that the bank can hold against its protected deposits. Such assets should have a readily ascertainable market value, and in some of these proposals should also be nearly capital certain.

In cases where assets have a known market value, but are not capital certain, insolvency and failure can still be ruled out by requiring the value of the deposit to vary pro rata with the value of the asset portfolio. This would transfer a traditional bank into a mutual fund with simultaneous payment facilities (for earlier seminal contributions, see Black, 1970 and Fama, 1980, 1983). With failure prevented by definition, there would be no reason for continuing concern with the possibility of contagious runs, or systemic externalities. There would, however, be some continuing need for credit-rating type agencies to assess and warn on the riskiness of individual fund portfolios.

Although there are examples of financial intermediaries handling (high net worth) client funds in the manner of a mutual fund bank, the idea has not caught on yet to any great extent. One reason why this is so, is that bank clients may prefer their assets to possess nominal certainty, so they know what potential outward cash flows they can meet without difficulty. Of course such nominal certainty does not provide certainty of real balance levels, but in the short run nominal bank deposits will have approximate real certainty. On the other hand, few depositors either keep an accurate running tally of their bank balances, or know exactly what their effective overdraft limit may be, so there will always be some residual uncertainty over the size of future payments that could be sustained from existing balances.

Be that as it may, an equity based, mutual fund bank would involve potentially large swings in the nominal value of deposits, so long as the numeraire remained as at present, in the guise of Central Bank legal tender currency. Given, however, the possibility of issuing interest-bearing competitive commercial bank currencies, one might envisage also making the value of the currency into a unit which represented the value of, was a claim on, a basket of top equities, the FTSE 100 or S & P 500 (see also Fama, 1983). In this case a passive fund, with payment provisions, would become nominally certain. Those financial intermediaries, whose portfolios did not replicate the chosen equity bundle, would, of course, still be issuing deposits whose value could vary in value against the equity basket.

The average price level in the case of an equity-basket numeraire would reflect shifts in the relative valuation of goods and services on the one hand and equities on the other. The events of 19 October 1987 would, in these circumstances, metamorphose into a sudden once-for-all upwards leap in the average price level. With equities generally incorporating capital gains under our existing monetary system, the analogue under an equity basket numeraire would be a tendency for a steady fall in average goods and services prices. On the other hand, in so far as the dividend process augments the equity currency base, this is equivalent to a rise in the money stock, and would lead to a general rise in the price of goods; I am indebted to Norbert Schnadt for this thought. An anchor for the stability of the system as a whole could be provided by the expected stationarity of the real return on equities.[8]

Even though the numeraire would itself be a claim to a basket of equities, there would still be a distinction between bonds (senior creditors) and equity (junior, residual creditors). Bond holders would be guaranteed either a return fixed in terms of the numeraire, or, if the promised return was not forthcoming, the right to seize the assets of the company via bankruptcy proceedings, while equity holders would receive the residual. This would have the implication that there would be little distinction between a mutual fund bank that was backed by a passive fund and one that was backed by bonds, since both would offer a relatively safe return in terms of the equity numeraire. In the case of the bond the interest rate would, however, be fixed, whereas the dividend process varies over time, and the returns of the two alternatives would also differ in the event of company bankruptcies. Nevertheless, given the close equivalence between the outcomes from these two strategies, it would become extremely difficult under such circumstances to provide any justification for a continuing fiscal discrimination between the tax treatment of bonds and equities. Indeed one of my colleagues with whom I exchange thoughts on these issues, Gordon Getty, in private correspondence and papers going back for some years, argues that it is the preferential tax treatment of debt that is largely responsible for the continuation of the present system of debt based, rather than equity based, banking, see, in particular Getty (1991, 1992).[9]

There remain, however, two major problems with proposals of this genre. First, equity values are so volatile, certainly in the short run, so that with the present numeraire, equity-based deposits would have sharply fluctuating nominal values; or, with an equity-linked numeraire, the average price level would reflect such severe volatility. Either way, to move our monetary and banking system onto an equity basis would seem to build asset-market volatility into the heart of that system (as pointed out by White, 1984 in a criticism of such ideas). Perhaps as Getty, in private correspondence, and Klein

(1974) suggest, the best approach would be to let such bank-mutual funds compete in trying to find the porfolios, of bonds, equities and other assets, which provide the most attractive combination of risk and return, though that still leaves open the question of what should serve as the numeraire.

The second question is what would happen to the financing needs of the smaller companies and individuals who cannot easily access the equity market. If the numeraire remained as at present, but banks moved onto an equity basis for their assets, such borrowers would have to look elsewhere. This, however, is a common problem, as we shall soon see, with most such narrow bank proposals. If the numeraire moved onto an equity-basket basis, then a fixed interest loan in terms of such a numeraire would imply a promise to provide a return related to equity outcomes in general. This would have the advantage that variations in the real rate of return, in terms of goods and services, would depend in some large part on fluctutations in general profitability. Thus 'interest' payments, in terms of command over goods and services, would rise in the equity-based system when equity prices were relatively high in real terms (i.e. goods prices had fallen relative to equity prices); under the present system the reverse is often the case; when real rates of interest are high, asset prices tend to be low. This is one of the main causes of financial fragility in our present system. Accordingly the real rate of interest faced by the majority of borrowers under the equity-based system would tend to be much more stable relative to their ability to pay (and much more so than the present system), although lenders would suffer from fluctuations in the price of goods relative to the equity basket.

Apart from the volatility that an equity-basked numeraire would impart to the general price level of goods and services, such a structural change would have much to recommend it. But it is admittedly a futuristic concept. Most other proposals for ensuring the safety of banks, or of some sub-set of bank depositors, assume the continuation of the present system, based on Central Bank currency remaining a zero-yielding monopoly note issue. The proposals differ in the degree of capital certainty that they require for the assets that are to provide the backing, or collateral see Pollock (1991),[10] for the protected set of assets. The more capital certain the assets, the less bank capital is needed as a buffer. Some of the more extreme of these proposals, e.g. with 100 per cent reserve banking, as once proposed by both Friedman (1959) and Tobin (1985), require virtually no bank capital at all. In the case of those proposals allowing banks to invest in marketable, but less capital certain, assets, such as bonds, commercial paper, etc. the bank is required to hold capital, with provisions for the prompt closure of such banks when its capital falls below some low, but still positive level.

These schemes generally preclude such 'safe' or 'narrow' banks from holding assets which do not have a readily ascertainable market value. Consequently a large proportion of the present asset portfolios of banks would have to be financed by another financial intermediary, separate from the 'narrow' bank.

A great deal of thought has gone into conceptualising how the 'narrow' bank might be organised (see Litan, 1987, and Benston *et al.*, 1989); much less has been applied to an analysis of the residual financial intermediary taking over the non-marketed, and without collateral probably non-marketable, loans to individuals and small to medium companies.

First, would such 'risky' banks be able to offer any payments' services on their deposits? If they were so allowed, then safe banks would often be in a net creditor position *vis-à-vis* risky banks at the clearing. Such interbank daylight loans would represent, by definition, a risky asset. Hence it might be necessary to confine the payments system to the network of 'narrow banks', or at least, require the 'risky' banks to pledge considerable collateral funds in order to participate. But this might reduce competition and innovation in the provision of payments' services.

Second, what interest rate, and/or percentage capital backing, would be required to make lenders prepared to place uninsured time deposits with 'risky' banks. All the risks of contagious failure would be concentrated in these banks. In the late nineteenth century in the USA, prior to the establishment of the Fed, FDIC, etc., many banks had capital ratios of the order of 20 per cent, or more (Kaufman, 1992). That might suggest that the spread, above the time deposit rate, would have to be about 1–1½ per cent greater (than now) to encourage the application of capital to such 'risky' banks. In so far as 'risky' banks wished, or were required by prudential regulation, to hold more of their liabilities in longer-dated time deposits, or bonds, in order to lessen their maturity mismatch, this would tend to raise their funding costs, and hence their lending rates, yet further.

Given that depositors always had the alternative of holding safe short-dated Government debt, such as Treasury Bills, so that banks had to pay a competitive rate for deposits, much of the benefit accruing to banks from explicit/implicit insurance, and hence lower capital ratios, may have been passed on in the form of more competition for, and hence lower spreads on, bank loans. As Kane (1992, p. 362) notes, also see Benston *et al.* (1986), 'the public benefits of guarantee programmes are typically conceived as interest rate reductions for targeted parties'. If so, though this conjecture requires empirical study, one effect of splitting the banking system into 'narrow' and 'risky' banks would be to worsen the terms on which small and medium borrowers could obtain external finance. In view of the other handicaps which these borrowers face, e.g. owing to economies of scale, this adverse shift in their borrowing costs could be regarded as undesirable, as also noted by Vives (1991). Let me be explicit. My argument is that much of the benefit from the putative underpricing of deposit guarantees by the authorities, in one form or another, may have gone largely to reduce loan charges to small and medium borrowers. Before changing the present system, we need to decide whether we can accept the likely consequences, of higher lending rates to such borrowers. There will, nevertheless, be an equilibrium set of relative interest rates that will induce an appropriate division of lenders at any time between 'narrow' and 'risky' banks. My third concern is that this differential will fluctuate over time, associated with a possibly destabilising shift of funds between the two sets of banks. Under normal circumstances yields must be higher, on both deposits and capital, in the 'risky' banks. When times are good, and fears of insolvency fade, there will be a tendency for funds to be transferred to the 'risky' banks, reducing the differential between the return on the safe assets held by the 'narrow' banks and the return on loans of the 'risky' banks. This transfer of additional funds to the 'risky' banks will lead them to expand additional loans more aggressively.

In fact the 'narrow' bank concept is not new. It was present at the very historical outset of banking. Even then, the higher return on loans, during good times, led to pressures to switch funds into riskier activities. Thus the Swedish Riksbank, founded by Palmstruch as a private bank in 1656, re-organised under the authority of Parliament in 1664, was organised on the basis of two supposedly separate departments, the loan department financing loans on the basis of deposits, and the issue department supplying credit notes on the receipt of coin and specie. Even when Palmstruch's private bank had been taken over by Parliament, 'A secret instruction, however, authorized the advance by the exchange department to the lending department of the funds at its disposal though on reasonably moderate terms' [Flux, 1911, p. 17]. Thus, as early as 1668, the pursuit of a 100 per cent reserve ratio collapsed in the face of commercial pressures.

But the effects of the split between 'narrow' and 'risky' banks would be even worse during periods of downturn and potential panic. The difficulties, loss provisions and possible failure of the 'risky' banks will lead depositors to switch funds back towards the 'narrow' banks. Under the present system, adverse economic conditions frequently lead commercial banks to be much more cautious about making *new* loans, but they very rarely call *existing* loans. If trouble causes a haemorrhage of funds out of 'risky' banks towards the safe haven of 'narrow' banks, the 'risky' banks, with a high proportion of loans on their books, may be forced to call existing loans.

Such shifts of funds between safe and 'risky' banks, and the danger of runs on 'risky' banks, would be mitigated, but not removed, by a likely shift in the liability structure of the 'risky' banks towards longer-dated time deposits, or bonds. The initial loss of funds in many recent bank runs has come from a difficulty in rolling over maturing, wholesale, CDs rather than from withdrawals of demand deposits. Again, as perceived riskiness increases, the incentive for lenders is to *reduce* the maturity of their funding (as banks did with LDCs), in order to facilitate possible withdrawal, and perhaps to assist with monitoring. So, as earlier noted, 'risky' banks might have to offer considerably higher rates to persuade lenders to provide longer-term fixed funds. Because 'risky' bank assets would not, in general, have an immediately ascertainable and exercisable market value, the various mechanisms for protecting claimants on pension funds and insurance companies from losses in bankruptcy, (e.g. requiring companies with 'defined benefit' pension funds to top these up), would be much more difficult or impossible to put in place. It is, therefore, perilous to seek to draw an analogy between 'risky' banks and these other specialised long-term financial intermediaries, i.e. pension funds.

Thus the division of the banking system into two parts, safe and 'risky', is likely in my view to enhance the variability both of the availability of credit, and the risk differential between safe and risky assets. This could exacerbate the extent of the cycle. Admittedly this judgement does depend on lenders having a tendency to overestimate the permanence of current circumstances, i.e. good times in a boom and continuing problems in a slump, but the shortness of life and the associated decay of memory makes this syndrome probable.

It is, of course, true that properly designed narrow banks need no support from a Central Bank Lender of Last Resort. Per contra, could a community comfortably stand a contagious collapse of its 'risky' banks? The narrow money supply might continue to grow at a steady, or even increased, rate, but how would the economy fare if credit to smaller and medium borrowers became extremely expensive, or non-attainable, or at worst had to be repaid? Would there not then still be a vital role for the Central Bank to maintain the systemic stability and health of the 'risky' bank group?

I am disturbed by reports that this concept of splitting the banking system into the separate components of 'narrow' and 'risky' banks is gaining adherents in the USA. While there is no harm in allowing bankers to establish narrow-type banks on their own volition, if they so wish – though note that few have done so, though there are no legal prohibitions[11] – the legally enforced separation of the system into two parts in this manner would seem to be a bad idea, and one likely to enhance rather than to dampen cyclical fluctuations.

2.4 CONCLUSIONS

I have concentrated in this paper on two main features of our system of money and banking. The first of these was the non-payment of interest on currency. Whereas this characteristic plays a fundamental role in much of our monetary theory, in terms of the determination of interest rates, the optimal rate of inflation and the monopolistic provision of cash by the Central Bank, I claim that this feature is not technically essential, and derives rather from a fiscal choice than from any inherent monetary condition. Consequently I have sought to explore, in a mental experiment, which aspects of theory would change if all monetary assets, except token coin, were interest bearing. In particular, the prohibition of competitive note issues by commercial banks could be lifted. Central banks could continue to control the short-term rate of interest, in such a competitive note-issuing system, with a more limited set of requirements essential for this purpose.

Central Banks are currently being given strict marching orders to use their power to control interest rates for the purpose of achieving price stability. There are those who are sceptical, largely in the light of Central Banks' chequered prior history, whether any managed system of monetary control would be satisfactory. So I have sought to explore, again primarily within the context of a system of competitive interest-bearing note issues, how the adoption of some differing numeraires would work, notably gold and an equity based system.

The need for a Central Bank does not derive solely, perhaps not even primarily, from its macro-level control over the monetary base, interest rates and prices. An inherent micro-level problem for the banking system, arising primarily from uncertainty and information asymmetry, is that the current market value of much of a bank's assets cannot be known.[12] This leads to the possibility of bad run equilibria. Central Banks play a micro-level role in preventing systemic failure. Again there are those who doubt whether the authorities either can, or do, play this role satisfactorily, in part because their role in providing implicit insurance can cause moral hazard. Consequently there has been considerable interest in schemes which limit the assets which can be held by banks as backing, or collateral, against some sub-set of bank deposit liabilities, notably those which are used in the payments' mechanism. In the final part of this paper, I have, however, argued that, rather than enhance the stability of the banking system, such a split into a narrow (or safe) part on the one hand and a 'risky' part on the other might lead to large-scale flows of funds between the two parts, as confidence shifted, and thereby actually worsen instability in the provision of credit. My conclusion, here, is that the 'narrow bank' idea is unsound.

NOTES

1. Some of the earlier theoretical studies on banking, such as those Fischer Black (1970) and Fama (1980, 1983), tended to overlook the asymmetric information problems that make valuation of a traditional bank's portfolio so intractable an exercise.

2. It is the absence of expertise in such credit analysis that provides a major barrier to the development of proper Western banking in Eastern Europe and the former Soviet Union.

3. The general public simply has no idea of the true costs of processing a cheque through the banking system, which may amount to about £1 per cheque. Indeed, the public seems to believe that it has a right to make payments without charge. In part, perhaps, because it has also been conditioned by economists to regard money as normally non-interest-bearing, such cross-subsidisation remains

more popular than the alternative of making appropriate service charges for payments whilst offering a more market-related interest rate on deposits. Such cross-subsidisation does, however, cause real distortions and costs. Payments systems which use less real resources, such as electronically operated debit cards, become harder to introduce, since the public, whose payments are already subsidised, can see little, or no, benefit in them, and indeed suffers the loss of the float during the period of cheque clearing.

It is extremely difficult to get any data on *costs*, partly because accurate costings may be hard to estimate, e.g. what is the appropriate share of overheads, and partly because the matter will be commercially sensitive. There are, however, some data on *charges*, though, as noted in the main text these are, probably, an underestimate of true charges.

The Committee of London and Scottish Bankers published a table (6.51, p. 56) in 1988 showing charges for cheques, when the account fell below the minimum for free banking. These charges ranged between 25p and 36p for all banks, except Girobank (85p), but needs to be approximately doubled to account for charges both on drawing *and* paying in.

A more recent article in the Financial Times (26 May 1992) by Jane Fuller on bank charges, 'Paying more than a pony', has NatWest making a charge, to small businesses, of 64p 'for every payment into or out of the account', Lloyds being 'the most expensive at 75p per credit or debit entry', Barclays charging 26p per cheque paid in, and 'a 30p charge to the customer writing a cheque for less than 50 pounds'.

4. Hall (1986) (see also Hall, 1983) suggested that 'The best step would be to grant all financial institutions the right to issue interest-bearing notes in small denominations. A note with a constant face value of 100 dollars could earn interest for the holder, which would be credited to that person's Visa account. Each time a bank paid a depositor with a note, it would record the fact electronically with Visa so that interest could be credited to the current holder'.

But McCulloch (1986) noted that 'Hall's method would not encourage the depositor to hold the bill unless the serial number of each bill were also laboriously recorded and flagged when it was cashed. Nor would it give subsequent holders of the bill any incentive to hold the bill, since they would not be receiving the interest on it.' Also the administrative and bureaucratic costs of Hall's scheme might be high.

5. Given that a government, or Central Bank, may seek to prohibit the payment of interest on currency, or currency substitutes such as travellers cheques, within its own boundaries, one question that still remains is whether a bank could issue interest-bearing notes, e.g. with accompanying lottery prizes, denominated, say, in US dollar's, but issued in other countries, e.g. Latin America or East European countries. If the bank involved had no physical presence in the USA, how could the Fed deter such a bank from competing part of its (external) seigniorage away? On the other hand, if such a bank had no physical presence in the USA, and no access to the Fed, would its 'implicit' promise to convert its own dollar notes into US legal tender currency at par carry sufficient credibility?

A somewhat similar suggestion, which I owe to Graham Bishop of Salomon Brothers, which would enable the banks involved to avoid direct competition with any *national* currency, would be for banks to issue private ECU notes, again possibly mainly, or entirely, outside the EC. Again these could offer lottery prizes.

6. Conditions in Hong Kong currently provide a reasonably close practical example. The note issue (non-interest-bearing) is provided by commercial banks (HSBC

and Standard) on a currency board basis (i.e they can issue more Hong Kong notes by paying over US dollars to the Exchange Fund). For various reasons note arbitrage (to take advantage of any discrepancy between the fixed HK $7.80 = 1 US dollars on note issue and the time varying market exchange rate) involves sufficient frictions to allow the market exchange rate to diverge somewhat from the linked rate.

In order, therefore, to support the exchange link, the monetary authorities in Hong Kong wished to be able to influence local interest rates. They could undertake open market operations to sell US dollars and buy HK dollars. Whereas in most other countries this would have reduced the monetary base (by reducing commercial bank deposits with the Central Bank), in Hong Kong the authorities, under the system prior to July 1988, had no practical alternative but to return the HK dollars which they had bought in the form of additional deposits to the Hong Kong commercial banks. There was, therefore, no limit to the extent that Hong Kong banks could go into debt to the Hong Kong monetary authorities: so their open market operations did note bite.

The solution to this problem was then found by requiring the main commercial bank (HSBC) to hold a minimum balance with the Exchange Fund, which could provide a fulcrum for the monetary authorities to enforce a net reduction in overall liquidity in the Hong Kong banking system through their operations. The practical details are somewhat more complicated than as set out here, and can be read in Freris (1991) and Yam (1991), but this gives the essence of the system.

Reverting from Hong Kong specifics, to the general case, also see Kneeshaw and Van den Bergh (1989); and the various Canadian papers, e.g. Bank of Canada (1991) and Longworth and Muller (1991) on operating monetary policy with zero reserve requirements.

There has been some general theoretical discussion on what the crucial features of a Central Bank depend, see for example Rymes (1989) and Galbraith and Rymes (1992). It has been argued that 'A central bank, constrained to pay competitive interest rates on reserves and to replicate other competitive conditions, is not a central bank' (Rymes, 1989, p. 372). My claim here is that a central bank can continue to control the level of short-term interest rates, and hence nominal conditions, while paying competitive interest rates on both its deposits *and* its notes. The essential conditions for such control are (1) commercial banks wish to maintain convertibility into some asset whose supply is effectively controlled by the central bank, (2) limitations on the ability/willingness of the commercial banks to obtain such assets by extending their debt position at the central bank, and (3) the central bank is non-profit-maximising.

7. One problem with a gold standard is that the price level will fluctuate depending on the accidents of shifts in the supply and the non-monetary demand for this single object of value. One proposed solution is to broaden the base to comprise a basket of goods, or even command over some standard length of labour time, as advocated by Thompson (1981, 1986) and Glasner (1989). Indeed, such a (basket) proposal formed the conclusion of a lead article in *The Economist* in February 1992. A problem with that is that bank creditors cannot easily enforce convertibility by swapping their notes or deposits for all the bits of the basket, even less so for some notional labour time. This problem was supposed to be answered by the adoption of indirect convertibility, whereby the bank creditor would exchange her notes for gold, but the amount of gold handed over would vary depending on fluctuations in the price of gold in terms of the underlying basket (see Greenfield and Yeager, 1989).

Schnadt and Whittaker (1993), however, claim that there is a flaw in such proposals for indirect convertibility. The difficulty is caused by the fact that instantaneous, continuous indirect convertibility will lead from time to time to a difference emerging between the *market* price of the base, say gold, used for such indirect convertibility and the price that the *bank* must set in order to keep its liabilities at par in terms of the basket of goods. (This assumes that the price of all the commodities and services in the basket can be continuously monitored). Consider a rise in the dollar price of one of the constituents of the basket. Then the bank has to lower its gold price (of its liabilities), i.e. the depositor gets more gold for its deposits, in order to maintain convertibility into the basket. But arbitrage will then drive the market price of gold down, which will cause a further fall in the bank's convertibility rate. Schnadt and Whittaker note that 'The bank would be able to continue practising indirect convertibility if and only if (a) there is a process by which the bank's changes in Rg_s [the bank's rate for selling gold to maintain convertibility of its liabilities against the basket] cause correction of the basket price P_{hs} back to unity, and (b) this process acts faster than the convergence of Pg_s [the market price of gold] on Rg_s'. For a further discussion, see Dowd (1992).

In fact there might be such a mechanism. The unlimited collapse (expansion) of the price of gold, envisaged in this story, would lead to an equivalent fluctuation in the effective availability of bank (gold) reserves, and hence to enormous fluctuations in interest rates, which would rapidly stabilise prices. But such huge volatility in interest rates and asset prices, which would similarly seem a necessary corollary of Black's (1987) proposal, would be a high price to pay for achieving greater stability in goods' prices. The point of Black's paper being that tiny changes in banks' gold reserves are accompanied with massive net open market sales; thus 'When the government buys a dollar's worth of gold, it must buy $1/\lambda - 1$ dollars' worth of bonds on the open market to keep the reserve ratio at λ. When it sells gold, it must sell bonds. When λ is near zero, the government buys and sells almost no gold. Stocks are met almost entirely through open market operations'. Indeed most schemes for monetary reform that promise robust and rapid price stabilisation (e.g. Hall, 1983, 1986) appear, on examination, implicitly to require huge fluctuations in interest rates to do the job. Is there a necessary trade-off in the economic system between the extent of stability in asset prices and in goods' prices, so that achieving absolute stability in one results in unacceptable instability in the other? Such a result occurs in the model by Fuhrer and Moore (1992) who note that, 'In the limit, as all of the weight in the reaction function is placed on asset prices, the real rate converges so rapidly that policy loses control of inflation' (Fuhrer and Moore, 1992, pp. 305–6).

Schnadt and Whittaker then argue that the instability of a process of indirect convertibility can be assuaged by making *periodic*, rather than continuous, adjustments to the gold price, as in Fisher's (1926) 'compensated dollar' scheme. A problem with this is that if the timing (and direction) of the price change is known in advance, then the return from holding the indirect asset (e.g. gold) rather than the bank liability, just in advance of the adjustment moves to + or − infinity. This would be so whether the Fisher plan or the Thompson/Glasner plan for periodic redemption was used (see Glasner, 1989, pp. 230–6). Accordingly the rule for adjustment must be of the form

$$\alpha Rg_s(t + i) = Rg_s(t)/Pb_s(t),$$
$$1 - \alpha Rg_s(t + i) = Rg_s(t),$$

where α is the probability of realigning at time $t + i$, if no previous realignment has occurred sine time t. So long as i is calibrated at a high frequency, say every ten minutes, then one can combine a probability of realignment at any point of time which will be approximately zero with a mean expectation of the realignment occurring, say, once a fortnight. This also has the advantage that the prices in the basket need only be monitored at a much lower frequency than used for the frequency of potential rebasing. Either way, as Schnadt and Whittaker state, 'this would not *precisely* maintain the desired currency value of the basket'. Indeed, their conclusion is that these problems arise fundamentally from 'the fact that indexing the value of the medium of account itself is impossible; it is impossible to index the dollar to the value of a basket of goods whose prices are expressed in dollars' (see also Yeager, 1983).

8. In a free banking system, without a Central Bank, there is a question of whether a unique banking equilibrium exists. Thus Galbraith and Rymes (1992) envisaging a system (with all bank liabilities and assets paying the same market rate and service charges imposed on turnover and close-of-day balances) organised around a Clearing House, argue that 'For the banking system as a whole we would observe a net increase in deposits and overdrafts without the net position in the House of either the individual representative bank or all the other banks taken together experiencing a net debit or credit position. Thus, the banking equilibrium is not unique in that if any individual bank contemplates an expansion or contraction of its loans, all other banks will behave in such a way that the total amount of loans and deposits in the banking system will expand or contract. Double all nominal values in the banking equilibrium, that is, all loans or overdrafts, all deposits, all the debits and credits, all service charges, all prices and nothing happens. No 'real' variable is affected. There is nothing to pin the nominal system down',

The analogous concern in the equity banking system, with an equity basket numeraire, would be that such banks, as a group, could expand their assets, thereby lowering the price level indefinitely (n.b. the value of goods would presumably be falling relative to the price of equities), without any check from a loss of an outside monetary reserve base. The hope, however, would be that the system would be stabilised by a belief in the stationarity of the real return on equities. If the price level fell too low (high) (i.e. equity prices rose (fell) too far in terms of goods), economic agents would want to get out of (buy) equities in exchange for goods. Agents, including banks, would want to contract (increase) their net credit position, and relative interest rates (or service charges) would adjust to facilitate that. The greater (less) the stationarity of the real return on equity, the more (less) stable would be an equity banking system.

9. The following quotes are taken from Getty (1992).

(1) Certain laws in the US and elsewhere tilt the debt-equity playing field toward debt. Thus borrowing is often artificially high. Money instability and the business cycle are both magnified by leverage, and a levelling of the playing field should help tame both. We can level it by repealing deposit insurance subsidies, bank regulation and the double tax while eliminating or counterbalancing home interest deductibility. I will speculate on the adjustments society might make to these reforms.

(2) Banks tend to be unstable not because they are mismanaged but because they are pathologically overleveraged. Their ratios of deposits to capital are often higher than ten to one, and in essence their depositors are their creditors. Such debt ratios, and the narrow spreads that go with them, leave too little room for bad guesses and bad luck. Mutual funds at the other extreme are typically unleveraged. They are for the most part diversified portfolios of

stocks or bonds, with expenses pretty much limited to portfolio management. In the absence of downright embezzlement, such a fund can hardly become worthless until every last issue it holds does. Therefore owners or 'unitholders' of such funds can expect maximum safety and a competitive market return as well. (3) Our four reforms need not mean the end of banks as we know them, but I assume it will mean a much smaller aggregate role for them. What then will people use for money? Most money today exists in the form of bank deposits. What will take their place? Certain economists have suggested that corporate securities might serve as money. Let's see how that could work. (4) We just saw that most money today is deposits, and that deposits are loans to the bank. Thus we live in an economy of what might be called debt money. Stocks and units in stock mutual funds are equities, and might be called equity money if stabilized and used to settle transactions. Now let us consider the ancient and vexing question 'what is money?' In the world we know, this pretty much boils down to the question 'what are debt instruments?' In a world of equity money, it rather boils down to the question 'what is equity?' I for one find the last question easier to answer. A stock is literally a share. For example a share of Exxon is a prorated ownership right in Exxon; it is Exxon divided by the number of shares outstanding. A bond on the other hand is typically a prior claim on earnings in the form of interest and repayment, plus a contingent claim on presumably distressed assets in the event of default. What then is its value? In the absence of default, it is the capitalized present value of a known future income stream of dollars or other currencies. Thus the definition of debt money such as a bank deposit is circular. It is a right to a growing bank deposit. We need not be surprised then that debt money is historically unstable. It is tied to nothing tangible except under default, and then to assets likely to be distressed.

10. Pollock (1991) has written:

Under a collateralized money system, all money deposits would be collateralized under a rule analogous to the SEC's rule 15c3–3 or that of the National Bank Act for bank notes, requiring maintenance at all times of assets with a market value of at least 100 per cent of the money liabilities. Every bank, while remaining one operating organization, would be understood and managed as what it in fact is, i.e. two functions: the Money Bank and the Credit Bank. These two functions do not need separate incorporation or separate organizations or complex holding company structures or bureaucratic agonizing over so-called 'firewalls'. They need collateral against money deposits of high quality marketable assets (plus deposits with the Federal Reserve and demand deposits due from other commercial banks). This needs daily measurement, and like 15c3–3, making managements responsible for immediate self-reporting of any shortfall. For clarity with the public it would be advisable for only these money liabilities to be called 'deposits'.

The rest of the bank should then be free to pursue any business its wholly at-risk creditors will finance. These other three-quarters of bank liabilities should be called what they are, namely investments, notes, debentures, commercial paper, bonds, participations, etc. They are not money. They are not riskless. They do not need nor should they have government guarantees or 'insurance'. The liabilities of the Credit Bank function need, like other investments offered to the public, appropriate disclosures of their nature and risks; they should be subject to SEC requirements. Some of them may need to be collateralized to make them saleable, just as some other investments do. Those bank employees who sell these to the public should have the same disciplines as other salesmen of investments.

The Credit Banks should then operate in markets freed from our current Gordian knot of price, product and geographic barriers to competition and without our current massive deposit insurance subsidies. However, given the inherent tendency of credit markets to periodic crisis, a Bagehotian lender of last resort to the market will continue to be necessary.

11. It is arguable that this has not happened in the USA because FDIC insurance has made virtually all bank deposits 'safe'. But it remains difficult to point to examples of successful 'narrow' banks being established in other countries, and at other times, when there were no such guarantees, or safeguards.

12. A colleague, L. Price, commented on an earlier draft of this paper that, 'the underlying problem is to reconcile the apparent preference of most economic agents to hold much of their wealth in capital-certain assets with the fact that the market valuation of the total wealth of the economy is susceptible to shocks and is quite volatile. Banks help solve this problem by holding a portfolio of non-marketable loans which is difficult to value. Swings in the underlying value of the portfolio are obscured by the lack of a market valuation so that the banks are able to offer more capital-certainty to their depositors than the portfolio may warrant. There are dangers in this, of course, for the day may arrive when a fall in the true value of the assets becomes too obvious to ignore. But until then depositors are happier with the apparent capital-certainty they are being given by the banks than they would be with possible alternatives such as mutual funds whose assets are continually marked to market.'

3 The Implications of Shifting Frontiers in Financial Markets for Monetary Control (1986)*

3.1 INTRODUCTION

The purpose of this paper is to try to weave the theoretical work of that emerging school of monetary economists who have espoused the 'Legal Restrictions' theory of the demand for money and monetary policy together with practical observations taken from the experience of the UK in recent years. Professor Neil Wallace, Professor of Economics at the University of Minnesota, coined this term, 'The Legal Restrictions Theory of Money', in a paper in the *Federal Reserve Bank of Minneapolis Quarterly Review* (1983). There had been forerunners of this approach in the literature much earlier, for example the article on 'Problems of Efficiency in Monetary Management' by Harry Johnson (1968), and in an extraordinarily prescient article by Fischer Black on 'Banking and Interest Rates in a World Without Money' (1970). More recently, this theoretical approach has been taken further by economists such as Fama (1980), Hall (1983), Kareken (1981), Sargent and Wallace (1982 and 1983), Wallace (1983), and other economists, with a centre in Minneapolis: the arguments and analysis of this developing school have been summarised and pooled together in a brilliant survey paper, 'A Libertarian Approach to Monetary Theory and Policy', by Jao (1984). This new school, which also has strong links with the 'new view' of money creation put forward by James Tobin (1963), ascribes both the particular characteristics of bank deposits, and also some special features of currency, together with the observed regularities between such money holdings and nominal incomes, to legal restrictions placed upon the banking system; they go on to suggest that such regularities will collapse as, and when, the restrictions are lifted, or eroded by innovation.

Let me provide some examples of their approach. First, Robert Hall, in his review of Friedman and Schwartz (1982), writes, 'The new monetary economics views the quantity theory as nothing more than an artifact of government regulation. An economy organised along free-market principles

* Chapter XX in D.E. Fair, *Shifting Frontiers in Financial Markets* (Kluwer Academic, 1986): 303–27.

could function without money at all (Fischer Black, 1970). It is true that the kinds of monetary regulations imposed by the American and British Governments of the past century create a more-or-less stable relation between a certain class of assets called money and nominal spending (Eugene Fama, 1980), but different regulations would alter that relation'.

Again, Jao (1983) writes, 'To sum up then, the libertarians' theoretical case against mainstream monetarism rests on the latter's uncritical acceptance of the various legal restrictions and regulations on money and finance. Without such restrictions and regulations, the distinctions between banks and other non-bank intermediaries would vanish, and the conceptual differences between various monetary aggregates would also become meaningless. With these foundations gone, the major components of the monetarist upper structure, such as a stable demand function for money, and a constant money growth rule, also fall to the ground' (p. 14). Later (p. 17), Jao writes, 'There is nothing unique about bank deposits. In an unregulated setting, competitive yields have to be offered on deposits; in principle, they can be issued by any other financial intermediary and acquired as portfolio assets by wealth-holders. Full competition will force banks to offer more portfolio management services, and non-bank intermediaries to offer more transactions services. The blurring of the distinction between banks and other intermediaries has already been mentioned. Thus, the term 'deposits' is now a rubric for all the different forms of wealth that have access to the accounting system of exchange provided by 'banks' defined in the widest sense'.

3.2   BANK DEPOSITS

In this section we will examine how far the erosion of legal, and conventional, restrictions on the banking system in the UK has already tended to disturb previous statistical regularities, and also ask whether that same process is still continuing. During the 1950s and 1960s, interest rates offered on bank deposits in the UK were, for the most part, determined in a conventional manner. Thus no interest was offered on sight deposits; the interest rate offered by the clearing banks on time deposits was related, by a cartel arrangement, to the administratively-determined Bank rate. Certain other non-clearing banks were offering more market-related interest rates on time deposits, but, although such banks were growing considerably more rapidly than the clearing banks, the proportion of time deposits held with them still represented a small proportion of total time deposits. Thus the own rate on sight deposits was fixed at zero, while the own rate on time deposits was relatively sticky, since it was conventionally related to an administratively-fixed Bank rate. The demand-for-money functions estimated around that time (see (Goodhart, 1970 and 1984) and the references in that paper to contemporary econometric work), indicated that both M1 and broader money, M3, were significantly related, inversely, to the level of competing interest rates. Own rates were rarely included in such equations: yet, despite that omission, the equations generally demonstrated stability.

Then in 1971, partly at the prompting of earlier academic and official studies, (Artis, 1968, National Board for Prices and Incomes, NBPI, 1967), the cartel was ended, with the intention of generating greater competition and efficiency, as one element of the package of reforms, described as 'Competition and Credit Control', introduced in 1971. The abolition of the cartel did, indeed, induce both the clearing and the non-clearing banks to compete much more strongly between, and among, themselves for deposits, by offering more market-related interest rates on a wider range of instruments, including Certificates of Deposits (CDs), following the practice and example of liability management developed by US banks during the preceding decade. It is difficult to be certain whether the previous stable relationship between the broad money aggregate (M3) and nominal incomes and interest rates broke down at that time because of the adoption of liability management, or for a range of other reasons. Nevertheless, following the adoption of such liability management, this relationship did collapse; in particular, with the banks now offering market-related interest rates on a wide range of wholesale deposits, the prior (inverse) relationship between the general level of interest rates in the economy and the growth of broad money totally disappeared (Hacche, 1974). Nevertheless, there did still seem to be a relationship between the growth of broad money and the *subsequent* development of nominal incomes, with broad money leading nominal incomes by about 8 quarters, or nearly two years. This relationship, shown in Figure 3.1, was, of course, particularly marked over the period 1972–75 but did appear to hold even outside that time period, up until the end of the 1970s (see Mills, 1982 and 1983b). One strand of thought ascribed this relationship to the effect of 'supply shocks' (e.g. resulting from surges in extending bank loans, notably following Competition and Credit Control; and/or as a consequence of large fiscal deficits), inducing temporary 'excessive' holdings of broad money, which subsequently, and more slowly, became absorbed into higher nominal incomes through additional expenditures. This 'buffer stock' analysis has been examined by Laidler (1983b), Goodhart (1984), Davidson (1984), Knoester (1979), and others. Whatever the cognitive attractions of the 'buffer stock' analysis may be, this latter 'lead' relationship between M3 pounds and subsequent nominal incomes also broke down comprehensively in the early 1980s, when a sharp rise in the growth rate of M3 pounds during 1980 and 1981 preceded quite rapid declines in the growth rate of nominal incomes over the two or three years, as can also be seen clearly in Figure 3.1. This latter experience is considered further below.

Meanwhile during the course of the 1970s the convention that interest would not be paid on sight deposits remained generally in force. Perhaps as a result, the demand-for-money function for M1 remained stable, with a signifi-

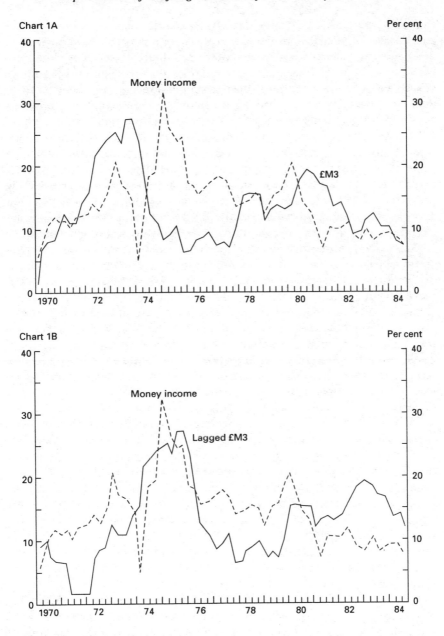

Figure 3.1   £M3 and money income (percentage changes on a year earlier –
seasonally adjusted)

cant and well-behaved interest elasticity (although the fit was never close and the predictive ability of the equation was rather weak). Nevertheless, in this area also competitive pressures, both from building societies, who have been increasingly offering transaction services on their interest-bearing deposits (and who have remained open on Saturdays for the convenience of their customers whereas the banks have (mostly) shut), and also competition from within the banking system itself, were inducing the banks to pay market-related interest rates first on wholesale sight deposits and more recently and increasingly on a wider range of available retail-type chequable sight deposits. The growth of such interest-bearing sight deposits has been remarkably fast over the last four years, and such deposits now represent an increasing proportion of total M1 (see Table 3.1). Under these circumstances what has remained surprising has been the relative *success* of the standard M1 demand-for-money equations in continuing to fit the path of M1, despite its growing share of interest-bearing deposits. Nevertheless we believe that an important structural change in the characteristics of retail-type sight deposits is in process, and we regularly expect the imminent break-down of the stability of its demand function – even though it has not yet happened.

As already mentioned, building societies in the UK are increasingly proving a range of transaction services for their depositors. Nevertheless, legal restrictions, notably on their ability to provide overdrafts, or even to lend on any security other than mortgages, have restricted their capacity to provide a full range of transactions and other financial services to their depositors. The Green Paper on building societies (1984) proposed to relax sufficient of these restrictions to make it prospectively possible for building societies to offer a wider range of financial services, including transaction services, notably via ATMs, to their personal depositors. Moreover, the transaction services that they already provide allow their depositors to choose among quite a wide range of alternative options of instruments with varying withdrawal facilities and interest rates. If the proposals in the Green Paper are promulgated as suggested, it will further blur the distinction between banks and building societies, at least for macroeconomic purposes. Together with the foreshadowed changes in the form and structure of the capital market, previous clear lines of distinction between separate types of financial intermediary are disappearing, as is also the distinction between transactions balances, e.g. M1, and saving balances.

Not only, therefore are these distinctions between financial intermediaries, and between chequable and non-chequable instruments becoming blurred, but also an increasing proportion of monetary assets, with the exception of currency, discussed further below, is bearing a market-related interest rate (though several of the facilities now being offered by the clearing banks which provide interest on chequable facilities do not incorporate any automatic adjustment of that interest rate in line with market variations). Under these circumstances, the choice of the asset-holder to shift between one asset

Table 3.1   Interest bearing sight deposits and M1 (£ million unadjusted)

		Interest-bearing sight deposits	M1	IB sight deposits as a percentage of M1
1980	1	4,332	28,979	14.95
	2	4,521	29,513	15.32
	3	4,263	29,567	14.42
	4	4,587	31,044	14.78
1981	1	4,678	31,441	14.88
	2	5,007	32,539	15.39
	3	5,516	33,090	16.67
	4	7,985	36,533	21.86
1982	1	8,279	36,341	22.78
	2	8,458	37,261	22.70
	3	8,659	38,205	22.66
	4	9,998	40,664	24.59
1983	1	10,320	41,723	24.73
	2	11,247	42,825	26.26
	3	11,186	43,269	25.85
	4	11,700	45,201	25.88
1984	1	13,309	46,835	28.42
	2	14,332	48,927	29.29
	3	15,544	50,394	30.84

and another depends on interest-rate *relativities*, where the relative own rate offered by each individual financial intermediary is *not* subject to the direct influence of the authorities, and cannot be easily made greater, or less, by the authorities seeking to influence the *general* level of interest rates, which latter they still remain capable of doing. Under such circumstances, and with the increasing financial sophistication of wealth holders, the elasticity of substitution, i.e. the speed and responsiveness of shifting between different assets in response to changing interest-rate relativities may well increase, but the authorities may equally find it increasingly difficult to exert much influence over such relativities. It is not moreover just the alternative interest rates on different *assets* that matters for the disposition of wealth holders' funds. The 'spread' between deposit and lending rates is at the same time a particularly important relativity, measuring, as it does the actual cost of financial intermediation.

When the cost of providing a service is relatively low, then one would expect that more use would be made of such services. A theoretical analysis demonstrating that additional use will be made of intermediation, with both bank lending and bank deposits increasing, when the cost of intermediation falls, has been provided by Sprenkle and Miller (1980). Effectively when the 'spread', or cost of intermediation is low, the cost of acquiring liquidity services, through borrowing, also declines to a point at which (large) wealth holders may find it desirable to increase borrowing for the purpose of adding to their wholly-owned deposit holdings. Various additional features, such as the tendency of banks to withdraw, or at least to query, overdraft facilities that remain unused, and fees on unused facilities, also serve to encourage large wealth holders to expand their borrowings and deposits simultaneously, as the spread narrows. The importance of the spread in this respect has been demonstrated by Johnston for the Euro-markets (1983), and, although there is no direct evidence domestically, it is also believed to have played some, possibly important, role in explaining the large-scale build up of both company sector advances and deposits by UK companies during the 1980s. Thus, the cost of intermediation to large borrowers, such as sovereign countries and large companies, has probably already fallen to a point at which the choice of whether to obtain funds by borrowing, or by running down deposits, or even under certain occasions to expand both borrowing and deposits simultaneously, may depend rather finely on apparently small changes in interest rate relativities.

Black (1970) considers the circumstances that would allow a world 'in which money does not exist'. A major requirement is that, 'Each bank is allowed to accept deposits under any conditions that it chooses to specify, and to pay any rate of interest on these deposits. In particular, the bank can allow transfers of credit by check between two interest-bearing accounts. Demand deposits will pay interest, and depositors are likely to be charged the full cost of transferring credit from one account to another. Almost all deposits will be in the form of demand deposits' (p. 10). In this world, 'An individual, business or government will simply have an account at a bank; there will be no need to distinguish between accounts with positive balances (deposits) and accounts with negative balances (loans). An individual may write a check that converts his deposit into a loan, or he may receive a salary payment that converts his loan into a deposit. So long as his loan does not come to exceed the maximum permitted by the bank, there is no need to make special note of these transactions' (p. 11). Abstracting from currency holdings, then 'there is nothing in this simpler world that can meaningfully be called a quantity of money. Some might say that the total value of all positive bank accounts is the quantity of money. But this makes a completely arbitrary distinction between positive and negative bank accounts. And it means that the quantity of money will change every time an individual transfers credit from his negative bank account to another individual's positive bank account. Others might say that the net value of all bank accounts, both positive and negative, is the quantity of money. But the net value of all the accounts in a bank is simply the capital of that bank. It is equal to the assets of the bank (its loans) minus the liabilities of the bank (its deposits). Thus, the net value of all bank accounts is equal to the aggregate value of all bank securities. We would hardly want to call this the quantity of money'.

Along similar lines, Wallace (1983) asks 'But what is so special about deposits subject to check and private bank notes? They are particular private credit instruments. If it makes sense to control their quantities, why not those of other credit instruments? For example, most economists would not favour a proposal to constrain the dollar volume of mortgages on single family residences to grow at a prescribed rate. Almost certainly, most would say that it is a necessary feature of a well-functioning credit system that the number of mortgages be determined in the market and not be set administratively. But if this is right for one set of private credit instruments, why is it not right for all? No satisfactory answer has ever been given' (p. 6).

Have we then reached the point in the UK at which the legal restrictions surrounding banking have been eroded so far that not only is it hardly feasible to give an unambiguous answer to the question 'What is money?', but also at which the econometric relationships that applied earlier are now comprehensively breaking down? The conditions described by Fischer Black as consistent with such a world do increasingly seem to hold for the UK at least. Such arguments would seem to have some considerable validity when considering the behaviour of the *wealthier* asset-holders at least. In particular, given the sensitivity of, for example, sovereign countries and large corporate treasurers in deciding on their disposition of their liquid financial assets and liabilities to the 'spread', or cost of intermediation, it becomes difficult to believe that their behaviour will be affected in a stable and systematic manner by their access to bank *deposits* only. Instead such wealthy asset holders may be more responsive to changes in their *net liquidity* position. As Davidson has pointed out (1984) (p. 265), however, the same is not necessarily true of persons. The imperfections of financial and capital markets are still such that the spread between the cost of borrowing and the return on deposits facing an ordinary individual can still be extremely large, and the absence of collateral may mean that a person in many circumstances is unable to borrow at all. When subject to financial constraints of this kind, an individual's expenditure may well be strongly influenced, indeed constrained, by his access to liquid assets, or even to more narrowly defined monetary balances. Thus the buffer-stock approach may be applicable to persons, but less so to the company or public sectors: indeed, that is why public sector (government) deposits are generally excluded from definitions of the aggregate money stock, precisely because they are thought to bear virtually no relation to the public sector's other general economic activities e.g. their expenditure.

If this is so, then an accurate sectoral analysis of incomes, and expenditures, together with sectoral holdings of money-like liquid assets (and short-term liabilities and facilities), would be important for macro-economic analytical purposes. Unfortunately, in the UK at least, the financial data on sectoral accounts exhibit very little coherence with the national income accounts for those same sectors. Thus, the quarterly data on the company sector surplus, or deficit, obtained from the national income accounts, shows little coherence

Table 3.2   Reconciliation of ICCs' surplus/deficit and net borrowing
requirement (£ million seasonally adjusted)

		Financial surplus/deficit (1)	Identifiable financial transactions* (2)	Balancing item (3)	Net borrowing requirement (4)
1982	1	−458	−443	−2,458	3,359
	2	234	−2,011	−456	2,233
	3	1,765	−1,111	−1,270	616
	4	2,880	−1,947	122	−1,055
1983	1	2,021	408	−1,418	−1,011
	2	1,497	−1,184	−1,175	862
	3	2,527	−1,764	−1,756	993
	4	1,827	−1,487	2,236	−2,576
1984	1	3,016	−698	−4,219	1,901
	2	2,396	−2,779	−1,894	2,277

* Including: Net unremitted profits, net identified trade and other credit, investment in UK company securities and investment abroad.
Columns (1) + (2) + (3) + (4) sum to zero.

Source: *Economic Trends* (1985), Table 62.

or correlation with the estimated data on net financial borrowing, as obtained from financial sources (largely from the banks). As can be seen from Table 3.2, the unidentified residual between these two has been huge and extremely variable over the course of recent quarters. The available quarterly sectoral national income data base is unfortunately poor, at least in the UK. If we are to make much headway in developing our understanding of behavioural responses to monetary stimuli, we may instead have to do much more work at the micro level, perhaps trying to develop additional sources of data. I continually hope to be able to persuade commercial bank economists to make more use of the micro data available within their own banks, despite problems of confidentiality. For ourselves, we are seeking also to push ahead with trying to develop understanding at the micro level by the use of an additional data source, in this case the annual balance sheet returns from a wide sample of companies as collected by Datastream. The nature of such data, obtained from annual balance sheets, will however condition and limit the general applicability of such research. It may be that economists from other countries would be able to obtain better data sources.

3.3   CURRENCY

Wallace (1983) argues that legal restrictions are also responsible for the peculiar nature of currency, notably its non-interest-bearing form. He notes that large-value, riskless, government-issued Treasury bills and bonds exist. Why cannot a financial intermediary issue much lower valued currency assets, bearing interest, against the backing of such riskless government debt, with a small interest margin to remunerate the intermediary for 'breaking bulk'? Wallace's answer is that such financial intermediaries would, indeed, develop but for legal constraints, (such as the 1844 Bank of England Act) which restrict other commercial banks, and other intermediaries from competing with the Central Bank in the production of small notes. It is, Wallace claims, such institutional constraints that explain the continuation of the monopoly, non-interest-bearing currency issue by Central Banks.

Two minor qualifications should, perhaps, be made at this stage. First, there are, on occasions, overtones from the 'legal restrictions' school that such restrictions were imposed on an unwilling public by governments keen to raise revenue from seigniorage. This is far from wholly true, as a study of 19th century monetary history would indicate. First, the unification of the currency via the Central Bank in countries such as Germany, Italy, and Swit- zerland was regarded not only as a welcome symbol of national unification, but ended years of inconvenience and public disaffection with often badly-working systems of pluralist note emission. Second, the centralisation of note issue in the Central Bank was regarded as a valuable prudential measure; as Leslie Pressnell has reminded me, in nineteenth century Britain there was a clear distinction, comparable with that between the external creditor and the equity holder in ordinary business, between notes and deposits. The ac- ceptor, and then holder, of notes had less choice, often facing a local, or regional, monopolist (or oligopolist), whereas the depositor acted virtually by free choice. The depositor was not normally protected in the case of a bank run, when, by contrast, local worthies would proclaim support for note holders. Restricting note issue to the Central Bank was widely seen as im- proving the security and general acceptability of the public's currency, and as such was generally popular, except among private note issuers facing a loss of property rights.

The second qualification is that there do remain some examples of 'com- petitive' private bank note issues, e.g. in Scotland and Hong Kong. In these cases, however, the banks, though benefiting from a small fiduciary issue, have to back any incremental issue, one for one, with non-interest-bearing legal tender (Bank of England notes in Scotland; US dollars now in Hong Kong). Nevertheless the banks obtain a benefit in that their till money be- comes costless, and they obtain some extra public recognition. Indeed, fol- lowing on the recent notification of the withdrawal of the 1 pound note in England, there was a query whether English banks could follow the Scottish example. However, note issue under such severe constraints, is not what Wallace, and others, have in mind for freely competitive note issue.

Anyhow, Wallace (1983, p. 4) predicts that 'the effects of imposing *laissez-faire* (would take) the form of an either/or statement: either nominal rates

go to zero or existing government currency becomes worthless'. That statement can be explained, and partly qualified, as follows. Any holder of non-
interest-bearing (nib) currency, issued by the Central Bank, could take such
notes to his (her) own commercial bank, and exchange non-interest-bearing
for interest-bearing (ib) private notes. The commercial bank, in turn, could
use the Central Bank currency to buy Treasury bills. The Central Bank could
force its own nib notes back into circulation, e.g. by open market purchases,
since these are legal tender, but they would only stay in circulation in the
return to the holder in going to exchange such notes for private ib notes
was low enough to make the exercise not worthwhile (i.e. interest rates on
privately issued notes would have to fall to low levels). Alternatively the
Central Bank's nib notes would be forced out of circulation, (which is not
quite the same as becoming worthless), and would be replaced by privately
issued ib notes.

   That analysis is based on the assumption, however, that privately issued
notes would provide equivalent transactions' services to existing Central Bank
currency. As already noted, there must remain a presumption that private
bank notes would, at least under certain circumstances, be perceived as carrying more risk. In addition, it is possible that currency enjoys such economies of scale and economies of information that it becomes a form of
'public good'. The wider the range over which a currency is used, and the
greater the trust attributed to the ability of the currency issuer to maintain
the value of that currency, the greater will be the usefulness, and use, of
that particular currency. Thus it may be that currency issue approximates to
a 'natural monopoly', and, as a monopolist, the issuer is not then under
competitive pressure to offer an interest rate. Claassen (1984) argues that
the objective of monetary integration, and the convenience of monetary union,
would seem to require a single currency, a 'natural monopoly', which then
conflicts with the objectives of achieving a greater degree of competition in
the provision of currencies. Others, Vaubel (1984), Salin (1984), agree that
economies of scale and information would restrict the number of potential
competitive issuers, but claim that the result of competition would be oligopoly,
rather than (governmental) monopoly, a state of affairs which they view as
preferable. Also see Klein (1974).

   Nevertheless, in a sense, there already exist competitive issues of pri-
vately-produced currencies by commercial entities in the form of Travellers
Cheques. For most practical purposes, a Travellers Cheque, such as an American
Express Check, is a form of currency. Interestingly enough, these also do
not offer interest.[1] Perhaps when a bank has reached a size and reputation to
make its Travellers Cheques widely acceptable, such issuers have already
obtained a sufficient degree of monopoly to enable them to make their 'currencies' acceptable *without* having to offer an interest rate.

   Another feature which is sometimes advanced as an explanation of the
absence of payment of interest on currency is the technical difficulties that

would be involved in doing so. In particular, if the currency issue included a coupon payable at a certain moment, or if the holder of the currency receives interest on a particular date, then the return to holding that currency would rise sharply as the date of interest payment neared. At the limit such currency issues, particularly of a higher face value, would be withdrawn entirely from circulation, as the date of payment drew near (an example of Gresham's Law). Nevertheless such technical difficulties could be circumvented, or at least mitigated, in certain respects. Thus, for example, the issuer of a Travellers Cheque could provide a randomised prize for the holders of such cheques based on the number on the cheque, akin to a premium bond in the UK, which would make the mathematical expectation of interest receipt the same as a regular interest payment, but would reduce somewhat the resultant disincentive to using such cheques as currency. Again, the arrival of 'smart' plastic cards might allow the funds represented by the remaining value of that card to be continuously (and slowly) augmented electronically at the going rate of interest. In the meantime, the spread of the ability of bank customers to draw, and redeposit, cash via ATMs from (to) interest-bearing deposit accounts, and the possible further step of making the ATM card usable in an EFTPOS system, will enhance the ability of customers to earn interest on all their liquid asset holdings for a larger proportion of the time.

Be that as it may, one can certainly imagine ways in which the technical difficulties of providing a yield, or interest, on currency instruments could be overcome. In that case, absent legal restrictions, could we expect commercial financial intermediaries to compete in making such instruments available, and what might be the consequences?

3.4 CONTROL

Wallace (1983), and Jao (1983), argue further that, not only does the stable relationship between certain forms of monetary deposit and nominal incomes and interest rates depend upon a particular set of legal restrictions, but that so also does the ability of the authorities to control the money stock. Wallace and Jao consider the case in which both government and private sector issue notes competitively side-by-side.

Thus Jao (1983) writes (pp. 18, 19):

Now suppose that government monopoly of currency issue and reserve requirement no longer exist, and a common constant-cost technology for the production and distribution of small-denomination bearer notes is available to the government as well as private intermediaries. Consider the same open market operation again, whereby the purchase of Treasure bills is made by issue of currency notes. This time, however, there is no increase in the money stock. For the private intermediaries simply scale down their note-issue operations, offsetting one-for-one the government issue in the open market operation. The resources thus released from private intermediaries are employed by the government to produce and maintain a larger stock of government currency. The said open market operation merely changes the location of a particular economic activity. Otherwise, nothing else is affected: neither interest rates, nor the price level, nor the level of economic activity . . . The re-interpretation and extension of the Modigliani–Miller theorem undermines the monetarist case in two ways. First, the theorem demonstrates that it is neither necessary nor possible to control bank intermediation and hence bank deposits. Second, government exogenous control of the money stock is an illusion, an illusion made possible only by an uncritical acceptance of a host of binding legal restrictions.

This claim, that the provision of privately issued (ib) notes in conditions of *laissez-faire* would undermine the authorities' monetary control, in my view goes too far, and is based on the implicit assumption that the authorities, in those circumstances, would peg the interest rate on their own notes at a *fixed* level. But it is already well established that, if the authorities fix the interest rate(s) on their own liabilities (e.g. Treasury bills), they cannot simultaneously fix the monetary quantities outstanding. Thus I argued earlier that, if the authorities offered only nib currency while private financial institutions offered ib notes, the two sets of notes would only coexist when the interest rate was driven low enough to make the utility of holding both at the same time equal at the margin. If the Central Bank then forced more nib currency into the system, it would tend to drive down real rates of interest by forcing up inflation or driving down nominal interest rates. That would induce private sector note issuers to reduce their own issues. If this process of substitution was virtually perfect, as Jao implies, there need be little change in the total volume of currency outstanding, etc.

But the authorities could, in these circumstances, restore their own grip simply enough. All that they would need to do would be to vary the interest rate that they themselves offered on their own currency. This would then provide the basis for the *general* level of rates, while the various costs of intermediation, maturity preferences, etc, would determine the *relativities* between rates. The authorities' control over the general level of rates would, in turn, influence the demand for credit and saving, and the general rate of expansion of nominal incomes and monetary expansion. Under the legal restrictions of the present regime the general level of rates is determined by the rate charged for *access* to cash. If such legal restrictions were removed (and the technical problems of offering interest on cash overcome), the general rate of interest would be determined by the rate offered *on cash* by the Central Bank. If the Central Bank issued notes providing the bearer with a risk-less return of X per cent, then that would provide the base-line from which all other rates would be determined. If technical means of providing and varying interest yields on cash could be developed, it might even offer an administratively-easier system of control for the authorities to operate than the present.

The above analysis assumes, however, not only that all legal restrictions, and technical obstacles, to the provision of ib currency by private intermediaries are removed, but also that the Central Bank competes in the provision of currency, the yield on which could, *and would*, be varied by administrative fiat. But what would happen in the (even more extreme) case in which, for one reason or another, the Central Bank in the country should cease to issue notes at all and passed over that function entirely to commercial banks? In such a circumstance, in which the note issuing function became entirely the responsibility of commercial banks, could the authorities subsequently maintain control over either interest rates or the money stock? In order to answer that question, it is necessary first to consider on what basis – or policy regime – banking would then be organised.

The first question is whether the bank deposits, and private note issues, would be convertible into a more 'fundamental' store of value, or would simply represent a proportionate share to the market value of the underlying assets held by the banks. The latter alternative would involve the commercial banks shifting towards a 'unit trust' approach. One of the major differences between banks and unit trusts, in their roles as financial intermediaries, relates to the nature of the valuation of their assets. The assets held by unit trusts are, for the most part, marketable; in the case of banks, the assets held by them are, for the most part, non-marketable (or, at least, are not marketed), and there is no market mechanism for establishing in a competitive and open fashion their true expected value. One of the more interesting questions about banking (to which no answer will be attempted here), is why any sizeable (secondary) market in bank loans, or at least loans of certain specific kinds, has not already developed; though there are currently some signs of developments in that direction.

So long as such markets in loans do not develop (and may in general perhaps not be possible to develop), thereby allowing a market price to be placed on the assets on the commercial banks, considerable uncertainty about the underlying asset values of the banks will persist (even after taking account of the effect of supervision, accounting, etc.). There would, therefore, in a world in which banks faced similar market and accounting practices as now, remain considerable uncertainty as to what the true value of a proportionate share in such assets would amount to. This would complicate the development of 'unit trust' banking. Furthermore, it would remain to be seen how popular such an institution would be; White (1984a) expresses certain reservations on this score. Nevertheless, certain institutions along such lines are beginning to emerge, which offer transactions services against a deposit holding which is, or can be, revalued continuously in line with the value of

institutions' own portfolio. For example, some of the fund management arrangements in the US, and also some aspects of Islamic banking – a neglected
topic among Western monetary economists – have similarities with the concept of 'unit trust' banking. Such an institution, with deposits which were
not nominally capital certain, could not, however, qualify as a 'bank' in the
UK, under the definition as set out in the 1979 Banking Act. Some recent
analysts have further envisaged a hypothetical future system in which both
the note and deposit liabilities of such 'unit trust' banks are valued in terms
of a numeraire consisting, perhaps, of (an indexed combination of) commodities, which no note/deposit holder would have any incentive to hold
directly (see Greenfield and Yeager, 1983). There are various problems about
the feasibility of such a world, e.g. how would the relative prices of the
commodities entering the numeraire be set themselves, or the practical likelihood of its development (see White, 1984a).

Nevertheless if we should accept the hypothetical possibility of such a
system, what role would then be left for a Central Bank, with no outside
currency in existence and, thus, no shifts between inside and outside money?
One important role that now exists is a banker to the government, and, as
we shall later again pick up, that function nowadays provides an even more
important reason for commercial banks to hold bankers' balances than the
need for access to notes: but that function could, in theory, also be transferred to, and among, competitive private banks. One major problem would,
however, remain within this commercial banking system. So long as deposits
are much more easily transferable between banks than are bank loans – because
arranging the latter requires specialised information and confidential arrangements – any large scale shifts of funds from one bank to another could
cause major difficulties for the borrowers of banks losing deposits, and would
require recycling. This will be discussed at greater length in my monograph
'The Evolution of Central Banks: A Natural Development?' (1985), subsequently published as *The Evolution of Central Banks* (1988). So a supervisory, recycling function would remain, but whether, in such a world, the
authorities would either wish, or be able, to maintain any control functions,
i.e. whether they would need, or be able, to influence interest rates, seems
obscure.

Let us assume, instead, that banks retain the particular feature of offering
liabilities which are fixed in value, i.e. convertible, against some other asset
(i.e. that they do not simply represent a proportionate share of the value of
the bank's asset book). Again we could imagine banks choosing to make
their liabilities convertible into differing stores of value, e.g. gold, a foreign
currency, another commodity, a basket of commodities, or perhaps an index
such as the RPI. If banks independently chose a whole set of differing stores
of value, into which to make their liabilities convertible, that would add
considerably to the inconvenience of the public. Thus the current values of
the banks' individual liabilities, would be continually shifting re the numeraire,

as the spot prices of the more 'fundamental' assets into which their liab-ilities were convertible fluctuated, and the interest rates offered by each of the independent banks would have to adjust as expectations of the relative future prices of their particular fundamental assets altered. So, there would be considerable advantages, economies of scale and information, of a public good nature, to encouraging all the various banks to adhere to the same brand of convertibility.

The present form of convertibility requires the banks to make their de-posits convertible into the legal tender non-interest-bearing notes issued by the Central Bank. Let us consider instead a convertible system, in which the banks make their liabilities, both deposits and notes, both of which bear a competitive interest rate, convertible into a commodity, say gold. If there was to be such a return to the gold standard, would there be any need for a Central Bank. Would it have a function? If such a Central Bank was estab-lished in a gold standard world, could it influence interest rates and the money stock?

As a factual matter of historical record, Central Banks in the main indus-trialised countries of Europe and Japan became established, and evolved a role, during the gold standard period. Although their influence over interest rates and monetary developments was subject to the constraints involved in maintaining the gold standard regime, they undoubtedly played a consider-able role in influencing the timing and extent of interest rate changes in their country, and also a role in fostering the development of financial in-termediation in their countries. It is, however, the argument of a number of monetary historians, who have adopted, in some large part, the legal restric-tions approach, that central banks were established primarily as a result of governmental legislative intervention, which unnecessarily and undesirably restricted the freedom of the financial systems. They claim that there was no necessary function for central banks within such a gold standard system, and, indeed, that such systems, as in Scotland, would have functioned better without them (see Cameron, 1967; Timberlake, 1978; White, 1984b).

In my longer paper (1985) and subsequent book (1988), I challenge this latest historical interpretation of the evolution of Central Banks. In this pa-per, I argue that there *are* natural reasons why a central bank would de-velop within such a convertible commodity system. Let me here give three reasons for this view.

First, the commodity, into which the deposits and the notes are to be made convertible, itself is barren, in the sense of being non-interest-bearing. There are, therefore, economies of reserve centralisation to be obtained by the individual banks, particularly in a unit-banking system, centralising their own reserves with a strong and trustworthy bank at the centre: Then the remaining banks can hold their own reserves in this central bank in the form of interest-bearing correspondent balances. Particularly if this central bank has the support of the government behind it, so that it need not be profit-maximising, such centralisation would allow the banks as a whole to maintain convertibility into the chosen commodity at a higher rate of profit than would otherwise be feasible.

Secondly, given the difficulty of observing the true value of each bank's assets, which has already been mentioned, the value attached by the depositor, and note holder, to a commercial bank's liabilities, will depend as much on confidence and trust in the bank's reputation, as on the available valuation (for what it is worth) of the bank's assets. There is a public good aspect to such reputation, in the sense that the failure, and/or revealed bad behaviour, of one bank, will throw doubt and distrust over the reputation of a wider range of other banks. Given this public good nature of reputation, there will be a felt need among banks for rules of good conduct to be followed. Owing to conflicts of interest, it would be difficult for commercial banks to act together to set such rules, e.g. for the criteria required to become a bank, or to monitor the adherence of each other to such rules, since that would involve at least some degree of opening of books, and exchange of confidentiality, with competitors. A solution to this latter problem is to shift such supervisory and control functions to an outside institution, such as a central bank, particularly since its lender of last resort function would seem to entail its close involvement in such matters.

Finally, the combination of the convertibility promise, together with the uncertainty about each bank's underlying asset value, allows, as history has shown only too clearly, the possibility of contagion of distrust to occur, in which the failure of one bank can trigger off doubts about other banks, leading to a crisis of illiquidity, and associated insolvency. So, there would seem to be a need for an institution which would be capable of stemming such panics by acting as lender of last resort in the traditional Bagehot manner.

For all such reasons, a Central Bank is likely to emerge, even when the liabilities of the private commercial banks are convertible into a commodity, rather than into fiat money, and even when the note issue within the country is provided entirely, or in the main, by the same private commercial banks. The essential functions of a Central Bank, as a central (efficient) repository of barren reserves and as a lender of last resort, bring in their train a (reasonably stable) behavioural demand among the commercial banks for balances with the central bank. This latter is the key to the influence of the Central Bank over the level of interest rates and the rate of growth of the monetary aggregates. Given this (stable) demand function for Central Bank balances, the authorities can undertake open market operations, to affect at the same time both the quantities of such balances and the rate of interest at which banks can obtain access to such balances. The question of whether the Central Bank should aim primarily to influence the quantity of balances held with it, or the level of interest rates at which the banks can obtain access to such balances, is, for this purpose, a secondary issue.

Nevertheless, within a regime of convertibility into a commodity, such as the gold standard, the Central Bank's influence on interest rates is both more direct, and more directly influential in affecting the inward and outward flow of gold into the country, than is its influence via control over the quantity of bank reserves: the relationship of bankers' balances at the Central Bank with the various wider monetary aggregates, is, in a free system, subject to the changing behaviour of the individual commercial banks. Variations in such reserve ratios, however, can be limited by making them mandatory. But if such required ratios then act as an effective constraint on bank behaviour, they must represent, to a greater or lesser extent, a burden, and therefore involve a tax on banking, which in turn the banks will try to avoid by innovation or disintermediation.

To conclude and summarise, the question of whether the Central Bank, or the commercial banks, provide the notes which are used as hand-to-hand currency is actually irrelevant to the question of whether the Central Bank can establish control. What is needed, and essential, is a relatively stable demand function by the banking system for the liabilities of the Central Bank. Wallace and Jao examined a case in which no such stable demand function existed, because Central Bank and commercial bank notes coexisted and were (perfectly) substitutable. Even then, I have argued, the Central Bank can simply restore its control over the general level of interest rates, and thence over monetary developments, by varying the rate of interest that it was itself prepared to offer on cash instruments. Moreover, even if the Central Bank completely abandoned the note-issuing function to the commercial banks, there would still be a stable demand for balances to be held with a Central Bank.

This latter was argued in the context of a system with deposits, and private notes, convertible into a commodity. The same would obviously be true within a fiat money system of the kind now generally existing. Indeed the need of the commercial banks to obtain notes and currency from the Central Bank currently represents a relatively small proportion of the cash flows influencing the commercial banks' overall reserve position on a day-to-day basis. A much larger proportion of the daily cash flows, affecting banks' reserve positions, is the result of transactions with the public sector. Indeed, as can be seen from Table 3.3, which reports the main cash flows in the UK in a recent, reasonably representative, week, the flows resulting from transactions with the government were very much larger than those arising from changes in the outstanding note issue. So long as the Central Bank is the government's bank,[2] and the government, therefore requires payment in the form of a claim on its own bank, i.e. on the Central Bank, there will be another important reason for the commercial banks to maintain reserve balances with the Central Bank. It is such banker's balances at the Central Bank, and not the note issue, which serves as the main fulcrum for establishing a Central Bank's control.

Table 3.3   Daily cash flows affecting banks' reserve positions

	(£mn s)	Exchequer transactions	Maturing assistance	Notes[1]	Other[2]	Total shortage
Monday	19.11.84	−55	−685	+279	+216	−245
Tuesday	20.11.84	+203	−349	+41	+23	−82
Wednesday	21.11.84	−221	−326	−102	+39	−610
Thursday	22.11.84	+269	−686	−36	+204	−249
Friday	23.11.84	+186	−707	−232	−243	−996
Total for week		+382	−2,753	−50	+239	−2,182

1. No figures available for coin but the sums involved are minute on a daily basis.
2. Includes bankers' balances brought forward, net gilt transactions, take-up of Treasury Bills, Foreign Exchange and miscellaneous.

3.5   CONCLUSION

The ability of a Central Bank to maintain its influence over interest rates, and a generalised pressure on the rate of monetary expansion, depends ultimately on commercial banks needing to retain balances with itself. That need would appear likely to continue so long as the banks themselves need to maintain the convertibility of their own liabilities, whether deposits or notes, into a more 'fundamental' store of value, whether that be (a basket of) commodities, or into fiat money. It does *not*, I have argued, depend to any important extent on the note-issuing function of the Central Bank, and, in the perhaps improbable circumstances that that latter function were to pass, in part or in whole, to the commercial banks, the Central Bank's power would not be seriously diminished. So, I do not myself believe that any of the many, far-reaching structural changes now underway (or indeed even if some of the more visionary changes were to take place in future), would seriously erode the present power of Central Banks to influence interest rates and the pace of monetary expansion.

The problems that the structural changes do bring are not that they diminish the Central Bank's power to control, but rather that the blurring of instruments and institutions make it more difficult to assess and to interpret financial developments, and thence to judge how to apply monetary controls. I have quoted assertions by others, and presented arguments that suggests that, in these circumstances, there can be no single, continuously reliable, unambiguous, and unchanging definition of money; and also that there are likely to be sizeable shifts between different forms of liquid assets by wealth holders in response to interest-rate *relativities*, which the authorities cannot control, although they can still influence the general level of short-term interest rates.

In such circumstances, if these are indeed a proper reflection of today's reality, it would hardly be possible, nor sensible, for the authorities to commit themselves *rigidly* to achieving a specified numerical growth rate for any particular definition of money over any period much longer than a year, or two. Nevertheless, in a fiat system world, there is an understandable fear that the growth of the money stock, and thence inflation, is driven by the short-term expedients of the authorities, which may not only have a bias to inflation, but also gives no basis for confidence about longer-term price stability, nor even what rate of inflation might be reasonably expected. As Leijonhufvud has shown, (eg. 1977), such general uncertainty can have most adverse economic effects. Against that background, there is an understandable and justifiable demand for the authorities to adopt a degree of pre-commitment, to submit themselves to certain clearly-defined rules, sufficient to allay fears about future uncertain inflation, and to provide the necessary basis of financial stability for the economic system to work effectively. It is the counter-balance between the shifting structure of the financial system on the one hand, and the need for rules and pre-commitment on the part of the authorities on the other, that makes it so hard to select an optimal form of monetary targetry, one that could retain underlying discipline, while at the same time allowing a sensible and flexible response to the rapidly changing form of the financial system.

NOTES

1. Issuers of such cheques do provide a service, to wit refund in the case of loss, which is not available from holding currency; on the other hand most purchas ers pay a commission to the selling agent when buying Travellers Cheques. I am indebted to Mr L.D.D. Price for this, and other helpful comments.
2. It might be argued that, in a *laissez-faire* world, the government need not necessarily place the handling of its financial affairs with the Central Bank, but with whichever bank offered it the best competitive terms. There would, however, be problems with this course. The government would be such a large customer that it might – or it might be feared that it might – use its market power to exert direct influence on the commercial banks with which it was dealing. Furthermore, switching banking operations from one bank to another, or dividing the operations between several banks, could well be less efficient than the present course: the Bank of England prides itself on the efficiency with which it handles the government's financial affairs. Again, the role of the government as the fiscal authority, and in some cases as the supervisory authority, might cause it to face conflicts of interest in the course of any direct commercial dealings with the privately-owned banks.

4 Central Bank Independence (1994)*

4.1 AN IDEA WHOSE TIME HAS COME

Until a few years ago, Central Banks were regarded as an integral part of the Government's central policy-making machine. The phrase, 'the Monetary Authorities', was coined and used to describe the combined operations of the Central Banks and Treasury, under the political leadership of Chancellor/Treasurer and Prime Minister. The idea that a Central Bank might, or should, be independent of Central Government was simply not considered as a serious issue in most countries. Yet this is now an idea whose time has most certainly come.

Central banks in a wide variety of countries, from Venezuela to Chile in South America, through South Africa to New Zealand, have already been given formal constitutional independence from the executive branch of government. Bills for the same purpose have been enacted in France and Mexico. The subject has been intensively studied both by a Select Committee of the House of Commons in the UK, and by a separate prestigious group of mostly ex-officials, businessmen, international Central Bankers, and academics, of whom I was one, under the Chairmanship of Eric Roll of Warburgs. The Report of our group, *Independent and Accountable: A New Mandate for the Bank of England*, was published by the Centre for Economic Policy Research (CEPR) on 29 Oct. 1993. The House of Commons Select Committee also reported early in 1994.

Moreover, the statutes of the European Central Bank are closely modelled on those of the Bundesbank, historically the most independent of all Central Banks. And other European Community nations cannot participate in the final stages of European Monetary Union and join the European System of Central Banks until these have been made independent of their executive Governments, no longer subservient and indeed even statutorily prevented from taking any instructions from Government. Hence all the major European countries are moving towards the degree of constitutional independence already enjoyed by Germany and Switzerland.

* *Journal of International and Comparative Economics*, 3 (1994).

This paper was initially given as an address to the Committee for the Economic Development of Australia (CEDA) in Melbourne on 1 November 1993. I am grateful to Jerome Stein for helpful comments. The usual disclaimers apply.

Why has this surge of support for the concept of an independent Central Bank now occurred? The purpose of the exercise is to improve economic performance, and, as might therefore be expected, the basic ideas which have driven the case for independence have been provided by economic theory. The first of these goes by the somewhat unfortunate name of the vertical Phillips curve. Bill Phillips, a New Zealand economist working at LSE, had earlier discovered in the 1950s that, using historical British data, when unemployment was high, the pressure of demand in an economy being low, then wage and price inflation had also been lower. This suggested that the authorities might be able to choose an optimal combination, or trade-off, between inflation and unemployment. And this is exactly what governments sought to do in the 1950s and 1960s. But in the 1970s, the rate of inflation consistent with a given level of unemployment kept on rising; we ran into stagflation.

Milton Friedman then explained that the problem was that the short run Phillips curve had depended on the existing stage of inflationary expectations. If the supposedly optimal level of inflation that the authorities wanted was above that which had been expected by the public, then the public's *real* wage and profit outcomes, which they had sought to achieve by their price setting agreements, would have been systematically inflated away. They would subsequently revise their inflationary expectations up, and at any given level of unemployment would demand higher wage, or price, increases. In short, if the authorities tried to keep the level of unemployment below the natural rate, which is, broadly, the rate that causes workers to seek that rate of real wage increase that their own productivity increases make available, then inflation will not be constant, but will rise without limit; in economists' jargon, in the longer term the Phillips curve is vertical. There is no trade-off in the medium, and longer, term between inflation on the one hand, and output, growth and unemployment on the other.

During the immediate post-war decades when economists and governments had worked on the basis of such an assumed trade-off, the choice of the 'optimal' balance between employment and inflationary objectives was seen, and rightly so, as an essentially political matter. Consequently, instruments of demand management, monetary and fiscal policies, needed to be coordinated and managed to achieve that balanced outcome. Once, however, the concept of the medium-term vertical Phillips curve was absorbed, it became apparent that one both could, and should, use monetary policy to control inflation in the medium and longer term without losing any benefits in the way of growth or employment over that same horizon.

But what that implied was that governments should use monetary policy as a *medium term* instrument to control inflation, while using (quasi-automatic) fiscal stabilisers, or supply side measures, to moderate shorter term shocks and cycles, *not* that the monetary policy instrument should be removed altogether from the hands of Ministers. And this is broadly what happened. Governments in the 1970s and early 1980s embraced monetary targets and medium-term financial strategies for bringing down inflation, and moved to 'supply side' measures to encourage growth.

This strategy had a mixed success. When sufficiently tough Central Bankers and Treasurers were in charge, at the Bundesbank, Paul Volcker at the Fed, Geoffrey Howe and Nigel Lawson in the UK, inflation was brought down, but often at a severe short-term cost in terms of higher unemployment. These costs were attributed, in large part, to a lack of credibility that the authorities would achieve, and then maintain, a regime of stable prices, of zero inflation. And this in turn was attributed to the short-time-horizons of politicians, especially in advance of elections. Even though in the longer term expansionary monetary and fiscal policies, lowering taxes and raising expenditures, would do no good to output and employment, and just raise inflation, in the short run, with expectations given, they would raise employment, induce a feel-good factor, and raise the probability of re-election. Economists incorporated all this into another jargon-rich model of behaviour, termed time-inconsistency, whereby a government's rhetoric would always be that its counter-inflationary determination was absolute, but its actual actions, whenever short-term pressures really mounted, or an election loomed, would be to accommodate, even to encourage, monetary expansion as a short-term palliative. However, the public, not being entirely mugs, would soon appreciate this and would therefore largely ignore and disdain the government's counter-inflationary rhetoric. The medium-term result would be higher inflation, no more growth, and a thoroughly cynical set of politicians and electorates.

Meanwhile, the problem of credibility had been made worse by the collapse in the stability of the relationships between monetary growth and inflation, is the increasing unpredictability of the velocity of circulation. Previously governments could publicly pre-commit themselves to a series of monetary targets, which would, it was hoped, lead straight through to lower nominal incomes and inflation. But these monetary relationships progressively collapsed during the 1980s in almost all countries. Hence operations to achieve stable prices reverted from being a matter of sticking to publicly announced monetary target rules back to the more discretionary use of the interest rate instrument for that purpose; that is to say interest rates had to be varied now to try to bring inflation back to its desired, say zero, rate several quarters, perhaps a year or more hence, when the interest rate adjustment would have had its full effect on expenditures and prices. This exercise requires technical expertise, good models of the economy, discretion, patience and long horizons, none of which government ministers as a collective, irrespective of personality, party or country, have been renowned for possessing. There is no doubt but that the popularity of the idea of an independent Central Bank has, as its flip side, a generalised distrust of politicians of all shapes and sizes.

Thus, the theory ran, if there is a need for a credible medium-term counter-inflationary policy, a solution would be for the government to delegate the objective of achieving price stability to a separate institution, an autonomous Central Bank, which should have both the requisite longer time-horizon and technical expertise to achieve that objective. Note in particular that the Central Bank is *not* independent with respect to the *objectives* that it should fulfil; indeed it may often, as in the case of New Zealand, be tied down rather rigidly to the achievement of a defined outcome. In that sense the Central Bank is autonomous with respect to the powers used to achieve its statutorily defined objective, but not *independent* to choose its objectives. By the same token an autonomous Central Bank can be *more* democratically accountable than a subservient Central Bank.

But the move towards an independent, or autonomous, (and I prefer the latter adjective) Central Bank was not only a matter of theory. A whole series of econometric/statistical tests have shown that countries with more independent Central Banks have had generally lower inflation rates, led by Germany and the Bundesbank. Recently countries that have adopted independent Central Banks, such as Chile and New Zealand, have moved from bottom of their class towards being best performers. Finally, but very important, the Germans are so enamoured of their independent Central Bank that they refused to counterance a move towards the European System of Central Banks and European Economic and Monetary Union, EMU, until all the other Community participants, and the European Central Bank, had installed independence along Germanic lines in their own Central Banks.

4.2 SOME QUALIFICATIONS

In section 4.1 I tried to explain why the enthusiasm for an independent, a more autonomous, Central Bank has arisen. This, therefore, involves setting out the case in favour of it. It is, however, a highly fashionable argument, very much the flavour of the month. Some even regard it as a painless panacea, the obvious way to restore price stability in our countries, without any offsetting loss to growth or output over the medium term. I, and my academic colleagues, teach the time inconsistency theory, and the benefit of an independent Central Bank to cohorts of aspiring young undergraduates and graduates. When there is such widespread enthusiasm for a new idea, perhaps especially in economics, it is as well to be wary.

Let us, therefore, turn to some of the qualifications, starting with the economic ones. First, the case for an autonomous Central Bank, statutorily committed to price stability, is predicated on the assumption of a natural rate of unemployment, a vertical Phillips curve. Whereas the theoretical underpinnings for that concept seem sound, in practice the natural rate itself does not seem stable, or stationary, either between countries or over time.

The unemployment rate consistent with a steady inflation rate appears to differ markedly between Japan, USA and Europe, and has steadily risen in Europe over recent decades from about 2½ per cent in the 1950s to perhaps around 8 per cent now. How far is the 'so-called' equilibrium, longer term, level of unemployment a function of the shorter-run path followed in the mean-time; to use another jargon term, does the natural rate exhibit 'hysteresis'? If so, there *may* be a longer term trade off between the level of unemployment and the measures taken to reduce inflation, for example its planned rate of change. But such a trade off, if it exists, would once again be a proper subject for political choice, not just a technical matter. Be that as it may, our present inability to understand, or influence, the factors affecting the time-variant natural rate of unemployment should make us cautious about policy proposals that implicitly assume that natural rate is either constant, or unaffected by the monetary policies adopted in the mean-time.

Keynes remarked that, in the long run, we are all dead. Even in the medium term our tastes change, we may get divorced and change jobs and homes. The short run matters, especially at times of great uncertainty and disturbance, such as political turmoil, civil unrest and wars. Some shocks are too massive to refuse any accommodation. Let me evidence German reunification, and the 1973 and 1979 oil shocks. If rules are drawn too tightly, with no let-outs for unforeseen contingencies, they can become unacceptable, and themselves incredible. Thus, there has to be *some* flexibility in the policy objectives proposed for the autonomous Central Bank. This, for example, is provided for the Bundesbank by carefully refraining from giving any precise definition, either in terms of index, quantification or date, to its objective of price stability. In the case of New Zealand, where the objective is both quantified and date-stamped, the flexibility is provided by the small-print in the contract and by the override procedure. Quite which mechanism for achieving the desired modicum of flexibility is better is a debatable matter. What is clear is that granting autonomy to a Central Bank does not, and should not, mean that complete priority is given to medium term objectives, with no attention to the short run. It involves a significant shift in the balancing of priorities, rather than a total change in regimes.

Let me go on to some of the more political qualifications. We have in a sense already noted a couple of these. The first is that Central Banks, under this proposal, are not really being given independence; indeed their objectives are in most cases, specifically in the New Zealand case, spelt out and defined much more closely than before. They have *autonomy* over the powers needed to achieve that objective, notably interest rate adjustment, but no more. Second, even their use of this limited autonomy will be constrained, either specifically by the retention of certain 'override' powers by the government, though these are intended to be used only in emergencies, or more generally by the Central Bank's need to retain, if not a political consensus, at least a sufficient degree of political support to maintain their position of 'independence'.

The establishment of the Central Bank's independence is generally done by a legislative Act, an Act of Parliament or Congress. What one Congress, or Parliament, has enacted, another can repeal. The independence of the Federal Reserve System is constantly under scrutiny, and sometimes under threat, from Congress. For example in the last few months Congressman Gonzalez of the House Banking Committee has sought to reopen the question of how the regional Federal Reserve Presidents are to be appointed. The independence of the Bundesbank is not part of the German constitution, but derives from an Act of the Bundestag. The independence of the Banque de France and, perhaps, of the Bank of England would not, could not, be absolute, but would be subject to the continuing pleasure of the legislature. In some respects the prospective independence of the European System of Central Banks is more profound since that will be based on the inter-governmental Treaty of Maastricht. Treaties can also be amended, or rescinded; it just takes rather longer.

Moreover, there is one key aspect of monetary affairs that Governments have never been willing to delegate to their Central Bank, whether formally independent or not, and this is the right to take the strategic decisions on the exchange rate regime. Despite the vaunted independence of the Bundesbank, the decision on establishing the Exchange Rate Mechanism (ERM) of the European monetary system, on the exchange rate for changing ost-marks into Deutschemarks, and on conditions for European monetary union, were all taken by the German politicians, in several of these cases against the clear advice and wishes of the Bundesbank. In the US, exchange rate decisions are a matter for the Secretary of the Treasury, not the Chairman of the FRB. Despite awarding an unusual degree of independence to the ESCB, the framers of the Maastricht Treaty kept exchange rate decisions in the hands of the politicians (Article 109). This can cause problems and frictions. Central Banks only have one major instrument, their ability to vary interest rates. As a generality this cannot be used to hit two objectives simultaneously, e.g. an external objective for the exchange rate and an internal objective for price stability, except by a fluke. In some cases, e.g. of small, open countries, or countries where domestic control may have been problematical (e.g. Luxembourg, Hong Kong, Argentina, Estonia), Central Banks have transformed their operations, into a currently board format, specifically to achieve an external rather than an internal objective. In other cases, the latitude allowed to a Central Bank to use its powers to achieve domestic price stability may prove to be conditional on the effects of that on the country's exchange rate. Alternatively, a Central Bank, whether formally independent or not, may find that its politicians have agreed to the establishment of an exchange rate regime that restricts its own freedom to act to meet its domestic objectives. Again, its only recourse would be to the court of public opinion, to persuade the wider public that the exchange rate regime change proposed by the politicians would be counter-productive.

In such an appeal to public opinion, the Central Bank has a reasonably good chance of succeeding. This is partly because of the wide-spread cynicism and distrust of politicians, whereas Central Bankers are, I believe, seen as relatively more disinterested technicians. Indeed, it is this cynicism about politicians, embodied for example in time-inconsistency theory, that is largely responsible for much of the enthusiasm for taking the levers of monetary control from them. In my view this cynicism has been exaggerated. It has been shown, for example, that the existence of a political business cycle, whereby the incumbent government pumps up the economy before the election, only to reverse engines once safely re-elected, is largely mythical. As Lincoln said 'you cannot fool all of the people, all of the time'.

The rationale for granting independence to Central Banks derives largely from the view that the continuance of inflation is due largely, if not entirely, to the self-interested short-termism of politicians. That is a very seductive concept, particularly since we like to think ill of those in power over us. But it is not necessarily true. I can certainly remember cases when the politicians in the UK were pressing the Bank of England to lower interest rates, but there have also been cases, e.g. in 1981 and 1982, when the Bank might have adopted, on its own, a more expansionary path than the politicians had chosen. On balance, I do accept that politicians usually have a somewhat shorter time horizon, and feel a greater need to respond rapidly to immediate distress, at a potential cost in longer-term stability, but the differences in priorities, and probably in performance, may not be nearly as great as the enthusiasts for Central Bank independence may believe.

In practice, the differences in priorities and performance between an independent Central Bank and a Chancellor/Treasurer *cannot* be all that great, because both ultimately have got to persuade and satisfy the general public that the policies are good. If not, the Central Bank independence would be repealed, just as the Treasurer would be voted out of office. There is, in some quarters, a view that enacting Central Bank independence would be to take monetary policy issues out of the political arena. That is absolutely wrong. What such enactment does is to put the Central Bank squarely *into* the political arena. Subservient Central Banks can always hide their advice and involvement behind the front of the responsible Minister, and claim that they offer only technical advice on which the government and Ministers put a political gloss. When they become independent, Central Banks have to justify their actions to a much greater extent, and that will involve the full gamut of political and presentational skills.

Indeed, sensible Central Bankers know that they have to forge, and maintain, a widely-based political consensus for the main thrust of their (counter-inflationary) policies. This is central to their success. If a major political party, likely to be elected shortly, campaigns on the basis of rescinding the independence of its Central Bank, what medium term credibility will the latter still have? It was the fact that the Reserve Bank of New Zealand Act was, and is, supported by both the main parties there, that has enabled the newly independent Bank there to start so well. Equally it is the fact that none of the main parties in Germany would want, or dare, to try to compromise the independence of the Bundesbank that gives it its real strength.

What this means is that an independent Central Bank will only retain credibility so long as it can maintain a broadly based political coalition of support for giving priority to using monetary policy for the medium-term control of inflation, despite the shorter-term pains that such a policy may, at times, involve. But there is something of a paradox here. If there is such a widely-based political coalition for giving priority to medium-term price stability, then you do not need an independent Central Bank, since the politicians would deliver much the same result, unaided. While if there is no such general support for counter-inflationary policies, granting a Central Bank independence probably will not work either. It is for this reason that one should take the historical correlations between Central Bank independence and low inflation with several grains of salt. The true underlying correlations may be between the underlying priorities of the electorate and the economic outturn. Both the independence of the Bundesbank and low German inflation may be symptoms of the abhorrence of Germans for inflation. It is quite possible, therefore, that Germany would have had relatively low inflation in recent decades whatever the status of its Central Bank. It is, perhaps, worth recalling that the German hyperinflation in the 1920s took place at a time when the Reichsbank was statutorily independent of the executive, as was also the Russian Central Bank, at least until Yeltsin destroyed the legislature. It is at least arguable that the constitutional status of the Central Bank is of second-order importance.

The argument, advanced here, is that what really matters in a democratic state are the priorities, perceptions and beliefs of the general public. If so, the passage of an Act to grant the Central Bank independence may achieve little unless it influences those same priorities and perceptions.

4.3   AN ASSESSMENT

Although it is, I believe, fair to argue, as I have just done in Section II, that the basic determinants of inflation reside, in a democratic state, in the general public's priorities and preferences, it is not valid to treat these as exogenously fixed, or independent of the institutional framework. The establishment of an independent Central Bank, with a mandate to achieve stable prices, provides a public protagonist for longer-term counter-inflationary policies. Politicians want simultaneously to provide higher real incomes (for their potential supporters) and stable prices (for all). Each party will tend to claim that its own policies can provide both; there is likely to be some self-deception in such claims, but, with all the political parties making somewhat similar claims, the electorate is likely to become confused. The addition of a player into the public arena, the Central Bank, with a more narrowly focused mandate, should help to improve the publics' understanding of the true alternatives. Even so, the Central Bank's ability to enter the public arena to help educate the public will be limited; if its advice appears to have a regular bias in favour of one, or another, political party's programmes, then it risks breaking the necessary wide consensus, and thus, perhaps losing its own independence.

Besides such educational functions, a Central Bank should be able, dependent on the strength and breadth of its political support, to give significantly greater priority in its monetary policy actions to the achievement of longer term price stability; it will have a longer time horizon. Subject to the earlier qualification about hysteresis, that would be advantageous in itself, since in the longer term no output growth is lost and greater price stability is achieved. Moreover, depending on its record, its constitutional position, and its political support, a Central Bank may hope to make its, and the nation's, future adherence to price stability more *credible*. To the extent that such credibility is achieved, private sector behaviour may help to make such stability self-fulfilling, (since a rise in prices would then become a signal to sell, not to buy more, before inflation worsens further); it may become possible for the Central Bank to offset short-term shocks to a greater extent without risking its longer-term credibility, and the costs in terms of short-term unemployment and output loss of reverting to price stability may fall. The achievement of credibility by the Central Bank for the maintenance of a stationary process of price stability is the Holy Grail of this exercise.

It is dubious whether this Holy Grail has yet been attained. Whereas countries with independent Central Banks do tend to have lower inflation, I have seen no evidence to indicate that their loss ratio, measured as the number of extra man-years of unemployment necessary to lower inflation by one per cent, has also been significantly or systematically lowered. Even so, there are likely to be *some* practical differences in credibility between countries, such as Germany and Switzerland, which have a proven reputation for maintaining low inflation, and those countries which may be enacting constitutional independence for their own Central Banks for the first time, in some part in the hopes of improving a relatively poor past inflationary performance. This suggests that the mandate for the achievement of low inflation may need to be more tightly drawn, and narrowly focused, for the newly independent Central Banks, as in New Zealand: the longer and better established independent Central Banks, with a stronger counter-inflationary track-record, can afford to be more accommodating to short-term shocks, since this will not immediately endanger their credibility. This was one of the considerations influencing the Roll Committee's judgement in the UK, whether a prospectively independent Bank of England should follow the Bundesbank or the New Zealand model.

In the UK context, with which I am, of course, most familiar, there have been two main arguments put up *against* independence for the Bank of England, which should be directly addressed. The first is to query the democratic accountability of an independent Central Bank; the second is to ask whether such independence would preclude a desirable degree of policy coordination: (this latter issue is generally raised *intra*-nationally, but could also be relevant in an *inter*-national context). Neither criticism is compelling.

The issue of democratic accountability depends on the exact model of the independent Central Bank under consideration. Under the New Zealand model, democratic accountability is clearly *enhanced*. The government is a party to the specific contract, and maintains an override. The public knows exactly what the Governor's objective is, and the Governor is accountable for that. I would agree that democratic accountability is formally lacking in the Bundesbank model, but that may be because, in the German context, there is such a strong, underlying coherence between the public, the political parties, and the Bundesbank on the appropriate (medium term) objectives that there is less need to formalise them. This suggests two conclusions. First, the question of democratic accountability is model specific. Second, it may be undesirable to seek to impose on other European central banks the German model, since the success of the latter may depend on circumstances and conditions particular to Germany.

The second question, of coordination, has been raised in the UK, not altogether surprisingly, by ex-Treasury officials. There is, however, nothing to stop fiscal policy still being co-ordinated with the given, counter-inflationary monetary policy. The argument is not really about co-ordination, but about which policy instrument should move first and have primacy. Under the Keynesian policy modalities of the 1950s and 1960s, fiscal policy had primacy; the fiscal deficit was decided first, and monetary policy then adjusted to achieve the desired level of interest rates, given the deficit. With an independent Central Bank, monetary policy is aimed at achieving stable prices. The government, and Treasury, can still vary fiscal policy as they prefer. But in so far as such fiscal measures are assessed by the Central Bank as affecting the future course of inflation, the Central Bank will vary interest rates in a countervailing fashion. Essentially the difference is that, without independence, the Treasury can bring about a change in the fiscal stance while ensuring that interest rates remain unchanged. With independence, a change in the fiscal stance is rather likely to induce an offsetting interest rate adjustment. While one can see why Treasury officials and Ministers may prefer the first set-up, it is equally self-evident why the latter is likely to be more consistent with price stability.

Indeed, one of the advantages of an independent Central Bank is that, once Treasury officials and Ministers lose the power to control short-term monetary policies, fiscal policy itself may become more disciplined. The coordination issue may, in truth, be an argument *for*, rather than against, Central Bank independence.

If I may sum up now, I do not think that the enactment of Central Bank independence will make an enormous difference; it will not be a panacea leading directly to price stability at little, or no, short term cost. The continuing (and perfectly natural and proper) political constraints on even the most independent Central Bank, concerns about the exchange rate, and the very complexity of the inflation process itself, will all serve to lessen the likely effects of such a constitutional measure. If people expect the world to alter greatly for the better immediately after such a change, they are likely to be gravely disappointed.

The adoption of Central Bank independence ought, instead, to be seen as an incremental step, leading to somewhat improved policy measures, in both the monetary *and* fiscal areas, aimed at a longer time-horizon, and to a better public understanding of policy issues. I would stress the latter. An independent Central Bank will fail and be rejected, unless it can establish broadly-based public support for its policies. The educational and presentational skills of an independent Central Bank will be as important as its technical and operational capabilities. To succeed it has to establish a broad constituency.

Will the present government in the UK propose a Bill to grant the Bank of England greater autonomy? That remains uncertain. The Select Committee (for the Treasury and Civil Service) of the House of Commons and the Roll Report have both proposed independence for the Bank advocating a modified form of the New Zealand Act. Both past Chancellors, Nigel Lawson and Norman Lamont, have endorsed the idea, but both the Prime Minister, John Major, the present Chancellor, Ken Clarke, and the Leader of the Opposition, John Smith, remain cagey, unwilling to reveal either their preferences, or their arguments, in any detail. Mrs Thatcher was broadly in favour of the idea when in opposition, but turned against it when in power. That is symptomatic of the main, but largely unspoken, reason for political objection, which is that it serves, and is intended, to reduce politician's hands-on power over the economy. It is always hard for any Prime Minister to cede any particle of his, or her, power.

It is the case, of course, that the UK could only participate in EMU if the Bank was to have become independent by the time of entry, but that is not currently a factor enhancing the likelihood of such an Act. After the travails of the ERM, the path to, and achievement of, EMU is seen as problematical. There are, moreover, so many passionate euro-sceptics in the UK that, should independence for the Bank of England be seen as part of the federal European program, it might endanger its chances of obtaining Parliamentary assent. In any case, as already noted, the Select Committee of the House of Commons and the Roll Report have recommended a modified version of the New Zealand Model, and that is not exactly consonant with the Maastricht

Treaty, which appears to require national Central Banks to adopt, more or less, the Bundesbank model.

Whether this, or a successor, government will introduce such a Bill, therefore remains uncertain. The worst reason for doing so would be to try to bind the hands of a successor from another party, though that may nevertheless be influential. The best reason for doing so would be because it becomes widely accepted that such independence would be beneficial to us all.

5 Alternative Monetary Standards (1992)*

5.1 INTRODUCTION

During the course of the past two decades the interplay of the pressure of events, together with the development of academic and informed thinking, led the major Central Banks of the industrialised world to experiment with various alternative methods of monetary management and control – different *monetary standards or regimes* as they are usually termed. In particular, Central Banks responded to the worsening inflation of the 1970s by adopting quantitative monetary targets as their main intermediate monetary objective. Such targets were 'intermediate' in the sense that they lay between the operational instruments of Central Banks (e.g. open market operations to vary either prices, i.e. interest rates, or quantities, the monetary base, in money markets) on the one hand, and the ultimate objectives of policy, especially the control of inflation, on the other.

As described further below, such targetry led to tight monetary policies in the early 1980s, which *did* result in a significant reduction in inflation, albeit at the expense of a severe, but temporary, recession (1980–2) and a longer-lasting problem of debt overhang among less developed countries. In the event, however, the relationship between monetary expansion and the growth of nominal incomes, i.e. the velocity of money, proved much less stable than had been expected, at least for the initially chosen key monetary aggregates (M3 pounds in UK, M1 in USA). Whereas the instability in the demand for money functions of certain other monetary aggregates (e.g. M0 in UK, M2 in USA) was somewhat less marked, there was diminished faith in the applicability of monetary targetry for the successful conduct of policy, just at a time, in the mid-1980s, when attention had been turning away from overriding concern with controlling inflation to other objectives, such as exchange-rate stability and the resumption of full employment.

This latter historical story is told in much greater detail in my survey paper on 'The Conduct of Monetary Policy' (1989), and Chapter 6 here. The distinction between that paper, and this chapter, is that the former paper is much more concerned with short-term macroeconomic policy matters, concentrating on issues of monetary policy and theory that were of particular importance in the context of the past two decades. By contrast the purpose

---

* Chapter 2 in K. Dowd and M.K. Lewis (eds), *Current Issues in Financial and Monetary Economics* (Macmillan, 1992): 15–41.

72

of this chapter, is to examine briefly major structural changes in monetary systems and methods of management and control stretching over several decades, even centuries.

5.2 THE MAINTENANCE OF CONVERTIBILITY

The *convertibility* of deposits into some generally accepted external source of value represents a fundamental cornerstone of bank intermediation. While the crucial development in early banking lay in the appreciation that a *proportion* of the specie (gold, silver) left with bankers for safe-keeping and convenience could be loaned out (with a prudently acceptable balance between greater profit and increased risk), the banker *had* to ensure that his clients would be confident of converting the bankers' notes and deposits back into specie on sight or at notice; otherwise they would withdraw their existing balances with the bank, and the contagious effect of such withdrawals could then precipitate a 'run'. A rigorous theoretical analysis of the conditions that lead to bank runs, in a modern rather than an historical context, is to be found in Diamond and Dybvig (1983).

Banks can provide money to needy borrowers either by using their own capital, or by making loans of the funds deposited with them. Governments have often found themselves in the position of a needy borrower, especially when wanting to finance an expensive war. In turn, governments have had the power to provide valuable favours to a bank, in exchange for funds, in the form of a (local) monopoly over note issue, a monopoly over the handling of tax revenues, a privileged ownership structure (e.g. being specially Chartered as contrasted with a private partnership). Thus the Bank of England and the Banque de France were originally established (1694 and 1800 respectively) by their governments to provide funds for them in exchange for such monopolistic favours.

Indeed, as has been shown by Cameron (1967), these early (pre-1850) government banks on occasions used their privileged, monopolistic position to hinder the establishment of other strong, competitive banks; this is one reason why the Scottish banking system, which had a separate, independent structure, proved more robust in the eighteenth and early nineteenth century than the English banking system. Moreover, at times of particular stress and need for funds under pressure of war, governments frequently called on these banks, which they had specially chartered, for such massive extra loans that the ratio of loans outstanding to specie reserves became unduly stretched. In the face of external drains of specie, as domestic monetary expansion turned the balance of payments adverse, and internal drains, as rising nominal incomes led to increasing requirements for coin, there would be an increasing danger of 'runs' even on the governments' own chartered bank, and subsequent financial panic and crisis.

In order to avert such a potential catastrophe the government would then decree that their own main chartered bank's notes were 'legal tender' for the payment of taxes, and release the bank from its obligation to maintain convertibility. The Bank of England went through just such a period of inconvertibility, and restriction of specie payments, during the years 1797 to 1821, and many other European government banks, e.g. in Belgium, France, Austria, Denmark, etc. were forced into temporary periods of inconvertibility by the urgent needs of war finance at one time or another during the nineteenth century.

Nevertheless, even when the pressures preventing the resumption of convertibility seemed endemic, it was always recognised that such convertibility into specie was the appropriate, proper regime for a bank. The episodes of war-time monetary expansion and inconvertibility were, almost invariably, accompanied by worsening inflation; while there was some controversy, e.g. the Bullionist controversy in England, about the extent of responsibility of monetary expansion, as contrasted with specific demand and supply side factors, for such inflation, the consensus was that the forced adoption of fiat, legal tender (the *cours forcé*) was a sign of political weakness and the harbinger of inflation.

Meanwhile, the strong, central position of the government's bank led (many of) the smaller banks and discount houses to keep their reserves largely in the form of notes issued by, and deposits with, this central bank. This had a number of advantages for the smaller banks who might obtain some benefits in the form of interest on deposits, or access to borrowing facilities, or clearing facilities, or other correspondent services, so that such reserve holdings with the central bank came, in their view, to be preferable to holding large quantities of (sterile) specie in their own vaults. In turn, the balances held by such correspondent banks with the central bank increased the latter's balance sheet position.

This led, without any official prompting, to a pyramiding of the reserves of the banking system, with the generality of banks keeping the majority of their reserves with the central, government-chartered, bank, and with the bulk of the whole system's reserves of specie (gold and/or silver) concentrated in this central bank. This naturally led to considerable discussion about what was the responsibility of the central bank for managing the system that had evolved in this way. These discussions gave rise to the debate between the 'currency' and the 'banking' schools of thought in the UK in the first half of the nineteenth century, leading up to the 1844 Bank Charter Act (see Fetter, 1965); in addition there was a third group which deplored both the privileged position of the central bank and the pyramiding and centralisation of reserves that had occurred, (as recorded by White, 1984b); while this latter group included several notable figures, a major problem (as Walter Bagehot, a convinced sympathiser, recognised in *Lombard Street*, 1873) was that the removal/abolition of the Bank of England was just not practical politics.

The currency school argued that monetary problems arose when the money supply, which this school defined as consisting of coins and bank notes, *but not bank deposits*, rose too fast relatively to the available specie reserve base. They argued that so long as the issue of bank notes was constrained to adjust automatically in line with the specie base, all would be well and that the central bank, in this case the Bank of England, need have no further responsibility for the working of the system as a whole – no systemic responsibility – and could revert to operating as any other profit-maximising commercial bank.

The banking school contested the concentration of the currency school on one narrow monetary aggregate, and argued that the central bank did have a responsibility to maintain both convertibility and the soundness of the banking system as a whole by the appropriate discretionary management of its portfolio. Thus it should ensure convertibility by maintaining a prudent balance between its earning assets and its gold reserves (a ratio that became known as 'the proportion'), and seek to ensure the prudential *quality* of bank loans by refusing to discount low-quality paper.

In the event the currency school won the immediate battle, since the 1844 Bank Charter Act was designed according to its precepts, including the division of the Bank of England into two separate Departments (Issue and Banking) – a division which had become an anachronism by the 1870s and continues to be a source of statistical confusion to this day, with the Issue Department treated as part of the public sector, and the Banking Department as part of the banking sector. But the banking school won the war. A series of financial crises in the mid-nineteenth century required the suspension of the 1844 Act, to allow an emergency increased issue of Bank of England notes, if they were to be allayed. The experiences seemed to demonstrate that the monetary and banking system needed to be managed in order to avoid crises. The monetary rule of the currency school was not satisfactory in practice.

The ultimate objective of the central bank, however, remained convertibility into specie. The main indicator which it watched was the proportion of gold reserves to earning assets. The main instrument which it developed, about which more is said in the next section, was to use its position as the main source of cash reserves for the commercial banking system to inject or withdraw further reserves (originally through a variety of devices, now primarily by open market operations) to control interest rates. When the central bank raised interest rates, it would make the deposit of specie and coin with commercial banks more attractive (higher interest rates being paid on deposits) and by the same token would make borrowing from banks more expensive, and hence less attractive: so an increase in interest rates would help to stem both internal, and external, drains of specie from the banking system. When the central bank's gold reserves declined, it would withdraw cash reserves and raise interest rates, and vice versa.

Ideally such variation in interest rates would not only maintain convertibility, but also stability in the banking system. In practice unforeseen shocks (or bad management) could still lead to financial crises developing. In such cases commercial banks facing runs to withdraw deposits into gold coin, or into central bank notes, would turn to the central bank for assistance. In such cases Bagehot emphasised that the central bank should lend freely to reputable and prudently managed banks, but at high interest rates.

Thus by the latter half of the nineteenth century, the gold standard regime was in place. Although its decisions remained discretionary, the central banks mostly followed the rules of the game, raising interest rates in the face of declining gold reserves, and vice versa. In addition it increasingly accepted a further responsibility for sustaining the health of the banking sector as a whole, and staving off financial panics by appropriate last-resort lending (see Goodhart, 1988 and several of the papers in Capie and Wood, 1991).

Even in those countries without a formal central bank, the natural evolution of the pyramiding of (smaller) bank reserves with, and the concentration and centralisation of specie reserves in, some set of major, central commercial banks, or bank, occurred, [as in the USA or in most countries, such as India or Brazil, prior to the formal establishment of central banks there]. In those countries where a single commercial bank dominated, it tended to assume quasi-central-bank functions. In those countries, such as the USA, where the pyramiding/centralisation went to a *group* of powerful New York banks, the Clearing House which they had established and run assumed certain quasi-central-banking functions, see Timberlake (1978, 1984).

The rules of the gold-standard regime required the central bank to tighten interest rates just at the time when increasing optimism was leading to faster monetary expansion, and hence a declining proportion of reserves to deposits. It was generally easier for central banks, which were by this time no longer seeking to maximise profits, to do this than for large commercial banks. The consensus was that, without a central bank to manage the monetary system, crises were more likely and more severe. So, by the start of the twentieth century central banks were in vogue, and by the middle of the century virtually every country had one.

The basis, the rules of the game, on which central banks had been operating, however, changed dramatically with the onset of war in 1914. As had happened in previous war-time periods, the exigencies of government finance rapidly led to such monetary expansion among the European combatants that they were forced off into inconvertible, fiat currency. Inflation, and in some cases hyperinflation, followed.

There was naturally a desire in the 1920s, to return to the pre-1914 gold age, but the disruption of the 1914–18 war had been so great that the return to the gold standard proved hard to arrange smoothly. Much of the world's gold reserves had been accumulated by the world's emerging leading creditor nation, the USA, during the war. Rectification of this imbalance required either inflation in the USA or deflation elsewhere. The structural upheavals caused by the war meant that the parities of 1914 would no longer be appropriate, but nevertheless attempts to go back to those in some countries – e.g. the UK – caused stagnation there while the adoption of more competitive parities elsewhere, e.g. France, meant that real exchange rates, and competitiveness, were not in line with their underlying equilibrium values. Beyond this, the dissension over German reparations and war debts continued to hinder international cooperation.

In this context the Federal Reserve Board (the 'Fed') in the USA did not have the previously relatively clear guidelines of the pre-1914 gold standard by which to steer. It hardly wanted to inflate consciously, simply because it had so much gold, yet it may have somewhat muted and delayed its contra-cyclical response to the stock-market boom of the late 1920s because of its concern with its international responsibilities. Thus Friedman and Schwartz (1963, p. 297 and Chapter 6) wrote that:

> Inevitably in the absence of any single well-defined statutory objective, conflicts developed between discretionary objectives of monetary policy. The two most important arose out of the re-establishment of the gold standard abroad and the emergence of the bull market in stocks.

Even worse was to follow. One of the reasons why the Fed failed to adopt a more expansionary, contra-cyclical policy when the initial downturn in 1929 moved into extremely severe recession, with large-scale bank failures and severe monetary contraction in 1931–3, was the outflow of gold, especially after the UK left the gold standard in September 1931 (see Friedman and Schwartz, 1963, Chapter 7).

A conclusion which Friedman and Schwartz drew from this débâcle was that a central bank's discretionary management is more likely to be inept when it seeks to achieve several, potentially incompatible objectives at the same time. In this case in the inter-war period there were certain conflicts between external and internal objectives. Yet it is by no means clear that the appropriate objective *should* necessarily be an internal one, e.g. domestic price stability, rather than an external one, e.g. holding the exchange rate pegged, or fixed, against some external source of value. If the latter external source of value can at the same time provide a reasonable guarantee of price stability, then the external objective would also provide the additional benefit of stable exchange rates.

Indeed, the breakdown of the gold standard in the early 1930s, and the increasing concentration of national central banks on inward-looking autarchic monetary policies, led to such chaotic exchange-rate movements and such restrictions on trade, as well as on capital movements, that the architects of the international monetary system at Bretton Woods in 1944 determined that a more structured system of exchange rates was necessary, in which these would normally be held pegged against gold, or the US dollar, but could be adjusted (revalued) in those cases in which a 'fundamental disequilibrium' was held to exist.

5.3   THE BREAKDOWN OF THE BRETTON WOODS SYSTEM

Indeed, at the end of the 1960s, the major countries of the world still adhered to the Bretton Woods system of pegged but adjustable exchange rates. Under such a system, the main requirement and objective of the central bank is to maintain the value of the domestic money stock in some nearly-fixed relationship to some other external standard of value; under the Bretton Woods system the external standard of value was initially gold, whose value in terms of US dollars was in turn held fixed. After a steady process of mild inflation in the 1950s and 1960s had led to the fixed dollar value of gold becoming unrealistically low in real terms, a run on (US) gold reserves developed. In 1968 the USA was forced to abandon pegging the gold price, and the Bretton Woods system became one of linking currency parities to the dollar, *de jure* as well as *de facto*: the interest rates available on dollar reserves had made them more attractive than gold for other central banks to hold, until there was a serious prospect of forthcoming gold revaluation, as Triffin (1960) had foreseen would happen.

As already noted, the maintenance of the convertibility of the domestic money stock into an external standard of value has been the normal procedure for *all* central banks (with the important exception of the US Federal Reserve System) for the greater part of their history.

As described in section 5.2, the primary instrument that they had developed for achieving this objective was their ability to control interest rates. When a tendency for the value of domestic money to depreciate relative to the external standard of value occurs, an increase in interest rates will not only have a deflationary effect on domestic credit expansion, output and inflation, but will also attract capital inflows from abroad. Both historical experience and economic theorists of all schools agree that the medicine will work.

Nevertheless the medicine is often unpalatable. Besides having the generally *desired* effect of maintaining the internal value of the currency, and restraining inflation, an increase in interest rates not only adversely affects the level of output but also, and perhaps more important, its composition, with a particularly severe effect on activity financed by borrowing, such as housing. This is politically unpopular.

In order to alleviate the adverse domestic consequences of such distributional effects on expenditures, while at the same time maintaining external convertibility, central banks have repeatedly been forced, often by outside pressure, to bring other more direct methods of control in support of, or even instead of, their traditional interest-rate adjustments. Exchange controls provide, perhaps, the most common example. They operate, however, by impairing the ability of the ordinary private citizen to take full advantage of the external convertibility that is otherwise formally preserved. In addition, direct-lending ceilings to limit and to redistribute domestic credit, and tariffs and export subsidies, are further mechanisms which can be used to try to maintain the convertibility objective at a generally lower level of interest rates than would otherwise be required. While in the short run the advantages of such direct controls may seem considerable, even self-evident, the inefficiencies and distortions that increasingly ensue, the longer such direct controls are kept in place, make their adoption questionable at all times.

Historical experience has abundantly demonstrated that the main threat to the maintenance of external convertibility and to price stability has come from governments being forced, usually as a result of war, defence expenditures, or the political unpopularity of explicit taxation, to resort to the printing press – that is to an inflation tax – to finance their actions. Monetarists would add to the list of inflation-causing factors the siren-song of Keynesian support for deficit budgeting whenever output fell below some, often over-optimistically estimated, full employment level.

The examples of countries being forced into inflation by the pressures of war, or by the attempt to maintain public-sector expenditures well in excess of governments' political ability to finance through taxation, have been historically obvious, even dramatic. What then became a more nagging worry in the post-war world has been the attempts of governments to encourage faster growth, or even just recovery in output, by means of fiscal and monetary expansion to an extent that endangers the pegged exchange rate, unless a fairly savage dose of deflation is applied. The problem then is that the relative inflexibility of labour and goods markets – that is of wages and prices – makes so much of the initial adjustment fall on employment and output, rather than on wages and prices. Faced with an exchange rate out of line with equilibrium, which may have resulted in the first place from excessive political pressures, how strongly can, or should, a central banker argue for the defence of its current level, if that would require domestic adjustment of a severity which might possibly threaten political consensus and even social stability? But, if financial stability is not maintained at an early stage, will not an even more difficult spiral of exchange-rate depreciation and worsening domestic inflation set in?

So, the maintenance of a regime of convertibility into an external standard of value, the historical commonplace for central banks, may sound easy. All it involves is varying interest rates inversely to the strength of the balance of payments. In practice, however, its conduct in the post-war world involved continuing arguments both on the weights to be placed on interest rates or direct controls as instruments, and on whether it was better to defend the existing exchange rate or to adjust its value to another level.

Despite these various difficulties the periods when the main industrialised countries of the world jointly adhered to a generally fixed exchange-rate system, that is, the gold-standard period, roughly from 1870 to 1913, and the Bretton Woods period, from 1945 to 1971, were the outstanding occasions of world economic success, combining generally low inflation, with little inter-country dispersion around the mean (thus it is often now forgotten that in the 1950s and 1960s the UK was a relatively low-inflation country), with relatively rapid growth, though the latter was not steady over time and varied quite sharply between countries.

Why, then, did the major countries of the world abandon a system of proven success in 1971–3, without the excuse of a major war as in 1914? Of course, the success of the Bretton Woods period is clearer in hindsight: at the time the discipline entailed in the pegged-exchange-rate system was felt to be irksome. The British disliked it, because the stop-periods in the stop-go cycle, enforced in order to maintain the sterling exchange rate, were held to prevent the achievement of a satisfactorily faster rate of growth: the Germans disliked it because the maintenance of a fixed exchange rate forced them to accept the faster rate of inflation being generated in the USA by the Vietnam War: the USA disliked it because the pegged-exchange-rate system allowed other individual countries to shift their peg on competitive grounds against them, but hardly allowed them, despite the high-level labours of the Smithsonian round, to adjust the dollar *vis-à-vis* everyone else: the French disliked it because it allowed the USA too much leeway to finance the Vietnam War by running a current account deficit, since other central banks had to hold dollars after the closing of the gold window. Rather more generally, academic economic opinion had become opposed to pegged exchange rates, with a strong theoretical attachment to free floating.

There was, in addition, a second reason. The development of an international capital market, with improved communications, etc, was vastly increasing the volume and rapidity of cross-country capital flows, especially when the market smelled the chance of chasing a central bank facing a one-way option. In 1972 a second-rate sterling crisis that hardly hit the headlines was nonetheless sufficient to denude much of our own usable reserves in the UK within a fortnight. In earlier years the size of central bank reserves, relative to potential market flows, allowed the authorities to use intervention as the short-time adjustment, allowing them more time to review whether, and by how much, a change in interest rates was required. The failure of central bank reserves to grow in line with the expanding international capital market was, however, in some part the result of conscious decision by policy-makers to restrain such international reserves out of fear of their possible world inflationary consequences.

Anyhow, as the size of the international capital market grew, relative to central bank reserves, even to the extent that these could be augmented by cooperation among central banks with exchange, etc. the extent of reliance that could be placed on (sterilised) intervention declined, until it is now widely seen as an instrument of strictly limited usefulness. Under such circumstances the maintenance of exchange-rate stability seems to imply a willingness to allow domestic interest rates to adjust rapidly to all shocks affecting the exchange rate, whether those shocks originate at home or abroad (except to the extent that exchange controls on capital flows can dampen the impact of such shocks on domestic interest rates). The virulence of external shocks in the 1970s, notably the oil shocks, however, was so great that it is debatable whether the fixed-exchange-rate system could have endured, even had there been a greater will to defend it. I shall review in section 5.5 present prospects for restoring such a system.

5.4 MONETARY TARGETS

For several countries, including the UK, the collapse of the Bretton Woods system was a semi-conscious rejection of financial discipline in pursuit of faster-growth objectives. The experience of the years, 1972–5, thereafter, however, confirmed the worst fears of those who claimed that the supposed trade-off between inflation and higher output was illusory, even possibly perverse, in all but the short-run (see Friedman, 1968 and various subsequent papers, and Phelps, 1972). While there remains debate about the wider question of how far the oil shock of 1973 was *sui generis*, or itself an inevitable response to more expansionary Western economic policies in 1971–3, and whether inflation which followed the oil shocks in 1973 could be attributed more to the oil shock or to those expansionary policies, there was a general consensus that those countries which maintained a relatively more expansionary policy through that period, such as the UK and Italy, did worse generally, on inflation and ultimately also on output, than those countries such as Germany that battened down the monetary hatches early on. The former group of countries subsequently had to reverse their relatively expansionary policies.

This experience pointed to an urgent need to establish an alternative bastion of financial discipline, to replace the exchange rate, as a constraint against over-expansionary policies, and as a guarantee against ever-worsening inflation and financial chaos. The case for the adoption of such an alternative domestic financial target, in the form of an intermediate monetary target, had long been pressed by monetarists. They argued that the medium-term stability of the velocity of money, the close relationship apparent throughout history between inflation and monetary growth, made a monetary target not only a necessary and sufficient guard against worsening inflation, but also a more efficient form of constraint than a pegged exchange rate, since it freed domestic monetary policy to control domestic inflation. Moreover, it was recognised that volatile expectations about future inflation made it increasingly difficult to use interest rates as a yardstick to judge the stance of monetary policy: the case for shifting the focus of attention for domestic monetary policy purposes from prices, in the form of interest rates, to quantities, in the form of growth rates of the monetary aggregates, seemed demonstrably established. Concerns over which monetary aggregate to choose and possible instabilities in short-run relationships between monetary aggregates, activity, inflation and interest rates were dismissed as second-order problems.

The general case for intermediate monetary targets was also accepted by many moderate Keynesians, at least outside the UK, partly on the grounds that velocity was sufficiently stable for monetary movements to represent a reasonable leading indicator of future movements in nominal incomes. In consequence, an interest-rate adjustment that would restore monetary growth to its target path should also help to restore nominal incomes to its target path. In addition, the adoption of a monetary target not only allowed central banks to argue the case for adjusting interest rates on apparently objective grounds, but even in some cases allowed them to operate in such a way – for example, through some version of monetary base control – as to be able to claim that the resulting interest-rate changes were nothing to do with them, but only the result of free-market actions, in a system where the central bank set the *quantity* of money and its *price* – i.e. the level of interest rates in the short run – was freely determined to equilibrate demand and supply. This latter had obvious 'political' advantages. Thus there was a sizeable constituency in favour of monetary targets, opposed really only by those who thought that financial discipline and the control of inflation was an undesirable constraint, or a strictly subsidiary objective, or could be achieved at less cost by prices and incomes policies.

Indeed, in some quarters the main subject of discussion was whether the public announcement of a commitment to a medium-term strategy for rapid monetary deceleration, supported by credible policies, would not allow for a faster deceleration of both monetary growth and inflation, without much, or any, accompanying depression of output and employment, because of expectational effects. Analogies were drawn with the monetary reforms which had terminated certain European hyperinflations without significantly worse unemployment then resulting (see Sargent, 1986, especially Chapter 3 on 'The Ends of Four Big Inflations' and Chapter 4 on 'Stopping Moderate Inflation: The Methods of Poincaré and Thatcher').

In the event, a more cautious gradualism was generally adopted. Even so, the effects on output and employment were as severe as the most old-fangled Keynesian economists warned. Some economists and commentators blamed this on a lack of commitment, and/or on inappropriate supporting policies, by the central bank and/or government, so that the promise of lower future monetary growth (and inflation) was not treated as credible. Other economists, including myself, argued that the normal market mechanisms through which wages and prices were set were not such as to allow government promises of future lower monetary growth to have much current impact on wage or price-setting decisions today. (The difference in hyperinflationary conditions is that normal market mechanisms for wage- and price-setting will already have largely broken down in chaos.) So monetary targets did not prove a painless panacea, but few had thought they would.

However, it was not so much the pain and stress of the severe (in the UK at least) recession in 1980/2 that led to a withdrawal from monetary targetry, but rather the comparative *success* of such tight monetary policies in bringing inflation down to levels (e.g. below 5 per cent) by the mid-1980s, at which its further containment no longer seemed of overriding priority. In these circumstances many pragmatic politicians, and even some central bankers, gave more weight to other issues, considerations and priorities, e.g. exchange-rate stability, the growth of employment, etc. Even so, had the link between monetary growth and nominal incomes remained predictable, it is extremely doubtful whether any major country would have abandoned targetry simply because inflation seemed less immediately threatening.

A more serious problem was that the vaunted stability of velocity was found wanting, at least in a number of countries for periods long enough to cause serious policy problems. The relationships between £M3 and subsequent movements in nominal incomes in the UK and between M1 and nominal incomes in the USA and Canada, have all been subject to such sizeable and unpredictable (at least unpredicted at the time) shifts, that the emphasis on the achievement of such single targets had to be relaxed. What has been increasingly appreciated is that the stability of the time-series relationships between any particular definition of money and nominal incomes depends on the institutional structure of the system. The very pressures, of worsening and more volatile inflation, that led to the adoption of monetary targets also encouraged innovation and competitive pressures that resulted in changes to the structure. Moreover, as some of us have noted, the adoption of a new target, to take advantage of an apparent statistical regularity, is liable of itself to result in changes to the structure of the system that will cause the prior regularity to collapse.

In particular, the onset of high and fluctuating inflation brought with it, as both lenders and borrowers tried to adjust, high and fluctuating market interest rates. Up until the 1970s banks had generally been prepared to set interest rates on their deposit liabilities in a passive, administered context. Demand/sight deposits were generally offered at no interest, while the rates provided on time-deposits were subject to various constraints through cartel agreements, legal certificates under Regulation Q, etc. This meant that the authorities, by shifting market rates relative to such passively-determined bank rates, were able to affect the flow of deposits into the banking system, and hence the volume of funds that the banks could lend themselves. Since the beginning of the 1970s, however, banks have reacted to external market pressures by offering a larger and larger proportion of their liabilities at market-related interest rates. Whenever a profitable outlet for additional lending could be identified and established, banks and other financial intermediaries would bid for funds, largely in wholesale markets, to finance such lending. Moreover, the demand by borrowers for loans from banks has itself turned out to be relatively insensitive to interest-rate movements, perhaps in part because of tax offsets generally allowed. In consequence, both the elasticity of the response of monetary aggregates, and the possibility of imposing a credit squeeze, following interest-rate adjustments, have diminished. Particularly in those countries allowing tax advantages and offsets for borrowers, the resulting volatility and average level of interest rates increased.

Another partial consequence of this was that much of the effect of domestic monetary targetry was transmitted through exchange-rate adjustments. There have been several examples in recent years of countries in which the confrontation between a tight monetary policy and expansionary pressures elsewhere in the same economy (e.g. UK, 1980–1; USA, 1982–5) was reflected in an appreciation in the real effective exchange-rate to levels that appeared grossly out of alignment with existing fundamentals.

As stated at the outset, a more detailed account of these recent events is available in my survey paper on 'The Conduct of Monetary Policy' (1989), Chapter 6 here. The aim of this chapter, instead, is to review a rather longer horizon, and to consider next the range of monetary regimes that we might possibly adopt in future.

5.5 WHITHER NOW?

There are, perhaps, some five possible alternatives now. In view of current steps towards economic and monetary union (EMU) in Europe, the first, most immediate, option for the UK is simply to stay in the Exchange Rate Mechanism (ERM) of the European Monetary System (EMS), currently a pegged but adjustable exchange rate system, but one which is now intended to move on to the adoption of irrevocably fixed parities, and then ultimately to a single European currency. (The UK joined the ERM in October 1990.) Whereas such a progression towards monetary union is underway in Western Europe, it remains hard to observe any significant progress towards the readoption of external, exchange rate, constraints on domestic monetary policy between the three main (G3) block centres, i.e. Europe/DM, America/dollar, and Asia/ Yen. Consequently the regime shift which is currently most relevant for the UK is not at present politically (or economically?) feasible at the world level.

The adoption of an irrevocably fixed parity against some external source of value, e.g. gold or the DM, does limit, though it does not completely remove, a central bank's powers of independent action, e.g. in prudential supervision, or lender-of-last-resort functions. Of course, a single European currency would require a single focus of monetary decision-making, a European System of Central Banks, as set out in the Delors Report of 1989. An even more radical option now canvassed by some theoreticians is not only to fix the money stock to some external source of value, perhaps a basket of goods or a labour standard as an 'ideal' index of value, but also to abolish central banks as such, and to rely on competitive forces, and/or on structural changes in the banking system, to maintain financial stability.

A third option would be to move on from monetary targets to nominal income targets. A fourth possibility would be to hope for a return to stable predictability in monetary velocity, so that monetary targetry, after the present hiatus, could be resumed. A fifth option would be simply to go back to the previous regime of purely discretionary monetary management. In practice, however, such discretion is conditioned by continuing observation and assessment of developments amongst both nominal income and monetary indicators, so the final three alternatives are not really distinct from each other, being more a matter of the balance of emphasis in the continuing conduct of domestic monetary policy, whereas the first two involve a clear shift in the locus of decision-making, sharing it with other countries in the first option and abandoning it altogether in the second.

Readoption of Fixed Exchange Rates

Although this alternative would undoubtedly severely limit national autonomy in conducting monetary policy (except for the central, hegemonic, country in such a system, e.g. for Germany in the EMS, or the USA in the Bretton Woods system), and would strictly limit the ability of national policy-makers to address purely domestic objectives, there is growing doubt about how valuable that freedom really is. Recent history now makes the 1950s and 1960s, when Bretton Woods still held, look like a golden age compared with the disturbances of the 1970s and 1980s, two decades of general floating. The causal connections, such as they may be, however are mixed; thus the disturbances of the 1970s and early 1980s may have forced floating on us willy-nilly; but the desire to return to an apparently more stable system is strong, particularly within Europe.

Moreover, practical experience has demonstrated that flexible exchange rates do not adjust smoothly. Not only is there much short-term volatility, though the real costs of that are probably limited and often avoidable by hedging, e.g. in forward and futures markets, but it is also the case that major exchange-rate relativities have moved in certain cases far from their apparent comparative price-competitive equilibrium. There is less doubt that such misalignments have involved serious costs, in terms of inefficient allocations of resources and increased risk and uncertainties, in the countries involved.

Moreover, analytical argument suggests that the supposed benefits of having domestic freedom for monetary control are not all that great. With the continuing development of a single world capital market, the elasticity of cross-currency capital flows has almost certainly increased and is almost bound to increase further. This will tend to force *ex ante* real interest rates into equality in all countries. All that the local central banker will be able to influence will be *nominal* magnitudes, e.g. the rate of inflation, the movements in nominal exchange rates and interest rates. The question then arises as to what great value it is to have one's own local man doing that rather than relying on Mr Greenspan or Mr Pöhl.

In general, countries with a dominant currency (and economic position), such as Germany within the EMS, have not objected if other countries have sought to link their currencies in some pegged (but adjustable) relationship to their own, so long as they themselves continued to be allowed absolute sovereignty and command to pursue their own national policy as they thought fit. Many smaller countries, for the reasons already considered, have thought that the benefits in greater external stability (and counter-inflation credibility) arising from such a link outweighed the loss of domestic autonomy. Greater problems arise when the countries considering an exchange-rate link are more equivalent in financial strength. In virtually no case, prior to the 1990s, had the country whose currency would seem to be the most obvious central anchor of the system, been prepared to cede any significant part in the decision-making process concerning its own national (sovereign) monetary policy to other countries making up that system. Now, however, the Delors Committee Report (1989) does envisage a significant transfer of power from national Central Banks, including the Deutsche Bundesbank, to a federal European System of Central Banks (ESCB), though an ESCB whose proposed independence from political oversight, constitutional prime objective (price stability), and structure would seem to be largely modelled on the Bundesbank itself. More controversially, the Delors Committee Report claims that an accompanying transfer of powers over other economic policies, e.g. constraints over budget deficits and incomes policies, to a federal European centre in Brussels would also be necessary if the further steps – Stages 2 and 3 – towards monetary union were to be successfully implemented.

Moreover, there remains some concern about the technical problems of running a pegged, but adjustable, system of exchange rates, e.g. the ERM and Stage 1 of the Delors Committee Report, without the support of exchange controls in those cases where the economies of the countries involved have not succeeded in achieving underlying economic convergence, e.g. with similar trends in unit labour costs. Underlying divergences in inflation trends would, at times, lead to the development of one-way options, or unless the realignments are made promptly and in quite small, frequent steps – which latter course undermines the objectives of stability and monetary discipline that the system is intended to provide. It is no accident that Mrs Thatcher insisted at the Madrid summit in June 1989 that the UK would only join the ERM when the UK's inflation had fallen into line with that in Europe, and it was demonstrated that the ERM could continue to function well even after the abandonment of exchange controls. (The fact that the UK then joined anyway is another matter.)

It will be hard enough to overcome the technical and political obstacles confronting the achievement, in stages, of monetary union within Western Europe. It would be even harder to achieve either economic convergence, or political consensus on appropriate policies, or on the distribution of adjustments necessary to achieve such policies, between the major block currencies, DM, dollar and Yen. With each bloc having relatively a free flow of labour and goods within themselves, with a comparatively small flow between the blocs, adjustment to imbalances in the balance of payments between these blocs would be difficult to achieve smoothly without the support of changing (real) exchange rates. Consequently there may be no real alternative to a relatively free float between major bloc currencies, (though the path of that float should be capable of some influences from inter-governmental cooperation). The world is not yet ready, economically or politically, for a single world currency. Indeed it remains to be seen whether Western Europe does manage to move to a single European Currency.

Free Banking

As was noted earlier, there were many commentators and economists, e.g. Bagehot, who argued that both the natural and proper condition for banking was one of free competition between many private banks, the number of which would depend on economies of scale in the business. Central Banks, they claimed, had been imposed on the banking system by the intervention of governments. Both the resulting monopoly position of such central banks, and their close involvement with government, were seen as deplorable in theory, and liable to lead to endemic inflation in practice. So proponents of this view (e.g. Hayek, 1976) advocate a new regime, or constitution, in which central banks would be abolished, and banks would be left free, hence the term 'free-banking', to operate according to the dictates of their own commercial objectives, subject only to the same kind of legal constraint, e.g. on mergers and the misuse of monopoly power as apply to any other industry.

The dominant impulse of the advocates of a new monetary constitution is the conviction that virtually all, perhaps all, inflation arises from political mismanagement, a view which a study of history demonstrates has to be taken seriously. Furthermore central banks are held to be compromised, either through being themselves subject to political pressures, or because their nature as a large public-sector bureaucracy makes their pursuit of the goal of price stability less than whole-hearted. I do not myself accept the latter argument; though I do recognise the strength of the view that the issue of how to ensure the stability of the currency in a democracy is largely a constitutional question. Be that as it may, the advocates of a new monetary constitution seek to remove the conduct of macro-monetary policy from the hands of the authorities, by in effect making it into an automatic system.

There are various forms of automatic system proposed – for example, a return to the gold standard, the adoption of a fancier kind of commodity-based scheme in which all monetary units would represent a basket of standard raw materials, or alternatively Friedman's suggestion of a monetary bureau that would expand the base, every working day, at a fixed rate. The idea of removing any political influence, or discretionary management, from monetary affairs may sound academic and impractical. Nevertheless one must always remember Keynes's dictum about those in authority distilling the lessons of previous academic economists. Moreover, the earlier establishment of the Gold Standard Commission in the USA by President Reagan suggested that, were it not for bitter divisions in the ranks of the more right-wing thinkers about *which* monetary constitution to adopt, there might well be a strong constituency, at least in the USA, for such a change to be attempted.

One of the common features of such proposals is that the government/central bank should cease to issue and provide money, e.g. Bank of England notes. Some economists of this view have argued that the resulting external sources of value into which banks should be free to make their deposits, and bank notes (under these proposals, commercial banks would regain the right to issue notes) could also be chosen freely, and competitively. In practice the confusion that would result if some banks pegged to gold, others to wheat, others to coal, others to a basket of goods, would disrupt the efficient operation of the payments system. Since this latter is a public good, there is a case for the government defining what the common external source of value should be, but not getting involved in issuing money against it. Just as the authorities define a yard, or metre, as a certain distance, so they could play a metric role, defining a dollar or pound as equal to a certain amount of a good (ounces of gold) or goods, e.g. a basket of goods.

The latter is preferable in principle since it reflects more closely what people actually buy, hence ensuring price stability, and reduces the impact of relative demand/supply shocks on a single monetary good, (e.g. the discovery of gold in California in 1849). But one could hardly exercise convertibility directly into a statistically appropriate basket of goods. Instead the community would perhaps revert to full-value gold or silver coins, but the market value of such coins in terms of both the dollar/pound numéraire, and also of bank deposits, would change continuously over time, as the value of gold shifted relative to the basket. This has sometimes been described as 'indirect convertibility', e.g. by Greenfield and Yeager (1983) and Yeager (1985). That would make it harder to use such full-value coins for transactions purposes, but a combination of (commercial) banks notes, credit/debt cards, and subsidiary (base metal) low-value coins would be used for such purposes instead.

Besides doubts whether governments would ever be willing to relinquish their monetary powers in this way (for three main reasons, (a) power is enjoyed by those who have it, (b) the issue of banks notes provides a small, but useful, command over extra real resources (*seigniorage*) in normal times, (c) the use of the printing press as the final available source of finance may be vital to a government *in extremis*), such a return to free banking raises two questions: first, how would interest rates be determined in such a system, and second, would the banking system be prone to 'runs', panic, etc. without a central bank?

First, assume that banks could/would pay interest on *all* their liabilities, notes and deposits. There *are* some possible technical ways of paying interest on notes, either by issuing notes in smart card form which incorporate a continuous compound rate of interest, or by holding a lottery based on the identifying serial numbers of the notes outstanding, so the expected mean return equals the market rate. In such cases with all liabilities bearing interest, competition would force such rates into equality, after taking account of normal business costs, etc., with the underlying market rate of interest determined by the forces of productivity (and investment demand) and thrift (the propensity to save). It is its monopolistic ability to issue legal tender, zero-interest money that gives a central bank its monetary command over nominal interest rates; and with sticky, sluggishly adjusting prices, also over real interest.

It has been argued (e.g. Wallace, 1983) that if commercial banks were left free to issue bank notes, but that they found themselves unable to, or prevented from, paying any interest on these, then they would go on issuing these until interest rates were driven to close to zero, that no profit could be made from printing more notes to buy up (riskless) government debt, thereby presumably causing hyperinflation. This argument would hold if the commercial banks' notes were legal tender.

Otherwise, as history shows, since there have been many earlier periods of free commercial notes issue, an increased issue of notes will raise the probability of notes being presented for redemption. The need to sell assets (e.g. government debt) to meet the drain of specie reserve would lower the price of such assets and raise the possibility of runs on the banks and their insolvency. Accordingly there would be an equilibrium trade-off between return and risk. Since risk cannot be fully eliminated, the equilibrium return would not be driven to zero.

This then raises the second question of whether a free banking system would be inherently stable, or whether, without a central bank to provide prudential supervision and lender-of-last-resort services, it would be more prone to runs, panics and financial crises than in the past. Some economists (e.g. Dowd, 1989; Selgin, 1988) have argued that the normal working forces of competitive markets would make the system stable. Others have argued that the appropriate structural reforms (e.g. limiting the assets that banks could buy, *or* requiring banks to revalue all their assets continuously to their current market values, i.e. 'mark to market', and increasingly constraining the banks' freedom to operate as their free capital became further eroded, *or* basing the payments mechanism on deposits, units, whose capital value varied instanteously in line with their asset portfolio) could easily make banks proof against runs in a free banking milieu, without a central bank (see Goodhart, 1990; Shadow Financial Regulatory Committee, 1989).

These latter structural reforms would, however, generally prevent banks from undertaking the fixed interest loans of a non-marketed, and perhaps inherently non-marketable, form, i.e. advance to small businesses and persons, which has been a staple of their activities. Given the problems such small agents would have in borrowing directly from capital markets (e.g. high transactions costs, information asymmetries) some financial institutions will still have to specialise in making such loans, and will need to issue fixed interest liabilities against their fixed interest assets, and will maintain the risk characteristics of existing banks. So, even if 'safe' intermediaries can be developed to run the payments system, we may still need banks' credit-creating operations and a central bank to support these.

Some features of this alternative are visionary, and currently mostly of academic interest. If we then exclude either of these first two alternatives, we then turn to variants of presently available methods of existing central banks to conduct monetary policy for the achievement of domestic objectives.

A Nominal Income Target

If velocity was exactly predictable, then a monetary target would be identical to a nominal income target, since velocity is *defined* in terms of the relationship between the money stock on the one hand and of prices and output on the other. Anyhow, the ultimate objectives with which the authorities are concerned, output, employment, and price stability, relate to nominal incomes, not so much to the intermediate monetary variable, since the monetary aggregate itself is a statistical abstraction of no direct or immediate concern to anyone. Particularly therefore in the aftermath of velocity having proved to be more unpredictable than expected, many moderate Keynesians (in the USA) and moderate monetarists (in the UK) are suggesting a shift to targeting the path of nominal incomes itself.

This, however, implicitly involves giving exactly equal weight to a percentage deviation of real output from its desired level as to a divergence of prices from the objective for the price level, since nominal incomes equals prices time output, $Y = P \times Q$. Hall (1986) has suggested an improved method of targeting in which the weights on output and price level deviations could be chosen in such a manner as to reflect more closely some social welfare function weighting of output losses (unemployment) and price level instability and uncertainty.

While this latter suggestion could represent a considerable improvement over a simple nominal income target, there remain several serious objections to the adoption of nominal income targets. For those central banks which are constitutionally independent of the executive government, such as the Federal Reserve Board and the Deutsche Bundesbank, such a move could lead them into an awkward relationship with government. What if the central bank and the government might want to set different nominal incomes objectives? Moreover, nominal incomes are influenced by fiscal and other policies, as well as by monetary policy. How could a central bank unilaterally commit itself to achieve a nominal income target, when many of the relevant policy instruments were controlled elsewhere? These problems, essentially relating to policy coordination, are less pressing in countries where all policy is already coordinated under central political direction.

But many problems remain. For example, a rise in nominal income is composed of an increase in output, which is a good thing, and an increase in prices, which is a bad thing. How can you combine a good and a bad into a single target? To put the same point better, one may well want to react to a shock to prices by encouraging, through policy measures, a (partial) offset to output, in pursuit of stability. But if there was a shock to output, say it fell suddenly on account of a bad harvest, would one consciously seek *higher* prices in order to attain a nominal incomes target? The problem above could be reduced by the sensible adoption of an improved, Hall-type, system of targets.

Indeed, the above is something of a debating point. Much more serious is the fact that the national income data are generally quite long delayed, of uncertain accuracy and subject to major revisions, and, above all, represent the *lagged* consequences in the economy to *previous* policy initiatives. What one needs for policy purposes is not an accurate measure of where the economy *was*, but a reasonable indication of where it may *go* in future if no policy action should be taken now. By their nature past and still unreliable indications of GDP cannot give you that: you need, instead, some information, some leading indicators about future developments; and here current financial developments, if carefully and sensibly assessed, may help. By their nature there is really no way in which quarterly observations of past GDP can help to guide and direct a central bank's *day-to-day* decisions on market operations in money and exchange markets.

Where it may, however, be sensible to place more emphasis on a nominal income path is, rather, in establishing and publicly explaining the longer-term strategy and framework of policy over a run of years, within which intermediate targets, and shorter-term operating rules, will still be needed for the conduct of policy through each year.

Monetary Targets

It was, indeed, one of the intended purposes of monetary targetry, that the course of the chosen aggregate should provide a reasonably clear leading indication of where the economy was currently heading. The problem is that they no longer appear able to do so in a sufficiently clear and reliable manner. In the case of those aggregates which seemed to have a leading, predictive relationship with subsequent nominal income movements, e.g. £M3 in the UK, the (velocity) relationship between them has become quite unstable. In those cases where the demand for money function still fits quite well, e.g M0 in the UK, the relationship is concurrent, so that the M0 statistic does little more than provide a noisy signal of what is currently happening to consumers expenditures in current prices, which one knows anyway from retail sales and RPI data.

It is certainly possible that the current disturbances to monetary relationships just reflect a temporary flood of innovations, and that stability and predictability will be restored. We will see. But for the time being monetary targetry has been largely abandoned.

Discretion

There appear, therefore, to be serious objections to all these alternative approaches *except* for Alternative (i), the adoption of an exchange-rate commitment, for the UK and other European countries. For the rest, in the absence of any clear and practicable alternative, central banks have reacted to structural change and to breakdowns of previously stable relations between money and nominal incomes by adopting a more pragmatic and discretionary approach. They take into consideration a wider range of variables in coming to a view on the stance of policy and its appropriate adjustments. In many ways this is congenial to central bankers, since they are at heart pragmatic people and their discretion is legendary. Nevertheless it is not an entirely comfortable position for them.

6 The Conduct of Monetary Policy (1989)*

6.1 INTRODUCTION

Nowadays the Central Bank of a country is the monopoly supplier of legal tender currency. The commercial banks are committed to making their deposits convertible at par into such currency. So the banks need to keep reserves in the form of currency and deposits at the Central Bank. The Central Bank primarily conducts its policy by buying and selling financial securities, e.g. Treasury bills or foreign exchange, in exchange for its own liabilities, i.e. open market operations. Academic economists generally regard such operations as adjusting the quantitative volume of the banks' reserve base, and hence of the money stock, with rates (prices) in such markets simultaneously determined by the interplay of demand and supply. Central Bank practitioners, almost always, view themselves as unable to deny the banks the reserve base that the banking system requires, and see themselves as setting the level of interest rates, at which such reserve requirements are met, with the quantity of money then simultaneously determined by the portfolio preferences of private sector banks and non-banks. This difference in perceptions is discussed again in section 6.4.

Whether the monetary policy operations of Central Banks should be viewed primarily in terms of quantity, or rate, setting actions, (though, of course, one is the dual of the other), these had allowed inflation, and inflationary expectations, to become entrenched by the end of the 1970s. A selection of representative statistics for a number of the leading industrialised countries is given in Table 6.1.

Table 6.1 indicates a common pattern, among the countries, of interaction between interest rates, inflation and the growth of output. The first period, 1969–78, is marked by high inflation, negative real interest rates, and slightly above average growth; the second period, 1979–82, by very high nominal,

* *The Economic Journal*, 99 (396) (June) (1989): 293–346. My thanks for help and suggestions in the compilation of this paper go to Mike Artis, Peter Bull, Victoria Chick, Jean-Claude Chouraqui, Keith Cuthbertson, Dick Davis, Hermann-Joseph Dudler, Kim Frame, Chuck Freedman, Eric Hansen, David Hendry, Richard Jackman, David Laidler, David Lindsey, Ian Macfarlane, Gordon Midgley, Mark Mullins, Peter Nicholl, Andrew Oswald, Robert Raymond, Yoshio Suzuki, Richard Urwin, and my referees, none of whom should be held responsible for my opinions or remaining errors.

Table 6.1   Representative statistics for some major industrial countries

		1969 Q_1 to 1987 Q4	1969 Q_1 to 1978 Q4	1979 Q_1 to 1987 Q4	1979 Q_1 to 1982 Q4	1983 Q_1 to 1987 Q4
\multicolumn{7}{c}{1 UK}
A	(£M3)	12.9	12.3	13.6	13.1	14.1
B	(Y)	11.9	14.0	9.6	11.6	8.0
C	(y)	2.1	2.1	2.1	0.3	3.5
D	(P)	9.8	11.9	7.6	11.4	4.5
E	(i_s)	10.7	9.4	12.2	14.1	10.6
F	(i_l)	11.7	11.6	11.8	13.6	10.3
\multicolumn{7}{c}{2 US}
A	(Mt)	7.4	6.2	8.9	7.8	9.6
B	(Y)	9.0	10.0	7.9	8.0	7.8
C	(y)	2.7	3.0	2.5	−0.1	4.5
D	(P)	6.2	6.9	5.3	8.1	3.2
E	(i_s)	8.5	6.9	10.4	13.1	8.2
F	(i_l)	9.0	7.2	10.9	12.0	10.1
\multicolumn{7}{c}{West Germany}
A	(CBM)	7.6	9.3	5.8	4.9	6.2
B	(Y)	7.3	9.3	5.0	5.0	4.8
C	(y)	2.7	3.6	1.8	0.7	2.5
D	(P)	4.5	5.6	3.2	4.3	2.3
E	(i_s)	6.9	6.7	7.0	9.3	5.2
F	(i_l)	7.8	7.8	7.7	8.8	6.8
\multicolumn{7}{c}{Japan}
A	(M2)	12.7	16.4	8.7	8.7	8.9
B	(Y)	10.4	14.4	5.9	6.5	5.4
C	(y)	4.9	5.7	4.0	3.8	4.4
D	(P)	5.2	8.4	1.8	2.6	1.0
E	(i_s)	7.0	7.5	6.5	7.8	5.5
F	(i_l)	7.3	7.6	7.0	8.4	5.9
\multicolumn{7}{c}{France}
A	(M2)	12.2	14.7	9.2	11.3	7.2
B	(Y)	11.8	13.4	10.0	13.1	7.4
C	(y)	3.1	4.2	1.8	1.9	1.9
D	(P)	8.5	8.9	8.0	10.9	5.4
E	(i_s)	9.7	8.4	11.1	12.6	10.0
F	(i_l)	10.3	8.7	12.1	13.5	11.0
\multicolumn{7}{c}{Canada}
A	(M_1)	8.2	10.3	6.1	5.3	6.4
B	(Y)	11.1	12.6	9.4	10.7	8.5
C	(y)	4.0	4.8	3.1	0.5	4.9
D	(P)	6.9	7.5	6.2	10.1	3.4
E	(i_s)	9.7	7.7	11.8	14.5	9.6
F	(i_l)	10.0	8.3	11.9	13.1	11.0
\multicolumn{7}{c}{Australia}
A	(M2)	12.9	12.9	12.9	11.6	13.7
B	(Y)	13.2	14.4	11.6	12.0	11.6
C	(y)	3.5	3.2	3.7	3.1	4.6
D	(P)	9.5	11.0	7.7	8.8	6.8
E	(i_s)	9.4	6.6	12.6	11.9	13.1
F	(i_l)	10.6	8.1	13.3	12.7	13.9

(A) Annualised mean % growth of key monetary aggregate.
(B) Annualised mean % growth of nominal income.
(C) Annualised mean % growth of real output.
(D) Annualised mean % growth of inflation.
(E) Annualised mean level of representative short-term (3-month) interest rate.
(F) Annualised mean level of representative long-term (10-year) interest rate.

and high real, interest rates, high (but falling) inflation, and very low output growth. The final period, 1983–7, is marked by much lower inflation, lower nominal, but still high real, interest rates, and a recovery in output growth, in some cases to above average rates. In contrast, the relationship in these countries between the growth of their chosen key monetary aggregate and nominal incomes appears much weaker; also see Clinton and Chouraqui (1987, esp. p. 7).

Whether measured in terms of monetary growth, or in terms of 'real' interest rates, i.e. after adjustment for prospective future inflation, policy during the 1970s had become quite slack. Such accommodative policy had been accompanied by higher inflation, than in previous decades, but not by particularly strong output growth. While it remained possible to argue, and was often so argued in the UK during the 1970s, that this conjuncture was caused by the adverse oil-related supply-side shocks of 1973 and 1979, the combination of the stagflation of this decade, together with the Lucas (1976) critique of Keynesian macro-models, as exemplified in the Friedman (1968)/ Phelps (1968) analysis of the irrationality and likely disappearance of a downwards sloping Phillips curve, led to a downgrading of Keynesian demand-management, and associated monetary policy, strategies, (Mankiw, 1988). In addition, the demonstration effect of the comparative success of the West German and Swiss economies, which first adopted overtly quasi-monetarist policies, in reviving from the 1973 crisis led to a shift towards targetry and monetary rules. So, at the close of the 1970s most major industrialised countries had committed themselves to following targets, sometimes stretching into the medium term, for a selected monetary aggregate, a particular definition of the domestic money stock. With each country choosing its separate *domestic* target, the *international* relationship between the currencies was, per force, flexibly determined through the foreign exchange market.

The power to conduct such monetary policy is not, however, concentrated solely in the Central Bank. In many countries, such as the United Kingdom, Australia and France, the Central Bank acts as the executive agent to carry out the strategic policy decisions of the Chancellor or Minister of Finance; meanwhile the Treasury and/or Ministry of Finance plays a major role in the formulation of such policy as well as the Central Bank. Even where the Central Bank is constitutionally independent of the Executive, as in the US and West Germany, the decisions of the Central Bank are not, and can hardly be, taken in a political vacuum. Havrilesky (1988) provides a recent example (and an excellent reading list) of the entertaining US literature examining the degree to which the Fed's actions are affected by pressure from the Executive or Congress. Two more substantial works on this politico-economic border-line are, for the USA, Wooley (1984) and, for the United Kingdom, Moran (1984); Greider (1988) has written a more popular recent book about the Fed, for the United Kingdom, see Fay (1987). For West Germany, see Willms (1983) and Filc *et al.* (1988); for France, see Aftalion (1983); and for a wider survey of several countries, see Hodgman (1983).

In practice, the balance of power to determine monetary policy between the political Minister, the Ministry of Finance or Treasury, and the Central Bank varies both between countries, depending often as much on the wider political context as on the precise constitutional position of the Central Bank – viz. the comparatively powerful role of the Banca d'Italia and Banca d'España, – and also over time, depending greatly on the accident of personalities. Nevertheless, there has been some interest in the question whether the comparative susceptibility of Central Banks to political pressures has been a factor in their performance, e.g. in combating inflation, see Mayer (1987), Burdekin (1986), and Frey and Schneider (1981). For the purpose of this survey, I shall not pursue this question further; instead I shall explore the acts of the monetary authorities, without too much concern for the internal balance between Central Bank and Treasury.

Nevertheless the failure of the monetary authorities, whether Central Bankers or Ministers of Finance, to stem inflation in the 1970s led to reconsideration whether they were selflessly working for the public good as implicit in much Keynesian theory or might be swayed by other political and bureaucratic objectives. Such public-choice theorising about the incentives affecting the decision-making process of the authorities was for many monetarists (Friedman, 1984a) at the root of their preference for 'rules' rather than discretion.

A more analytically rigorous, and persuasive, reformulation of the arguments against discretionary intervention appeared somewhat later, in the guise of the 'Rules vs. Discretion' literature initially developed by Kydland and Prescott (1977), Calvo (1978), and made more accessible to the generality of economists by Barro and Gordon (1983a, 1983b), and Barro (1986); also see McCallum (1987, 1988) and Isard and Rojas-Suarez (1986). In such models, if the authorities either assume (incorrectly) that expectations are relatively inflexible, or place excessive weight upon the short run, e.g. because of approaching elections, they will be led to introduce an expansionary (inflationary) policy which they would have previously pledged to abjure (time inconsistency). Unless the authorities are deterred from such actions by penalties arising from a loss of reputation in the future, leading to a reputational equilibrium, the ultimate outcome of discretion will be a higher inflation/same unemployment (time consistent) equilibrium than could be achieved by sticking to a monetary rule. It is doubtful how far those in charge of monetary policy followed the finer points of this analysis. But the general thrust of the importance of credibility, commitment, sticking to (simple) rules undoubtedly struck a resonant chord among them then at the end of the 1970s.

So, at the outset of this decade (1980s) there was a considerable degree of concordance between (most) policy-makers and (most) academic economists. Monetary policy should be based on the achievement of monetary targets predicated on an assumed long-term stable relationship between the money stock and nominal incomes. Apart from setting and maintaining such quantitative monetary targets, the authorities should refrain from market intervention, e.g. in the foreign exchange market, since in conditions of efficient financial markets, in which agents were informed by rational expectations, such intervention could only destabilise the market to no good end.

By the latter part of the 1980s, however, the more *technical* elements, (as contrasted with the broader politico-economic ends), of this experiment were deemed, by the generality of policy-makers, to have comprehensively failed. The policies adopted in the early 1980s did, however, allow the authorities freedom to raise interest rates to levels that did subdue inflation, and the accompanying check to output growth, though severe, was indeed temporary. In terms of the mechanics, as contrasted with the ultimate objectives, of the policy, however, the crucial *long-term* relationships, i.e. the relationships between the money stock and nominal incomes (velocity), and between prices in two countries and their nominal exchange rate (purchasing power parity), appeared far more fragile than expected.[1] The extraordinary movements (misalignments) in foreign exchange markets and the Crash of October 1987 put major question marks over the rational expectation, efficient market hypothesis.

Yet a large wing of mainstream (mostly US) macro-theoretical economists appear to have taken little notice of such historical experience in recent years, driving ever deeper into an artificial (Arrow/Debreu) world of perfectly clearing (complete) markets, in which money and finance do not matter, and business cycles are caused by real phenomena, e.g. Kydland and Prescott (1982), Long and Plosser (1983), King and Plosser (1984). Moreover, in a number of analytical studies of this kind, e.g. Lucas (1972), Sargent and Wallace (1975), the only reason why monetary policy may affect real variables is owing to an informational imperfection, which would seem simple and worthwhile to overcome. This leaves something of a gap between state-of-the-art macro-theory and practical policy analysis, see Laidler (1988*a*, 1988*b*).

It is not the function, or purpose, of this paper to examine the recent development of macro-economic theory, on which two recent surveys, (Fischer, 1988; Mankiw, 1988), can be consulted. Both note the increasing divorce between theory and current practice. Thus Fischer (p. 331), comments that 'there is greater not less confusion at the business end of macroeconomics in understanding the actual causes of macroeconomic fluctuations, and in applying macroeconomics to policy-making'. Instead, the main aim of this paper is to document how, and why, policy makers in the main moved decisively away from the ideological (pragmatic monetarist) position adopted at the outset of the decade.

For this latter exercise I shall begin by examining the actual historical record of what policy makers have said and done (section 6.2). In this section, I shall somewhat arbitrarily divide up the recent decade into four periods:

(i) The Shift of Policy towards Monetarism up till 1979; (ii) The High Tide
of Monetarism, 1979–82; (iii) The Return to Pragmatism, 1982–5; (iv) The
Increasing Concern with Exchange Rate Regimes, 1985 onwards.

A severe problem, occasioned by space limitations, concerns which countries' experience to record. Naturally, we focus primarily on the UK, but we
must also review developments in the USA, not only since it has remained
the central economic power, but also because US experience shapes the views
of the dominant body of (American) monetary theorists.[2] Nevertheless, a
number of references to papers on the experience of other countries will be
added, in order to provide students with an entree to the literature available
on other major developed countries: there is no discussion of the monetary
policy problems of LDCs.

The main reason for the progressive withdrawal of the monetary authorities from a public commitment to a pre-set monetary target was that such
targetry was predicated on the existence of a predictable, and preferably
stable, relationship between monetary growth and (subsequent) growth of
nominal incomes. The previously estimated econometric relationships between movements in the money stock and in nominal incomes increasingly
came apart at the seams during the course of the 1980s, though less dramatically in some countries, such as West Germany and France,[3] than in
others, such as UK, USA and Canada. Since the purpose of monetary targetry
was to seek to compress the rate of growth of nominal incomes, (to a rate in
line with the underlying potential rate of real growth), (see Lawson, 1986),
the inability to predict what rate of growth of money would be consistent
with the preferred path of nominal incomes removed the rationale for the
authorities choosing, and seeking to maintain, some particular numerical target
for monetary growth (Leigh-Pemberton, 1986). We record the main features
of this story in section 6.3.

The breakdown of existing econometric relationships, e.g. in the form of
demand-for-money functions, and the difficulties of replacing these earlier
relationships with superior, and *credible*, more stable alternatives can be
easily retold. What remains much harder is to explain just how, and why,
such breakdowns occurred. During the last two decades, however, theoretical economists have emphasised that statistically estimated equations, such
as demand-for-money functions, are not true, 'deep', structural equations,
but are conditioned on the institutional structures and policy regimes – and
the behaviour and expectations that these induce. The last decade has seen a
wave of financial innovations (Solomon, 1981), again more so in the Anglo-
Saxon countries than in continental Europe, in part in response to the various pressures within the financial system brought about by the earlier policy
regime switch towards monetary targetry, and 'practical monetarism' (as
described by Richardson, 1978). This is discussed in the second part of section 6.3.

One of the more important of such financial innovations was the spreading practice of banks offering market related interest rates on deposits that had earlier borne zero interest (i.e. sight/demand deposits), or whose interest rates had been administratively constrained. The increasing scope for liability management limited the authorities' capacity to control the volume of bank deposits by varying the general level of short-term interest rates, since they could no longer thereby control the relative differential between rates on deposits and on non-monetary assets. At the outset of the 1980s the ability of the authorities to control the money stock by this traditional method (interest rate adjustment) was the subject of sharp debate, and the alternative policy of monetary base control (mbc) was strongly advocated, and, subject to some qualifications, partially adopted in the US. We discuss such control issues in section 6.4. As policy makers came to place less weight on the achievement of monetary targets, public concern with the techniques of monetary control abated. Even so, reliance on interest rate adjustments, (whether occasioned directly by the authorities or indirectly through the market under mbc), in order to stabilise monetary growth, appeared to entail sizeable fluctuations in such rates. There remained, therefore, some interest in other possible methods of monetary control, notably the policy of 'over-funding' which was peculiar to the UK.

Nevertheless, especially following the removal of exchange controls (abolished in the UK in October 1979, see Lawson, 1980 for the rationale) and other barriers to the free movement of capital between countries, it became generally accepted that adjustments to the general level of short-term interest rates formed just about the only effective monetary instrument, viz. for the UK, Leigh-Pemberton (1987) and Lawson (1986, 1988); for France, Conseil National Du Credit (1987), Banque de France (1987); for Japan, Suzuki (1988) and Bank of Japan (1985). With monetary targets falling out of favour as key intermediate objectives, concern shifted away from the question of how interest rate adjustments might affect the monetary aggregates back towards the more traditional question of how they might affect nominal incomes and inflation.

This latter is considered in section 6.5, but only briefly and mainly by reference to other survey papers. The subject of the transmission mechanism of monetary policy is both too large, and impinges too much on general macroeconomic issues, to cover adequately here. Even so, we regard it as important to distinguish in this respect between the standard Keynesian, IS/LM, approach, (which views the transmission mechanism as being restricted to a limited channel running from short-term interest rates, to long-term interest rates and equity prices, and hence to expenditures), and both the monetarist and neo-Keynesian approaches, wherein monetary/credit shocks can directly affect expenditures, e.g. by relaxing market imperfections. While most economists would probably now accept some aspects of this latter position, there remains great uncertainty on the relative importance of credit and monetary shocks.

So, this Chapter has the following structure; Section 6.2: Historical Overview; Section 6.3: Demand for Money; Section 6.4: Supply of Money; Section 6.5: Transmission Mechanism.

The paper is intended for the general, non-technical reader. Some technical references to current econometric methodology creep into section 6.2, but, even so, the literary description is meant to give everyone some understanding of what is afoot.

As evidenced in section 6.2, policy-makers became increasingly concerned, as the 1980s progressed, with the wayward behaviour of the foreign exchange market, and concerned to re-establish co-operative exchange rate regimes, either regionally (EMS) or internationally (e.g. at the meetings of the G7 Finance Ministers), to restore some 'order' to the international system. Although germane, and indeed increasingly central, to the story of the conduct of monetary policy in these years, space limitations have regretfully precluded a satisfactory coverage of this further extensive subject here.

6.2   AN HISTORICAL OVERVIEW

The 1970s: The Policy Shifts

During the course of the mid-1970s, the monetary authorities in a growing number of countries adopted published monetary targets, starting with West Germany late in 1974, and then quite rapidly followed by US, Switzerland and Canada in 1975, and UK, France and Australia in 1976, see Chouraqui *et al.* (1988, Table 3, p. 45), Hoskins (1985), and Foot (1981). Nevertheless the commitment of the authorities in a number of these countries remained doubted by sceptical commentators. Indeed, 'Judged solely by whether or not the targets were met, the results [in the earlier years were] generally poor', (Foot, 1981, p. 28). In the USA the authorities initially shifted the target period forward one quarter at a time until the end of 1978, when, under the terms of the Humphrey–Hawkins Act of that year, targets were generally set for a full year at a time. The earlier approach in particular proved fertile ground for 'base drift', the practice of starting the new target from the actual (higher) money stock obtaining at the end of each quarter, rather than from the previously desired objective position (Friedman, 1982; Broaddus and Goodfriend, 1984; Wang, 1980). The Bank of Japan did not provide a public announcement of the future path of M2 until 1978, and even then these have continued to be termed 'forecasts' rather than targets (Tamura, 1987). In the UK, the authorities had been targets (Tamura, 1987). In the UK, the authorities had been required to accept ceilings on Domestic Credit Expansion by the IMF in the course of dealing with the exchange rate crisis of 1976: while the associated adoption of published monetary objectives by the UK government was an independent decision, it is doubtful whether they would have taken that step without the external pressures. Moreover, whereas the Prime Minister (Callaghan) (in 1976) and Chancellor (Healey) did appreciate that the pursuit of some level of employment, or output growth, beyond that consistent with equilibrium would lead to accelerating, and unacceptable, inflation, it was doubtful how far the Labour Party as a whole was willing to absorb that argument, or still believed that some refurbished incomes policy could reconcile both nominal and real objectives. The Bank of England's wavering attitude to the proper balance between monetary targets and incomes policies is apparent in Lord Richardson's Mais Lecture (1978).

Be that as it may, the second half of the 1970's saw only limited further improvements in the reduction of inflation, following those achieved in the post-1973 deflation. Nominal interest rates remained in many countries below the concurrent rate of inflation, and even reached the ridiculously low figure of 5 per cent in the autumn of 1977 in the UK as the authorities strove to maintain the competitive advantage for their manufacturing industry of the low exchange rate occasioned by the crisis in 1976 – a scenario that was to be replayed with a different cast in 1987/8. Inflationary expectations remained entrenched.

The overthrow of the Shah of Iran, causing fears of a shortage of oil, then led to the second oil shock in 1979, with crude oil prices more than doubling, to about 29 dollars a barrel, by the beginning of 1980. Besides the direct effect of this on prices, the apparent weakness of President Carter led to growing fears about American policies more generally, and for the longer-term outlook for US inflation. The dollar had weakened sharply in 1978, and remained weak, despite official support in 1979: moreover, during 1979, there was a remarkable surge in the prices of precious metals, gold and silver, which, following the Russian intervention in Afghanistan, reached an extraordinary peak in early 1980.

This was the backdrop to the newly appointed Chairman of the Federal Reserve Board Paul Volcker's announcement of a new approach to monetary control on Saturday, 6 October 1979. Previously, the Fed had operated by controlling the level of the Fed Funds rate. While they could hit their chosen rate virtually exactly, various pressures, such as the natural tendency to limit changes under conditions of uncertainty, and the political unpopularity of upward movements in interest rates, had limited the flexibility with which the Fed felt able to vary such rates. From 6 October the Fed moved to control non-borrowed reserves – a modified form of mbc, see Section III below – allowing interest rates to vary, within wide and unpublished limits, as market forces might dictate. This single step transformed monetary conditions around the world, and was quite largely responsible, along with concurrent shifts to more deflationary policies in other major countries, for the shift from the generally inflationary conditions of the 1970s to the generally deflationary conditions of the 1980s.

Meanwhile in the UK the General Election of May 1979 had led to a Conservative victory. The new Conservative leaders had interpreted the inflationary upsurge of 1974/5 as being the direct consequence of the explosive increase in the broad money stock, £M3, in 1972/3. From the outset, in his first Budget on 12 June 1979, the Chancellor, Sir Geoffrey Howe, reaffirmed the government's commitment to controlling the growth of the monetary aggregates as the centrepiece of monetary policy (Howe 1979). At the same time, however, he presided over measures that would make such control more problematical. First, he raised the general level of VAT sharply, from 8 to 15 per cent, thereby at a stroke increasing the margin between the current rate of increase of prices and of nominal expenditures on the one hand, and the target rate of monetary growth on the other. Second, he set in motion the removal of exchange controls, which was fully effected in October 1979; this allowed such obvious possibilities of disintermediation from the direct control over monetary growth then in operation, the 'Corset' – for an account see Bank of England (1982*a*) – that there was no alternative but its speedy abandonment, with occurred in June 1980.

Concurrent and retrospective policy analyses of this 1979–82 period indicate that there were significant moves towards stricter monetary control in other countries at the same time (see BIS, 1983; for Italy, see Barbato, 1987). Some of this alleged pervasive movement towards greater monetary discipline may have come from the influence that U.S. monetary policy had on the rest of the world, but some of it simply may have emerged simultaneously as an idea whose time had come (Laney, 1985).

1979–1982: The High Water-Mark of National Monetarism

In the face of the upsurge of prices, and of nominal incomes, in 1979, with the RPI year-on-year reaching a peak of 21.9 per cent in May 1980, the Bank of England ran into immediate problems in trying to hold £M3 down to the re-affirmed target of 7.11 per cent. Bank lending rates were increased to 17 per cent in November. Despite such operational problems, the Chancellor adopted a Medium Term Financial Strategy, announced in the March 1980 budget, in which a pre-set declining target path for £M3 was made the centerpiece of the government's strategy, and whereby the fiscal policy decision, on the size of the Budget deficit, the Public Sector Borrowing Requirement (PSBR), was subordinated to the need to achieve the monetary target at acceptable levels of interest rates.[4] Thus 'there would be no question of departing from the money supply policy, which is essential to the success of any anti-inflationary strategy' (*Financial Statement and Budget Report* (FSBR) HM Treasury, 1980/1, p. 19, para. 16).

Given the extent of instability already evident in UK demand-for-money studies (e.g. Hacche, 1974), there were grounds for concern whether the relationships between (any particular definition of) monetary growth and nominal incomes were too fragile a basis for such a long-term commitment. A number of commentators, e.g. the Treasury and Civil Service Committee (1981), expressed such doubts. Perhaps because of differing views about the existing evidence, more likely because of a belief that it was worth taking risks in order to establish a convincing picture of credible commitment, such worries were brushed aside by the Government. Such commitment was welcomed by a number of influential commentators (e.g. Brittan, 1980), who believed that it could so alter expectations as to allow a decline in inflation with less associated unemployment. The *locus classicus* wherein the authorities' strategy was outlined was the speech given in Zurich on 14 January 1981 by Lawson, then the Financial Secretary (Lawson, 1981; also see Lawson, 1980, 1982, 1985) who is generally held to be the architect of the MTFS.

In that summer, June 1980, the 'Corset' control ended. An immediate upsurge in bank deposits, and in bank lending, had been forecast, as re-intermediation became possible. In the event the upsurge was over twice what had been expected, and the growth of £M3 shot through its upper limit, causing considerable embarrassment and annoyance (mostly aimed at the Bank) in the Government, especially coming so shortly after its prior public commitment. Interest rates were kept at the high level of 16 per cent, and there was intensive consideration of the merits of moving to monetary base control (mbc).

At the same time (in 1980), however, the combination of the UK's new found role as a major oil producer, the high level of interest rates, and the credibility of Mrs Thatcher's anti-inflation commitment, led to a dramatic rise in the UK's nominal, and even more in its real, exchange rate,[5] see Buiter and Miller (1982, 1983).

Despite the embarrassment of accepting a large overshoot in the first year of the MTFS, a further tightening of monetary policy, in the form of higher interest rates, beyond 16 per cent, at such a time was unacceptable, and, indeed, rates were reduced to 14 per cent in November 1980.[6] Even so, the deflationary pressure from the increased real exchange rate was intense, with industrial production falling by 10 per cent (1980 Q4 on 1979 Q4) and unemployment rising by over a half, from 1.3 to 2.2 million during 1980 (January/January).

Moreover, during the autumn of 1980 Alan Walters took up position as economic adviser to the P.M. He doubted, on analytical grounds, whether £M3 was the most appropriate monetary aggregate to target, and noted that the stance of monetary policy appeared much tighter if one looked at narrower aggregates, M1 or M0, instead (Walters, 1986). A colleague from Johns Hopkins, Prof. J. Niehans, was encouraged to do an academic study of this issue. His paper, widely circulated though not subsequently published in a journal (Niehans, 1981), was influential.

Nevertheless, if monetary and nominal income growth were to be reduced in line with the target, without any further upwards ratchet in interest and exchange rates, it was thought that the PSBR had to be kept tight. The continuing commitment of the Chancellor to the MTFS, and his refusal to allow even the automatic stabilisers to bring about an increase in the PSBR at a time of severe cyclical downturn, brought down upon his head the outrage of the (Keynesian) economic establishment in the UK, as the famous *Times* letter from the 364 economists attests (31 March 1981), organised by Hahn and Nield (also see Healy, 1987). The publication date of the letter coincided fairly closely with the low point in the cycle. A combination of world-wide deflation and, beyond that, the rise in the UK exchange rate were helping to bring about a sharp decline in import prices,[7] which began to feed through into declining levels for the RPI and for nominal wage increases. Moreover the latter did appear sensitive to movements in (short-term) unemployment (Hall and Henry, 1987; Layard and Nickell, 1986). It is also arguable that the 1981 Budget decision, whether, or not, strictly necessary within the MTFS framework, provided a dramatic manifestation of the government's shift to counter-inflationary commitment away from Keynesian demand management, and hence helped to break the inflationary psychology of the time.

During the first half of fiscal 1981, a Civil Service strike led to delays in the receipt of certain taxes, so the course of monetary growth was distorted. With the rate of growth of nominal incomes declining quite sharply, while monetary growth remained quite strong, with £M3 growing by about 14.5 per cent in 1981/2, the pressures imposed on the system by the MTFS were somewhat relieved, and interest rates, having been raised sharply in the autumn of 1981 to counteract downward pressure on the pound, were steadily reduced in 1982 to a trough of 9 per cent in November.

Meanwhile, in the US the authorities did not flinch from allowing interest rates to adjust flexibly in response to market pressures emanating from the revised operating procedures, whereby they sought to achieve a chosen level for the non-borrowed reserve base (see further below in section 6.4). It was, however, a bumpy ride. The volatility of interest rates (both short and long term) increased by a factor of about five to eight times as compared with the pre-October 1979 period (Dickens, 1987; Walsh, 1982; Evans, 1984: though for qualifications see Rosenblum and Storin, 1983). This was not entirely the result of the change in operating procedures, since the (ill-considered) imposition and subsequent withdrawal of direct controls on personal credit in spring 1980 led to sharp fluctuations in monetary growth and in interest rates.

Some considerable increase in the volatility of short-term interest rates had always been viewed as a likely concomitant of a move towards mbc. Simulations of constant monetary growth rules have tended to indicate extreme interest rates volatility, e.g. Anderson and Enzler (1987). What was more surprising was that this was accompanied by an increase in the volatility of monthly and quarterly (i.e. short-term) rates of monetary growth and in long term interest rates, (see further section 6.4). Despite these greater short-term fluctuations, the Fed did get close to the *annual* targets for monetary growth (M1) that it had set.

Certainly the Fed in general, and its Chairman Paul Volcker in particular, established credibility for their anti-inflation commitment. Such credibility was probably based more on their demonstrated willingness to accept a painfully high level of (real) interest rates and a sharp downturn in output, rather than on the achievement of a particular monetary target (Solomon, 1984), as may also have been true in Switzerland (Bomhoff, 1983, 1985) and in the UK. Even so Central Bankers appreciated the function of a monetary target in providing them with 'a place to stand' in warding off calls for a premature easing of policy (Bouey, 1982*a*). Also Fforde (1983) commented that, 'it would scarcely have been possible to mount and carry through, over several years and without resort to direct controls of all kinds, so determined a counter-inflationary policy if it had not been for the initial "political economy" of the firm monetary target'.

Much of the pain of the monetary deflation fell, however, on producers of raw materials – except where protected, e.g. European agriculture, – for whom the combination of falling output prices and sharply rising interest rates proved devastating. The summer of 1982 saw the conflation of the onset of the LDC debt crisis, growing success and credibility in the domestic (USA) struggle against inflation, and a growing difficulty in interpreting (or controlling) the increasingly wayward path of M1. The consequence was that the operating procedure, of targeting *non-borrowed* reserves, was (quietly) shelved, and replaced by one of targeting *borrowed* reserves (see section 6.4), which had the effect of accommodating unforeseen shifts in the demand for money, and allowed the authorities to reintroduce more stability into interest rate movements (see Axilrod, 1985).

For an account of how Central Bankers, not only in the USA and UK but also in a selection of other major countries, viewed the conduct of monetary targets at about this time (1982) see Meek (1983). For further details on the policy and experience of the Bank of Japan, see Suzuki (1986), and Hamada and Hayashi (1985); a discussion of the Bundesbank's practices and experience is provided by Dudler (1984); a useful chronology and account of monetary policy in Italy is provided by Barbato (1987); for France refer to the annual reports of the Conseil National Du Credit. For a more general survey of several countries' experience, see Argy (1988), Hoskins (1985) and Johnson (1983).

1982–5: The Return to Pragmatism

Apart from 1972/3, the years of the Barber 'boom' and monetary surge, the path of velocity of £M3 in the UK remained steadily upwards, i.e. nominal incomes growing faster than £M3, from the 1960s through till 1979. This historical trend, quite naturally, provided the main basis for choosing the target rates of growth of £M3 in June 1979 and March 1980. Initially the overshoots in 1980/1 and 1981/2 led to fears that there was a resulting excess 'overhang' of money which would lead to a subsequent reemergence of inflation.

On the other hand more immediate measures of inflationary pressure, e.g. the exchange rate, asset prices, wage increases, various measures of inflation itself, e.g. RPI or GDP deflator – let alone real variables such as output and unemployment – were indicating the continuing presence of deflation. Initially, up till March 1982, an uneasy compromise resulted. The target for £M3 was extended on the assumption that the historic trend in velocity would be reestablished, but no attempt was made to claw back prior overshoots, despite initial hopes/intentions to do so, (Lawson, 1982 and FSBR, 1981/2, p. 16, para. 11). Meanwhile, pressure was maintained on the Bank of England to achieve the target growth rate, but interest rates were not allowed to vary without limit in pursuit of that target.

But as time went by, it became increasingly difficult for the authorities to believe that they fully understood, or could predict, the path of velocity, and/or the demand for money (see section 6.3). This erosion of confidence in their ability to interpret the signals given by their prior chosen main target and indicator, £M3, led the authorities to extend the range of monetary and other variables, including notably the exchange rate, that they would consult in assessing the stance of policy,[8] and hence in deciding on how to vary interest rates. Thus, in the March 1982 Budget, (see FSBR 1982/3), targets were set for two additional monetary aggregates, M1, a narrow definition, and PSL2, (Private Sector Liquidity, Second Definition) an even broader aggregate than £M3: for an account of UK monetary statistics, see Bank of England (1982*b*, 1987). Outside commentators complained that this would give the authorities a greater chance to hit at least one target; insiders worried that the markets would concentrate on whichever indicator/target was currently doing worst.

Meanwhile, the demand by the private sector for bank loans continued to grow at persistently high levels, due initially to the needs of industry to overcome the financial squeeze in 1980/1, and then increasingly to the (apparently almost insatiable) demand for mortgage finance from the personal sector. Such demand for bank loans appeared to be, both from casual and econometric evidence (Goodhart, 1984; Moore and Threadgold, 1985), highly interest *inelastic*. Even as early as the autumn of 1980, the government shrunk from the option of pushing up interest rates high enough, (and what level would that be?) to close off such lending directly. In order then to prevent such rapid increases in bank lending coming through in a commesurate increase in bank deposits, the authorities had to reduce bank lending to the public sector, (see n. 4 above); they did so by selling more public sector debt to the non-bank private sector than necessary to finance the PSBR, i.e.

'overfunding'. They achieved this in part by a number of innovations which made public sector debt more attractive to the private sector, e.g. part-paid issues, convertibles, index-linked issues, in part by an assiduous concern with maximising sales in the light of existing market conditions. At no time did the authorities seek to force some prearranged quantum of gilts upon an unwilling market. Moreover, while overfunding may have *resulted* in some twist to the yield curve, (though no rigorous evidence to that effect is available), it was not brought about by the authorities acting directly on the yield curve for that purpose.

In practice, the Bank of England was remarkably successful in this exercise. But with bank *credit* continuing to grow at a very rapid pace, some commentators wondered whether mopping up bank deposits by selling a larger volume of gilts, public sector bonds, was a somewhat contrived, even artificial, way of holding monetary growth nearer to its target level. With growing uncertainty about the central relevance of £M3, and with its control in the years 1982–5 more subject to the influence of 'overfunding' than of interest rate changes, this then left the question of what factors determined the choice of short-term interest rates during this period. This became increasingly pragmatic, involving a combined assessment of a range of monetary indicators, of direct measures of domestic inflation, even on occasions with a glance at real variables, but increasingly attention became drawn in practice to exchange rate fluctuations. It was no accident that the main occasions from 1981 through to 1986 on which interest rates were jerked upwards, (in October 1981, January 1983, July 1984, January 1985 and January 1986), all coincided with periods of pound weakness on the forex market.

Whereas some aspects of this story are peculiar, even unique, to the UK, e.g. the use of 'overfunding' to seek to attain a broad monetary target, other aspects were also reflected abroad. In particular the timing, and scale, of the bend in the trend in the growth of the key monetary aggregate (M1) in the USA and in Canada coincides very closely with UK experience, even though the coverage of the monetary aggregate concerned differed. Possible causes for this are discussed further in section 6.3.

The consequences, and reactions, were – not surprisingly – much the same in the USA and Canada, as in the UK. Until 1982 (see Lindsey, 1986), the USA authorities kept M1 as the main target, viewing disturbances to the demand for money function as possibly temporary, or owing to transitory shocks such as the introduction of NOW accounts nation-wide in 1981 (see the series of papers by Wenninger and associates in the 1980s, e.g. Radecki and Wenninger, 1985). Then, in the face of the continuing unpredictability of velocity, (while some considerable success and credibility had been achieved in the containment of inflation), the Fed moved, at broadly the same speed as in the UK, down the road of widening the range of monetary targets/ indicators, and returning to a more discretionary and pragmatic mode of determining money market rates. In Canada the switch from the regime of monetary targeting to discretionary interest rate adjustment appeared rather more abrupt (see Bouey, 1982*b*; Freedman, 1983); as also in Australia, (Keating, 1985; Johnston, 1985).

Moreover, velocity tended to fall, although not perhaps as dramatically, and there were (unpredicted) increases in the demand for money, in certain other countries around the same time, for example Japan (see Bank of Japan, 1988*a*, Chart 15) and Australia (Stevens *et al.*, 1987).

This experience, of unstable velocities, was not, however, universal: in particular in West Germany, and in France, there were no clear signs of any break in the trend of velocity at this juncture. Consequently the Bundesbank exhibited greater persistence with targetry than other Central Banks, though, even so with some greater flexibility in operating methods, (see Schlesinger, 1984, 1988; Deutsche Bundesbank, 1985).

Elsewhere, apart from West Germany, e.g. in Japan and Australia, the achievement of an intermediate monetary target had not been elevated to be the centrepiece of monetary policy in quite such a committed manner. Consequently the subsequent withdrawal towards a more discretionary policy mode was also achieved with less public drama.

1985 Onwards: Increasing Concern with Exchange Rate Regimes

The misalignment of the pound during the years 1980–2 had had a devastating impact on the UK manufacturing sector, but had not impinged seriously on the Western world more widely. The subsequent misalignment of the US dollar, however, reaching its apogee in early 1985, greatly affected all the major countries. This latter experience led to growing doubts among policy-makers whether it really was the case that the forex market did adjust prices efficiently, (or at least more efficiently than policy makers could), and rapidly into line with some 'fundamental equilibrium'. 'Governments have to come to terms with the behaviour of the foreign exchange market. Left entirely to its own devices, we have seen in recent years how destabilising and destructive that behaviour can at times be' (Lawson, 1988).

The combination of growing doubts about the predictability of domestic velocity, and increasing concern about medium-term forex misalignments, led to a tendency for medium-sized countries, e.g. Sweden, Canada, UK, Australia to conduct their own monetary policy in practice[9] largely with a view to stabilising their exchange rate, in some cases bilaterally with a larger neighbour, USA or West Germany, (see Crow, 1988) but on occasions against a basket of currencies, (for Australia, see Hogan, 1986): for a more general assessment, see Atkinson and Chouraqui (1987).

This option was not really open to the three main economies, USA, Japan and West Germany. In this latter case academic interest turned to the possibility of applying cooperative monetary policies (among the three majors) for the joint purpose of stabilising both international exchange rates and world inflation. Suggestions to this end were put forward by Williamson (1983); Edison *et al.* (1987); McKinnon (1984) and McKinnon and Ohno (1988), among others. For a commentary and a critique, see Frenkel and Goldstein (1988). Although a series of meetings of Finance Ministers, starting with that at the Plaza in New York in September 1985, was held with the aim of establishing whether there was scope for enhanced international coordination, it is debatable how much actual difference such meetings have made to the policy steps the protagonists would have adopted independently anyhow (see Feldstein, 1988). This should not be read as implying that exchange rate movements had no influence on the domestic monetary policy decisions in Germany and Japan; clearly the German and Japanese authorities adjusted the fervour with which they pursued their domestic monetary targets in the light of external developments, but rather that such adjustments were autonomously decided, and not undertaken in order to preserve international cooperation and amity.

Be that as it may, doubts about the central significance of £M3, and concern whether 'over-funding' was leading to some artificial distortions in both relative interest rates and in the growth of the aggregates, led the Chancellor to aim at 'full-funding' – but no overfunding of the PSBR – and to downgrade £M3 as a target variable during the course of 1985 (Lawson, 1985). The virtual abandonment, by 1985, of the monetary variable chosen to be the centre-piece of policy in 1979/80 represented a considerable volte-face. It was, however, too much for the Chancellor, who in 1980/1 had opposed virtually any intervention to check the giddy rise of pound, to make the further step of linking monetary policy formally to exchange rate developments (see Lawson, 1986, 1988), and also politically difficult for him to do so in the context of the Prime Minister's opposition to the UK's joining the Exchange Rate Mechanism (ERM) of the European Monetary System (EMS).

In any case financial innovations, that were held to be largely responsible for the break-down in the statistical relationships between the various monetary aggregates on the one hand and nominal incomes and interest rates on the other, (see section 6.3 and Leigh-Pemberton, 1986), appeared to be causing relatively *less* disturbance to the relationship between the monetary base (M0) and nominal incomes in the UK (Johnston, 1984): nevertheless, technological and social changes, e.g. the spread of automated teller machines (ATMs), electronic funds transfers, EFTPOS (point of sale, or place of work, etc.), home banking, etc. threatened potential instability here too (Hall *et al.*, 1988). Such instability has, moreover, occurred recently in West Germany, leading the Bundesbank to shift from their prior Central Bank Money to an M3 target, (Deutsche Bundesbank, 1988; Holtham *et al.*, 1988).

Moreover, M0 is overwhelmingly (99 per cent) represented by currency outstanding, in the hands of the public (84 per cent) or in banks' vaults/tills (15 per cent). Such currency is provided automatically on demand by the

Bank of England. While there *are* reasons why one might believe, (see section 6.5, that monetary/credit shocks would have subsequent effects on the economy, most outside commentators in the UK reckoned that movements in M0 were no more than a concurrent measure, with additional noise, of consumer expenditures. The Chancellor disagreed, and he emphasised that he regarded M0 as an *'advance* indicator' of money GDP, (Lawson, 1986, p. 12); the econometric basis for this claim is uncertain, (and is not to be found in Johnston, 1984).

Nonetheless, perhaps out of a belief in its economic significance, perhaps out of a presentational desire to stick with *some* monetary target aggregate, (and one for which technological/social changes were still leading to comparatively low growth figures), the Chancellor and Treasury have since maintained an annual target for M0 as *the* monetary target[10] for the conduct of monetary policy. In practice, however, interest rate adjustments during the course of 1986 appeared to depend on the same pragmatic blend of discretionary response to monetary developments, (more generally than just M0), on current domestic inflationary indicators, and on exchange rate developments, as already described.

Then, sometime in the early Spring (March?) in 1987, policy appeared to shift, in part perhaps influenced by the understandings in February reached between Finance Ministers at the Louvre meeting, though without any formal, public announcement – indeed the monetary target set out in the Budget Redbook (1987) continued to be expressed in terms of a growth rate for M0. However, from March 1987 to March 1988 the value of the pound remained held in a narrow trading range against the DM, and whenever the pound tended to rise above 3.00 DM[11] overt policy action, either in the form of intervention or reductions in interest rates, was taken to prevent it breaking that limit. There was still room for intra-marginal interest rate adjustments, e.g. the upwards hike in August 1987 owing to general concern with inflation, and the post-October-crash (internationally concerted) reductions. Even so, the parameters within which such discretion could operate appeared to have become more closely restricted by this new policy of 'shadowing' the DM in the forex market.

Early in 1988 this caused a problem. Boom conditions in the UK gave rise to fears about incipient worsening inflation, such that higher interest rates appeared domestically prudent. But there was already a yield differential *vis-à-vis* German interest rates that made capital inflows profitable, so long as the expectation remained that the peg to the DM would remain in place. The scale of capital inflows put upwards pressure on the sterling sufficient to force large intervention by the Bank of England to maintain the peg, and this in turn tended to expand the money stock even faster.

This gave rise to a policy dilemma, (a dilemma condition that Walters (1986) had warned would be endemic in such instances), to hold the external peg and suffer worse short-term inflationary pressures, or to abandon the peg and lose the medium-term (counter-inflationary) support of maintaining a DM peg. There were reports in the newspapers of high-level ministerial conflict over which choice to make; in the event the second was adopted. Thereafter, for some three and a half months, policy seemed to move onto a new tack, of varying the balance between the exchange rate and interest rates so as to maintain a constant pressure upon nominal incomes. The (econometric) finding of HMT's forecasting model, whereby a 4 per cent, appreciation of the sterling, e.g. from 3.00 DM to 3.12 DM, would have its deflationary effect on nominal incomes offset by a 1 per cent reduction, e.g. from 9.5 per cent to 8.5 per cent, decline in short-term interest rates, found its way into the Press. Whether, or not, this was an accurate report, from March until July 1988, it was noted that every five/seven pfennig appreciation (depreciation) in the pound/DM Spot exchange rate was counterbalanced by 1/2 per cent cut (hike) in interest rates.

In turn this period, of appearing to balance interest rate adjustments against exchange rate adjustments, so as to achieve a constant pressure (of demand) on nominal incomes, seemed to conclude in early July. A series of indicators revealed continuing strong output, worsening inflationary pressure and a weakening balance of payments. The authorities then raised interest rates, (though initially in steps of only 1/2 per cent at a time), quite sharply through the course of the summer: the strength of the US dollar and some appalling UK trade figures enabled the authorities to do so without incurring any further appreciation of pound, which became increasingly subject to weakness.

With national monetarism, plus flexible exchange rates, having effectively broken down in the first half of the 1980s, the Chancellor appeared to be looking for an alternative (coherent) strategy of international monetary cooperation and coordination, involving more or less formal linkages within regions, e.g. the ERM in Europe, and closer cooperation between the G3 (the Group of Three, USA, Germany and Japan). In the event in early 1988 this objective conflicted with the government's overriding commitment to containing domestic inflation causing a policy dilemma. The latter objective took priority, (as it also has in similar dilemmas in West Germany), but exactly how the conduct of monetary policy can best be calibrated under present conditions to achieve this objective remains a subject for debate.

6.3 THE UNSTEADY RELATIONSHIP BETWEEN MONEY AND NOMINAL INCOMES

The Demand for Money

Studies of the demand for money usually start from a presumption that there exists a long-term equilibrium relationship between private sector money holdings and certain other aggregate macro-economic variables, such as the price level, real incomes (or expenditures), (some set of) interest rates and, perhaps, wealth and the rate of inflation. The relevant variables, to appear as arguments in this long-run (equilibrium) relationship, are normally initially chosen on the basis of *a priori* theory, whether deriving from Keynes' suggested motives for holding money (i.e. transactions, precautionary, speculative), from a Tobin–Baumol inventory theoretic analysis, or from Friedman's more general portfolio choice approach (Friedman, 1956). In most earlier studies the variables, considered to be relevant in the long-term equilibrium relationship, were then imbedded in a short-run demand-for-money function, via some, often *ad hoc*, partial adjustment mechanism; and then tested directly against the data. Indeed this is still the most usual approach in the USA, for recent surveys see Roley (1985) and Judd and Scadding (1982).

More recently econometricians have sought to examine and test for the presence of such a long-run equilibrium relationship between variables directly, (*before* imbedding them in equations which also explore short-run dynamic adjustments), by testing whether such variables are cointegrated. If such a long-run relationship does exist between variables X and Y, which may well both be non-stationary and trended in levels, but stationary in differenced form, i.e. they are both I(1) series, then in the simple linear relationship between the series in levels.

$$Z_t = X_t - aY_t,$$

Z_t (the residual from an OLS regression of X on Y) will be stationary, (i.e. an I(0) series), and this can be easily tested (see Engle and Granger, 1987), though problems may still arise since the cointegrating vector need not be unique. It is, however, minimal information to know that X and Y are cointegrated. One does not know why and in what relationship that appears; in a multi-equation context it would not even tell one which linear combinations of which cointegrated variables constituted the long-run relationship of interest. So it is necessary to proceed, as Hendry argues, (e.g. 1985, 1988), to model jointly the long-run and the short-run to establish in which equations the error corrections appear and hence to identify them.

In more behavioural terms, if an equilibrium long-run relationship exists between variables X and Y, say of the linear form $X = aY$, then any deviation from this relationship will induce pressures to drive either X, or Y, or both, back towards the equilibrium. The implication of this is that equations to examine short-run adjustment should include an error-correction mechanism, along the lines proposed by Granger in more theoretical work, e.g. (1981), and by Hendry in a series of more applied studies, e.g. (1979, 1985, 1988).

This approach involves no preconditions, either about the nature of the shocks that may disturb the long-run equilibrium relationship, or about whether the resumption of the equilibrium involves a re-adjustment primarily in X or

Y, or whether they both adjust. Thus, in the context of the relationship between money holdings and nominal incomes, the existence, if indeed it does still exist, (see further below) of a long-run relationship between them (i.e. a predictable and stable velocity) implies no prior conditions on whether the shocks that disturb the relationship occur primarily to money holdings or to nominal incomes, nor whether the subsequent return to equilibrium occurs via an adjustment in money holdings or in nominal incomes. In particular, the money stock may well be largely endogenously determined, as economists such as Moore (1988*a*, *b*) and Kaldor (1982) have argued, and it can still be the case that shocks to the money stock, which disturb the long-term equilibrium, may lead to subsequent adjustments in nominal incomes. The latter is an empirical question, which does *not* depend on the money stock being exogenous with respect to nominal incomes.

There is quite a close connection, though it has not been widely recognised, between the cointegration/error correction mechanism and the buffer stock approach to monetary analysis (see Laidler, 1983*b*, 1986). Like the former, the latter depends on the existence of a stable long-term relationship between money holdings and nominal incomes. Various shocks, especially those affecting bank credit expansion, e.g. on the occasion of deregulation, then drive actual money balances away from their long-term equilibrium level, a divergence that people are willing to tolerate temporarily because money balances are particularly well suited to act as a buffer to such shocks. But this divergence (from long-term equilibrium) then sets up forces that will affect both monetary variables, (i.e. the demand both for loans and deposits), *and* nominal expenditures. Models along this line began with 1976 Reserve Bank of Australia model, (Jonson *et al.*, 1977), and (generally small) models have since been constructed for several countries, including the USA (Laidler and Bentley, 1983), Netherlands (Knoester and Van Sinderen, 1982) and the UK (Davidson, 1987; Davidson and Ireland, 1987). The literature on buffer stock money is now becoming large: for recent contributions see Cuthbertson and Taylor (1987) and Muscatelli (1988). Again this approach has not been widely adopted in the USA, with certain exceptions, e.g. Carr and Darby (1981) and Judd and Scadding (1981), in part because critics such as Milbourne (1987) have queried the micro-foundations of the approach, and in part because the concept that agents may allow themselves to be driven temporarily off their demand function is alien to the dominant US model of (relatively) perfect clearing markets.

Be that as it may, early empirical work (see Goldfeld, 1973, for the USA; Laidler and Parkin, 1970, and Goodhart and Crockett, 1970, for the UK) soon established that money holdings appeared to adjust to the arguments in the long run relationship rather slowly, i.e. with long lags. In most US literature such lags were modelled by the adoption of a partial adjustment mechanism applied either to real or to nominal money balances, (see Roley, 1985 and the Comment thereon by Hafer, 1985). In the UK, again under the influence of David Hendry, the recent tendency in such econometric work has been to put as few prior restrictions on the form of the dynamic adjustment model as possible, but to test down from very general models to more 'parsimonious' equations, using restrictions, e.g. excluding variables, that are data consistent. So there is quite a marked disparity between the Granger/Engle/Hendry approach (i.e. start by examining the stationarity characteristics of the time series; next test for cointegration; then imbed the resulting error correction variable(s) into a general short-term adjustment model, which is tested down to a more parsimonious version), and the more common single equation, partial adjustment, standard demand for money function.

Either approach, however, is liable to leave one with a 'preferred' equation including lags of the monetary aggregate serving as dependent variable and, possibly, lagged values of the other arguments, which generally imply a lengthy adjustment period. This has been criticised on several scores. First, it would seem to suggest that, should there be 'exogenous' shocks to the money stock, certain other variables, e.g. interest rates, would have to overshoot. Second, the length of adjustment seems to be too long to be readily accounted for by costs of adjustment, see Laidler (1985) and Goodfriend (1985). Third, it is not generally clear whether these lags, and the error correction feedback mechanism, are consistent with rational expectations. Cuthbertson (1988*a*); Cuthbertson and Taylor (1987); Lane (1984) and Dutkowsky and Foote (1988), among others, have explored a two stage approach, whereby a 'model consistent' estimate of expectations is constructed in stage one, and these forward-looking variables are then entered into a demand-for-money function, in conjunction with backwards-looking variables including error-correction mechanisms.

Hendry (1988) has argued that, should the expectations generating process shift during the data period, it should be possible to discriminate between feedback and 'feedforward' mechanisms (also see Hendry and Neale, 1988). While he clearly demonstrates that interest rates and real output movements are so hard to predict, being close to random walks, that there can be little power to feed-forward mechanisms, even he expresses surprise that apparently the data suggest that agents 'ignore the predictability of inflation in adjusting their M1 balances' (p. 146). Cuthbertson (1988*b*) has responded by arguing that Hendry's assessment, and claimed refutation, of the Lucas critique is weakened by the fact that, in a finite sample, the marginal model for the forward looking variables is likely to be highly inefficient, but if such marginal models, including in this case Cuthbertson's own equations, are so inefficient how can any *confident* forward-looking expectation be established?

But this is not a survey of demand-for-money studies, even less of their econometric technicalities. Policy makers were, in the main, less concerned with the academic details of the studies than with the ·question of whether the relationships uncovered were sufficiently robust to serve as a basis for conducting monetary policy. As already noted, the early work on such relationships, undertaken in the years until 1973, did in the main appear to demonstrate, circa the end of the 1960s, that the demand for money was a predictable function of a few variables. That predictability then suffered some knocks, however, during the disturbed years in the early mid-1970s, notably with 'the case of the missing money' (Goldfeld, 1976) in the USA.

Nowhere else, however, did the prior stability of the (short-run) demand for money function exhibit such a comprehensive collapse as in the case of £M3 in the UK in 1972/3. A surge in bank lending to the private sector (and a large public sector borrowing requirement) was funded by a massive increase in wholesale bank deposits, as the banks bid aggressively for funds. This drove £M3 far beyond the level that would have been predicted on the basis of previously calculated equations: even when attempts (Hacche, 1974; Smith, 1978, 1980) were made to account for the banks' new liability management practices, the refitted equations could not account satisfactorily for the monetary surge in 1972/3 (for an exception, see Taylor, 1987). The consensus remains that the demand-for-money function for £M3 broke down in 1972/3, and has remained unstable ever since; (this break-down is most evident in the case of company sector holdings of £M3; indeed Lubrano *et al.* (1986) report that the *long-term* relationship for the *personal* sector remained fairly stable, at least until 1981). At one time a study by Grice *et al.* (1981) – (also Grice and Bennett, 1984), did suggest that a stable function for £M3 could be obtained by relating £M3 to a measure of gross financial wealth and an estimate of expected returns on gilts (i.e. government bonds), but not only did this formulation entail some inherent problems (e.g. in taking bank lending as exogenously determined), but its out-of-sample forecasting properties soon disappointed. For a recent survey, see Holtham *et al.* (1988).

This might provoke the question why this break-down did *not* discourage UK policy makers from placing so much reliance on £M3. The crucial reason is that the subsequent upsurge in prices and nominal incomes in 1974/5 appeared to confirm the monetarists' historical/policy claim that major monetary shocks caused *subsequent* nominal income changes. Thus the breakdown of the (*short-run*) demand for money function in the UK signalled to many monetarist economists (and policy makers) here that we had been running these regressions the wrong way around, rather than that the *long-run* money/ nominal income nexus was fragile and unreliable.

First steps at transforming the equation to make £M3 into an independent, right hand side variable were taken by Artis and Lewis (1976), but initially they took the level of interest rates, rather than nominal incomes as their dependent variable, (also see Andersen, 1985). Subsequently Mills (1983*b*) examined the extent to which various measures of the UK money stock appeared to be able to predict movements in nominal incomes, once the pattern of auto-regression in nominal incomes had been taken into consideration, and concluded that £M3 represented the best guide; for a broadly similar study on West Germany, see Geisler (1986).

The UK experience in the mid 1970s was, however, unusual. In several other countries the earlier fitted equations had had some predictive problems in the mid 1970s, but these had been quite minor, relative to the shock in the UK, and normal econometric running repairs had encouraged Central Banks in most major countries to base the technical choice of their chosen money stock target numbers on their preferred demand-for-money function.

As recorded earlier in section 6.2, policy shifted in late 1979 onto a much more deflationary tack, initiated by the major change in the monetary control regime in the USA. From that point onwards, velocity trends shifted, and the monetary aggregates grew more rapidly relative to nominal incomes than in the past. This experience occurred at roughly the same time, though to different degrees, in most Western countries, and in Japan (Ueda, 1988).

Lucas (1976) had earlier demonstrated why a regime change might well lead to instability and parameter shifts in previously estimated 'structural' equations. The adoption of new operating procedures in the USA on 6 October 1979 represented a major policy regime change. American economists soon noted that the prediction errors in the demand for money functions could have resulted from such regime changes (Judd and Scadding 1982). Indeed, Gordon (1984) called for the abandonment of efforts to estimate *short-term* demand-for-money functions, since the appropriate form of short-run relationships that may be estimated between the monetary base, the money stock, interest rates and nominal incomes may depend more on the (changing) form of the policy regime than on the (changing) nature of behavioural responses of the private sector.

Even though a number of economists, especially in the USA, have continued to argue that at least some definitions, especially the monetary base, of) the money stock still exhibits a well-behaved demand-for-money function,[12] the extent of predictive failure subsequently went beyond the ability of most (US) economists to explain in terms of regime change, or of (UK) economists to explain in terms of a buffer-stock (disequilibrium) response to monetary shocks. The inherent problem with these approaches has been that they seek to, and can only, explain *short-term* deviations of velocity. Thus a monetary surge, caused, say, by the abolition of the 'corset' control in the UK in 1980, will lead to a temporary fall in velocity; or alternatively the changed monetary regime, as in the USA in 1979, could lead people to expect an initial monetary overshoot, relative to the target, to provoke a future rise in interest rates, as the authorities react, and hence cause the private sector to wish to hold more, not less, monetary balances on speculative grounds (see Vaciago, 1985).

So, there are quite a number of (partly related) grounds for explaining short-term fluctuations in velocity, and short-term instability in the demand-for-money function. But such approaches, (notably including the buffer stock/ disequilibrium models), generally incorporate an assumption of a stable *long-run* equilibrium relationship between money holdings and nominal incomes. Indeed it is the divergence of the short-run, (credit-counterpart determined), money stock from the stable long-run desired level that drives expenditures in these models. In more policy-oriented terms, economic advisers in the UK were waiting with trepidation for the built-up 'overhang', or excess money balances, to spill over into higher expenditures in 1981, 1982, 1983, 1984. Eventually they tired of waiting, and accepted that there must have been some change to the underlying *long-term* demand for money (though see Artis and Lewis, 1984, and Budd and Holly, 1986, for a graphical illustration of its prior stability). Similarly in the USA and Canada, the change in the trend since 1979 has gone on too long to explain as a purely short-run phenomenon. For an illustration of the long run changes in velocity in the various countries discussed in this paper, see Figures 6.1–6.7 on p. 118–21.

Put in more formal terms, both Engle and Granger (1987) and Miller (1988) have demonstrated that, over the last couple of decades in the USA, the various monetary aggregates have *not* been cointegrated with nominal incomes, with the possible exception of M2, i.e. velocity has been generally non-stationary. The latest empirical studies undertaken within the Federal Reserve Board now also lead to a preference for M2, over M1, as a monetary target, (Moore *et al.*, 1988); the same preference also currently holds in Canada, (Crow, 1988). This longer term departure of velocity for US M1 from prior trends has been nicely illustrated by B. Friedman (1988*a*), also see Wenninger (1988).

In such circumstances a number of US economists have advocated running demand-for-money equations in first difference form (without error-correction-mechanism), see Cover and Keeler (1987), but, while this may allow accurate short-term forecasting, it enables velocity to wander without limit over time. See Roley (1985, pp. 620–1), for a review of economists who have proposed that the equation be specified in such a first differenced format.

Replications for the UK of the Engle-Granger tests of cointegration between monetary aggregates and nominal incomes during recent decades are currently being undertaken (Ireland and Wren-Lewis, 1988; Hall *et al.*, 1988) – for an earlier exercise covering a longer data period see Hendry and Ericsson (1983). Although these results are still provisional, the general finding in the UK is that the monetary aggregates are *not* currently simply cointegrated with nominal incomes: however, the addition of certain other variables, e.g. wealth, can allow cointegration to be restored. Be that as it may, bends in the trend of velocity of monetary aggregates have appeared in several countries during the 1980s, often in that aggregate chosen to be *the* national intermediate target, and have often proven difficult to explain, (though Mayer (1988) has argued that the extent of such 'breaks' has often been exaggerated).

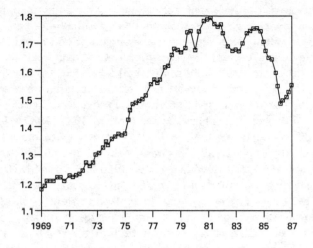

Figure 6.1   USA, velocity of M1

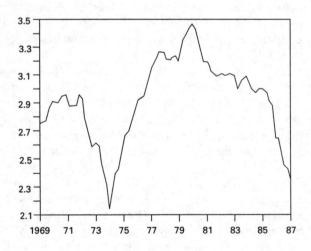

Figure 6.2   UK, velocity of M3

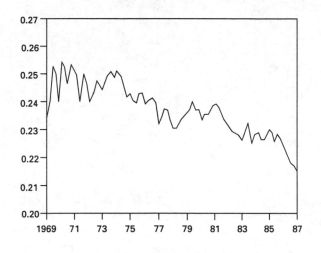

Figure 6.3 West Germany, velocity of GBM

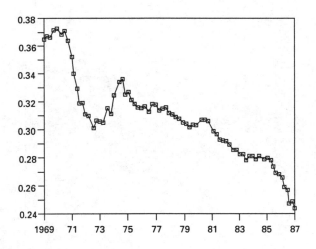

Figure 6.4 Japan, velocity of M2

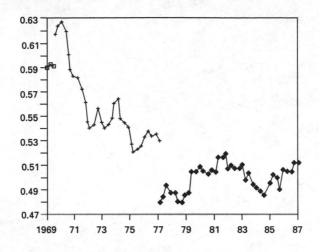

Figure 6.5   France, velocity of M2: □ 1969 unadjusted; ◇ 1977:4–1987 M2;
+ 1970–7:3 M2 R

Figure 6.6   Canada, velocity of M1

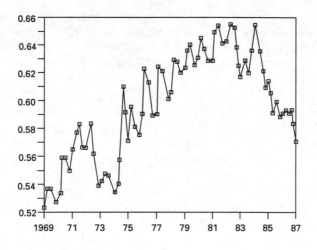

Figure 6.7   Australia, velocity of M2

Some Explanations of the Shifting Path of Velocity

So, why did the trend bend? There are a variety of suggested answers, none of them fully satisfactory, though all of them may possess some validity. First, it may be that econometricians had previously failed to estimate the effect of certain interest rate relativities correctly. As already noted, the period 1979–82 was marked by extreme interest rate volatility in the USA. One would expect an increase in the variance of key asset prices, around a given mean level, to raise the (speculative and precautionary) demand for money (Tobin, 1958; Buiter and Armstrong, 1978; Walsh, 1984). There is some econometric evidence to this effect, e.g. Baba *et al.* (1987), Ueda (1988) but the decline in velocity continued after 1982 whereas interest rate volatility reverted to lower levels.

Second, the 1980s represented a period of declining inflation, and (rather more slowly) declining nominal inflation rates. It may be that earlier studies underestimated the elasticity of response of desired money balances to inflation and/or nominal interest rates. In those cases where financial innovation led to the payment of interest rates that were either *fixed* or had an upper ceiling on certain monetary aggregates – as with NOW accounts in the USA until January 1986 – it is possible that the elasticity of such balances to changes in market interest rates increased (Heller, 1988; Simpson, 1984). The question of whether financial innovations led to an increase in interest elasticity, or not, has provoked a sizeable literature in the USA, see Hafer and Hein (1984), Brayton *et al.* (1983), Akhtar (1983), Wenninger (1986), Darby *et al.* (1987), etc. Greenspan (1988) appears confident that 'the aggregates have become more responsive to interest rate changes in the 1980s'. The same is apparently also the case in Japan, (Bank of Japan 1988*b*, 1988*c*).

If such elasticities should be higher, than previously thought, this would then intensify certain consequential problems for monetary targetry, commonly described as 'the re-entry problem' (see Simpson, 1984; Blundell-Wignall and Thorp, 1987 and Budd and Holly, 1986). The difficulty is that a successful counter-inflationary policy would entail lower inflation and nominal interest rates; this would so raise the demand for money that either the resulting target values would *look* lax, or, if a continuing hold was kept on the target numbers, then the intermediate target objective could prove unduly restrictive.

Third, the increase in competitive pressures in the financial system, among banks, and between banks and other financial intermediaries, in the 1980s has led to a paring of spreads between lending and deposit rates, with interest rates on deposits being made more attractive, while the cost of borrowing to the personal sector, e.g. on mortgages, has been reduced in a number of countries, notably in the UK. The private sector, both the company and the personal sectors, has increased both its indebtedness to, and claims upon, the banking sector enormously. Although the micro level data make it hard to estimate whether the borrowers are the same, or different, entities as the depositors, (note, though, that more assured access to bank borrowing facilities could have been expected to reduce precautionary holdings of deposits), there is no question but that the scale of bank intermediation has increased dramatically; for an analysis of the UK personal sector, see R.B. Johnston (1985), and for the UK company sector, see Chowdhury *et al.* (1986). The best measure of the cost of intermediating through (some part of) the financial system is the spread charged therein, (see Miller and Sprenkle, 1980; Johnston, 1983). As Miller and Sprenkle argued, the scale of intermediation may respond elastically to reductions in the spread.

A further factor tending to raise the demand for liquid assets, in general, will have been the massive increase in the value of non-human wealth, e.g. equities and houses, during the bull market of the early eighties (up till 1987/8) and an associated upsurge in the volume of financial transactions, see Ueda (1988) and Grice and Bennett (1984), though Wenninger and Radecki (1986) doubt whether the growth of financial transactions had much effect on M1's growth in the USA.

This first set of suggestions all point to the possibility that the response of desired money balances to certain interest rate relativities may have been underestimated. The second set of suggestions, *not* in any way mutually exclusive with the first, cover the possibility that the characteristics of bank liabilities and assets were upgraded by financial innovation making them more attractive to hold (Hester, 1981; Akhtar, 1983; Artus, 1987; Tamura, 1987; Leigh-Pemberton, 1986; de Cecco, 1987). The term, financial innovation, tends to make most people think of exotic new instruments, e.g. options, futures, options on futures, forward rate agreements, swaps, etc. but the financial innovations of key importance for the conduct of monetary policy have been rather more prosaic. The controls imposed by the authorities, both 'prudential' and direct credit controls, and in several countries the oligopolistic nature of the banking industry, had restricted the range and variety of lending facilities and the payment of interest on deposits, available to the private sector, *retail* customers, (the effect of financial liberalisation in stimulating the growth of the money stock has been a regular theme recently of the Bank of Japan, e.g. (1988*a*, 1988*b*)), – the *wholesale* customer had benefited from the 1960s onwards from the bench-mark competition provided by the euro-currency markets.

Anyhow, the extension of variable rate lending in mortgage form made relatively much cheaper credit available to personal sector borrowers in the UK. The rapid expansion of bank credit to the private sector in most countries throughout the 1980s, in part a supply-side shock, required the banks to act more aggressively to fund the additional demand for loans and the continuing process of de-regulation allowed them to do so. This need for funds, the increasing competition in the industry and the trend towards de-regulation[13] then combined to induce banks to pay higher – than previously –, often market-related, interest rates on categories of deposit that had previously by custom or by regulation, borne zero interest, e.g. checkable, sight deposits, or where the rates had been administratively pegged.

The payment of market related interest rates on certain categories of checkable deposits naturally made them much more attractive to hold. Assets jointly held in a portfolio will provide, at the margin, the same utility. If one asset offers the same rate of interest as another safe, but non-monetary asset, but also provides certain extra liquidity or transaction services, then both assets will only be held simultaneously if the demand for the transactions/liquidity services of the first asset is completely satiated. So the provision of market related interest rates on a wider range of bank deposits would lead to a surge in demand for them, until the demand for their extra liquidity services became approximately satisfied, and, at the margin, such deposits were held as interest-bearing safe assets, rather than as 'money'.

In that case the rate of growth of the monetary aggregates will have overstated, possibly considerably, the rate of growth of true 'money', since the money-like characteristics of the interest-bearing deposits will have declined. This is the argument, and analysis, preferred by those who advocate the use of a Divisia index, whereby the 'moneyness' of a deposit is represented by the divergence between its own rate and that on a non-monetary safe asset. There is now quite a large literature on this topic, see Barnett *et al.* (1984), Barnett (1982); for the UK, Mills (1983*a*). The use of a Divisia-index to measure money can go some way to explain recent trends in velocity, insofar as the innovation process is reflected in shifts in relative interest rates. While in principle this approach would seem to have much to recommend it in a period of rapid shifts in deposit characteristics, in practice the use of such monetary indices in the USA would have provided 'little clear improvement in terms of either demand equation or reduced-form equation performance' in the 1980s, Lindsey and Spindt (1986). And, despite much of the academic research on it having been done under the aegis of Central Banks, senior officials have been reluctant to give the concept much public prominence or any policy role.

Competition may well drive banks towards offering a fully market-related interest rate for deposits, while at the same time charging full economic costs for their payments and transactions services. If so, the above analysis would suggest that deposit holdings would increase until the demand for liquidity was satiated, and would be perfectly substitutable for non-monetary assets of the same maturity. If so, what, if anything, would remain of the distinction between money and other assets of a similar maturity? Is one particular characteristic of money, as Tobin (1963) has earlier suggested, that the interest payable on it is externally restricted? And could the distinction between monetary and non-monetary assets become further blurred by an extension in the range of assets that can be monetised, and/or the range of intermediaries offering, perhaps limited, payments services on the back of electronic technology? It might seem that, with the extension of market related interest rates to a wider range of deposits, the only essential 'money' left might be currency outstanding, or the monetary base, (see Solomon, 1981). But the demand for such currency is affected by cross-border holdings (e.g. for DM in Eastern Europe, and for dollars around the world, (Greenspan, 1988 and Board of Governors, 1988, Appendix on Monetary Base), and by the 'black economy' (Thomas, 1988); thus surveys of currency holdings can only account for a fraction of the amount outstanding, see Avery *et al.* (1987) and Porter and Bayer (1983); (though econometric studies for the UK (Johnston, 1984) and for the USA (Dotsey, 1988) have continued to show generally stable demand for currency functions, unlike West Germany where the demand for currency function has recently become unstable, (see Deutsche Bundesbank, 1988; Holtham *et al.*, 1988). Moreover, techniques are available whereby interest *could* be paid even now on currency, (McCulloch, 1986), though they are unlikely to be adopted, since seignorage represents an attractive and simple source of taxation. While such receipts are small in most developed, non-inflationary countries (Buiter, 1981), they are large enough in several southern European countries to cause certain problems in the process of convergence to a unified, non-inflationary European Monetary System, (see for example Grilli, 1988).

6.4 MONETARY CONTROL METHODS

Debates on Monetary Base Control (1979–82)

The advent of liability management weakened the ability of the authorities to use their traditional mechanism, of interest rate adjustment, to control monetary growth, because the banks would compete with the Central Bank for funds, leading to an upwards spiral in interest rates, so long as they could continue to intermediate profitably, i.e. to lend out such funds to borrowers at a margin above (wholesale) deposit rates (Moore, 1989). And the demand for bank loans has proven notably interest inelastic. Moreover there had always been certain other difficulties in using this approach.

Even before the adoption of liability management, the interest elasticity of demand for bank deposits was subject to considerable uncertainty, so the authorities could not calibrate at all exactly how much interest rates had to change to bring about a desired adjustment in the money stock. Moreover, the authorities only had occasional, once a month or once a quarter in most countries, snapshots of the money stock, which were frequently distorted by temporary disturbances, e.g. a large new issue, or a take-over bid, or a strike, or even bad weather disrupting the normal course of bank clearing: so it was always hard to distinguish temporary from more permanent monetary movements. Given such uncertainty, and the 'political' dislike of raising interest rates – interestingly enough more clearly apparent in the USA where the Fed is independent of the Executive than in the UK where it is not – there was a natural tendency for interest rate adjustments to be (or to be perceived to be) 'too little and too late', as was recognised in the Green Paper on *Monetary Control* (1980), also see Friedman (1982, 1984*b*).

There were, therefore, inherent reasons to suspect that Central Banks' traditional methods, of interest rate adjustments, would not operate satisfactorily to achieve adequate monetary control, and that such deficiencies would be particularly marked at times of severe inflationary pressures, when lags in the process of interest rate adjustment would induce the authorities temporarily to accommodate each inflationary shock to the demand for money until they had both managed to observe it *and* come to a decision to offset it. With monetary control becoming the centrepiece of many governments' policies at the end of the 1970s, it was therefore inevitable that intensive consideration would be given to an alternative method of monetary control, namely monetary base control, or mbc.

Banks need to maintain high-powered cash reserves (R) in order to honour their commitment to maintain the convertibility of their deposits (D) into currency (C). If the ratio which they maintain of such reserves to deposits is stable, and if the general public maintains a stable currency/deposit ratio, then the multiplier linking the money stock (M) to the high-powered reserve base (H) will also remain stable via the identity $M = H(C/D + 1)/(C/D + R/D)$.

Empirical work tended to demonstrate that these ratios were generally stable and quite closely predictable for the USA; Johannes and Rasche (1979, 1981); Balbach (1981); Hafer *et al.* (1983); Rasche and Johannes (1987); Dewald and Lai (1987); and also for West Germany, van Hagen (1988); but less so in the UK in recent years, Capie and Wood (1986); or in Australia, Macfarlane (1984). So the argument was straightforward. The Central Bank can control H, which incidentally represents its own liabilities, by open market operations. Given the predicted values for the two key ratios, (which might, indeed, be sensitive to interest rates, but one could attempt to measure such sensitivities), the authorities could set H in a manner that would deliver any desired M. Of course, the determination of a quantity M implies the determination of a dual: In the short term, while the general level of prices is slowly adjusting, this would be reflected in changes of flexible asset prices, in particular of nominal interest rates. But it was the excessively sluggish adjustment of nominal interest rates that was (it was claimed) part of the problem with the traditional mechanism, and much more variable short-term interest rates would be an acceptable price to pay for better monetary control, especially since longer term asset prices might show *greater* stability than in the past because inflationary expectations would be stabilised.

After a pre-emptive counter-attack by the Bank of England on these arguments, (Foot *et al.*, 1979), the Government established a Bank/Treasury working party to study the issue, and their report, in effect, was published in the Green Paper on *Monetary Control* (1980). In this, the working party accepted much of the case against mbc. Briefly it runs as follows. The historical stability of the banks' reserve ratio had depended on the willingness of the authorities always to supply extra cash on demand at an interest rate chosen by the authorities. If the authorities should shift the operational form of the system, by refusing banks' access to cash freely at any price, the banks' desired reserve ratio might experience a major shift, and could then become much more variable. There would be a long transition period, from regime to regime, in which it would be hard to select an appropriate level of base money, and the variability of the banks' reserve/deposit ratio under the new system could be so large as to prevent any improvement in monetary control, while at the same time losing grip on interest rates.

The above arguments referred essentially to a system of *mbc* operated without any mandatory controls on required bank reserves. If, however, the banks were required to hold a mandatorily required reserve ratio, then there would be a (somewhat) firmer fulcrum, with a more stable reserve/deposit ratio. But this alternative option ran into some technical problems over the accounting base for the required reserves, that has plagued the Americans in practice. If the required reserves were to be based on a previous, known deposit base, a lagged accounting rule, then there would be nothing the banks could do by their own actions, e.g. by running down current assets, to lessen their need for reserves. Under such circumstances the authorities really have no alternative to giving them the reserves the banks require, as in the case, for example, in West Germany, see Kloten (1987); they can only choose the interest rate, or penalty, for providing the required reserves, (for an authoritative account of the operational practices of the Bundesbank, see *The Deutsche Bundesbank*, 1987). But this would then just be a throw-back to the traditional system (see M. Friedman, 1982). Owing to the difficulty of estimating deposit levels except at the close of business, operational lags, etc. moving to a current accounting basis does not really avoid this prior difficulty.

A more radical solution to this problem, advocated in a few quarters, (see Laurent, 1979; Kopecky and Laurent, 1984), was to move to a system of forward accounting, whereby the permissible volume of deposits at future date $t + x$ would be dependent on the volume of reserves held at time t. An inherent problem with this approach, as with the even more radical suggestion, (Duck and Sheppard, 1978), of selling the commercial banks (non-monetary) permits to expand deposits, is that it would have the effect of artificially raising the cost of *banks'* intermediation, when restrictive pressure was applied, relative to costs via other financial channels and would thus promote large-scale ('cosmetic') disintermediation.

Since the arguments, pro and con, in the UK depended largely on claims about how banks, and other agents, in the financial system might behave in the *hypothetical* conditions of a change in the regime to (some version of) *mbc*, it was not really possible to *demonstrate* the superiority of one set of arguments over the other. The protagonists on either side in the UK, who met to discuss it under official auspices, in the improbable venue of Church House in Westminster on 29 September 1980, stuck generally to their prejudices. One argument that did, however, sway some of those in positions of power and influence was that it would be difficult to steer the system clearly through the transitional learning period: thus 'we in the UK have very little idea of the size of cash balances the banks would wish to hold if we were to move to a system of monetary base control', (Lawson, 1981); moreover the ratio of £M3 to base money was not stable or predictable, so there was 'little or no point in trying to use the MBC system to control £M3', (Walters, 1986, p. 123). These considerations, combined with the convinced opposition to *mbc* from the Bank of England, the commercial bankers and the City of London, persuaded the monetarists not to push more strongly for *mbc*, although remaining unpersuaded of the contrary case, in the early years of the MTFS, e.g. in 1980–2. Thereafter, the progressive withdrawal from monetary targetry has relegated the associated/subsidiary issue of *mbc* to the very back of the policy burner.

In the USA the constraints on a flexible use of traditional interest rate adjustments were even more severe than in the UK. Accordingly the authorities *did* decide to shift their operating procedures, on 6 October 1979, into a form with a number of the characteristics of *mbc*. The approach adopted, to control *non-borrowed-reserves*, was ingenious. Although the accounting system remained on a lagged basis, so the banks *had* to obtain a *given* total of required reserves, they could do so by *borrowing* reserves from the Fed, given the volume of non-borrowed-reserves. The US system of borrowing at the discount window is such that additional borrowing would be stimulated by a rise in the margin between market rates and the (administratively pegged) discount rate, though the relationship involved some inter-temporal complexities (see Goodfriend, 1983). Hence an expansionary monetary shock impinging on an unchanged non-borrowed-reserve total would lead to a quasi-automatic market increase in interest rates until enough extra borrowing was induced to allow the banks to satisfy their required ratio (Axilrod and Lindsey, 1981; Federal Reserve Staff Studies, 1981). Thus interest rates would adjust much more rapidly and flexibly in the face of monetary shocks, but would not spiral away without limit: as a further safety measure the Fed set (un-published) interest rate bands, whereby at the upper (lower) limit it would intervene directly to inject (withdraw) reserves to prevent excessively wild interest rate movements.

In the event, however, these bands were set quite widely and often adjusted into line with market movements, so they only rarely came into play (Sternlight and Axilrod, 1982). The change in policy immediately, and dramatically, increased both the level and volatility of market interest rates, with volatility in the period 1979/82 being some 4/5 greater than before 1979, (see Evans, 1981, 1984; Walsh, 1982; Mascaro and Meltzer, 1983). The effect of such high, and variable, interest rates, and the determination of Paul Volcker to continue with the medicine, undoubtedly played a major role both in shifting the US and World economy from a generally inflationary to a generally deflationary tack, and in stemming inflationary expectations and psychology.

A number of technical operating problems did, however, arise (see the papers presented at the Conference on 'Current Issues in the Conduct of U.S. Monetary Policy', republished in the *Journal of Money, Credit and Banking*, November 1982). First, although the Fed did broadly achieve its annual M1 targets, the shorter-term, quarter to quarter, time path of M1 became even more variable than before 1979. Second, whereas some greater variability of short-term interest rates had been expected (though no one was sure in advance of the scale of the increase; see Walsh (1982) for a comparison of the outcome with earlier studies), the concomitant increase in volatility of longer-term bond yields had not been predicted (Volcker, 1978; Spindt and Tarhan, 1987). Monetarists ascribed both failings to a lack of zeal in the Fed, and to the modifications from full *mbc* outlined above, and advocated such measures as a shift to current accounting, (adopted in 1984), and closure of, or greater penalties from using, the discount window, and/or a shift from using non-borrowed-reserves to a total reserves or monetary base operating target, viz. Poole (1982), Friedman (1982, 1984*a*, *b*), Mascaro and Meltzer (1983), McCallum (1985), Rasche (1985), Brunner and Meltzer

(1983), Rasche and Meltzer (1982). The Fed often advanced particular conjunctural explanations for each short-term surge, or fall, in M1, (see the studies by Wenninger and associates from 1981 onwards, e.g. Radecki and Wenninger, 1985), and Bryant (1982) provided econometric evidence to support the claim that little, or no, improvement in monetary control could have been obtained by changing the operational basis, e.g. to a total reserves target, see Lindsey *et al.* (1984), and Tinsley, *et al.* (1982). Others regarded such fluctuations as the inevitable result of trying (too hard) to impose short term control on a monetary system wherein there were lengthy lags in the adjustment of the demand of both deposits and advances to interest rates (instrument instability) (e.g. White, 1976; Radecki, 1982; Cosimano and Jansen, 1987, but see Lane, 1984 and McCallum, 1985 for an attemped rebuttal).

Be that as it may, the adoption of this operating procedure led to a very bumpy ride over the period 1979–82.[14] In the summer of 1982, a combination of falling inflation in the USA, and the onset of the LDC debt crisis, (in some large part triggered by the change in US monetary policy, see Congdon, 1988), induced the Fed to move away from *mbc*. This took the form of shifting from a target for *non-borrowed-reserves* to a target for *borrowed* reserves (see Wallich, 1984*a*). At a superficial glance this still sounds like a reserve base objective. However, as already noted, the demand for borrowed reserves is a function of the margin between market interest rates and the discount rate, so a target for borrowed reserves implicitly represents an interest rate objective, and also implies that monetary shocks would be accommodated by accompanying movements in non-borrowed-reserves at given borrowed reserve/interest rate levels. As in the UK and elsewhere, the withdrawal from monetary targetry in the USA has meant that this area of argument has gone quiet there too, though not as moribund as here. Moreover, the success of both the Japanese (see Dotsey, 1986) and Germans in achieving more stable growth (than in the USA), both for the monetary aggregates and for nominal incomes while still using interbank market interest rates as their policy instrument, (Fukui, 1986; Suzuki, 1988 for Japan: Deutsche Bundesbank, 1987 for Germany), suggests that it has not been operating procedures that have distinguished the differing macroeconomic outcomes of monetary policy.

For a recent account of such procedures, see Suzuki *et al.* (1988) for Japan; Willms and Dudler (1983), Kloten (1987) for West Germany; Conseil National Du Credit (1986) for France; Dotsey (1987), Macfarlane (1984) and Reserve Bank of Australia (1985) for Australia.

Subsequent UK history

Although the UK Government did not seek to impose *mbc* in 1980/1 on a banking community that deeply opposed the idea, one of the features of *mbc* that had attracted the Government was that it removed the determination

Financial Systems

of nominal interest rates from the hands of the authorities, and gave it to the market. At that time it was one of the tenets of the Conservative government that prices were set much more efficiently in markets, than by the decision of some group of policy makers. So, even though the Government did not insist on *mbc*, they wanted to introduce a system which gave more scope to the market, and equivalently less to the Bank of England, to set interest rates.

Previously, the Bank of England had organised the pattern of the weekly Treasury Bill issue, so as to leave the market normally slightly short of its desired cash reserve levels (Bank of England, 1984*b*, Chapter 6). Since the market would have then regularly to sell paper to the Bank to obtain cash, it would facilitate the Bank's control over the price the market would receive for such paper, i.e. over nominal interest rates. In mid-1981, the government and the Bank agreed that this practice would henceforth cease. The Bank would aim, at its weekly Treasury Bill tender, to leave the market in balance. On those days – expected to be in the majority – when the market was roughly in balance the Bank could withdraw from the market, leaving rates to be determined in the free market. The authorities remained, however, concerned not to allow freedom to become entirely untrammelled, and thus stated that they would set (unpublished) bands, which would represent those levels of interest rates beyond which the authorities would intervene to prevent further market-driven movement of interest rates.

In the event, however, this system never came into operation, and the concept of market freedom within unpublished bands proved chimerical. The reason was as follows. During the years 1981–5, the authorities continued to aim to achieve a target for £M3. But at the same time the authorities had lost faith in their ability to achieve such a target by an (acceptable) adjustment in the level of nominal interest rates, and were beginning to vary interest rates in the light of the (pragmatic) blend of concern with monetary conditions, domestic indicators of inflation and exchange rates, described earlier. Meanwhile, with interest rates thus determined, bank lending to the private sector continued to grow at around 20 per cent p.a., compared to a target for £M3 nearer 10 per cent p.a. The authorities, the Bank taking the lead, sought to resolve this conundrum by offsetting the faster rate of growth of bank lending to the private sector by inducing a fall in bank lending to the public sector. They did this by selling more public sector debt to the *non-bank* private sector than needed to fund the PSBR, thus making the banks *systematically short of cash* in their transactions with the government via the Bank. The commercial banks then relaxed their cash shortage by allowing their short-dated public sector debt to run-off, or by selling their longer dated public sector debt. But this effectively forced the Bank again to determine the interest rate level at which it would resolve the systematic cash shortage by buying in the banks' paper, (see Bank of England, 1984*a*).

This policy was remarkably successful in reconciling continuing extremely rapid bank credit creation with a much lower monetary target. By about 1981, however, a technical problem ensued. The commercial banks effectively ran out of public sector debt to sell back, or run off. This problem was then resolved by the Bank of England buying private sector commercial bills from the commercial banks. This resolved the problem, but only temporarily till the bills matured, when the whole process had to be rolled over. So, on each occasion of overfunding, the 'bill mountain' steadily grew, leading in time to an almost farcical situation of vast quantities of bills maturing on each day, huge resulting cash shortages in the banking system and the Bank needing to purchase 'wheelbarrows' full of further commercial bills from the market to balance the books. This raised numerous questions. The authorities were selling long dated securities, and buying back short-dated bills. Did this make commercial sense?[15] In order to generate the wheelbarrow loads of commercial bills they needed to buy (to square the books),[16] interest rates on commercial bills were reduced below interest rates on alternative assets. This led to some arbitrage opportunities. Indeed, the authorities aimed to induce borrowers to shift to bill finance out of loan finance. But it was claimed that the need to generate the vast additional amounts of bills at times caused bill rates to fall to a level that could encourage various undesirable forms of 'hard' arbitrage, which could inflate both bank lending and deposits. More generally, did a programme of selling longer-dated debt and buying shorter-dated bills tilt the yield curve in a way that would encourage private sector borrowers to seek funds from banks rather than from capital markets, which was one cause of the original problem? More fundamentally yet, was a technique that allowed bank credit expansion to continue roaring ahead, but restrained the growth of bank deposits, achieving any proper purpose, or was it just another 'cosmetic' device?

It has never been easy to answer these questions, and they continued to raise nagging doubts at the time. As the emphasis given to controlling £M3 lapsed, (and such control was largely achieved by over-funding), so the Chancellor decided in mid 1985 to abandon the policy of over-funding, to shift to a policy of fully funding the (rapidly falling) PSBR outside the banking system (Lawson, 1985); a similar full-fund policy was also adopted in Australia (Johnston, 1985) and New Zealand (Reserve Bank, 1987a). Quite how this (full-fund) policy might be operated now that the public sector has moved into increasing surplus[17] remains to be seen. In the event, the abandonment of over-funding did have the predicted effect of bringing about a jump increase in the growth rate of £M3, broadly into line with that of bank lending, at about 20 per cent p.a. in 1987/8, compared with a growth of nominal incomes of about half as much.

Whereas the Government, that had claimed in 1980/1 that £M3 was the absolute centrepiece of policy, treated such expansion with apparent unconcern, the Bank remained concerned that, though the messages from the broad monetary aggregates might be hard to decipher, it was wrong to ignore them entirely.

6.5   MONETARY TRANSMISSION MECHANISMS

The Effect of Interest Rates on the Domestic Economy

The unification of financial markets, especially following the abolition of exchange controls, has lessened the efficacy of direct *credit controls*, or other constraints on intermediation, imposed on one segment of that (international) market. In any case the conventional wisdom is that such direct controls on financial markets are generally undesirable. This has left the authorities' discretionary determination of (short-term) market interest rates as the chief, virtually the sole, instrument of monetary policy[18] (see Leigh-Pemberton, 1987).

The main effect of interest rate adjustment probably works through its influence on external capital flows and exchange rates, but space limitation precludes us from considering that here. Instead, in the remainder of this sub-section, we shall review briefly how interest rate adjustments are perceived to affect domestic nominal expenditures and incomes. This topic, however, is, perhaps, more a part of general applied macroeconomics; although it is a subject of major concern to monetary policy makers, it is one where they turn mainly to specialist economic advisors for advice and assistance, rather than a subject where they feel responsible for reaching, and defending, a conclusion themselves. Accordingly I shall refer briefly to some general surveys, rather than more specialised papers.

A suitable starting point is the OECD paper by Chouraqui *et al.* (1988) on 'The Effects of Monetary Policy on the Real Sector: An Overview of Empirical Evidence for Selected OECD Economies', which explores the evidence from some thirty large-scale national and international macro models. For a recent study concentrating on the effect of changes in interest rates in UK macroeconomic models, see Easton (1985), and for a review of such effects in the USA, see Akhtar and Harris (1987).

Chouraqui *et al.* begin by noting that an initial decline in interest rates, associated with a rise in the monetary base, *can* lead to such flexible adjustments in inflationary expectations and in prices that any systematic, or anticipated monetary policy becomes impotent to affect real output, following the arguments of the new classical economics, of which Sargent and Wallace (1975) represents the prototype. They then examined the evidence of whether rational expectation, structurally neutral (RESN) conditions appeared to hold in practice. One of the tests of this, following Barro (1977; 1978), is whether real output reacts to *unanticipated* monetary changes, but not to *anticipated* monetary movements. They survey some *seventy* empirical studies of this question, covering seven countries (Table 13), and note that 'the number of studies claiming refutation of the proposition that only unanticipated monetary policy matters is running ahead of corroborative ones', p. 27. For this, and other reasons, e.g. 'the apparent dependence of the current price level on its own past values', p. 24, and that 'Evidence from survey data on expectations does not generally support the idea that expectations are formed rationally', (referring to Holden *et al.*, 1985 for a comprehensive survey of studies of data on expectations surveys), they reach the conclusion that 'On the whole, the evidence on models which combined market clearing and rational expectations is not favourable to their relevance in current circumstances. Market clearing and rational expectations have little or no empirical foundation, the weight of evidence providing more support for a macroeconomic framework in which prices adjust slowly'.

Be that as it may – and it is not a function of this survey to attempt further adjudication – the major macro-economic models, to which policy makers turn for a quantification of the effect of interest rates changes, do incorporate a sluggish adjustment of prices and of future inflationary expectations. Although this does imply that administered interest rate adjustments, whether anticipated or not, would not be impotent, the effect of such changes on the various categories of (domestic) expenditures, e.g. business fixed investment, residential investment, consumption, inventory investment, varies quite widely not only between countries, but even more markedly between models. Even so, Chouraqui *et al.* comment that 'One thing that does emerge from recent evidence compared with studies of earlier vintage is the finding of significant interest rate effects' (on domestic expenditures) (p. 13), perhaps because the recent high level of real interest rates has made agents more conscious of interest costs and because the more competitive and more nearly perfect financial markets spread their effects more widely. Even so, 'The diversity in the size of the reported multipliers and the widely varying structure of the models, the parameters of which are often subject to large revisions, means that the short-run response of real sector variables to changes in financial conditions cannot be known with any degree of confidence' (*ibid.*, p. 22).

Even though both the strength of the effect of interest rates on domestic expenditures, and the time lags involved, are uncertain, at least the direction of effect appears unambiguous.

But in the *short* run the relationship between increases in interest rates and in price levels can be ambiguous, in part because interest rates represent a business cost – and pricing may be of the cost-plus form – and in part because of the curious manner in which mortgage interest rates enter into the RPI in the UK (also see Reserve Bank of New Zealand, 1987*a*). As already noted, however, the main impact of changes in interest rates is, however, perceived to work through its effect on international capital flows, and hence on the exchange rate. 'More immediate, and more powerful, channels through which interest rate changes influence demand work through induced movements in real competitiveness', Miles and Wilcox, (1988). If this latter channel is allowed to work freely, any short run adverse domestic effect on inflation of higher interest rates should be more than countered by an appreciation in the exchange rate.

Other Possible Channels

An unhelpful dichotomy, between the theory and the reality of Central Bank operations, was introduced into macro-economics by the IS/LM codification of Keynes' *General Theory* (1936), and has been continued by Friedman (1970, 1971) among others. When either of these two great economists would discuss practical policy matters concerning the level of short-term interest rates, they had no doubts that these were normally determined by the authorities, and could be changed by them, and were not freely determined in the market, (putting the US experience 1979–82 on one side). Whether, or not, this was the most appreciate operating procedure is another question; this was how it has worked in practice.

But when they came to their more theoretical papers, they often reverted to the assumption that the Central Bank sets the nominal money stock, or alternatively fixes the level of the monetary base. If then the goods and labour markets were somewhat sticky, so that the general level of prices did not adjust immediately, the demand and supply of money would be equilibrated in the short-run, in this theoretical framework, by market-led adjustments in nominal interest rates. With equilibrium between the demand and supply of money being thus restored by adjustments in nominal interest rates, subsequent effects on nominal incomes/expenditures would seem to *have to work* entirely via such interest rate movements, (see, for example, Crow 1988 for a restatement of this 'mainline' view), unless one made some auxiliary assumption, e.g. using the buffer stock/disequilibrium money type approach, that the equilibrium achieved in the money market was less than perfect.

All that remains a subject of continuing debate. If, however, one sticks to the real world in which the authorities set the level of nominal interest rates, then the question of the additional effects on the economy, beyond that working via adjustments in interest rates, of monetary and credit shocks is much easier to comprehend. With a given, discretionarily determined, level of short-term interest rates, there can, of course, be all kinds of shocks to the credit and money markets, which will cause the aggregates to change, without there being any (necessary) change in short-term money market rates. How much do these latter changes in the aggregates matter? Moreover, in section 6.4, we noted how 'overfunding' could divorce bank credit shocks from monetary changes. Although money and (bank) credit usually vary together, they need not do so, and as Brunner and Meltzer have continued to argue (1972*a*,

1972*b*, 1988), they are not the same thing: On this same subject also see Greenfield and Yeager (1986) and Kohn (1988). Which matters most?

In a world characterised by *perfect* markets, expenditure decisions would be determined by the budget constraint in the form of the present value of human and non-human wealth, the current and expected future levels of prices, etc. It is not clear why monetary, or various credit, aggregates should play a strategic role. Thus Gertler (1988) comments that 'Most of macro-economic theory presumes that the financial system functions smoothly – and smoothly enough to justify abstracting from financial considerations. . . . The currently popular real business cycle paradigm proceeds under the working hypothesis that financial structure is irrelevant.[19] Indeed in a world of perfect markets, which presumably implies costless information, complete trust, etc. it is dubious whether there is any need for money in its role as a means of exchange, (without the introduction of *ad hoc* imperfections, such as a cash in advance constraint, which would be inconsistent with the conditions otherwise allowing perfect markets to exist), though there would still be a need for intertemporal stores of value; the literature on all this is, of course, vast; for a formal treatment see Gale (1982, 1983).

Accordingly, a key function of credit/monetary expansion, given the level of interest rates, may be in allowing certain market imperfections, owing to imperfect, or asymmetric, information to be overcome (Kohn and Tsiang, 1988). There has been considerable theoretical interest in the question of whether credit rationing may exist when the financial system is in 'equilibrium', e.g. Jaffee and Russell (1976), Stiglitz and Weiss (1981), Gale and Hellwig (1985), (as well as when such rationing occurs as a result of slow, or restricted, adjustment of interest rates, see Fry, 1988; McKinnon, 1973; Shaw, 1973). Such studies, in which Stiglitz has been a major contributor, have extended to both theoretical and empirical analyses of how changes in credit conditions can affect the economy (Blinder, 1987; Gertler, 1988; Gertler and Hubbard, 1988; Bernanke and Gertler, 1987; Greenwald and Stiglitz, 1988; Woodford in Kohn and Tsiang, 1988, etc.).

A practical current example of this in the UK has been the move of banks into mortgage lending,[20] the greater competition between banks and building societies in (mortgage-backed) personal lending; and the surge in such lending following the end of the Building Societies' cartel (Meen, 1985). The effect of this can be seen in Table 6.2. This has raised the question of what effect this supply-side shock has had on the real economy, e.g. consumer demand, house construction, housing prices, etc. (see Drayson, 1985).

During the early 1980s, the effect of this credit surge on the broad money supply was offset by the policy of overfunding. As noted in Section I, this involved offering terms on gilt-edged securities that would shift wealth holders out of bank deposits into gilts. Whereas it is comparatively easy to see how certain market imperfections may be assuaged by relaxations in credit market conditions, (or *vice-versa* following the imposition of credit controls), it

Table 6.2 Mortgage lending by banks and building societies

	1976	1977	1978	1979	1980	1981	1982	1983	1984	1985	1986	1987
Increase in lending (%)	15.9	17.7	19.6	20.1	17.8	21.1	24.1	21.1	18.6	17.8	18.7	18.2
to persons (£ bn)	4.1	5.3	6.9	8.5	9.0	12.6	18.0	19.5	20.7	24.8	29.4	33.8
Of which												
Building societies (£ bn)	3.6	4.1	5.1	5.3	5.7	6.3	8.1	10.9	14.5	14.6	19.4	15.3
Banks (£ bn)	0.5	1.2	1.8	3.2	3.3	6.3	9.8	8.6	6.2	10.2	10.0	18.5
Of which latter,												
mortgage-based (£ bn)	0.1	0.1	0.3	0.6	0.5	2.3	5.1	3.5	2.0	4.2	4.7	10.0

is somewhat harder to see why expenditures should respond directly to portfolio shifts between monetary deposits and other assets, *except* in response to the shift in wealth and in the pattern of interest rates thereby generated. Now that proviso is, of course, of vital importance. Friedman has argued that the linkage between (some definition of) the monetary aggregates and nominal incomes and expenditures has been sufficiently stable and strong that no significant extra explanatory power would be achieved by considering the nature of the credit counterparts to that expansion. For example, in the context of the policy-oriented discussion of overfunding, it is arguable that, had that been continued after 1985, with £M3 correspondingly lower, there would have been less money directed towards UK housing, property and equity markets, so that non-human wealth, expenditures and nominal incomes would all now have been lower.

All this is now a subject of both theoretical and empirical debate. In his survey paper, Gertler (1988) notes that earlier 'the theory of liquidity preference and the time series work of Friedman and Schwartz (1963 and 1982) provided motivation for the preoccupation with money'. (Moreover 'the widespread use of vector autoregressions to analyse time series shifted the focus back to money as the key financial aggregate', e.g. Sims (1972). But now, Gertler claims, there is a revival of interest in studying the financial, and especially the credit-related, aspects of the business cycle, both at the theoretical level, e.g. Williamson (1987), and at the empirical level, e.g. Bernanke (1983), Gertler and Hubbard (1988), Hamilton (1987), (but for doubts about the empirical relevance of the credit view, see King (1986).

Although B. Friedman had reported (1980*a*, 1982) that a credit aggregate could be found in the USA which gave just as stable a relationship with nominal incomes, as did M1 for example, the weight of argument in the 1970s persuaded most Central Bankers that it was, indeed, the (most appropriate definition of the) money stock that should be the centre of policy, rather than some more pragmatic blend of concern with interest rates, monetary *and* credit expansion, asset prices, etc. Now, of course, that earlier, (always somewhat fragile), confidence in the stability (predictability) of the velocity of money has gone, and Central Bankers' traditional (see M. Friedman, 1982) concern with credit (rather than, or as well as, money) has resurfaced; even though the stability of the credit aggregate relationship has fared no better econometrically (B. Friedman, 1988*a*).

But in this somewhat confused state (of economic argumentation), what exactly, besides the level of nominal (and real) interest rates does/should a policy-maker look at, and how does one arrive at a policy judgement?[21]

To conclude and summarise, the (pure Keynesian) route for assessing the effect of money upon the economy, using the IS/LM paradigm, usually has money market interest rates determined by the interaction of the demand for, and (Central Bank) determined supply of, the (high-powered) money base; then short-term interest rates affect longer-term rates, equity yields, etc. and hence via Tobinesque q effects and standard interest elasticities, then affect expenditures; and thereby influence nominal expenditures. This approach ignores the effects of credit and monetary shocks, at given levels of interest rates, in relaxing certain market imperfections, as even erstwhile committed Keynesians now accept, e.g. Dow and Saville (1988). *Per contra*, the monetarist approach wrapped up all the various channels of possible influence in its concentration on the direct (econometric) relationship between money and nominal incomes. The weakening in the predictability of such relationships has now made policy makers reluctant to continue to base policy on any further revised and warmed-up econometric findings in this field.

Instead, policy makers are tending to look directly at domestic indicators of nominal incomes, and of inflation, and to vary nominal interest rates in the light of these, while continuing to cast a rather anxious glance at both credit and monetary aggregates, and also at asset prices (e.g. equities and houses mainly). This is sometimes partially formalised into a 'check-list' approach, (Johnston, 1985; Reserve Bank of New Zealand, 1987*b*), whereby Central Bankers record the list of indicators which they take into account. Supporters would describe it as sensible pragmatism; detractors as a reversion to a muddled discretion, which, once again, allows the authorities more rope than is good for them, or us.

6.6 CONCLUSIONS

During the course of the 1970s, economists and policy-makers came to view the economic system as based on a number of long-term equilibrium conditions. Among the most important were: (i) the natural (equilibrium) level of output and unemployment; (ii) the long-run relationship between the money stock and nominal incomes, a predictable long-term velocity; and (iii) the long-run relationship between prices of tradeable goods among pairs of countries and their bilateral exchange rate, purchasing power parity.

A whole variety of shocks, on the demand or supply side, induced by natural causes or by human agents, could divert the economy temporarily from its long-run equilibrium, but market forces would tend to restore the economy to that equilibrium. The speed with which market forces would operate to restore the economy to its full equilibrium would depend on the extent of market imperfection, and consequential price sluggishness, and there was, and remains, considerable debate on how extensive such imperfections might be. Nevertheless, given that agents could anchor their longer-term expectations on the restoration of such fundamental equilibria (a tranversality condition) and dependent on the assumed extent of shorter run price stickiness, it should, in principle, be possible to trace out the (rationally expected) intervening future path for the economy in response to current shocks. In this context it was hard to see any useful role for the authorities apart from setting a medium-term target (rule) for monetary growth, so as to anchor long term expectations of price inflation, and also acting to eliminate current market imperfections (supply side economics).

The main problem with this view of the economic system is that experience in the 1980s has demonstrated that there appears to be little tendency for the economy to revert with any perceptible speed to a (unique) equilibrium. Unemployment in the UK rose sharply at the start of the 1980s, and remained high – only falling markedly in 1987/8 without apparently causing much sustained downwards pressure on wages and prices. More important for our own story, previously predictable long-term relationships between the money stock and nominal incomes appeared to fall apart, while exchange rates proved capable of diverging both massively and for long periods from PPP.

Under these circumstances the anchor given to forward expectations by such long-term equilibrium conditions, or by the (in the event temporary) adoption of monetary targets by the authorities in the early 1980s, was not firmly set. During this last decade speculation based on an expectation of a (rapid) reversion of velocity or exchange rates to their prior norm would not have been generally financially rewarding, and indeed speculation based on such longer-term fundamentals was rarely visible.

If the natural forces driving the economy back to a (unique) equilibrium are, in practice, much weaker than earlier expected – or even at times nonexistent, or offset by other market considerations – then there is much more room for intervention, and much more need for discretion, by the authorities, since they cannot just sit back and leave affairs to rational agents operating in efficient markets.

In the main, policy-makers, even some of those most captivated by the earlier vision, such as Lawson, have accepted that practical lesson. We do not live in a world in which one can confidently rely on market forces to restore the economy to a stable (unique) equilibrium, so long as the authorities themselves do not rock the boat. In this context, the authorities have reverted to discretionary intervention. Their current main problem is how to operate so as to balance the (occasionally conflicting) objectives of external and internal price stability, but that is another, continuing story.

Many macro-theorists are apparently loathe to accept any dilution of their earlier image of the economy, partly because it raises questions about the adequacy of their models, and the meaning of such accepted concepts as rational expectations. As noted in the Introduction, this has led to an increasing divide between state-of-the-art macro-theory and practical policy analysis. On this my own sympathies are firmly on the side of the policy maker, who has to cope with reality and cannot retreat to the more tractable and elegant models of the theorist.

NOTES

1. For a reconsideration of rules for targetry in these new circumstances, and an advocacy of their reformulation in terms of a feed-back rule from nominal incomes (or some combination of price and output behaviour) to base money, see McCallum (1988) and Hall (1986). For a continuing critique of such rules, see Summers (1988), Tobin (1983) and Lamfalussy (1981).
2. The continental parochialism of US economists is remarkable. Purely as an example, without wishing to impugn an otherwise admirable paper, B. Friedman's (1988b) bibliography of approximately 100 citations has no reference to experience outside North America, and cites, by my count, only a couple of economists not primarily resident there.
3. Au fil du temps, l'évolution à longue terme de la vitesse de circulation de la monnaie a été suffisamment stable, en France, pour qu'un simple analyse de tendance fournisse une approximation correcte de sa valeur future (Bordes and Strauss-Kahn, 1988).
4. The association between monetary and fiscal policy can be most easily seen via the credit counterparts approach. Assume that, with flexible exchange rates, the expected change in banks' net foreign assets is zero, and also ignore any possible change in banks' non-deposit liabilities. Then, the following accounting identities will hold: $\Delta D = \Delta A$; $\Delta A = \Delta BLPub + \Delta BLPS$; $\Delta BLPub = PSBR - DS, NBPS$; where D is £M3, A banks' holdings of domestic assets, $BLPub$, bank lending to the public sector, $BLPS$ bank lending to private sector, DS, $NBPS$ are (net) public sector debt sales to the non-bank private sector.

    With both $BLPS$ and DS, $NBPS$ being functions of interest rates and a vector of other assets, so that $\Delta BLPS = F(i, X)$, then given X, a desire to achieve both the target for ΔD, *and* some preferred level of i, constrains the size of the PSBR. 'Too high a PSBR requires either that the Government borrow heavily from the Banks – which adds directly to the money supply; or, failing this, that it borrows from individuals and institutions, but at ever-increasing rates of interest, which places an unacceptable squeeze on the private sector. From these two facts comes one conclusion, and one conclusion only – that the PSBR is too large', (Lawson, 1980). Also see *Financial Statement and Budget Report* (FSBR redbook) 1980–1, page 16, para. 4). For a more sceptical view of the strength of the *behavioural* relationships involved, see Treasury and Civil Service Committee (1981), and Dow and Saville (1988). Indeed despite these accounting identities, the strength of the relationship between public sector deficits and interest rates, and between public sector deficits and the growth of monetary aggregates, has usually been found to be weak when the data are tested, see Dwyer (1985). This finding caused this aspect of the MTFS to be criticised both by British Keynesians, e.g. Kaldor (1982), and by US Monetarists, e.g. Friedman in his evidence to the Treasury and Civil Service Committee.

5. It proved remarkably difficult to sort out the proportional responsibility of these different factors, and none of the attempts appears really convincing, see Bean (1987) and Niehans (1981) among others.

6. The Bank of England's Minimum Lending Rate, MLR, was suspended in August 1981: thereafter interest rates in the UK refer to the London Clearing Bank base rates, unless otherwise specified.

7. Papers arguing that the reduction in inflation in the 1980s has been largely due to a fall in commodity prices, not to the (direct) effect of monetary restriction (Beckerman 1985), can be misleading in so far as such declines are themselves the indirect consequence of monetary tightness (see Lawson, 1986).

8. There was some subsequent reinterpretation of the degree to which the government had tied itself to the single target, £M3, (Lawson, 1982), together with the beguiling concept, (later formalised in some of the academic literature on policy games, see for example Persson, 1988 and Driffill, 1988), that the more committed the authorities appeared to be to monetarism in theory, the more discretionary they could be in practice. Thus, 'If, on the other hand, the discretion is being exercised by those whose commitment to the policy, and to the overriding need to maintain financial discipline is beyond doubt, then there is no cause for such misgivings' (Lawson, 1982, p. 5).

9. In principle, however, some of these countries e.g. UK, France, retained domestic monetary targets as their formally declared intermediate objective.

10. There was no suggestion, however, in this latter period that the authorities should also shift their control mechanism, and adopt mbc. Indeed this latter option was publicly dismissed (Lawson, 1983).

11. Because the pound remained generally strong during this period, the associated (unpublished) lower limit could not be so easily ascertained.

12. For a recent example see Rasche (1988) who states that 'The research cited here suggests strongly that a very simple demand function specification can account for a large portion of the observed variation in all of these [monetary] aggregates, and that with only two exceptions this function appears very robust over the entire post accord period. The two exceptions are the monetary base and M1 for which there is a significant change in the constant term of the first difference specification around the beginning of 1981 (p. 58). Also see Hamburger (1983) and Baba *et al.* (1987).

13. A dramatic switch occurred in New Zealand in 1984/5, see Spencer and Carey (1988) and RBNZ (1986).

14. For an analysis of some of the consequences of greater interest rates volatility, see B. Friedman (1982) for its effects in US capital markets; Enzler and Johnson (1981) for its effects on output and prices; Black (1982) for its effects on exchange rates; Walsh (1984) for its effects on the demand for money.

15. In fact the yield curve was downwards sloping for much of the period, and the authorities may well have made a commercial profit from the exercise.

16. By this time the authorities' effective money market dealing was almost entirely in commercial bills. Treasury bills could have been completely phased out. The only reason for continuing with a residual TB market, and weekly tender, was the educational function of keeping market-makers familiar with an instrument which might some day regain an important role.

17. In the introduction, we described how the adoption of the MTFS led the fiscal decision on the size of the PSBR to be subordinated to the requirements of monetary policy. With the progressive abandonment of monetary targetry, the influence of such monetary considerations on the fiscal decision weakened.

Indeed, exactly what balance of Keynesian, monetarist, long-term structural, or yet other concepts and ideas, either does, or should, now influence the choice of the size of public sector deficit/surplus in the UK remains unclear, but to follow that murky issue further would take us outside the scope of this paper.

18. Some economists worry over the question whether, and how, the Central Bank can set interest rates, e.g. Dow and Saville (1988). In practice, on a day-to-day basis the Central Bank's monopoly control over the high powered monetary base enables the Central Bank to dictate the price, the short-term interest rate, at which it will provide the banking system with the cash that it requires, (see Bank of England, 1984*b*, Chapter 6). In the medium, and longer term, however, the Central Bank's ability to determine the nominal, and even more so the real, interest rate is constrained by a wide range of both political and economic considerations.

19. In this same paper (p. 10), Gertler commented that, 'the methodological revolution in macroeconomics in the 1970s also helped shift attention away from financial factors, in a less direct but probably more substantial way. The resulting emphasis on developing macroeconomic models explicitly from individual optimization posed an obstacle. At the time, the only available and tractable model suitable for pursuing this methodological approach, the stochastic competitive equilibrium growth model, developed by Brock and Mirman (1972) and others was essentially an Arrow-Debreu model, and thus had the property that financial structure was irrelevant'.

20. For practical examples concerning the USA, see Wojnilower (1980).

21. A good example of such uncertainty can be found in policy makers' reaction to the Crash of 19 October 1987. It was argued that the fall in asset prices might have a deflationary effect or various reasons. First, it might cause insolvencies and a contagious collapse in the financial system; second, and related to the first, it might cause a weakening in 'confidence' and hence in both business and personal expenditure; third, through the wealth effect, it would cause some reduction in consumers' expenditures. With the benefit of hindsight the (rather slight) effect of the last factor appears to have been well captured by the models. But was the subsequent absence of the first two effects due to a (correctly) expansionary monetary policy then adopted by the authorities, or were the fears always exaggerated?

7 Banks and the Control of Corporations (1993)*

7.1 INTRODUCTION

The chief executive, the head, of an enterprise, a firm, is in a position of power. Indeed, the hierarchy, the institutional form of a firm, is established in part to provide the head of a firm with the ability to manage the coordination of the various factors of production (Coase, 1937). That power can be misused. Even when the head of the firm is a primitive entrepreneur with 100 per cent ownership over the residual profits, the entrepreneur will enter into a series of explicit, or implicit, contracts with his labour force, outside suppliers, sales outlets and providers of external (debt) finance. Such a primitive entrepreneur will, indeed, have an incentive to maximise profits, since they all accrue to him, and to remain efficient and minimise costs. But he may also have an incentive to pass on the ownership within the family, irrespective of natural ability; to maintain control long after the most sensible retirement date; to defraud those with whom he has a contractual relationship, e.g. Maxwell's pension fund, if he thinks he can get away with it; or to behave in other ways inimical to the best interests of those with whom he has some form of (contractual) relationship, and to whom he owes some duty of care.

There are, moreover, a number of well-known reasons why a successful firm started by a primitive entrepreneur will generally mutate into a publicly owned firm run by managers. Problems of the inheritance of managerial ability mean that only a few families, such as the Rothschilds or Sainsburys, are willing and able to pass the management of large corporations down from generation to generation; the desire to reduce risk by diversifying wealth away from concentration in a single, and therefore risky, firm adds to the pressure on successful entrepreneurs to dilute their initial ownership and control, whereas success often requires raising additional (outside) equity.

Thus the typical large capitalist firm will be run by a manager, whose own share-holding in the firm will usually be small, and who will be paid largely through a fixed salary, as contrasted with the residual claim of an

* *The Cyprus Journal of Economics*, 6 (2), (December, 1993): 91–108; also published in *Note Economiche*, 2/3 (1993), Riviste del Monte dei Paschi di Siena.

142

entrepreneur on the profits of a firm. This involves, then, a standard principal – agent problem. The agent, the firm's manager, is responsible to the ultimate owners, the share holders of the firm, but does not have the direct incentive of access to the residual profits to push him to maintain efficiency and to minimise costs. The managerial agent is bound to act to some extent in his own personal interest, and his own utility function will include variables, such as empire building, power, perks and leisure, whose pursuit will often be inimical to the best interest of the principal equity share-owners of the firm, and of the others (contractually) involved with the firm to whom the manager has some responsibility (Hart and Moore, 1993; Grossman and Hart, 1982).

Such principal – agent problems are central to the modern theory of the firm, and have led to a vast literature from Jensen and Meckling (1976) onwards, on incentive structures, the appropriate design of contracts, etc. which is well beyond my own specialised field or interest or my technical capacity. What I want to establish at this juncture is simply that there needs to be some mechanism for limiting the misuse and abuse of power by managers of firms, whether that misuse is due to incompetence and inefficiency, to principal – agent problems, or to wilful fraud.

It is, instead, the main thesis of this lecture that such controls over the misuse and abuse of managerial power have largely been undertaken by banks, see also Gorton and Kahn (1993). This has been so, not only under capitalism, but also, in a more limited fashion, under socialist/communist regimes. I shall argue in section 7.2 that many of the problems of the transition from communism to a market economy have come about because the control mechanisms over the firms/enterprises in the communist system have broken down *before* the alternative mechanisms of a market economy, based on commercial law, property rights and bankruptcy could be established, thereby making it difficult, or impossible, for the fledgling banking systems in such countries to control either their large enterprise customers, or even their own balance sheets. Blommestein and Spencer (1993) cover similar ground.

There is, therefore, an urgent short-term problem of how to restore and reinforce (bank) control over enterprises, especially the huge, monopolistic state owned enterprises (SOEs), in these countries. There is, however, also a longer term question of which model of bank/corporate (control) relationships the formerly communist countries should be advised to adopt. There are, of course, two such models on offer, the Anglo–Saxon market-based, arms-length model, in which the bank maintains a purely commercial relationship with its corporate clients, without direct ownership connections, and the Japanese/German model of much closer relationship banking, often with direct equity/ownership involvement. The choice between these models, e.g. for those countries moving from socialism to a market economy is, briefly, discussed in section 7.3, briefly because there is already a large, and continuing, literature on the relative merits of the two models.

First, however, in the remainder of this section, I want to consider *why* banks have played such a large role in exerting outside control over the exercise of managerial power. The first requirement for the exercise of control is adequate information. Unless the outsider (the principal) knows what the factual situation actually is, she is in no position to control it effectively. Banks, in general, have an informational advantage in dealing with their clients relative to all others involved in contractual relationships with an enterprise. It is relatively costly to provide information to the myriad individual investors in primary capital markets, and the information provided becomes public knowledge. When a corporation deals with a bank, it is dealing with one institution and a small number of bank employees. Exchanges of confidential information between bank and customer are generally protected against enforced public disclosure by law, or by custom and practice, with a few exceptions, e.g. money laundering, where failure by a bank to disclose is now becoming a legal offence in the UK. For its part, the commercial bank has an opportunity, indeed a duty to its own depositors and shareholders, to acquire information about the economic prospect of those clients to whom it lends money.

Indeed, the bank is acting as an agent on behalf of its depositors in assessing and monitoring the prospects of its clients. One reason why such intermediation becomes worthwhile, despite the inevitable resulting principal/agent problems that this also entails, is that the banker can specialise and develop an expertise in assessing the economic condition of prospective borrowers (Diamond, 1984). Moreover, the banker will usually have some added informational advantage from undertaking transactions/payments services on behalf of customers, and may therefore be in a position to observe unusual shifts in the regular pattern of payments. The longer a borrower has been servicing its loans, the more likely it is a viable business and its owner is trustworthy (Diamond 1991). For all such reasons the channels for communicating information between banker and corporate client are likely to be much better than with others with a contractual relationship with an enterprise.

It might be argued that a firm's accountants are in an even more privileged position on inside information. Possibly so, though the bank will be more interested in future prospects, and the accountant in past historical data. Moreover, the accountancy firm is hired by the firm, paid by the firm, and, as the Caparo case in the UK underscored, owes its primary allegiance to the firm, see Gwilliam (1992), Power and Freedman (1991) and Woolf (1993). The obligations of the auditor to outsiders, whether regulators, shareholders, or other interested parties are, by contrast, ill-defined and insubstantial. Consequently the auditor is in a much more subservient position, *vis-à-vis* the firm, than is the bank to the company which is indebted to it.

In this discussion I have been making the implicit assumption that each corporation maintains its checking accounts with, and borrows from, a single commercial bank. Except where the corporation has a physical presence in places where its main bank cannot serve it, or requires some special financial expertise, say on mergers and acquisitions, economies of scale and economies of information would suggest that corporations would concentrate their business with a single main commercial bank. The costs of transferring the account from one bank to another, especially of establishing a new informational relationship, can give a bank a degree of monopoly power (see Sharpe 1990 and Rajan 1992) and firms may seek to switch banks as a means of bargaining for lower bank charges and lower margins over the cost of wholesale funds.

Alternatively firms may seek to switch banks, or to establish a borrowing relationship with a number of other banks, because the firm's main bank is unwilling to lend to the firm as much as it wants. Thus the desire to switch banks, or to open up numerous bank borrowing relationships, can be a danger signal that the initial main bank was concerned about the prospects revealed by the information provided to it. It may, moreover, be in the interests of an enterprise, especially when desperate for outside funding, to dissemble about the nature of its other financial commitments when approaching a (new) bank with a borrowing request. Not surprisingly, therefore, there is evidence that, in the USA, 'Attempts by a firm to widen its circle of relationships by borrowing from multiple lenders increases the price and reduces the availability of credit' (Petersen and Rajan, 1992a). Consequently, banks in many countries, often with the support of the authorities, maintain registers of the borrowing commitments and debt payment histories of borrowing customers, (see Padilla and Pagano, 1993). In part, the purpose of the exercise is to prevent the degradation of information available to any one bank which client firms, especially when running into difficulties, may seek to achieve by providing partial information to a number of banks.

So, a bank is likely to be comparatively well informed about the circumstances of its corporate customers. Even so, except when a client approaches the bank with a borrowing request, providing an opportunity for deeper investigation, the bank still generally remains at a remove from direct continuous information on corporate performance. However, the structure of the lending relationship gives it a quasi-automatic entry for monitoring and reviewing its control actions if and when an enterprise's condition seriously worsens. As Diamond (1984) has demonstrated, when continuous monitoring of corporations' true economic condition is difficult or very costly, the optimal contract is in fixed interest debt format. So long as the interest is regularly and promptly paid, the bank can relax its monitoring. Once interest fails to be paid as per contract, and the loan becomes non-performing, the bank will have both the signal of serious problems, the occasion to seek intensive information, and the power to enforce bankruptcy and liquidation in order to recover its debt.

Given a bank's ability to drive a defaulting borrower into bankruptcy, one might think that an enterprise would always seek to pay the bank before other current creditors, e.g. suppliers, labour force. But these latter have the power, if not paid, to withdraw their input into the production process, thereby bringing output to a physical end. Failing to pay the (bank) lender, or the government's revenue authorities for taxes due, does not itself *directly* threaten production, (and indeed saves precious cash). It is, perhaps, for this reason that banks, and the revenue authorities, are given senior creditor claims, with a general floating lien over corporate assets, and are the two institutions that generally initiate bankruptcy proceedings. Bankruptcy, with the attendant possibility of liquidation, implies a severe deterioration in company affairs. Cannot others, notably shareholders, involved with a firm take earlier action to control, and perhaps change, an ineffective management before such a serious stage is reached? The difficulty here is partly one of obtaining sufficient information, and partly the free-rider problem that any one (small) shareholder seeking to correct the situation will bear all the costs of that action, whereas the benefits go to the class of shareholders as a group. It will often be cheaper to sell the share, and vote with ones' feet. Whenever the shareholding is sufficiently large to overcome the free-rider problem, the attempt to intervene directly to alter the independent course of management will often involve both being in receipt of insider information and exercising some degree of executive responsibility. As will be discussed in section 7.3, this is regarded as inappropriate for financial intermediaries in the Anglo–Saxon financial model, but has formed a central plank of the functions of universal banks in the German–Japanese model. We shall defer further discussion of this issue to section 7.3.

Bankruptcy tends to involve sizeable, dead-weight costs, notably to pay for the time of the various professionals called in. Moreover, given the firm-specific nature of both the human and the physical capital of a firm, the going concern value of a company would generally be in excess of its break-up, liquidation value. Furthermore, existing management will inevitably blame failure on a combination of bad luck and once-off temporary problems rather than endemic managerial weakness. Consequently in most individual cases of ex post default, there will generally be a strong case for a reorganisation involving some deferment, or forgiveness, of interest and capital by the bank.

But if the bank is perceived to be likely to accept such reorganisations, then its supposed hard debt, senior creditor position becomes transmuted, in practice, to a junior creditor, equity position in reality. This is a standard time inconsistency situation, whereby the bank's rhetoric *ex ante* is that it will drive any defaulter into liquidation, but its practice ex post is to agree to reorganisations with debt forgiveness. There are a number of institutional conditions which have been established to enable banks to take a more hard-nosed stance. First, bank loan books should be diversified with no loan to any individual borrower amounting to more than a small fraction of its overall loan book. If so, a bank can be prepared to take a tougher line on any individual case, since the loss from the immediate write-off is relatively small, while it has preserved its reputation for ex ante toughness with potential future defaulters. As the saying goes, if you owe the bank 100,000 dollars you are in trouble; if you owe the bank 10 billion dollars, the bank is in trouble. This obviously raises the question of how best to organise bank/borrower relationships when the potential borrower is very large relative to any individual bank, an issue that we shall again defer till later.

The second institutional condition is that the senior creditors, the bank and the tax authority, have a prior claim, a first charge on the assets of the defaulter. Even if reorganisation as an on-going concern would provide a higher present value than liquidation, the senior creditors might find it cheaper and simpler to liquidate, realise asset sales sufficient to cover their own claim, and enable them to walk away whole, leaving the excess real loss from their action to be divided among junior creditors, e.g. bond holders, trade debtors, equity holders. Against the possibility that the structure of bankruptcy laws might induce senior creditors to take *too tough* a line, with an inefficient loss of social value, Aghion, Hart and Moore (1992) have suggested a bankruptcy arrangement, notably for Eastern Europe, whereby more junior creditors or outsiders always get an option to buy out the debt claims of more senior creditors at full value. Hence if reorganisation was better than liquidation, more junior creditors, or outsiders, should find it worthwhile to buy out the claims of the banks and tax revenue authorities. But this takes us rather deeper into the modern theory of the relationships between banks and corporations than we need to go. For my present purposes, the objective was just to establish that banks play a key role in maintaining some outside control over the use, and occasional abuse, of managerial control.

7.2 THE TRANSITION FROM COMMUNISM TO A MARKET ECONOMY

In the opening section I have been taking the market infrastructure of a capitalist economy, including private property rights, commercial law, bankruptcy, etc., as given. But even in a communist system the banks played a key role in maintaining control over companies. In this case, however, their role was rather different, being that of a somewhat mechanical scorekeeper (rather than having direct powers to initiate a relaxation of the hard budget constraint by making (new) loans, or not as the case may be, as in capitalist systems).

Instead, the main discussions, e.g. on inputs, outputs and investment, were taken by the planners in real terms at the central planning authority, e.g. Gosplan, and turned into nominal values by application of controlled prices. This would then imply a consequential, consistent set of monetary flows, payments for inputs and receipts from sales to other enterprises or final sales to consumers. The role of the bank was simply to check whether the payments flows, in and out, was consistent with the plan. Although investment decisions, both on fixed capital and inventories, might be taken by the planners after assessment of relative present values with the aid of some notional discount rate, once investment decisions had been taken, often following bilateral discussions between planners and head of enterprises, they were also part of the plan, and were not generally subject to review by the banks. The actual interest rates offered on deposit and charged on loans by the banks were kept low in real terms, and had virtually no effect on the allocation of funds between potential borrowers, or on the aggregate level of investment. Such interest rates had, instead, some limited effect on the aggregate distribution of incomes and savings patterns between workers, enterprises and governments.

Since the key decisions, e.g. on investment, were regarded as appropriately the function of the Central Planners, in discussion with those directly affected at regional and enterprise level, the banks took little, or no, part in the assessment of projects for which, in effect, bank loans were to be extended. Whereas credit assessment, the monitoring of ongoing client projects, etc., provides the heart of Western banking, Communist bankers played little more than a minimal savings bank role, taking in deposits, operating the payments system (inefficiently) and reporting back to central authority whenever actual enterprise financial flows deviated significantly from those planned. This has meant that there was no tradition, or experience, of market-oriented commercial banking, with its emphasis on credit assessment, in the previously communist countries once they embarked on the path to a market economy. See Blommestein, (1993).

Even within the confines of such a limited savings bank model, with all important credit decisions taken elsewhere by the planners, there remained plenty of room for improvement in the provision of their limited financial services, e.g. in competition through higher interest rates and improved services to depositors, in improving the payments system, in making small loans, e.g. to cooperatives to buy trucks, etc. Such improvements were generally not made, or only sluggishly, partly because of the dead hand of the communist methodology and partly because of the insistence, on both ideological and security grounds, with central control. Improvement of the payments system was impossible if all cheque payments had to be routed physically through the Central Bank as a further control device, as in Russia, rather than netted through local Clearing Houses. Most other improvements, e.g. extension of small loans, would depend on local initiative, and the more the local initiative, the greater might be the chance of an erosion of central control.

Not surprisingly, therefore, the standard banking system in such communist countries had a unitary framework, with a single main bank undertaking both Central Banking functions, such as note issue and interest rate setting, and rudimentary commercial bank functions, though both were to be subject to, and consistent with, the overall national plan. The limited number of other separate banks were usually specialised by function, e.g. a specialist export/import bank like the Moscow Narodny, and possibly specialist banks for Construction, Agriculture, Heavy Industry, or whatever. Such monopoly provision of banking services further reduced incentives for greater efficiency, e.g. in developing payments systems, in this field, (see Folkerts-Landau, Garber and Lane, 1993).

One of the many difficulties of a centrally planned system was the sheer technical problem of assembling and coordinating the necessary information. Partly in order to simplify and enhance the control system, partly out of an, often unwarranted, belief in the availability of economies of scale, there was a tendency in most communist countries to centralise manufacturing output in huge plants, and many state owned enterprises consisted of one, or just a few, such massive plants. These individual giant plants often provided virtually the only source of domestic production of such products, often in turn an essential input into other domestic production processes. Frequently these plants would provide the majority of employment opportunities for the middle-sized towns in which they had been placed, and in many cases the enterprise provided many of the main social service functions, e.g. organising the provision of sick pay, the allocation of housing, in the town. Consequently the livelihood and well-being of the giant plant and town were much more closely tied together than has normally been the case in the West.

Particularly when the nominal exchange rate is misaligned, and/or foreign exchange too scarce to replace domestic production by imports, the strategic position of many giant SOEs in formerly communist countries, strategic both in the domestic production matrix and in the livelihood of their immediate localities, means that they can hardly be closed down. So, they had a 'soft budget constraint' (Kornai, 1980).

Standard Western bankruptcy procedures, even if in place, which, outside Hungary, is not yet the case (Fries and Lane, 1993), could hardly be applied to these institutions, which still represent a large proportion of output in many formerly communist countries. Consequently they cannot have a hard budget constraint, and commercial banks, willy-nilly, *cannot* control their managers and activities through standard Western banking procedures. No doubt over time, with the extension of privatisation, growing competition, the application of commercial and bankruptcy law, this condition will slowly fade, (see the Section on 'gradual privatisation' in Hay and Peacock, 1992, pp. 40–2), but the transition may take a decade, or more, and in the meantime problems with inflation, which ultimately reflect a variety of *control* problems, continue (see Blommestein and Spencer, 1993).

These control problems would be bad enough if the nascent commercial banks in the transitional economies were entirely independent of the giant SOEs. In practice, they often have not been so. Perhaps the easiest virtue of capitalism for communists to grasp is the advantages of competition, e.g. in encouraging efficiency. Even Lenin understood the benefits of competition. Consequently, in addition to hiving off most of the branches of the previously unitary main bank to form one, or usually a number of supposedly independently competitive, commercial banks, many of these countries encouraged the formation of further 'commercial' banks primarily from domestic resources, there being some hesitations on both sides (outside East Germany) to encouraging the advent of Western banks. But which bodies had access to the resources and capital needed to start up such banks? In many cases, notably in Russia (see Ickes and Ryterman, 1992, 1993; Long and Talley, 1993), the answer was precisely these same giant SOEs, or alternatively regional and local governments one of whose main concerns was to foster and succour their own local SOEs. So, rather than exercising an outside control of the managers of SOEs, such 'commercial' banks have often been little more than a conduit of extra funding for them, relaxing the soft budget yet further![1]

Even where the 'commercial' banks are not dominated by, and run for the benefit of, some enterprise or regional group of enterprises, the previous structure of the system means that the 'assets' of these banks are largely filled with loans to such SOEs. For a variety of reasons, which are important but not germane to the central theme here, a large proportion of SOEs have shifted from being cash cows and major tax-revenue sources under the old centralised system to becoming deficit, loss-making entities during the transition, McKinnon (1991a and b). Many are effectively insolvent, but for the reasons outlined above cannot be closed down.

The result is that many of the loans, a large proportion of the assets, of the 'commercial' banks in these countries in transition are bad, are not worth their face value; EBRD officials 'estimate that bad debts represent more than 60 per cent of the balance sheet in some of the largest east European banks', Gillian Tett, *Financial Times*, 3 August 1993. Consequently many of the commercial banks in these countries have at best impaired capital, and at worst are insolvent. Given the central position of commercial banks in the payments and financial systems in Western economies, capitalist monetary authorities are generally not prepared to envisage the bankruptcy and closure of any significant parts of their own banking system. By extension, one could hardly expect the Eastern transitional economies to close their bankrupt, or capital-impaired banks.

Instead, as noted earlier, we get reorganisations, e.g. with government bonds replacing defaulted loans. This means, of course, that banks too are on a soft-budget basis. The route to survival and success is not so much profit maximisation, which is hardly possible so long as loans to loss-making SOEs remain a major element of banks books, but rather maintaining good bureaucratic relationships with those likely to be influential in future reorganisations. See Fries and Lane (1993) and Summers (1992). Under these circumstances an adjustment of interest rates is unlikely to provide an effective limit to the demand for external credit from soft-budget SOEs. Indeed Ickes and Ryterman (1992) report that 'less successful enterprises are often charged lower rates of interest than more successful ones' (p. 347) to help prop them up. Moreover, even if the banks appreciate that the SOEs are unlikely ever to be able to repay such loans, with or without interest, their own soft-budgets mean that they have to balance the political effect of refusal (plus the effect of recognising the effect of such refusal on the accounting value of their existing loans to such enterprises), against the economic advantage of shifting more of the allocation of lending elsewhere, e.g. to small cooperatives and the private sector. Given their historical background, it can hardly be surprising if commercial banks in such circumstances in transitional countries allocate credit more on the basis of the political clout of those seeking such funds than on any market-based credit assessment, see Frenkel (1992) for a particularly gloomy assessment of banking in the CIS; Johnson, Kroll and Horton (1993) have a more optimistic viewpoint.

Consequently an increase in interest rates, though it will generally be desirable to have rates which are positive in real terms, may reallocate credit from the more efficient private sector towards less efficient SOEs, because of the softer budgets of the latter. Moreover, the effect of such interest rate increases will be less effective, since they do not impact on a sizeable proportion of borrowers. The standard answer in such circumstances has been for the Central Bank to seek to ration credit directly, by direct limits on Central Bank credits, by imposing quotas on new commercial bank lending, etc. But this too has been only partially effective, at best.

Because their strategic position makes them impervious to bankruptcy, an SOE denied direct credit by its bank simply does not pay its supplier, or writes a cheque which it has no funds to meet. The denial or direct bank credit just leads to an offsetting ballooning in inter-enterprise debts, which has happened time and again, whenever the Central Bank, or the monetary authorities, have tried a direct credit squeeze in such circumstances (Begg and Portes, 1992). Given that the delay between initiating a payment and its final settlement is several weeks in Russia, the commercial banks have little clear, immediate idea of the present true 'liquidity' position of their SOE customers. (Also see the discussion of Poland's 1991 Art B scandal in Folkerts-Landau, Garber and Lane, 1993). What can they do if a payment order comes in taking the SOE customer above its quota limits? If they do insist on its meeting its credit limits, then (involuntary) trade credit will just replace the forbidden bank credit. Ultimately, if you are not prepared to enforce bankruptcy and closure on a firm, you cannot control it by financial means. (See Ickes and Ryterman, 1992; Sachs and Lipton, 1992).

Most of the attempts to deal with the resulting problems have tried to respond to the *symptoms*, for example reorganising the asset structure of the commercial banks, replacing bad loans by government bonds, and by a netting process to collapse the pyramid of inter-firm trade debt, plus, perhaps, a further injection of (Central) bank credit to internalise the remaining net trade debt within the banking system (Ickes and Ryterman, 1993; Fries and Lane, 1993). While such measures may be desirable in themselves, they fail to meet the crucial point which is that commercial banks should not be allowed to lend *at all* to firms which they cannot control through a hard budget constraint.

What economies in transition to a market economy should do is largely as follows. First, Central Government should decide which plants and enterprises could not be allowed to close as a consequence of bankruptcy. These then should subsequently be reabsorbed, financed and controlled, as best as possible, through the central budget mechanism and direct central control, until privatisation can be accompanied by acceptance of potential closure of the individual privatised entities. *Banks should not be allowed to lend anything to soft-budget strategic SOEs.* This proposal is quite close to that already made by McKinnon (1991a, 1992, 1993) and Perotti (1992). Banks should not be allowed to make any connected lending, i.e. loans to their owners. Banks should not be allowed to make loans in amounts greater than a small, specified proportion of capital. The aim is to put banks in a position where they can exert external control on their corporate borrowers. Long and Talley's (1993) proposal for an 'International Standard Bank' programme for Russia goes some of the way, but fails to take the crucial step of separating those SOEs who cannot, or will not, be allowed to fail altogether from the commercial banking system.

This would mean that a large proportion of existing commercial bank business, with existing SOEs, would disappear from their balance sheets, being reabsorbed by the Central, or regional, Governments. Instead, banks would lend at arms length only to smaller, and non-strategic, SOEs, cooperatives and the nascent private sector, whom they can control. Such lending might represent only a limited proportion initially of their funds, the rest being channeled directly to Central, or Regional, Government. The successful application of bank finance depends on its ultimate ability to exert control through a hard budget constraint. Whenever banks cannot do that, external financial and direct control should revert to the ultimate political authorities. If they, too, cannot exert effective control, chaos will ensue.

7.3   WHICH WESTERN MODEL?

There are, of course, two differing capitalist models of bank–corporate relationships, the Anglo–Saxon (AS) and the German–Japanese (GJ) models. In both models the bank exerts control over its corporate client borrower, but through rather differing mechanisms. In the AS mould, bank control is sporadic, and triggered either by a default or a request for the extension of new loans. Otherwise relationships between bank and corporate client are at arms length, and the firm manager's power is otherwise limited by the influence, such as it may be, of his Board of Directors, his shareholders and the effect of fluctuations in the price of the company's equity on his hold over power, in the face of potential take-overs, shareholder revolts, etc. Benston (1993) presents a discussion of the relative advantages and disadvantages of the two systems.

In the GJ model the (universal) bank often has a closer and continuing relationship with the corporate client, frequently involving an equity stake, and even the ability, whether directly or by the exercise of proxy votes, to achieve a strategically commanding position in corporate Board decisions. For a study of the system in Germany, see Francke and Hudson (1984), and in Japan, Morishima (1993). Such relationships require a sizeable commitment on the part of the bank. Scott (1993) queries whether there is sufficient managerial capacity available to banks in transitional socialist economies to make the GJ universal bank model suitable for them. As noted earlier, when a bank has much of its free capital tied to the economic results of a client, it may find its ability and willingness to take hard decisions compromised, and may be persuaded after a bad outcome to propose reorganisation rather than liquidation. Similarly, with such large exposures, the bank may itself be dragged into failure by the losses of a few of its main clients, as happened in Italy in the inter-war period.

There are two responses to this. First, the model has typically been based on an oligopoly of extremely large universal banks (e.g. Mitsui, Mitsubishi, Sumitomo, Deutsche, Commerz). The size and profitability of the bank at the centre of the industrial enterprise group (Keiretsu) is such that the involvement of the bank with any one of its associated corporate clients, with whom it is closely inter-twined, is sufficiently small that its own fortunes remain independent of that single company's success. The GJ model requires a banking structure that fosters extremely large and strong (oligopolistic) banks.

The second response is that the closer equity links, between bank and corporate client, in this model is beneficial precisely *because* it does tend to make banks act more softly, at times of bad outcomes, and exhibit a preference for reorganisation rather than closure. It is argued that the weakening in hardness of the debt claim of the bank in such cases is more than counterbalanced by its privileged position in obtaining (inside) information on corporate prospects and, because of its strategic position on the Board, can act on that information to influence the direction of management (see Petersen and Rajan, 1992b; Pozdena, 1987). In return, the bank can, and usually does, use that same strategic position to protect its client company from outside takeovers. Fluctuations in equity prices, and the attitude of non-strategic shareholders, therefore have much less resonance in the GJ than in the AS model.

The advantage of this model is that encourages the regular maximum flow of accurate confidential information between corporation and strategic main bank, see Hoshi, Kashyap, and Scharfstein (1990). Bank control is continuous, rather than sporadic as in the AS model. Since the transfer of information will be confidential and restricted to a few bankers, there are fewer costs and more advantages to the corporate manager in providing it. The corporate managers have an incentive to provide accurate forward-looking information, since they may be moved from office if their forecasts for the future turn out ex post to have been too optimistic, of if their forecasts are currently ex ante so pessimistic, that the banker allocates funds elsewhere. Equally the main bank has both the incentive and the ability to act, e.g. by controlling corporate management, in order to maximise the present value of its stake in the company. This strategic control limits managements' ability to act in a self-interested way, beyond the level tolerated by the culture of the main bank, and thereby bank claims on the client are less hard, and more junior, and more postponable in practice, than under the AS model, as Hart's theory (1993) would predict.

With better information flows, more junior and postponable debt, and a tendency towards *ex post* reorganisation, rather than liquidation, the GJ model involves incentives for the main bank to nurse ailing companies through difficult periods, so long as inside information suggests a reasonable prospect for a recovery. This model is often hailed as encouraging long-term commitment and the pursuit of long-term strategies, that may nevertheless maximise expected net present value. Gerschenkron (1962) argued that the GJ banking model played a central role in enhancing the rapid industrial development of the emerging economies at the end of the nineteenth century. By contrast, the AS model is criticised as short-termist, overly concerned with current performance and equity prices, subject to considerable dead-weight costs in avoidable bankruptcies and take-over battles, etc. In part, this is due to the likelihood that main bank–corporate information flows will be better, more revealing and more accurate in the GJ model; and, in part it will be due to the institutional structure, of the AS model which both encourages banks to be relatively hard-nosed when defaults in interest payments do put them to control, and otherwise places few effective restrictions on managerial power beyond those deriving from a falling equity price.

The GJ model, therefore, does possess considerable advantages, and it is, therefore, little surprise that many Anglo–Saxon economic analysts (Mayer, 1988, 1990; Cable, 1985; Bisignano, 1991, 1992; Porter, 1991; Benston, 1993; Bhide, 1993) see it as preferable. But it depends on the main bank being clearly placed in a privileged, strategic, *inside* position, both for information and managerial control. The effect of that will be to weaken primary capital markets, to place banks sometimes in a position of conflict of interest with their depositors, and to sustain a culture in which insider information will be regularly used in asset trading. See, for example, Steinherr and Huveneers (1990). It is uncertain whether (the advantages of) the GJ system could survive a shift to a more competitive, transparent, set of asset markets with a level playing field for investors, so that any investor, including a main bank, would be precluded from the use of inside information in equity deals.

If we assume, as I do, that there is strong momentum towards such level, transparent asset markets, then the future would seem to belong to the AS bank model, despite its relative disadvantages outlined above. I conclude, therefore, by wondering whether our theorists, the Oliver Harts and John Moores, can find some way to combine the best features of both bank/finance models.

NOTE

1. The situation in China is healthier. The average size of state enterprises is much lower than in East Europe (Qian and Xu 1993, p. 25), though loss-making SOEs are still bailed out, rather than closed (Qian and Xu, p. 36). Most of the growth in recent years has been in smaller scale collectives, township and village enterprises, (TVEs), and even lately in privately owned businesses, which do face a harder budget constraint (Qian and Xu, p. 36). Although this growth, even in the so-called non-state sector, has been largely driven by initiatives from provincial and local government officials, and property rights are 'fuzzy' (see Weitzman and Xu, 1993) most of the financing has come from self-raised funds, including local budgetary sources, a kind of communal equity, rather than bank loans. Moreover a large proportion of such bank loans have been for working, rather than fixed, capital see Yusuf, (1993), especially Tables 8, 9, and 11. Furthermore, 'Although banks were still owned by the state, each regional branch of the specialized banks was required to link their total credit extension to deposits collected within the region (cundai guagou) (Qian and Xu, 1993, p. 24). Also see McKinnon (1993).

8 The Political Economy of Monetary Union (1995)*

8.1   100 LUMS IN A DRAM

In the last few years, while Western Europe has been preoccupied with its fitful progress toward economic and monetary union, previous monetary unions to the east have been unraveling. Wherever political unity and central control have ended in Central and Eastern Europe, monetary separation has rapidly followed. This was true in Czechoslovakia, where political division was comparatively friendly and peaceful, as well as in Yugoslavia, where it has been hostile. Despite a Czech-Slovak agreement, on 29 October 1992, to use a common currency for an unspecified period after formal separation, Slovaks rushed to get rid of Czech banknotes almost as soon as the break occurred on 1 January 1993, and the Czech and Slovak central banks began overprinting bank notes in preparation for the new separate currencies (Reuters, 11 January 1993). In Yugoslavia, not only were the Slovenian tolar and Croatian dinar established separately from the Yugoslav (Serbian) dinar, but separate new dinars were planned for Muslim-held parts of Bosnia-Herzegovina and the self-proclaimed 'Serbian Republic of Bosnia-Herzegovina'. Thus, Sarajevo radio announced on 15 August 1992, that the old Yugoslav dinar would be scrapped in favour of a new Bosnian dinar, pegged to the German mark at 350 to 1 (Reuters, 15 August 1992).

It is the former Soviet Union (FSU), however, that has spawned the greatest number of new and projected new currencies. My own favourite is the proposed Armenian currency, which will have banknotes worth between 1 and 500 drams and coins worth 10 lums to 10 drams. A dram will contain 100 lums (Interfax, 4 September 1992). Other republics have moved varying distances toward introducing separate currencies; the range and state of play in May 1993 is shown in Table 8.1 (see pp. 158–9). Of the countries listed, only Estonia had managed a full transformation to an independent currency. Latvia, Lithuania, and Ukraine were using temporary coupons or currencies

---

* In P. Kenen (ed.), *Understanding Interdependence: The Macroeconomics of the Open Economy* (Princeton University Press, 1995).

My thanks are due to those participating in discussions of this paper at Columbia, Liverpool, and Princeton Universities; to Michael Artis, Andrew Crockett, Phillipa Gaster, Dieter Guffens, Rosa Lastra, Jacques Melitz, Robert Nobay, Lionel Price, and Christien Schluter for help and suggestions; and to Benjamin Cohen, Alberto Giovannini, and Andrew Hughes Hallett for acting not only as discussants, but also as friendly advisers. They are not, however, to be chided for my opinions and errors.

intended to supplant the Russian ruble, and Azerbaijan and Kazakhstan were using new currencies side by side with the ruble (Hansson, 1993).

No one suggests that the defections from the ruble area occurred because the region was too large to be an optimal currency area (OCA). Indeed, the preference of Soviet planners for huge centralised plants serving, in some cases, the whole Soviet Union and the other members of the Council for Mutual Economic Assistance (CMEA) made the single-currency area more efficient than not, and it has greatly increased the real economic cost of the region's breakup (Havrylyshyn and Williamson, 1991; Williamson, 1992a). Political, not economic, events have caused the monetary changes in Central and Eastern Europe; economic considerations, although important, have been secondary.

It is probable that those favoring monetary unification within the European Community (EC) are also motivated mainly by political considerations,[1] although the change in the monetary constitution, set out in the Maastricht Treaty, has been discussed largely in economic terms. The Zollverein may be remembered as an example of monetary unification being used as an important stage, even a precondition, for political unification (Holtfrerich, 1988, 1992).

Evidence that politics determine currency questions has generally been sought from recent or prospective examples of changes in existing circumstances. We might consider also the status quo. How many economists seriously argue that the great federal countries, Australia, Brazil, Canada, the former Soviet Union, and the USA, are too large to be optimal currency areas and that they should be disbanded? How many argue that certain small nations using the dollar, such as Liberia and Panama, belong optimally to the US currency area? Does anyone suggest that OCA considerations have determined the use of the dollar in countries with hyperinflation (for example, Argentina and Russia)? At the opposite end of the size spectrum are Iceland, with a separate currency for about 250,000 people, and Liechtenstein, San Marino, and Monaco, whose economies are so closely joined to their neighbours that having separate currencies would be economically inefficient. Size alone seems not to be the most important criterion.

Many countries peg their currencies to others, of course, often so irrevocably that the currencies are accepted as interchangeable (Hanke and Schuler, 1990, 1991; Hanke, Jonung and Schuler, 1993; Walters and Hanke, 1992; Newlyn and Rowan, 1954). Even so, the smaller pegged countries generally maintain separate bank notes in order to enjoy prestige and seigniorage (when the backing is in the form of earning assets) and, just possibly, security against a day when the 'irrevocable' ceases to be unalterable, as, for example, when Luxembourg broke with the Belgian franc or Ireland ended a half-century of equivalency with sterling (Walsh, 1993). No independent country, however, has unilaterally abandoned its own note issue for another's currency. There was some discussion in Israel, during a period of severe inflation,

Table 8.1 The status of currencies in the former Soviet Union, May 1993

State	Currency	Current position	Comment	Reuters date
Russia	Ruble	Existing	On verge of hyperinflation; may need currency reform	4 December 1992
Turkmenistan	Manat	Introduced August 1992	Parallel with ruble	15 December 1992
Azerbaijan	Manat	Introduced January 1993	Manat and ruble used side by side	11 December 1992
Latvia	Lat	Phased introduction planned from March 1993, alongside Latvian ruble	Lat and Latvian ruble initially to be used side by side; Latvian ruble devalued 25 per cent in October 1992	30 November 1992
Ukraine	Hrivnya	Coupons (karbovanets) deemed only legal tender, November 1992	Coupons in halfway stage to new currency	12 November 1992
Lithuania	Litas	Coupons (talonas) termed 'zoo tickets', because of animal motif, issued at end September 1992; sole legal tender since October 1992	Coupons is halfway stage to new currency	October 1992
Tatarstan[a]	Ruble	New national coins ordered from Yugoslav supplier	To enable citizens to buy bread	14 September 1992
Armenia	Dram	Planning stage only	Unprofitable to leave ruble zone at present	2 September 1992

Tajikistan	Ruble	Order given to Canada's Bank Note company to print new money; possibly to be called 'somon'	At early planning stage	10 August 1992
Kazakhstan	Tanga	Introduced August 1992 for limited groups, e.g., pensioners	Tanga and ruble used side by side	22 May 1992 5 August 1992
Estonia	Kroon	Introduced June 1992	Pegged to deutschemark; backed by prewar gold	21 June 1992
Uzbekistan	Ruble	Early planning stage		3 June 1992
Belarus	Rubel	Interim currency issued June 1992; sole legal tender since November 1992	1 Rubel = 10 rubles	16 May 1992
Moldova	Lei	Already printed in Romania, but *not* then issued		9 May 1992
Kyrgyzstan	Som	Introduced May 1993 as sole legal tender[b]		
Georgia	Ruble	Plans to introduce for new currency, the 'Lary' arranged		

Source: Reuters reports, 1992 and 1993.

Note: I thank Phillipa Gaster for enabling me to update this table to May 1993.

[a] It is interesting that Tatarstan may now be moving towards introducing a national currency. Whilst there have been several manifestations of its desire to become more independent over the last year, it is currently still technically a part of Russia (being one of the 20 autonomous republics within Russia), and thus required to comply with Russia's monetary policies. The attempt, albeit modest as yet, partly to nationalise the currency is probably quite significant in terms of whether or not Russia will fragment. It will be interesting to see what other Russian republics decide to do.

b See also John Lloyd, 'IMF Watches as Kyrgyzstan Fights the Battle of the Som', *Financial Times* (21 May 1993).

of stopping the inflation by replacing the shekel with the US dollar. Imaginative as the cure was, however, it was quickly dismissed as both too radical and too politically humiliating to be acceptable (Glasner, 1989; see Chown and Wood, 1992–3, for a somewhat similar proposal in Russia). There are many instances of currency substitution and dollarisation during inflationary processes (Fischer, 1982), of course, but national authorities have generally seen these as threats to their ability to generate seigniorage.

The evidence therefore suggests that the theory of optimal currency areas has relatively little predictive power. Virtually all independent sovereign states have separate currencies, and changes in sovereign status lead rapidly to accompanying adjustments in monetary autonomy. The boundaries of states rarely coincide exactly with optimal currency areas, and changes in boundaries causing changes in currency domains rarely reflect shifts in optimal currency areas.

Section 8.2 asks why currency questions have such political resonance. It examines the symbolic significance of national currencies as emblems of sovereignty, the role of seigniorage, particularly as revenue of last resort, and the economic benefits of monetary autonomy. But can we really believe these issues are so important? Symbols are, after all, just symbols; the use of seigniorage to obtain control over real resources is, and should remain, low in most stable, industrial countries; and, if monetary autonomy is beneficial in, for example, adjusting to asymmetric, local shocks, why has no federal country considered the adoption of a multiplicity of currencies for its constituent states? Will political considerations, in fact, hinder or even preclude the prospective move to Economic and Monetary Union.

Section 8.3 examines the reasons and incentives to move to EMU and reviews the European Commission's analysis of the economic benefits and costs of EMU within an OCA framework (Commission, 1990). The Commission compares largely unquantifiable gains from greater microeconomic efficiency in the functioning of money as a medium of exchange and unit of account with more tangible losses in the authorities' ability to conduct macroeconomic demand management (Krugman 1993). Neither the benefits nor costs appear to be large (Bean, 1992). Moreover, judging by the usual criteria of convergence, frequency of asymmetric shocks, and flexibility of labor markets, it is doubtful that the EC is an OCA at all, at least outside the core area of north central Europe (Austria, Denmark, France, Germany, Switzerland, and the Benelux countries); it is equally doubtful that several existing EC states (reunified Germany, Italy, Spain, and the UK) are OCAs. It can also be argued, however, that, if there is no long-term trade-off between inflation and output, if there is considerable real-wage rigidity throughout Europe (Jackman, Layard, and Nickell, 1991), and if exchange-rate adjustment is not the appropriate response to many (perhaps most) shocks, then abandoning the exchange rate as an instrument of demand management may involve no serious cost (Artis, 1991; Melitz. 1993a).

If it is difficult to make a strong case for EMU along OCA lines, and, if the political concerns seem trivial, what is all the fuss about? To answer this question, section 8.4 returns to an earlier line of argument, pioneered by Kenen (1969), that there is an essential interaction between the currency domain and the domain in which certain other policies can effectively operate. Kenen emphasises the interaction between the monetary and fiscal domains. Most assessments of EMU ask whether some significant fiscal centralisation is a necessary adjunct to a currency union, and this issue is reviewed here, but the point stressed by Kenen and often overlooked is that a considerable degree of currency stability may also be necessary if a federal fiscal system is to work satisfactorily. This reverse causation, from currency stability to federal fiscalism, is assessed in the second part of section 8.4.

Not only do currency and fiscal domains interact, but the currency domain also interacts with the relative freedom of trade and the free movement of factors of production. The influence that the degree of economic openness has on the case for monetary union and on OCA theory has been clear in the literature from the start (Mundell, 1961; McKinnon, 1963). What I emphasise in section 8.4 is the reverse causation whereby the nature of the currency and exchange-rate regime may influence political decisions on the future of the single market. Anglo–Saxon commentators often assert that an open single market with common minimum standards is perfectly consistent with flexible exchange rates and autonomous monetary policies; continental European commentators usually take the opposite tack.

The history of the European Monetary System (EMS) shows that it has been possible to move to a single market before achieving a single currency. Although it is uncertain that the benefits of the single market can survive freely floating exchange rates within the EC, the events of 1992 have thrown into doubt the proposed transition to EMU whereby a single currency will eventually supplant ever more tightly fixed, then irrevocably locked, nominal exchange rates. Much of the early discussion of EMU took place either in terms of comparative statics, involving the comparison of the benefits and costs of different but established exchange-rate systems, or under the assumption that the transition would follow the orderly process laid down by the Delors Committee (Committee, 1989) and amended in the Maastricht Treaty (Council, 1992).

Some of these transitional issues are examined in section 8.5, which considers three main issues. First, it examines the long-standing dispute between the 'monetarists' and 'economists.' The monetarists believe that early moves toward monetary union will put pressure on members to converge in other economic respects; the economists hold to the German 'coronation' theory and maintain that monetary union can be securely achieved only as the culmination of a general process of convergence. Second, it examines the likely costs and disturbances of moving from Stage 3A, with irrevocably locked exchange rates between national currencies, to Stage 3B, with a single currency (Melitz, 1993a; Gros and Thygesen, 1992). Advocates of EMU have been largely silent, and occasionally cavalier, about these costs and disturbances, which are potentially severe. A variety of proposals for reducing them are discussed. Third, section 8.5 argues that Stage 3A may last longer than is generally expected, perhaps up to four or five years, and it examines the operational problems that may arise with respect to the functioning of the financial system and the conduct of monetary policy.

8.2　THE POLITICAL IMPERATIVE

The Symbolism of National Currencies

From the earliest days of minted coins, images on currencies have celebrated sovereign majesty and power. A strong currency is in itself grounds for national satisfaction, and devaluation is seen as a humiliation, a sign of national weakness. When decimalization was introduced in the UK (from 1967 to 1971), the authorities retained the pound as the main unit, rather than switch to the mathematically more convenient ten shilling note. This was partly a matter of national prestige, for the pound was the heaviest, most valuable monetary unit among the industrialised nations.

In several EC countries, and especially in Germany, the public is concerned about losing their national note issues under EMU and having to accept an unfamiliar and perhaps less stable currency, produced and controlled by foreigners. Because currency is the most tangible and commonly used claim to goods and services, the significance attached to its imagery and control is not so surprising. The seigniorage derived from note issue, moreover, can be an important source of revenue for countries, especially in times of war or other crises, when revenue from taxes or bond issues is difficult or impossible to raise. It is, therefore, understandable that emerging countries like Slovenia or the Baltic states should regard as a top priority the establishment of national currencies and the concomitant demonetisation of the dinar and ruble (Williamson, 1992b; Havrylshyn and Williamson, 1991; Hansson, 1993). Even the Archbishop of Canterbury, Dr George Carey, is reported to have 'draw[n] the line at the idea of monetary union leading to the head of his Church disappearing from English pound notes. . . . 'I want the Queen's head on the banknotes,' he is quoted as saying. 'The point about national identity is a very important one. For me, being British is deeply important. I don't want to become French or German' ('Interview,' *Financial Times*, 15 February 1993).

Seigniorage

David Glasner (1989, p. 31), in his chapter on 'Money and the State,' asks why money, of all goods and services, has led governments of all types to try to control its production and supply. His answer is that state monopoly of money 'was founded on security considerations . . . [as] an instrument of wartime finance.' There is thus 'a real, if only historical, connection between control over money and the protection of sovereignty, . . . [a connection that] would also explain the otherwise surprising fact that counterfeiting was a treasonable offence under English law,' and that the primary duties of the secret service in the USA are protection of the president and prevention of counterfeiting.

Glasner's hypothesis has a number of testable implications. One (p. 36) is that 'governments most likely to relinquish control over the creation of money are ones with no defense responsibilities.' This fits the early American experience, Glasner argues, and, certainly, it fits current European experience. The political cement of the EC has been the determination of the French and Germans to end their rivalry and the series of European wars. If the nations of Western Europe no longer expect to wage wars among themselves, they no longer need national instruments of wartime finance. Moving to a single EC currency therefore represents both an actual and a symbolic renunciation of any anticipated need to finance the protection of national, as opposed to EC, sovereignty. In Central and Eastern Europe, the reverse is true. Political upheavals have caused concern about the status and nature of independence, and continuing hostilities in the former Yugoslavia and potential rivalries between former Soviet republics (Ukraine and Russia, Armenia and Azerbaijan, Georgia and Abkhazia, for example) have naturally led the new Eastern states to consider all possible means of reinforcing their recently won independence.

Another testable implication (p. 39) is that the national-defense rationale 'implies that governments optimally exploit the monopoly by avoiding inflation in peacetime. If they don't avoid inflation, they risk being left defenseless in wartime.' This accords well with the history of the nineteenth century, when nearly all governments and central banks strove to maintain a non-inflationary monetary rule in peacetime but readily abandoned it for inflationary note finance in times of war. It fits less well with the largely peaceful years since 1945, during which both inflation and currency devaluation have been frequent. Perhaps a nuclear-age war is considered so remote, or so apocalyptic, that the need to hold monetary finance in reserve for such an occurrence is perceived as much reduced or even pointless. Glasner explains this by the currently fashionable theory of time inconsistency. Thus (p. 39). 'One disincentive to investing in the monopoly over money in peacetime is that the government decision makers have a limited tenure in office and have no transferable property rights in the assets [low inflation expectations] they create while in office.' Notwithstanding the popularity of this theory, evidence for the existence of a regular Nordhaus political business cycle is surprisingly weak (Alesina, 1989). History may record that the genesis of the inflationary upsurge in recent decades, especially in the 1970s, was much more specific to the context of the period, combining a continuing belief in a potential trade-off between inflation and output along a declining Phillips curve with specific inflationary oil shocks.

A state must nevertheless be able to undertake certain costly functions to ensure its own survival. Even in peacetime, the maintenance of civil authority requires a variety of expenditures, including disbursements to avert disaffection, disobedience, and insurrection. At times of crisis, when a government is not fully in control and its ability to raise funds from taxation and bond issues is reduced, it may well revert to issuing notes. Such monetary expansion leads to inflation, of course, which erodes still further the government's access to ordinary funding sources and leads inevitably to hyperinflation (Havrylyshyn and Williamson, 1991).

The time-inconsistency model suggests that the use of seigniorage as a means of government finance will be inversely related to the stability of the national government; the weaker the government's authority, the greater its reliance on seigniorage as an instrument of finance (Leijonhufvud, 1992). Thus, asking whether seigniorage is at an optimal level in some absolute sense is misguided, because the question must be conditioned on the strength and ability of the government to tap alternative sources of finance. Italy, for example, might be concerned that the reduction of the national debt required by the Maastricht Treaty, combined with a simultaneous reduction in seigniorage and the loss of monetary autonomy, could lead to so great an increase in tax rates or so significant a reduction in public-sector expenditures that the cohesion of the Italian state could be put at risk (Dornbusch, 1988; Grilli, 1989; Giavazzi, 1989; Gros and Thygesen, 1992).

Monetary Autonomy

The value of seigniorage to a stable country with low inflation is small, and the arrangements made under the Maastricht Treaty for returning seigniorage to the constituent national central banks suggest that the net loss or gain to most EC states will be of secondary importance. The considerations raised above may therefore be regarded as of relatively minor importance for EC countries, although this assessment would surely not hold for most of the states in Central and Eastern Europe.

The main cost perceived for the EC states is the loss of monetary policy as a national instrument for demand management. Monetary policy can be used, at least in the short run, to control interest rates or exchange rates, key prices within any economy. It cannot by itself, however, achieve differing and separate objectives for both of these rates without the deployment of another instrument, for example, exchange controls. The attempt in the Maastricht Treaty to assign exchange-rate decisions to politicians and to assign the operation of monetary policy to an independent European System of Central Banks (ESCB) has therefore generated considerable concern (Kenen, 1993; Goodhart, 1992b; Begg *et al.*, 1991).

It can be argued that national governments should not, and in some cases cannot, optimally control nominal interest rates and exchange rates in a discretionary fashion. The ability to engineer short-term increase in output, whether by exploiting agents' misperceptions or temporary rigidities, carries with it the cost that private-sector agents will be led to revise upward their expectations of inflation. Given that the long-term optimal position is to maintain near-zero inflation at an unemployment rate consistent with nonaccelerating inflation, the best long-term monetary policy would be to stick to a noninflationary path, unless the rigidities were extensive and very long lasting or the time-discount rates of private agents were very high. The danger is that governments, particularly when seeking reelection, will have higher rates of time discount than those of the public and will therefore be tempted to undertake expansionary policies that risk re-igniting both inflation and inflationary expectations.

Concern over this problem has been central in the drive to achieve independence for central banks. Even when governments deny that they have pursued expansionary policies, they are worried about the perceived lack of credibility attaching to their counterinflationary commitments. One solution would be to transfer to an independent central bank the power to determine the *tactics* of monetary policy, but to restrict the bank's *strategic* objectives to the primary, overriding task of achieving price stability. This has been done in the Reserve Bank of New Zealand Act and suggested to, but rejected by, the current U.K. government; it is the scheme adopted in the Maastricht Treaty for the prospective European Central Bank (ECB).

A second solution was sought by governments participating in the Exchange Rate Mechanism (ERM) of the EMS. They hoped that their commitment to the ERM would reward them with the reputation for maintaining low inflation already enjoyed by the Bundesbank. This commitment was modest before 1983, however, requiring only that realignments be less than sufficient to recoup the prior losses of competitiveness caused by higher inflation rates. With the increasingly successful operation of the ERM, the commitment progressively hardened, until, from 1987 to 1992, there seemed to be a strong preference for avoiding any realignments.[2]

Insofar as the ERM had hardened by the end of the 1980s, and members' strategies were based on holding their ERM parities against the deutschmark, adherence to the ERM tightly constrained the use of monetary policy and, in particular, the level of interest rates. The discretion of member governments became more and more limited, especially as exchange controls were progressively abandoned. It is arguable that, having accepted ERM membership in this context, governments had already abandoned discretionary monetary policy and that there would be virtually no economic cost in doing so formally and completely by moving to a full monetary union. This issue is examined further in Section 5.

8.3   STEADY-STATE ECONOMIC BENEFITS AND COSTS OF MONETARY UNION

The Economic Benefits

The economic gains from monetary union would accrue primarily in the form of increased microeconomic efficiency. As listed by the Commission (1990, pp. 63–84), these are:

(1) *Reduction in transactions costs*. EMU would allow the redeployment to more profitable uses of the resources used in exchange-rate transactions. Transactions savings are calculated to be 4 per cent of Community GDP, with smaller countries and trading companies benefiting more than larger ones. Associated improvements in cross-border payments facilities would provide additional savings.

(2) *Reduction in the risk of realignment and devaluation*. EMU should result in a reduction of the risk premia currently included in the interest rates of most EC countries, relative to German rates. These can be large in countries whose peg to the deutschmark is threatened. If, in turn, that threat is perceived as greater when undesirable economic outturns (such as high unemployment) would result from maintaining the peg, these risk-premia may be larger in the intermediate ERM stage than in a managed float or with a single currency.

The existence of such risk premia is clear. Compare, for example, French, Danish, or Spanish real interest rates in the winter of 1992–93 with those of Germany. The average long-term level is less certain, however, and the Commission's (1990, pp. 63, 77–83) estimates of the long-term effect on real incomes of reducing the premia seem optimistic: 'Preliminary estimates show that even a reduction in the risk premium of only 0.5 percentage points could raise income in the community significantly, possibly up to 5–10% in the longer run.' The Commission would count as yet another gain from EMU the more buoyant expectations of business leaders following the successful achievement of EMU. The possibility that a differential 'default' premium on government (for example, Italian) bonds may replace some part of the prior devaluation-risk premium is not addressed (see also Baldwin, 1991).

(3) *Efficiency gains to trade and capital movements*. Gains should result from both the reductions in exchange-rate uncertainty and the greater price transparency that EMU would bring across EC countries, but these are difficult to quantify. Without good regional trade data and the opportunity to regress trade flows on both distance (gravity-model) variables and exchange-rate volatility, it is hard to tell how far monetary separation and volatility reduce the scale of the market. The studies quoted by the Commission (1990) concerning the effect of exchange-rate variability on trade are inconclusive and suggest that the effect is small (see also Feldstein, 1992).

(4) *Stable prices.* Stable prices are clearly beneficial, but it is difficult to say whether they should be ascribed, if achieved, to EMU or to the structural and constitutional foundations of the ESCB, which mandate the Bank's independence from political influence and require that its overriding objective be to 'maintain price stability' (Treaty, Article 105, 1, and Protocol on the ESCB Statute, Article 2; Currie, 1992; Fratianni and von Hagen, 1990). If such structural and constitutional amendments were introduced at the national level, would the effect not be the same? What, if anything, does EMU add beyond the establishment of an independent central bank? Hughes Hallett and Vines (1993) estimate the additionality to be minuscule. Indeed, the continuing confusion over the relation between external exchange-rate policies, to be left in the hands of the politicians, and monetary policy, to be controlled by the ESCB, may suggest that the added European dimension could have adverse effects on price stability (Treaty, Article 109; Commission, 1990; Kenen, 1992a; Goodhart, 1992b; Begg *et al.*, 1991).

(5) *Internationally stronger currency.* The Commission (1990, pp. 178–198) argues that a single, unified European currency would have more authority than the sum of the currencies of middle-sized European countries (sec. 7.1) and that the change would allow Europe a stronger voice in negotiations with the USA (secs. 7.2 and 7.3; see also Alogoskoufis and Portes, 1991). This argument appeals particularly to those in the EC who are jealous of the dollar's predominant role in international finance and of the asymmetric power of the USA in international conclaves. The Commission makes the curious conjunction of claims that EMU would enable the EC to match the USA in international weight and that this could lead to greater harmony and coordination. Risks that antagonistic trading blocks could develop are noted but dismissed as negligible (Commission, 1990, p. 196). Recent history of the EC's trade negotiations with the USA in the GATT and with Central and Eastern Europe gives little reason for optimism in this respect. The final two arguments for EMU, that it may be necessary for the continued success and development of the single market and that it is a prerequisite for further fiscal federalism, are taken up below.

The Costs of Monetary Union

The main cost of moving to monetary union has generally been identified as the loss of an instrument of national demand management, domestic monetary policy, and of the associated ability to adjust exchange rates. As noted above, the loss is less if the ability to use monetary policy has already been constrained by membership in the ERM. Indeed, the Commission (1990, Chapter 6, and Chapter 2 especially section 2.1.2 on 'Alternative to EMU', p. 40) reduces considerably its estimates of this cost because it assumes the existence of the 'EMS and the 1992 Single Market.'

Leaving to one side the problem of deciding how far national authorities

still retain control over monetary policies in the initial regime, the cost of
losing this instrument will depend, in part, on (1) the extent to which the
participating nations and regions are likely to suffer asymmetric shocks, (2)
the speed and flexibility of the adjustment process whereby disequilibria
can be resolved by wage flexibility and the migration of the factors of production, especially labour, and (3) the extent to which fiscal policy, at either the national or federal level, can, and should, serve as an alternative to
the use of monetary policy to foster adjustments. The need for fiscal policies that are more active than in recent years raises the question of how to
fund deficits that may be disproportionately large in some regions; this is
discussed below.

The founding fathers of OCA theory, Mundell, McKinnon, and Kenen,
identified three main criteria to define an optimal currency area. The first,
emphasized by McKinnon, is the openness of the economies involved to
trade among themselves. This is discussed in section 8.4. The second criterion, emphasised by Kenen, concerns the susceptibility of the constituent
economies to asymmetric shocks. The third criterion, emphasized by Mundell,
pertains to the flexibility of adjustment to such shocks (Melitz, 1991b, has
a slightly different approach). As De Grauwe and Vanhaverbeke (1993, p.
111) state, 'this theory says that when regions or countries are subjected to
different disturbances (asymmetric shocks), the adjustment process will require either real exchange rates to adjust, or factors of production to move,
or a combination of these two. In the absence of real exchange-rate flexibility and factor mobility, regional or national concentrations of unemployment will be inevitable.' This analysis has led to a burgeoning of empirical
research comparing the incidence of common and idiosyncratic shocks with
the extent of nominal- and real-wage flexibility and of labour and capital
mobility between and within the countries in Europe and the regions of the
USA (Eichengreen, 1992b).

The Commission (1990, p. 147) argues that asymmetric shocks 'are likely
to diminish with the disappearance of trade barriers through the completion
of internal market[s],' but that they still exist within the EC. They are notably less, however, for the core countries of northern Europe, Austria, France,
Denmark, Germany, and the Benelux nations, than for the peripheral Mediterranean and British Isles countries. For the core countries, the ratio of
common to idiosyncratic shocks is higher between themselves than between
them and the USA (Cohen and Wyplosz, 1989), and it is broadly similar to·
the ratio between US regions (Bayoumi and Eichengreen, 1992; Bini-Smaghi
and Vori, 1992; De Grauwe and Heens, 1993).

Taken by themselves, these results suggest that the structures of the EC
core countries have converged sufficiently for monetary union to be feasible. Whether the peripheral countries can reach an adequate level of convergence without severe adjustment difficulties is much more problematic.
Yet, as Gros and Thygesen (1992) and Malo de Molina (1992) point out,

the advantages of EMU for the peripheral countries may be greater, in terms of lower transactions costs, lower risk premia, and greater price stability, than for the core countries.

There is also a question whether the dynamic effects of EMU are likely to make regions more similar, because they will become more 'converged,' or more dissimilar, because they will become more specialised. The Commission believes that economic integration in Europe will make local economies more similar and thus subject to fewer asymmetric shocks (Spahn, 1992; Gros and Thygesen, 1992); some economists, arguing in part from American experience, claim the reverse (Eichengreen, 1992b; Feldstein, 1992; Krugman, 1992). The literature must be read, however, with a significant caveat. Since 1989, Germany has suffered a massive idiosyncratic shock as a result of reunification. Because of Germany's position as the anchor country, this has been particularly damaging to the ERM and a major cause of the setbacks to EMU in 1992 and 1993. How should one view this event when looking to the future – as a unique shock that will never happen again or as a striking example that effectively destroys the validity of earlier work on the ratio of common to asymmetric shocks among the core countries?

There has been an enormous amount of work in recent years on rigidities in nominal and real wages, mostly at the national level, but also at the regional level. Although this research has chiefly tried to explain the persistence of high unemployment levels in Europe (Layard, Nickell, and Jackman, 1991; Bini-Smaghi and Vori, 1992; Drèze and Bean, 1990; Bruno and Sachs, 1985), the findings are significant for EMU. In general, the conclusions are that EC countries, especially the UK, suffer from considerable real-wage rigidity but little nominal-wage rigidity, whereas the USA shows more nominal-wage stickiness but much less real-wage rigidity.

This finding can be used to argue both for and against EMU. It supports EMU in that the existence of real-wage rigidity makes improved competitiveness through nominal devaluations much harder to achieve and maintain. It opposes EMU in that the sclerotic workings of European labour markets make it unlikely that wage adjustment can play a significant role in alleviating regional disequilibria. De Grauwe and Vanhaverbeke (1993, pp. 123–4) challenge this argument, observing that 'the regional variability of output is relatively well correlated with the regional variability of the real exchange rates. . . . that this correlation is stronger and more significant at the regional than at the national level. This suggests that, although the regional variability of real exchange rates is relatively small, it nevertheless plays a significant role in regional adjustment.' They point out that 'the correlation between the variability of real exchange rates and employment is much weaker. . . .' but that the evidence is only suggestive, and that correlation coefficients say nothing 'about the direction of the causality. These correlations can also be interpreted to mean that relative price shocks cause variability in output and employment.' They stress, in addition that 'there is evidence . . . that real exchange-rate changes have also been quite important in the adjustment process of individual EMS countries that have chosen to limit the changes in their nominal exchange rates. Countries like Belgium and the Netherlands, for example, allowed significant real depreciations of their currencies of 20–30 per cent to occur during the early part of the eighties' (see also Poloz, 1990).

There are, furthermore, disputes about the effect that EMU, a regime change, would have on the future interregional flexibility of wages. The optimists think that abandoning the option of national monetary management and exchange-rate adjustment would force workers and unions into greater local flexibility. The pessimists perceive that the greater transparency of international differences in nominal wages following the adoption of a single currency would likely lead, through demonstration effects, to less flexibility in labour markets than now exists (Doyle, 1989; also Horn and Zwiener, 1992, who model the effects of differing wage regimes in Europe). The demand in the former East Germany for nominal-wage parity with West Germany within a few years, largely irrespective of productivity differentials, supports this view. Certainly, special factors are involved in Germany, but can we be confident that monetary union in the EC would not lead to similar tendencies?

De Grauwe and Vanhaverbeke (1993, p. 111), perhaps echoing the belief that a single currency would promote a single labour market with insufficient regional flexibility, claim that 'The theory of optimum currency areas has also established a presumption that in a monetary union the adjustment mechanism will rely more on factor mobility than on real exchange-rate flexibility.' This is certainly true in the USA (Blanchard and Katz, 1992).

The largest question, therefore, about identifying the EC as an optimal currency area arises from the empirical studies revealing that labour migration in Europe is minuscule in comparison to that in the USA, and that any large increase would cause political problems (Doyle, 1989). Eichengreen (1993, p. 131) notes that, 'in comparison, little systematic attention has been directed toward the analysis of labour mobility. Previous studies cited in Eichengreen (1991) indicate that observed migration rates are lower in Europe than in the US. Not only are migration rates between European nations relatively low, but so are migration rates within those nations. Americans move between US states about three times as frequently as Frenchmen move between *départements* and Germans move between *länder*. If Europeans move little among regions of European nations within which culture and language are relatively minor barriers to mobility, they can hardly be expected to move between European nations once statutory barriers to migration are removed. On the basis of this evidence, Mundell's second criterion also suggests that the EC is less of an optimum currency area than the USA.'

Eichengreen (1993) follows prior work by Pissarides and McMaster (1990) and by Attanasio and Padoa-Schioppa (1991) and models the propensity of labour to migrate between regions in Italy, in the UK, and in the USA in response to changes in relative regional unemployment and wage levels. He concludes (p. 150) that 'the models estimated here confirm the tendency for inter-regional labour flows to respond to economic conditions. In all three countries, immigration is encouraged by relatively high wages and relatively low unemployment. But the elasticity of migration with respect to wage differentials is very much larger in the USA, US labour exhibits a greater tendency to move in response to regional unemployment differentials. This, then, is systematic evidence in support of the presumption of greater labour mobility in the US.' As Eichengreen realises, this latter finding poses an important question, because Italy and the UK *already are* single-currency areas, yet his evidence suggests that the low level of mobility *within* these countries makes them, *prima facie*, unsuitable to be so. Apart from political stirrings in Lombardy and Scotland, however, nobody has seriously suggested dividing these countries into separate currency areas.

In addition, using a cointegration approach, Eichengreen (1993, p. 155) finds that regional labour markets in Italy and the UK, and to a lesser extent in the USA, tend to revert quite quickly to a normal relation with aggregate unemployment (that is, the series are cointegrated), although this 'normal' relationship implies that some regions remain worse, and others better, than average.[3] Idiosyncratic shocks, however, do not appear to make regional unemployment deviate indefinitely from the average, as in a random walk. Even if labour-market forces, real-wage adjustment and mobility, are comparatively weak within Italy and the UK, other factors, 'perhaps including relative wage adjustments, inter-regional capital mobility, and government policy,' appear capable of providing a spatially unifying effect. The implication is that these factors could work as powerfully in EMU as in Italy or the UK to offset the inflexibility of labour markets. One such possibility is that capital mobility might substitute for labour mobility, with new firms and new investment being attracted to areas of available, low-wage labour, and that EMU would thereby bring particular benefits in cheaper capital to the smaller peripheral regions (Bayoumi and Rose, 1993).[4]

Much current research on capital mobility has asked whether the financial equity markets in the EC have become more integrated in recent years. (Fraser and MacDonald, 1993; Sentana, Shah, and Wadhwani, 1992; Atkeson and Bayoumi, 1993). The results are inconclusive, but financial-market integration may be a necessary, although insufficient, condition for capital mobility to preserve the cohesion of a monetary union. Indeed, a strong body of academic argument sees unification as likely to exacerbate regional divergences by attracting investment and activity to the already successful regions rather than to the comparatively unsuccessful periphery (Masera, 1992).[5]

Masson and Taylor (1993), who have looked at the issue in the US context, compare the regional deviations of real output per capita within the USA with the national deviations within the EC. Regional disparity in the

USA was markedly less than in the EC and fell over time, whereas the dispersion of real output per capita among EC nations remained roughly constant, except for Greece, Portugal, and Spain, where output per capita diverged sharply until the early 1970s and converged somewhat thereafter. Masson and Taylor (1993, p. 31) note that, 'there is certainly no presumption from the US data that currency union makes convergence of living standards difficult. However, how much of the convergence was facilitated by fixity of exchange rates – encouraging both capital and labour mobility – and how much was due to fiscal transfers from richer to poorer regions, . . . is unclear.'

This is one of the problems facing empirical econometric work in this field. The domain of a single currency has generally had the same boundaries as its central political and fiscal system, and areas with independent currencies have likewise had separate political and fiscal centers. It is therefore difficult to distinguish between the roles played by monetary union and by the redistributive role of the federal fiscal center in bringing about convergence. I turn now to this interaction between monetary and fiscal policies.

8.4   INTERACTIONS BETWEEN THE CURRENCY DOMAIN AND THE FISCAL AND TRADE DOMAINS

Most modern federal countries, (Australia, Brazil, Canada, Germany, the former Soviet Union, the USA, and Yugoslavia) have had strong central political institutions, single currencies, and central control over most of the fiscal flows. Switzerland, with the least centralisation, still has several orders of magnitude more central power than that proposed for the EC (Schneider, 1993). It is therefore not surprising that many economists have looked at existing federal states when trying to decide whether EMU can survive without comparable fiscal centralisation. This issue goes back to the Werner Report (Council, 1970), which made more ambitious proposals for an associated EC fiscal function than did the Delors Report (Committee, 1989) or the Maastricht Treaty (Council, 1992, and see Gros and Thygesen, 1992, Chapter 1).

Is Federal Fiscalism Needed to Support a Single Currency?

Insofar as the main economic cost of abandoning separate currencies lies in losing control over monetary policy, it would appear that more weight should be placed on alternative mechanisms of demand management, such as fiscal policy. The two main concerns about EMU are that parts of the union might suffer from asymmetric shocks and that unification might lead to a divergence, rather than a convergence, of economic performance (Giersch *et al.*, 1992). Fiscal measures aimed at both stabilisation and redistribution could mitigate these concerns.

As Goodhart and Smith (1993) emphasise, these two fiscal functions should be carefully distinguished, although many measures, such as income taxes and unemployment benefits, simultaneously stabilise and redistribute. Stabilisation is concerned with dynamic changes in economic conditions. It involves changing fiscal flows (expenditures and revenues) in response to economic changes relative to the normal trend, irrespective of initial levels. Redistribution adjusts expenditures and taxes in response to relative levels of economic activity, irrespective of the direction or extent of previous change. If asymmetric shocks are the primary concern, stabilisation policies should be emphasised; if regional divergence is anticipated, redistribution should be stressed.

Virtually all stabilising and redistributive fiscal functions in the EC are currently undertaken at the national level, with the monetary and fiscal authorities having the same boundary. Why, when the monetary boundary is enlarged to replace national currencies with a single currency, cannot the fiscal functions of stabilisation and redistribution be left at the national level and, if necessary, be pursued at that level more vigorously than before?

There are several arguments for shifting these fiscal functions partly to the federal center. Specific to the EC is the conflict between national needs and the restrictions imposed on national autonomy. The Maastricht Treaty (Article 104c, 2, and Protocol on the Excessive Deficit Procedure, Article 1) established reference values to limit both the ratio of national debt to income and the government deficit, with the normally acceptable limit for the planned or actual government deficit set at 3 per cent of gross domestic product. In the course of the 1993 recession in Europe, however, every EC member except Luxembourg expected, indeed planned, to exceed the 3 per cent limit. This implies that the ability of national governments to undertake countercyclical fiscal stabilisation could be seriously constrained by strict adherence to the Treaty (Buiter, 1992).

Insofar as fiscal constraints designed to counter budgetary indiscipline could yield insufficient scope for national stabilisation, a case can be argued for transferring the function to the federal level. A more general argument for centralising fiscal functions at the federal level is that fiscal-policy measures in one area may spill over into neighbouring areas. Some overspills, such as those resulting from a high marginal propensity to import, may make a national or regional authority less fiscally active than desirable (see Knoester, Kolodziejak, and Muijzers, 1990, with respect to the smaller EC countries). Other overspills, such as the reduced effect of national fiscal policies on national interest rates and exchange rates, and their effect, instead, on the general level of EC interest rates, may encourage national fiscal policymakers to be less disciplined. The Delors Report (Committee, 1989) and the Maastricht Treaty (Article 104c) have given enormous emphasis to this problem and to the necessity of avoiding 'excessive' governmental deficits.

Overspills can, of course, be internalised by appropriate coordination, without shifting actual operational control and responsibility to the federal center.

The Maastricht Treaty (Article 103) requires that 'Member States shall regard their economic policies as a matter of common concern and shall coordinate them within the Council.' But, beyond publicity (Article 103, 4), the Council can impose no penalties on a state that refuses to coordinate its fiscal policies for the common European benefit. It is therefore unlikely that there will be much effective coordination of national fiscal policies at the EC level. Moreover, to the extent that national policies are effectively coordinated at the federal level, a key policymaking role is transferred de facto to the federal level.

A second argument for centralising fiscal functions is that their continued exercise at the national or regional level is likely to affect not only current levels of public-sector expenditures and tax rates, but also expected future levels. The achievement of EMU may not only require a high level of factor mobility, at least in theory, but may also induce greater future mobility in response to differing tax rates. It is already increasingly difficult within the EC to impose differential taxes on highly mobile tax bases like financial transactions, savings, or corporate profits. If labour should also become highly mobile, it would be difficult to differentiate nationally benefits to, or taxes on, labour. With levels of labour mobility remaining low, however, this constraint is of academic interest only (Eichengreen, 1990; Bean *et al.*, 1992).

A third argument for centralising these functions is to insure against having to meet locally the full costs of an asymmetric downturn or of a shock producing a more permanently depressed economy. This involves some moral hazard, however, in that policies might become more reckless or that natural market adjustments might be more muted. Moral hazard could be much reduced, however, by a specialised stabilisation scheme (proposed by Goodhart and Smith, 1993) that would tie stabilisation more closely to random asymmetric shocks. Each participating nation would then have an almost equal chance of benefiting, and transfers would be triggered only by a worse than average downturn and would be strictly temporary (see also Italianer and Vanheukelen, 1992; Van Rompuy, Abraham, and Heremans, 1991; and van der Ploeg, 1991). Redistribution, by contrast, is usually a function, not of accidents, but of a need for predictable long-term transfers, so moral hazard would be much increased by its centralisation (as reported for the Canadian Maritimes by Courchene, 1992, or for the Mezzogiorno by De Nardis and Micossi, 1991; and Micossi and Tullio, 1991). The insurance argument is consequently best applied to well-designed stabilisation mechanisms with minimal redistributive content (Persson and Tabellini, 1992a, 1992b).

The fourth, and most powerful, argument for centralisation refers to the condition of 'social union,' when people in a particular area agree that all of them should be treated alike. Assuming that the benefits go to people who are dependent, unemployed, or poor, and that taxes are raised on the usual principles relating to personal expenditure, income, or wealth, there will generally be, often without much public notice, spatial transfers from more prosperous to less prosperous regions (for example, from northern European to Mediterranean regions). Within the EC, however, there is not now, or in sight, an agreement that all area inhabitants should have broadly the same menu of benefits and taxes. Indeed, there is scarcely accord on minimum standards for the provision of public goods. Insofar as redistribution takes place at all, it occurs through the more covert mechanism of structural, or cohesion, funds, which are themselves subject to a variety of operational problems.[6]

Any new steps in the direction of social union will be either voluntary, in response to a stronger feeling of common citizenship and solidarity than is currently apparent, or forced, if the international mobility of people interferes with national attempts at interpersonal redistribution. Neither prospect looks likely in the foreseeable future. Steps taken so far have been to set down conditions for raising the volume of interregional transfers and for making them unconditional. But, because equity normally relates to the reduction of interpersonal, not interregional, income disparities, interregional transfers have two disadvantages (Prud'homme, 1993). They will not automatically narrow interpersonal differences, for poor people in rich regions may end up supporting rich people in poor regions. Similarly, aid to a region may not be used to support its most needy inhabitants. For these reasons, regional policies in several federal and unitary countries have been scaled down to put greater emphasis on 'people-oriented' instruments.

Considerations of interpersonal equity obtain, in principle, in the EC as well, but they need to be set beside the powerful political-economic arguments against a large role for central government in interpersonal redistribution (Forte, 1977; Tresch, 1981). A large central role can be contemplated only when altruism has taken on so strong a European dimension that nationality is dominated by solidarity, and national preferences for redistribution have closely converged. Until then, redistribution in the EC will continue to be limited, disguised, and somewhat inefficient.

Virtually no stabilisation is achieved through the current federal EC budget. The gross flows are very small relative to national budgets; the form of the expenditures, mainly through the Common Agricultural Policy (CAP), and of the taxes, mainly through the value added tax, are not highly responsive to economic fluctuations; and the EC cannot, by law, run a deficit.

Does this matter for the success of EMU? How extensive are federal, 'automatic' stabilisers in existing federal countries? Sala-i-Martin and Sachs (1992) argue that such stabilising flows offset about 35 to 44 per cent of divergences between regional income levels in the USA, and they suggest that attempting to move to EMU without a similar supporting fiscal mechanism in the EC would be difficult. Their findings are criticized by von Hagen (1992), partly on the grounds that their percentages relate to redistribution rather than stabilisation. When von Hagen repeated the exercise in first-difference form on state-level data, he found much lower figures, about 10 per

Table 8.2 Estimates of the degree of interregional income redistribution and regional stabilization through central public finance channels in selected federal and unitary countries

Country	(%)	Interregional redistribution	(%)	Regional stabilization
Australia	50	(Commission, 1977)		—
Canada	30	(Commission)	17	[Bayoumi and Masson (1991)]
			24	[Goodhart and Smith, 1993]
France	53	(Commission)	37	[Pisani-Ferry, Italianer, and Lescure, 1993]
Germany	35	(Commission)	33–42	[Pisani-Ferry, Italianer, and Lescure (1993)]
Switzerland	15	(Commisssion)		—
United Kingdom	34	(Commission)	34	[Goodhart and Smith (1993)]
United States	35–44	(Sala-i-Martin and Sachs, 1992)	10	[von Hagen, 1992]
			28	[Bayoumi and Masson (1991)]
	25	(Commission)	20	[Goodhart and Smith (1993)]
			17	[Pisani-Ferry, Italianer, and Lescure (1993)]

Source: Adapted from Commission, 1993, table 9, p. 37.
[a] Income data.
[b] Tax side only.

cent for the tax offset to changes in incomes. Since then, a number of studies have given generally higher figures for the extent of regional stabilisation (for example, Pisani-Ferry, Italianer, and Lescure, 1993). These are summarised in Table 8.2.

I conclude from these various studies that both stabilising and redistributive functions have been actively carried out through existing federal fiscal systems. It would be reckless to dismiss the potential importance of these activities for the cohesion and success of such monetary unions,[7] but it is reasonable to ask if the fiscal authority carrying out such functions needs to be a federal center (von Hagen, 1993; Bean, 1992). As noted earlier, there is no likelihood whatsoever of transferring overt, unconditional redistributive functions to Brussels. That is ruled out by the principle of 'subsidiarity,' by the fact that regional disparities within EC countries, for example, Italy, Spain, and the UK, are greater than most disparities between those countries, and, above all, by the lack of political cohesion.

That the scheme proposed by Goodhart and Smith (1993) will be seen as a welcome and useful supplement to existing national systems of automatic stabilisation is doubtful. Some oppose on broad political grounds any further transfer of fiscal powers to Brussels. Melitz and Vori (1992) argue against the adoption of any federal insurance scheme, given those already available at the national level. They believe that the likelihood of sizable asymmetric shocks and the benefits of federal insurance are both too small, and that there are large risks both of moral hazard and of a benefit being triggered by an event that could be held to be a nation's own fault (a strike, a mistaken policy). How would other EC members have reacted, for example, to a call in recent years to transfer funds to East Germany?

A final argument for adopting some federal stabilisation insurance scheme is, again, unashamedly political. It is that, once Stage 3 is achieved, politicians and commentators will rightly or wrongly, blame the severity of cyclical downturns on monetary union. They will argue that, without such a union, monetary policy would have been relaxed. So long as the downturn is symmetric over the entire EC, the answer will be straightforward, but, in an asymmetric, particularly adverse situation, how can a supporter of EMU counter the accusation that monetary union involves a sizable net disadvantage? A significant, timely, and visible fiscal federal transfer to temporarily disadvantaged countries could help to sustain political support for EMU at especially difficult times.

Is a Single Currency Needed to Support Fiscal Federalism?

In many, perhaps most, of the large federal countries, there are regions that are both distant from the industrial heartland of the country and specialised in production, often in certain primary commodities. Examples are Western Australia, the oil-producing states of the USA, and Alberta, Canada; no doubt similar examples can be found in Brazil, the former Soviet Union, and elsewhere. Given the separation and specialisation of these divergent states and regimes, there would seem to be *prima facie* grounds, according to OCA theory, for them to have currencies separate from those of the states to which they belong. Does Western Australia, for example, form an OCA with the rest of Australia? Yet these large federal nations never choose to maintain a multiplicity of currencies. Why not?

In section 8.3, I stated that microeconomic efficiency gains from currency unions were mostly unquantifiable and, quite probably, relatively minor. If they are not minor, however, and those gains in economic efficiency explain the maintenance of currency unions in huge federal states, why is it so rare, and apparently difficult, to combine several sovereign countries in a currency union? The more political considerations addressed in section 8.2, symbolism, seigniorage, and the power to control a key economic instrument, are no longer such compelling reasons.

If there are economic benefits to having more currencies and monetary authorities, from being able to offset asymmetric shocks, for example, why not enjoy these within a larger federation? Yet no stable, autonomous, federal government has voluntarily chosen to allow separate currency areas and regional central banks within its own domain. How can American economists, such as Feldstein (1992), advise European countries against monetary union, while appearing entirely content with their own even wider monetary union?

The answer, as Feldstein puts it, lies in the interrelations between monetary policy, on the one hand, and fiscal and trade policies, on the other.[8] Yet I have just argued that it might be possible to operate EMU with a strictly limited transfer of stabilising and redistributive functions to the federal budget; the bulk of these functions could remain at the national level. By the same token, Western Australia, the southwestern states of the USA, and the western provinces of Canada could look after their own internal stabilisation and redistribution. The adoption and implementation of a carefully focused and cost-effective stabilisation scheme in the EC would, of course, alleviate short-term adjustment pressures after the advent of EMU. Nevertheless, it is hard to prove that such a comparatively limited scheme is essential to the success of EMU.

A move to comparatively fixed exchange rates, however, may be necessary for the success of any centralised fiscal domain; that is, the thrust of causation may run opposite to that normally discussed. Certainly, the problems of trying to run the system of levies and subsidies that constitute the CAP were made so complicated by flexible exchange rates that the agreement nearly collapsed. The political process that sustains agreements like these requires centralised payoffs. This concern played a major role in the establishment of the ERM; as Giavazzi and Giovannini (1989, p. 7) note, 'the common market [in cereals under the CAP] could only function if intra-Community exchange rates remained stable.'

The response can be made that such arrangements require no more than the adoption of pegged but adjustable exchange rates, not a move all the way to a single currency. Indeed, the subsequent experience of the EC suggests that currency adjustments in member states would not impede the continuation of the CAP, the progress toward a single market, or any further transfer of fiscal responsibilities to Brussels, so long as two conditions are met: first, that the adjustments are infrequent, and, second, that the sizes and occasions of the adjustments are subject to multilateral oversight and agreement, for example, within the Monetary Committee of the EC.

Thus, the move toward a single market in Europe may have been conditional on the continued perceived success of the ERM. If so, a policy dilemma arises. A system of pegged but adjustable exchange rates is well known to be fragile under the 'unholy trinity' of free movement of goods and capital, stable exchange rates, and autonomous monetary policies (Cohen, 1993b). What is surprising about disturbances in European exchange markets in 1992 and 1993 is not so much their occurrence, but that the ERM had operated so successfully for so long (from 1987 to 1992) without such disturbances. To revert to more flexible exchange rates would make the system less susceptible to such 'speculative' attacks, although not necessarily less prone to medium-term misalignment. But would such flexibility in exchange rates dampen political enthusiasm for a single market and for greater centralisation of fiscal and political powers?

The fragility of pegged but adjustable exchange rates in the absence of exchange controls suggests that the continuation of such a regime for an extended period may not be viable. But, even if it were, there are reasons for doubting whether any regime with periodic exchange-rate adjustments is consistent with sizable transfers of fiscal responsibility to a federal center. Such doubts become more pronounced the more flexible the exchange-rate regime is, whether a float, a crawling peg, or, as advocated by *The Economist* ('Can Europe. . . .,' 1993), an arrangement with soft bands.

The first argument is largely presentational, though not less important for that. It is that the existence of separate national currencies facilitates the calculation of the net fiscal transfer between the member states, indeed almost requires such calculations when transfers involve conversions between domestic currencies and ECUs. Partly in consequence, the identification of net fiscal winners and losers within the EC is regularly made in terms of the overall position of each country, rather than of diverse groups of individuals within the whole of the EC. This means that, despite the best preventive efforts of the Commission, the identification of 'gainers' or 'losers' from the majority of EC economic measures is made largely in terms of the effects the measures have on separate countries. Thus, the battles over EC fiscal policies in Brussels are not about how these affect the welfare of the representative European, but how they change the net position of each separate state. Although it is possible to estimate the net benefits to Queensland, Indiana, or Manitoba from a change in the federal budgets of their respective countries, the existence of a single currency tends to shift the focus of debate toward the effect on the representative agent defined by type, for example, age, income, and job, and not by geographical locality.

It is true that US senators support the interests of their own states within the USA, just as heads of member states do in the EC, but they do so to a somewhat lesser extent, I believe, and not so single-mindedly. As Giovannini (1993) stated in his comment on this chapter, it is often difficult to identify exactly who the gainers or losers are from a switch to a single-currency regime. Thus, 'the political debate on EMU . . . is not characterised by the confrontation of those [intranational] constituencies that gain or lose from the introduction of a single currency, since these constituencies do not have a clear identity.' When the fiscal assessment concentrates on type rather than geographical residence, moreover, the perceived gainers or losers will only occasionally be concentrated in any one locality and, when they are, will often constitute producer groups, such as miners or farmers, whose political clout far outweighs their numerical strength. The rise of the Lombard League as a political power in Italy is an interesting exception to this generalisation. Its rallying cry is partly that heavy tax burdens are placed on Northern Italian taxpayers to finance (corrupt) expenditures in Rome and the Mezzogiorno.

Because the continuation of separate currencies encourages the calculation of benefits and costs in national terms, it exerts a centrifugal force, causing national politicians to fight for 'our money,' the *juste retour*, and so forth. By contrast, calculations that concentrate on a similar treatment of similar types of agents, irrespective of location, exert a centripetal force. Adopting a single currency would be an important step in moving in this latter direction.

I argued earlier that the development of certain centralised, federal powers, for example, fiscal powers, could ease the strain of asymmetric shocks and localised disturbances in a coherent, cohesive federal country. It is far from certain, however, that the analogy can be directly applied to Europe, where there is as yet little fundamental cohesion. Would transferring more powers to the center not just result in more disputes and bickering over the division of political rents between nation states? See Aghion and Bolton (1990), Buiter and Kletzer (1991), and Persson and Tabellini (1992a, 1992b) for theoretical analyses of cooperation under heterogeneous preferences.

Whenever fiscal expenditures are financed by taxes, some regions will gain and some lose. If each fiscal decision were considered on its own and each region had a veto, it would become impossible to reach any agreement, because the losers on each issue would veto it. Some political scientists therefore ask how the EC has achieved as much agreement and cohesion as it has. One answer (Martin, 1993, p. 127) is that 'international organizations such as the EC facilitate stable linkages among issues that are not inseparably intertwined for functional reasons.' As Keohane (1984, p. 91) put it, 'clustering of issues under a regime facilitates side-payments among these issues: more potential *quids* are available for the *quo*. Without international regimes linking clusters of issues to one another, side-payments and linkages would be difficult to arrange in world politics.'

Cohen (1993a, p. 200) suggests that the very factors determining 'the sustainability of EC monetary cooperation under the Maastricht Treaty' would, no doubt, affect fiscal cooperation. He claims that 'studies of currency integration that principally emphasize either economic variables (Masson and Taylor, 1992 [here 1993]) or organizational characteristics (Griffiths, 1992) miss the main point. . . . The primary question is whether there is likely to be either a local hegemon or a fabric of related ties with sufficient influence to neutralize the risk of time inconsistency.'

There is no single hegemon in Europe. Moreover, differences in language, culture, history, legal systems, and so forth, often divide countries. The attempt to find unity through diversity is, in addition, not particularly well served by the political process at the European center, whereby decisionmaking remains firmly in the hands of national politicians. Thus, the European federal political system is *indirectly* democratic, rather than *directly* accountable to the European people. Europeans do not vote for the appointee to the presidency of the Commission. The Council has the power, whereas the European Parliament is largely a cipher (Martin, 1993).

Cohen (1993a, p. 200), referring to the Scandinavian monetary union of 1873 to 1931, notes that, "given the density of existing ties, creation of a common currency system seemed not only natural but almost inevitable." The concern of a European federalist must be to extend and strengthen ties between European states. Adopting a single currency in the EC would seem to be a potent measure for this purpose, for it could refocus the attention to gainers and losers on the status of the agent involved, rather than his or her country of residence.

As Cohen points out the process of currency union is mutually interactive. Sharing a single currency could so shift perceptions that it would encourage federalism in other, notably fiscal, spheres. This would, in turn, reinforce a network of other existing ties that could support the single currency. The combination could bring about a markedly different, and preferable, balance to the discussion concerning the level of authority – local, regional, state, or federal – at which fiscal measures should be undertaken.

Some groups fear and oppose EMU as an important step in the path to a federal Europe in which the power and identity of the nation states would be much reduced. Lady Thatcher is an example. For these opponents, the pros and cons of monetary union are a secondary matter. The hidden agenda is federalism and the locus of political sovereignty. I agree with much of their analysis, although not with their prejudices. Other groups, especially in Germany, believe that monetary union cannot easily survive unless it is accompanied by greater fiscal and political federalism. They fear that the loss of national control over monetary policy would enable local politicians to blame federal European constraints for any future severe or persistent national depression. On this view, more political and economic cohesion and integration must be achieved at the federal level for monetary union to withstand the centrifugal force of nationalism.

There is, thus, a division of opinion between those who believe that monetary union can work only if it is, or already has been, accompanied by a transfer of political and fiscal powers to a federal center, and those who believe that monetary union can precede any such large-scale transfer. This division pits the German coronation theorists (or economists), who support the first view, against the monetarists, who support the second (Gros and Thygesen, 1992; Bini-Smaghi, Padoa-Schioppa, and Papadia, 1993). Most of the monetarists also hope, however, that monetary unification would accelerate the transfer of fiscal powers. This conflict goes back to the time of the Werner Report (Council, 1970). Thus, Giavazzi and Giovannini (1989, p. 25) record that, at the Hague Summit in 1969, 'the six EEC countries agreed on the principle of monetary unification, but expressed divergent opinions on how to implement the transition.... The French wanted the immediate abolition of fluctuation bands, and the transition to irrevocably fixed exchange rates; the Germans thought that precondition for a monetary union was the convergence of macroeconomic policies and performances, and the transfer of powers in the area of economic policy-making to the EEC Commission. The French thought that a clear commitment to irrevocably fixed rates would be sufficient to force policy convergence; the Germans thought instead that irrevocably fixed rates were incompatible with decentralised policy-making, and put forth a program of step-by-step transition toward supranational decision making first, and currency unification later.'

These differences have led the proponents of EMU and the Maastricht Treaty into some difficult policy dilemmas and areas of argument. The Commission finds itself in a delicate position between those who bitterly oppose the 'hidden agenda' of federalism and those who believe that monetary union without federalism is not viable. Should the Commission try to pacify the Danes and UK eurosceptics, by claiming that EMU need not imply any further federalism in, for example, defense, political processes, and fiscal affairs? This argument would cause those who hold to the German view to be even more sceptical about the viability of a monetary union pushed ahead of supporting federal measures. The conflict helps to explain why the Commission (1990, p. 32) has embraced the principle of subsidiarity, which asserts that policies should be decided at the lowest effective level of government: 'In the Community context, the application of this principle should ensure that a policy function is assigned to the Community level only when it can be performed in a more efficient way at that level than by national or local governments.' This is a clever compromise.[9] It enables politicians to address the antifederalists by stating that powers will be transferred to the federal center only when it can be clearly demonstrated that they can be used more efficiently there. It also enables them to respond to the federalists by asking them whether they would really argue for a transfer to a higher level of government of powers that can better be exercised at a lower level.

In addition to providing an intellectual balance between two strongly opposed pressure groups, the principle of subsidiarity shifts the continuing argument from the general to the particular. On what grounds, and by what criteria, can one decide whether a function can be handled 'more efficiently' at one level of government rather than another (Adonis and Tyrie, 1990)? There are methods for so doing in the area of fiscal federalism (Oates, 1972; Walsh, 1992; von Hagen, 1993), but how would one decide in the fields of defense, diplomacy, or law and order?

In one sense, the principle of subsidiarity provides an intellectual smokescreen behind which the ongoing decisionmaking process in the EC can result in a series of pragmatic determinations leading either toward or away from greater federalism. For the time being, general questions about the relation between monetary union and the appropriate extent of federalism are being purposefully masked as being both too difficult and too potentially inflammatory to attempt to answer directly.

Should there be any significant shift of sovereignty to the federal center, however, involving diplomacy or defense, heavy expenditures would be required and would need to be financed. There would then be a problem with multiple currencies, varying flexibly against each other within the federation. The comparative regional benefits and costs of the central fiscal policy would be disturbed and distorted by the monetary fluctuations. At best, this would lead to great complexities; almost certainly, it would lead to dissatisfaction resulting, perhaps, in dissension and the progressive division of the federal state into its component parts. Even under a pegged, but occasionally adjustable, exchange-rate regime, a realignment would alter either the real fiscal impact on individual member states, if monetary transfers (fiscal expenditures and receipts) were denominated in terms of a federal currency such as the ECU, or the real fiscal outturn for the federal budget, if transfers were denominated in national currencies. And what would happen if the realignment were to occur partway through the fiscal year, with more accruals than disbursements completed?

One of the main questions raised by Kenen (1969) is whether the currency and fiscal domains need to have identical boundaries. It is difficult to answer this question empirically, because there are virtually no instances of single, unified fiscal authorities spanning a multiplicity of currency domains connected by flexible exchange rates. Indeed, one of the few available examples is the early EC, which had extremely limited federal fiscal powers. This is, in itself, suggestive. Note, for example, that, in the FSU, responsibility for fiscal policy has accompanied the shift to separate currency regimes among the independent former republics.

Interactions Between Currency Regimes and Trade Policies

The extent to which two regions with initially separate currencies are linked by sizable trade flows has been a main criterion for currency union since the earliest discussions of the subject (for example, McKinnon, 1963, and Melitz, 1993a). I shall take this strand of the literature as given and simply consider the influence of the currency regime on trade policies. Does the existence of a single market depend on the existence of a single currency? The argument largely follows that on the need for a single currency to support a unified federal fiscal system. Giavazzi and Giovannini (1989), for example, give even greater weight to the role of exchange-rate stability in maintaining trading relationships within the common market than to its role in maintaining the viability of the CAP.

Although currency adjustments, properly controlled, would not likely impede progress toward a single market, I would argue that the adoption of a single currency supports free trade and the free movement of labour and capital far more effectively than a regime of pegged but adjustable rates. No one would suggest the erection of artificial, internal barriers to free trade or the free movement of factors within a single country with a single currency. It is much less certain, moreover, that the EC countries would be prepared to continue with a single market if some participants were viewed as engaging unilaterally in competitive devaluations. Few doubt the overall benefits of a single market within the EC, but there is reason to doubt that a single market, with no exchange controls, and with free movement of factors, will be compatible with the ability of its constituent members to vary exchange rates autonomously and sharply. If exchange rates can be shifted independently of the desires and welfare of the other members, the continued cohesion of the single market, as well as other joint federal activities, may be threatened. The political response in France, for example, to Hoover's move from Dijon to Scotland, suggests that the combination of a single market and floating exchange rates is untenable.

If it is also accepted that pegged but adjustable exchange rates are fragile in the face of political unwillingness to realign promptly, and unstable in the face of speculative attacks on currencies seen as realignment candidates, the only way to guarantee the continued success of the single market may be to move rapidly on to EMU. The recent disturbances in the ERM have led to many proposals for accelerating the transition, at least for the core countries that more or less meet the convergence criteria (Broder, 1992; de Largentaye, 1992; Malo de Molina, 1992; Levitt, 1992b; Steinherr, 1992).

The same analysis can be applied to the FSU. The monetary arrangements adopted by the former republics will have a large influence on trade policy among them (Williamson, 1992b; Havrylyshyn and Williamson, 1991). Maintaining a ruble zone does not guarantee, indeed has not guaranteed, the continuation of free trade between the participating republics. Neither does the adoption of separate currencies and autonomous monetary policies necessarily lead to the abandonment of a single market or of free trade and unimpeded factor movements within that market. Nevertheless, Havrylyshyn and Williamson (1991, p. 74) note that, 'it is also a worry that in establishing its own currency each republic will feel compelled to control, if not close, its borders, thereby unleashing a damaging beggar-thy-neighbor trade war.' Certainly, one of the crucial issues concerning advisers on currency reform in the FSU was whether a move to separate currencies and adjustable or floating exchange rates *vis-à-vis* the Russian ruble would or would not result in policy measures that would seriously impede trade among the former republics (Gros, 1991, 1993; Bofinger and Gros, 1991; Williamson, 1992b; de Largentaye, 1992).

In a note in the *Financial Times*, Boulton (1993) reported two developments that are not entirely unrelated; (1) 'The [Russian] government is also finally forcing other former Soviet republics to drop the ruble as their currency unless they coordinate monetary and credit policy with it,' and (2) 'The country is now even building proper borders with other republics which should help it implement foreign exchange controls.' Boughton (1993, pp. 101–102), analysing the success of the CFA franc zone, notes that, 'the positive factor. . . . is that membership in the zone has given these countries access to France and to Europe.... First, and foremost, it has generated a great deal of trade.... Access to Europe has enabled the countries in the zone to maintain currency convertibility and open capital movements, which has further promoted the growth of trade and output.'

The experience of the formerly socialist countries, especially those of the FSU, exemplifies many of the disadvantages of independent floating currencies. Leaving the value of a currency to market forces does not prevent misalignment, as was evident with respect to the US dollar in the mid-1980s. Because it is so difficult and contentious to fix the value of a currency, the measurement of misalignment cannot be made clearly and objectively. Even so, it is arguable that the misalignments occurring under the comparatively free float from 1979 to 1985 were as pronounced as any under the various pegged but adjustable systems. The current misalignment of the Russian ruble, relative to fundamentals, is extreme, however, and values the labour of a Russian worker at a ridiculously low dollar level (Boone, 1993, Table 4).

Moreover, a currency that is neither supported by sizable reserves nor based in an economic system run on a known and credible set of economic policy rules, is subject to extreme and volatile movements that may reinforce domestic inflationary pressures and relative price distortions. It is no accident that the most successful independent new currency in the FSU is the Estonian kroon, which is controlled by a currency-board mechanism supported by Estonia's restored prewar gold hoard. Even so, Estonia had a price increase of about 75 per cent between June and December of 1992. Although this was comparatively low by FSU standards, it underlines the problems of trying to maintain a currency-board mechanism under such difficult circumstances.

What, then, are countries like Ukraine and the other non-Russian FSU states to do, with virtually no foreign-exchange reserves and no real prospect of a counterinflationary nominal anchor? The prospects of trying to maintain a unified currency with Russia are slight. Russia itself has few reserves, has a central bank that is sufficiently independent from the executive branch of the government to reverse all the established correlations between independence and price stability, and has severe problems of credit control (both with respect to monopolistic state enterprises and to the central government).[10] The probability of hyperinflation in Russia is high (Skorov, 1992–93), but the economic prospects of monetary and economic independence may be even worse, especially when Russia acts antagonistically, for example, by withholding oil and gas supplies from its neighbors.[11]

The existing ruble zone has virtually broken up, with local central banks issuing their own rubles to finance their newly national governments. In order to prevent even worse inflationary pressures from unchecked local seigniorage spilling across borders, cross-border payments in, say, Georgian rubles, are not being accepted by shippers of goods in, for example, Kazakhstan. Instead, the so-called ruble area has degenerated into a barter system. In this context, the adoption of new national currencies may be no more than a de jure confirmation of a de facto breakdown (Williamson, 1992a and 1992b; Sachs and Lipton, 1993).

If separate currencies were to be introduced by regions within a sovereign nation, would trade barriers develop? Would federal nationalism give way to regional nationalism? This is a controversial question. In theory, the existence of flexible exchange rates between regions could facilitate the removal of trade barriers, because it would provide a market means of adjustment to imbalances. Indeed, Anglo-Saxon economists often take the line that an open single market with common minimum standards is perfectly consistent with flexible exchange rates (Wood, 1990; Feldstein, 1992). Continental European economists generally disagree (Giovannini, 1992a; Masera, 1992). Gros and Thygesen, 1992, p. 3) quote the dictum attributed to Jacques Rueff: 'L'Europe se fera par la monnaie ou elle ne se fera pas.'[12] The Association for the Monetary Union of Europe (1992, p. 3) flatly asserts that, 'so long as the possibility remains that exchange rates within the European Community will change, barriers to trade will not be eliminated.'

The Anglo-Saxon argument is further supported by reference to the North American Free Trade Agreement (NAFTA), an agreement that includes no mutual surveillance of exchange rates. This would seem to counter the European claim that a single market requires a single currency. But there are differences between NAFTA and the EC. Recall the argument in Cohen (1993a) that the existence of a hegemon reinforces international agreements. The USA is so large relative to Canada and Mexico that it may be able to play the role of Stackelberg leader. There is no such hegemon in the EC. We must wait to see, moreover, what complaints there will be under NAFTA if there is great volatility in the exchange rates of its members.

NAFTA and the EC differ in yet another respect. European commentators concerned with the effect of floating exchange rates on the single market assume that the current account, national competitiveness, and employment will be variables influencing the monetary authorities' policy decisions; national interest rates or monetary growth rates may be used to bring about short-term effects on trade and output. The pure theory of international trade usually assumes that the money stock is exogenously given or influenced by some rule that does not involve a feed-back link to the current account. In North America, by contrast, the central banks of both Canada and Mexico have been focusing more on achieving price stability in recent years than on maintaining competitiveness. Indeed, the obligation to achieve price stability will be included in the proposed statute that will grant independence to the Central Bank of Mexico. Whether or not floating exchange rates are compatible with a single market may therefore depend on the policies and rules adopted by the monetary authorities in the countries involved.

The apparent reluctance of national authorities to accept constraints on the conduct of domestic monetary policy raises questions about the path to a single currency proposed by the Delors Report and Maastricht Treaty.

Table 8.3

Exchange rate	Stable without exchange controls	Consistent with a federal fiscal system	Consistent with a single market
Free float	Yes	No	Doubtful
Pegged but adjustable	No	Doubtful	Yes
Single currency	Yes	Yes	Yes

Might there be a different way of making the transition? Before turning to that question, we can summarize the discussion in Table 8.3. The benefits of a single currency for the EC seem to be clear. It is these, I claim, rather than OCA analysis, that provide the drive toward EMU.

8.5　THE TRANSITION TO MONETARY UNION

The Intermediate Stages

Most of the plans for, and studies on, EMU have assumed that monetary union would be reached through a series of stages progressing closer to union. Thus, the EMS began with an ERM with frequent realignments (1979 to 1983), which progressed to occasional realignments (1983 to 1987), then, to virtually fixed rates (1987 to 1992). From that point, the system was to have moved in 1994 to Stage 2 of the Delors process, with all EMS countries in the narrow band, to the irrevocable fixing of parities by 1999 at the latest, and, finally, to a single currency.

Advocates of monetary union saw a number of advantages in this phased plan. It not only made each step appear less radical, but it also enabled supporters to compare monetary union, an end point that had many economic and political advantages, to the ERM, a middle stage that shared most of the economic costs of EMU with few of its economic advantages. Thus, the peripheral members of the ERM largely gave up monetary autonomy and independence, so long as they sought to maintain their peg to the deutschmark anchor; they could adjust their exchange rates only on infrequent occasions, either by a realignment or a temporary float, both of which would severely strain the ordered conduct of macroeconomic policy. In addition, they had to guard against the possibility of future devaluation or float by maintaining their nominal interest rates at a significant premium over those in Germany. Given asymmetric shocks, most notably German reunification, the level and structure of interest rates appropriate for German conditions would not necessarily be suitable for the rest of the EMS.

Those pressing for monetary union therefore claimed that its main cost, the loss of monetary sovereignty, had largely been incurred in the early stages of the ERM, whereas the benefits to the peripheral members would only accrue at the final stage of EMU, when the devaluation- and inflation-risk premia on interest rates would end and monetary policy would be set on an EMS-centered, rather than a German-centered, basis. This argument, which was central to much of the Commission's reasoning, was largely valid within the context of its own assumptions, but it had a number of weaknesses. First, none of the arguments held for Germany. As the anchor country, with the highest credibility, Germany's loss of monetary sovereignty was, as yet, negligible, even under the 1987 Basle-Nyborg rules governing intervention in the ERM; Germany suffered no interest-rate premium (rather the reverse), and the ERM tended to make German exports supercompetitive within Europe (Melitz, 1988). The transfer of power to an ESCB, however, would result in a potentially serious loss of sovereignty to Germany and, in particular, to the Bundesbank.

What, then, has been the German response to EMU? First, the Bundesbank has been one of the main centers of euroscepticism. Second, the Bank, and most Germans, have insisted that the transfer of control over monetary policy to the ESCB must not impose any serious losses on Germany. To this end, they have tried to ensure that the ESCB should perform for the larger community exactly as the Bundesbank does for Germany. This would be achieved by drafting the constitution of the ESCB along the lines of, or more rigidly than, that of the Bundesbank with respect to independence, the overriding priority of price stability, and the absence of significant responsibility for the stability of the banking system. In addition, they have favoured strict criteria to prevent EMS countries from joining the ESCB until they have achieved economic convergence with Germany. Even so, Germans would feel much happier about EMU if there were clearer indications, even if largely symbolic, of continuing German sovereignty; if, for example, Germany were host to the European Monetary Institute (EMI) and, subsequently, the European Central Bank (ECB), and if the common currency were given a Germanic, rather than Francophone, name (Waigel, 1992).

What benefits do Germans see in proceeding with EMU? The arguments are largely political and suggest a conscious, and preferred, shifting of political and economic powers to a federal center in order to prevent a rerun of the political and economic disasters of the last two centuries. A move to a single monetary and currency system to reinforce the European single market and a transfer of political and fiscal powers to the center would be important manifestations of such a shift. It has also been argued that Germany stands to benefit more than other members of the EC from both the single market and the enlargement of the EC to incorporate Eastern European countries (Padoan and Pericoli, 1992; Collins and Rodrik, 1991). Insofar as the single market and its expansion may be conditional on the successful achievement of EMU, Germany would then have an incentive to accept the package as a whole (Martin, 1993).

With the benefit of hindsight, it can be seen that the main weakness of the Commission's arguments, and of the proposed path through various stages, is that they assumed the successful continuation of pegged but adjustable exchange rates, a system known to be susceptible to, and fragile in the face of, speculative attack. This is what occurred in the second half of 1992.

Whether and how the ERM will continue remains now uncertain. One widely drawn conclusion is that the phased route to EMU may have been misdesigned. If the German coronation thesis is correct, countries should seek, instead, to achieve sufficient convergence while retaining residual exchange-rate flexibility. Once such convergence has been achieved, a sudden, complete step to immediate monetary union might then be taken. Stage 2 is not only superfluous and otiose; it is positively dangerous. In this sense, the events of 1992 can be held to represent a defeat for the view shared by France, Italy, and the Commission that increasingly fixed exchange rates will generate the convergence required by the German view. This conclusion, however, has a number of implications for the balance of the argument. It means that the alternative to full monetary union can no longer be taken to be the halfway house of a rigid ERM, in which monetary sovereignty has already been partly relinquished. It needs to be compared, instead, with floating exchange rates or a much more flexible ERM, perhaps like that of the 1979–83 period. In this latter case, national authorities would maintain much more control over domestic monetary policies.

Given the possibility that national governments will pursue time-inconsistent policies, what then would provide the nominal anchor, and what guarantee, if any, would there be of a convergence that might allow a subsequent jump to full monetary union? A plan proposed by Fratianni, von Hagen, and Waller (1992), Begg *et al.* (1991), and Giovannini (1991) would be, first, to transfer the power to determine national monetary policies to independent national central banks that would be required by statute to achieve price stability (see also Hughes Hallett and Vines, 1993). Kenen (1992b, p. 59) makes a somewhat similar suggestion that the monetary policies of EC countries should be coordinated during the transition by the EMI, which would bring about convergence and show 'the sceptics, especially in Germany, that a common monetary policy for Europe does not jeopardise price stability.' Convergence would thus be compatible with exchange-rate flexibility for an interim period. France, Italy, and Spain have introduced legislation to provide more independence to their central banks, but, in the United Kingdom, the prime minister and chancellor took advantage of the appointment of the next governor of the Bank of England to reaffirm the bank's political subservience.

When I have argued the case for some such alternative transitional sequence, the most forceful counterargument has been that experience with floating exchange rates since 1973 suggests that they are not solely, or even primarily, determined by the economic fundamentals of relative prices and monetary policies. Thus, even if independent central banks were to deliver price stability to a common degree in each EC country, there would be no guarantee either of relatively stable exchange rates or of properly aligned exchange rates. The critics of this alternative approach therefore argue that some official intervention in the exchange market is a necessary precondition for moving to Stage 3.

We are left with a dilemma. It may be extremely difficult to move directly from a float to irrevocably fixed rates, and it may be equally difficult in the face of speculative attack to operate a system of pegged rates for any length of time. This would seem to suggest that, whenever the political will to move to a single currency is present, the step should be taken as quickly as possible, from whatever the initial starting point may be. The crucial factor may well be the time interval involved, not the precise nature of the intermediate steps. It should be noted, however, that any sudden, unannounced move to monetary union could cause large capital gains and losses to borrowers and lenders. This would be not only unfair, but, because of asymmetries, probably deflationary. A second problem, that of a 'two-speed Europe,' in which only a subset of EC countries will have met the minimum convergence requirements and desire to move quickly to a single currency, raises issues that must await another discussion.

The problem that I shall tackle now is that there may have to be a long interval between the irrevocable locking of parities (Stage 3A) and the general adoption of a single currency (Stage 3B). It would be relatively simple during this interval for countries to withdraw from EMU. In addition, even though the ECB would begin operations at the start of Stage 3A, continued use of separate currencies for domestic retail purposes could complicate the operations of the emerging monetary union. For both of these reasons, there may be some concern about the viability of Stage 3A, which could continue to exhibit at least part of the fragility of pegged but adjustable rates.

The Costs of Changing Currencies: Dissolution and Unification

Most studies of the benefits and costs of monetary independence or union have focused on the static, steady-state alternatives. This is certainly true of the Commission's 'One Market, One Money' (1990). There are, however, significant transitional costs in moving from one currency to another.

The disturbance to information sets is one of the main costs in changing currencies, whether in unifying multiple currencies or in dissolving single-currency systems. In many historical, and current, examples of currency-area dissolution, separation has occurred when some event has already diminished the information value of the shared currency within the separating region or state. Hostilities between regions are one such factor. The inhabitants of the region without control of the single central bank may query the future acceptability of the unified currency in their own region and may seek to substitute into a more highly regarded store of value.

Separation can also occur when the unified currency has become so inflationary that it cannot act as a reasonable nominal anchor. This is clearly the case in both the former Yugoslavia and the FSU (Skorov, 1992–93). At the introduction to the EBRD's first annual economic review, Jacques Attali, (*Financial Times* 12 February 1993) said, with regard to the FSU, that 'establishing separate national currencies or smaller currency zones could improve the prospects for production and trade among the republics.... The EBRD said the ruble zone had been undermined by inadequate control of credit and cash creation which had brought its members to the brink of hyperinflation. [It] suggested that some republics, once outside the zone, would opt for more prudent fiscal and monetary policies' (Gros, 1993; Williamson, 1992; Hansson, 1993). If a monetary system is primarily a device for organising information, the value of any unified system will depend on whether it is undertaking this function satisfactorily. Under conditions of civil war or hyperinflation, it cannot do so, and the cost of monetary separation will therefore be lessened.

Even apart from informational disturbances, there will be the transitional costs of establishing a new central bank, of designing and printing new notes, of establishing a mint or buying in new coins, and of adapting to the new currency. Many of the larger costs of introducing new currencies, such as altering coin-operated vending machines, changing bank software, and revising automated payment systems, will be much the same whether one is separating from, or moving to, a unified system. These costs are discussed below.

A common problem in cases of amicable currency dissolution[13] is how to divide up the fiscal and monetary assets and liabilities of the previous unit. This is not a problem in hostile conditions; the separating state will renounce responsibility for all liabilities and grab any assets it can. But, what should be the responsibility, if any, of an Armenian government with a separate currency for the liabilities of the former Soviet Union (Williamson, 1992b; Armendariz de Aghion and Williamson, 1993)? If Quebec were to secede and to establish a separate central bank and currency, what share should it take of Canadian federal assets and liabilities? In practice, as occurred in the FSU, formulas can be negotiated for such divisions, given a modicum of good will.

When the information content of an existing monetary system has *not* already been severely diminished, the transitional cost of replacing it is perceived to be quite large. This is borne out by the reluctance of several countries to reform low-value currency units simply by knocking off several zeros.[14] The benefits of such reforms seem obvious. Entering fewer digits at each transaction would lessen the chance of decimal-point errors. Informational efficiency would clearly be enhanced, and the transitional costs of a decimal change would be much lower than for any other redenomination. Yet even so simple a reform is rarely made in the absence of prior hyperinflation. The last instance I can recall in a Western industrialised country, is de Gaulle's replacement of the old franc with the new franc in 1958.

There are, nevertheless, immediate transitional costs that may be perceived to outweigh the long-run, steady-state benefits. The physical costs of printing and substituting new notes would not be very large. More serious could be fears that such a substitution would be used by a government as a device either for refusing to exchange high-value hoards of old currency (a wealth tax on currency hoarders) or for asking questions about fiscal or possible criminal activity that may have led to the accumulation of such hoards. And time-inconsistency problems could also arise. A good example of this occurred in the Soviet Union in January 1991 (Havrylshyn and Williamson, 1991).

Even such simple reforms as knocking zeros off currency units could cause costly problems. All written contracts, financial arrangements, wills, and electronic software programs dealing with payments would have to be changed. Suppose that the lira is rebased by a factor of 1,000 to 1. Your granny wrote a will before the reform giving you a bequest of 15,000 lire. She dies two days after the reform. Is your bequest valid in law for new or old lire? There are, of course, ways of dealing with such problems, but the change will inevitably cause confusion and legal complexity. For all these reasons, the program for currency reform in Italy is moving very slowly, even though it is widely accepted (De Vecchis, 1990).

Another sort of currency reform is the 1967–71 British shift from nondecimal to decimal coinage (from 20 shillings to the pound, 12 pence to the shilling, and so forth, to 100 new pence to the pound). Not only did the main unit (the pound) remain unchanged, but several of the subsidiary coins continued in use; thus, the previous florin (2 shillings) became 10 new pennies, and the existing shilling, 5 new pennies. The value of the reform is clear to those of us who spent our early childhood years doing sums such as, 'You have two pounds six shillings and fourpence in your pocket. Chocolate bars cost three shillings and sixpence halfpenny each. How many can you buy?' Yet more than five years were taken in planning and executing the reform; the costs of adjusting vending machines, and so forth, were large; and the public outcry was great.

Economists use the concept of menu costs. A change in subsidiary coinage involves the simultaneous imposition of the required menu cost on every single pricing arrangement involving coins. One reason for the public outcry in England was that the reform required a rounding up or down of all menu prices previously set at a level not immediately translatable into new-penny integers. Not only did most people claim that prices were more frequently rounded up than down, but many accused sales outlets of using the conversion to raise prices surreptitiously. Although I know of no rigorous academic support, a widely held hypothesis at the time was that the introduction of coin decimalisation caused an upward blip in inflation. The idea that a currency reform will leave all relative prices unchanged is untenable. The confusion provides a perfect cover for sellers to raise prices, and consumers will expect them to do just that.

The costs of UK decimalisation would be dwarfed by the costs of changing to an ECU system. Yet these costs have hardly begun to be considered with respect to EMU. There is virtually nothing about such problems in the studies of the Commission, and, among academics, only Giovannini (1991) and Melitz (1991a, 1993b) have yet commented on them. The best and most complete treatment is in Mazzaferro's (1992) San Paolo Bank report. Various working groups of central-bank governors are now addressing these issues, but little has been revealed publicly:[15] some of the studies and options under consideration are, however, outlined in the annual report for 1992 of the Committee of EC Central Bank Governors (1993).

Compare the switch to the ECU with the 1958 French rebasing. Under rebasing, the new franc was worth 100 old francs, and information sets could adjust relatively easily. Assume, for the moment, that the ECU replaces the French franc at the franc's February 1993 ECU parity. Each new ECU is then worth 6.54988 previous francs, each prior franc, worth 0.1526746 ECU. Apart from the enforced need to change all contracts, payment systems, and software programmes involving money, consider the shock to our information systems.

Again, compare ECU unification to British decimalisation. In the British case, several coins were common to both regimes, so both the real cost and informational loss were reduced. The proposed ECU, however, does not equal a round number of any national unit and is commonly expressed to the nearest six figures. If we were to switch on the present basis to a unified ECU system, all coins in all currencies participating in EMU would have to be replaced by completely new, totally unfamiliar subsidiary coins. Menu costs may sometimes seem small; but not these.

At least three proposals have been put forward to reduce some of these costs. The first is that the value of the new common currency should be made equal to that of the most widely held existing currency. In this case, 1 ECU would be made equal to 1 deutschmark, and the subsidiary coin (a pecu?) would be equal to a pfennig. This would eliminate any transitional costs in Germany (Giovannini, 1991; Lehment and Scheide, 1992). Lord Cobbold, 'How to make the ECU user-friendly' (*Financial Times* 12 May 1993), has recently proposed a variant, whereby an ECU would be valued at exactly 2 deutschmarks, rather than its current rate of 1.953 deutschmarks. Because many businesses would be more familiar initially with the deutschmark than with the ECU, this adjustment would reduce information costs outside Germany. Because the deutschmark also has the greatest credibility among existing EC currencies as a store of value, its close link to the ECU would launch the new currency in the best possible manner. The economic arguments for this method seem incontrovertible. Nevertheless, it will probably not happen. The French may block it on purely political grounds, and the British, and others, may block it on commercial grounds. Mazzaferro (1992, p. 71) notes that this technique would be illegal under Article 109J of the Maastricht Treaty, but, more important, 'that the German financial system will have been offered a lead which it will never lose.' For this reason, he states, other countries will not accept it.

A second way to reduce transitional costs would be to have one final realignment to shift the ECU value of each participating EC currency onto a user-friendly fraction. Giovannini (1991) suggests one such realignment (see also Neumann, 1992). There are two problems with this method. The first is that a final realignment might not be consistent with the Maastricht convergence criteria, unless it were done more than two years before Stage 3, when currency parities are to be irrevocably fixed. The conflict might be avoided, however, if the realignments were made on the initiative of the EC, rather than that of the member states. Second, Articles 109g and 109l, 4 of the Maastricht Treaty state that 'from the start of the third stage, the value of the ECU shall be irrevocably fixed.' There could well be a small window of opportunity for realignment between the end of the two-year convergence period and the start of Stage 3, but any such opportunity would be perceived by the markets, which would react in advance with speculation.

A third proposal to reduce information costs would be to phase in gradual stages the replacement of national currencies by the ECU (Spahn, 1992). To this end, Mrs. Thatcher proposed that a 'hard ECU' might be introduced and adopted by private agents in an evolutionary manner (H.M. Treasury, 1989; Richards, 1990). But this might not have led to any appreciable currency unification; indeed, many feel that its expected failure to do so was exactly what some of its antifederalist British proponents wanted.

An alternative proposal would be to introduce actual ECU notes in three stages. In the first stage, the round number of the national currency would be on one side and the equivalent ECU value, on the other. Such notes would be legal tender in all participating countries, but the information costs of making change could still lead holders to acquire the host country's notes when traveling abroad. In the second stage, notes in round numbers of ECUs would be introduced, with the equivalent national value on the reverse side. At first, both sets of notes (national round-number notes and ECU round-number notes) would circulate side by side; subsequently, national round-number notes would be withdrawn. In the final stage, the preunification national equivalent on the reverse side would be omitted, although it would still remain possible to design notes displaying national features for initial emission in a particular country. Thus, ECU notes issued in England would have the Queen's head on them, although Dutch notes with Queen Beatrix would be just as good for payment purposes. Even so, would the Spanish find it acceptable to have a large part of their note circulation in 'British' and 'German' ECU after every tourist season? If not, they would have to find means for sorting perhaps seven or eight different denominations of bank notes from seven or more countries, and either destroying or repatriating 'nonlocal' notes, a complex and expensive task.

Such dual-valuation printing of notes has occurred in the past.[16] Whether an accompanying procedure could be achieved for subsidiary coins, however, is another question. Subject to possible rounding to a user-friendly fraction, the reverse-side stamping of coins (initially ECU, subsequently national) would presumably have to be an approximation, for, as Mazzaferro (1992, p. 12) notes, 'national coins will be non-decimal multiples and submultiples of the Ecu.' A fine calculation would have to be made to balance the need for informational simplicity against the opportunities for arbitrage (Gresham's Law). If a graduated process for subsidiary coins is not possible, however, and the changeover had to be done on a single big-bang day, the arguments for phasing in notes would become much weaker.[17]

One argument for having a single changeover day is that, until national currencies are completely replaced by the ECU, the costs of reneging on the Maastricht commitment will not be perceived as prohibitive (Mazzaferro, 1992); devaluation premia in nominal national interest rates may remain, increasing the temptation for national politicians to withdraw. Those who favour unification therefore want to complete it as quickly as possible once Stage 3 has begun. Moreover, it is arguable that, if such a major break is to be made, it is better to make it cleanly and quickly on a chosen day for which everyone can be prepared in advance. The chaos on, and immediately after, changeover day will be indescribable, but the present discounted value of the costs may be less than if the changeover is organised in stages, with some businesses and accountants operating on a national-currency basis while others have shifted to the ECU. Levitt (1992b, pp. 32–3), for example, claims that 'a parallel currency, favoured by some politicians and experts, would add to the problems' and would double some of the costs facing banks. It is, however, quite possible, perhaps probable, that monetary operations in Stage 3A will require the banking systems in the EC to combine a wholesale system denominated in ECUs with a retail system in national currencies. If so, banks may be unable to avoid running two sets of books, at least for the transitional period.

Insufficient appreciation has been given to the length of time required to prepare for the changeover day, and there has been little discussion of the time that is likely to elapse between the start of Stage 3A, with an irrevocable fixing of parities, and the subsequent achievement of a single currency among the participating counties (Stage 3B). It is also unclear which countries will participate and when Stage 3A will begin, although we have a *terminus ad quem* of 1 January 1999. People will consequently be disinclined to spend much time, or to incur many preparatory costs, in advance of an event that might not happen to them at all.

In light of the British experience with decimalisation, my guess is that Stage 3A will have to continue for at least three years and may, as all the complexities become apparent, need to last for up to six years. Assuming that Stage 3A begins on 1 January 1999, this would put the changeover day somewhere between 1 January 2002, and 1 January 2005.

Is there not an inconsistency here? It is commonly suggested that the transitional costs of monetary dissolution are much greater than those of monetary union; yet the monetary unions of the former Yugoslavia and FSU are breaking up rapidly. Although their dissolution has involved much disturbance, it does not seem to have been on the same scale as the dislocation suggested for the changeover to the ECU. The answer to this apparent paradox is threefold. First, the political imperative for dissolution in Eastern Europe has been greater than the public and political enthusiasm for currency union in Western Europe. Second, the monetary system, and the associated hardware and software, is technically much more rudimentary in Eastern Europe than in Western Europe, so that there has been less to change and it has been easier so to do. Third, the information function and nominal stability provided by the dinar and the ruble had already been dissipated.

The Interregnum between Currency Regimes: From National Currencies to EMU

The Delors Report originally envisaged Stage 2 as a transitional step en route to a single currency. Under the Maastricht Treaty, however, domestic monetary arrangements are to remain effectively unchanged during Stage 2 and under the sole control of national central banks. Although the convergence criteria, subject to any amendments, revisions, or reinterpretations that may be introduced, will exert an influence over the economies of EC members during Stage 2, the monetary regime will remain essentially unchanged until Stage 3. There will be nearly no shift to ECU usage, no significant currency substitution at the domestic level, and possibly very little substitutability at the wholesale level. Currency usage, payment and settlement systems between and within EC countries, structures of financial markets and central-bank operations are likely to look much the same at the end of Stage 2 as they look now. Although these assertions may appear to be incidental, substantive changes to market structures, payment mechanisms, and so forth, take years to plan and bring into effect. If they are to occur before the start of Stage 3, due by 1999 at the latest, where are the present plans for them? What evidence is there of growing currency substitution, or greater ECU usage, especially after the setback in 1992?

By much the same token, we can imagine relatively easily what the single European currency regime, Stage 3B, will look like when it is fully operational. There are several problems to resolve. How will the ECB and the national central banks balance their operations in money markets to bring into effect the single European monetary policy and to ensure systemic stability in the European payment mechanisms and financial system? Financial markets and payment systems within EC countries currently function on the basis of differing technical systems, for example, gross versus net payment systems. How much harmonisation will be necessary or desirable for Stage 3B?

We can nevertheless characterise the larger picture. All transactions within and between EC countries will be undertaken in ECUs, all asset prices, including the various government bonds, will be denominated in ECUs, a single ECU interest-rate structure will obtain, and so on. The question then arises, how do we get from here to there? In practice, this transition will occur during Stage 3A, at which point currencies are separate but irrevocably fixed. As noted above, this stage is more important and will take much longer than is generally realised.

During the Maastricht negotiations, the transition to the ECU was shifted from Stage 2 to Stage 3A, and the details of the transition were relegated to the various committees established by the EC central-bank governors and, once the EMI was in place, to the institution (Treaty, Article 109f, and Protocol on the EMI Statute). The EMI's main function, in fact, will be to plan the transition. Thus, the transitional arrangements have become the province of a few financial experts drawn primarily from the national central banks and monitored where possible and advised and criticised by a limited group of outside academics (Kenen, 1992a; Melitz, 1993b) and practitioners (Levitt, 1992a, 1992b).

The key features of Stage 3A are that, from day one, the parities between the separate national currencies and the ECU must be absolutely exactly fixed, and that there will be a single monetary policy across all the member countries. As Monticelli and Viñals (1993, p. 12) state, 'a necessary condition for the conduct of monetary policy in Stage Three is the establishment of an integrated market for central bank money.' If the market is to be integrated, its business will have to be conducted from the start in the single currency, the ECU. In order to participate in the ECU funds market, the participating banks will need to be able to exchange ECUs for their domestic currencies without limit at par with their national central banks. A wholesale payment and settlement system in ECUs will need to be in place from the start to settle such transactions in the ECU funds market. Finally, in order to hedge and adjust their ECU positions, banks will need to be able to transact in large, liquid ECU financial markets; these can best be provided, perhaps, if the central governments of the participating countries irrevocably guarantee from the start the ECU value of some portion of their debt (both interest and principal). Note that this guarantee would also represent a strong precommitment to moving on to Stage 3B.

Kenen (1992a, p. 34) sets out six proposed requirements for day one: (1) The balance sheets of the ECB and the national central banks are denominated in ECUs; (2) credit institutions hold ECU balances with their national central banks. They may or may not be *required* to hold them; (3) an ECB funds market is in place, in which credit institutions can make or take interbank loans and thus lend or borrow ECU cash balances held at the national central banks; (4) governments have attached 'ECU endorsements' to all of their marketable obligations, guaranteeing to redeem them in ECUs; similar endorsements are attached to all other instruments used in open-market operations; (5) a unified market for all securities bearing ECU endorsements is in place, in which interest rates on individual issues differ only insofar as the issues themselves differ in default risk, liquidity, and taxability; and (6) firms and individuals hold and deal in securities with ECU endorsements, although they also use their own national currencies. Because national central banks will still have national note issues as their main liabilities, it may be decided that all national central-bank assets need not be denominated in ECUs, but, given an ECU endorsement to central-government debt, this is a minor issue.

Commercial banks will need to operate simultaneously in two currencies during Stage 3A, in ECUs for wholesale transactions and in national currencies for retail transactions. Various working parties are studying the technical forms of the ECU wholesale payment and settlement systems and the links with the continuing national retail systems, which will still be denominated in national currencies during Stage 3A. A number of papers are becoming available by, for example, the Commission (1992a, 1992b, 1992c), the Committee of Governors (1992), the CEPS Working Party (1994), and Giovannini (1992a).

Monticelli and Viñals (1993, p. 13) suggest that the achievement of same-day ECU payments and settlements 'does not require the centralization of payment and settlement systems at the EC level. . . . the examples of the United States and Germany show that decentralized systems are compatible with a single monetary policy. What is required instead is the linking of national payment systems to ensure that interbank funds can be transferred across borders and, once transferred, can be used for final settlements within the same day. To achieve this result, some harmonization of central-bank practices in the operation of payment systems is needed; in particular, common technical standards on operational reliability and compatibility must be defined together with an agreement on the time of the final clearing. These measures are sufficient to create an integrated interbank market and thus permit the conduct of a single monetary policy. Unfortunately, they do not ensure the safety of the interbank payment and settlement systems. Safety requires measures to reduce liquidity, credit, and systemic risks (such as collateral requirements, caps on exposure, the definition of the conditions of access to the system), as well as common legal provisions regulating the finality of payments (bankruptcy laws, "zero-hour" clauses) and the revocability of payment instructions.'

Unification will also require, even at the outset of Stage 3A, the establishment of a single interest rate (at each maturity on instruments of identical character) throughout the participating countries in the EC. The present structures and types of money markets, however, and the operational mechanisms of central banks, are different in the various countries (see Schnadt, 1994, on money markets in London, Frankfurt, Paris, and New York). There could, therefore, be a conflict between the desire for subsidiarity and national continuity enshrined in the Maastricht Treaty, Protocol on the Statute of the European System of Central Banks and of the European Central Bank (Article 12.1, indent 3) and the need for integration and central control (Melitz, 1993b).

The Treaty (Protocol on the ESCB Statute, Article 12.1) states that, 'to the extent deemed possible and appropriate, . . . the ECB shall have recourse to the national central banks to carry out operations which form part of the tasks of the ESCB.' Among those tasks would be open-market operations to achieve a common European interest rate and monetary growth rate. But central banks currently intervene in different ways at different times and frequencies and leave different degrees of latitude to market forces. Might there not be a likelihood of dissonance and financial turmoil between markets, and even of noncooperative behaviour deteriorating possibly into disguised discord, between national money markets and the national central banks that back them. Melitz (1993b) is concerned about this. How far the structure of national money markets and the technical mechanisms of central-bank money-market operations will need to be harmonised has not yet been fully assessed and agreed.

Finally, the Maastricht limitations (Treaty, Article 104, and Protocol on the ESCB Statute, Article 21) on direct finance of governments by central banks suggest that certain existing financial arrangements between government bodies, especially the central government and the central bank, will have to be changed. If government bodies should continue to want access to short-term bank finance (overdrafts, ways and means advances), they would need, under these circumstances, to approach commercial banks, not their central banks (Goodhart, 1992b). This may have to occur in advance of Stage 3 for all countries except the UK, which has been granted an opt-out; for the others, the prohibition on central-bank financing will take effect at the beginning of Stage 2 (Committee of Governors, 1993, p. 58).

This short summary suggests that the following prerequisites will need to be in place and ready to operate on day one for those countries participating in Stage 3: Each national government will have to guarantee the ECU value of a significant proportion of its outstanding debt and to negotiate any desired loan facilities with commercial banks. Commercial banks will have to be prepared to operate simultaneously in ECU wholesale markets and domestic-currency retail markets. The EMI, ECB, and national central banks will have to establish wholesale payment and settlement systems in ECUs and link them with domestic-currency payment systems; to agree on the prudential supervision and regulation of such systems, particularly responsibility for the proper working of the wholesale payment system: and to decide on the modus operandi for central-bank operations in money markets. They must be able and ready to put into place such structural changes as may be required to achieve the minimum harmonisation needed for these purposes.

## 8.6	CONCLUSIONS

My objectives in this discussion have been to probe the political and economic issues linking independent countries with separate currencies. This is particularly important in the context of EMU, for EMU represents a potential counterexample to the one country one currency format. What considerations that normally make nations want to have separate currencies may now induce EC countries voluntarily to move toward a single currency?

First is the connection between autonomous currencies and international constraints on the flows of goods, capital, and other factors of production. Does the maintenance of a single market require either a single currency or, at least, strict limitations on the autonomous use of national monetary policies among the partner countries? Could the European single market survive a reversion to floating exchange rates? Will the breakup of the ruble area be followed by the building of barriers to interstate trade? How much sovereignty over national monetary policies must be relinquished to gain the benefits of a single market? In theory, a single market is possible among countries with separate currencies, autonomous monetary policies, and floating exchange rates, but would such a market work, given the tendency of governments to manipulate their monetary and exchange-rate policies to achieve competitive trading advantages?

A second consideration is the form and nature of the relations between monetary and fiscal policies. Is it practicable and feasible to carry out the fiscal functions necessary for the existence of a sovereign state without having a single currency over the whole of that state? If not, one can understand why nations do not consider having several currencies within their boundaries. If the autonomous republics with Russia should insist on having their own currencies, would that presage the further dismemberment of Russia's sovereignty? Can sovereignty and fiscal functions remain largely at the national level within EMU, while a single currency is shared with the other EC nations, decisions on monetary policy are taken independently of national governments, and decisions on exchange-rate policy are taken jointly among governments?

I have grave doubts whether this can work. Fiscal-policy decisions at the EC level will be subject to nationalistic haggling, and central cooperation and coordination will be limited by each country's desire to avoid a net loss nationally. Fiscal policy at the national level, which already faces many constraints, will be further shackled by the fiscal limits set by the Maastrict Treaty. Monetary autonomy will have been abandoned. Consequently, the inhabitants of each member nation are likely to suffer a reduction in their ability to control their own economic destinies. At times of pressure and cyclical downturn, they might perceive this loss as greater than the gain from preserving the single market by remaining within the monetary system.

Economists have become used to the concept of choosing the appropriate *sequence* of steps to achieve a major regime change, most notably in moving from socialist to market regimes in Eastern Europe. What is needed is a similar analysis of the best sequence for moving toward a federal Europe. Whether it is sensible in this context to push monetary union so far ahead of fiscal and political union is, perhaps, the final and most crucial question.

NOTES

1. Fratianni, von Hagen, and Waller (1992, pp. 1–2) concur: 'Although there are surely economic benefits to be expected from a monetary union, the main driving force for its [EMU's] resurgence remains the quest for the political integration of Europe, . . . The main objections to monetary union have also been largely political.'
2. This is an oversimplification. The core countries, France, Denmark, and the Benelux group clearly renounced any further realignment against the deutschmark. The problem for the peripheral countries was that they would have been willing to participate in a general realignment against the deutschmark but were unwilling to do so individually, as that would have demonstrated weakness and diminished their credibility.
3. Note that, for the time being, such 'normality' has ceased to hold in the UK.
4. Thus, Spahn (1992, p. 12) states that, 'the benefit is, of course, greatest for the smaller, peripheral monies, the escudo, the Krona. Portugal and Denmark, by their belonging to the Ecu zone, would thus automatically appear on the map for Japanese institutional investors; and this would lower their costs of raising money and capital to a considerable degree.'
5. A discussion of whether monetary union is more likely to lead to convergence or divergence in per capita incomes in the constituent regions has been omitted from this section to economize on space.
6. Although a definitive judgment has to await the completion of the Commission's evaluation that is currently underway, the reform of the Structural Funds may need to be carried beyond the stage reached in 1988. If not, the Structural Funds, which are meant as conditional specific-purpose grants, risk remaining a set of disguised block grants, which, because their implementation procedures are rather convoluted, may produce neither an efficient nor a fair outcome.
7. A counterargument is that the gold standard operated successfully without any such international fiscal transfers. A recent book by Panić (1992) specifically considers what lessons the gold standard may hold for EMU. The gist of Panić's conclusions was that the success of the gold standard was the result of unrepeatable, serendipitous circumstances and cannot serve as a useful analogy or basis for assessing the probable outcome of EMU. Eichengreen (1992a) concurs.
8. Feldstein's other arguments for leaving the US monetary union intact are historical inertia and the 'reputation' of the US dollar. I find these less convincing.
9. Not perhaps surprisingly in this context, the British government has also been

pushing the concept of subsidiarity, but it supports the principle only when it is applied between Brussels and Westminster. The government appears aghast when anyone asks that the same principle be applied between Westminster and the local authorities in Scotland and Wales.

10. Boulton (1993) reported that the Central Bank of Russia proposed what must be the world's highest monetary target, '20 per cent a month.'

11. Ukraine's oil quota in 1993 was 1 million tons less than Russia promised Belarus, which is one-fifth the size of Ukraine but which had acceded to all of Russia's political and military demands. Russia's deputy prime minister, Viktor Shokhin, said in February 1993 that Russia will tie the continued supply of fuel to military and political conditions, including the stationing of Russian military bases in Ukraine. 'I cannot understand the Russian position,' Kuchma said, 'It can only be seen as pressure on Ukraine, motivated by something beyond economic considerations. This is a conflict in which there can be no victors' ('Reform Club's New Member,' *Financial Times*, 23 February 1993).

12. David Marsh, in a note on ' "Franc fort" Set to Survive French Poll,' quotes a top French official as stating that, if the franc had to float, 'this would mean the end of the EMS, of the Maastricht Treaty, of the single market and the Treaty of Rome itself' (*Financial Times*, 18 March 1993).

13. A close observer of the Czech-Slovak breakup comments that he is 'not sure than an amicable currency dissolution is actually possible.'

14. For example, Portuguese, Spanish, and Italian currency exchange rates against the US dollar in February 1993 were 214 escudos, 167 pesetas, and 2,200 lire.

15. I understand that, among the subcommittees established to prepare for Stage 3, there is one, set up in May 1992, 'to supervise technical preparation of Ecu bank notes.'

16. The *Financial Times*, (9 September 1992) noted that, 'Lord Younger, the Royal Bank chairman, has been dipping into the history books to make a separate point about the design of European banknotes if Emu one day became a reality. For about a century after political and monetary union between England and Scotland in 1707, one pound sterling banknotes north of the border carried the inscription that they were equivalent to 12 pounds Scots. Lord Younger has been presenting EC Commissioners with facsimiles of 200-year-old Scottish banknotes to show how future European notes could carry the names both of the prospective single European currency and of the old national units. If the Community really wanted to ease popular misgivings about the abandonment of francs, pounds and D-Marks then, the Royal Bank chairman suggests, it could copy this ancient example'.

17. The problem of dealing with coins may well turn out to be even more troublesome than harmonising bank notes. Mazzaferro (1992, p. 9) notes that 'the second paragraph of Article 105 underlines that a series of measures *may* be adopted in order to "harmonize the denominations and technical specifications...." The adoption of such measures is optional...; this might therefore lead to a situation in which coinage was not standardized'.!!

Part II

Central Banking

9 What do Central Banks Do? (1989)*

9.1 EARLY HISTORICAL DEVELOPMENT

When the first Central Banks were founded, for example the Swedish Riksbank, the Bank of England, the Banque de France, they were neither expected, nor intended, to perform the functions of a modern Central Bank. Instead, they were established by the government of the day in a position as the main commercial bank in the country, with special privileges provided to them by their original Charter. In particular, they were generally given the privilege of the monopoly of the note issue in certain areas, for example in the London area or in the Paris area. Moreover, you should recall that in these early years the majority of bank liabilities were in the form of notes, rather than of deposits inscribed onto the bank's books, so this monopoly of note issue effectively provided them with a virtual monopoly of the provision of banking facilities in the capital city. Naturally, the government wanted something in return, and, as you will imagine, this was additional finance. In return for the original Charter, the Bank of England and the Banque de France both subscribed large amounts of their initial capital to the purchase of government bonds, thus relieving the financing problem of the government in that year; in addition, every time the Charter came up for renewal, this led to some additional subscription for extra government bonds. Besides such occasional lump-sum payments, the role of the main central Chartered bank, as the commercial bank with closest direct links to the Government, meant that in times when the government was having particular difficulties in financing a deficit, notably at times of war or civil strife, this central bank would be expected to make additional loans to the Government; and, if such 'politically forced' lending should lead to a drain of gold reserves from the central Chartered bank, then the Government, desperate for funds, would normally declare the note liabilities of their central Chartered bank to be legal tender, and to accede to a suspension of the convertibility of the central commercial bank's note into gold, a convertibility commitment that would otherwise be crucial to the reputation and standing of the bank.

The above potted history represents, quite closely, the actual historical experience of the Banque de France and the Bank of England, in the latter

* Chapter 6, 'Role of Central Bank', from Visiting Specialists' Papers, presented to the 17th SEANZA Central Banking Course, October–November 1988, Sydney, Australia, reproduced as a Supplement to *Issues in Central Banking* (Sydney: Reserve Bank of Australia, 1989).

case remembering the suspension of convertibility during the Napoleonic Wars, 1797–1819. As a slight digression, and to reinforce the claim that the foundation of what later became Central Banks should not be seen as such in the earlier decades, I would just turn to the early history of the Swedish Riksbank. The best known fact about the Riksbank is that it was founded in 1668, 26 years before the Bank of England, and thus is the oldest established Central Bank. While this is strictly the case, in another sense it can be said to be misleading. First, the bank was actually initially founded as a private institution in 1656 under Charter granted to a certain Jan Palmstruch. This ran into difficulties in 1664; the Government, perhaps because of a number of loans made by that bank to some of its members, wished to support its continued existence, and, after a period in which the Government continued the bank's operations as a supposedly temporary expedient, it was re-organised under the authority and supervision of Parliament in 1668. It was not, however, called the Riksbank until 1867, but rather Rikets Standers Bank, the Bank of the Estates of the Realm. It was not in any sense under the control of the executive, the Crown; indeed its independence from the Crown was jealously guarded. Instead, the bank operated effectively as a commercial bank, with two peculiar features. First, for almost all the period from its foundation in 1656 until the 1830s, it was the only bank in Sweden as well as the primary source of notes. Second, as already noted, it was owned and supervised by Parliament.

The grant, by the Government of such special privileges, indeed of a local monopoly in note issue, to their specially chartered, main commercial bank with strong links with the Government, had, however, some initial social and economic disadvantages. Since the infant central banks saw themselves as commercial banks with a normal profit motive, they naturally used their advantageous monopoly position, at any rate in the earlier years of the nineteenth century, to limit and prevent competition from other privately owned commercial banks with a less favourable position. The Bank of England tried, eventually unsuccessfully, to maintain its monopoly of joint-stock banking in the London area. The Banque de France actively sought the downfall of commercial bank competitors in other areas in France. Such unfair monopolistic competition almost certainly weakened the early development of private banking in both England and France. The greater strength of earlier Scottish banking was largely based on the absence of any prohibition on the establishment of larger joint-stock banks in Scotland, a prohibition extended within England in order to support the position of the favoured Bank of England. Many eminent nineteenth century contemporary observers, such as Bagehot, and subsequent economic historians such as R. Cameron, have suggested that the formation of specially favoured government banks, with monopolistic privileges built into their Charters, acted as a blight and baleful influence on the development of commercial banking more generally in such countries, at any rate in the first half of the nineteenth century. Indeed, it was quite widely argued that a system of free banking, free in the sense of not being constrained by the existence of a specially chartered central government bank, would be naturally superior. Bagehot, however, recognised that it would be politically impossible to abolish the Bank of England, because of the advantages that this institution provided to the Government.

Besides its role as the government's bank, the other crucial commitment which the central government bank had, as did also the other commercial banks at this time, was always to stand ready to convert its liabilities, both notes and deposits, into specie, gold, on demand, at least for sight deposits. Moreover, the comparative great strength and central position of the central chartered bank was such that most of the smaller, provincial banks, came to hold their own reserves in the form of deposits with this stronger central bank. When there was a local run upon a provincial bank, it would turn its own deposits at the Bank of England into gold, which it would then transfer back home. Such a centralisation of bank reserves, through a spreading system of inter-bank deposits, obviously provided the central chartered bank with a larger deposit base. It also provided additional services to the local provincial bank, sometimes in the form of explicit interest on such inter-bank deposits, but also in the provision of various services and facilities, in the clearing of settlements, the handling of bills on London, normal banking introductions, etc. Thus, over a period of time, the chief responsibility for the maintenance of the gold standard, the continued convertibility of all bank notes and deposits, from the whole banking system of the country, into gold, came to fall on this main central chartered bank, even though it still was primarily a profit-oriented commercial bank. Exactly the same process of reserve centralisation, and the effective devolution of responsibility for convertibility onto the main central commercial bank, or occasionally as in Canada and in the USA, onto a group of the main commercial banks gathered together into the Clearing House, can be seen in many other countries. Indeed, it remains to this day in those few countries without central banks; as, for example, in the case of the Hong Kong and Shanghai Bank.

Thus, in a manner that had not been foreseen, nor really intended, in the course of operating these central government banks, such banks found themselves undertaking the responsibility of having to bear the main role in maintaining the convertibility of bank liabilities generally into gold. The question then arose how they should best undertake this responsibility, and how that responsibility would fit in with their normal commercial profit orientation.

This question formed a major theme in the seminal and famous discussions about monetary regimes and Central Banking principles that took place in England in the first half of the nineteenth century. The outstanding historical exposition of these issues is that by Henry Thornton, whose *Enquiry into the Nature and Effects of Paper Credit* was written in 1802; it remains outstandingly well-worth reading to this day. A recent re-examination of the monetary debates of this period has been undertaken by L.H. White in his book *Free Banking in Britain: Theory, Experience and Debate, 1800–1845 (1984)*. White identifies three distinct schools of thought. First, there is the 'free banking' school, which claimed that monetary stability would be greater if each individual bank had the responsibility for maintaining its own individual reserves. They argued that monetary instability was caused by the capacity of the central bank, the Bank of England, to undertake inappropriate expansionary, or deflationary, measures without immediately running into reserve losses or gains. Their solution was to abolish the Central Bank.

The second school was the 'Currency School'. They argued that the cause of monetary instability should be attributed to the capacity of all banks, whether the Central Bank or otherwise, to vary their note issue, in such a way that this note issue might expand out of line with the availability of gold. Their response was to restrict the note issue of all commercial banks, by centralising it in the Issue Department of the Bank of England, and only allowing the Bank to issue notes in accordance with the additional inflow of gold. With the note issue thereby determined by a 'rule', somewhat reminiscent of some of the rules recently advocated by monetarists, the advocates of the Currency School argued that the remainder of the Bank of England's operations, as separated into a Banking Department, could operate as if it was just another ordinary commercial bank, seeking to maximise profits.

Finally, the 'Banking School' argued that the concentration of the advocates of the Currency School upon the note issue was misplaced and exaggerated. Instead, what mattered was the overall rate of expansion of bank assets and liabilities, whether the latter were in note or in deposit form. The Banking School paid much more attention to the quality of bank loans, and the overall pace and nature of bank expansion. Moreover, they argued that the control of commercial bank expansion, and of quality of bank loans, could not just be left to the operation of the free market – as the advocates of Free Banking had claimed. Instead, those supporting the Banking School argued in favour of a central authority, a central banking institution with the capacity and power to influence both the quality and volume of bank expansion.

If this latter control over the operations of other commercial banks was to be undertaken, however, it would require the Central Bank, when carrying out this role, to undertake operations that would be naturally resented by its commercial rivals. These actions would include returning their notes for conversion into gold of banks which were expanding their note issue too rapidly; or alternatively, of refusing to discount certain kinds of paper which the Central Bank regarded as of insufficient quality; or of operating in markets in order to raise interest rates at a time when the commercial banks were otherwise engaged in (excessively rapid) expansion. So, the authority to intervene, which the Banking School advocated, would put the central commercial bank into a position of some authority over its rival commercial banks.

9.2   THE DEVELOPING RELATIONSHIPS WITH OTHER COMMERCIAL BANKS

At first, however, the Currency School triumphed. The Bank of England Act in 1844 effectively adopted the tenets of the Currency School. The note issue was to be determined by a fixed rule, and for the rest, the rump of the Bank of England, its Banking Department, was to operate as a commercially minded profit-maximising commercial Bank. This quickly turned out, and proved, to be a mistake. The analysis of the Currency School was flawed. It was the overall expansion of bank assets, not the rate of growth of the note issue, that mattered for economic developments in general, and for the maintenance of gold reserves in particular. Even though the note issue was tightly controlled under 1844 Act, periods of growing bank expansion and bank deposits led to drains on the gold reserve, and, when it appeared that the Bank of England would be unable to expand its note issue, and make reserves more widely available at times of crisis, the monetary system threatened to come to a complete halt. The 1844 Act had to be suspended on a number of occasions. It soon became appreciated that, if the Bank was to protect its gold reserves, and the convertibility commitment, it had to do so mainly by varying interest rates in a contra-cyclical manner. So, the Banking School lost the battle in 1844, but, soon came to win the war!

But, as I have earlier indicated, the assumption of such a role of discretionary authority, in order to protect the specie reserve, tends to lead the bank at the centre into a degree of conflict with commercial banks whose expansion it is trying to control. The protection of central specie reserve requires the bank, or banks, charged with this responsibility at the centre to prevent over-expansion of the commercial banks on the periphery. The conduct of this responsibility by the bank at the centre, particularly when it is still a profit-oriented, competitive commercial bank, tends to induce feelings of rivalry and jealousy from the commercial banks around the periphery. Essentially this was the reason why the smaller State Banks in the USA campaigned for the non-renewal of the Charter of the two Banks of the USA.

Consequently two conflicts of interest occurred. The first was between the profit-maximisation motivation of the central bank, and its responsibility for managing the banking system, and maintaining convertibility, on behalf of the greater national welfare: the second conflict was between the commercial activity of the Central Bank, and its role in authority over the commercial banks outside, with which it was competing. Effectively what then happened during the course of the latter half of the nineteenth century was that the central banks effectively became non-commercial, and non-profit-maximising, thereby eliminating the conflicts of interest, and transforming these banks into true Central Banks.

Thus, in order to lessen the concern of these newly constituted Central Banks for profit, the financing, both of the traditional central banks and of those newly founded during this period, were transformed in a fashion that left the central bank with a fixed sum of money each year to pay its shareholders, (with the fluctuating profits, or seignorage, which depended on the variations in the rate of interest, going to the Treasury, the Government). With the Central Bank thus becoming non-commercial, it enabled them also to become non-competitive; to stand above the commercial fray. Once this transformation occurred, Central Banks totally ceased to use their advantageous monopoly position to do down their competitors, as had happened earlier, and instead moved to use their power to support the continuing general health of the banking system. So, during the latter part of the nineteenth century Central Banks developed a prudential concern for the health of the financial system, and started their role of operation as Lender of Last Resort. The first major occasion when this was done in England was in the Baring Crisis of 1890. However, the Bank of England was simply following the example of the Banca d'Italia, and of the Banque de France, which had earlier shown the way by using their powerful position and capacity to lend to salvage certain banks, and financial institutions in trouble.

9.3   THE ROLE OF THE CENTRAL BANK IN FINANCIAL DEVELOPMENT

As I have already recorded, the banking systems of the countries where central (commercial) banks were first established, for example in England, France and Sweden, developed in some part in spite of, not because of, the role of such banks. Thus, the first central banks played, at any rate in the earlier decades, very little developmental role at all. During this period, the weakness of the remaining commercial banks, and the frequency of panic runs on such banks, in particular with note-holders seeking to redeem the bank notes of banks now seen as potentially fragile, led these banks to be notably cautious in the composition of their assets, to maintain a large proportion of liquid assets, and to limit their loans to supposedly short-term self-liquidating projects, with also some protection from collateral. Thus, bank loans were more generally applied to the financing of working capital, inventories, rather than to the financing of fixed capital. Since the countries which first developed banking systems, such as England and France, were the most developed economically, there were some alternative sources of external long-term funds, besides retained profits. In addition to the funds that could be obtained from family and close friends, there was some possibility, which grew during the nineteenth century, for raising long-term funds through capital markets, particularly in the form of debentures, through the infant Stock Markets in those countries.

There were fewer sources of external capital available in other less developed countries at the time, such as Germany, Russia and Japan. There was less private wealth that might be tapped, and there were no capital markets on which private entrepreneurs could hope to obtain long-term funds. Moreover, the banking system was generally fragmented and barely established. In these cases one of the functions which the Central Bank was formed to undertake was to strengthen the financial system, and, in particular, to increase the ability of that system to facilitate industrial growth; in part because there was no other source of outside funding. In one respect, the Central Banks in these countries had an advantage in encouraging their banks to extend longer-term financing loans to industry. Because the banking system in these countries was in its infancy, there was less use made of banks for payments. The greater bulk of transactions were paid in currency; and paper transfers, i.e. cheques, were rarely used. In turn, the liabilities of banks largely took the form of time and saving deposits, rather than sight deposits. So, with their deposit base being largely funded through time deposits, there was less need for banks in these other countries to maintain such a high proportion of liquid assets, and they were able to respond to the desire of the growing industries for longer-term funds rather more easily than could be achieved in England.

So, besides a number of structural reforms to improve and unify the payments mechanisms, for example by setting up clearing houses, and through the unification of the note issue, (in such countries as Germany and Switzerland where a bewildering variety of notes of varying qualities had been exchanged at fluctuating exchange rates), Central Banks also encouraged the development of a range of long-term and specialised lending institutions, of which the Industrial Bank of Japan is now perhaps the greatest continuing example.

9.4 THE CENTRAL BANK'S RELATIONSHIP WITH GOVERNMENT

As noted at the outset of this session, there has always been a very close relationship between the Central Bank and the Government; indeed the initial Charters were granted to the Bank, ultimately becoming the Central Bank, in order to provide mutual benefits. The Bank got special privileges from the Government; while the Government got additional financing from the new bank. But, equally, the relationship has remained uneasy. Initially, the main focus of conflict lay between the bank's commitment to maintaining the gold standard, and the pressures upon Government finance, especially during wartime.

Indeed the conflict between providing financial support to the Government on the one hand, and both the macro-economic objective of maintaining the internal and external value of the currency on the other, together with the financial development function of Central Banks, can still to this day be well illustrated, e.g. by the Chakravarty Report. Thus, when the tax base and ability to borrow from the general public remains low, the enforcement of high (and rising) required cash and liquidity ratios, in order to mop up what would otherwise amount to an excess currency issue, must be seen as a tax and additional burden on the banking system. Such burdens and taxes, in the form of high-required reserve ratios, together with the imposition of restrictions on what interest rates can be charged and offered, the direction of credit though central directives, and other limitations on the free competitive development of the banking system, all tend to hinder the efficient long-term structural development of the financial system.

During the course of twentieth century, the links between Central Banks and Governments in the conduct of macro-policy have become very much closer. Earlier in the nineteenth century, the maintenance of the stability of the value of the currency, by linking it to gold, or in some cases to silver, was generally accepted as being the main macro-economic responsibility of the Central Bank. Direct, enforced, finance of government expenditure by the Central Bank was clearly seen as potentially inflationary, dangerous, and likely to break the convertibility commitment. So, except at times when the financial pressure of war and other crises overrode the convertibility commitment, it was accepted that the Central Bank should not generally finance Government. Again, the economy at large was seen as naturally self-stabilising, and the shocks that disturbed the stability were frequently seen as being largely financial in character, and certainly temporary. Accordingly the Government was regarded as having little remit for undertaking demand management, or even contra-cyclical policy. Instead, its main function was to raise tax funds in order to carry out a limited range of expenditures, for which there was some comparative advantage in having them provided publicly by the state. Thus, apart from war-time crises, the respective roles of Central Bank and Government were quite clearly separate.

That such separation should cease to hold during the course of war-time, was immediately illustrated in World War I (1914–18). This had been expected. What was not, however, expected was that the old pre-war structure, of the Central Bank maintaining its convertibility commitment to the Gold Standard, the private economy generally exhibiting a reversion to long-term stability, and Government intervention in the economy restricted to a limited range of special expenditures, was not thereafter re-established; indeed it broke down. Keynes argued that the economy was not naturally self-equilibrating, and that the authorities must undertake demand management, in order to equate the level of demand with the potential supply which could be provided by the available factors of production, notably including the labour force. Otherwise there would be unemployment. In particular, Keynes argued that if a fixed exchange rate, for example against gold, was set at an inappropriate level, then internal prices would not be flexible enough to allow balance of payments equilibrium to be restored without the danger of unemployment arising. Although there were some advantages in the maintenance of fixed exchange rates, nevertheless the danger remained that these would be incompatible with domestic full employment. Accordingly, Keynes wanted demand management to be aimed at an internal balance between real demand and supply, while the option should always be open for the external exchange rate to be varied in order to be consistent with the combination of domestic full employment and external equilibrium.

Consequently, the single-minded objective of Central Banks in maintaining the external commitment of the Gold Standard was abrogated. Instead, the main function of the authorities, more generally, comprising both the fiscal and monetary authorities, was to manage demand in order to achieve full employment domestically. In principle, such demand management might have been undertaken primarily either through fiscal or monetary policies. However, in practice the experience of the inter-war, wartime and immediate post-war period, persuaded most commentators and observers that the power of fiscal policy, to influence aggregate demand, was much greater and more reliable than the power of monetary policy. Accordingly, fiscal policy became the main instrument of demand management, while monetary policy was relegated to a residual function. The general objective of the use of monetary policy was to keep interest rates as low as possible, in the interests of encouraging more domestic investment, subject to the need to vary interest rates in order to influence capital flows, to maintain external stability, and sufficient external Gold and Dollar reserves, during the periods in which the exchange rate remained pegged.

In turn, however, the primacy of the Keynesian paradigm itself came under severe attack during the course of the 1970s. It had always been recognised that, if the authorities tried to run the economy at a higher level of demand, they would have to suffer a higher level of inflation; the relationship between the two being traced out by the well-known Phillips Curve. What had not, however, been earlier realised was that the short-run Phillips curve would not remain stable, if the authorities tried to run the level of demand at a point consistently below the Natural Rate of Unemployment. As Milton Friedman and Phelps then proved in the course of the 1960s, the attempt by the authorities to retain 'too high' a level of employment would lead to ever-accelerating inflation. This appeared to fit with the worsening inflationary experience during the 1970s. The lesson that was drawn that the authorities could not independently choose an appropriate pressure of demand for the economy, and keep the economy at the point, without running the danger of ever-worsening inflationary developments. Moreover, the relatively good experience of the Germans and Swiss in bringing down inflation after the 1973 oil shock by the tight monetary policy, without experiencing significantly worse unemployment than other countries which tried to accommodate the oil shock by more reflationary measures, led to the view that the authorities could not effectively, and usefully, seek to control the level of real demand. This was akin to a disavowal of the Keynesian view that the economy could reach an equilibrium significantly below full employment, and a reversion to the earlier Classical view that the economy would become self-stabilising, reverting to its natural equilibrium, if not disturbed by inappropriate Government policies. Under these circumstances, with the Government being thought not able to manage real demand beneficially, all that was left was its ability to vary monetary developments, so as to achieve the appropriate degree of price stability. This was the context in which, during the late 1970s and early 1980s, many governments resiled from the exercise of demand management, and instead encouraged their Central Banks and monetary authorities to establish monetary targets, and longer-term programmes for decreasing monetary growth, in order to revert to price stability.

This belief in the ultimate self-stabilising characteristics of the economy had been a feature of the earlier Classical school of economics, which dominated before Keynes. Indeed, the new dominant school of American economists has frequently been called the Neo-Classical school. One difference between the precepts of the Neo-Classical school, and the earlier classical approach, was that the anchor of nominal price stability had been given, pre-1914, by the Gold Standard. In the 1970s and 1980s, the dominant school of monetarists argued that domestic monetary policy should be more directly aimed at the achievement of internal price stability, through the adoption of rules and pre-commitment to the achievement of a certain, declining monetary growth path. With each major country following such domestic policies, the proposal was that exchange rates should be left to float freely, adjusting quite sensitively to variations in relative national purchasing power parities (PPP), allowing real exchange rates to remain relatively stable.

Thus, the new policy programme was based on the view that there existed a limited number of key stable medium or long-term relationships within the economy. These were:

- that there was a natural rate of unemployment, to which the economy would revert;
- that nominal exchange rates would adjust quite sensitively to relate domestic purchasing power (PPP); and
- that the relationship between the growth of some (preferred) monetary aggregate and nominal incomes, (ultimately prices), would remain stable.

Given such long-term stable relationships, and the ability of rational agents, operating in efficient markets, to predict the way that the economy would revert to such long-term equilibrium states, the role of the Central Bank was clearly to establish a monetary rule for monetary growth which would allow for the medium-run attainment of price stability. There was no role for governmental demand management, nor for intervention on the exchange rate. Fiscal policy once again should be limited to conducting such expenditures as only the public sector could more efficiently carry out.

In the event, however, these nostrums have also run into practical difficulties in the course of recent experience, and have thus encountered more general criticism. The long-term equilibrium conditions, to which the system was supposed to revert, have tended to fall apart. Velocity has proven unstable, even in the medium-term; exchange rates have been misaligned, remaining far from their PPP equilibrium by considerable margins, and over long periods, in a way that has caused great industrial disruption. The level of the natural rate of unemployment, in so far as it can be ascertained at all, has appeared to vary considerably, and in ways that are difficult to explain, even with hindsight. Meanwhile, developments both in foreign exchange markets, and also in Stock markets, such as the Crash of 19 October 1987, have led to increasing doubt both about the view that agents always assess all available information rationally, and that markets work efficiently.

In particular, the breakdown of the stability of the velocity of money, of the relationship between money and nominal incomes, has undermined the rationale for the continuing adoption of publicly-announced monetary targets. We have moved back towards a regime of greater discretion, and of greater Central Bank intervention in markets, notably in the foreign exchange market. But we have not reverted, in policy terms, all the way back to the Keynesian system. In this respect, there still remains great doubt whether it is either possible, or desirable, to try to aim for some particular level of real demand within the economy. In this context, currently the prime objective for which Central Banks adjust their discretionary instrument, notably their command over short-term interest rates, remains the control and limitation of inflation. That, broadly, is where we are today.

10 The Objectives for, and Conduct of, Monetary Policy in the 1990s (1992)*

10.1 MACRO POLICY

A Consensus on Macro Policy

In contrast to the previous two decades, there is presently, at the outset of the 1990s, a considerable degree of consensus about the appropriate objectives and functions for a central bank in the conduct of macro monetary policy. During the late 1960s and 1970s there was a ferment of discussion about theoretical aspects of monetary policy, with conflict between the various schools of Monetarists and Keynesians. The decisive battle in that conflict was won by the Monetarists with the general acceptance that there was no medium- or longer-term trade-off between inflation and output growth, and that expectations, if not perhaps as fully informed as some theoreticians might propose, would at least not be subject to systematic error. Hence the medium- and longer-term Phillips curves were vertical, and the appropriate medium-term financial strategy for any monetary authority was to reduce inflation steadily towards the achievement of price stability; though the optimal dynamic path to price stability was, and remains, a contentious subject, to which I shall revert.

Consequently, by the end of the 1970s virtually all central banks had become converted to pragmatic monetarism, and the discussions in the first half of the 1980s revolved primarily around operational issues. Which monetary aggregate had the most predictable relationship with nominal income? Which aggregate(s) should be chosen as the target(s)? How should the target aggregate be operationally controlled; through the adjustment of interest rates or via some form of monetary base control? It was an era when econometric studies of demand for money functions multiplied like rabbits. Rarely have so many equations been claimed to have stable and satisfactory properties one moment, and have collapsed the next.

The sceptics who doubted the efficacy of rule-based monetary targetry

---

* In A. Blundell-Wignall (ed.), *Inflation, Disinflation and Monetary Policy* (Sydney: Reserve Bank of Australia, 1992): 314–33.

won that particular battle, though the German rear-guard still holds fairly firm, despite being forced to shift ground from central bank money to M3 as their icon. Indeed, monetary targetry became so discredited, that many of the initial zealots, such as Nigel Lawson and the British Treasury, somersaulted from the claim that control of a broad monetary aggregate (£M3) was an essential and almost infallible route to price stability to the opposite position of asserting that there was *no* useful information at all to be gleaned from movements in broad money aggregates.

Yet the core of the monetarist position remains untouched, or has even strengthened. There has been no serious challenge to the claim that the medium- and longer-term Phillips curve is vertical, and hence that monetary policy should focus, primarily, if not solely, on controlling the level of some intermediate nominal variable, so as to anchor the rate of inflation at zero, or some very small positive number. Moreover, the ever increasing international mobility of money, combined with the patent greater success of free market economies (as compared with more centrally planned, controlled economies), has led to deregulation, and the abandonment of structures of direct controls, (exchange controls, quantitative controls over lending, etc.). Under these circumstances, it has become generally accepted that the central bank's primary policy instrument, (we shall discuss later whether secondary instruments do exist), lies in its ability to vary money market interest rates; it can do so via open market operations to alter the amount of base money available to the banking system, relative to a reasonably stable demand for such reserves by the banking system. I shall discuss later whether there are any potential threats to the central bank's control over short-term interest rates. (Note that the time frame here is relatively short, in terms of weeks, quarters or a few years. In the long term, nominal interest rates will be determined by real (international) forces and the expected rate of inflation.)

Thus the current consensus is that the central bank should use its (short-run) control over money market interest rates to achieve price stability. There remains some considerable discussion whether the central bank should use its powers of interest rate control *directly* to restrain inflation, or should still aim at some intermediate (nominal) target, such as some monetary aggregate or the exchange rate, (as in the Exchange Rate Mechanism in Europe). I shall discuss this shortly.

Nevertheless, most of the discussion has currently shifted to more institutional and constitutional issues, such as how best to design the constitution of the monetary authorities, and their incentives, so as to induce them to focus on the medium-term achievement of price stability and worry less about shorter-term concerns over employment, output and growth. Discussion over the optimal *structure* for the European System of Central Banks (ESCB) was central to the deliberations of the Intergovernmental Conference on European Monetary Union (EMU) leading up to the Maastricht Treaty last year, whereas questions on how the ESCB should actually *operate* in markets were put on one side and deferred for consideration by the European Monetary Institute (EMI) over the next four years.

All this has led to a delightful, but not notably conclusive, academic literature in which the statutes of the various central banks are reviewed in order to draw up an index of their constitutional characteristics, notably their independence from political control, and then such an index is regressed against the average national rates of inflation. Long studies by Cukierman *et al.* (1992) and Cukierman (1992) are the most comprehensive to date; also see Alesina and Grilli (1991); and Grilli, Masciandaro and Tabellini (1991). Since this debate is familiar, I can perhaps, be allowed to leave it at that.

Be that as it may, central banks around the world are being increasingly put on their mettle to deliver price stability. If this outcome is not achieved, without some overriding and publicly-accepted rationale for failure in this respect, within the next couple of decades, academic commentators may increasingly question whether there is some inherent fault in the basic concept of entrusting sole control over base money to a single monopoly provider, subject to various institutional constraints and incentives. The alternative, which a number of radical economists have already put before us, is to limit the intervention of the state to the definition of the monetary unit, e.g. in terms of (some basket of) commodities or assets, and then to leave commercial banks completely free to issue their own notes and deposits defined in terms of, and ultimately convertible into, such real assets. While this may sound implausibly futuristic, should central banks fail to achieve price stability, despite being given detailed instructions to do so, the attractions of a system that is designed to achieve (an approximation to) price stability *automatically* might come to seem considerable.

Whereas the upward *trend* in prices, and indeed in inflation until recently, (the question of whether one needs to difference prices once, or twice, to achieve stationarity has been finely balanced), has been worrying, the volatility of *short-term fluctuations* in most economic variables, both nominal and real, around their longer-term growth rates has been quite low in recent decades, (apart from 1972–6). There is, in my mind at least, a question whether a free banking system, without central bank support, would exhibit a higher degree of systemic instability. It was, after all, micro-level concerns about such instability, and contagious bank failures, that led to widespread introduction of central banks in the latter part of the nineteenth and early twentieth centuries, e.g. the Federal Reserve Act of 1913 was a direct consequence of the 1907 banking crisis in the USA. This was, it will be remembered, at a time when macro-policy was largely determined by the constraints of the gold standard. So, while I do not entirely dismiss the possibility of a reversion from a fiat monetary system to one in which the monetary unit is defined in terms of (some basket of) real assets, I doubt whether this would, *ipso facto*, spell the death-knell of the central bank. I shall revert to the topic of these micro-functions of the central bank later.

Another nightmare which occasionally troubles central bankers is that their ability to control,(over the short and medium term), the level of nominal interest rates might increasingly erode. Would the advent of the cashless society cause the basis for, and stability of, commercial banks' demand for the monetary liabilities (base money) of the central bank to disappear? Alternatively, how long can the central bank prevent commercial banks, or other financial institutions, from issuing interest-bearing notes (e.g. by offering lottery prizes based on their serial numbers)? In fact, such fears are largely chimerical. The cashless society is unlikely ever to appear, so long as we prefer, or find that it leads to cheaper transactions costs, to make certain payments on an anonymous basis. Even if there was a cashless society, the monetary authorities could still ensure a well-defined demand for their liabilities so long as some payments, e.g. taxes, had to be made in such form.

The old concept, enshrined in many text books, that money is, or should be, non-interest bearing has increasingly been eroded. Only cash is now seen to be such, and, as noted above, currency notes could easily be given an expected yield. The reason that this is not done is fiscal; seigniorage is a nice, steady source of revenue for the government. There is no monetary reason why the central bank need prevent the issue of (competitive) interest-bearings notes. Since it is non-profit maximising, unlike the commercial banks, it can always drive up interest rates, notably by offering higher interest rates, e.g. on its own notes, or drive down interest rates, by open market purchases of assets, making it unprofitable for commercial banks to offer high interest rates. Neil Wallace (1983) claimed that restrictions on competitive commercial bank issues of notes were necessary to enable the central bank to control nominal interest rates. But this is so only when the central bank chooses to fix the yield on its own currency notes at zero. When the central bank is, itself, willing to offer a competitive rate of interest on its notes, then the necessary conditions for its maintenance of control over nominal interest rates are relaxed. These are that the central bank is prepared to undertake non-profit maximising operations, and that commercial banks have an incentive (e.g. caused by a penalty rate), or a direct constraining requirement, to limit their net indebtedness to the central bank beyond some given limit, see Goodhart (1992a).

But this latter is, indeed, an academic digression. Let us return to present policy issues, and the choice of intermediate target for the central bank.

The Choice of Intermediate Target

A Monetary Aggregate

The failure of equations intended to model the relationship between a money stock and nominal income, usually in the form of demand for money functions, to predict the future path of velocity has been notorious, especially when the aggregate involved became the chosen target for the country's monetary authority. Although there are a variety of reasons for such breakdowns, including some exaggeration of the reliability of the initial econometric findings, (and it is impossible to allocate the share of the blame with any accuracy), there is some general agreement that financial innovation has been mainly responsible.

In particular, deregulation and greater competition, both from non-banks and overseas banks, has led to the provision of higher, market-related interest rates on a wider range of bank deposits, which has led to large shifts in velocity. The only monetary aggregate not subject (yet) to such competitive pressures on yields has been the monetary base, where nominal interest rates have remained zero. As noted above, it is technically possible to pay interest on base money, obviously so for commercial bank deposits at the central bank, and the reasons for not doing so are primarily fiscal. I would note, *en passant*, the emergence of a minor dispute in the European Community (EC) about whether the seigniorage receipts of a future ESCB should be allocated to the member central banks on an (arbitrary) formula basis, or go to the EC central budget, as a Committee of Experts, on which I was a member, has advocated. Be that as it may, not only is the monetary base potentially subject to various other (technical) innovations, automatic teller machines, plastic cards, etc., but in certain countries, notably Germany, there have been sharp fluctuations in the demand for hard currency (high value) notes in substitution for the depreciating currency of collapsing centrally-planned economies. Surveys in the United States can only identify the resting place of a fraction of the outstanding stock of currency.

Nor are there good grounds for believing that such innovations were once-for-all, and that, having happened, we need only wait for a while until a stable relationship is re-established. On the contrary, the commercial banking sector has been having a difficult time. Greater competition, and bad debts, in part the result of the use of monetary policy, i.e. high nominal and real interest rates, to control inflation, have reduced the profitability, capital backing and credit rating of commercial banks in many countries around the world. This has led to some renewed concern whether it is appropriate to entrust the operation of the payments system entirely to such fragile financial intermediaries. On the one hand, this has resulted in attempts to boost capital adequacy, the Basle Agreement, and to constrain bank activity to be dependent on the relative level of such capital, as in the draft bill, 'The Financial Institutions Safety and Consumer Choice Act of 1991', proposed (but not in the event enacted) by the US Administration. Such measures are bound to affect the interest rates that banks can pay on deposits, their relative competitiveness, and the rate of growth of both assets and liabilities.

On the other hand, there is an increasing awareness that payments facilities, even if perhaps on a limited basis, e.g. plastic cards, electronic transfers, high value paper transfers, can be provided by a much wider range of intermediaries than commercial banks. Such payments services are now being routinely provided by the building society/saving and loan/mortgage bank system, and there is no reason why this should not spread further into the mutual fund/unit trust/undertakings for collective investments in transferable securities field, or beyond. As payments services become provided much more widely, the question of the definition of money, or of a bank, is likely to become increasingly blurred.

Against the background, the statistical definition and calculation of monetary aggregates (other than M0) on a 1/0 basis, (i.e. either all deposits in that category are included in the definition, or all are excluded), seems increasingly hard to defend. Quite why central bankers have been so adamant in their refusal to consider improved indices of moneyness, e.g. based on comparative interest rates (such as the Divisia index), or on comparative turnover, remains unclear to me. I do not suggest that such indices would, at a stroke, provide a stable relationship between money and nominal incomes, but, despite their complexity, I believe that they would add to our general information in a world where the relative competitiveness, interest rates paid and payments services offered by the various component elements of our shifting financial structure are continuously adjusting, and will go on doing so.

Against such a background of on-going structural change and financial innovation,there seems, therefore, little reason to expect (or hope) to find a monetary relationship (velocity) predictable enough to serve as a basis for a credible pre-commitment. Even in those cases where a modicum of econometric predictability may have remained, (M0 in the UK, M2 in the US, M3 in Germany?), the authorities, well aware of prior problems with monetary targetry in other circumstances, have paid much more attention to a set of other indicators of inflationary pressure (e.g. exchange rates, wage increases, asset prices, retail prices), than to their continuing monetary target, (with Germany providing a partial exception). Indeed in the UK the continued role of M0 as a monetary target, (quintessentially so, now that we are in the ERM), has been an example of pure lip service to the concept of targetry. I cannot identify any monetary decision since 1985 in which the growth rate of M0 has played a significant part, and I can imagine the cynical laughter in the Chancellor's room were M0 to be mentioned during a discussion of interest rate policy.

What, however, does worry me is that the failure of the monetary aggregates to provide an accurate prediction of the movement of nominal income by themselves at all times has been taken by many authorities, notably in the UK, as a rationale for claiming that there is no useful information to be obtained from analysing the growth of the monetary aggregates at any time. In particular, the collapse in the growth rate of bank credit and in broad money in many countries in the last couple of years has provided a strong indication, to those who would look, that the depression would be longer, and the recovery more delayed and weaker, than those many official groups using standard Keynesian macro-models had expected. Until 10 April, many of us had expected that the UK Treasury's failure to factor such monetary conditions into their model would cost the Conservatives the 1992 election. Quite why that expectation, and the UK polls, were so wrong remains an interesting question for political scientists. Nevertheless, my message here remains. Despite the failure of monetary targetry, full analysis of monetary conditions should remain prominent, a constituent element in any central bank's set of information variables.

An Exchange Rate

The simultaneous failure, around the mid-1980s, of monetary targetry to provide predictable control over nominal incomes in many countries, and of floating exchange rates to provide stable and appropriate real exchange rates, enhanced the perceived advantages of pegging the exchange rate to whichever neighbouring major country could be expected to provide price stability. The mutual international links and surveillance, notably for example in the ERM, gave a degree of firmness and credibility to the exchange rate peg that no amount of domestic rhetoric about holding onto the monetary target could equal. Moreover, an exchange rate target is more tangible and understandable than a number (how obtained) for some (how and why chosen) abstract 'M'.

There is, however, an important distinction between joining the ERM, which is but one (major) element within the wider context of the European Community, and a unilateral decision of a country to peg its exchange rate against another currency. The multilateralism of the ERM enhances its credibility well beyond that achievable by a unilateral, and hence more easily revoked, commitment. Australia, for example, cannot, if only for geographical reasons, join the European Community. If it was to commit to peg its exchange rate against the DM, or the ECU, it would *not* have the same effect as in the case of the UK joining the ERM.

Depending, therefore, in part on the degree of multilateralism involved, an exchange rate target can enhance the degree of commitment and credibility. Subject to differences in the rate of growth of productivity in tradeable goods and services, (a significant qualification emphasised in the Scandinavian theory of comparative inflation in fixed exchange rate systems, as Japan found out under Bretton Woods and Hong Kong is currently experiencing), the rate of growth of prices in the dependent country will approximate in the longer run to the rate of inflation in the anchor country.

The long-term trend outcome is fine so long as the anchor country does provide satisfactory price stability. But what happens if the anchor slips? Inflation in the USA in the 1960s was a major cause of the chaotic collapse of the Bretton Woods system. There are some worries that the disinclination of the German authorities to raise taxes to finance re-unification could threaten its record of price stability. If so, could the European Community switch, if necessary prior to Stage 3 of EMU, to an alternative anchor, e.g. the French franc, without massive disturbance? In the past the anchor country has generally been hegemonic, combining a good price stability record (if not necessarily the best in the system) with overall economic leadership, (the UK in the Gold Standard, the USA in Bretton Woods, Germany in the ERM). Does that *have* to be so, or can the anchor country be one of the smaller nations, e.g. could Germany ever anchor onto Switzerland, or does it always have to be vice-versa?

Even if the anchor country does continue to provide appropriate *longer-term* stability, pegging the exchange rate to another currency is likely to provide a bumpy ride when the (cyclical) shocks in the anchor country are not synchronised (are asymmetric) with those in the peripheral country (or countries). Let me take two current examples. German re-unification imparted an inflationary shock, exacerbated by their government's fiscal response, to Western Germany, requiring a strong hike in German interest rates. The resulting need to hold nominal, and real, interest rates high in the remainder of the European Community to hold the ERM peg intensified the recession there. Again, the low interest rates that have been appropriate in the depressed cyclical conditions pertaining in the USA have not been exactly right for the booming conditions in Hong Kong.

This asymmetry may result in a time path for real interest rates in the peripheral countries that is markedly inappropriate to their own short-term conjunctural needs, (otherwise known as the Walters critique of pegged exchange rates). Such potential asymmetries imply that, *ceteris paribus*, the road to price stability may be somewhat smoother when countries travel alone rather than by hitching their monetary policy to another's control and direction. But other things are not always equal. As in Europe, closer economic integration, in which exchange rate stability and subsequently currency union plays a major part, may be highly prized for its own sake. The credibility and security given by a currency link may, particularly for a small country facing a difficult future, vastly outweigh the inconvenience of temporary periods of inappropriate interest rates.

Finally, if monetary and exchange rate policy is to be predicated to the maintenance of an exchange rate peg, (and thereby to the same long-term rate of inflation as in the anchor country), can fiscal policy be used more aggressively to stabilise the peripheral countries against asymmetric shocks, e.g. those coming from the anchor country? To revert to my previous two examples, could the rest of the European Community have expanded their fiscal deficits to offset German-led higher real interest rates, and could Hong Kong have raised its budget surplus (by more than it actually did)? These examples show quite clearly, that whatever may be possible in theory, in practice much more aggressive use of fiscal policy, (and larger year-on-year fluctuations in the size and sign of the Public Sector Borrowing Requirement

(PSBR)), would be fraught with serious political and economic problems.

In my view there needs to be a major politico-economic argument in favour of exchange rate pegging, e.g. to achieve wider economic integration or to maintain credibility under especially difficult circumstances, to justify the transfer of monetary policy control to another country, whose own needs and objectives will, in the shorter run at least, at times be out of line with your own. In the examples quoted, the EMS and Hong Kong, such justification clearly exists, but it will not hold as a generality.

The Direct Targeting of Inflation

Monetary targetry has failed. Exchange rate pegging is only to be advised in special circumstances. Yet central banks are being are being charged with particular responsibility for achieving price stability. How then should they achieve this? The most general answer is that they should use their main instrument, the control of short-term interest rates, directly to target inflation.

This involves a number of problems. Chief among these is the presence of (long and variable) lags, slow response/adjustment processes, within the economic system. In a world without lags, where nominal incomes and expenditures reacted instantaneously to movements in (real) interest rates, and where inflation reacted instantaneously to the pressure of demand, monetary policy would be vastly easier. Even in the face of stochastic shifts in economic relationships, the instantaneous nature of the relationships would enable the authorities to adjust their policy response quite closely to immediate needs.

The main problems are caused by the interaction of uncertainty about, and stochastic shifts in, the underlying economic relationships and the long and variable lags. Our best estimates suggest that domestic expenditures react quite slowly, building up over a number of quarters, to changes in interest rates. Meanwhile inflation, perhaps particularly asset price inflation, (notably housing and property prices), may also have a dynamic of its own.

Let me illustrate with a heuristic model of the inter-relationship between lending to finance real property, and property prices:

$$L_D = f(E\dot{P}, i), \text{ where } f_1 > 0, f_2 < 0 \tag{1}$$

$$L_s = f(P, i), \text{ where } f_1 > 0, f_2 > 0 \tag{2}$$

$$P = f(P_{t-1}, L), \text{ where } f_1 > 0, f_2 > 0 \tag{3}$$

$$E\dot{P} = f(P_t - P_{t-1}), \text{ where } f > 0 \tag{4}$$

where L_D, L_s are the demand and supply of loans for real property, P, the price level of property, $E\dot{P}$, its expected rate of appreciation, i is the nominal rate of interest, and the signs of the partial derivatives are as shown.

Thus, the demand for loans is a negative function of the own real interest rate; the supply of loans is a positive function of the price level, (since this raises the available collateral), and the yield on such loans, and the price level responds to credit expansion. Finally, we assume a less than perfectly rational, backwards-looking expectations function.

Obviously if an equilibrium, $P_t = P_{t-1}$, is disturbed, instability results, since both P and $E\dot{P}$ enter positively into both L_s and L_p, and L adjusts to reinforce the disturbance. In this kind of model, if the authorities are slow to spot what is happening, i may have to be varied very sharply indeed, in order to offset increasingly strong expectations of future price changes. But once the authorities do manage to brake the expansion, then a given *nominal* level of interest becomes an increasingly severe *real* level of interest rates, as buoyant expectations first falter and then reverse.

Not only in the UK, but in quite a number of industrial countries, the last cycle of boom and subsequent recession has been much influenced by the path of real property prices, (especially housing in the UK), and the associated time path of bank lending connected with that. Housing and property prices rose steadily in the late 1980s fuelled by buoyant bank lending (with associated rapid growth in broad money). Asset price inflation preceded retail price inflation, but the growth in personal wealth in the UK surely had some considerable responsibility for the decline in the saving ratio, which drove up the pressure of demand and inflationary pressure in 1988–90. Checking this boom took a long time. Interest rates went to 14 per cent in May 1989 and 15 per cent in October 1989, but the economy did not decisively turn till Q3, 1990. Subsequently, of course, the reversal of the previous dynamics in the property and banking sectors, and the need to keep nominal interest rates high to support sterling within the ERM, induced a deep and lengthy recession, from which an anaemic recovery is only just beginning.

While much of this (unhappy) story is particular either to the UK, and/or to the special characteristics of the end of the 1980s , there are some more general issues. First, what exactly does one mean by inflation? This is usually measured by the Retail or Consumer Price Index (RPI, CPI), or, sometimes, by the estimated GDP price deflator. But should the authorities also concern themselves with asset price inflation/deflation, either for its own sake or because it may be a leading indicator of the CPI? Say that the authorities were in a position, much like that in Japan, with the CPI rising at 4 per cent per annum, but equity and property prices collapsing. What is the true rate of inflation in such circumstances, and how should monetary policy be adjusted then? In part, this question relates to the paper, by Blundell-Wignall *et al.*, presented to the same Conference at which this paper was initially given, which asks whether asset-price and commodity-price inflation, (among others), may be leading indicators of RPI inflation. But even were there no such interconnecting links, should the authorities be concerned for asset-price inflation, (and deflation), as well as for the RPI?

Given that monetary policy's primary function is to achieve price stability, then interest rates are likely to (need to) be raised as, and when, inflation worsens. But the rise in inflation is almost bound to be accompanied by a worsening of inflationary expectations. Hence, in order to raise real interest rates, nominal interest rates must be raised significantly more than the prior increase in the annualised rate of growth of the RPI. In order to nip an inflationary spiral in the bud, the initial increase in interest rates needs to be rather dramatic, and once the down-turn comes the subsequent dismantling should also be rapid.

But the need for a sharp interest rate response to the early stages of inflationary/deflationary spirals goes right against a central banker's innate caution, reinforced by uncertainty not only about the future, but also about the present state of the economy. Moreover, whatever the constitutional position of the central bank, there will be a wider political need to justify interest rate changes to the general public. This need also tends to make the authorities hesitate too long.

It was quite largely to avoid such pressures for the interest rate response to be too little/too late that the authorities embraced monetary targetry. This gave an additional rationale for interest rate adjustments (we had to raise them as M was growing too fast), hopefully at an early stage (i.e. was M growth a leading indicator of inflation?): some even used it as a smokescreen, (i.e. 'we try to control M, or non-borrowed reserves, and it is the market, not us, that varies interest rates'). The smokescreen was of great use in the early 1980s, notably to Volcker to enable him to raise interest rates sufficiently violently to check the worsening inflationary trend in the USA.

The record in the UK, (prior to its entry into the ERM, which changed the rules of the game), suggests that some continuing strengthening of the authorities' backbone against 'too little, too late', would still be desirable. But how can one factor that into a system in which the authorities act judgmentally, against a set of information variables, in order to achieve price stability? One route has been to consider changing the constitutional position, and incentive structure, of the central bank as a backbone brace. Might there be other routes? I have sometimes wondered whether, starting from a presumed equilibrium with zero inflation and 3 per cent nominal interest rates, there should not be a presumption that such interest rates should rise by 1½ per cent for each 1 per cent that inflation rises above zero, and that the Governor should be asked, say twice a year, to account for any divergence from that 'rule'. But I fear that any such rule would be too mechanical; and hence it would be too easy for a Governor to justify, and commentators, politicians and the public to accept, lower interest rates.

Back in the early 1980s, when inflation threatened to stay in double figures, there was much discussion about the optimal speed of adjustment of price inflation, (gradual or as quick as possible). Now, with inflation commonly under 5 per cent in many industrialised countries, the more immediate question is exactly how do you define price stability? From its peak in 1979–80 many industrialised countries managed to reduce inflation to around 2–4 per cent by 1986–87, (aided by falls in oil/commodity prices). Then many finance ministers proclaimed victory over inflation, (prematurely, as evidenced in 1989–90), and turned to other matters. But that experience suggests that the public stomach for continuing (monetary) restraint may weaken below some low positive number. And is the calculation of inflation sufficiently reliable, (e.g. taking proper account of quality changes, etc.) to make it worthwhile to get the rate down to a somewhat arbitrary 0 per cent, especially if wringing out the final few percentage points involves a high cost in lost output? Exactly what do we mean, how should we define, 'price stability'? It is an important, and quite difficult, question; and a question which the drafters of the Maastricht Treaty comprehensively burked.

Given the sources of dynamic instability, and the long and variable lags, within the economy, I have argued that the monetary authorities need to be brave in the face of uncertainty, and be prepared to vary interest rates earlier and more violently than their natural caution would normally entertain. If they are to follow this advice, it will have implications for interest rate risk. Acting early, rather than late, will make it harder for the private sector to predict such actions, and a larger movement will have a greater impact on those in an exposed position. Of course, there should be a *quid pro quo*, in that decisive early action should prevent the need for much larger, longer cycles; but that thought may be little solace to those on the receiving end.

These latter are not just randomly distributed among all economic agents, but the adverse effects are likely to be concentrated amongst certain sectors, among possibly fragile financial institutions and certain classes of borrowers. The sudden explosion of house repossessions from mortgage defaulters was a particularly painful aspect of the recent recession in the UK. Insofar as the continuation, and perhaps intensification, of interest rate risk will be a feature of a monetary system dedicated to the achievement of price stability, do the monetary authorities have a need, possibly a responsibility, to ensure structural adjustments to the financial system, (to its markets, instruments, conventions, e.g. on collateral, and institutions), that will enable it to absorb such interest risk satisfactorily? I shall try to address such micro-level structural concerns subsequently.

Secondary Instruments and Objectives

In prior decades, the objectives of a central bank, when spelt out, were usually held to be several, including protection of the external and internal value of the currency, high employment, financial stability, etc. with the trade-offs between them left unspecified. As noted in (a) above, there is now a consensus that absolute primacy must be given to the achievement of domestic price stability. But this does not mean that central bankers are urged to concentrate entirely on only one variable, price stability. Rather their objective function is to become lexicographic; i.e. they can consider all these other subsidiary issues, e.g. external balance, growth, financial stability, etc. so long as it is consistent with the prior achievement of price stability.

This is made plain in Article 2 of the Statute of the ESCB (1992): 'The primary objective of the ESCB shall be to maintain price stability. Without prejudice to the objective of price stability, it shall support the general economic policies in the Community with a view to contributing to the achievement of the objectives of the Community . . .' So there are to be subsidiary objectives, given the primary objective. If so, are there secondary instruments of *monetary* policy usable for that purpose, given that the main instrument will have to be predicated to controlling domestic inflation (or, *pro tem*, within the ERM to holding the exchange rate peg)? What are these instruments?

I shall discuss two sets of such subsidiary instruments. The first of these is debt management; the second, direct (prudential) controls. Let us start with debt management. In order to control short-term money market interest rates, sufficient open market operations must be undertaken to operate on and determine the reserve base of the banking system. This, however, leaves considerable freedom to use debt operations to influence the maturity structure of the outstanding debt and to attempt to sell more, or less, debt to the various counterparty sectors, the banking sector, non-bank private sector and the external sector. Such techniques can be used either to try to twist the yield curve, 'Operation Twist', or to influence monetary growth, given the level of short-term interest rates. Exactly this latter was attempted in the 'overfunding' exercise in the UK, 1981–85. More gilts were sold to the non-bank public than necessary to fund the PSBR, so reducing bank deposits (and £M3); and the resulting cash stringency and upwards pressure on short-term interest rates were then relaxed by the Bank of England buying short-term (commercial) bills from the banks.

The general idea is that, when you want to ease monetary conditions (prices and quantities) relative to your, otherwise determined, short rates, you underfund, and vice versa. Indeed, with short rates in the United Kingdom now largely determined by German rates (within ERM), a number of economists, especially those focusing on broad money aggregates, such as T. Congdon, are imploring the Chancellor consciously to underfund, in order to relieve the severe monetary squeeze, see, for example, Anthony Harris' column in the *Financial Times* (20 June 1992).

While I support this latter proposal to some considerable extent, there is obviously a major question whether such debt management is at all a powerful secondary weapon. 'Operation Twist' in the United States was not found to be notably successful, and studies of the effect of relative debt supplies (at the long, medium and short end) on the yield curve have not found any strong, significant effect. There is better evidence that overfunding in the United Kingdom did hold down the growth of £M3s by several percentage points per annum, but it did not lower the growth rate of bank lending to the private sector, or narrow money. Moreover, its (beneficial) effect on £M3 was achieved at the cost of causing certain tensions, and potential sources of arbitrage, in money markets. So the demise of this policy in 1985 was then regretted by only a few.

Not only are there doubts about the effectiveness of such debt management as a monetary instrument, there are also queries whether it should be operated by the monetary authorities at all, but rather should be controlled by the fiscal authorities. It is so in most countries, and to use debt management for monetary purposes would then require some coordinating accord. Those charged with formulating the Maastricht Treaty had such a terror of the ESCB being forced to provide monetary finance to (any sector of) government, that they insisted that the ESCB not participate in any *primary* public sector debt markets. Although the ESCB could still advise on debt management (and operate in secondary markets), the effect of Maastricht will be to reinforce the allocation of debt management responsibility to the Ministry of Finance.

Be that as it may, there will be continuing interest over the potential effects of debt management (given the level of short-term interest rates) on monetary conditions. From time to time some commentators and economists will advocate its use as a monetary instrument.

The use of my next set of instruments as secondary mechanisms for achieving macro monetary ends is even more contentious. These are direct controls over banks. In general, in this age of the triumph of free markets and of internationally mobile factor resources, such controls are eschewed. They are interventionist and anti-competitive. They lead to boundary problems, disintermediation, avoidance and evasion, distortion, moral hazard and to all the curses of the Pharaohs. Nevertheless, we have them in banking. They are usually for prudential reasons, e.g. capital adequacy requirements, minimum collateral requirements, liquidity requirements, etc. In one case, that of required reserve ratios, the advocates of such ratios also point to their fiscal results and their purported effect in facilitating monetary control. This latter is going to prove another contentious issue in EMU, where the Maastricht Treaty gives the Governing Council of the ESCB the right to set common reserve ratio requirements, Article 19 of the Statute of the ESCB, but the initial national levels (and use of) such ratios varies from none in the UK to high in certain Southern European countries.

The application of the Basle (and EC) capital adequacy requirements in recent years has revealed that from a conjunctural, cyclical standpoint, they are counterproductive. During recessions, bad debts will be high, profits low. Capital adequacy requirements will bite, prolonging the downturn, weakening the recovery. Per contra, they will be slack in booms, and have no constraining effect. The same feature will tend to hold more, or less, for most other prudential requirements, e.g. collateral margins, liquidity requirements, etc.

Suggestions have been made, e.g. by the Bush Administration, that the severity of the application of the capital adequacy requirement be relaxed in this recession. But it is possible to go much further, as the Labour Party was indicating, before the last general election in the UK, and make *variations* in direct controls (e.g. in margin requirements for house mortgages), which have a primarily prudential purpose, into a secondary monetary instrument. It is quite possible that a future ESCB might vary reserve ratios for a similar purpose.

There are, of course, problems with this tactic. Would it work? While one may hope to obtain world-wide agreement to a common prudential level, e.g. of capital, getting such agreement to co-ordinated contra-cyclical *variations* in the level seems most improbable. Hence, there are bound to be considerable problems of disintermediation across boundaries, avoidance, non-level-playing fields, etc. The Channel Islands must be looking forward to high EC reserve ratio requirements with great relish.

Although cyclical variations in such requirements *can* be defended on prudential grounds, e.g. it makes some sense to raise margins when housing (stock exchange) prices are cyclically high, there are nevertheless many problems. In an efficient market, how can the authorities infer when prices are (cyclically) (too) high? Could one deal with this by adjusting such controls in response, not to the level, but to the rate of change of prices, (but what is the average trend rate of increase?). Moreover, once attempts are made to adjust the level of such prudential requirements for cyclical reasons, might not there be pressures that could drive the average, over the cycle, away from its appropriate level. For example, an individual country might use such an excuse to gain a quasi-permanent regulatory arbitrage advantage. Having lowered, say, capital adequacy requirements on (valid) cyclical grounds, lobbying from its banks might prevent any return to the prior (agreed) level, whatever the circumstances. Alternatively, once having imposed tougher requirements, the authorities might be afraid to relax them, perhaps because of a fear that the resulting expansion could be unduly large, or merely because, in a world where inflation is the regular enemy, it is difficult ever to find a good time for an explicitly expansionary signal. For such reasons the monetary authorities in the UK persisted with direct controls over bank lending far too long in the 1950s and 1960s.

For all such reasons, the attempt to piggyback on prudential controls, to use them as the basis of a secondary conjunctural monetary instrument, is quite likely to pervert the initial prudential intention. Yet, as already noted, constant prudential controls are likely to exacerbate cyclical fluctuations. What conclusions does one draw from all this? One conclusion that I draw is that fashions change, partly in response to historical events. Booms and busts in asset prices (equity, housing) tend to make variations in collateral margins (equities, post-1929; housing, post-1990?) appear more sensible, whereas in other circumstances they are seen as, at best, *otiose*. Some decades ago, (variable) required cash/liquidity ratios were the *dernier cri*; now it is capital adequacy ratios. Even the most free-market, anti-intervention econo- mists (e.g. the Shadow Open Market Committee in the USA) are advocating a direct constraint over the permissible business activities of banks in ac- cordance with a (somewhat arbitrarily defined) ladder of capital availability.

Such problems, and debates, which will persist, arise originally because some prudential intervention is seen as required. If intervention is necess- ary, then its conjunctural effects will have to be assessed, and perhaps har- nessed and utilised. But is such intervention necessary in the first place? This is the subject of the final section.

10.2   MICRO POLICY

Whereas there is now something of a consensus on the main lines of macro policy, there is less agreement on micro policy, by which I mean the central bank's concerns with the structure and stability of the banking system. Not only are there growing doubts whether there are clear dividing lines be- tween those parts of the system (e.g. banks), for which the central bank *should* have the lead regulatory responsibility, and those for which it should *not* (e.g. capital market institutions), but also there are those who would transfer (all) such regulatory, structural micro functions to another body.

Indeed in the Maastricht Treaty sizeable barriers, e.g. in the shape of a *unanimous* agreement in the Council (Article 105 para. 6 of the Treaty), must be overcome to allocate any regulatory responsibility, beyond that of advising, to the European Central Bank (ECB). Meanwhile, the individual national European central banks have quite widely differing *formal* consti- tutional responsibilities for supervision and regulation in their own coun- tries. There is, however, more difference between the formal positions than in reality. Even when a separate body is constitutionally responsible for banking supervision, insurance, closure, authorisation, etc. as in Germany, it must, and does, work in practice closely in concert with the central bank.

The desire to separate the macro from the micro functions of central banks springs from several sources. Given that the ESCB was to be independent of political control, there may have been some reluctance to give the ECB micro-structural powers as well, lest it seem too powerful relative to the democratic, political process. Probably more important, there may have been (in my view groundless) fears that concern with micro-level banking stability might divert the central bank's focus from its primary responsibility of achieving price stability, and that micro-level action, notably Lender of Last Resort lending (LOLR), could infect monetary policy in an inflationary fashion. (Exactly why such targeted LOLR support could not be offset in its overall market effect by generalised open market operations has never been clear to me.) Finally, there may have been a view that regulation and supervision *could* be done at the national, rather than the European, level and hence, under the principle of subsidiarity, should so be done. This concentration, in the Maastricht Treaty, on the macro-functions of central banks, and the implicit willingness not only to downgrade their micro-functions, but perhaps to hive off such functions to some extent to some other, constitutionally separate, body runs counter to the historical record. The establishment of the central banks before 1914 was done in a context in which the price level, and the main elements of monetary macro policy, were set by the operation of the quasi-automatic gold standard. The function of the central bank was to prevent micro-level banking disturbances, banking crises and panics, from disturbing the macro-economy. Moreover in the then developing countries, e.g. Germany, Russia, Japan, the central bank was perceived as having an extremely important role in developing the *structure* of the financial system to underpin industrial and economic growth. The idea that the central banks should concentrate on the aggregates, and ignore the development of the constituent parts, and the *structure* of the financial system, is alien to the historical record.

Moreover, it is doubtful whether such a division of responsibilities, (macro to the central bank, micro to some other bodies), is feasible or viable. Banking crises have usually involved sizeable deposit withdrawals, or runs, from banks whose solvency was subject to doubt. In those circumstances other banks would not lend to such risky brethren. The decision, whether or not to provide last resort loans in such cases, is traditionally that of the central bank. Who could replace it? The argument is sometimes made that *no* such lending is desirable, particularly since such runs are often (well justified) symptoms of insolvency. So long as the central bank looks after the aggregates, let the chips fall where they may for the individual institutions, or so it may be argued. That proposal strikes me as extremely dangerous, given the contagious nature of confidence and panic, and the effect on asset prices of such changes in mood. Moreover, once panic should take hold, it could radically alter the structure of financial institutions, with a flight to those institutions perceived as relatively safer.

The central bank will have concern for systemic stability. One key feature of the financial system is the continuing smooth working of the clearing, payments and settlements systems. I find it difficult to envisage how such systems can remain secure under all circumstances without the involvement, support and guarantee of the central bank. If the central bank is to provide its guarantee, e.g. by providing daylight overdrafts to banks with net debt positions, it is going to want to ensure that their financial conditions remain satisfactory. Hence, concern with the central payments mechanism would seem to imply that the central bank retain a direct supervisory, and regulatory, oversight over the main monetary institutions in the country.

Once, however, we establish that a central bank's concern with systemic stability will make it want to maintain its regulatory oversight (and LOLR functions) with respect to *some* banks, is there any clear, or convenient, outer limit,or boundary, to the central bank's field of authority. Most financial boundaries have become fuzzy. Many of the large banks are now international, and the BCCI affair has underlined both the importance, and difficulties, of international regulatory (and accounting) co-ordination. The acceptance of the universal banking principle in Europe, the erosion (and possible future repeal) of Glass–Steagall in the USA and Article 65 in Japan, is blurring the distinction between banks and non-banks. As earlier noted, not only are banks entering capital market activities, but non-banks may increasingly compete by offering certain (perhaps limited) payments services.

It is no longer as clear, as it used to be, which are the set of (banking) institutions which should come under the central bank's protective wing, and which should be the responsibility of other regulators. That raises the question of which parts of the system really need such support, and why, and whether those parts within the safety net can, or should, be effectively separated from other associated activities. There have been suggestions to restrict deposit insurance and protection to those banks whose permissible asset holdings would be narrowly defined, e.g. Litan's narrow banks (Litan, 1987). But deposits with such 'narrow' banks would presumably yield less than deposits with other financial intermediaries. Would it be acceptable to prevent these latter from offering payments' services on their *uninsured* deposits? Moreover, such 'narrow' banks would presumably only be able to lend money to the private sector, if at all, through purchases of high-grade marketable commercial paper. Ordinary loans and overdrafts to the rest of the private sector, (apart from fully collaterised mortgages), would have to be made on the basis of uninsured deposits. Could, should, a central bank stand quietly by while any significant proportion of such credit creating capacity collapsed?

Thus, the appropriate boundary for central banks' micro-level responsibilities has become unclear and fuzzy. By the same token, the extent of the central bank's responsibility to support the system is, and should remain, ambiguous. One hundred per cent insurance , whether explicit as in the USA, or implicit, causes severe moral hazard problems. One of the major problems facing central bank regulators is that the 'too big to fail' syndrome is commonly believed to hold in all major countries. Not only does this involve some moral hazard for the large banks, who are perceived as invulnerable, but it also provides a marketing advantage to them relative to their smaller competitors.

It is, perhaps, the 'too big to fail' syndrome that gives the main edge to the proposals that banks should be required to value their capital on a 'mark-to-market' basis, so that increasing controls can be placed on their operations, including, if need be, enforced sale, or merger, while their residual capital value is still positive. But can this really be done?

While I have clearly only been able to sketch in a few of the micro issues facing central banks, I hope to have demonstrated that, unlike macro policy where something of a consensus now holds, there is great uncertainty about the appropriate ambit and functions of a central bank at the structural, regulatory level. Such problems and issues will continue to confront them through the 1990s, whatever degree of success they may achieve in taming inflation.

10.3 CONCLUSIONS

There is a general acceptance among economists that the medium, and longer, term Phillips curve is vertical. Hence, there is no trade-off in the longer run between growth and inflation. Consequently, there is now also a consensus that the primary macro-policy objective of a central bank should be price stability. Given the consensus on the objective, much current discussion has shifted to structural questions on how best to design the constitution of, and incentives for, the monetary authorities so as to induce them to focus on the achievement of price stability.

In part owing to the collapse of the stability of demand-for-money functions, there is also now a general acceptance that the monetary authorities' main instrument lies in their control of short-term interest rates, rather than monetary base control for example. Yet given the demise of monetary targetry, on what basis should the authorities set such interest rates? The option of pegging the exchange rate, and hence interest rates, to that of another (presumably more counter-inflationary) country has the disadvantage that, when the cycles in the centre and periphery are unsynchronised, the time path of the real interest rate in the peripheral country will become inappropriate. Except where there are supplementary advantages from exchange rate pegging, the best option would seem to be for the central bank to target inflation, or the growth of nominal income, directly. But the long and variable lags of the operation of monetary policy, and uncertainty about, and changes in, the structure of the economic system make that difficult. The authorities have to use a set of information variables, including the growth rate of the monetary aggregates themselves, as their (partial) guide.

An upsurge in inflation is quite likely to cause a worsening in inflationary expectations. This is, perhaps especially so in the case of asset prices; the links between asset price inflation and general inflation deserve careful consideration. Consequently, following such an upsurge, nominal interest rates need to be raised sharply, if there is to be an increase in real interest rates. But, once inflationary expectations are damped, that same level of nominal interest rates could imply a sharply rising level of real rates. Central bankers need to brave their innate caution and be prepared to vary nominal interest rates sharply, both up and down, over the cycle. But such interest rate volatility impinges primarily upon a relatively small portion of the economy, which may require structural reform in order to absorb such volatility.

With interest rates, the central bank's primary instrument, being predicated to the control of inflation (or of exchange rates), its primary objective, are there any secondary instruments that could be employed in the pursuit of secondary objectives, e.g. encouraging investment? Two such potential instruments are considered; the first is debt management, mainly in the form of over-, or under-funding, whose effect on the economy is assessed as rather weak; and the second is the application of prudential controls to macro-policy, cyclical objectives, which may pervert their primary prudential purpose and whose value in this role is contentious.

Indeed, unlike monetary macro-policy, where there is now a general consensus, the whole issue of the role of the central bank in prudential micro-policy supervision has become a matter of debate. There is no agreement, or common view, on the extent and nature of a central bank's appropriate responsibilities in this field, and which financial institutions, if any, the central bank should supervise. The costs of compliance, the moral hazard arising from (implicit) insurance, particularly the 'too big to fail' syndrome, regulatory failures (BCCI), are all deplored, but there is no agreement on a better way forward.

11 Advising the Bank of England (1992)*

'You are not here to tell me what to do. You are here to tell me why I have done what I have already decided to do.' Montagu Norman, the longest serving (1920–44) and most famous Governor of the Bank of England, is reputed to have greeted one of the first economic advisers to be appointed to the Bank with this memorable phrase. There was, and remains, some considerable truth in the claim that part of an economic adviser's job in any official body is to provide the best possible academic gloss to policy decisions which have been taken for a wide variety of other reasons, and in which decision-making process the economic adviser's role is often relatively small. In any case most immediate policy decisions are primarily determined by the interplay of the pressure of events with the ideologies and prior beliefs of those in power. Moreover, nobody in authority, certainly no politician, is likely to continue to accept advice happily from someone, however well qualified professionally, who openly reveals fundamental disagreements with such ideologies and priors.

Central banks and government ministries hire economists to suit themselves, and some part of any economist's role in government, or indeed in business, is, comparatively high-grade, PR. Yet one should not be too cynical. As Keynes, and many others, have noted, there is little as powerful as an idea whose time has come. Within Central Banks and economic ministries many of these key ideas are economic. Whereas it is often hard for an economist to point to his input into most individual current decisions, yet the economists in such an institution can, and should, act as a kind of filter, extracting emerging ideas from the academic world and packaging them effectively for internal consumption by non-economists, and, in reverse, seeking to appreciate the practical arguments of colleagues, in my case of Bank officials, and relaying these in proper, reasonably rigorous academic dress to one's academic colleagues.

The Bank had become, in the late 1950s and 1960s, worried that this second transfer, of the Bank's ideas to the academic world, needed further strenghtening. So, they instituted a scheme of relatively short-term (two year) secondments of academics specialising in money and banking into the Bank. Several economists, including Roger Alford who has just retired from LSE, had done this, before I was approached – partly through the good offices of

* London School of Economics and Political Science, in J. Mayall (ed.), *Annual Review* (1992): 14–17.

Professor Richard Sayers – to do so, on secondment from my position here as Lecturer (1966–8).

It was, however, a fortuitously good time to act as a filter for ideas. The new doctrine of Monetarism was spreading in from Milton Friedman in Chicago, and given some further impetus from Harry Johnson and Alan Walters during their years at LSE. The Bank became aware of the growing power and influence of such new ideas, but most senior officials, at any rate initially, found them hard to comprehend, and alien. My main job initially was to try to interpret Monetarism for the Bank, and to assess within the operational context of the Bank what its strengths and weaknesses might be. Much of the fruits of that appeared in the *Bank of England Quarterly Bulletin* article (1970) 'The Importance of Money', written under the supervision of Kit McMahon and Leslie Dicks-Mireaux.

One of the key conclusions of that paper was to reaffirm the empirical findings of those years that the demand for money in the UK appeared to be stably related to movements in nominal incomes and interest rates, thereby overturning the assertions of the Radcliffe Committee. This not only led towards acceptance of the view that 'the appropriate objective of monetary policy was control of the growth rate of the monetary aggregates, but also suggested that this could, and should, be done through the instrument of varying interest rates, thereby enabling the Bank to persuade a (reluctant) Treasury to get rid of the long persistent and constraining direct controls on bank lending. Hence Competition and Credit Control. It would be entirely wrong for me to take either the plaudits, or blame, for CCC, but I was part of the filtering process through which these ideas were transmuted into policy. If not me, then another, because the development and absorption of (academic) ideas into general (and official) acceptance is a (fascinating, but dimly understood) process, in which few individuals play any separately crucial role. But it was fun to be a part of that process, so by then I had transmuted my initial short-term secondment into a permanent position, which was to last seventeen years.

The debacle of CCC in the expansionary boom of 1972/3, pricked by the 1973 oil shock and the fringe bank crisis is well known. What went wrong? Our internal Bank view was that the main cause was that the commercial banks, during such a boom, were prepared – once given their competitive head – to bid up deposit rates to any levels necessary to fund the demand for lending, and that such loan demand proved much less sensitive to interest rates than we had hoped; (in partial exculpation it should be recalled that such lending had been constrained by direct controls previously, so we had little empirical experience to go on). We had failed to predict the extent of both these forces. We were impelled, by a dictate from above, to revert rather shamefacedly to some form of direct control, and the particular design of the 'Corset' control, (part of whose function was simultaneously to control growth of bank lending and broad money while obfuscating the reality that it was such a direct control, and virtually a reimposition of the old ceilings), was one of the exercises in which I did play a large role.

We were, however, told by the Monetarists that this debacle was the fault of an analytical and operational error. We were, in the Bank, trying to control money, and credit, by varying interest rates. The Monetarists argued that this was a faulty mechanism; instead we should seek to apply a quantitative control over the high-powered-monetary base. This, however, was a subject on which the operational experience of the Bank conflicted head-on with these academic ideas. Academics tended to believe both that the money stock was adjusted by injections, or withdrawals, of such base money, and that this was the correct process. Whereas Central Bankers knew that their own banking system was constructed on the basis of a system whereby banks could *always* get additional reserves at the interest rate set by the Bank. It would have caused mayhem to change the system. This was a major analytical battlefield in the 1970s, and particularly in the early 1980s, where my role, enthusiastically undertaken, was to try to make the academics understand the arguments of the Bank. Perhaps the finest hour in this battle was the publication of the Green Paper on 'Monetary Control', Cmnd 7858 (March 1980), a joint Treasury/Bank working paper, which came out against a switch to Monetary Base Control (MBC), despite the exercise having been set up by the incoming Conservative government which had strong ideological leanings towards Monetarism in all its manifestations.

I have concentrated on the key role of the economist as a filter for the exchange of ideas between the academic and the operational worlds. I certainly believe that that is our main function in such an advisory role, and that it is more than, though it can, at times, degenerate into, high-grade PR.

This is not, perhaps, the main role seen by many outsiders, who focus instead on the economist's role in forecasting. Once upon a time, there were indeed many who believed not only that the combined availability of relatively good economic data series with sufficient computing power to chew these over would enable us to learn enough about the workings of the economy to forecast the (short-term) future with some degree of accuracy, but also that we could advise on the setting of the levers of economic management well enough to achieve an *optimal* outcome, conditional on the social preferences of our political masters. Those hopes have been largely exploded both by bitter experience and by more advanced analytical reasoning (the Lucas critique). It remains, of course, necessary to attempt to construct a systematic picture of what the future might hold (on a policy unchanged basis), but a continuing difficulty for economists is to persuade their operational masters of the uncertainties and large margins of error involved in a forecast involving row upon row of seemingly accurate numbers. The danger is that non-economists tend to veer from placing exaggerated reliance on such forecast numbers, to the opposite of believing that all forecasts are worthless, when they inevitably go awry. Perhaps all senior officials and politicians should be forced to attend a training course on 'The Use and Mis-Use of Forecasts'. A measure of economists' loss of confidence in their forecasting abilities is that back in the 1960s and 1970s we used to reckon that our econometric equations for variables like investment, consumption, etc. could outpredict expectational surveys; no longer!

Such a forecasting function, therefore, plays a (deservedly) rather minor role in the life of most economists in the Bank (or Treasury). Instead, the key role is to participate in the development, transfer and assimilation of economic ideas. In this exercise the economist in the Bank is doing much the same as the economist in academe. But it has to be said that working conditions in the Bank are far better than in higher education. There is much more money for (often) less work; the availability of support staff is much greater; and the burden of administration has become *far* greater in academic life than in an organization like the Bank. So, why did I come back? As I enter my third year as Convener of the Economics Department facing umpteen requests to fill up forms, applications to the ESRC, personal references, promotion forms, help construct innumerable codes of conduct, try to assess teaching and research outputs, etc., I sometimes wonder.

12 The Operational Role of the Bank of England (1985)*

12.1 THE POLICY FRAMEWORK

Every morning at 11 o'clock in the Bank, senior officials meet with the Governor. By long tradition, the meeting opens with reports on conditions in the three major markets in which the Bank operates: the money market, the gilt market, and the foreign exchange market. Of course, nowadays information on current developments in such markets can be, and is, disseminated electronically, but the meeting provides opportunity to give supplementary information, for example on the underlying strength of market movements and their perceived causes, and to discuss future contingency plans. The precedence given to the reports of the market operators does, however, effectively symbolise the central importance in the Bank's activities of its role as market operator for the Government in these crucial financial markets.

The objectives, which the Bank's market operators are seeking to achieve, are not decided by the Bank itself, but form a component part of the Government's overall economic strategy. These strategic decisions on the policies to be adopted condition the direction and nature of the Bank's market operations, and also the relative weight that may be placed on market operations as compared with more direct intervention and controls on financial activities.

For example, prior to 1971 and the introduction of Competition and Credit Control, credit expansion, especially bank lending, was primarily constrained by direct controls (i.e. ceilings) rather than by interest rates affecting the cost of credit; and, until 1979, the freedom of UK residents to transfer funds abroad was limited by exchange controls. Such direct controls over banks were also administered by the Bank, until they were abolished in 1979–80.

Since 1976 the main feature of the policy framework, within which the Bank's operations are undertaken, has been the adoption of monetary targets. The first paper in this series, by David Savage in September 1984, provided a short history of subsequent experience with such targets. This experience, as Savage records, was not entirely successful, particularly in the earlier years. A major cause of these difficulties, as David Llewellyn records in the third paper in the series entitled 'The difficult concept of money', has been that structural changes and innovations have tended to

* The Economic Review (May 1985): 23–7.

'change the assets which can legitimately be included in any particular category, and this in turn will change the relationship between that category of "money" and the level of spending'; so, 'it is universally agreed that there is no constant or predictable relationship between any single definition of money and national income or inflation in the short run'.

Indeed, the UK's monetary system is currently in a transitional phase during which it is subject to rapid structural changes. These changes are likely to continue for several years yet, under the influence of developments that will alter the role of the building societies *vis-à-vis* the banks (as indicated in the recent Green Paper on building societies) and also change the inter-relationships between banks and the capital market. Under these circumstances you might well ask why the authorities persist with monetary targets. In practice, however, the authorities apply such targets reasonably pragmatically, and try to take account of the effects of these structural changes and innovations on, for example, the changing relationships between nominal incomes and monetary developments.

Moreover, this question raises the wider topic of the proper balance between the adoption of rules of monetary conduct and allowing the authorities to exercise their untrammelled discretion. Over the greater part of the Bank's history, its conduct of monetary policy has been constrained by the need to maintain sterling at a fixed rate against an external standard, for example the gold standard in the nineteenth century. This represented a form of monetary rule. When the Bretton Woods system, involving us in pegging the pound against the US dollar, broke down in 1971–72, the subsequent experience persuaded many central banks of the case for the adoption of an alternative rule to place some limits on domestic monetary expansion.

Although the issue of rules versus discretion is a lively and fascinating topic, involving a range of considerations that extend beyond pure economic analysis, it is outside the scope of this article. The subject has, however, been recently discussed by the Governor in a lecture published in the *Bank of England Quarterly Bulletin* (December 1984). Instead, the purpose of this paper is to describe how the Bank actually operates within the context of the overall economic strategy adopted by the Government of the day.

12.2   THE FOREIGN EXCHANGE MARKET

It is, perhaps, in the foreign exchange market that the decisive influence of the chosen policy regime on the role of the Bank's market operators is most immediately obvious. The crucial importance of the decision whether to maintain a pegged exchange rate or to float, more or less cleanly (i.e. with more or less intervention by the Bank's operators in the foreign exchange market), for the conduct and transmission mechanism of monetary policy has been described by David Laidler in the fourth paper in this series, 'Monetary policy in an open economy', notably in Section 5. In those periods when the Government has determined that the value of the domestic currency, the pound sterling, should be maintained at a fixed rate against an external standard (as it was during the Gold Standard; and again under the Bretton Woods system from 1945 to 1972; and as it would be again if we were to join the Exchange Rate Mechanism (ERM) of the European Monetary System (EMS)), the foreign exchange operators in the Bank would have to be ready at all times to intervene in this market in order to maintain such a commitment. The priority then given to this commitment would make the assessment of current market developments in the foreign exchange market, and of the choice of appropriate reaction by the Bank to exchange rate fluctuations, of prime concern.

Even when there is no such external peg and the currency is 'floating', as it has been since 1972, the exchange rate representing such an important variable, certainly for a small open economy such as the UK, that its movements are regarded as an important factor in the overall assessment of financial conditions. Also it still remains possible for the authorities, even when 'floating', to intervene more, or less, in the foreign exchange market, in order to offset undesired market developments or to reinforce desired developments. In recent years, however, such intervention has been increasingly limited, partly because of doubts as to whether the authorities have any superior ability to foresee appropriate equilibrium values and sustainable trends in the foreign exchange market, and partly because of doubts as to whether intervention would, by itself, be effective anyhow, particularly in a world where the volume of potential capital flows between currencies has become so much larger than the authorities' effective reserves.

This latter consideration means that the authorities, when facing pressure on an exchange-rate commitment, would be quite rapidly required to adjust interest rates in order to maintain the peg. If so, the authorities could not then simultaneously vary interest rates in order to seek to influence the path of domestic monetary aggregates, which is their objective under the present policy regime. This illustrates the dictum that one cannot, at least in the long run, simultaneously achieve two objectives with the use of only one instrument.

12.3   THE MONEY MARKET

There are two major questions in relation to the Bank's money market operations that deserve discussion. the first is what influence the operators in the Bank have upon money market interest rates (this is quite separate from the issue of what objectives determine *the use* of this influence). The second is how far these operators should concentrate their influence upon the *quantity* of cash in the system (leaving interest rates free), rather than directly upon interest rates.

To analyse the Bank's influence over short-term interest rates, we must first establish the 'mechanics' of the present arrangements which were put in place in 1981. Each day, large amounts of cash flow from government (which banks at the Bank) to others (who use commercial banks), and vice versa. (What follows is a simplified summary of what actually happens. Full details are given in the March 1982 *Bank of England Quarterly Bulletin*, pp. 86–94.) At the end of the day, the clearing banks (including the Bank) settle their net differences with each other. Then, if Barclays customers are found to have made payments that day worth 500 million pounds in favour of the Government but have received payments from Government totalling only 400 million pounds, the difference is settled by a debit of 100 million pounds from Barclays account at the Bank. During the day, each clearing bank therefore keeps a running forecast of its likely cash position; it also maintains operational balances at the Bank to meet any necessary debit at the end of the day. These balances yield no interest. Each bank consequently has an incentive to monitor its cash position closely, so as to minimise the amount it needs to hold at the Bank. No amount of effort will enable the bank to dispense with all balances, however, because it will inevitably be unaware of many of the payments made or received by its customers until these payments appear in the clearing.

When the arrangements were put in place in 1981, it was the Bank's intention broadly 'to offset daily cash flows between the Bank and the money markets' and to abandon the previous technique 'of creating initial shortages in the money markets which the Bank then acts to relieve'. The Bank's operation aim was 'to keep very short-term interest rates within an unpublished band which would be determined by the authorities with a view to the achievement of their monetary objectives'. (The quotations in this paragraph all come from a Notice on 'Methods of monetary control' issued by the Bank on 24 November 1980, and reproduced in the Bank's *Quarterly Bulletin* for December 1980).

In practice, a variety of factors, but particularly the heavy sales of government debt described below in the section on the gilt-edged market, have caused regular and substantial daily shortages of cash in the banking system. To the individual banks this translates into a prospective shortage in the day larger than it can safely meet from its balances at the Bank. Then, the bank will drawn upon a portfolio of very liquid assets, either calling back deposits placed with others – notably the discount market – or selling assets such as bills. This action may solve an *individual* bank's problem, but only because the shortage has been passed on. Consequently, under present arrangements, the Bank stands prepared to receive offers from discount houses to sell (Treasury, local authority or eligible bank) bills when it looks as though the system as a whole will be short of cash. The terms on which the Bank will operate, by buying assets or lending money, constitutes the prime 'mechanical' source of the Bank's ability to influence short-term interest rates.

The way in which open-market operations by the Bank have a 'mechanical' influence upon short-term interest rates can be seen by assuming that the Bank provides cash to the system by buying three-month bills. In this situation the supply of cash has been increased relative to the demand, affecting the interest rates for very short-term money, while the demand for three-month bills has been augmented (by the Bank) relative to the supply, affecting this rate too. But, more apparently, the Bank's actions are likely to be read as having policy implications and, as such, will be one of the influences affecting market expectations about the future course of interest rates, expectations which in practice are a key determinant of the level and relative pattern of all short-term interest rates.

The frequent and substantial shortages of cash in the banking system have meant that the 1981 arrangements have not operated quite as intended. The cash flows between the Bank and the money markets have been offset, but only by the Bank being a regular and heavy buyer of bills. As a result, the Bank's influence on interest rates has, at times, been both visible and substantial; but there are strict limits to how far the Bank can influence interest rates contrary to the market's expectations. Thus, suppose that monetary growth appears to be rising quite rapidly, but that the authorities are reluctant to let interest rates rise (perhaps because they think that the growth in money is purely temporary). Then, the Bank could conduct open-market operations on terms which made it clear that it wished short-term interest rates to remain unchanged. But if the market became increasingly pessimistic about the outlook for interest rates, this policy would become increasingly difficult to sustain. More and more short-term assets would be offered for sale to the authorities and, especially if the market judged that the Government's policy was likely to lead to higher inflation, the value of sterling and of long-term bonds would tend to fall sharply. All this would set up additional tensions and potential arbitrage possibilities that would put extra pressure on the Bank to adjust.

Suppose now, to turn to the second question posed at the beginning of this section, the Bank sought to concentrate its influence on the *quantity* of cash rather than on short-term interest rates. The 'mechanical' background would be much as before. As now, the amount and direction of cash flows through the financial system each day would remain somewhat unpredictable. At the same time the banks would not only have to hold sufficient cash reserves to maintain the convertibility of their deposits into cash, but also continue to wish to reduce their surplus holdings to a minimum, in order to economise on their holdings of such costly (because non-interest-bearing) assets. This combination of unpredictably fluctuating cash flows with a strictly limited, but strictly necessary, demand for cash, makes it difficult to envisage how the Bank could manage to control more closely than it currently does the actual total of cash in the system on a day-to-day operating basis. Nevertheless, one could envisage changes in the operational

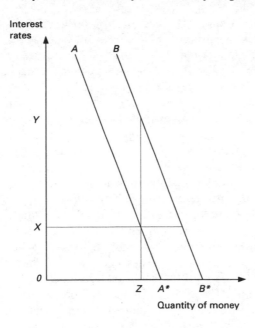

Figure 12.1   The banks' demand for cash

methods that would enable the Bank to place more emphasis in its operations on the (cumulative) developing cash position, thereby leaving the determination of interest rates more to the free play of market forces.

So long as interest rates are broadly pegged by the authorities, say at level X in Figure 12.1, then shifts in the demand for money (and also for credit, since an increased demand for credit will encourage banks to bid more aggressively for deposits), say from *AA** to *BB**, will be passively accommodated by the Central Bank. The proponents of a change to Monetary Base Control (MBC) argue that not only will money then vary pro-cyclically during those intervals in which the interest rate is held pegged, but also that the 'political' difficulties of consciously and overtly taking steps to raise interest rates mean that there is a bias for delay. The defenders of the present system would argue that not only is the adequacy of existing interest-rate levels, in the light of current and prospective experience in achieving the monetary targets, under continuous detailed review, but also that the role already given in the present UK system for market forces to put pressure on the authorities represents an effective antidote to the 'bias for delay'.

In turn, those who doubt the advantages of moving further towards MBC emphasise the inelasticity, at least under the present system, of the demand for cash. If, then, the volume of cash was held fixed at Z, when there was a change in demand for cash from *AA** to *BB**, the level of interest rates would jump from X to Y. The adoption of MBC might, therefore, be expected to result in much more volatile interest rates, as did, indeed, appear to occur in the USA after the shift in the operating procedure of the Federal Reserve system in October 1979. Proponents of such a change to MBC would argue, however, that not only did the Federal Reserve system fail to adopt MBC properly, so that experiment was flawed, but that the system would adjust to MBC in such a way as would moderate the resulting interest-rate volatility. In any case, they would argue, such additional volatility of interest rates as might occur would be a relatively small price to pay for achieving greater monetary control.

One of the main problems facing the authorities in trying to achieve monetary control is the apparently sluggish response of the demand both for money and credit to interest rates. This raises the question of whether one is trying to control the monetary aggregates via operating on the *demand* for money and credit or, more directly, via trying to control the supply of money and credit through restricting the monetary base. Either way, the interest rate would have to rise until the demand and supply are brought into equality. If the response is highly inelastic in the short run, and slow and uncertain in the longer run, control will inevitably prove difficult, and is liable to involve sharply fluctuating interest rates.

12.4 THE GILT MARKET

In practice, the authorities have not felt able to rely solely on their influence over interest rates to provide a sufficiently satisfactory means of achieving their domestic monetary objectives. In addition, they have sought to vary their funding operations in the gilt-edged market as a supporting instrument for achieving monetary control.

Perhaps because of the massive accumulation of debt during the two world wars, there has been a lengthy history of using debt management in the UK, not just to fund fiscal deficits but also for monetary purposes. The conversion of war debt in 1932, and the attempt by Chancellor Dalton to drive down long-term interest rates immediately after the Second World War, are two such earlier examples. Throughout the 1950s and 1960s a paramount consideration of the operators in the gilt-edged market in the Bank was to keep gilt-edged debt sufficiently attractive to the investing public, in order to prevent such debt becoming monetised on redemption. Thereafter, since the mid-1970s, the monetary task of the debt managers in the Bank has been sharpened further by the assumption of a large part of the obligation to restrain the rate of broad monetary growth.

Thus, when bank lending to the private sector has been growing at a faster rate than is consistent with achievement for the target of £M3, the Bank, besides seeking to raise interest rates to levels that in the medium to longer term should serve to restrain bank lending to a more moderate rate, has sought in some degree to offset the immediate impact on the monetary aggregates by overfunding, that is by selling more public sector debt to the non-bank private sector than would be necessary solely for the purpose of financing the public sector borrowing requirement. Such open market sales have the effect of reducing both bank deposits and banks' cash equally. Whereas the reduction in bank deposits is the intended purpose of the exercise, the Bank's operators in the money markets then have to find ways of offsetting the cash squeeze on the banking system; otherwise there would be a massive shortage and interest rates would rise sharply in the scramble for cash.

In passing, it is worth noting that the particular history and circumstances of the UK have given the Bank an operating role in the gilt-edged market. This is a feature that is not shared in many other European and North American Central Banks, where the Treasury or Finance Ministry typically undertakes its own debt management. One result of the British approach is a closer interrelationship between interest rate and debt management policies.

12.5   THE VIEW FROM THE BANK

The main function of the Bank is to operate in these three key financial markets. Due to the nature of these markets, and in particular the slow, uncertain and inelastic response of the demand for money and credit to variations in interest rates, the Bank's operators do not attempt to achieve a predetermined change in the outstanding amount of monetary base, nor of any other monetary aggregate, on a day-to-day basis. Thus phrases such as David Laidler's 'We assume that the monetary authorities can, and do, control the stock of money', and the analysis of Monetary Base Control, as faithfully reported by Mike Artis, appear other-worldly and 'academic' to a central banker. Instead we see ourselves as operating within an uncertain market context, fitfully illuminated by unreliable forecasts of other influences on monetray growth, to influence the level and pattern of interest rates and the volume of debt sales in such a way to help to achieve the Government's monetary objectives – since 1976 publicly announced monetary targets.

Among such other influences on monetary growth, two are particularly important in the present context: the fiscal deficit and the volume of bank lending to the private sector. A third influence – external monetary flows – would become more important if the authorities were intervening more extensively in the foreign exchange market. These relationships are described at greater length by Mike Artis in his section on 'The dominant approach'.

The market operations of the Bank and the fiscal actions of the Treasury are coordinated within the ambit of the overall policy strategy of the Government, as currently exemplified by the medium-term financial strategy

(MTFS), in the context of various forecasting and policy review rounds, each with differing horizons. Thus, against the background of the Treasury's economic forecast (the National Income Forecast, or NIF), which has the longest horizon, the Government decides on its fiscal policy changes. The NIF incorporates complete Flow of Funds forecasts, albeit in a somewhat judgmental manner, which suggest how each sector may finance its forecast financial surplus/delicit. The forecasts for such sectoral financial surpluses and deficits, together with projections for the level and structure of interest rates, provide a (rather unsure) basis for forecasting future bank lending. As described by Professor Artis in his earlier paper on 'Monetary control in the United Kingdom' (1984), it is then possible to use the counterparts approach (also requiring an assumption about external monetary flows since these will not necessarily be zero even under a free float) to estimate the volume of net public-sector debt sales required to meet the monetary target for £M 3 incorporated in the MTFS. The calculated size of such sales, relative to the capacity of the gilt market, then serves as an overall check on the consistency and coordination of fiscal and monetary policy.

The second forecasting round, with a much shorter horizon, occurs monthly. In this round, the recent developments of the monetary aggregates are reviewed and examined, and attempts are made to predict their development over the next few months. Over the shorter horizon, fiscal developments are taken as effectively predetermined, but the exercise provides an occasion for reviewing, and considering changes in, short-term interest rates and funding policy.

Finally, and with the shortest horizon of all, every morning at 11 o'clock the senior officials of the Bank gather together with the Governor to consider the course of market operations during that working day . . . which is where we began!

13 Money Supply Control: Base or Interest Rates? (1995)*

13.1 ANALYTICAL ANTECEDENTS TO THE COURSE OF THE MONEY SUPPLY CONTROL DEBATE

Commercial bankers have traditionally seen themselves as playing a passive role in the money supply process. Bankers argued that, in general, they only lent out money that had first been deposited with them. There were two major flaws in this argument. First, the loan made on the basis of cash initially deposited generally led to the funds being redeposited in another bank. Creation of deposits was restrained by the banks' need to keep reserves in the form of specie and/or Central Bank notes and deposits, in order to maintain the convertibility of their own liabilities into cash. Thus *assuming* a constant desired reserve/deposit ratio (D/R), the initial injection of one unit of reserves into the banking system would, if there were no subsequent drains of such cash reserves from the system, lead to an ultimate multiple increase in deposits of D/R, in reserves of 1, and in other bank assets (e.g. loans) of $D/R - 1$.

Second, a banker could choose to behave in a more, or less, aggressive fashion, in particular by altering the bank's reserve/liquidity ratio. Many banking cycles and panics of the last two centuries have been ascribed to cycles of optimistic over-lending, followed by liquidity crises with bank runs, and subsequent retrenchment.

People use cash as well as commercial bank liabilities as money. Central Banks in virtually all countries came to monopolise the provision of bank notes. Where this is not so (e.g. Scotland and Hong Kong) both the conditions of note issue and seigniorage are controlled by the monetary authorities. An expansion of the money supply leads to some increase in the non-bank public's demand for cash, a reduction in reserves, and further attenuation of the money multiplier. These factors are formalised in the famous monetary multiplier:

$$M = \frac{H(1 + C/D)}{(C/D + R/D)} \tag{1}$$

* In K. Hoover and S. Sheffrin (eds), *Monetarism and the Methodology of Economics* (Edward Elgar, 1995).

where M is the money stock, H high-powered money (reserves and currency), C is currency in the hand of the public, and D is commercial-bank deposits.

If there are differing kinds of deposits, or financial intermediaries with differing reserve ratios, the multiplier formula can become complex and messy. Moreover, the cash drain is *not* the only drain of reserves from the banking system. In a monetary expansion, reserves may drain abroad, at least in an open economy with a fixed exchange rate. Similarly, if the monetary expansion leads the non-bank private sector to buy government debt or to incur higher taxes, cash will be transferred to the Government. Such drains of cash reduce the high-powered money (H), available to the private sector.

Equation (1), is an identity, which must hold at all times.[1] One cannot quarrel with an identity. Analytical differences arise when we, first, ascribe a direction of causation to an identity which, of itself, implies no presumption of causation; and, second, when we attempt to imbed such an identity into a choice-theoretic analysis in which banks, the non-bank public, and the monetary authorities try to maximise their utilities subject to market constraints.

In particular, in earlier descriptions of the money multiplier process, the banking system and the non-bank public react to an exogenous change in high-powered money (H), which, in turn, drives changes in M. The influence of the banks and of the non-bank public appears limited to their choices of desired R/D and C/D ratios. But what happens if, for example, the public's demand for bank loans rises? There are two sides to a commercial bank's balance sheet; why should the interest rate that equilibrates the money market, with the money supply equal to money demand, also equilibrate the demand for credit, bringing the demand and supply of loan into equilibrium?

Is it correct, in current institutional circumstances, to treat H as exogenously given? If not, then causation may run from M to H. If so, what determines M? What part, irrespective of the exogeneity of M, or H, do the behaviourial decisions of the banks and non-bank public play in this? And what are the adjustments that ensure that the assets and liabilities of banks are both at their desired levels, and that, simultaneously, the balance sheet identity is respected.

To start these questions, it may be helpful to give a shortened, simplified reprise of the historical regimes of money supply determination during that last 150 years.

13.2   AN HISTORICAL REPRISE

Under a specie standard, the monetary base consists primarily of the available stock of monetary gold or silver, (ignoring distinctions between a full metallic standard, an exchange standard, a 'limping' standard, etc.). The Central

Bank under a specie standard aims to maintain convertibility of local money into specie according to 'the rules of the game' (see Bloomfield, 1959). These were simple: the Central Bank should raise interest rates, when the Proportion of metallic reserve to its own notes and deposits was falling, and vice versa. (For an account of the importance attached by the Bank of England to 'the Proportion' as a key indicator, see Beach, 1935; Goodhart 1972; Dutton 1984; Pippenger 1984).

Because of its strong and privileged position as the government's bank, the Central Bank was the last available source of liquid funds when other potential lenders were seeking to conserve their liquidity in a crisis. Following Bagehot (*Lombard Street*, 1873), the Central Bank also came to accept a duty for maintaining the stability of the banking system, determining to whom it would lend and on what terms.

Under the gold standard the causal relationships between H and M could be complex. There could be exogenous shocks in H driving M. There could be shocks to M, (eg a reduction in the R/D ratio), affecting H inversely, and/or shocks to M, which, eg via changes in the Central Bank's interest rate, could bring about a positive change in H. Either way, the influence of the Central Bank on H was indirect: a Central Bank, under such a metallic standard, cannot create gold (or silver), but it can attract reserves by using its open market operations to adjust relative interest rates. Indeed, a central concern of Central Banks under the gold standard was to ensure their effective power to control interest rates (Sayers, 1936).

A further objective of the Central Bank was to help finance the government on acceptable, but non-inflationary, terms. During the decades of low government expenditures before World War I this objective was not much of a burden. During the World Wars and the immediate post-war years government finance became an over-riding concern for virtually all European countries, though much less so for the USA.

The government financing identity implies that the growth of high-powered money depends on the size of the borrowing requirement (i.e. fiscal policy) and the extent to which this can be funded without recourse to the 'printing press', (i.e. funding policy). Facing *massive* government deficits, the Central Bank can hardly 'control' H. Rather, it adjusts interest rates and otherwise attempts to encourage the non-bank public to hold public sector debt directly in order to limit excessive growth in the monetary base and the money stock. In so far as the non-bank public did not absorb sufficient public sector debt, the banking system would provide residual finance. Central Banks tried to ensure that bank funding of the public sector did not lead to excessive build-up of bank liquidity, and multiple expansion of loans and deposits. Central Banks then used direct controls: first, banks were required to hold a large proportion of their assets in government paper; second, direct controls were placed on bank lending to the private sector, so banks had no alternative but to use excess funds to purchase government paper.

In so far as credit controls then effectively constrained bank lending, interest rates were largely influenced by three considerations: first, the need to keep longer term rates high enough to encourage public-sector debt sales to the non-bank public; second, to keep short-term interest rates high enough to maintain the exchange rate; third, to keep interest rates low in order to finance the government deficit cheaply.

There was no attempt under *such* circumstances to vary interest rates as a means of influencing either the demand for money, or the demand for bank loans. Nor, despite the money multiplier identity, would it be sensible to describe that system as one of monetary base control. Instead, the three main credit counterparts to a monetary expansion, the budget deficit, public sector debt funding and bank lending to the private sector, were each influenced by specific policies, fiscal policy, funding policy and credit control.

The subsequent abandonment of direct credit controls threw greater weight on the use of interest rates to control monetary expansion. At this stage it might have been possible, *in theory,* to have moved towards a true system of monetary base control, in which the authorities control the amount of available banks reserves, letting the market determine the level of interest rates. As we shall see, with a few possible exceptions, no Central Bank did so in practice. Instead, they sought to control the level of interest rates in order to affect the rate of monetary expansion indirectly.

As already noted, commercial banks were largely force-fed public sector debt during major wars and their immediate aftermaths. They, therefore, entered the 1950s with an 'excessive' holding of such debt. With the combination of low real interest rates, active funding policies and the relaxation of credit control then leading to the demand for money growing slower than private sector demand for credit, the banks ran down their portfolio of such Treasury bills and bonds to meet the excess loan demand, at the level of interest rates determined by the authorities.

This asset management mechanism could last only so long as the banks were prepared to allow their holdings of public sector debt to decline as a proportion of total assets. Once their holdings were reduced to the level where they were positively desired for their liquidity attributes, this buffering mechanism became exhausted. Commercial banks, starting in the USA in the mid–1960s, then turned to managed liabilities (i.e. to wholesale money market instruments, such as CDs and euro-deposits), to finance any excess of desired lending over the available inflow of retail deposits.

So long as monetary control was focussed on a narrow aggregate like M1, consisting primarily of retail deposits with pegged own interest rates, (e.g. pegged at zero for demand deposits (current accounts)), liability management initially caused no additional control problems. Interest rates on alternative assets, including wholesale bank liabilities, could be raised by the Central Bank causing substitution out of retail deposits, and thereby allowing the growth of M1 to be reined back.

A combination of worsening inflation in the 1970s, deregulation and enchanced competition led to market-related interest rates being offered on an increasing range of retail deposit instruments. This led to major shifts in liquid asset holdings both within and between the somewhat arbitrary definitions of the various monetary aggregates. This poses a serious problem for monetary control using interest rates. The key variable within the demand function for money is no longer just r_{st} (the general level of short-term interest rates that the authorities can control); it is now $r_{st} - r_{bd}$ (the differential between the general level and the rates offered by banks on their various deposit liabilities). The authorities *cannot* control that differential. So long as there is sufficiently strong demand for bank loans by the private sector, the banks will go on bidding for funds to meet that demand. Consequently, the Central Bank must now use interest rates either directly to reduce the demand for loans, or indirectly to reduce nominal incomes and *hence* the demand for both loans and deposits, if it is to limit the rate of monetary expansion.

Both these routes are fraught with uncertainty. The demand for loans appears to be, in the UK at least, highly inelastic to changes in the general level of interest rates, perhaps because most such loans are on a variable rather a fixed rated basis. Instead, such demand appears to be more responsive to interest rate differentials; but, once again, the Central Bank cannot control these in a regime of liability management. Furthermore, if nominal incomes are the ultimate target, and the monetary aggregates an *intermediate* target, it seems a cack-handed method to control monetary aggregates via the effect of interest rates on nominal incomes. Why not just concentrate on the interest rate/nominal income nexus?

13.3 PROBLEMS OF INTEREST RATE MANAGEMENT

The use of interest rates as the main mechanism of monetary control, therefore, entails several serious problems. First, as noted above, while the Central Bank can control the general level of interest rates, it cannot control *differentials,* between rates on deposits and rates on other assets/liabilities, notably the loan/deposit spread (Miller and Sprenkle, 1980; Cuthbertson, 1993; Chowdhury *et al.,* 1989). Furthermore, variable mortgage/deposit rates reduce inter-temporal substitution effects and enhance income effects on borrowers/depositors. Under a variable rate system, it is less important to time the moment of making the loan or deposit correctly; conversely the change in the interest rates will affect the cash flow of a larger number of agents and may, therefore, make interest rate adjustments more politically sensitive.

Second, lags between changes in interest rates and in the response either of monetary or of wider economic variables are long and variable. In so far as substitution effects act more quickly than income effects on general expenditures, a variable rate system may lengthen the lag between the change in interest rates and its observed effect on the economy.

Why such lags exist is uncertain. McCallum (1985, pp. 583–4) notes that 'past values of interest rates should not have *any* direct effect on asset demands. That is because interest rates (or other prices) prevailing in the past would seem to fall clearly in the category of bygones – and the irrelevance of bygones is of course one of the most fundamental principles of monetary economics'. There may be several reasons why such lagged effects nevertheless appear. McCallum suggests possible mis-specification, e.g. of the demand for money function. Another reason, already noted above, is that the indirect, income effects of interest rate changes may be the more powerful.

A more likely explanation is, perhaps, that during a boom, prices, and expectations of future inflation may be revised upwards. Confidence in future real profits, incomes, employment, etc. will be increasing. Against that background some increase in *nominal* interest rates is necessary just to hold correctly calculated real interest rates constant.

If nominal interest rates are raised far enough to halt the boom, price expectations and confidence will become dented, and a given nominal level of interest rates may have an increasing real effect. Without having any clear measure either of expectations, or confidence, and of what expectations and whose confidence is most important, we cannot measure 'real' interest rates accurately, and changes in nominal interest rates may then appear to have long and variable lags. Nevertheless, all this leads to great uncertainty. The impact effect of interest rates is generally found to be low on real expenditures and asset demand. The long-run effect is now widely believed to be considerable and important, (whereas this was doubted in the 1950s and 1960s), but it is not clearly quantified.

Such uncertainty has caused political hesitation in using this instrument expeditiously and vigorously. Increases in interest rates cause immediate dismay to large segments of the population, e.g. recent house-buyers on variable rate mortgages, small businessmen reliant on bank credit, etc. It is, therefore, politically unpopular. Against such patent unpopularity, the economist or Central Banker cannot state with any confidence how any level of interest rates will affect the monetary aggregates or the economy over any particular period. So, action tends to be deferred until the need is more clearly discerned with the natural result that interest rates are varied 'too little, too late'.

13.4 THE DEBATE INTENSIFIES

The consequence of 'too little, too late' was that the monetary aggregates have generally varied procyclically. With stagflation in the 1970s, governments became increasingly disillusioned with discretionary demand management. Following the example of West Germany in 1975, most developed countries then adopted monetary aggregate targets.

Targets were, of course, predicated on the belief that econometric estimates of the relationship between the targeted monetary variable and nominal incomes would remain stable. The intermediate target would then give an early indication of where nominal incomes were heading; and the deviation of actual money growth from its target might provide a quicker, clearer signal for counter-cyclical policy.

But this just transferred the problem of the uncertainty about the effect of interest rates on the economy as a whole to their effect on the monetary target. Monetarists argued that the uncertainties involved were so great that interest rate control mechanisms could never work effectively (e.g. Friedman, 1980). Moreover, they demonstrated in the 1970s that many countries failed to hit their targets using such control mechanisms.

In particular, the adoption of monetary targets in the USA from 1975 did *not* reduce monetary growth by mid 1979. In the early years, the target base was allowed to drift continuously. More fundamentally, the Fed chose to vary the Federal Funds rate, its key instrument, only in discrete steps of 25 basis points (see Lindsey, 1986, Figure 5.1; Friedman 1982). This, of course, internalised 'too little, too late'.

With the economic crisis of 1979, the Fed accepted some of these criticisms and changed its control regime. On 6 October 1979, Chairman Volcker introduced the non-borrowed reserved base system. Its name suggests a move towards monetary base control; but, in practice, features such as lagged reserve requirements, and an administered discount rate meant that it was more a quasi-automatic mechanism for forcing quicker and larger adjustments in interest rates whenever actual M1 growth deviated from desired growth.

Non-borrowed reserve control introduced volatility in interest rates 4 or 5 times as great as under the previous regime (see Walsh, 1982, 1984). Moreover, the average level of interest rates (1980–2) was much higher. Such high and volatile interest rates, however, succeeded in reducing monetary growth, inflation, and nominal incomes.

But it was bumpy ride. Short-term volatility in monetary growth increased to the highest level for any three years during the post-war period (M. Friedman, 1984). Some argued (e.g. Mascaro and Meltzer, 1983) that volatility in money growth increased the volatility of short and long-term interest rates, strengthened their positive correlation, and altered the relationship between M1 (which went on growing rapidly in 1982) and nominal incomes (whose growth rate declined sharply).

A 'purer' method of monetary base control, they argued, would allow more predictable and steadier growth of the monetary aggregates. The debate in the USA focused on whether alternative versions of monetary base control could improve monetary control. All sides agreed that the pre-1979 regime had led to 'too little, too late'.

In the UK in 1971 financial deregulation, part of the Competition and
Credit Control reform, led to a surge in bank lending and broad money
(£M3). Unlike M1, £M3 did not seem to respond much to (politically acceptable) increases in interest rates. Rates were nonetheless raised to 13 per
cent in 1973, but no one could be confident what further increase might be
required to halt the expansion. In the event the authorities reverted to a
revised form of credit control, 'the corset', which, in effect, penalised banks
which used liability management to fund additional lending. (On these episodes, see Bank of England, *Development and Operation of Monetary Policy,
1960–83*, esp. Chapters 2 and 6). The 'corset', a downturn in the economy
(1974/75), and an external sterling crisis in 1976, which brought in the
IMF, restrained monetary growth until 1978. Sterling M3 and inflation had
both begun to accelerate ominously again before the Conservatives were
returned to power in May 1979. As they had pledged, the Conservatives
abolished exchange controls (an adjunct to direct credit controls; needed to
avoid external disintermediation) in October 1979, and the 'corset' in June
1980.

Without the 'corset' how was the new Government to achieve control
over £M3, the centrepiece of its Medium Term Financial Strategy?[2] The
experience of 1971–3 did not augur well for control by interest rate variation. Several influential advisers of the incoming Conservative government,
notably Griffiths and Pepper, were Monetarist by inclination (Griffiths and
Wood, 1981), and favoured adoption of some form of Monetary Base Control. Pepper was then Editor of Greenwells' Monetary Bulletin, an influential monthly survey of monetary matters, published by a City firm. He wrote
several issues, advocating a switch to monetary base control in January and
February 1977, and March and July 1979.

The Bank of England opposed monetary base control. Foot, Goodhart and
Hotson outlined the major arguments against monetary base control, in a
Bank of England Quarterly Bulletin article in June 1979. The Bank was
supported by much of the City, and also most, predominantly Keynesian,
economists in the UK. Caught between the proposals of its own academic
advisers and its preference for a rule-based approach, leaving interest rate
determination to market forces, on the one hand, and the opposition of the
Bank and most of the City on the other hand, the Government asked for an
internal study, a Green Paper on 'Monetary Control', which appeared in
March 1980, Cmnd 7858 (H M Treasury and Bank of England).

13.5   ELEMENTS IN THE DEBATE

It is difficult to isolate the main elements in the monetary base control debate in an uncontroversial manner, partly because there are several variants
of monetary base control mechanisms.

One variant uses movements in the monetary base as an indicator guiding subsequent discretionary adjustments in interest rates, or by a rule (e.g. if the base deviates by X per cent vary interest rates Y per cent). No attempt is made to control movements in the base directly. The Deutsche Bundesbank (1980, 1985, 1987; also see Dudler, 1980a, 1980b, 1984) viewed its Central Bank Money target in this light. The evidence is more mixed on the operating procedures of the Swiss National Bank: Rich and Schiltknecht (1980) reads as implying pure monetary base control, but Rich and Beguelin (1985) and Kohli and Rich (1986) suggest a monetary base indicator system. After abandoning broad money targets in 1985, the UK government targeted the monetary base (MO); but, unlike the Germans and Swiss, the British government did not take the path of their base money targets seriously as a guide to interest rate adjustment. In all such circumstances there is no change in the control mechanism, which continues to use discretionary adjustments in interest rates. As indicator mechanisms, targets for Central Bank Money or MO are no different than intermediate targets for M1 or M3 or any other M. Here, however, we wish to concentrate on monetary base *control* proposals, not monetary base indicator (target) systems.

A preliminary issue involved is the connection between monetary base control mechanisms and the reserve requirement system. Most countries calculate reserve requirements using data on the deposit base over some *past* period. Such lagged reserve requirements were usually introduced for prudential reasons. But lagged reserved requirements present a severe hurdle for monetary base control. Since the deposits on which the reserve requirements are based are history, the banks cannot possibly reduce the amount of reserves that legally they must hold. Consequently the authorities must either connive at banks missing their requirements or provide the needed bank reserves at a price of their own choosing. The latter amounts once again to a discretionary choice of interest rates by the authorities.

The Green Paper on *Monetary Control* (1980) in the UK emphasised the difficulties of adopting any system of *mandatory*[3] base control (pp. 10–11, 23–26). Henceforward I focus mainly on a comparison of discretionary interest rate control with a *non-mandatory* monetary base control. Even with a non-mandatory system we must still consider problems of net shortages of reserves within the system that may force a commercial bank into borrowing from the Central Bank. The Bank in that case must decide what interest rate it would charge on such an overnight overdraft. We assume that the Central Bank charges a severely penal rate. We also assume that commercial banks cannot avoid incurring penal rates through the use of cosmetic accounting devices.

It is easier to analyse historical experience, than to judge what might occur hypothetically. Thus, the problems of using interest rates as a major instrument for monetary control, and the 'too little, too late' syndrome are generally understood. Furthermore, the actual time path of the C/D and R/D ratios is known. In the United States and West Germany, these ratios had generally been stable and predictable (Johannes and Rasche, 1979, 1981; Rasche and Johannes, 1987; Dewald and Lai, 1987; von Hagen, 1988). They have been less so in the UK and Australia (Capie and Wood, 1986; Macfarlane, 1984). Where the base is non-mandatory, the R/D ratio can, however, become more variable, weakening the link between changes in H and the targeted M, at least in the short run. Nevertheless, given the ability of the Central Bank to vary H in the short run, and sophisticated statistical techniques (e.g. Kalman filtering) for predicting the levels of the R/D and C/D ratios, their variability might not prove, if best practice is followed, a serious handicap to the adoption of monetary base control.

In the USA under the non-borrowed reserve system there was an increase in the short-run (quarter by quarter) volatility, both of monetary growth, and of short and *long-term* interest rates. Over the *medium term,* M1 was fairly well controlled; interest rates were on average much higher; and a strong deflationary shock was applied to the US (and World) economy. Was this vastly increased short-run volatility (1) the chance effect of a series of unconnected shocks (e.g. the imposition and removal of the Carter credit controls, financial innovation) (see, for example, Wenninger and Radecki, 1986); (2) the direct consequence of moving towards monetary base control, which might be further exacerbated by a 'purer' form of monetary base control, (i.e. in which total H, or total bank reserves, not just non-borrowed reserves, were strictly controlled); or (3) the consequence of failure to control total bank reserves, or H, sufficiently closely. These issues have never been convincingly resolved.

Five questions remain about how a system might operate under a (non-mandatory) monetary base control system.

What Would Happen to Interest Rates?

Within any system, to each equilibrium price corresponds an equilibrium quantity. To try to control monetary aggregates, the authorities had to accept large variations in interest rates. In 1979–81 they reached the limits of political tolerance. Would forcing monetary control upon a system, seemingly unresponsive to variations in the general level of interest rates, make interest rates even more volatile? If so, by how much?

How Might the Control Mechanism Itself Change?

In the UK opponents of monetary base control argued that monetary policy operated through interest rates. Consequently, they saw monetary base control just as a means of forcing more violent interest rate adjustments on the system. Proponents of monetary base control argued that, if banks knew in advance that additional reserves would not be made available or made available only at extremely penal interest rates, to accommodate an 'excessive' expansion, they would be less aggressive during boom times. Proponents saw the regime change as stabilising the behaviour pattern of the banks themselves.

Would Closer Control of H Deliver Closer Control of M?

Proponents of monetary base control pointed to the past predictability of the monetary base multiplier. Opponents attributed this stability of the R/D ratio to the confidence of banks that they could always obtain additional reserves at a predictable, non-penal, rate. A regime change that shattered this confidence might shift the level and increase the volatility of R/D. To a lesser extent, volatile interest rates and doubts about the convertibility of deposits into cash, might also shift the C/D ratio.

Would Monetary Control be Achieved Cosmetically?

A non-mandatory system would be less prone to disintermediation than certain other variants of mandatory monetary base control, e.g. forward reserve requirements (see Laurent, 1974; Kopecky and Laurent, 1984). Even so, a system which caused short-term volatility in interest rates might develop mechanisms for shifting financing flows between banks and non-bank intermediaries. In consequence, monetary growth rates might be stabilised while inducing greater variability in the relationship between money and nominal incomes. Proponents of monetary base control dismiss this possibility.

How Would the Structure and Stability of the Monetary System Change?

Opponents of monetary base control claim that the structure of the present system (e.g. the overdraft system, money market arrangements, bank desired asset portfolios) presumes that additional cash reserves will always be made available on reasonable terms, and that circumstances when interest rates are adjusted abruptly (e.g. foreign exchange crises) are few, widely understood, and often predictable (e.g. the ERM crisis in September 1992). Opponents claim that there could be severe transitional problems in a regime change. During the transition the banking system might be unstable and, even after the new system had settled down, it might be more fragile. Proponents claim that this is just scare-mongering.

Recall, however, that both proponents and opponents of monetary base control, more or less, agree that discretionary interest rate control is fallible and problematic. So, acceptance of some of the points made by opponents does not necessarily settle the argument.

13.6 THE DEBATE RECEDES

Quite remarkably, and unusually, there actually were *formal debates* over monetary base control in the UK and the USA. In the UK, the Green Paper on 'Monetary Control', prepared by Bank and Treasury (1980) officials, argued strongly against the adoption of any system of monetary base control. It concluded: 'Using the basic weapons of fiscal policy, gilt-edged funding and short term interest rates, the monetary authorities can achieve the first requisite of control of the money supply – control, say, over a year or more' (para. 1.9).

British proponents (e.g. Pepper, 1980) were neither convinced, nor impressed, by the analysis in the Green Paper. To see if any meeting of minds could be achieved, an official debate was held on 29 September 1980. As might have been expected, the protagonists stuck to their prejudices, and the event created more heat than light.

Nevertheless, the government had to reach a decision on whether to change the monetary control system. They decided *not* to do so, although many of those closely influential in reaching that decision (e.g. both Lawson and Walters) were sympathetic to the case for change. The prospective difficulty of steering the system clearly through the transitional period seemed to be the deciding factor: 'we in the UK have very little idea of the size of cash balances the banks would wish to hold if we were to move to a system of monetary base control' (Lawson, 1981); moreover the ratio of £M3 to base money was not stable or predictable, so there as 'little or no point in trying to use the monetary base control system to control £M3' (Walters, 1986, p. 123). These considerations, combined with opposition from the Bank of England, commercial bankers, and the City of London, persuaded the monetarists not to push more strongly for monetary base control.

In the USA, in addition to several conferences held on the monetary control regime (e.g. the American Enterprise Institute Conferences in February 1982 and February 1985; see *Journal of Money, Credit and Banking* 1982b, 1985), a formal debate was held on 30 April 1981, on the motion 'Is the Federal Reserve's Monetary Control Policy Misdirected?', with Rasche and Meltzer for the Affirmative, arguing for the adoption of a 'purer' form of monetary base control, and Sternlight and Axilrod for the Negative, for persisting with non borrowed reserve control (JMCB, 1982a).

In the event, the Fed's monetary control system was to be changed again, in the early Autumn of 1982, but away from, rather than towards, a purer monetary base control. The Fed adopted a 'borrowed reserve base' target, (see Wallich, 1984). Since borrowed reserves were largely a function of the differential between the Federal Funds rate and the discount rate (Goodfriend, 1983), the borrowed reserves target implied a reversion to targetting interest rates.

Among the reasons for abandoning non-borrowed reserve control were the LDC crisis and its potential implications for banking fragility in the USA, and the recession in nominal incomes. Inflation ceased to be enemy number one. But more important, the growth of M1 no longer behaved consistently with the time path of nominal incomes and interest rates.

In both the US and the UK in the early 1980s nominal incomes declined sharply, more or less as planned, while the intermediate monetary aggregates (£M3 and M1 respectively) continued to grow faster than targeted. Both countries unsuccessfully sought alternative monetary targets with more predictable characteristics, and by the mid-to late 1980s monetary targetry was effectively abandoned in most Anglo-Saxon countries, (see B. Friedman, 1988), though not in West Germany or Switzerland.

That effectively ended the monetary control debate. If the links between monetary aggregates and nominal incomes were loose and unstable, intermediate monetary targets seemed pointless. Whereas interest rates remained important, irrespective of the collapse of monetary targetry, because of their direct links with exchange rates, incomes and expenditures, the only function and purpose of the monetary base multiplier was to link movements in H and M.

Only sporadic calls are still made for a reconsideration of monetary base control. Central Banks have been left to run their traditional operational mechanism of discretionary adjustments in short-term interest rates. Although interest rate control remains subject to all the same technical problems noted earlier, economists now appear less concerned about such operational problems.

13.7   MAY THE DEBATE REVIVE?

In the absence of monetary targets the debate over monetary base control appears historical. But in an analytical sense the debate also mirrors a fundamental, continuing discussion about the process of money supply determination. Central Bankers, and their supporting economists, see the driving force of monetary expansion as deriving from the demand from the public and private sectors for *credit*. While narrow monetary growth remains best explained within the context of a demand for money function, broad money growth in this view is, in the short run, a consequence of the credit counterparts via liability management (and buffer stock adjustments). Again, on this view, the monetary base multiplier is a not particularly important identity.

All this remains anathema to many American monetary economists, (much less so to monetarists in other countries). To them the essential causal direction remains from the creation of base money by the Central Bank, via the multiplier, to the determination of M. They accept that, in practice, the discretionary choice of short-term interest rates by the Fed makes H an endogenous variable, but for analytical purposes they still tend to focus on its movements to help to explain changes in M.

NOTES

1. It can be obtained by a simple manipulation of the identities:

$$M = C + D$$
$$H = R + C$$

   which hold at all times. The equilibrium condition, however, is that:

   R/D (Actual) $= R/D$ (Desired)

   and

   C/D (Actual) $= C/D$ (Desired)

2. The advent of the Reagan government in the USA in 1980 had less of a cata-lytic effect on the debate there. This was partly due to Volcker having preempted and shaped the discussion by shifting to NBR in October 1979, and also partly to the constitutional separation of powers in the monetary policy field between the Fed and the Treasury.
3. Pepper 1990, esp. p. 61 (note 1), also prefers a non-mandatory system for its flexibility and lack of distortion in response to shifts between deposits with differing ratios.

14 Price Stability and Financial Fragility (1995)*

14.1 INTRODUCTION

If asked to provide a practical, quantitative definition of price stability, most people would offer something like a rate of increase in the RPI, or the GDP deflator, of 0–2 per cent. This is the kind of numerical objective which those Central Banks with a direct inflation target, e.g. New Zealand and Canada, are aiming to achieve. While I have great sympathy for such an approach, I want to start by arguing that the standard measures of inflation used in such targets may be incorrect, at least in principle. Such measures concentrate on current service flow prices, and ignore future service flow prices, changes in which are indicated by changing interest rates and asset prices. This thesis was cogently argued by Alchian and Klein in a paper in 1973; they put the case so well then, that I felt that I could do no better than repeat it. So, much of section 14.2 consists of selections from their earlier work.

Asset prices do move differently from current service flow prices. In recent years they have had a much more violent cycle of boom and bust. The focus on current service flow prices as the sole index of inflation has been one of the main reasons why monetary policy has been systematically mishandled in several countries, too lax 1988–90, too restrictive thereafter.

This asset price cycle has been closely related, with strong causal links operating in both directions, with a cycle in bank credit expansion, in broad money, bank profits and in banking (and financial) fragility. In section 14.3 I argue that one would normally expect to find a link between banking fragility and asset price deflation, though which sets of asset prices are most important for the banking system may vary over time. Consequently, occasions when the banking system needs support are likely to be periods of general (asset price) deflation, when the achievement of price stability

* In *Financial Stability in a Changing Environment*, Proceedings of the Bank of Japan Conference (28–29 October 1993) (Macmillan, 1995).

My thanks are due to Horst Bockelmann, Franco Bruni, Stan Fischer, Jerry Jordan, Mervyn King, Ian Macfarlane and Hiroo Taguchi for helpful comments; to Niral Maru for research assistance; and to the participants of the Bank of Japan Conference on 'Financial Stability in a Changing Environment' (28–29 October 1993) and of the Conference on 'Financial Stability', at the H.C. Coombs Center for Financial Studies, Sydney (31 October and 1 November 1993) for their many views and suggestions. I have not, however, always followed these in my revision, and responsibility for all remaining errors remains, as always, with me.

might anyhow indicate a more expansionary monetary policy. On this view there is no normal, or necessary, conflict between the two objectives. As noted in section 14.4, however, there *is* a conflict between the prudential regulations imposed by the authorities, e.g. the Basle capital adequacy ratios, and the macro-economic objectives of monetary policy, since the former will usually only bind during periods of deflation.

Be that as it may, the recent period of asset price deflation has been accompanied by an upsurge in actual, or potential, bank failures over a wide range of countries. Central Banks, in these circumstances, have pursued their traditional policies of lender of last resort and arranging rescues. I note in section 14.4 that most classical monetary economists oppose such activities; they would limit LOLR lending strictly to cases of illiquidity, and would instead use general market measure to sustain a steady expansion of certain monetary aggregates. But in my view it is both safer and more efficient to nip contagious panics in the bud by such Central Bank rescues.

I end this section with a brief glance at the use of 'narrow' banks and deposit insurance as a way of preventing systemic panics. I am doubtful about both, as a remedy against contagious failure. However, the allocation of responsibility for (limited) deposit insurance to 'home' monetary authorities, as contrasted with 'host' banking supervisors, might help to prevent multi-national banks flying under flags of convenience. In Appendix A we discuss international cooperation and coordination among Central Banks in dealing with cases of distress in multi-national banks. Most large banks now have branches or subsidiaries in several countries outside their domestic base. Section 14.5 draws some conclusions.

14.2 'ON A CORRECT MEASURE OF INFLATION'

It is remarkable that, at a juncture when so much of macro and monetary economics has been recast in terms of dynamic *inter-temporal* utility maximisation (e.g. Sargent, 1987), that the same has rarely been done for the analysis of price inflation.[1] This is so despite a cogently argued plea for this to be done in an excellent, but rarely referenced, article, by Alchian and Klein, whose title I have taken above as the heading for this section, written some twenty years ago (*JMCB* February 1973). They note that the price indices that 'dominate popular and professional literature and analyses', e.g. the Bureau of Labour Statistics' Consumer Price Index and the Commerce Department's GNP deflator only measure 'current consumer service flow price inflation'. Such indices are 'inappropriate' for a broader assessment of inflation and 'result in significant errors in monetary research, theory, and policy', (quotes from pp. 173, 174, 186).

They start by noting that, 'For many situations we are interested in measuring the *money* cost of a fixed welfare or constant utility vector of goods as money prices change . . . However, as early as 1906, Irving Fisher (and others earlier, we conjecture) pointed out that an iso-utility vector included claims to future consumption'. They further refer to Fisher's (1911) comment that 'To base our index number [of purchasing power] for time contracts solely on services and immediately consumable goods would therefore be illogical' (p. 174).

They continue,

Assume, initially, that markets exist for every consumption service flow to be delivered at every moment of time. At any moment an individual is assumed to be constrained by a scalar W(wealth), which he allocates over claims to present and future consumption flows at present prices quoted on these markets. If at each (current and future) moment there are n consumption services, then

$$W_A \equiv \int_0^\infty \left[\sum_{i=1}^n q_A\,(i,t)\,p_A\,(i,t) \right] dt$$

where W_A is the individual's current nominal wealth, (i, t) is the current rental price of the ith consumption service for moment t (i.e., present prices include prices of present claims to future consumption) and $q_A\,(i, t)$ is the magnitude of the ith consumption service flow at moment t which at the current price vector and wealth level maximizes the individual's intertemporal utility. All of these values are described as given under condition A.

Let present flow prices, including present prices of future consumption services, change and describe this new state as condition B. The question we are asking is whether prices, measured by a constant-utility index, have risen or fallen. We can, in principle, compute at the new set of present prices, $[p_B\,(i, t)]$, the cost of an iso-utility consumption service vector, $[q_B\,(i, t)]$. If, for example, the new cost under price condition B, W_B, is greater than under the initial price condition A, we can say that the money cost of an iso-utility vector of goods has risen. The iso-utility price index implicit in this can be represented by

$$P_{AB} \equiv \frac{W_B}{W_A} \equiv \frac{\int_0^\infty \left[\sum_{i=1}^n q_B\,(i,t)\,p_B\,(i,t) \right] dt}{\int_0^\infty \left[\sum_{i=1}^n q_A\,(i,t)\,p_A\,(i,t) \right] dt}$$

where $q_B\,(i, t)$ represents the (i, t) element in the minimum cost consumption vector that yields the same condition A utility at the new condition B price vector. If P_{AB} is greater than one, the nominal money cost of condition A utility has increased; an inflation has occurred.

To emphasise the intertemporal nature of this price index and the fact that it does not refer solely to the cost of the current moment's consumption it could less misleadingly be called the current 'cost of life' index. Current instantaneous prices of current consumption flows enter this index, but insignificantly.

* * *

The major difficulty in making our index operational is that separate futures markets or contracts do not exist for all future consumption services. As a result, some futures prices required for a complete iso-utility price index will not be directly observable in explicit market prices. But since assets are sources of future services, asset prices provide clues to prices of present claims on future consumption. Current wealth can be represented by the sum of all asset values, or, equivalently, interpreted as the sum of all present valued claims to all consumption service flows over time. Symbolically, if there are m assets, wealth is denotable by

$$ W_A \equiv \sum_{j=1}^{M} P_A(j)\, Q_A(j) \equiv \int_0^\infty \left[\sum_{i=1}^{n} q_A\,(i,t)\, p_A\,(i,t) \right] dt $$

where W_A is the individual's current nominal wealth and $[Q_A\,(j)]$ is the current vector of asset quantities that would yield intertemporal utility – maximising consumption service stream, $[q_A\,(i, t)]$. If assets are standardised in terms of their present and future service flows, the current vector of asset prices, $[P_A\,(j)]$, can therefore be used as a proxy for current futures prices, $p_A\,(i, t)$.

When relative prices change, one can, in principle, determine the vector of assets, $[Q_B\,(j)]$, which will yield the minimum cost iso-utility consumption service stream $[q_B\,(i, t)]$ at the new set of asset prices $[P_B\,(j)]$ and implicit futures prices $p_B\,(i, t)$. Current asset prices can therefore be used to construct our constant welfare price index

$$ P_{AB} \equiv \frac{W_B}{W_A} \equiv \frac{\displaystyle\sum_{j=1}^{m} P_B\,(j)\, Q_B\,(j)}{\displaystyle\sum_{j=1}^{m} P_A\,(j)\, Q_A\,(j)} $$

where W_B is the nominal cost of the vector of assets that will yield a flow of present and future consumption services equal in utility to the initial condition A consumption service stream.

It is crucial to emphasize that the vectors $[Q_A(j)]$ and $[Q_B(j)]$ must include all assets-consumer and producer, durable and nondurable, tangible and intangible, financial and non financial, human and nonhuman. All sources of present and future consumption services must be considered. The vectors do not represent the actual assets held by the representative individual, but the asset combination that would yield the individual's desired consumption service flows. An individual may hold some assets that yield the exact pattern of consumption service flows that he demands over time, e.g. a house that yields his present and future desired housing service flow. But, more generally, due to transaction costs individuals will hold some assets not because they yield services that coincide with their consumption plans, but because they are an efficient form in which to hold wealth. The services from these assets or the assets themselves are later sold and exchanged for desired consumption services. Human capital is the most obvious example.

Since our asset price index is not constructed on the basis of assets actually owned by an individual we are therefore not measuring whether the individual is better or worse off after a change in prices, only whether he requires more or less money to reach the same utility level.

A money prices index based on considerations we have outlined is fundamentally different from the CPI, which is constructed on the basis of prices of *current* consumption services. The CPI considers the prices of only a part of the utility function and is therefore inadequate in principle as a constant utility money price measure. The CPI attempts to measure changes in the cost of only the iso-utility current consumption flows and therefore supplies an answer to a question distinct from whether the present money cost of consumer utility has changed.

Current service flow prices are related to asset prices by implicit real rates of interest and therefore our iso-utility price index is logically equivalent to an index based on current service flow prices and a broadly defined interest rate vector. If our representative individual moved to a new society where current service flow prices are identical but where real interest rates are higher, our iso-utility price index would fall. The individual would substitute future consumption for present consumption and his money cost of life would decrease (pp. 174–8).

Here we get to the crux of the matter. The first point is that, in a correctly defined price index, a higher real interest rate implies a *lower* price level, *ceteris paribus*. Although the treatment of housing in price indices still varies considerably from country to country, it remains the case that in some countries a higher (nominal) interest rate feeds through positively into measured current housing costs, and hence is associated with a *higher* calculated price level. Second, this analysis provides an academic basis for the view that asset price movements *should* be taken into account in any proper, overall assessment of price stability. If current consumer flow prices are steady, but equity, land and housing asset prices are plummeting, then price stability has *not* been achieved. I follow Alchian and Klein in believing that, *conceptually*, asset prices and real interest rates should enter into assessments of inflation.

One major problem is that there are massive *practical* difficulties in combining asset prices and current flow prices to construct an acceptable 'cost of life' index. We cannot observe their 'broadly defined interest rate vector'. Asset markets are notoriously incomplete. Even where asset markets operate, 'surprisingly little reliable information exists on current prices of assets and given the assumed importance of these prices in the transmission of monetary impulses, some effort in this direction would seem to be clearly economic. Collection of transaction price data on land, commercial and residential property, producer and consumer durables, and other tangible and financial assets and the construction of a crude quarterly wealth price index would probably be worthwhile' (p. 187), and they applaud proposals by Stigler (1981) and Snyder (1928) to move in that direction (n. 27).

Besides the considerable problems in obtaining the basic data, there are far greater difficulties in adjusting for *quality* changes than when a current flow price index is used. If an equity price rises, is this because of

(i) a change in the price of an unchanged future service flow from the asset, (ii) a shift in preferences for this asset's service relative to other assets, (iii) a shift in preferences for present consumption relative to future consumption, or (iv) a change in the anticipated magnitude of service flow from the asset. Any or all of these changes are likely to be occurring simultaneously and therefore the cause of a change in a particular asset price is difficult to determine. Changes (ii) and (iii) represent a shift in tastes while (iv) represents a change in asset quality; however, they are not conceptually different from the problems encountered in constructing the presently used indices (p. 188).

* * *

The empirical problems involved are enormous. But whatever efforts may be made in this direction and whatever the results, we believe it is an error to assign all of the change in common stock and other asset prices to changes in anticipated future service flows with no change in present prices of such future flows . . . which is what is implicitly done now in commonly used price indices that ignore asset prices (p. 189).

Next, there is a problem of perception. Inflation is treated not only as a measure of the change of the real current value of the monetary unit, but more generally as an index of the loss of welfare and purchasing power of someone with a given nominal income. This latter view may be associated with the fact that normally the expected flow of nominal income over a year is much larger than the initial inventory value of current consumer goods. Only if one is a producer does the rise in the price of one's product, relative to other products, become positively desirable. All this alters when we turn to asset prices. Many of us, especially the cohort aged 50–65 who usually dominate policy decisions, are relatively long on owned assets, equities, bonds, houses, land. An increase in housing prices, when I already own two, quite large houses, improves my own welfare. So I do *not* assess a change in housing prices in the same, uniformly hostile, light as I do current inflation.

Alchian and Klein ask

> But why, then, isn't there a demand for a price index that includes asset prices and why do movements in the CPI appear to be politically important? Within the context of our model it is difficult to find a rationale for the fact that rising consumer service flow prices are generally unpopular while falling asset prices are generally unpopular. The relevance of our intertemporal iso-utility index appears to be seriously questioned by common attitudes. One possible explanation may be that individuals fail to recognize that price changes of assets they do not own may significantly affect their money costs of life and their welfare. While individuals that, for example, own houses are aware of the decrease in their wealth when prices of houses fall, individuals that do not own houses do not appear to recognize that such a price change also affects them by lowering future housing service prices. Individuals are more fully aware of changes in their nominal wealth than of changes in the nominal cost of future consumption, possibly because an intertemporal consumption index is not now published (p. 186).

Such perceptions are economically important. It is arguable that a fall in the price of (financial) assets arising from an increase in the interest rate at which future, assumed unchanged, dividends are discounted should have a *positive* wealth effect. Those already holding such assets can look forward to an unchanged future service flow; those short of such assets can now obtain them more cheaply. In practice, however, we believe that the wealth effect of lower asset prices will be negative, whereas that of lower goods prices will be positive. King, in his Presidential address to the European Economic Association (1993), emphasises the asymmetric distributional effects of shifts of wealth between creditor and debtor households. Indeed, one of the curiosities of the 1987 stock market crash was why the anticipated negative wealth effect did not appear. Besides the fact that this was an occasion in which monetary policy was adjusted appropriately in the face of asset price movements, one reason that is often given for the resilience of consumer expenditures was the shift of equity holdings from individual investors to financial intermediaries, e.g. pension funds and insurance companies. When an asset is owned on my behalf by such an intermediary, or by the State, and the change in the present value of my future claims, consequent on the current asset price change, is uncertain and perhaps hard to calculate, my response is, perhaps, likely to be much more muted than when I am the immediate beneficial owner.

There are, therefore, many problems involved in constructing, or interpreting, an *intertemporal* price index. But the existence of such problems is not, of itself, a justification for concentrating solely on an objective which is expressed only in terms of current consumer flow prices, ignoring asset prices. The failure to take into account asset price changes will lead to misspecification and errors, both theoretically and in policy operation.

Thus Alchian and Klein note that

the use of the GNP deflator as the relevant price variable in the demand for money function remains theoretically unjustified. Money is used to purchase assets of varying durability and age. The demand for money therefore cannot be dependent solely on the prices of current output flows which represent only a part of what money can buy. Hence, within the context of a transactions demand framework or a wealth portfolio choice framework, the GNP deflator is incomplete and the purchasing power of money could be more meaningfully measured in terms of our more inclusive price of wealth index (p. 182).

But their greater concern was with resulting policy errors. In my view, this same syndrome has been repeated in recent years, *mutatis mutandis*; so I shall restate their conclusions incorporating my current amendments in square brackets.

Reliance on these biased numbers as an indicator or target of monetary policy makes it difficult for the monetary authorities to know what they are doing, let alone what they should be doing. And action on the basis of these numbers can lead to inappropriate decisions; policy changes will often come too late and move too far. Recent monetary policy provides an instructive example. The authorities' preoccupation with the movement of inappropriate flow prices indices to the almost complete exclusion of asset prices was partially responsible for a monetary policy that was too easy for too long a period (1967–68) [1988–9] and then a policy that was too tight for too long a period (1968–69) [1991–2] followed by a policy that was once again too easy (1979–early 1971) [1994?]. A crude modification of the CPI, with, say, an index of stock prices [housing and property] would have provided a much more useful indicator and target for price level stability (p. 185).

(Most of the comments and discussion at the two Conferences at which I presented this paper concentrated on this part of my presentation, the Alchian/Klein definition of inflation. Some argued that this was theoretically incorrect, though I was not convinced by their points. Others proposed that 'price stability' should imply certain constraints on the *expected future* time path for current consumer flow prices, e.g. that this should not be a trended, (I 1), series. While they agreed that movements in current consumer flow prices today might give an unsatisfactory impression of the expected future time path of such prices, they felt that movements in asset prices were far too noisy, and affected by quality changes, etc. to be used in any *formal* assessment of the expected future time path of current consumer flow prices. The practical difficulties of incorporating asset prices into a price index (e.g. their noisiness, the impossibility of adjusting for quality changes, the problems of providing associated inter-temporal quantity indices), were widely stressed. *None* of those present, who spoke, would have been happy to have an Alchian/Klein/Shibuya index used as the *main* measure of inflation. Some would be interested to see such an index regularly calculated to see if it would have any significant (lead) relationship with more conventional price indices; others felt that such an index could be dangerously misleading.

By contrast, however, almost all the participants did agree that movements in asset prices often could contain valuable leading information on potential future goods price changes, since asset prices were comparatively flexible whereas prices of current goods and services exhibited inertia. In the longer run, asset and goods prices should be cointegrated, so a marked deviation in asset prices could be expected to be followed *either* by a resultant shift in goods prices (as in the early 1970s), *or* a reversal of asset prices (as in the boom and bust cycle of 1988–92). Either result, following an asset price explosion, could cause problems to the monetary authorities. It was generally agreed that there was no mechanical method for taking account of asset price inflation, but that attention and care should be given to it, perhaps more so than in recent years, but that this would still have to be done in a broadly subjective and discretionary fashion.)

Another of the problems of taking asset prices into account for policy purposes is that the identity of the key asset market(s) that link monetary policy to the real economy appears to shift over time. Alchian and Klein give the equity market preeminence in their account of the 1969–71 cycle that they study. In a number of countries, Scandinavia, UK, Australia, USA?, the swings in housing and property prices were more important in the last cycle, 1988–93. In Japan, equity and land prices moved quite closely together (see Nakajima and Taguchi, 1993 and Shimizu, 1992). In the UK in

1979–85, the link between monetary developments and the exchange rate was probably the main transmission mechanism.

Such shifts in the importance (for monetary policy) of differing asset markets may, in part, reflect changing patterns of asset ownership (e.g. the rise in the importance of owner-occupation, the switch from personal to institutional ownership of equities). It will also reflect shifts in the importance of differing asset markets for bank (lending) business. The switch of bank loan portfolios away from lending to large corporations, whose credit rating and direct access to (wholesale) funds, e.g. via the commercial paper market, has become relatively stronger than that of the banks themselves in recent years, has been much remarked (e.g. Boyd and Gertler, 1993, also see Yoshino, 1993, for Japan). In their place banks have tended to substitute mortgage lending and loans to persons and small businesses, often collateralised by, or related to, housing, construction and property, see Nakajima and Taguchi, 1993. Black, de Meza and Jeffreys (1992) have noted that the main influence on the rate of start-up of new businesses in the UK has been the level of housing prices, in some large part presumably because this represents the main source of equity available as collateral for outside (bank) funding.

Thus it is possible that housing/property prices have become relatively more important, and equity prices less so, in relation to bank loan business, both as an influence on the demand for loans, as collateral for such loans, and as a factor determining the rate of bad debts. It would be nice to have some direct measure of the proportion of loans which is housing/property related, or equity connected, but given the difficulty of obtaining data on what is used as collateral, inter alia, that would be difficult, and time consuming to do satisfactorily. See Yoshino (1993) and Shimizu (1992) for data on this for Japan.

Instead, what I have attempted is to explore whether the data can give us any indication of the relative, changing influence of housing/property and equity prices on bank lending to the private sector, in both the US and the UK. The data for the USA are annual, from 1919 to 1991, and for the UK annual from 1939 to 1991. The data set consists of a measure of bank lending to the private sector, and indices of prices (CPI), real output, stock market prices and the price of houses, and interest rates on Treasury Bills.[2] The most problematic series is the housing price index. Not only is this complicated by the heterogeneous characteristic of housing, and questions of quality changes, but also we failed to obtain a single consecutive index for the USA. Instead we spliced together data for prices of existing houses, (1919–47) and of new houses (1947–91); we were only partially comforted by finding that, in the period 1970–89 when these two series overlapped, the correlation between them in levels was 0.985, and in first differences 0.467.

We were forced to use a shorter data period for the UK, since 'In the inter-war there is as yet no detailed record of house prices, though the material with which to construct it may still exist in building societies' records'

(Holmans, 1990, p. 112). The index used here, from 1939 till 1991, is taken from the same source, (Holmans, 1990, pp. 113–14). In practice, however, owing to direct controls over both prices and bank lending, we generally omitted the years 1939–45, starting in 1946.[3]

All these series, with the exception of interest rates in the UK, which are also on the borderline in the USA, are trended, I1, series. Taking the US exercise first, we began by examining whether bank lending was cointegrated with prices (CPI) and real output.

The ADF value of the residuals was −4.60, compared with a 95 per cent critical value of −3.86. Next we ran the same regression in first difference form, with the result:

$$\text{dBLP} = 0.027 + 0.222 \text{ dOUT} + 1.077 \text{ dPRI}$$
$$\quad\quad (0.009) \quad (0.133) \quad\quad\quad (0.162)$$

With the coefficient on the percentage change in the price index being insignificantly different from unity, we took as our dependent variable, the real change in bank lending to the private sector, dRBLP. This was then regressed against the percentage changes in real output, stock prices and housing prices, plus current levels of interest rates, (trying this both in nominal and in real terms, i.e. after subtracting the current rate of CPI inflation), the residuals from the cointegrating equation, and with, and without, a lagged dependent variable.

The main problem, from an econometric point of view, with this equation, is that neither housing prices, nor the stock price index, nor some of the other variables, can be considered independent of the current annual change in bank lending. Our concern, however, was *not* to examine the determinants of bank lending, but to explore for indications of changing *two-way* relationships between bank lending and equity and housing prices.

Our basic equation, over the period, 1920–91, was as follows:

$$\text{dRBLP} = 0.008 + 0.095 \text{ dOUT} + 0.330 \text{ dPHS} + 0.122 \text{ dPEQ}$$
$$\quad\quad\quad (0.011) \quad (0.137) \quad\quad\quad (0.131) \quad\quad\quad (0.044)$$
$$\quad + \quad 0.002 \text{ RInt} \quad -0.000 \text{ ECM}$$
$$\quad\quad\quad (0.002) \quad\quad (-0.000)$$
$$R^2 = 0.22 \text{ DW } 1.27$$

The coefficients on the percentage change in the housing and equity indices were significant. However, there were clear signs of auto-correlation in the error term, with a low DW ratio for an equation in first differences. When a lagged dependent variable was introduced, the coefficient on dPHS fell sharply, and became insignificant, as follows:

$$\text{dRBLP} = \begin{array}{llll} -0.001 + & 0.140 \text{ dOUT} + & 0.112 \text{ dPHS} + & 0.136 \text{ dPEQ} \\ (0.010) & (0.123) & (0.119) & (0.038) \end{array}$$

$$+ \begin{array}{lll} 0.002 \text{ Int} + & -0.000 \text{ ECM} + & 0.496 \text{ dRBLP}_{t-1} \\ (0.002) & (-0.000) & (0.097) \end{array}$$

$$R^2 = 0.440 \text{ Lagrange multiplier test } 1.07$$

Our main interest, however, is whether this relationship has exhibited changes over time. For this purpose we reran both regressions over separate sub-periods, and did a rolling regression, starting with 1919–39, and extending the period by one year at a time. We chart the coefficients for dPHS and dPEQ from the second equation, i.e. with a lagged dependent variable, with their associated one standard deviation bands in Figures 14.1 and 14.2. The coefficients, and associated standard errors, from four selected different sub-periods are shown in Table 14.1 below.

These results suggest, somewhat tentatively, that the relationship between equity price movements and bank lending remained relatively important and stable over the early years of this period, but may have diminished in strength recently. By contrast the relationship between conditions in the housing market and in bank lending was comparatively strong in the inter-war period and in recent years, since 1979, but was weak in the intervening years, 1940–79. In any case there does seem some evidence, especially in the bank lending-housing nexus, of changing relationships over this, quite lengthy, data period.

When we turn next to the UK data, the strength of the relationships between bank lending and housing prices, over our shorter data period, appears generally stronger and more stable than in the USA. We found it, however, hard to obtain a cointegrating equation between bank lending in the UK and real output and CPI inflation. When housing prices were added as an additional regressor, it was clear that this was the dominant variable, with a *t* value of over 30. Indeed, with housing prices included, the coefficients on output and CPI inflation became negative. Even so, their inclusion 'improved' the cointegrating equation, though it remained pretty unsatisfactory and marginal; over the period 1939–91 the ADF was –4.36, (–4.32 being the 95 per cent critical value), over the period 1946–91 the ADF fell to –4.13, (compared with –4.36 at the 95 per cent critical value).

Unlike the USA, there was no evidence in the UK of an X per cent rise in the CPI being matched by a similar X per cent rise in bank lending to the private sector. Hence in our equations the per cent change in nominal bank lending is the dependent variable, and both the per cent change in the CPI and in nominal interest rates are entered separately as regressors. Otherwise the form of the equations (including lagged dependent variable) are the same as tested for the USA.

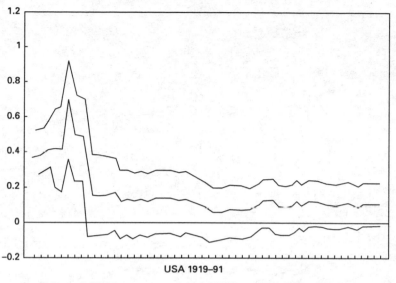

USA 1919–91

Coefficients of dPHS from a regression of dRBLP on dOUT, dPHS, dPEQ, REALINT
ECM, dRBLP(–1).

Figure 14.1   Effect of changes in housing prices on bank lending, USA, 1919–91

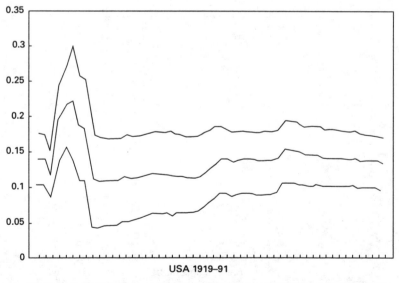

USA 1919–91

Coefficients of dPEQ from a regression of dRBLP on dOUT, dPHS, dPEQ, REALINT
ECM, dRBLP(–1).

Figure 14.2   Effect of changes in equity prices on bank lending, USA, 1919–91

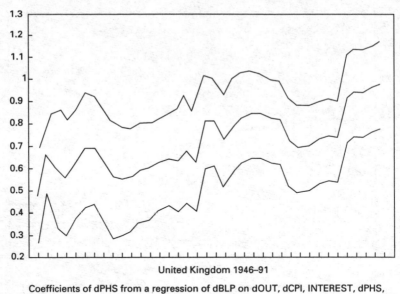

United Kingdom 1946–91

Coefficients of dPHS from a regression of dBLP on dOUT, dCPI, INTEREST, dPHS, dPEQ, ECM, dBLP(−1).

Figure 14.3   Effect of changes in housing prices on bank leading, UK, 1946–91

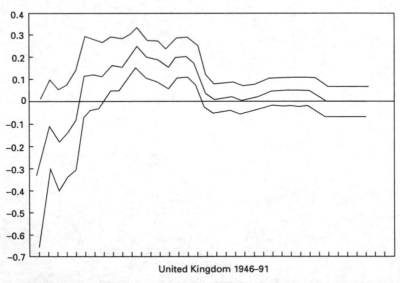

United Kingdom 1946–91

Coefficients of dPEQ from a regression of dBLP on dOUT, dCPI, INTEREST, dPHS, dPEQ, ECM, dBLP(−1).

Figure 14.4   Effect of changes in equity prices on bank lending, UK, 1946–91

Table 14.1   Determinants of bank lending

UNITED STATES 1919–1991
Regression of dRBLP on dOUT, dPHS, dPEQ, REALINT, ECM

Period	dPHS		dPEQ	
	Coeff.	t ratio	Coeff.	t ratio
1919–91	0.330	2.526	0.122	2.788
1919–1939	0.331	1.340	0.131	1.990
1939–1955	−0.096	−0.237	0.061	0.333
1955–1979	−0.181	−0.756	0.129	1.674
1979–1991	0.645	2.081	−0.087	−0.977

Regression of dRBLP on dOUT, dPHS, dPEQ, REALINT, ECM, dRBLP(−1)

Period	dPHS		dPEQ	
	Coeff.	t ratio	Coeff.	t ratio
1919–1991	0.112	0.940	0.136	3.634
1919–1939	0.378	3.046	0.139	4.086
1939–1955	−0.180	−0.355	1.003	0.432
1955–1979	−0.241	−1.040	0.143	1.935
1979–1991	0.552	1.707	−0.068	−0.739

UNITED KINGDOM 1946–1991
Regression of dBLP on dOUT, dCPI, INTEREST, dPHS, dPEQ, ECM, DBLP (−1).

Period	dPHS		dPEQ	
	Coeff.	t ratio	Coeff.	t ratio
1946–1991	0.966	5.016	−0.001	−0.012
1946–1963	0.550	2.144	0.116	0.685
1963–1979	1.200	4.423	−0.151	−2.370
1979–1991	1.428	1.544	−0.133	−0.220

The results are shown below:

$$dBLP = 0.058 - 0.872\ dOUT - 0.329\ dCPI$$
$$(0.037)\quad\ \ (0.693)\qquad\quad (0.409)$$

$$-0.02\ INT + 0.966\ dPHS - 0.001\ dPEQ - 0.000\ ECM + 0.205\ dB1P_{t-1}$$
$$(0.004)\qquad (0.193)\qquad\quad (0.058)\qquad\quad (0.000)\qquad\quad (0.141)$$

The coefficient on the per cent change in housing prices is highly signifi-cant, more so than in the US case, but the coefficient on the per cent change in the equity price is insignificant, and even negative.

Again we wanted to examine the stability over time of the relationships between asset prices and bank lending. Data for sub-periods are shown in Table 14.1, and the rolling regression, from the second equation, in Figure 14.3 and 14.4. These results suggest that housing prices have developed a stronger association with bank lending, since the immediate post-war period, whereas the relationship between movements in the equity index and bank lending has been weakening.

The tentative conclusion of this, broad-brush and rough, preliminary statistical exercise is that the nexus between housing prices and bank lending has been strengthening in recent decades, and forms the major link between asset prices and bank lending in the UK. By contrast, earlier stronger relationships between equity prices and bank lending, especially strong in the USA, appear to have weakened recently.

14.3 FINANCIAL FRAGILITY AND ASSET PRICE INSTABILITY

The relationship, in both directions, between the banking system and the real economy is primarily via asset prices. In Keynesian analysis the transmission mechanism from a monetary impulse to the real economy runs primarily through a specified, and limited, set of financial assets, short rates on Treasury bills, long rates on bonds, equity yields (Tobin's q) onto investment. Whereas monetarists deny the validity of such tight restrictions (Friedman and Meiselmen, 1964, e.g. p. 217), in their formulation also monetary impulses pass through to the real economy via a shift in the relativity of generalised asset prices *vis-a-vis* current flow prices (see Friedman and Schwartz, 1963, pp. 229–31; Alchian and Klein, 1973, p. 179).

In turn, movements in asset prices, as noted in the previous section, affect the demand for, and bad debts on, bank loans. In particular, bank crises and financial fragility are generally connected with the collapse of certain asset prices, rather than a fall of current consumer flow prices, (through, as will be discussed further, the two sets of prices are usually positively correlated). This is not invariably so. The LDC crisis in 1982, and the following years, was in some large part related to the fall in commodity export prices from those countries rather than any specific LDC asset prices.

Nevertheless we could look back to the gold standard period of the 19th century as a time when the general current price level was fairly firmly anchored by the exchange rate regime. This did not avert banking crises, and these were mainly related to, and triggered by, some asset price decline. Some documentation of this claim is given in Appendix B.

Asset price instability is generally associated with bank instability, with the causation running strongly and simultaneously in both directions. A bubble economy will normally be accompanied by a surge in bank lending, and perhaps to a lesser extent in broad money, on the upswing, and the collapse of the bubble will equally result in a welter of bad debts and a drastic slowing of credit and monetary expansion. We can think of recent occasions. This general type of analysis has been put forward by Fisher (1932), Kindleberger, Minsky, etc.

Wherein, however, lies the conflict, if any, between the pursuit of price stability and financial stability? One aspect of the recent property/financial cycle was that the authorities did not react quickly, or strongly, enough to

Table 14.2   Correlations between current flow and asset price series

	USA					
	Levels			*1st difference*		
	CPI	*HSN*	*EQ*	*CPI*	*HSN*	*EQ*
CPI						
HSN	0.993			0.436		
EQ	0.950	0.963		0.223	0.259	
	UK					
	Levels			*1st difference*		
	CPI	*HSN*	*EQ*	*CPI*	*HSN*	*EQ*
CPI						
HSN	0.958			0.103		
EQ	0.951	0.984		0.006	0.132	

the housing/property price surge in the latter years of the 1980s, because they did not factor it into their assessment of inflation, incorrectly as we have already argued. If asset prices had been taken into account in assessing potential inflation, monetary policy would have been less accommodative prior to 1990, and more expansionary recently. Such action would have helped not only to stabilise the banking system, but also to achieve greater price stability on an Alchian-Klein 'life cost' index basis.

If movements in asset prices, and in current consumer flow prices, were uncorrelated, or negatively correlated, then a recommendation to give some weight to the former, in interpreting the objective of 'price stability' would, perhaps, be more controversial. In practice, however, current consumer flow prices and asset prices have been positively correlated, though not strongly so, over the years.

In Table 14.2 the correlations between the levels and the per cent changes in the indices of current consumer flow prices (CPI in both the US and the UK), housing prices and equity prices, are reported for the USA and UK.

Next we examined the temporal, 'causal', structure of relationships between these three sets of asset prices by regressing the per cent changes of each price series on its own lags, and the lagged changes in the other two series; two lags were taken in each case. The results for the USA, in Table 14.3 below, indicated that CPI inflation was strongly autocorrelated, and Granger caused by housing inflation and, with a negative sign, by changes in equity prices lagged two years; this latter, however, was largely due to outliers in the early 1930s. Housing inflation was rather more mildly autocorrelated, and equity prices not significantly different from random walk.

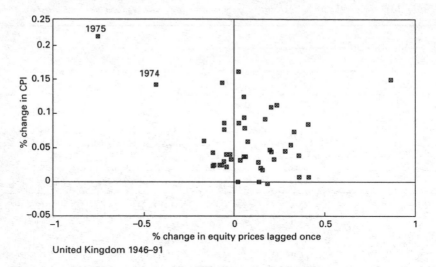

United Kingdom 1946–91

Figure 14.5   Relationship between the CPI and equity prices, UK, 1946–91

The results for the UK, over the shorter period 1946–91, are broadly similar. CPI inflation has been strongly autocorrelated, and Granger caused by housing price inflation. Again, as in the USA, there is a significant negative relationship between CPI inflation and prior changes in equity prices, and, once more, this is due to a couple of outliers, though in this case to high inflation rates in 1974 and 1975 following sharp reductions in equity prices in 1973 and 1974 respectively (see Figure 14.5). Housing inflation is also strongly autocorrelated, with some slight signs of Granger causality from CPI inflation; finally, equity prices show no indications either of autocorrelation, or of Granger causality from these other variables.

Overall, therefore, one would expect that bank failures, and prolonged periods of financial fragility, would take place during periods of disinflation, when the rate of change of asset prices was (sharply) declining, and with asset price levels perhaps even falling; and that the same would be true, though to a less marked extent, for current flow prices. This is difficult to test in the UK since, within the oligopolistic British system, bank failures have been so sporadic. It does, however, fit the case of the most serious post-war example of financial fragility in the UK rather well, to wit the secondary banking crisis in 1973/74. This occurred at a time when a surge in asset prices in equities, housing and property peaked and then sharply reversed, whereas the rate of inflation in current flow prices showed more inertia. This is shown in Figure 14.6 for 1971–6.

Table 14.3   Granger causality studies on consumer, housing and equity prices

	US		
Dependent variable	*dCPI*	*dPHS*	*dEQ*
t value on constant	0.57	2.20	1.08
dCPI - 1	8.12	1.44	−0.55
dCPI - 2	−3.15	−0.27	0.80
dPHS - 1	2.65	2.71	−1.37
dPHS - 2	2.61	1.30	1.96
dEQ - 1	0.19	1.08	1.46
dEQ - 2	−2.93	−1.59	−1.88
	UK		
Dependent variable	*dCPI*	*dPHS*	*dEQ*
t value on constant	1.99	1.71	2.16
dCPI - 1	4.26	−1.83	−0.53
dCPI - 2	2.26	2.14	1.74
dPHS - 1	4.75	5.82	−1.74
dPHS - 2	−3.70	−1.87	−0.37
dEQ - 1	−5.04	1.03	−1.69
dEQ - 2	−2.45	−1.25	−1.55

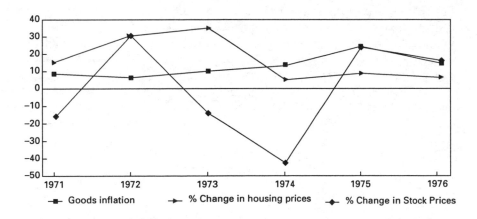

Figure 14.6   Annual changes in inflation, housing and equity prices, UK, 1971–6

Source: CSO, *Economic Trends*.

It is easier to examine the relationship between bank failures and inflation in the USA, where any tendency to oligopoly has been limited by branching restrictions.

Figure 14.7 shows the relationship between the per cent change in the rate of inflation, i.e. the second difference of prices, in the USA and the number of banks failures, as a per cent of the total number of banks. This indicates that bank failures tend to be more frequent when the rate of inflation is subsiding. This chart excludes the outlying years of 1930, 31, 32 and 33. They are off the scale. In two of these years the second difference of prices was positive, so if all years, including these outliers, were taken into account, the negative relationship shown in Figure 14.7 would disappear.

Figure 14.8 shows the relationship between bank failures and the per cent change, i.e. first difference, in housing prices. This has a somewhat less marked negative correlation of -0.30310. In this case, however, the relationship with the outlying four years was also negative. A regression of bank failures on the change in house prices, with and without the outliers, gave the following result (A without outliers, B with outliers):

A % Failures = 0.78 −0.043 dPHS
$\quad\quad\quad\quad\quad$ (0.14) (0.017)

$R^2 = 0.078$

B % Failures = 2.69 −0.275 dPHS
$\quad\quad\quad\quad\quad$ (0.49) (0.060)

$R^2 = 0.22$

Figure 14.9 shows the relationship between bank failures and the per cent change, first difference, in equity prices. The relationship, both with and without the four outlying years is far less close; indeed in similar equations to those above the coefficient on d*PEQ* is insignificant without outliers, and just significant with these years (Case B):

A % Failures = 0.46 + 0.006 dPEQ
$\quad\quad\quad\quad\quad$ (0.11) (0.006)

$R^2 = 0.004$

B % Failures = 1.52 −0.049 dPEQ
$\quad\quad\quad\quad\quad$ (0.043) (0.021)

$R^2 = 0.055$

In general, though not invariably, bank failures will be high when asset (especially housing and property) prices have peaked, and have started to decline, and when the rate of inflation of current flow prices is starting to decline. Wherein, therefore, lies any conflict between the achievement of price stability and the preservation of financial stability? Resisting the asset price boom in the upswing, and supporting the banking system in the downswing are both likely to assist price stability.

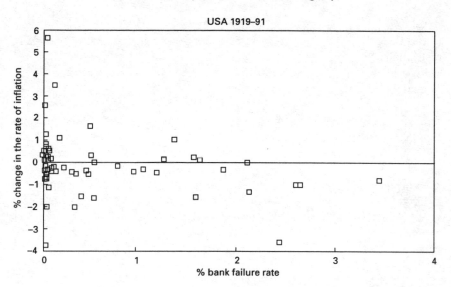

Figure 14.7   Relationship between bank failures and changes in the rate of inflation, USA, 1919–91

Source: Bureau of the Census, *Statistical Abstract of the United States.*
Not including observations on 1930, 1931, 1932, 1933.

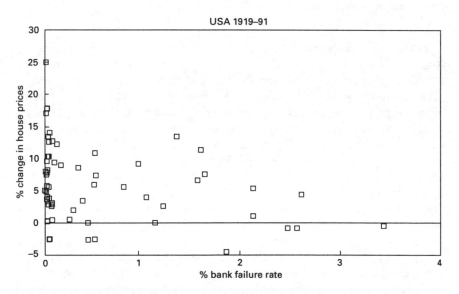

Figure 14.8   Relationship between bank failures and changes in house prices, USA, 1919–91

Source: Bureau of the Census, *Historical Statistics Colonial Times to 1957*; *Statistical Abstract of the United States.*
Not including observations on 1930, 1931, 1932, 1933.

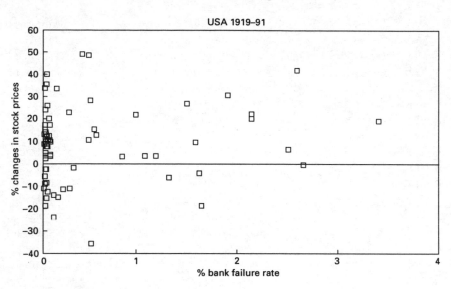

Figure 14.9 Relationship between bank failures and changes in equity prices, USA, 1919–91

Source: R.J. Shiller, *Market Volatility* (Cambridge, MA: MIT Press, 1989); Bureau of the Census, *Statistical Abstract of the United States*.
Not including observations on 1930, 1931, 1932, 1933.

There are, perhaps, two main junctures at which such conflict *may* arise. The first is that the increase(s) in interest rates necessary to puncture the inflationary surge (in current service flow and/or asset prices), or to achieve other macro-economic objectives, (e.g. adherence to an Exchange Rate Mechanism), may imperil the solvency of financial and banking firms, both directly and indirectly via the effect on asset prices more generally. If the monetary authorities were able to raise interest rates sufficiently *quickly* and vigorously, to avert the asset price bubble, in a perfect world such a potential conflict should rarely occur, since the bubbles would not be allowed to expand to dangerous dimensions in the first place. When it does, however, a Central Bank can not let itself be constrained by the threat of potential future financial fragility from taking appropriate action to achieve its macro-economic objectives. Otherwise it could be blackmailed into immobility by the threat of systemic financial dangers ahead. The eventual cyclical outcome, the boom and bust, would most likely be *worsened* by any such constraints on the freedom of Central Bank action.

A recent study of Central Banking in a game theoretic context, Cukierman (1992) has suggested (Chapter 7) that Central Banks are more likely to smooth interest rates, relative to the appropriate level for the achievement of price stability, when they are most concerned with the fragility of the banking system, i.e. when bank profits are low. When low profits herald problems with systemic stability, so he conjectures, Central Banks may refrain from raising interest rates sufficiently to offset inflationary shocks, and hence may have to restrain interest rate decreases more during downturns in order to regain counter-inflationary credibility. I sought to give a first-pass test of this hypothesis by examining the correlation between average bank profitability and the variance of inflation.

The data for the USA are taken from the Statistical Abstract, and cover the period 1919–91. The data from the UK, from the BBA, Annual Abstract of Banking Statistics, cover a shorter period, 1969–91; prior to 1969 both profits and capital were reported after undisclosed transfers to hidden reserves, and are generally regarded as potentially seriously biassed. In both cases, we compared the average ratio of bank profits to bank capital against the calculated standard deviation of inflation in non-overlapping windows of 5, 7 and 9 years for the USA, and five years for the shorter UK data period. The results for the UK, with only four data points, were indecipherable, but the results for the USA appear to be the reverse of that hypothesised by Cukierman (see Figures 14.10–14.13). Of course, all that this indicates is that the level of bank profits has not *by itself* been negatively correlated with the variance of inflation. If the variance of inflation was conditioned on a more complete set of variables, then the partial effect of bank profitability on the variance of inflation *might* be perceived to be negative.

An associated problem is that structural changes, e.g. deregulation, which may be desirable in themselves, may disturb the extent of competition, profit margins and risk assessment, and hence lead to financial fragility. Davis (1992, p. 216) notes that

> periods of financial instability, which may culminate in crises, are often preceded by changes in conditions for entry to financial markets. Such developments lead to heightened competition in the market concerned, whether due to actual new entry (tending to perfect competition), effects to potential new entry on the behaviour of incumbents (heightened contestability), competitive responses of incumbents to the threat of entry (strategic competition), or indeed 'managerial' growth maximisation. Such heightened competition may provoke reductions in prudential standards (which may be manifested in lower prices and higher quantities in credit markets, as well as declining capital ratios), especially in the absence of appropriate prudential supervision. This in turn can lead on to financial instability. In effect, the market may overshoot the level of competition which is sustainable in long-run competitive equilibrium, and various market imperfections and distortions (many of which are discussed in the existing literature on financial crisis) can be adduced to explain this.

The analysis of the causes of recent instability in banking systems around the world in Nakajima and Taguchi (1993) is closely similar.

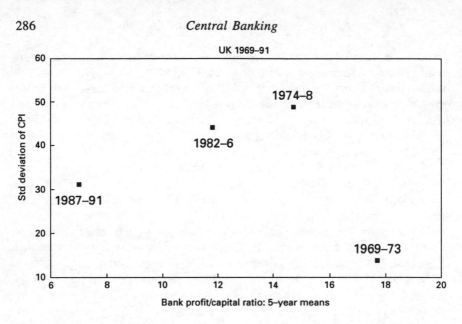

Figure 14.10   Bank profitability and the variance of inflation, UK, 1969–91, 4-year means

Source: British Bankers' Association, *Annual Abstract of Business Statistics*; CSO, *Economic Trends*.

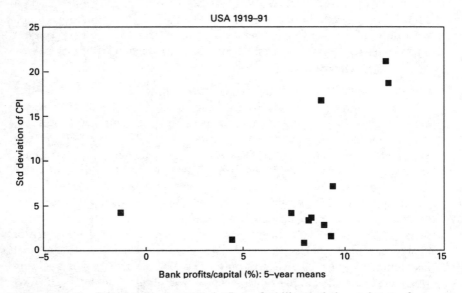

Figure 14.11   Relationship between bank profitability and the variance of inflation, USA, 1919–91, 5-year means

Source: Bureau of the Census, *Historical Statistics Colonial Times to 1957*; *Statistical Abstract*.

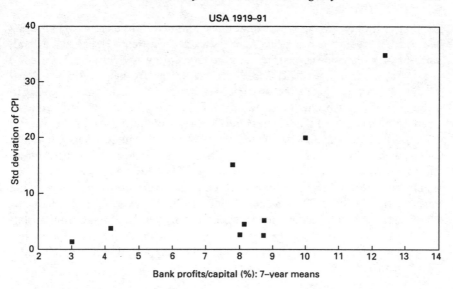

Figure 14.12   Relationship between bank profitability and the variance of inflation, USA, 1919–91, 7-year means

Source: Bureau of the Census, *Historical Statistics Colonial Times to 1957*; *Statistical Abstract*.

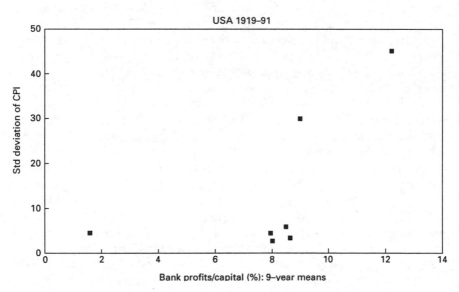

Figure 14.13   Relationship between bank profitability and the variance of inflation, USA, 1919–91, 9-year means

Source: Bureau of the Census, *Historical Statistics Colonial Times to 1957*; *Statistical Abstract*.

Be that as it may, I have argued that bank failures will generally occur *after* the asset price cycle has peaked and started to retreat. Hence once bank failures actually appear, restrictive monetary policy will usually have done the major part of its job. Hence, there should rarely be a serious macro-economic problem about the provision of support for a banking system in which serious, potentially systemic, bank failures are occurring. It is difficult to make a strong case that Central Bank rescues of failing banks, e.g. in the recent crises in Scandinavia, New England, etc., in the secondary banking crisis in the UK in 1973/74, etc. have had any significantly adverse effect on macro-economic, or price, stability. The more obvious cases of macroeconomic instability occurred when banks were *not* rescued, as in the case of the USA, 1907 (Goodhart, 1969), 1929–33, especially the Bank of United States, (Friedman and Schwartz, 1963, Chapter 7), or the Credit Anstalt (1931). Academic disputation has not focused so much on the need for *overall* support in such cases, but rather on how that support should be delivered. We turn to that next.

14.4   HOW TO SUPPORT A FRAGILE BANKING SYSTEM

There are two common nostrums among more classically-oriented monetary economists about bank rescues. The first is that Central Bank assistance ought only be given to commercial banks which are illiquid, but not insolvent. This has a heritage going back to Thornton and Bagehot, see Humphrey (1975) and Humphrey and Keleher (1984). The second is that systemic support should be provided by open market operations to the banking system as a whole, and not channelled via discount window, or other special lending facilities, to individual weak banks, (Goodfriend and King, 1988). On this view, the objective should be to keep the rate of growth of certain key quantitative monetary aggregates steady, and not the incidence and frequency of bank failures as such.

Neither nostrum is valid. The first is invalid, because (except in exceptional cases of technical difficulty, e.g. the Bank of New York computer failure), an illiquid bank will, almost always, be able to borrow additional liquid funds to meet a short-term liquidity problem from wholesale, (often inter-bank), money markets – at a rate cheaper than (unless such lending is specifically subsidised), and without the adverse reputational effects of, last resort lending – unless the market already suspects its solvency. A bank which cannot borrow from the money market to meet its liquidity needs is, almost by definition, a bank whose solvency is suspect in that market. Those suspicious may, of course, be more, or less, well-founded. Nevertheless many, perhaps most, rescues which start out, and will usually be presented as, temporary liquidity problems by the commercial bank in distress, will turn out to involve longer term solvency concerns. The two conditions are, given the present structure of (money) markets, closely inter-twined. A Central Bank will sometimes find itself faced with an ultimatum that bank X will close on the next working day, unless supported, and with next to no time to sort out the 'true' valuation and solvency position of the bank involved. Often it takes weeks, rather than days, to obtain a clear view of a distressed commercial bank's balance sheet, and time is not on the side of Central Bankers in such cases.

At this point the second nostrum comes to the fore. On this view, if Central Banks have *any* doubts about the solvency of the applicant bank, they should refuse assistance. If failures then take place, they should be offset by open market operations aimed at maintaining aggregate, macro-level stability by achieving a continuing, steady-state rate of growth of the monetary aggregates. While I understand the theoretical grounds for such an argument, I believe that it fails in practice. The reason is the Lucas critique. Any major failure, with adverse effects on depositors' wealth (we shall discuss deposit insurance later), which is widely publicised, is likely to change prior behaviour patterns. Normal ratios, of reserves, or currency, to deposits, of differing kinds of liquid asset to income (or wealth), normal risk premia, etc., are all likely to shift if a contagious panic takes hold. Recall how Kaldor (1983) criticised Friedman on the grounds that the rate of growth of base money *accelerated* during 1929–33. Although ex post there may, perhaps, turn out to be surviving stable relationships between certain monetary aggregates (and/or interest rates) and the economy during a severe panic, ex ante one must suspect that crises and panics will disturb and disrupt the prior pattern of statistical (econometric) relationships. Amidst a flurry of failing banks, screaming headlines in news stories, can anyone be confident that the monetary guideposts (weak as they have been) may not shift some considerable way further? How much easier then, how much less disruptive, how much more *efficient* to nip the panic in the bud, to prevent the contagion before it gets hold, by organising a rescue. And that is exactly what Central Bankers have traditionally done. The probability, and exact form, of the rescue, therefore, depends mainly on two factors, first the potential solvency gap to be filled as a consequence of the mismanagement or fraud of the previous bank management, and second the splash that would be made if that bank were to be allowed to fail. Bigger bank failures make larger waves; hence 'too big to fail'.

Such a typical Central Bank approach is widely condemned by the classical monetary economist as short-term, myopic and conducive to moral hazard. The high probability of depositor rescue means that depositors will not monitor bank safety, (through the ability of ordinary depositors to do so has always been doubtful), so that high risk banks will continue to be able to attract depositor funding (e.g. by offering slightly higher interest rates, as BCCI did). In such circumstances bank managers will be tempted to adopt higher-risk strategies, especially where their capital is already impaired. The analysis is well known and valid. In addition, the too-big-to-fail syndrome is either inequitable, in that it gives a competitive edge to larger banks, especially when, and if, small banks are perceived to fail: or alternatively, if competitive equity is to be retained, leads to the complete rescue of all banks.

A partial solution to both problems has been provided by the American proposal enacted in the FDICIA (1991), which come into effect in 1993, for a graduated response to an erosion of capital ratios. Benston (1993) describes these as, 'capital requirements with structured early intervention and resolution (SEIR) rules', also see Benston and Kaufman (1988) and Shadow Financial Regulatory Committee Statement 41 (1992). Outside the USA, such SEIRs are in the process of being adopted by New Zealand (Dale and RBNZ, Financial Regulation Report, June 1993). One of the main problems with any ratio procedure, whether it is a reserve ratio or capital ratio, *à la* Basle, is what to do if a bank fails to meet its ratio. An on/off trigger ratio, whereby a bank is allowed to do as it likes if it meets the ratio requirement, but is closed if it drops an iota below, involves a non-credible threat.

The precise definition of appropriate ratio levels, and the associated measurement of such ratios, is always going to be somewhat arbitrary. It is, in my view, much more important to work out a credible *sequence* of responses to progressive capital erosion than to worry whether the appropriate level is 8 per cent, or 10 per cent. The Basle capital adequacy requirements totally failed to do this, whereas the American proposals incorporate such a graduated sequence as their main new idea. If adopted, such measures should check the danger that managers would be tempted to undertake higher risk policies, as their capital became eroded, by placing increasing limitations on their freedom of action as their capital position weakens. Even so, this will not check the consciously fraudulent, a continuing source of failure.

Whether the proposal to make bank asset values more accurate, and balance sheets more transparent, by valuing on a mark-to-market basis, as best as possible, would help to check fraud, is not clear to me. It is certainly difficult to be opposed to greater accuracy, or transparency. If asset price movements were normally distributed, I would have no qualms in this respect. Unfortunately kurtosis, very large price jumps, is a phenomenon of such markets. If a system of progressive responses to capital ratio erosion, combined with mark-to-market asset pricing was to be established, I would advocate giving the Central Bank the right to 'override' the otherwise automatic stages of the graduated capital ratio, preferably for an identifiable group of banks, but possibly even, in extremis, for a single named bank.

When one thinks of sudden major shocks, such as the LDC crisis in August 1982, the Stock Market collapse in October 1987, the ERM crisis in 1992/3, would one really want large segments of one's banking system suddenly shifted into immobility, restrained from further lending? The counter-argument, presented by participants at the Conferences at which this paper was presented, is that the existence of such a potential 'override' would weaken the credibility of the existing ratio requirements, and leave the Central Banks open to political pressures to use, or misuse, this facility.

Dewatripont and Tirole (1993, p. 73) note that

> Unlike historical cost accounting, market value accounting makes the solvency measure very volatile and generates inappropriate transfers of control rights. We argued in favor of an intermediate method of accounting, in which, as under historical cost accounting, market specific fluctuations are not reflected in the solvency measure, but in which, unlike historical cost accounting, an automatic adjustment of the net worth offsets the change in the shareholders' incentives.

If the flexibility to respond to such shocks by accounting procedures is to be removed, should not the responsible authorities be provided with an alternative source of flexibility? If the Central Bank should invoke such an override, it would have to do so openly and be prepared to justify it publicly. It could be obliged to obtain legislative support for any extension of the initial override beyond, say, six months.

Much of the opposition to the flexible use of accounting procedures, as a means of adjusting to shocks, is their partially covert nature. A Central Bank might be excessively *reluctant* to use a transparent over-ride for fear of the public criticism that might ensue. I doubt whether there is any analytical way of deciding whether any such over-ride would be over, or under-utilised, in advance of experience.

Dewatripont and Tirole (1993, pp. 72–3), take somewhat the same line.

> Because [bank] managers (by definition) do not control macroeconomic shocks, their welfare, and therefore their compensation and the interference they face from outsiders, should be insensitive to such shocks. Because interference by shareholders depends on the bank's capitalization, the macroeconomic shock should be perfectly offset by an equal distribution of dividends if the bank's performance exceeds the minimum solvency ratio.
>
> Conversely, if the macroeconomic shock puts the bank's solvency below the minimum ratio, managers are unduly punished if control shifts to debtholders, or (in the context of voluntary recapitalization as in the Basle agreement) if shareholders refuse to recapitalize and leave control with the regulator. On the other hand, a mere adjustment in the minimum solvency ratio to the average solvency of banks is too lax a policy, as shareholders are more prone to take risk [sic] when the bank is poorly capitalized.
>
> This reasoning thus calls for a recapitalization requirement softened by some contribution of the regulatory agency in bad times, for example through pro-cyclical deposit insurance.

The problem with this is that an objective measurement of the effect of an 'exogenous' macro-economic shock is hardly possible, while the introduction of 'some contribution' from the regulatory agency in 'bad times' would be politically contentious. In my view a discretionary 'override' of limited duration would be more practicable.

Most measures aimed at encouraging more prudent bank behaviour are liable to be pro-cyclical in the short run, whereas, as argued earlier, Central Bank actions to support banks through crises are likely to be anti-cyclical. During periods of falling asset prices, bank profits are down, and bad debts are up. Capital ratios are under pressure, and new equity issues unpopular and difficult. Regulatory measures, e.g. capital ratios, whether graduated or not, tend to bite during (asset price) depressions, and are more commonly non-binding during (bubble) looms.

This has been so with (the introduction of) the Basle capital adequacy requirements recently. Falling asset prices, bad debts and low bank profits have meant that such requirements have become more binding on the size of bank books than had been expected. There is a sizeable literature on the putative responsibility of such supply-side constraints for the sharp fall in bank credit expansion that have been experienced, (e.g. Wojnilower, 1980; OECD, 1991; Bank of England, 1991; Bernanke and Lown, 1991; Federal Reserve Bank of New York, 1993). It is extremely hard to distinguish, and identify, the relative effects of demand and supply factors. I do not have the time or the facilities to add to this literature, but it would in my view be hard to deny that these prudential requirements had *some* additional restrictive effect.

There is, therefore, an inherent conflict between attempts at counter-cyclical monetary policy and the pro-cyclical effect of prudential/regulatory controls. For an account of a similar earlier (1938) conflict, see Simonson and Hempel, (1993). My answer to that is threefold, (i) only relax the automatic operation of graduated capital ratios by an override in cases of severe asset price shocks, (ii) continue, whenever banks still seek rescues, with present Central Bank policies, and (iii) pay much more attention in the tactical design of monetary policy to the course of asset prices, as well as current service flow prices.

The pro-cyclical nature of most mechanisms for regulating bank risk would be exacerbated by narrow-bank schemes, whereby only those banks investing in a restricted set of liquid, safe assets would be (100 per cent) insured. Narrow banks would, therefore, be compelled to offer much lower rates of interest than risky banks. During cyclical upturns, and periods of high confidence, there would be large transfers of funds, on relative interest rate grounds, from narrow to risky banks, and vice versa during periods of asset price declines, on relative risk grounds. As I have warned elsewhere (Goodhart, 1993) the narrow bank proposal would make cyclical fluctuations more, rather than less, extreme.

Let me turn finally, and briefly, to deposit insurance. If such insurance is 100 per cent, the adverse moral hazard effect has been made clear by the S & L debacle. Even so, a much more limited scheme, with partial pay-back, e.g. 80 per cent, or in other words co-insurance, can prove helpful in allowing the authorities to *countenance bank failures*, in conditions where the political outcry, about the losses to widows, orphans and other innocent depositors, might otherwise impel a full rescue. It is at least arguable that the limited deposit insurance scheme adopted in the UK helped to strengthen both the Bank of England's and the UK government's resolve to let BCCI fail. It is surprising that so much effort has been put into trying to devise risk-weighted premia, which is notoriously difficult to do, and so little into assessing the optimal amount of co-insurance, which can easily be put into operation.

But this brings us to the final subject of this session, the optimal design of international cooperation, since the allocation of deposit insurance to the host, or home, country is one of the current issues in this field. This discussion has been put into an Appendix, since the material is somewhat tangential to the main themes of the paper.

14.5 CONCLUSIONS

During the last few years many nations in the industrialised world have experienced a dramatic boom and bust in certain asset markets, notably housing and property, associated with the milder cycle in the goods markets. Current service flow prices exhibited more inertia, with their rate of inflation being slower to rise than asset prices, and dropped back in the last year, or so, to low positive levels rather than becoming negative.

The asset price cycle was both driven by, and drove, an accompanying cycle in bank credit expansion, and to a somewhat lesser extent in broad money. The collapse of these asset markets after 1990 was associated with a widespread rise in bad debts, in the need for bank provisions and in a fall in bank profits. In many countries banks either failed, or exhibited considerable distress. Prudential regulations, e.g. the Basle capital adequacy ratios, bit more tightly, and will, to some largely unquantifiable extent, have aggravated the constriction of bank credit. Central banks in these circumstances held to their last, and sought to support their banking systems by organising rescues, lender of last resort action, and various other stratagems. They did not, however, seek to abrogate the introduction of the Basel prudential requirements. Although banks failed in several countries, in the sense that their debts were greater than their asset values (negative equity), the banks were, in most cases, e.g. in the Nordic countries, kept open for business, and contagious panics were prevented.

How does one score this recent record of monetary policy and Central

Bank activity? In my view macro-policy has been systematically mishandled. The monetary authorities were far too lax in the late 1980s, 1988–90, and too restrictive thereafter. This was partly because they were concentrating on a limited index of inflation, current service flow prices, and ignoring the message about inflation given by asset prices. This misjudgement was exacerbated, in some countries, by a disinclination to give much weight in policy judgments to the rate of growth of bank credit and broad money, whose drastic decline in the early 1990s was not taken seriously enough.

The monetary authorities, therefore, share responsibility, along with the commercial banks, for the recent asset price/banking cycle. Having helped to bring about the fragility in the banking system, they then at least helped to pick up the pieces by behaving in their traditional way to prevent contagious panics by providing much needed support to their banking systems. There was no conflict between price stability and the provision of support to an ailing banking system.

There is an inbuilt conflict, however, between the imposition of generalised prudential regulations and macro-monetary stability, since the former, almost by definition, must bite harder at times of (asset price) deflation, and hence must, to some extent, aggravate the accompanying credit contraction. But it would make a mockery of such regulations, and negate their impact, if they were to be regularly relaxed at such times; though I would advocate that Central Banks should have a, carefully restricted, right of override of these regulations at times of severe, unforeseen shocks. Faced with this conflict, the correct response for the Central Banks is to take more aggressive expansionary action during such deflations, while still using their traditional rescue policies, to prevent systemic panics, in the time-honoured fashion.

APPENDIX A (WITH D. SCHOENMAKER)

International Cooperation Among Central Banks

As with other financial services, commercial banking has become multi-national (Benston, 1990; Gardener, 1991; Fingleton and Schoenmaker, 1992). Most of the largest commercial banks have branches, or subsidiaries, in a variety of financial centres outside their home country. The main response of Central Banks and bank supervisors has been to try to identify a single lead supervisory body, who takes overall responsibility for the health and solvency of each banking entity; the intended effect is to focus the responsibility for dealing with financial fragility on a single, identifiable 'home' authority, thereby reducing the need for international coordination and cooperation. As noted below, this does not remove the need for such coordination in dealing with liquidity and solvency problems that arise between parent bank and foreign-based subsidiary and/or branch, or from the operation of payment systems (see Folkerts-Landau, 1990, and below), but otherwise it is not clear that there should be any particularly serious problems in this context arising out of concerns with financial fragility.

Whereas bank supervisors have focused, to some extent, on how far it is either necessary, or desirable, to impose common prudential standards, e.g. a level play-ing-field (the Basle Accord on Common Capital Requirements, agreed in 1988, is a prime example of this), methods to deal with fragile banks of banking sectors differ widely across countries both in their composition and use (Goodhart and Schoenmaker, 1993). Such measures to deal with bank failures include deposit in-surance schemes, lender of last resort actions, and assisted bank mergers or take-overs. International cooperation among lenders of last resort has, therefore, to be analysed in conjunction with other parts of the safety net. Rather than harmonising these different domestic practices, the key issue is, in our opinion, whether the costs of bank failures can be internalised at the 'home' authorising and supervisory authorities, e.g. to make them responsible for the payment of deposit insurance in the event of failure. Home supervisory authorities (and Central Banks) of interna-tional banks may then have an additional incentive to supervise conscientiously, i.e. to prevent bank failures, and may be better situated, if such failure happen, to make informed decisions on the proper course of action, i.e. rescue versus closure.

Most banks will be registered and head-quartered in the country where their main domestic operations are undertaken. The banking supervisor of that country, whether Central Bank or specialist institution, (for a discussion of whether super-vision is, and should be, undertaken by the CB or a specialist, see Goodhart and Schoenmaker, 1993), is then, under the Basle Concordat of 1975, revised in 1983 (see Table 14A.1), designated as the lead supervisor, responsible for examining, and satisfying itself, about the solvency and the adherence to prudential standards, of the *bank as a whole*. So long as each bank has an *effective* lead supervisor, responsible for its consolidated supervision, there would seem to be little call for any international body to undertake lender of last resort functions: for discussions on possible roles for an international lender of last resort, see Humphrey and Keleher (1984) and Guttentag and Herring (1983).

Table 14A.1 The assignment of supervisory responsibilities in the two Basle Concordats

Type of bank	Supervisory issues	
	Solvency	Liquidity
1975 Concordat		
Branches	parent	host
Subsidiaries	host	host
Joint ventures	host	host
1983 Concordat		
Branches	parent	host/parent
Subsidiaries	host/parent	host
Joint ventures	host*	host

* When one bank is a dominant shareholder, then possibly host/parent.

Source: Gardener (1991, p. 112).

Where the bank has branches abroad, the host country will be responsible for operational controls, e.g. maintenance of liquidity ratios and codes of conduct, e.g. on money laundering, etc. but the home country will retain responsibility for solvency and overall capital ratios (see Table 14A.1). Within the EC, authorisation will be for the home country; more normally authorisation is for the host country in discussion with the home country. Branch closure may be by the host country, e.g. for transgressing the legal code. If the bank as a whole is closed, the branch will automatically follow.[4]

The situation is somewhat more complicated when the bank has separately established subsidiaries abroad. The host country of that subsidiary (i.e. the country of incorporation, which can be regarded as its 'home' country) will authorise it, monitor its capital adequacy and adherence to prudential standards, and clearly has the legal locus to close it down. But the reputation and the credit rating of the parent bank and its subsidiaries are so closely interlinked, that the Central Banks, and separate bank supervisors if such exist, of *both* the subsidiaries and the parent bank must coordinate before any closure/bankruptcy is imposed. Moreover, the parent bank can shift assets from foreign subsidiaries to other subsidiaries or to the parent in ways that are difficult to detect for host supervisors (Benston, 1993). This problem can be met by reliance on the parent supervisors, which stresses the need for cooperation between host and parent supervisors of subsidiaries (e.g. in the form of exchange of information or joint examinations), as introduced in the 1983 Concordat (see Table 14A.1). There may also be concerns among the supervisors of improper electronic fund transfers between the parent and subsidiaries for nefarious purposes (Scott, 1992).

In particular, both the parent bank, and its Central Bank/supervisor, must be given an adequate opportunity to avert a potential failure in a subsidiary, initiated by its local Central Bank/supervisor. Otherwise, a major international commercial bank could suffer a serious weakening in its reputation from the aggressive action of a small country supervisory authority. More rarely, perhaps, but still a practical possibility, subsidiaries, and their local Central Bank/supervisor, need to be given a chance to preserve their legally separate status and continue trading after the collapse of the parent bank. For example, an attempt was made to salvage BCCI, Hong Kong, even after BCCI had ceased trading elsewhere. On these legal aspects, see Key and Scott (1991).

The position, however, becomes much more complicated when there is no obvious single lead Central Bank/supervisor, and/or when the lead bank supervisor is unable to undertake full, coordinated unified surveillance over the bank as a whole. Both of these conditions appertained to BCCI. It was formally registered in Luxembourg, but its main business, and de facto Head Office, were in London. It carefully constructed its business, and organised its own audits, in order to prevent any single outside body getting proper unified surveillance over the condition of the bank as a whole. It is a normal phenomenon for business entities to register in states, where the regulatory costs are least, and the protective benefits greatest, e.g. Panama and Liberia for shipping, Delaware in the USA for company charters, etc.

In the aftermath of the BCCI collapse, banking supervisors have undertaken action on two lines to close these regulatory loopholes. The first such action is aimed at identifying, beyond doubt, the lead supervisor responsible for consolidated supervision and ensuring a *transparent* group structure. To this purpose the Basle Supervisory Committee reformulated and extended some of the principles of the earlier Concordats (which have the status of recommended guidelines) as minimum standards in June 1992. The basic requirement is that host countries should not permit foreign branches unless the parent bank is capably supervised on a consolidated basis by the home country. If the bank is structured in such a complex way that unified supervision is difficult to conduct, host authorities have to satisfy themselves both by communication with the home authority and, if felt necessary, also directly, that proper unified surveillance of the commercial bank as a whole is possible, and is being so conducted by the home authority. Furthermore, the creation of cross-border banking establishments would need the prior consent of both the host and home country and supervisory authorities should establish bilateral arrangements for the exchange of information. However, the standards do not provide any safeguard against the possibility of inadequate supervision by host supervisors, as Dale (1992b) argues. The EC Commission (July 1993) has recently made similar proposals, amending the Second Banking Directive, to reinforce prudential supervision.

The second line of action is to make the lead supervisor liable for the costs of bank failures in order to provide this supervisor with an incentive to supervise adequately. This proposed approach is not without problems and is, therefore, still very much under discussion. A major problem is that, for example, deposit insurance payouts, organised on a home country basis, will give rise to different levels of deposit protection. To date deposit insurance schemes are organised on a national basis (i.e. the host country principle) which guarantees equal treatment of depositors. Another problem is that, in a regime of self-contained national banking systems, bank rescues, organised by the Central Bank and financed by the domestic banking industry, may still be viable, but it is less likely to succeed if it involves the bailing out of foreign establishments. But it can be argued that such CB led rescues, financed by the domestic banks, have anyhow become more difficult to organise because of the breakdown of strong bank cartels, owing to international competition and deregulation (Goodhart and Schoenmaker, 1993).

What follows from all this for international cooperation among lenders of last resort, the theme of this Appendix? Although classical monetary analysis views the lender of last resort function as connected with liquidity supervision, largely the domain of the host supervisor (see section 14.4 above, and Table 14A.1), we argue, as Guttentag and Herring (1987) do, that it is more connected with solvency supervision, mainly the domain of the parent (i.e. home) supervisor.

Foreign branches are an indistinguishable part of the main, or parent bank and, hence, they can borrow, if they experience liquidity problems, under the parent brand name and credit rating or, alternatively, parent banks can borrow (in their markets) and swap it to their foreign branches. As the solvency (and liquidity) of a branch is thus basically as good as that of its parent and the parent country is responsible for supervision, it follows naturally that lender of last resort responsibility, for a foreign branch (and its parent), will be assigned to the parent Central Bank. Although the parent Central Bank will then have prime responsibility for lender of last resort actions, if any, cooperation among parent and host Central Banks may be required in the form of providing information to the parent Central Bank or helping the parent country to perfect their legal claim to the bank's assets in order to arrange a collateralised loan (Guttentag and Herring, 1987). Moreover the host Central Bank may provide emergency liquidity assistance on behalf, and at the risk, of the parent Central Bank, when the parent bank or Central Bank cannot provide timely assistance, e.g. because their market is closed, and liquidity problems at the foreign branch are so pressing that the host Central Bank would feel compelled to support this branch, e.g. when the branch faces settlement problems at the close of the payment system, as discussed below.

Foreign subsidiaries are separately capitalised and incorporated in the host country. As they are mainly subject to host country supervision, host Central Banks could be assigned as lenders of last resort to these subsidiaries. However, as argued above foreign subsidiaries and their parents are closely interlinked, and the revised Basle Concordat considered the supervision of solvency as a joint responsibility of both host and parent authorities (see Table 14A.1). As a result cooperation among the supervisors and lenders of last resort is required. The US authorities, for example, apply the source-of-strength doctrine which requires foreign banks seeking to establish banking operations in the US to serve as a source of strength to their banking operations in the US (Key and Scott, 1991, p. 31). Another example is the Bank of England requiring 'comfort letters', written acknowledgements from overseas parent banks that they accept a moral responsibility for their banking subsidiaries in London that goes beyond the narrow limits laid down by laws of limited liability (Guttentag and Herring, 1983, p. 15).

This all means a gradual shift of lender of last resort responsibility towards the parent Central Bank. The question is whether Central Banks would (and could) be prepared to back the worldwide operations of their international banks.[5] Although powers to provide temporary liquidity are set out in Central Bank statutes or laws, the modalities and rules for activating such powers are usually not specified and publicised on the grounds that the existence of an explicit commitment for implementing them could result in undue reliance on such facilities (Pecchioli, 1987). A formal statement regarding the international division of lender of last resort responsibilities is thus not to be expected.[6]

Turning again to deposit insurance, the EC (Commission, June 1992) put forward a proposal to make deposit insurance the responsibility of the authorising home country.[7] All bank branches should then publicly be required to exhibit on their bank counters the details both of their depositor insurance arrangements, which would hence differ from bank to bank depending on country of residence, and which country and Central Bank/agency was responsible for meeting such insurance claims. Whether depositors would find the insurance guarantees of supervisory authorities of convenience credible, and whether the Central Banks of large countries would avoid the time inconsistency temptation to step in in place of a failing supervisory authority of convenience, would have to emerge from experience.

The widely differing levels of deposit protection within the EC at present appears to be the main obstacle for adopting the Directive. The Commission chose to solve this problem by requiring a minimum level of deposit protection of 15,000 ECU (which was subsequently increased to 20,000 ECU by the European Parliament) without setting a maximum level. However, if host countries had a higher insurance pay-out than home countries, home country branches could be at a competitive disadvantage in host countries. It would be for discussion whether a top-up to host country levels would then be allowed, and, if so, which authority/scheme would be responsible for the extra slice. In the original proposed EC directive home country deposit insurance could *voluntarily* be topped up by the host country scheme if the latter is higher. A fundamental objection to host country topping-up is that the principle of no deposit insurance without supervision, established implicitly by the introduction of the home country principle, would be partially abrogated, since the host country would not get any supervisory powers. Furthermore, difficulties could arise when a bank branch is a member of two schemes, e.g. one scheme might prefer to reorganise the bank, while the other might prefer to close it and make the payments under its part of the guarantee. Disputes about the problem of which national scheme should be permitted to apply for the topping-up and the degree, if any, of coresponsibility in the insurance have stalled the progress on the EC directive (Stanhope, 1993).

The question of deposit insurance for home country bank *subsidiaries* in host countries is quite tricky. If the home country is to be responsible, as with branches, for deposit insurance, whereas the host country takes closure decisions, then the home country's supervisory authority/insurance scheme can be put at risk by an action of the host's supervisory authority which it disputed. And what would happen then if the home country refused to pay out of its scheme. *Per contra*, if the host country was responsible for insuring depositors in subsidiaries, then the likelihood of failure would be enhanced if the home regulator allowed that parent bank to flout proper prudential standards and subsequently went bankrupt. All these, and other conundrums, relating to the home/host deposit insurance decision are rehearsed in Schoenmaker (1993) and Key (1992).

The purpose of recent regulatory efforts in this field is to try to ensure both that it is transparently clear who has the lead responsibility for decisions concerning prudential oversight, rescues and closure of every banking entity, irrespective of location, *and* that each regulating authority has an incentive, through the requirement to make deposit insurance a home country obligation, to do the job to proper international standards. Even so, there will be many occasions when international communication and cooperation is essential, particularly where banking subsidiaries are involved.

A problem that may yet arise, which is not dealt with by the above formulation, is where an entity established in country *A*, which is a non-bank in that country, wishes to set up a banking business, presumably as a separately established subsidiary in country *B*, and possibly also further such subsidiaries in countries *C* and *D* as well. Presumably, the host country in each case would have to take responsibility for deposit insurance, if any, and whether to authorise the bank in the first place. Under the EC regulations, however, a non-bank registered in say, the C.... n Islands might obtain authorisation to establish a bank subsidiary in Luxembourg or Greece. Once that was done that subsidiary could branch, or set up secondary subsidiaries, in all other EC countries. That might prove a loop-hole. The point is not trivial, since investment banks prevented from doing commercial banking in the USA under Glass–Steagall, may wish to do a wider range of banking business under the more relaxed universal banking regulations in Europe.

At the moment, however, the exercise is primarily one of allocating primary responsibility clearly to a single national monetary authority in each case, and for organising ad hoc 'colleges' of supervisors when problems between parent bank and foreign subsidiaries/branches make such communication and coordination desirable..

There are, however two further, interconnected, areas where there will be debate about the allocation of international responsibility for supervision/regulation. The first concerns surveillance and potential lender of last resort responsibility in (inter)national payment and settlements systems. The second involves the division of responsibility between the European Central Bank and the national Central Banks, should EMU and the ESCB come into operation. The second issue is of particular European concern, and may, perhaps, be ducked for the purpose of this Conference; useful references are Folkerts-Landau and Garber (1992), Giovannini (1992 and 1992a) and Monticelli and Viñals (1993).

A problem, as discussed above, can arise when a foreign branch participates in the payment system of the host country. If such a branch faces liquidity problems and neither the parent bank nor the parent Central Bank can provide timely liquidity assistance, because, for example, the home money market is closed, the host Central Bank may have to advance liquidity to avoid disruptions in its payment system. A possible solution is to deny foreign branches direct access to the payment system, as the Banque de France, for example, does. Alternatively the host country can impose special limits on the settlement positions of foreign branches or require that these positions be fully collateralised (Scott, 1992). The problem can be stated more generally by asking whether foreign banks should be required to be incorporated (as a subsidiary) before they can start banking operations in the host country. The USA is moving in this direction and the FDIC Improvement Act of 1991 has authorised a study by the US supervisory authorities into this question (Scott, 1992).

One of the risks in payment systems used for the settlement of foreign exchange deals is Herstatt risk, i.e. that the two legs of the transaction are settled at different times in different localities. There is, therefore, a risk that a bank will close between the times of the two transactions, and delivery versus payment (DVP) cannot be exactly achieved. One proposal is to transform such international payments, at least for all payments bilateral with the US dollar, onto a 24 hour real time, gross settlement basis, and to establish links between these payment systems to ensure that settlement of one leg cannot be made without settlement of the other. If so, it would effectively end the fiction of banks being closed outside formal market hours. Central Bank officials would have to be prepared to take rescue and lender of last resort decisions on a 24 hour a day basis, with true market breaks occurring only at the week-end. While this would not exactly enhance the present pleasures of the life of Central Bank officials, and could on occasions force them to make even more instantaneous decisions, than now, it does not seem at first glance to us to cause any enormous difficulties of principle.

Concluding Remarks

Whereas international coordination among supervisory authorities started with establishing the home country principle, recent efforts are aimed at reinforcing *effective* consolidated supervision to close regulatory gaps, which were highlighted by the BCCI collapse. We have argued that the responsibility for, and costs of, dealing with banking fragility should also be based on the home country principle (to link it with supervision) and, consequently, be assigned to the lead supervisor of international banks. Each regulatory authority would then have an incentive to do the job properly or, alternatively, to refuse authorisation. This approach would also require cooperation among Central Banks/supervisors, as at present. The main problem would be that organising the safety net (i.e. lender of last resort actions, deposit insurance, and assisted bank mergers) on a home country basis would give rise to different levels of deposit protection within a country (mainly reflecting differing national philosophies about the appropriate level of Central Bank/government intervention in banking). However, these differences have to be accepted, if the costs are to be internalised at the home supervisor.

APPENDIX B

In the USA, Sprague (1910) quotes (pp. 36–7) the *Commercial and Financial Chronicle* about the events leading up to the crisis of 1873, 'This suspension [of Kenyon, Cox & Co., a stock broking house], although important in stock circles, was of far less general influence than that of Messrs Jay Cooke & Co., which occurred on Thursday [18 September], and of Fisk & Hatch, which was announced on Friday morning, and followed by the failures of a number of smaller stock-brokerage firms during the day ... The excitement and general distrust which followed this [Jay Cooke & Co] suspension caused a general and rapid calling in of loans, ..., and with the great fall in stocks produced the other disasters ... The excitement in Wall Street and vicinity was intense, and was heightened by a run on the Fourth National Bank and the Union Trust Co'. Again in 1884, the panic followed 'breaks in prices on the stock exchange' (p. 109) followed by brokerage firm failures, and 'a considerable further decline in the stock market' (p. 110). In contrast to the crises of 1873 and 1884, the 1890 stringency in New York was caused primarily by events in London, and gold outflows causing pressure on bank reserves. While stock prices fell, in response to rising interest rates, 'The disturbance. . . . was of short duration and did not at any time get beyond control' (p. 142). This contrasts with the longer-lasting 1893 crisis. The first stage in May was marked by 'a severe stock panic' connected with the failure of the National Cordage Company and the Philadelphia and Reading railroad, and the third stage by the failure of the Erie railroad, while 'the stock exchange suffered the worst decline of the year' (p. 176). In 1907 confidence had been weakened by the 'rich men's panic' in March. 'Never before or since have such severe declines taken place on the New York stock exchange'. The banking system weathered that, and the actual collapse was triggered by losses by supposedly bank-related copper company speculators (pp. 247–51).

Matthews (1954) addresses trade cycles in the UK between 1833 and 1842. Referring to the collapse of the boom of 1837 in the USA, he writes (p. 59)

> Despite the easing of credit conditions after the suspension, the year 1837 in the United States was one of violent recession in the financial sphere. Security prices and commodity prices fell catastrophically. The speculative real-estate boom came to an end, . . . The volume of domestic trade fell a good deal less severely, but it too was affected. The prostration of banks was widespread, especially in the South. The speculative nature of the boom determined largely the character of the crash. So long as funds are ample and confidence is not impaired, there exists no inherent force tending to bring to an end real-estate or commodity speculation based on expectation of ever rising prices. The analogy is rather to a stock-exchange boom than to a boom based, for instance, on industrial investment.

Meanwhile in the UK there was 'a railway mania' in 1836, 'a promotion boom, not a construction boom'; 'share speculation was rife', and the consequence was that confidence first 'passed, and had turned first into recession and then, in the early summer of 1837, into something near panic' (pp. 111–12). This boom was further intensified by the rapid growth of joint stock banks in 1836. 'There is plenty of evidence that the joint-stock banks actually intensified the boom by relaxing security requirements and pressing loans on their customers in an attempt to increase their business. In this way the supply of credit, so far from imposing a brake on the growth of activity, actually acted as a destabiliser' (p. 198). This was partly because the Bank of England, responding to the condition of its gold reserves, rather than to asset prices, allowed discount rates to soften in 1835 and the first half of 1836 (Chapter XI). 'It could of course be argued – as it was argued by Tooke and others – that the Bank *should* have brought about financial tightness in 1835 and early 1836 . . ., but . . . for the Bank to have deliberately brought about a rise in interest rates at a time when the exchanges were actually favourable, merely on the grounds that they might subsequently become unfavourable, would have been to go well beyond its avowed policy' (p. 172) *Plus ça change* . . .

NOTES

1. Perhaps not surprisingly, the main recent exception is to be found in an article by a Japanese economist, H. Shibuya (*Bank of Japan Monetary and Economic Studies*, 1992), who also references Pollak (1975) Carlson (1989) and Shigehara (1990). I am grateful to Hiroo Taguchi for drawing my attention to this paper.

2. The data from the USA were taken from the Bureau of the Census, *Historical Statistics: Colonial Times to 1957*, subsequent *Statistical Abstracts of the United States*, and the Federal Reserve Board, *All Bank Statistics*. The series used for bank lending to the private sector was column 22 in Table X20–41 on p. 623 in *Historical Statistics*, and conformable date from subsequent Abstracts. The indices for prices and real output were taken from B.R. Mitchell, *International Historical Statistics: Americas and Australia*. The index of stock market prices was constructed by Shiller in *Market Volatility*. The series for interest rates was found in X 311 in the *Historical Statistics*, suitably extended.

3. The housing price data are from Alan Holmans, 'House Prices: Changes through time at National and Sub-National Level', UK Government Economic Service Working Paper, no. 110, (1990). Data on the CPI are taken from B.R. Mitchell, *International Historical Statistics: Europe 1750–1988* (Macmillan, 1992). The equity price index is the Barclays de Zoete Wedd Equity Index. Data on bank lending are from B.R. Mitchell and P. Deane, *Abstract of British Historical Statistics*, (Cambridge University Press, 1962), and from IMF, *International Financial Statistics*, (IMF Publication Service, Washington, DC). Output data are from F. Capie and A. Webber, *A monetary history of the United Kingdom, 1870–1982*, (George Allen and Unwin, 1985); suitably extended. Interest rate data are from CSO, *Annual Abstract of Statistics* (HMSO).

4. One murky legal area is what are the respective rights of home and host countries to control over bank assets situated in their country on the advent of failure. For example, if the BCCI branch in Tokyo transfers funds to a BCCI branch in USA to invest in US Treasury bills what are the proper legal rights to such assets, after closure, of the creditors (prior depositors) of BCCI in USA, Japan, UK, Luxembourg, elsewhere. Scott (1992, p. 507) argues that the bankruptcy procedures need to be aligned with those for deposit insurance, i.e. either (1) host-country deposit insurance and host-country bankruptcy jurisdiction over the assets of insured branches, or (2) home-country deposit insurance and home-country bankruptcy jurisdiction over the worldwide assets of failed foreign banks.

5. In a national context Bisignano (1992) discusses the problem of a widening of central banks' responsibilities due to a shift of banking business to non-bank financial institutions and other markets, such as the commercial paper market. He notes the reluctance of Central Banks to assume wider responsibilities, and their response with demands for greater bank capital.

6. The revised Basle Concordat of 1983 states this explicitly:

   The report deals exclusively with the responsibilities of banking supervisory authorities for monitoring the prudential conduct and soundness of the business of banks' foreign establishments. It does not address itself to lender-of-last-resort aspects of the role of central banks.

7. In the USA the problem is tackled in a somewhat different way (Scott, 1992). The FDIC Improvement Act of 1991 requires that in future foreign banks that 'accept or maintain' deposits of less than 100,000 dollars (so-called retail deposits) do so through insured subsidiaries rather than through insured branches.

15 A European Central Bank (1992)*

15.1 THE CENTRAL BANK GOVERNORS' DRAFT STATUTES

The Current Position

During 1990 the Committee of Governors of the Central Banks of the Member States of the European Economic Community, henceforth called the Central Bank Governors Committee, prepared a draft Statute for the proposed European System of Central Banks (ESCB) to be put before the Inter-Governmental Conference (IGC) on Economic and Monetary Union (EMU), commencing in December 1990. In fact this draft was completed on 27 November, and presented to the Community Finance Ministers meeting in Italy on Sunday, 2 December 1990. The draft Statute then became generally publicly available during December. Most of section 1, and much of the rest of this chapter, represents a commentary on this Statute. Note that the Governors refer to this document, divided up into 41 Articles, as a Statute (singular), whereas more common English usage might be to refer to the document as presenting draft Statutes (plural). By the time this book is published, the IGC may well have decided to amend and revise the Statute. Other developments, economic and political, may have altered views on how the proposed ESCB might function. The current speed of change in Europe is such that any commentary rapidly becomes dated, but that cannot be helped.[1]

The ESCB is to consist of a central body, the European Central Bank (ECB), and the 12 national central banks. The main decision-making body of the ECB is to be the Council, comprising the President, Vice-President, the four other members of the Executive Board and the Governors of the 12 national central banks, all (with some minor qualifications relating mainly to internal financial matters) having one vote each (Article 10). The Council will normally meet monthly. In between Council meetings, the ECB will be run by the Executive Board, whose members will be appointed, for eight-year terms, by the European Council after consultation with the European Parliament for the President and Vice-President, and with the ESCB Council for the other members (Article 11). There remains some disagreement among the Governors, indicated in the Statute by the use of alternative drafts for certain clauses, in square brackets, about the relative responsibilities of the Board and Council (in particular Articles 12.1 and 14.4), with the

---

* Chapter 2 in A. Mullineaux (ed.), *European Banking* (Blackwell, 1992): 12–43.

Bundesbank apparently having argued for greater centralisation of power in the Executive Board, while most other Governors wanted to leave the main levers of power with the Council.

The time scale, as proposed at the European Council in Rome in October 1990, was to establish the ESCB and to enter Stage 2 of the Delors Committee Report by 1 January 1994, with a view to moving on to Stage 3 by 1 January 1997, if that step was then supported by at least eight members of the EMS in the European Council. This proposal was accepted by all heads of government at the summit, except the UK's. Mrs Thatcher denounced it. Since then, however, possibly as a result of representations from the Bundesbank, the German submission to the IGC has suggested delaying the formation of the ESCB until the extent of economic convergence has made the move to Stage 3, and to EMU, prospectively much closer.

Before turning to the remaining contents of the Statute itself, it is, perhaps, worth noting that there remains some controversy over the nomenclature of the proposed European central banking system. The Governors would prefer to emphasise the (voluntary) union of member central banks into a single system, the European System of Central Banks, with a unity of purpose and policy springing from a multiplicity of constituent members. Most other observers prefer the shorter phrase, Eurofed, partly because it is simpler and partly because the Federal Reserve System in the USA has provided the obvious model and analogy (see, for example, Thygesen, 1988). The Commission also tends to prefer to use the term Eurofed (e.g. in 'One market, one money'), perhaps because it likes the implication of federalism. No doubt part of the Governors' dislike of the term Eurofed arises from their wish to emphasise (a) that the ESCB is not simple imitation of the Fed in the USA, and (b) the continuing important role of the member national central banks. The use of words has a dynamic of its own (remember the UK Conservative Government's failing attempt to call their 'poll tax' a 'Community Charge') and, while one may sympathise with the Governors, I would expect Eurofed to become the common usage.

Independence

The draft Statute insists that the ESCB must be completely independent of the 12 national Community governments, and of all other Community and other political bodies. The draft also requires that all national central banks, and members of their decision-making bodies, cut their political dependence on governments and function independently. 'The Community and each Member State undertake to respect this principle and not to seek to influence the ECB, the national central banks and the members of their decision-making bodies in the performance of their tasks' (Article 7). All EC member states must ensure that their legislation, including that governing their own central banks, is compatible with the Statute. Governors of national central banks can be appointed only after consultation with the Council, and must hold office for not less than five years. A Governor cannot be sacked except for personal misconduct (Article 14). In this draft the Central Bank Governors have re-emphasised their insistence on their independence from political control, which was so prominent in the earlier Delors Report (1989, para. 32). Indeed, in requiring that the ESCB Council be consulted on the appointment of Governors of national central banks, this draft goes even further.

In his initial report on the draft Statute, Binyon (1990) records his view that the extent of independence requested for the ESCB 'is a clear victory for Karl Otto Pöhl, the President of the Bundesbank'.

Governance

The ESCB will be governed by a Council and an Executive Board. The Council, comprising a President, Vice-President, four other members of the Board and the 12 Governors of the national banks, will take decisions by simple majority, with the President having a casting vote. It will meet at least ten times a year, and its proceedings will normally be secret unless it chooses to publish (Article 10). The Executive Board, a full-time body, will comprise a President, Vice-President and four other members of recognised professional expertise. The President and Vice-President will be appointed for a period of eight years by the EC leaders meeting at their summits, after consultation with the European Parliament. A member can be sacked only by the European Court of Justice on grounds of serious misconduct. The Council's duty will be to formulate the monetary policy of the Community, including decisions relating to intermediate monetary objectives, key interest rates and the supply of reserves in the system, and to establish the necessary guidelines for their implementation. All but one of the Community central banks are of the opinion that the necessary operational powers for implementing the monetary policy decisions and guidelines should be delegated by the Council to the Executive Board, according to the reported Commentary accompanying the Statute. This legal construction would mean that the Council would have the right to revoke such powers, but would then immediately have to delegate a revised set. The Bundesbank, however, believed that the Executive Board should be allocated specific functions, and that the Statute should clearly assign to the Executive Board the task of implementing the monetary policy in accordance with the Council's decisions and guidelines. Exactly how far apart these two positions actually are is difficult for an outsider to gauge. Both Council and Executive Board meetings will be chaired by the President or Vice-President. He, or she, will also represent the bank overseas.

There was considerable discussion in the Central Bank Governors Committee on the proposed voting mechanism. In the event agreement, somewhat unexpectedly, emerged that each central bank Governor should have one vote, as will the additional six Executive Board members. In the event of a tie, the President will have the casting vote. Thygesen (1990, pp. 10–11) comments that,

> One point on which agreement has unexpectedly emerged in the preparations for the Intergovernmental Conference and which should reinforce this independence, is that each central bank governor will have one vote, as will the additional 5–6 members to be nominated for the Council at the European level. A system of weighted voting as in the Council of Ministers – or on the Executive Board of the IMF, including rules for blocking votes by minorities – would have fostered the thinking that the governors were just national representatives and not equal members of a collegiate body charged with formulating a common policy.
>
> Yet the enthusiasm for the principle of one member, one vote has made the designers of the ESCB overlook a danger. The votes of the national central bank governors will always tend to outweigh those of the European-nominated members. And the size of the Council could become excessive, as membership in the EEC and in EMU expands, as it seems likely to do in the next decade or two, potentially to even twice the present number. In this eventuality, or well before, either thought must be given to a system of constituencies (as in the IMF) where smaller countries merge into one voting area, possibly with rotation inside such a group as to who exercises the voting right, or nearly all authority is vested in the Board (or the Direktorium), the group of European-nominated members. It is worth noting that the Bundesbank, now faced with an enlargement of its already sizeable Council through the accession of the five Länder of the former German Democratic Republic is discussing how the number of decision-members can be reduced to assure efficiency in policy-making.

My own view, as will be discussed later, is rather different: that the proposed method of voting will mainly have the effect of strengthening the hand of the directly appointed Executive Board, at the expense of the wider Council. Whether or not this is desirable is a contentious issue.

Objectives and Functions

The Bank has three *objectives* (Article 2):

1. Its primary objective 'shall be to maintain price stability'.
2. 'Without prejudice to the objective of price stability, the System shall support the general economic policy of the Community'.
3. 'The system shall act consistently with free and competitive markets'.

Given these objectives, the Statute defines the ESCB's main tasks, in Article 3, as follows:

- 'to formulate and implement the monetary policy of the Community;
- to conduct foreign exchange operations in accordance with the prevailing exchange rate regime of the Community;
- to hold and manage [the] official foreign reserves of the participating countries;
- to ensure the smooth operation of payment systems;
- to participate as necessary in the formulation, coordination and execution of policies relating to prudential supervision and the stability of the financial system.'

In implementing the monetary policy laid down by the Council, the Executive Board will give the necessary instructions to national central banks.

The ESCB must be consulted on any draft Community legislation and any international agreements envisaged in the monetary, prudential, banking or financial field. This is known as 'national competence'.

The ESCB Council will have the exclusive right to authorise the issue of notes within the EC, and these will be the only ones to have legal tender. Coins will also be put into circulation by the ECB and/or the national central banks, their volume and denomination being determined by the Council (Article 16).

The ECB will be entitled to require credit institutions to hold minimum reserves on accounts with it and with national central banks. The Council will lay down what the minimum reserves should be (Article 19).

The ECB and national central banks will be entitled to establish relations with banks and financial institutions in third countries, and with international bodies such as the IMF. The ESCB will be entitled to acquire and sell spot and forward all types of foreign exchange assets and gold. The bank will also conduct all types of banking transactions with third countries, including borrowing and lending (Article 23).

Each national central bank will transfer to the ECB its foreign reserve assets, other than Community currencies and ecus. 'The Council shall decide upon the proportion to be called up by the ECB at the entry into force of this Statute and the amounts called up at later dates' (Article 30.1). Each national central bank will be credited with a claim equivalent to its contribution, and the Council will determine how such claims are remunerated. The ECB may accept the pooling of IMF reserve positions and SDRs (Article 30.3 and 30.5).

There may be some constitutional and political difficulties in the proposed transfer by constituent members of their gold and foreign exchange reserves to the ESCB. Thus, in the UK the reserves are held by the Exchange Equalisation Account (EEA), which is formally under the control of the Treasury, not of the Bank of England. At least until the establishment of a single currency, and perhaps thereafter, the transfer of foreign exchange reserves to the ECB would leave any member country considering reversion to adjustable, or floating, exchange rates powerless to manage its foreign exchange rate. (Once a single currency has been established, there are other, equally formidable, barriers to prevent such a regressive step.) While this may represent, therefore, a powerful form of pre-commitment to irrevocably fixed rates, and be supported by many as such, it would be seen by others, such as the UK, as a further significant abandonment of sovereignty. Not surprisingly, therefore, the Bank of England has doubts as to whether it is strictly necessary to transfer the ownership of foreign reserve assets to the ECB and considers it sufficient that each central bank agrees to make available a predetermined amount of reserves to be at the disposal of the ECB.

If note issue in EMU is to be the sole responsibility of the ECB, the assets currently backing national note issues will have to be transferred to it. These assets mainly take the form of interest-bearing claims on national central governments. Both these and the bulk of foreign exchange reserves earn interest, whereas there is no suggestion that the ECB's note liabilities should be interest earning (though in principle they could be). The ESCB, and within it the ECB, will consequently be a highly profitable organisation, since all the seigniorage from European note issue, and perhaps from the imposition of (common) reserve ratios, will accrue to it.

Such seigniorage will provide it with financial independence, with room to spare. Thygesen (1990, pp. 11–12) comments on this approvingly:

> Financial independence in the sense of determining its own salary structure and audit system is a non-negligible part of central bank autonomy, as one might infer from observation of the Federal Reserve System which is subject to externally imposed ceilings on remuneration and to government audit. This is thought to be one reason why the Fed has occasionally experienced difficulties in retaining Board members and top staff. The founders of the ESCB appear well aware of such dangers.

But even the most lavish salary structure, (and I shall comment on the design of this later), cannot make much of a dent in the likely flow of seigniorage receipts. The extent of such seigniorage revenues has been estimated by the Directorate-General for Economic and Financial Affairs (1990, pp. 120–3). How they will be used, e.g. transferred to the European Community or divided among member countries – and if so on what formula – presumably remains to be decided in the IGC, and was left on one side, 'to be drafted', in the draft Statute (Article 32).

15.2 THE TRANSITIONAL PERIOD

Which Constituent Central Banks?

In their recent deliberations and policy documents the Community institutions have frequently had a more clearly defined vision of the terminal steady state to be achieved than of the intervening transitional period. In the Delors Committee proposal, for example, the final, third stage, especially when the single currency and single ESCB have been achieved, is easier to comprehend and more clearly spelt out than the somewhat nebulous intervening Stage 2. The same is true for the ESCB. The transitional provisions for the ESCB have been left blank in the Committee of Governors' draft, still 'to be drafted'. As noted in section 15.1, it is envisaged that all constituent central banks should be independent of their own central governments and, in particular, should refrain from financing their governments' debts. Suppose, however, that by the date of the start of operational activities by the ESCB (say on 1 January 1997) not all member central banks have met these requirements. Would the still dependent central banks be unable to sit on the ESCB Council? Or would they be allowed to sit, but be unable to vote?[22]

It currently seems likely to me that the forthcoming IGC on EMU will lay down certain criteria, which could serve as preconditions for the move to Stage 3. Writing in advance of the meetings of the IGC, I would expect four such criteria:

1. convergence of inflation rates;
2. adequate control over public sector finances;
3. independent national central banks;
4. the absence of realignment over some previous period.

If such an approach were to be adopted, the technical details to allow observers to determine when the criteria were achieved by each separate country would need to be carefully and rigorously spelt out. The point of relevance here, however, is that the different countries of the EC could be expected to achieve such criteria with differing speeds.

If one was to wait until the final country (perhaps Greece) of the present members of the EC had met all such criteria before proceeding to Stage 3, the delay could be too long to be acceptable. It seems improbable that Germany, France and Benelux (the Schengen Five who first pulled down international customs and immigration posts), would be willing to wait that long. Moreover, if Stage 3 is to be deferred until all Community countries can move together, it will mean either further indefinite waiting or refusal to allow further countries, e.g. from East Europe, access to the Community.

It appears more likely to me that objective criteria will be established to decide which countries can move to Stage 3 by some starting date, perhaps 1 January 1997. On that date those countries that have achieved the criteria, and also agree in their own national parliaments to do so, will move first to irrevocably fixed currencies, and then to a single currency. This implies a multi-speed move to EMU, with those countries not achieving the criteria, or not being politically minded to take that policy regime step, only being able to move to Stage 3 at some later date when both these preconditions are met. The latest reports from the opening session of the IGC in December 1990 suggest that Stage 3 will not be adopted until at least eight member countries vote to do so in the European Council. The number is important because there are currently seven member states of the EC who could move quite quickly to EMU on the above criteria: the Schengen Five, Denmark and Eire. So one of the presently laggard states would have to be able to meet all the criteria before Stage 3 could commence under this rubric.

It is not really the function of this chapter to detail the advantages of such a multi-speed approach (see Dornbusch, 1990) or its disadvantages, as set out for example by the Financial Secretary of the UK Treasury, Francis Maude (1990). It is enough to note here that many of the leading German protagonists at the Bundesbank seem to favour such an approach, and that it seems quite likely to be adopted.

If so, some of the 12 constituent central banks will be in Stage 3, while others remain in Stage 2. What happens to the laggard central banks? They will still be running their own national monetary policies, with a possibility of realignment, when the others have merged their policies and moved on to a single currency and single ECB. Will the central banks remaining in Stage 2 send their own Governor as a participant to the Council, as an observer without a vote, or not at all? The members of the Executive Board, directly appointed by the European authorities, will be key personnel in policy decisions. Will the Community feel it appropriate to appoint to the Board only nationals of countries already in Stage 3? Would the same hold for senior officials of the ESCB?

If some central banks remain in Stage 2 when others have moved on to Stage 3, those in Stage 2 will need to maintain command over (some of) their foreign exchange reserves. So a multi-speed approach to Stage 3 would also imply a multi-speed arrangement for the transfer of respective national central bank assets, both foreign exchange and domestic, and liabilities, such as note liability and deposit liability, to national commercial banks and to non-EC central banks. One consequence of national central bank independence would presumably be that the central government of that country would transfer its main (deposit) account(s) to other commercial banks. It could legally still keep an account with its central bank, but the legal prohibition on any overdraft in that account would seem to make that somewhat unattractive.

Which Monetary Functions in the Transition?

The present mechanisms for the conduct of monetary policy by national central banks within Stage 1 of the ERM are reasonably clear. So is the nature of the mechanisms that will be in place once the final state of Stage 3, with a single currency and single ESCB, is ultimately achieved. But what about the intervening transition period? Let us start by assuming that, during Stage 2, the ESCB is established (say, in January 1994, as proposed at the Rome European Council summit in October 1990) and serves as a meeting point for member central bank Governors to discuss and coordinate policies, but otherwise undertakes no market operations. Then let us assume that on the appointed date of the start of Stage 3 (say January 1997) those countries making the regime change to Stage 3 announce that their currencies are irrevocably fixed, and transfer some proportion of their foreign exchange and domestic assets to the ECB in return for (deposit) claims on the ECB.

What happens next? Does each member (Stage 3) national bank then immediately cease all normal open market operations? (I shall defer discussion of the question and location of lender of last resort operations until section 15.5.) If so, in which market or markets (and in which currency or currencies, presumably either ecu or the currency of the domestic market involved) will the ECB undertake its open market operations? Are the (inter-bank) connections between (national) money markets sufficiently good to enable ESCB to operate in only one market and/or currency? The answer to this might be 'yes' if that one money market was London, since there are so many banks from other EC countries with branches there already, a broad money market, etc. But the UK may not have met the criteria for joining Stage 3 at its inception. Even if the UK has joined, will the present one-hour difference in time zones cause operational problems? If the UK has not joined Stage 3 at the start, will there be an alternative single centre with sufficient trans-EC linkages to establish a common single interest rate (on identical instruments; I shall discuss which instruments in section 15.4) over all the member countries in Stage 3? Or will the ESCB have to operate simultaneously in several (or all) of the main financial centres, and currencies, of the member countries?

During the period of irrevocably fixed parities, but before a single currency is established, the ESCB would have to decide whether to require par clearing between cheques denominated in the differing currencies of the Stage 3 member states, or it would have to intervene to limit exchange rate variations between the Stage 3 member countries within a minuscule range. The first option would presumably require the ESCB to establish, and run, some mechanism for (international) cheque clearing and settlement. How quickly and easily could that be done? Would it be possible or practical to have such a European settlement system up and running on day 1 of Stage 3.

If the alternative – mechanically somewhat easier perhaps – of tight intervention was preferred, the ESCB would have to be prepared to offer to buy and sell one member currency against another at the tight band without limit. Say there was a net excess market demand for French francs balanced by a net excess supply of Deutschmarks and Belgian francs. Presumably the ECB would order the Banque de France to create French franc deposits to the order of the ECB, against a claim on the ECB. Similarly the ECB would use Deutschmarks obtained to retire claims on itself held by the Bundesbank. If the ECB was going to achieve credibility for the tight irrevocable linking of member state currencies, this would have to be in force 24 hours every day. So the ECB would need to put in place some mechanism, perhaps via correspondents, to ensure that band margins did not widen, for example in Asian time zones.

This process would, however, mean that the currency constitution of the ECB's liabilities might rapidly diverge from the currency make-up of its assets. In the above example the ECB was becoming a net French franc debtor and a Deutschmark creditor. This would not matter so long as the parities were *really* fixed irrevocably, with a rapid transition to a single currency, and with a single common European interest rate, but it could cause some nervous moments in the meantime, particularly if speculative attacks caused a major divergence in the currency constitution of assets and liabilities.

Assuming that this system had operated successfully, with zero or minuscule exchange rate bands, and a single common interest rate among all Stage 3 members, then the switch to a single currency should be relatively simple technically. Each member country would stop printing additional national notes, and when retiring existing notes would exchange these for ECB ecu notes, transferring the asset backing to the ECB at the same time. The ECB would pass its own newly printed ecu notes along to each member central bank (perhaps with a distinctive print issue for each country), for onwards transmission to local commercial banks, much as the Bank of England now uses its branches for the local distribution of new notes. There would be a question of whether the ECB would use existing national note printing centres, in which case it would have to ensure common quality standards, or would centralise in a single plant, which would have minor resource and employment implications in the centres involved.

The question of which markets might be chosen by the ESCB for intervention, both in money and foreign exchange markets, may be quite important for relative market developments within Europe. If the UK was not to be among the first set of member countries in Stage 3, then it would hardly be possible for the ESCB to use the London money market as its main centre for open market operations; though it still could, and possibly would, choose to undertake its (main) foreign exchange operations through London.

In contrast, the question of where the head office might be sited, which could be entirely separate from its main intervention markets – as in the case of the Fed in the USA – seems of less economic importance except that the views of Board members might be influenced by the ambience of their host country and town. Apart from this latter consideration, the attention given to this issue of the location of the Board seems far out of keeping with its true economic significance. This decision was also among those ducked by the Central Bank Governors Committee: Article 37, on the seat of the ECB, remains 'to be drafted'. The assumption made until now in this section is that the ESCB would be formally established at the start of Stage

2, but would not begin open market operations until day 1 of Stage 3. Some participants in the debate have seen that transition on day 1 from talking-shop to main money market operator (among Stage 3 initial members) as being too sudden and sharp to be conducive to the successful subsequent conduct of monetary policy in the early – irrevocably fixed parities – months of Stage 3. They have suggested that the UK's hard ecu proposal,[3] or some variant of it, would provide useful training for ECB market operators during Stage 2, making the transition less abrupt.

While it may be that the IGC, partly out of deference to UK sensibilities, will accept some version of the hard ecu proposal for operation in Stage 2 (as long as the UK in turn accepts the ultimate goals of EMU), it is hard to see the hard ecu becoming widely used in the short interval which several Community countries will want to agree for the introduction of Stage 3 for those countries meeting the requisite criteria. Once these countries have established a common currency among themselves, it is hardly possible to see any further role for the hard ecu among member states remaining in Stage 2. Indeed, as Thygesen has pointed out, the hard ecu would then become virtually indistinguishable from the common or single currency of the core group. Consequently, it is doubtful (in my view) whether there would be sufficient advantages in terms of training ECB officials in market operations to offset the disadvantages (of complexity, division of responsibility, etc. as set out by Pöhl, 1990) to make adoption of the hard ecu, or some variant of that, a useful contribution to the transitional process.

15.3   GOVERNANCE AND CONTROL

Independence

The key concept in the design of the ESCB is that the ECB and its constituent member central banks should be *independent* of political control. This is currently a most fashionable idea. What is the provenance of this notion? The argument runs as follows. Inflation is a monetary phenomenon. The central banks can control the rate of monetary growth. So the central bank could restrain inflation, but it is subservient, usually, to the politicians. The politicians want to be re-elected and hence, as elections draw near, will require the central bank to engineer a (partially unanticipated) monetary expansion, with lower interest rates. The public will soon revise up their inflationary expectations, despite the fervent promises of the politicians (once safely elected) to restrain inflation in future, leading to even higher (anticipated) inflation and the need for even more expansive policies to create successive booms at pre-election times.

Among economists this argument is usually cast in terms of the game-theoretic approach, with buzz words such as 'time inconsistency' (see, for example, Melitz, 1988; Carraro, 1989; Giavazzi and Giovannini, 1989). Among central bankers the claim that their job could, and would, be done much better if only the politicians were taken off their back naturally finds a certain audience. Moreover, there is some empirical evidence that those countries with a more independent central bank, such as Germany, have succeeded in maintaining price stability better than those with central banks that are more subject to the control of their central government, such as the UK (see, for example, Grilli *et al.*, 1991).

There is probably some considerable truth in these arguments, and I am personally a supporter of giving more independence to central banks. But all fashionable ideas are likely to be both exaggerated and misleading, at least in part, and it would be sensible to be extremely wary of the idea that the (technically simple) act of granting the ESCB independence from political control will guarantee a much better record of appropriate economic achievement by the central bank. Again, the current consensus is that the overriding appropriate economic objective for a central bank should be the achievement of price stability. I support this view, but just being the current consensus does not make it into an eternal verity. Other occasions and situations, of war and internal rebellion, of financial collapse and massive unemployment, have led to differing ideas about the appropriate aims for a central bank. We will revert to the question of the choice of objectives for the ESCB further below.

Let me revert meanwhile to the issue of whether independence is an essential ingredient for a successful policy of price stabilisation. The empirical evidence is not clear-cut. The timing of those expansionary policies that are said, with the benefit of hindsight, to have caused subsequent worse inflation, e.g. 1971 to mid-1973, 1986 to 1988 in the UK, does not generally accord well with the re-election boom hypothesis (see Alesina and Roubini, 1990). The evidence on the relative performance of central banks is also mixed: the Bank of Japan is comparatively subservient to the Ministry of Finance, the Fed is comparatively independent of the US Treasury, but in recent decades Japan has had a better record on inflation than the USA. In the studies relating central bank independence to contra-inflationary performance, too little account has been taken of simultaneous and reverse causality. It is perfectly possible that those electorates that give their central banks independence are precisely those that give high priority to price stability. If so, the act of granting independence to a central bank to pursue policies *unwanted* by the public may cause severe political problems in a wider sense. In particular, granting independence to the ESCB will not so much take monetary policy out of politics, but rather will politicize the institution and its every step!

Much of the pressure for creating an independent central bank comes from a right-wing, Hayekian, distrust of governments and politicians. They are viewed not as Olympian pursuers of the public good, but as self-seeking individual maximisers only too happy to con the public if it keeps their snouts in the trough for a few minutes longer. While the earlier view was hopelessly idealistic, has not the balance swung too far towards utter cynicism? The game-theoretic argument has inflation generated by a conscious attempt of the authorities to trick the public. If you contrast this hypothesis with the alternative that the public generally have understood and supported exactly the policy mix that they actually got, which would get most support? But let us accept, for the time being, the argument that the incentives on politicians, such as re-election, are such that monetary policy is best removed from their control. By the same token it would behove the public to be equally sceptical and concerned about the incentives, sanctions, etc. applied to independent central bankers. We shall turn to that issue shortly.

Before then, however, we should consider further the meaning in this context of 'independence'.One element is clearly independence from government control, but as Isaiah Berlin described, in his famous lecture on *The Two Concepts of Freedom* (1958), there is also the question of what such independence is to be used for, and to what ends. Here the statutes lay down three objectives (see section 15.1):

1. To maintain price stability.
2. *Without prejudice to the objective of price stability* to support the Community's general economic policy.
3. To act consistently with free and competitive markets.

What is not yet entirely clear is how the ESCB should proceed if these objectives might clash. Assume that the Community wants to lower unemployment at a time when there is still some inflation. Should the ESCB be deflationary or expansionary? Presumably, the clause in italics in point 2 implies that the first two objectives, at least, are to be regarded as a lexicographic ordering, i.e. only when objective n is fully achieved can one move on to seeking to meet objective $n + 1$; or is there to be some trade-off in achieving these various, and at times possibly conflicting, objectives?

Three points may be noted about this set of objectives. First, as already stated, there is no apparent consideration given, or mechanism established, against the possibility (likelihood?) that some future generation of public and Community politicians might want to revise the priorities and objectives to be followed by the ESCB. Should some such override mechanism be in place? One can argue this on either side, with the need for precommitment on one side, against the need for democratic control on the other. What remains unclear is how far, if at all, the amendment procedures, which are foreshadowed in chapter IX of the Statute, but not yet drafted (e.g. Article 40 on 'Simplified amendment procedure' is still 'to be drafted'), might allow for some such override. Thus the accompanying Commentary notes that 'Some flexibility, however, needs to be preserved for amending provisions of a more technical nature in response to changing circumstances . . . Chapter IX will introduce a simplified procedure to amend those provisions which do not embody the fundamental principles of the System (Article 40)'. While the dividing line between technical and fundamental issues is always fuzzy, it is hard to see how the absolute primacy given to the objective of price stability in the Statute could be regarded as anything other than fundamental. If so, it could only be revised by the long and complex EC Treaty revision procedure. What would then happen if there was a war, or a major financial collapse, or if the ministers of finance decided to change the exchange rate regime, perhaps to a fixed rate system (which as we shall see remains a possibility), is unclear.

Second, there is as yet no precise definition of what is meant by 'price stability'. I turn to this in the next sub-section. Third, there is no specific objective relating to any responsibility on the part of the ESCB for the health and efficient functioning of the monetary, banking and financial systems. Many central banks, though not the first German central bank, the Reichsbank (see Goodhart, 1988), took on the micro-function of seeking to preserve the health of their national banking systems as an early and important element in their central banking functions. So its omission from the current list of objectives is, like the dog that did not bark in the night, to be observed. I shall discuss this further in section 5.

Accountability

As noted earlier there is no precise definition yet of what is meant by price stability. Thygesen (1990) suggests three possible measures: (a) an index of average prices for traded goods and services in the EC; (b) a weighted index of consumer prices; (c) an average of value-added deflators in the production of tradeables. The choice of index is both important and difficult. It would be desirable to use an index that was simple and widely understood, which would suggest the common consumer price index (CPI) rather than the value-added deflator; but, on the other hand, one would prefer an index which excluded the effects of (a) indirect taxes, (b) exogenous raw material (especially oil) price shocks, and (c) any direct effects of higher interest (mortgage) rates themselves, and this would suggest either the value-added deflator or a specially adjusted CPI. Moreover, there are lags of several months before value-added deflators become available, and the data only occur quarterly and are subject to revision over time. There are some differences between the frequency, timing, reliability and conceptual approach (e.g. in measuring the housing component) of consumer and retail price indices in the various countries. A task for a technical, statistical working party could usefully be to decide on appropriate measures of European inflation, in some large part to serve as an index of how well the ESCB was meeting its objective.

Let us assume that this not especially difficult task has been done. Then it would be possible to set out the objective for the achievement of price stability in numerical terms. In New Zealand the Government signed a contract with the Governor of the Reserve Bank (Mr D. Brash) that he would deliver 0–2 per cent inflation on the (specially adjusted) RPI by 1992, now extended to 1993 by the incoming National Party. If he fails to deliver (by a significant margin?), the clear implication is that he will not be re-appointed. Consideration was also given to relating the Governor's and a handful of other senior officials' salaries to the achievement of the inflation out-turn, but it was thought in the event that an increase in the Governor's salary for a deflationary measure (e.g. a rise in interest rates) throwing people out of work (even if only temporarily) would be too politically inflammatory and divisive.

Contrast the position in New Zealand, having (a) the possibility of a transparent political override, (b) a clear numerical objective and (c) some limited sanction (i.e. no re-appointment), with the proposals for the ESCB. There is, as yet at least, no numerical target; there are no specific sanctions or incentives on the ESCB members – apart from professional honour and the plaudits of history – to meet the objective; there is no possibility of governmental override; and their appointments are to be so long and so secure (only be dismissed for personal misconduct) that the threat of not being re-appointed is somewhat hollow.

Consider an analogy. The Minister of Arts is convinced that governmental interference in the theatre is undesirable. So he establishes an independent Board of National Theatre Directors. He hands over a massive financial grant (seigniorage), and allows the Board to decide its own salary structure and scale. He proposes the objective that the Board provides good theatre, but there is to be no explicit measure of goodness, e.g. in terms of reviews or seats sold. There is no specific contract of performance, and a Board member cannot be sacked unless he or she murders the leading lady on stage at a children's matinee. Then whatever the Board does, the Minister cannot override its judgement. It may be that a careful initial choice of Board members, and their subsequent professional honour, would indeed produce 'good theatre', but would an independent observer reckon that this was an optimal way to structure the constitution for such a Board? Yet at the moment this is essentially, as far as can be observed, the nature of the constitution that the Central Bank Governors Committee has proposed in the draft statute for the ESCB. And naturally so, A Theatre Directors Committee would, in turn, have proposed the above constitution for itself as well.

What is proposed, instead of any system of precise measurement and incentives and sanctions for success or failure, is that the ESCB should prepare an annual report and present it to the European Council, the Council of the European Communities and the European Parliament, somewhat following the example of the Fed and the US Congress. In addition the ECB shall draw up, and publish, 'reports on the activities of the System at regular intervals' (Article 15). It would be wrong to dismiss the threat of a *mauvais quart d'heure* before such bodies as of little influence. Such reporting responsibilities are usually taken enormously seriously by the institutions subject to them. But much of the effort, naturally, is taken up with *ex post* justification and rationalisation of past deeds; moreover, human nature leads us to believe our own justifications and rationalisations. There are considerable advantages in relating incentives and sanctions to an agreed (preferably precise) measure, whether or not its achievement is made easy or difficult by chance, whether or not those in charge have been devoted and skilled. But by the same token there is also a case for the wider public, and their political representatives, to have the chance to reset the precise objective that they want their central bank agents to pursue.

I should confess to having a personal interest. I was an adviser on a small scale on the adoption of the Reserve Bank of New Zealand (RBNZ) Act, and appeared in public before the select committee considering that Act. There are major differences in the constitution proposed between that Act and the Statute for the ESCB. Wherever there is such a difference, in my view the constitution of the RBNZ is preferable to that currently proposed for the ESCB.

The question of how to achieve appropriate democratic accountability for the various institutions of the EC is of a more general nature, and does not relate just to the ESCB. The parallel IGC on Political Union is likely to concern itself with such matters.

Who Will Run the ESCB?

Trying to revise the RBNZ Act was simpler than drawing up a Statute for the ESCB, since the latter is not only a new institution, but also involves bringing together into a single federal system 12 previously separate bodies. In this respect much attention has been given to the voting system to be adopted in the ESCB Council, of one-member-one-vote, irrespective of size of country and banks. A lengthy quote from Thygesen, pointing out that this should reinforce the collegial nature of the Council and reduce the likelihood of the Governors seeing themselves as national representatives, has already been given in section 15.1.

By the same token, however, the decision of the Governors not to adopt weighted voting is likely to increase the power and influence of the directly appointed Executive Board members, relative to the individual central bank Governors, at the monthly Council meetings. With weighted voting, a coalition of, say, the Governors of France, Germany and the UK or Italy could normally have determined the outcome. With single votes, the only natural coalition, and one made easy to achieve by personal communication, will be that of the Board members. Aided by the ability to set the agenda, choose the secretary and write the minutes, the President will dominate any single central bank Governor. Moreover, the central ECB staff will develop a greater Europe-wide competence than the economic staff of the individual national central banks. As happened quite naturally in the USA, but was not intended at the outset in 1913, the voting system will lead to the centralisation of power in the hands of the directly appointed Board. Power will pass from the Governors to the Board.

15.4   MACRO MONETARY POLICY FUNCTIONS

Open Market Operations

Central banks have generally now accepted that, in a free market system (the support and maintenance of which is to be the third objective of the System), open market operations will be the main instrument for the conduct of monetary policy. Consequently the first paragraph in chapter IV of the Statute, on 'Monetary functions and operations of the system' (Article 18.1), reads: 'In order to achieve the objectives of the System and to carry out its terms, the ECB and the national central banks shall be entitled:

- to operate in the financial markets by buying and selling outright (spot and forward) or under repurchase claims and marketable instruments, whether in Community or in foreign currencies, as well as precious metals;
- to conduct credit operations with credit institutions and other market participants [with lending being based on adequate collateral]'.

The square brackets in the final clause reflect some disagreement, very likely based on differing present national procedures about whether all lending should be collateralised, or not. The monograph by Hoffman and Keating on the ESCB (1990), notes that 'Some central banks (for example the Bundesbank and the Banque de France) do not lend in the course of open market operations other than through repurchase tenders, therefore always have collateral. Others (for example the Bank of England) do lend on an unsecured basis. . . . Which system the ECB should adopt, and whether all central banks should conform to that, seems to be the issue here.' One question that the present draft might raise is whether the definition of 'buying outright (spot and forward)' might exclude operations in other derivative markets which have not been specifically named, such as the futures and options markets.

   The draft does not seem to specify, or to limit, the maturity, risk-rating or other characteristics of the issuer of the financial instruments in which the ECB may operate, except to reinforce its determination that the ESCB shall never be under any compulsion to monetize the debt of national, or EC, governments. Accordingly, under Article 21.1 the draft states that, 'The ECB and national central banks shall not grant overdrafts or any other type of credit facility to Community institutions, governments or other public entities of Member States or purchase debt instruments directly from them'.

The adverb 'directly' is important here, since it is intended to prevent ESCB members from buying newly issued public sector debt, but to allow them to buy, and sell, existing public sector debt in the secondary markets. It is dubious whether the wording of the present draft necessarily achieves that. In a market intermediated by market makers and brokers, the counterpart seller of debt is often not known to the buyer. Public entities might be the counterpart seller in the secondary debt market and that, in the normal usage of words, might then seem to be a direct purchase by the ESCB from them. No doubt a form of words to allow the ESCB to operate in the secondary market for public sector debt, even without knowledge of the identity of the counterpart seller, can be found. Thygesen has suggested adding the words 'at issue', which leads directly on to the wider point below.

The deeper question is whether Article 21.1 actually makes much sense. If a national or EC government was to collude with (a member of) the ESCB to avoid it, then support by the ESCB of the secondary debt market for instruments which are close substitutes for the new issue will have virtually the same effect as buying the issues itself. If, for example, the ESCB should buy or promise to buy Treasury Bills one day after issue at a fixed, high price, it effectively underwrites the new issue price. In order to prevent any risk of avoidance, or evasion, it would logically be necessary to ban the purchase of (any form of) the public sector debt of any public entity (in current deficit). This would prevent the ESCB from operating in many of the major money and debt markets, and would be operationally restrictive, though there is no essential reason why ESCB purchases of financial instruments should not be limited to the debt of private-sector issuers.

Given the ease with which Article 21.1 could be avoided, if the ESCB member was minded to do so, there is a case for substituting a broader phraseology specifying the objective – that the ESCB shall refrain from giving any special support to the debt of public sector entities or willingly participate in monetising such debt – using the provisions of overdrafts and underwriting new issues more as examples of practices to be best avoided.

One obvious and immediate implication for the UK is that the Bank of England would have to cease its historical function of managing and operating the gilts market on behalf of HM Treasury. This would be a wrench for the Bank, not least because its monopoly of direct access to financial markets (relative to the Treasury and the Chancellor) gave it power to argue for, or against, particular policies on the grounds of its interpretation of 'market opinion'. On the other hand, the chance to obtain direct control over the funding programme would be some recompense to the Treasury to offset its loss of authority over domestic monetary policy to an independent Bank.

One of the questions presently ducked in the draft statute is the location of the market(s) in which the ECB (and national central banks) might operate. As already noted in section 2, this will be a vital issue for the health and development of the markets concerned. The US example would suggest that the most efficient mechanism would be a massive single market in one place connected to all other centres by an effective inter-bank federal funds market. That could probably be quickly established if the market was to be located in London, since it already is host to branches of most large EC banks and has a complete set of large financial markets, domestic and foreign exchange. If the UK is not an initial participant in Stage 3, it would be uncertain whether either the scale and scope of financial markets anywhere else, or the inter-bank linkages, would be such as to enable the ESCB to concentrate its market dealig in one centre, or whether it would have to attempt the operationally difficult task of market intervention (simultaneously?) in several different markets in several different cities.

Beyond such operational questions, there is the problem of how to manage the main instrument of policy, open market operations, to achieve the ultimate objective(s), primarily price stability (subject to my strictures in section 3 of no attention yet being paid to its precise measurement). A major question is whether the ESCB should adopt any intermediate targets. Besides indicating that the choice of targets should be properly the decision of the Council, the draft Statute is eclectic on this point. Thus in Article 12.1, 'The Council shall formulate the monetary policy of the Community including, as appropriate, decisions relating to intermediate monetary objectives, key interest rates and the supply of reserves in the System, and shall establish the necessary guidelines for their implementation'.

The question of the usefulness of intermediate targets is too large and general for this chapter. A recent volume of papers on *Intermediate Targets and Indicators for Monetary Policy* has been published by the Federal Reserve Bank of New York (1990). In his 'Introduction to the issues' (1990) Davis notes that

In general, however, confidence that there exist financial measures that can replace in part or in whole a basically judgmental, pragmatic, and eclectic approach to policy seems currently (1990) at a rather low ebb. Virtually without exception, the results reported in this volume support such a sceptical outlook. Nevertheless . . . the issue is far from closed. Indeed, interest in the problem of devising and implementing 'intermediate' guides for policy is likely to prove a hardy perennial in the years ahead.

Other Instruments

In many European countries national central banks still require certain minimum reserve ratios to be held against various categories of deposit; and in some countries, such as Italy and Spain, these ratios have been high, often over 10 per cent, occasionally over 20 per cent. Although such reserve requirements once had some prudential rationale, it is now widely accepted that this has lapsed, and been succeeded by other techniques, including capital adequacy ratios, liquidity ladders, etc. In countries with inefficient money markets, there may also have been a need to vary reserve ratios in order to improve control over domestic interest rates. But nowadays open market operations are just as capable of achieving any desired level of financial tightening, and publicity for announced changes in central bank operating rates can give just as clear a market signal, as changes in reserve ratios.

In so far as reserve ratios have a different effect on the financial system from open market operations (designed to achieve the same level of interest rates), it is because reserve ratios impose a differential (tax) burden on banks, and therefore can lead to disintermediation, and similarly provide additional (tax) seigniorage revenue to the authorities. Once exchange controls are fully removed as part of the 1992 process, and capital becomes even more mobile, differing reserve requirements (tax burdens) imposed in different countries would give a competetive advantage to banks with low burdens within the EC. Indeed, with exchange controls having already been removed in most European countries, including France, Italy and Belgium, there are already signs of pressure for lower required reserve ratios in countries where they have been comparatively high.

Consequently, there is a strong case for the harmonisation of required reserve ratios, and the ECB has been 'entitled to require credit institutions to hold minimum reserves on accounts with the ECB and national central banks. Regulations concerning the calculation and determination of the required minimum reserves shall be established by the Council' (Article 19). There is no strong case in theory for establishing other than the lowest possible common required reserve ratio, zero. There is no strong case for burdening Community banks relative to banks more favourably placed (e.g. in off-shore tax havens, perhaps the Channel Islands), or relative to other financial institutions. Nor is there a strong case for taxing banks in this special and covert manner.

An argument for the retention of reserve requirements in the EMS, which I owe to the editor of the book, Dr Mullineux, is that the politicians might require the ESCB to vary interest rates to help to achieve some external target, such as to hold the exchange rate against the dollar within some limit. If so, then the ability to vary the tax on banks, via variations in reserve requirements, might be used for domestic stabilisation purposes.

In practice, the shock to the fiscal systems of the Southern Cone countries from the entry requirements for Stage 3 is likely to be large – and there remains a curious attachment to the use of reserve ratios as a credit instrument among a number of high-level protagonists (e.g. Ciampi, in the Delors Report 1989; Thygesen, 1989) – so that an immediate move to a common zero, or very low level, reserve ratio is improbable. Instead, there is likely to be a compromise to some intermediate level, and the best to be expected is a subsequent common scaling-down of this level over time. Since this will create additional seigniorage receipts, notably in countries with currently below-average reserve ratios, this will further intensify the issue, already discussed in section 15.2, of the division of seigniorage between institutions (e.g. national central banks and the ECB) and between countries.

Apart from open market operations and minimum reserve requirements, no other instruments of monetary policy are specifically mentioned. In particular there is no reference to direct credit controls. However, there is a let-out clause, since under Article 20, 'The Council may decide, by qualified majority of two-thirds of the votes cast, upon the use of such other operational methods of monetary control as it sees fit.' It would, though, be difficult to square the adoption of exchange controls (with non-EC countries) and direct credit controls domestically with objective 2.3, to 'act consistently with free and competitive markets.' The two sets of controls are usually linked together since domestic credit controls can (increasingly) be avoided by disintermediation abroad in the absence of exchange controls.

Foreign Exchange Operations

Whereas the intellectual case for transferring the control of domestic monetary policy to an independent central bank has been widely accepted, indeed probably oversold, as suggested in section 15.3, the question of the appropriate division of responsibility between the politicians and the central bank in the area of international monetary policy remains contentious. In particular, politicians want to maintain their ability to determine the exchange rate regime, and to take the lead in *international* monetary policy meetings, such as those at the Plaza (1985) and Louvre (1987).

Yet the choice of exchange rate regime can circumscribe the ability of the central bank to achieve its primary domestic objective, of price stability. Clearly if the politicians were to decide on a fixed exchange rate with, say, the USA and Japan, then it would be difficult, if not impossible, for the ESCB to maintain both the exchange rate target *and* a lower rate of inflation than that prevailing in the other two countries. Indeed, even a less binding commitment, such as one requiring the ESCB to intervene in the foreign exchange market to defend some (even time-varying, unpublished and soft) bands could cause conflicts between their domestic obligation laid down by Treaty in the Statute, and the external obligation placed upon them by the political authorities.

The potential conflict of duties is obvious. Yet the present draft Statute fails to address it, unlike the Reserve Bank of New Zealand Act, wherein the political decision to peg the exchange rate would be a prime candidate for using the override clause (which is yet another example of why an override clause is needed). The draft Statute requires only that 'The ECB shall be consulted with a view to reaching consensus, consistent with the objective of price stability, prior to any decision relating to the exchange rate regime of the Community, including, in particular, the adoption, abandonment or change in central rates [or exchange rate policies] *vis-à-vis* third currencies' (Article 4.3).

Hoffman and Keating (1990) in their paper on the ESCB claim that

> The Bundesbank was not able to persuade the Governors to agree to replicate its own powers in the field of intervention in those of the ECB. [Hence the square brackets denoting disagreement in the final sentence of Article 4.3.] Article 4.3 is thereof a fudge. Most of the 12 Governors want the Community's exchange rate policy *vis-à-vis* third currencies to be decided by Governments. Others (presumably including the Bundesbank) think that such policy should be subject to the ECB's consent.

I doubt, however, whether the question is what the Governors 'want', rather what they think is practicable politics for their own countries.

In any case Article 4.3 appears to recognise that, once some consultation with the ECB has been undertaken, the actual decision on exchange rate policy remains with the political authorities. What might happen if that decision is not such as the ECB regards as 'consistent wiht the objective of price stability' is not made clear. Once the decision has been made, however, the ECB and national central banks must conduct foreign exchange operations in accordance with that decision. Thus in Article 3, the System will 'conduct foreign exchange operations in accordance with the prevailing exchange rate regime of the Community as referred to in Article 4.3', and in Article 31.2, 'All other operations in foreign reserve assets remaining with the national central banks after the transfers referred to in Article 30 shall be subject to approval by the ECB in order to ensure consistency with the exchange rate and monetary policies of the Community.'

Fiscal Policy

Not only might there be a clash between the ESCB's pursuit of price stability and the international monetary framework which the politicians have decided, but also there remains a possibility that fiscal policy, remaining largely under national political control, may be varied in a manner antithetical to the thrust of monetary policy. The governors have sought to meet the problem by insisting that the ESCB should never be required to monetise public sector debt, and that there should be no bail-outs of public sector bodies, including national governments, which cannot meet their debt obligations.

The (contentious) question remains, however, of how far national autonomy over fiscal policy should be constrained, in the interest of maintaining price stability, by the adoption of binding rules, or somewhat softer mutual surveillance, over certain national fiscal parameters, such as debt–income ratios, coverage of current public sector expenses by tax revenues, PSBR – income ratios, etc. It is likely that some such limits will be adopted in the course of the current IGC, but how hard or soft, and to what fiscal parameters they will apply, remains to be seen.

15.5   MICRO MONETARY POLICY FUNCTIONS

Lender of Last Resort?

There is no mention of any specific objective to sustain the health and effective functioning of the banking and financial systems among the objectives set out in Article 2. Moreover, there is no reference to the possible role of the ESCB as a lender of last resort (LLR) to be found anywhere in the draft Statute. It is not, however, necessarily ruled out. One of the tasks for the ESCB in Article 3 is 'to ensure the smooth operation of payment systems.' A justification of LLR operations has often been that bank failures would endanger such 'smooth operation.' Moreover, the final task for the ESCB is 'to participate as necessary in the formulation, co-ordination and execution of policies relating to prudential supervision and *the stability of the financial system*' (emphasis added here). This draft, however, clearly ducks the question of who is to decide what is necessary, an issue to be discussed shortly. Under Article 18.1, the System, both the ECB and national central banks, can 'conduct credit operations with credit institutions and other market participants', although there remains – as already noted – some dissension about the need for collateral backing for such lending.

Whereas the macro-functions of central banking are effectively indivisible within a single currency, or irrevocably fixed parity, the same is not true for the micro-functions of central banking, such as direct lending, prudential supervision, oversight of payment and settlement systems, etc. So it is in this micro-area that questions of subsidiarity, the division of responsibilities between the ECB and national central banks, become of great importance. Here again there is still some dissension among the central bank Governors, as indicated in the alternative drafts proposed for Article 14.4. The first draft would maximise the devolution of responsibility to national central banks. 'To the full extent possible in the judgement of the Council, the national central banks shall execute the operations arising out of the System's tasks.' Note that the decision would fall to the *Council*, where national central banks have a majority, and, remembering the discussion in section 15.3 above, they might be expected to vote together on such issues to keep the power to maintain micro-functions at the national level.

The alternative draft, leading to much greater centralisation, is: 'The Executive Board shall, to the extent possible and appropriate, make use of the national central banks in the execution of the operations arising out of the

System's tasks.' Again note that the deciding body would be the central Executive Board, or Direktorium, who need only delegate what they wish. The clear implication is that they would keep all important powers to themselves. Another possible inference is that the Executive Board would give comparatively more weight to the achievement of price stability, and less to the continuing smooth functioning of (national) commercial banks and financial systems, than would the individual central banks. Indeed it is possible that, should the second draft of Article 14.4 be adopted, The ESCB would renounce the function of LLR, at least until a financial collapse might become so intense as to force some response.

There is clearly a conflict between those who believe that the operation of LLR is not only generally unnecessary, but can also weaken the pursuit of price stability, and those who believe that the history of financial crises, and of central bank responses to these, indicates the necessity of maintaining some LLR function. Within the central bank Governors the Bundesbank was apparently in the first camp. Hoffman and Keating (1990, p. 9) state that 'One major difference between the Governors' blueprint and that of the Bundesbank is the extent to which the ESCB should be a "lender of last resort" in times of financial crisis. The Bundesbank draft implicitly rejects such a role. The German representatives at the Governors drafting meetings apparently maintained that it could raise moral hazard and the potential for inflation.'

Hoffman and Keating's own view appears to be that the LLR function should be within the province of the ECB, even though, or perhaps because, the ECB would act as such more sparingly than national central banks. Thus they continue (pp. 9–10):

> Someone will need to be the lender of last resort in Europe. Otherwise depositor confidence in the system will evaporate, and deposits will simply migrate elsewhere. The only practicable candidate other than the ECB is the national central banks. But logic suggests that such an arrangement would both detract from the ECB's credibility in monetary policy and exacerbate the moral hazard problem. Markets would perceive the chance of battles between the ECB on the one hand, anxious to meet its monetary target, and the national central banks on the other, their earlier antipathy to bailouts now tempered by their lack of direct monetary policy responsibility. Furthermore for the ESCB Members to keep the lender of last resort function goes directly counter to the Bundesbank's insistence on the 'indivisibility' of monetary policy. It opens up the possibility of the ECB draining liquidity at the same time as a central bank is injecting it to ward off financial panic.

In my view these last points are invalid. Assume that the ECB wants an aggregate withdrawal of X ecus of reserves. Then a national central bank injects Y of direct lending 'to ward off a financial panic'. But the ECB, which will be informed of the amount Y of direct lending, need only undertake net open market sales of $X + Y$ to achieve its own aggregate monetary objective. The two functions are compatible!

Prudential Control

Hoffman and Keating would wish to centralise any remaining LLR functions with the ECB and the Executive Board. But then they argue that 'If the ECB is to be Europe's lender of last resort, it has to have the last word on at least those supervisory questions with potential to trigger a bailout'. A differing argument in favour of the centralisation of prudential regulation is the need for 'level playing fields' and the risk of disintermediation. This latter argument, however, suggests that the optimum area of common regulation is the world, and not just the Community. To some large extent the logic of that has already been accepted, with the work of the Committee on the Supervision of Banks, set up by the central bank Governors' meeting under the aegis of the Bank for International Settlements (BIS) at Basle, to explore means of harmonizing bank regulation, and with the establishment of the International Organisation of Security Commissions and Security Organisations (IOSCO), which has much the same brief as the BIS in the field of security markets. Indeed the main effect of the formation of the ESCB in this respect may be procedural, in that the representatives of the Community at the BIS meeting may be reduced from 12 national central bankers to one ESCB Board member.

The conduct of prudential regulation of banks in some countries, such as the USA, has been split among several bodies, and in some countries, such as Germany and Canada, primary responsibility for such regulation is allocated to an authority separate from the central banks. This latter division of responsibilities is, however, only superficial. The need to be able to call upon lender of last resort support in crises has meant that the relevant authorities, in the central bank and the nationally separate supervisory body, have always had to work very closely together, and have normally done so.

Nevertheless the draft Statute demonstrates a somewhat reluctant approach towards its possible prudential duties. Thus the final entry in the list of tasks of the ESCB is 'to participate as necessary in the formulation, coordination and execution of policies relating to prudential supervision and the stability of the financial system'. Then in Article 25, on supervisory tasks, the draft goes as follows:

25.1 The ECB shall be entitled to offer advice and to be consulted on the interpretation and implementation of Community legislation relating to the prudential supervision of credit and other financial institutions and financial markets.

25.2 The ECB may formulate, interpret and implement policies relating to the prudential supervision of credit and other financial institutions for which it is designated as competent supervisory authority.

The approach of the draft is permissive, in that the ESCB, and within it the ECB, *may* if it so decides take the lead in designing and implementing the regulation of the Community's financial system, but is not mandated and required so to do. There is no discussion in the text of the appropriate nature and form of such supervision.

Settlement Systems

There is no discussion in the draft Statute of the role of the ESCB in improving, operating and safe-guarding the payments system, though one of its tasks is 'to ensure the smooth operation of payment systems'. It was argued earlier, in section 2, that the ESCB will need to consider the establishment of an intra-European cheque-clearing settlement system as a necessary part of the process of tying together the system of irrevocably linked parities, in the process of moving towards a single currency; indeed the ECB may need to operate such an intra-European clearing system itself.

Some academic consideration has already been given to this subject (e.g. Scott, 1990). This and other operational problems are barely touched on in the draft Statute, but their resolution will no doubt form part of the transitional process in Stage 2 and the early years of Stage 3. Indeed, the EC Central Bank Governors Committee set up, in January 1991, a sub-committee on payments and clearing mechanisms.

NOTES

1. The speed of evolution towards a single central banking system within Europe is now very rapid. This means that the contents of any commentary are greatly influenced by the precise timing of the date of writing, which in this case is December 1990. This chapter is therefore distinctly different from one that would have been written in November, before the outline of the draft Statute became available, and would no doubt have needed revision later in the winter as the IGC proceeded, had the publishing timetable allowed. In particular the immediate availability of this draft Statute tempts one to write a detailed commentary on it, a commentary that will soon look dated as time passes and the draft is revised, and new arguments and issues arise. I have been aware of the need to try to stand back from the detail and look at the larger issues, but I doubt if I have entirely succeeded.
2. In principle, according to the conclusions of the Presidency of the Rome European Council of 27–28 October 1990 (which so angered Mrs Thatcher), the formal *founding* date should be 1 January 1994. But national central banks would clearly not be expected to have met (all) the requirements for full eventual

membership by this date. I am indebted to N. Thygesen for this information.
3. The hard ecu proposal was unveiled by Chancellor Major in June 1990, and
then described in greater detail in various Bank of England and Treasury documents (see, for example, Leigh-Pemberton, 1990). The original idea, however,
emanated from Mr P. Richards of Samuel Montagu, and was then taken up and
advocated to the authorities by Sir Michael Butler of Hambros Bank. Both the
Bank and the Treasury then added certain extra elements to the scheme before
it was publicly presented.

The key feature of the hard ecu is that it should never be realigned downwards (devalued) against the currency of any member of the ERM. At any realignment, the hard ecu would automatically have its central value increased in
line with the currency appreciating most. Between realignments the hard ecu
could, and would, move under the pressure of market forces within the narrow(est)
bands then in force in the ERM.

Hard ecus would be made available from a new body, a European Monetary
Fund (EMF), only in exchange for the currencies of a member country of the
ERM, so there could not be any net monetary creation. Since at a realignment
some currency assets of the EMF would fall in value against the hard ecu, the
EMF would have the right to require a country whose policy the EMF felt to be
inflationary to redeem its own currency (held at the EMF) with harder currency
assets (e.g. to replace pounds with Deutschmarks). In addition, the proponents
hoped that the EMF would be able to develop a money market in hard ecu
denominated instruments, and become able to influence interest rates on such
instruments. By the use of these techniques the proponents felt that the EMF
could:

1. maintain and extend the contra-inflationary discipline and convergence to
   the most stable;
2. provide the nascent ESCB with a purpose, function and ability to learn during Stage 2;
3. give, indeed, a more concrete role for Stage 2;
4. still allow national authorities ultimate control over monetary policy and the
   final ability to realign during this stage.

While most commentators felt that the scheme was technically viable, and
indeed had some unusual and fascinating features, such as acting as a form of
currency option, it was not only complex but also added to, rather than reduced,
the existing plethora of currencies. Since the Deutschmark had continuously
been the strongest currency in the ERM, it was hard to see how the addition of
the hard ecu would, in practice, bring extra benefits, *unless* it was being argued
that German contra-inflationary determination would erode. By the same token
it was hard to see why people should want to hold, or trade in, this new, un-
tried and complex asset when the Deutschmark was already available. Finally,
if the EMF did succeed in making hard ecu markets of any significance, it
would complicate the question of who was responsible for the conduct of monetary policy. Although there were some signs of support, either for the hard ecu
or for some other method of hardening the ecu, among certain other EMS countries (e.g. Spain with the Solchaga proposal), the above considerations meant
that the weight of European opinion, especially in the Bundesbank in Germany,
was firmly opposed.

Part III

Financial Regulation

16 Institutional Separation between Supervisory and Monetary Agencies (1993)*
(with Dirk Schoenmaker)

16.1 INTRODUCTION

The early history of Central Banking led to the functions of monetary management and the role of Lender of Last Resort being combined within the nascent Central Bank (see Goodhart, 1988). Where established, (e.g. in Sweden, UK, France, Italy), the Central Bank was the government's bank, and, until the latter part of the 19th century, generally the largest bank within the economy. As such, it was assigned the overall responsibility, explicitly or implicitly, for maintaining currency convertibility into specie, the prime function of macro-monetary management until 1913.

Because of its role and power, the Central Bank had the finest credit standing in the country. Consequently, when all other channels were closed, desperate financial institutions would turn to the Central Bank as Lender of Last Resort. Much of the best writing, and thought, about the role of the Central Bank, (e.g. Thornton, 1802; Bagehot, 1873), was concerned with the appropriate responsibility of the Central Bank in this role.

Bagehot (1873) wrote *Lombard Street* in the aftermath of the Overend Gurney crash (1866) when there was some suspicion, at least, that the unwillingness of the Bank to support that House was due to commercial rivalry. While it was accepted that the Central Bank should only attempt to assist those banks which could expect to be (or to regain) solvency under normal (non-panic) conditions, the point was clearly made that a Central Bank should seek to act for the public good, and not simply as a private competitor for business; see, for example, Chapter VII of *Lombard Street*; especially the final two pages.

Indeed, it was the willingness of Central Banks to take the lead in bank rescues during the late nineteenth century that helped to establish their role as a quasi-official monetary authority. The Bank of England's rescue of Baring Bros, 1890, is probably the best known, but both the Banque de

* Chapter 1 in F. Bruni (ed.) *Prudential Regulation, Supervision and Monetary Policy* (Centro di Economia Monetaria e Finanziaria 'Paolo Baffi', Università Commerciale Luigi Bocconi, 1993): 353–439.

France and the Banca d'Italia were similarly involved in crisis management and bank rescues. Thus, from an early date, the functions of macro-monetary policy and of micro crisis management were jointly carried out within the Central Bank.

Yet this latter function, of crisis management, was limited in scale and scope. It was limited in scale, because the amount of Central Bank's shareholders' funds, (the shareholders in the Bank of England being in the private sector until nationalisation in 1946), which could be applied, and possibly lost, without causing a scandal and a public outcry, was strictly limited. Hence the Bank of England, and most other Central Banks in such circumstances, acted (and continue to act) in most such circumstances where the sums at risk are considerable as a *primus inter pares*, organising and leading a joint rescue party of the relevant group of banks. Except in cases involving relatively small amounts, the Central Bank has rarely been able, or willing to act on its own. In that respect the rescues orchestrated by the Central Bank, but largely financed by the other associated commercial banks, are not dissimilar to those arranged by a collectivity of commercial banks acting jointly in a Clearing House, as used to occur in the USA, see for example Timberlake (1984). The difference is that the leader of the orchestra has been allocated that role in advance, and is in a non-competitive position *vis-à-vis* both those institutions to be putatively rescued, and those being asked to put up the money. Again, the analogy of such a rescue mechanism with those organised by the IMF for the continuation of commercial bank lending to certain LDC borrowers is obvious.

Not only was the potential scale of Central Bank crisis management limited by the size of its balance sheet, (NB, it could generate *cash* without limit by its open market operations, but the size of *losses* it could absorb was limited by the size of its free capital), but the scope of its regulatory and supervisory involvement was also, at least initially, restricted. At any rate until 1914, (and to some large extent thereafter, and still), Central Banks saw themselves primarily as banks, albeit of a rather special kind, rather than as official agencies, or public sector bodies. While it was regarded as appropriate for them, as for any other commercial banker, to assess the quality of the paper offered by other banks on the market, and to use standard, generally available, techniques for assessing (potential) counterparties' creditworthiness, the idea that the Central Bank should have a formal duty to inspect and to give regulatory orders to the other commercial banks would have been anathema both to those banks and to the Central Bank at any time prior to 1914. Consequently the adoption of a Lender of Last Resort function did *not* imply any large scale exercise of supervisory or regulatory operations.

Until the secondary (fringe) banking crisis in 1973/74, the supervisory functions of the Bank of England were largely limited to ensuring that the central money market, through which additional liquidity was channelled, would be in good working order in all eventualities. To this end one senior official in the Bank, the Principal of the Discount Office, undertook relatively strict supervision of the handful of comparatively small Discount Houses who were the central institutions in that market, and somewhat looser supervision of the merchant bank members of the Accepting Houses Committee, whose acceptances (bills) were traditionally the main instruments traded in that market, along with Treasury Bills. Following this crisis, the extent of (informal) supervision exercised by the Bank increased considerably. Even so, until the first Banking Act (1979), there was no *formal* mechanism for the regular supervision of banks, though banks had to apply, to a variety of official bodies, for initial recognition to undertake various functions, and also had to apply to the Clubs involved to be accepted as members, e.g. the Finance Houses Association. The Bank of England would often be consulted in such cases, but this hardly represented regular, formal supervision.

Given, then, that from around the 1880s until 1914, there was some implicit guarantee that (potentially solvent) banks would be saved by an organised rescue, whereas there was virtually no formal system of supervision and regulation in most countries with Central Banks, how was moral hazard avoided? Part of the answer was that the likelihood of rescue remained highly uncertain. Investors were aware that bank failures could, and still did, occur. Moreover, since any rescue was likely to be a joint exercise, even if orchestrated by the Central Bank, the bank to be rescued needed to be a member in good standing of a club of banks that would be prepared to rally around to provide help. Those outside the club, e.g. British building societies before 1914, could expect no such help, (as was also true of Trust Companies in New York in the crash of 1907). The need to be a member of a specific club, with certain accepted rules of conduct, (which rules were, however, not always in the interests of the general public), in order to stand much chance of a concerted rescue, again acted to contain moral hazard. The other club members, being in the same line of business, would be as likely to spot aberrant, and excessively risky, behaviour as quickly as any external supervisor, (in part because they knew that they might be asked to share the cost of rescue), and would be expected to make their views clear to the Central Bank if later asked for support.

In effect, this was largely a system of self-regulation, through cartelised banking (financial) clubs, under the leadership of the Central Bank. This system subsequently ran into increasing difficulties for a variety of reasons. First, deregulation and fierce (international) competition led to a collapse of the cartelised banking clubs with their restrictive practices. This tended to lead to some diminution in the willingness and ability of the system to apply mutual surbveillance, but much more important has led to far greater reluctance of the members of a club to use their own funds on the rescue of competitors. The Bank of England had great difficulty in persuading other banks to share in the rescue of Johnson Matthey Bankers in 1984. Where deposit insurance is financed primarily by the contributions of the member financial iinstitutions, there are great difficulties in obtaining any agreement on the appropriate coverage, or premium charges, to be applied. The break-down of the dividing lines between the previously distinct clubs, the result-ing fuzziness of the structure of the financial system, has made any sef-regulatory system that much more difficult.

In addition, this fuzziness poses major problems for the effective regula-tion of the emerging financial conglomerates. The question can be raised whether separate regulators for banking, securities and insurance activities (perhaps with a lead regulator, like the Bank of England in the UK for institutions which are jointly supervised by the Bank of England and the Securities and Investments Board) are still effective. One of the rationales for mergers between banks and insurance companies is a better match of assets with liabilities than can be obtained in the individual cases (banks have largely long-term loans and short-term liabilities, while insurers carry mostly marketable securities against long-term liabilities). Moreover, some banks are looking for alternative sources of funding as the availability of 'cheap' (i.e. almost non-interest bearing) retail deposit is decreasing. An-other rationale can be found on the marketing side: the retail outlet of banks, which is becoming less and less important for banking business, can be used for selling insurance products.

These rationales for merging show that the bank and insurance parts are not likely to stay separated, not even in a holding structure with legally separated subsidiaries, but will try to integrate to reap such benefits. Fur-thermore, in a holding structure the decision making power may be found at the level of the holding company, rather than at that of the subsidiaries. To 'level' the regulators, they might have to join forces and to supervise both at the subsidiary *and* holding levels. A single agency for bank, securities and insurance supervision might be the answer rather than intensified coop-eration (see, for example the complex, and to date fruitless, attempts of bank supervisors (BIS) and securities supervisors (IOSCO) to establish common capital standards for securities activities). Denmark, Norway and Sweden have already merged agencies for overall regulation and supervision (see Appendix 1a).[1] An argument can be made for placing such a combined regu-latory agency outside the Central Bank,[2] e.g. to avoid expectations of Lender of Last Resort assistance for the entire financial conglomerate rather than only for the banking subsidiary.

Second, the scale of funding necessary in many cases (e.g. the USA, Scan-dinavia, Japan) has gone far beyond the sums which the Central Bank can provide from its own resources, or which the other commercial banks (financial institutions) are able, and /or willing, to provide themselves. Consequently there has been no alternative in many cases but to resort to the deeper pockets of the tax-payer (as in the USA for the banks, 1932/3, or the S&Ls re-cently; and as in Scandinavia in the last few years). When the government has been providing the funds, either directly to rescue the banks, or indirectly via institutions established to support the banking system, it is likely to wish to have a final oversight in the operation of the regulatory system. He who pays the piper, calls the tune. As the rescues are increasingly being financed by the tax-payer, so the responsibility for supervision and regulation of the system – in order to avoid excessive calls on such tax-payers' funding – has been passing more and more from Central Banks to separate agencies established under the aegis of the authorities.

Indeed, in our view the question of where the final responsibility will lie for supervision and regulation of the banking system will largely depend on the essentially mundane issue of who pays if, and when, things go wrong. It is, of course, true that, in the majority of cases when the Central Bank is a public sector body, losses absorbed by the Central Bank in the course of rescues ultimately lower the wealth of tax-payers. But, as will be documented below, Central Bank rescues are frequently jointly undertaken alongside other private-sector banks, and the accounting procedures leading to a change in the Central Bank's own capital are *perceived* as being quite different from a direct transfer of tax-payer's money.

There is one strong body of academic thought that argues that there should be no such protection of insurance for depositors, apart perhaps for some limited co-insurance for the small depositor, and/or that such protection should be limited to depositors of a subset of (narrow) banks, whose asset portfolio would be constrained to holding only safe assets. They argue that the protection (insurance) of depositors (almost inevitably) is mis-priced and hence generates so much moral hazard that the need for rescues is largely self-inflicted. In practice, however, (as documented in Appendix 3, which presents our cross-country survey of bank failures), the authorities have been manifestly unwilling to follow such academic promptings. In the majority of cases, 73 out of 104, the failing bank has been rescued, and in the remaining 31 cases of liquidation, in 22 the depositors, at least the small, suffered no substantial loss. In any case, our remit in this paper is to discuss whether there should be a separation between the Monetary and the Supervisory Agencies, not whether the latter should be abolished *sine die*. It would take us too far from our main subject to reopen the general issue of whether bank regulation, and rescue, is desirable or self-defeating. Our maintained hypothesis is that it will continue to be done. The question directly at hand is, if so, should it be undertaken in house in the Central Bank, or in a separate purpose-built institution.

There is no generally accepted answer to this question. In Appendix 1a we provide a listing of monetary and supervisory agencies. In about half the cases the functions are combined within the Central Bank; in about half the cases they are separated. In several cases, e.g. France, the precise division of responsibilities is somewhat blurred, see notes to Appendix 1A. There are no immediately obvious characteristics distinguishing countries with

combined, from those with separated functions. The German tradition has
historically been for separation, while the British was for combination. Countries
more closely under the influence of Germany in this respect (Austria, Switzerland, Scandinavia, possibly USA) have separate bodies, while countries
with UK links (Australia, New Zealand, Hong Kong, Ireland, but Canada is
an exception) combine them.

A feature of the last decade has been the rapid expansion of deposit insurance schemes to new countries. Of the deposit insurance schemes reported in Appendix 1B, 14 out of 23 have been established since 1980, or
are in preparation. Furthermore, the European Commission has made a proposal for a Directive to require all EC countries to introduce a common
scheme of minimum insurance levels for (most) depositors,[3] beyond which
individual member States can extend protection levels, if they so wish. This
current expansion of deposit insurance schemes may appear, on the face of
it, surprising in view of the well publicised problems of the FDIC and FSLIC
in the USA, the evident role of the resultant moral hazard in the USA in the
S&L debacle, and the growing chorus (especially in the USA) of academic
condemnation of (mispriced) deposit insurance.

In part, the recent practical popularity of deposit insurance, at least in
official quarters outside the USA, has been achieved since the organisers
have learnt from that experience *not* to allow 100 per cent unlimited insurance, but to require some form of co-insurance and/or to put an effective
ceiling on the size of deposits to be protected. Moreover, the purpose of
such (European) deposit insurance is somewhat different. It is *not* intended
to stop bank runs, but to provide some limited consumer protection. Indeed,
one purpose of the latter is to make it easier for the Central Bank, (and/or
the supervisory agency involved), to enforce a closure of a delinquent bank
with less of a subsequent public outcry. The authorities in the UK (Bank
and Government) have, properly, remained adamant that the losses of depositors in BCCI, beyond those deposits specifically covered by the scheme,
should *not* be recompensed in whole, or in part, from official sources.[4]

Such schemes have become more needed in those countries where rescues
were previously organised in a more ad hoc manner by the Central Bank,
acting in conjunction with the appropriate group(s) of commercial banks. In
large part because the growing competition within, and fuzziness of boundaries
of, the banking system has become so much greater, hence the ability of
Central Banks to organise and to co-ordinate rescues of banks (and of their
depositors) on a generally acceptable self-regulatory basis has been slip-
ping. So there has been a greater need for prior codification of the rights
and responsibilities of all concerned in such crisis circumstances.

Although our view is that the control of supervision and regulation will
depend, aside from national tradition, largely on the positive matter of who
is ultimately going to pay for any such rescues, there are a number of, perhaps, more normative issues about whether the monetary and supervisory

functions *should* be separated. We deal with three such issues in the following sections.

First in section 16.2, we address the question whether the combination of monetary and regulatory function under one roof leads to conflicts of interest; in particular whether concerns for the micro-level health and stability of (parts of) the banking system might distort the aim of the Central Banks' conduct of monetary macro-policy. If so, this would be an argument for separation.

Then in section 16.3 we turn to two arguments raised *against* separation, for keeping the functions combined. The first is that the Central Bank must have a concern for the efficient working of the payments system. If so, does it then follow that the Central Bank must also supervise, and regulate, at least the main money-market commercial banks at the heart of this system? Second, we address further the question of rescues, in the context of a cross-country survey of how some 104 major bank failures have been handled. Such failures have frequently occurred suddenly, and have needed, or have been perceived to need, some swift injection of cash, unless there was to be immediate closure, with whatever contagious consequences might, or might not, then follow. Whichever institutions might be formally responsible for regulation and supervision, and whichever bodies ultimately pay for the costs of rescue, is there any alternative to the Central Bank as provider in its Leader of Last Resort role, of immediate extra liquidity? If not, will then the Central Bank frequently get sucked into rescue cases, willy-nilly, and become a participant in any rescue? If so, is a *formal* division of responsibilities sensible, given that the *reality* will generally require joint, combined involvement?

16.2   ARGUMENTS FOR SEPARATION: A CONFLICT OF INTEREST

A major argument for divorcing the monetary from the bank regulatory authority is that the combination of functions might lead to a conflict of interest.

Sometimes this conflict is supposed to bring about a bias towards extra injections of high powered reserves into the banking system. In so far as the Central Bank lends to an individual bank, in its role as lender of last resort, it will alter the net flow of reserves to the system. The implied concern is that such lending (to a troubled bank) will increase the net inflow of reserves. In this simple guise this argument is unconvincing. The Central Bank knows exactly the amount of lending, and, even if the assistance is made too late in the day to offset immediately, the conduct of open market operations can be rapidly adjusted, e.g. on the next working day, to maintain the initial desired amount of reserve injection.

The assumption will be that the lender of last resort action will have changed the *distribution* of reserves among banks. Otherwise, why would the Central Bank have been asked to assist (at a rate generally less advantageous than in the market)? And the main purpose of the exercise, where the identity of the recipient bank is crucial, will have been to lessen the likelihood of contagious failure, leading to systemic problems. So LOLR actions, when exactly offset by a net reduction in OMO purchases will not leave the monetary system unchanged. *But* there is no good reason to believe that such actions need distort the aim of those Central Banks seeking to steer the system by means of a quantified target for the *overall* growth of the reserve base.

In fact, however, with a few exceptions, such as the USA in the era of the non-borrowed reserve target, 1979–82, Central Banks steer the monetary system by choosing an *interest rate* at which to inject, or withdraw, reserves. In these circumstances the rate of growth of the monetary base may be regarded as a most important information variable, (the Swiss National Bank), a somewhat useful information variable (the Bank of England since 1985), or be totally disregarded.

Within this more usual context, the conflict of interest may arise between the monetary authorities, who wish for higher rates (e.g. to maintain an exchange rate peg, to bear down on inflation, or to reduce the pace of monetary growth), and the regulatory authorities who are frightened about the adverse effects such higher rates may have upon the bad debts, profitability, capital adequacy and solvency of the banking system. It is in this guise that the conflict has, indeed, from time to time occurred. Moreover, the combination of functions might lead to *expectations* on the part of those setting prices that the Central Bank might be concerned with financial system stability considerations when determining monetary policy. However, with the discussions usually internalised either within the Central Bank or within the monetary authorities, it is extremely hard to document either the existence and number of such occasions, or the extent, if any, to which interest rates were kept lower as a result. In any case, the experience of the UK, an example of a country with a Central Bank which is strictly dependent on the political authorities, suggests that conflicts of interest between regulatory and monetary objectives (in holding interest rates below the level desired for monetary reasons alone) are an order of magnitude less important than conflicts between purely monetary objectives and political imperatives.

Moreover, the regulatory authorities' concern with the 'health' of the banking system is only in some part due to the natural affinity ('capture') that may grow up between the regulated and the regulators. For a variety of reasons, in part because occasions of systemic failure are both rare and usually occur in conditions exhibiting other unusual occurrences, most macro-economic models, and macro-economists, do not include variables such as bank failure rates, etc., in their models, usually regarding some vector of interest rates and, perhaps, monetary growth rates as providing a sufficient measure of monetary influence. Other economists, e.g. trained in a more historical mode, or with somewhat differing models, economists as diverse as Kindleberger, Minsky and Bernanke, would argue that banking crises and failures would have a significant effect on economic activity even when conditioned on the same set of interest rate and aggregate monetary variables. To this extent the 'conflict' between the monetary and regulatory arms of a monetary authority may not be between 'objectives' at all, but rather between differing (implicit) models of how the economic system works.

A more general point is that the cyclical effects of micro (regulatory) and macro (monetary) policy tend to conflict. Macro-monetary policy is supposed to be counter-cyclical, while the effects of regulation, e.g. capital adequacy requirements, tend to be pro-cyclical; it is harder to increase capital in a slump when bank profits are low and bad debts high. The pressures arising from this conflict may fall on supervisors to relax their regulation in a recession. On these grounds it may be argued that separation might, on the face of it, strengthen the resolve of the regulator to resist such pressures. But if separation puts the supervisory agency more directly under the thumb of the politicians, then the question of which structure will leave the regulators in a stronger position remains moot.

Be that as it may, there have been a number of instances when it is believed that interest rates were held down, in some large part because of concern with the 'health' of (parts of) the monetary system, when purely monetary considerations might have suggested higher rates. The effects on US monetary policy of the weakness of S&Ls, caught with a massive maturity mismatch between long-term loans at fixed rates and short term liabilities has been thoroughly documented (Vittas, 1992). Again from the USA, it is widely believed that Volcker was under pressure to abandon the non-borrowed reserve base scheme in Summer/Autumn 1982 because of the effects of the level/volatility of interest rates upon both LDC debt problems and the solvency of the major money-market-centre commercial banks in the USA.

A further illustration of such problems may have been provided by the events of September 1992. It has been rumoured in the City that one of the considerations, though probably a minor one, leading the monetary authorities to abandon the ERM and to float, was the fear of what 15 per cent, and possibly higher, base rates might have done to the solvency of certain City institutions. For an account of such concerns see Fildes (1993). The authorities were certainly extremely worried by the effects of higher interest rates on the economy, but their concern was as much for the effect of possible bankruptcies outside the financial system feeding back to financial intermediaries, as vice versa.

A speculative attack upon a currency, in a pegged but adjustable exchange rate system without exchange controls, can place extreme pressure upon short-term interest rates, if such an attack is to be repelled. Should the market, for example, come to believe that there is a 25 per cent chance of a 10 per cent realignment within the next week, then the expected return from the switch is positive unless the offsetting one week interest rate differential is about 130 per cent (0.25 × 10 × 52). Indeed, short-term money market interest rates, (e.g. in Sweden in September 1992, or in Norway in November 1992), in those countries which attempted to repulse the speculative attack by purely market measures, were actually in this ball-park (with overnight rates of 500 per cent in some cases).

This raises the question of what damage such sky-high short-term interest rates may do, first to the banking system, and second to the economy. Obviously this depends on how long such interest rates are likely to last. But, beyond that, it may depend importantly on the structure of the banking system, on both the liability and asset side of the balance sheet. Those banking systems which are primarily financed by a retail deposit base, whose interest rates are unlikely to follow, or can be restrained from so doing, the massive gyrations of money market wholesale rates, would be better able to ride out such a storm. Again, where bank loans (mortgages) are made on a variable rate basis, the system may be more sensitive, both economically and politically, to *temporary* periods of sky-high rates, than when such loans are on a fixed rate basis. The comparative fragility of variable, versus fixed, rate systems may well, however, be reversed in cases when the interest rate adjustment is more long-lasting. Furthermore, those banking systems which were effectively nationalised, or where the authorities can (quietly) transfer rents to the banks, or where the banks run a profitable cartel, will be inherently better placed to ride out such (temporary) volatility, since their solvency would be less at risk.

This example suggests that the potential for conflict between 'regulatory' and 'monetary' objectives depends to some large extent on the structure of the banking and financial systems. The more such a system involves intermediaries financing maturity mismatch positions through wholesale markets in a competitive milieu, the greater such dangers of 'conflict' are likely to be. This may, perhaps, suggest a paradox. It is the German tradition which exhibits the greatest concern about conflicts of interest, and the greatest desire for a separation of responsibilities; yet it is the German system, dominated by an oligopoly of enormously powerful universal banks, with relatively under-developed, competitive wholesale financial markets, in which such 'conflicts' of interest will be *least* bothersome (see Bisignano, 1992).

As earlier noted, such conflicts may not really be so much between objectives, as between rival models of how the economy and financial system interact. A conflict of this kind is generically different from the standard principle-agent analysis in economic theory. Certainly differences in incentives for personnel with differing responsibilities may often play a role. But one can easily envisage occasions where officials in charge of monetary policy, fearful of systemic stability, will want to rescue a bank which officials responsible for regulation will want to close, e.g. to avoid moral hazard.

Such conflicts are genuine and cannot be resolved by institutional rearrangements. Indeed, there are some, including some Central Bankers, who see the need to resolve such conflicts as an argument in *favour* of maintaining regulatory and supervisory functions within the Central Bank. Rather than institutional separation, clear statutory guidelines for the responsibilities of those entrusted with delegated authority for the several functions of monetary and supervisory management might be more useful.

It is, at least, possible to argue that where such conflicts really become important (in an open, competitive, market-driven system), they have, in order to obtain an efficient resolution, to be internalised within a single authority.[5] Indeed, when there is separation, conflicts can occur not only because of differences of objectives, of information sets, or of preferences, but also as a result of simple administrative complications (a cock-up).[6] Where such conflicts have been less pressing, because of a differing structure, (e.g. Germany, Japan) it is easier to maintain the 'luxury' of a separation of responsibilities.

One of the reasons why such separation may be regarded as a 'luxury' is that the function of regulation has rarely received plaudits from the public or the politicians. The Bank of England's reputation, prior to the 1973/74 secondary banking crisis, was, perhaps, a counter-example; but that can be viewed, with hindsight, as praise for having avoided virtually *any* prudential regulation without this having led to any major collapses.

Regulation is otiose, unless it forces financial intermediaries to do what they otherwise would not voluntarily have done. Therefore unless the regulatory body is largely an advisory, counselling body, it will be resented by its clientele, and given few thanks for hypothetical, averted crises, (except where these are obvious, as when the Fed calmed the situation on, and after, October 1987). Again, the public and politicians will blame the regulatory authority for the crises that do occur (BCCI and Johnson Matthey in the UK case), while taking the regulators for granted otherwise. Moreover, there may often be, and is certainly so perceived in the UK, a gap between the expectations of the public about the roles of a (banking) supervisor (that no one should ever lose any part of their deposit as a result of a (bank) failure), and the objective of the supervisors (i.e. to prevent systemic collapse and to alleviate asymmetric information by the partial protection of ill-informed clients).

Consequently, it has been argued that the reputation of the Central Bank is more likely to suffer, than to benefit, from the joint conduct of both functions. Moreover, such is the political and public 'flack' from a major collapse that much, perhaps far too much, of senior officials' time and energy is taken up with 'damage control' under these circumstances. Certainly the mood within the Bank of England has appeared to change under the baneful influence of the BCCI affair. Whereas in earlier years it regarded the regulation and prudential supervision of the banking system as a natural, core, function, more recently it has come to view the possible devolution of this function to some other official agency with some equanimity, or even relief. The potentially adverse reputational effect on the Central Bank as an institution that may, almost necessarily, be incurred as a consequence of conducting banking regulation and prudential supervision is now becoming widely recognised, at least among Central Banks. It may well be that, in future, the balance of 'proving' the case may shift from those wishing to separate the functions to those wishing to combine them.

In the past in those countries where the Central Banks were dependent, with the key monetary decision being taken in Ministries of Finance, there may have been some bureaucratic tendency for Central Bank officials to give more weight to fields in which they could still take the lead, often including more micro-level, structural relationships with financial intermediaries and markets. Heller (1991) has a table comparing the inflation performance of banks without a supervisory responsibility, relative to those with such a responsibility, to the detriment of the latter. (In Appendix 2 we have recomputed, extended and further commented on this table.) The point here is that there may be some correlation also between the dependency of the Central Bank for monetary decisions and its leadership in financial regulation; and it may be the former, rather than the latter that drives the relative inflation performance.

Anyhow, there are some indications that the process of transferring more independence to the Central Banks within the ESCB for the conduct of monetary policy may be being accompanied by a reverse shift of responsibility for micro, structural, regulatory policies back to official agencies under the aegis of some political Ministry. The politicians may be averse to too large a transfer of power to (unelected, independent) Central Banks, while the Central Bankers, for their part, may be quite happy with the exchange of obtaining more control over macro-monetary decisions while divesting themselves of a supervisory responsibility, which is becoming perceived as increasingly problematic and occasionally downright embarrassing.

It is, perhaps, surprising that those who argue for a formal separation appear to believe that the supervisory function will thereby be carried out better, with less regulatory cost and burden, fewer bail-outs and less use of tax-payer money. This seems to us to be a 'Grass is greener on the other side' syndrome. The alternative to Central Bank regulation is generally an agency more closely under political control. It is at least arguable that the closer the supervisory agency is to the political system (OCC and FDIC, to a lesser extent, in the USA) the more tax-payers' funds are used for bail-outs. The responsibility of the Bank of England for the banking system may well have strengthened Ministers' hands in refusing calls for extra payments to BCCI depositors. Furthermore, possibilities for the corruption of independence may become greater with multiple regulators for the (banking) lobbyists to approach, and with their proximity to politicians. A better answer to problems raised by such conflicts may be greater statutory clarification of objectives, rather than institutional separation.

16.3 ARGUMENTS AGAINST SEPARATION

Payment System

The massive intra-day credit exposures in most large value payment systems at present could give rise to settlement failure(s), which in turn could easily generate a systemic crisis. Settlement risk has therefore increasingly become an area of supervisory concern over the last decade.[7] Whereas we will deal with the broader concern of the Central Bank for systemic stability in the next section, we will focus here on the appropriate role of the Central Bank in the payment system, a key channel for the potential spread of contagion risk. Put differently, is there a role for the Central Bank in the payment system beyond that of settlement agent?

In net settlement systems participants send payment instructions over a period of time which are only settled at the end of this period. This arrangement exposes the participants to significant credit risks as they extend credit to each other. The settlement of payments, by the delivery of reserves at periodic, usually daily, intervals is therefore a key test of the solvency of the participants (Folkerts-Landau, 1990). Unless the clearing house (i.e. central bank or private clearing association) provides for settlement finality, it has to unwind payment instructions in the event one or more participants fail to settle their debit positions.[8] However, an unwinding may in practice be impossible, with potential consequences that may increase systemic risk rather than reduce it. Under settlement finality the non-defaulting participants have to cover the shortfall at settlement according to some kind of loss-sharing agreement, possibly backed by collateral posted at the clearing house. But collateral posted in support of loss-sharing agreements which are organised on the basis of 'the survivor pays' may, if used, so weaken existing participants that they may only be able to settle at the end of a given cycle and be unable to open for business the next day/period. Although no Central Bank would say so, a Central Bank as lender of last resort might feel compelled to support the failing participant in such cases of unwinding or loss-sharing which could endanger the liquidity and solvency of the non-defaulting participants in order to avoid systemic 'knock-on' effects. The Central Bank would then assume (part of) the liquidity and credit risk of the net settlement system and would become effectively the *implicit* guarantor of the system.

Domestic net settlement systems[9] are usually backed (and sometimes owned) by a Central Bank, whereas the private ECU clearing and settlement system is a net settlement system without a Central Bank. The BIS acts only as a settlement agent and does not provide liquidity support if needed. For this reason some EC Central Banks, i.e. Bank of England, Banque de France and Banco de Portugal, may provide secured borrowing facilities to ECU clearing banks.[10] However, the question of who would finally bail out the private ECU system if needed (in case the facilities were not enough) still remains open.[11] This highlights the need for a Central Bank for the ultimate credibility of a net settlement system.

In a gross or continuous settlement system each payment is immediately settled at the settlement institution. An important distinction is whether daylight overdrafts are allowed, or not. Gross settlement systems with daylight overdrafts, e.g. Fedwire in the USA, preserve the liquidity and, hence, the efficiency in the same way as net settlement systems. However, in the absence of collateral for these overdrafts the clearing house (e.g. the Federal Reserve for Fedwire) assumes the full amount of credit risk till the overdrafts are eliminated. Collateral requirements, or even more stringent no overdrafts, minimise the credit risk, but could also significantly reduce the liquidity of the system. Payments on 'credit' are no longer possible, and reserves (or collateral) need to be available before a payment can be effected. If funds are not available, payments are usually put in a queuing batch till sufficient funds are raised. This may in turn delay other payments, and eventually lead to gridlock in the system.

In SIC, the Swiss gross settlement system without daylight overdrafts, the level of reserves held by SIC participants with the Swiss National Bank declined significantly after the abolition of reserve requirements in January 1988. Although improvements, such as splitting up large payments, changing the input sequence and setting a fee structure which favours early initiation of payment orders, increased the daily turnover of reserves, Vital (1990) reports that in the second half of 1989 and in the first quarter of 1990 still about 25 per cent of all transactions (representing about 50 per cent of the value of payments) were not settled within three hours of having being entered. Such long settlement delays may create significant liquidity risks. He further raises the question whether the above mentioned improvements will be capable of preventing the transaction demand for non-interest bearing reserves from dropping to the gridlock level.[12] He suggests that the alternative is to consider the reimposition of binding liquidity requirements.

Be that as it may, an economist's answer would be to do a cost-benefit analysis. In a gross settlement system without overdrafts, the full cost of foregone interest falls on the reserves maintained, while a collateralised system only involves an opportunity cost since the collateral is tied up. However, the Central Bank assumes the credit risk associated with the collateral it acquires in exchange for the overdrafts, i.e. the provided liquidity, while it assumes no credit risk at all in the system without overdrafts. In the latter case, the Central Bank could therefore pay interest on reserves, as is done in countries like Ireland, Italy, the Netherlands, Portugal, Greece and New Zealand, although below the market rate (EC Commission, 1992b). Moreover, an intra-day credit market might emerge, as in Japan. But while an intraday credit market can facilitate the adjustment of banks' reserve positions, it does not provide an incentive to keep 'sufficient' reserves in the banking system.

A Central Bank needs to use the payment system in order to inject (or drain) reserves into (from) the banking system. However, for the shortage (e.g. payments to the government or conversion of deposits into currency) to be known and relieved, there is no need for a Central Bank to operate the payment system, so long as it can obtain sufficient information with real-time monitoring. Banks need reserves for settlement purposes and/or for meeting reserve requirements. The level of reserves that would be needed to ensure sufficient liquidity in a gross settlement system are not necessarily the same as these for monetary control purposes. The scale of such reserves and the period over which they need to be maintained or assessed may differ. Although reserve requirements are *not* essential for the conduct of monetary policy, they can play some role in facilitating transfers in the payment system. The decision to implement reserve requirements, or not, for EMU may depend in some part on this consideration.

The Central Banks' growing awareness of the liquidity and credit risks in net and gross (with uncollateralised overdrafts) settlement systems and their implicit or explicit assumption of these risks, have initiated several risk reduction policies. The most direct measure used to be, and still is, to control access and monitor the participants, which we will discuss in more detail below. More recently, work is under way to improve payment finality in order to reduce or eliminate the need of unwinding procedures. In this respect bilateral and/or multilateral caps have been put on the size of overdrafts by Central Banks in their own systems and by banks in private sector payment systems (very often persuaded or forced by Central Banks to do so). However, such an accounting measure does not provide incentives to reduce overdrafts further than the limits which are set. A market based approach would be the pricing of daylight overdrafts (Mengle *et al.*, 1987), perhaps together with some kind of caps.[13] This would be the natural counterpart of paying interest on reserves. With the present state of technology, i.e. real-time payment systems, the calculation of interest on credit and debit positions for short time periods, say ten minutes, should be no problem.

On top of these short term measures to reduce risk, there is a long term trend towards domestic gross settlement systems without daylight exposures to minimise credit risk.[14] However, the significant decrease in credit risk established by such gross settlement systems without daylight exposures may go hand in hand with an increase in liquidity risk. Increasing settlement delays can eventually lead to a gridlock of the payment system, as noted earlier. It should be noted that Central Banks are very much aware of this latter problem and are actively addressing it in devising their systems.[15]

It may be thought that gross settlement without daylight overdrafts, or even collateralised overdrafts, minimises credit risk (though not liquidity risk) and, hence, reduces the role of the Central Bank as explicit or implicit guarantor of the payment system. However, payment systems do not operate in isolation. Large value transfers are mainly initiated in foreign exchange trading, securities transactions and interbank transactions. The main risk in

forex or securities transactions is that one party settles its part, while the
other party fails to do so. The two 'legs' of a forex deal have to be settled
in the payment systems of the different currencies. The so-called cross currency settlement (or Herstatt) risk is largely due to the difference in the
time zones of central banks, which can prevent same time settlement, and is
clearly illustrated by the failure of Herstatt in 1974 (see case 38, Appendix 3).
Netting arrangements (provided it is done on a sound legal basis) can reduce, but not eliminate, the size of cross currency settlement exposures. In
securities transactions an equivalent risk, called principal risk, appears when
the seller of a security delivers but does not receive payment or vice versa.
The solution for this problem is delivery versus payment as recommended
by the Group of Thirty (1989).

While the improvement of payment systems may reduce banks' exposure
to each other within the payment system, banks can still have large, short-
dated, exposures on the interbank market (in section 16.2 we discuss the
implications of banking systems quite largely financed by wholesale deposits).[16] Rumours about a possible deteriorating creditworthiness of a bank
can easily lead to a run on wholesale deposits and, hence create a liquidity
or funding crisis, as Continental Illinois experienced in May 1984 (see case
98, Appendix 3). Due to growing concerns about interbank credit risk (which
usually lacks the safety of collateral), the scale of traditional interbank activities (e.g. interbank deposits and certificates of deposits) has recently declined
to the level of banks' basic funding needs. Interbank activities beyond this
level have been replaced by more efficient derivatives and other off-balance-sheet instruments for hedging and position-taking purposes (BIS, 1992).
A major advantage of the use of off-balance-sheet instruments is the reduction in credit risk.[17] It is important to note that credit exposures in the interbank
market (and in agency relations) are voluntarily taken on by banks on the
basis of choice and assessment of counterparties, and hence should be controlled within the general supervisory framework. However, in payment systems banks may have no choice over their counterparties as the payments
arise out of the decision of their customer's customer. The resulting interbank
credit exposures are therefore fundamentally different from the traditional
exposures which banks face on the money, and interbank, markets.

The access of banks to Central Bank reserves enable them to make payments under all market conditions (Folkerts-Landau, 1990). Moreover, Folkerts-
Landau, Garber and Weisbrod (1991) argue that the ability to mobilise reserves
more easily than competing financial institutions establishes banks as the
cheapest source of liquidity in the economy. They back their argument with
the observation that corporations which issue commercial paper maintain
credit lines, representing access to the liquidity of the banking system. Corporations can fall back on these credit lines when they experience difficulties
in the commercial paper market, e.g. during times of liquidity stress in the
market, to issue or roll-over commercial paper. As a result Central Bank
liquidity support for banks implicitly extends official support to other insti-

tutions that rely on liquidity provided by these banks (Folkerts-Landau, 1990).

As far as Central Banks guarantee the payment system and provide liquidity support if needed, control on access, in the form of restricting the participation to banks which are eligible for this support, is justified and even necessary. However, the Central Banks' attempts to reduce the need for liquidity support caused by payment problems via moving to gross settlement systems without daylight exposure, can in turn lead to looser controls on access. The basic argument is that with daylight exposures, a participant's creditworthiness is only tested at the end of the business day, while in gross settlement systems without such daylight overdrafts every participant's solvency is continuously tested. Moreover, a potentially 'weak' or less capable institution would be spotted before it can cause problems in the payment system as it will be prevented from executing a payment order if it has insufficient funds (i.e. reserves or collateral) up front.

The integrity and reliability of a payment system is essentially dependent on the quality of the participants, the specific clearing and settlement arrangements, and the possible backing by a Central Bank. The oversight of payment systems, to date done by the Central Bank in most countries, is therefore concerned with the participants (e.g. the quality of their risk controls and of their computers and back-up facilities), the clearing house, and the network technology for messages (e.g. SWIFT is the main vehicle for sending international payment messages). Such oversight differs considerably from the usual supervision of banks, which focuses primarily on the solvency and liquidity position. To assess and monitor a bank's liquidity, the supervisor has to know its short term claims and obligations. A payment system operator can gather information on a bank's flows through the system, but has no information on a bank's underlying assets and obligations. However, this latter information is crucial for a payment system operator when a net-debit bank experiences (settlement) difficulties (e.g. the knowledge that the bank has enough saleable Treasury bills would alleviate the problem considerably).

Whilst it should be the responsibility of Central Banks to initiate or to cooperate in the development of safe and stable payment systems *and* secure linkages with other payment systems and securities settlement systems, it does not follow that they should also operate them.[18] Put differently, we see a clear regulatory, but not necessarily an operational, role for Central Banks in the payment system.[19] As long as Central Banks have to assume significant credit and liquidity risks, in particular in net or gross settlement schemes with uncollateralised overdrafts, an additional oversight and monitoring role can not be denied to them. The latter role would become less urgent if we were to move to a safer payment environment with, e.g. gross settlement without daylight exposures, sufficient funds in the settlement accounts, delivery versus payment, synchronisation of time periods for forex settlements (which implies 24 hour settlement), etc. However, such 'safe' payment systems are still far away.

Systemic Failure

A distinction that is frequently made in the literature relating to a Central Bank's Lender of Last Resort function is between those circumstances in which a commercial bank is illiquid, but not insolvent, and those cases in which a bank is insolvent, and may, or may not, be illiquid. In much of this literature from Bagehot to Humphrey (1975) and Humphrey and Keleher (1984), the argument is made that it is appropriate for the Central Bank to use its LOLR function in the first case, but *not* in the second, e.g. because of moral hazard problems.

In our view that distinction can not, usually, be maintained. With an efficient money, and inter-bank, market a commercial bank that is generally believed to be solvent, can, almost always, obtain sufficient additional money to meet its liquidity difficulties. There have been some exceptions, notably when some technical failing in the clearing, or money market, system leads to a bank making out-payments, but unable to obtain offsetting in-payments; this occurred in the well-known Bank of New York case in 1985, (case 99, Appendix 3). But such cases are rare. In general, a bank that cannot borrow, on current market terms, to meet temporary liquidity difficulties, finds itself in that position because potential counterparty lenders are suspicious and uncertain about its potential solvency, as, for example, in the case of Continental Illinois, (case 98, Appendix 3).

Thus, the exercise of the Lender of *Last* Resort function, as contrasted with lending as part of standard money market practice, will generally occur in circumstances where the solvency of the borrower is subject to doubt. Frequently, perhaps usually, there will not be time to examine the books of the supplicant borrower sufficiently carefully to tell whether the bank, or other financial intermediary, is insolvent, or not.

While there is, as noted in the Introduction, a strong school of academic thought that believes that official intervention in such circumstances is misguided, we simply record here that the revealed preference of monetary authorities has been to rescue banks running into difficulties, so long as there appeared to be any risk of a systemic knock-on effect. Even when the possibility of contagion related to a rather narrow sub-set of banks, and a relatively minor market, as in the case of Johnson Matthey Bankers in 1984, (case 93, Appendix 3), where contagion was feared with the other banks connected with the London gold market and the survival of that market itself, the authorities, the Bank of England, nevertheless stepped in to rescue, though its judgement in so doing was later questioned.

Appendix 3 contains a cross-country survey of 104 bank failures in 24 countries and covers the 1980s and early 1990s, with a few important cases taken from the 1970s. The selection of countries corresponds largely with the set of countries of which institutional details are provided in appendix 1a (monetary and supervisory agencies) and 1b (deposit insurance agencies).

The main sources for these data are country reports of banking systems compiled by IBCA (a London based rating agency), the *Financial Times* and the Economist.[20] The criteria for including reported bank failures from these sources are the availability of conclusive information on the method of handling the bank failure and the funding of a possible rescue. We do not claim that this Appendix provides a complete coverage, least of all for the USA, where their banking system, limiting cross-State branching and encouraging small (undiversified) unit banks has resulted in a proliferation of failures. We hope that we have, nevertheless, provided relatively comprehensive coverage of the larger failures over a wide range of developed countries.

Some troubled banks continue on a stand alone basis after a rescue package in the form of emergency aid or a capital injection has been provided, while others are taken over by one or more banks. A third way of rescuing banks is putting them under a special regime administered by either the deposit insurance fund or the government. Related to this is the creation of a special fund to deal with a set of bank failures or with the whole of a troubled bank sector. Examples of such a special fund can be found in the USA, Norway, Finland, Sweden and Japan. Finally, a failing bank can be put in liquidation. Four sources of funding can be identified: banks, the Central Bank, the government or deposit insurance. Deposit insurance is usually financed through regular or ad-hoc contributions from the participating banks with contingency funding arrangements backed by the government (see Appendix 1B). In some cases banks are liquidated or taken over by another bank without any external funding.

The results of this survey are summarised in Tables 16.1–16.4 below. In some cases a combination of several methods is applied as in case 18: this troubled bank was finally taken over after an initial rescue package in the form of credit lines granted by the Central Bank and other commercial banks appeared to be insufficient. Funding can also be provided by more sources. We therefore give a breakdown of the results for the cases in which two methods or two funding sources are used. We do not specify the cases in which three or four sources of funding are used since such a further breakdown will not provide much additional information. Only the numbered cases are included in the tables, while other cases provide additional information which either reappears in following cases or does not provide enough details to be included. Note that the numbers in the tables do not add up, since more than one method or source is used in some cases.

We also distinguish, in the following Tables 16.1–16.4, between those cases in which the Central Bank of the country combined the functions of monetary management *and* banking regulation, and those cases where this was not so. The purpose of this is to provide some preliminary indication whether such combination led to any obvious differentiation either in the method adopted for dealing with a failing bank or with the resulting choice of funding.

This procedure is virtually bound to lead to severe under-sampling of the occasional failures of small banks, especially in the USA where the literature on their somewhat idiosyncratic system is, however, already rich. Such failures are not likely to precipitate systemic failure, and so leave the authorities the greatest room for exercising more severity in response. So a simple calculation of the number of failing banks *not* rescued from our sample in the Appendix will understate the total population of failing banks not rescued.

Even so, there is an obvious inequity involved in rescuing *all* depositors in large banks, but not in small banks. The application of a 'too big to fail' doctrine, though widespread in practice, does lead to an uncomfortable discrimination, a discrimination which leads to resentment, and may be challenged by those involved, e.g. on grounds of bias, see the case of the Freedom National Bank in the USA, (case 101 in Appendix 3).

It is not true that *all* large banks, or financial intermediaries, will be rescued, but the best known examples where there has been no rescue, i.e. BCCI and Drexel Burnham Lambert, have occurred when the bank (intermediary) was an 'outsider', i.e. had become somewhat excluded from the rest of the system, so that the failure, despite being large in itself, nevertheless could be regarded as having relatively minor, and containable, systemic implications.

Be that as it may, out of our sample of 104 bank failures, 73 resulted in a rescue, and 4 of the final 31 liquidations were only undertaken after initial attempts at a rescue had been tried. There are, of course, some borderline cases, which are difficult to classify. The recent arrangement whereby the Japanese authorities have allowed banks to transfer non-performing property loans to a special reference agency has been treated as a single example of rescue, whereas the number of banks thereby protected from failure may never be known with any accuracy (see case 57 in Appendix 3). Again the many cases, notably in the USA and in the Spain, where the deposit insurance plays a large role in dealing with failing banks, the fund splits the loan book of the failing bank into a 'bad' part, where it assumes the loss, and a 'good' part, which is on-sold to another bank. We have treated such cases as representing 'rescues'.

What the data in our Appendix demonstrate is that it has been the revealed preference of the monetary authorities in *all* developed countries to rescue those large banks whose failure *might* lead to a contagious, systemic failure. While there is a strand of (liberal) economic argument that regards this state of affairs as deplorable, our maintained assumption is that it will continue. The authorities find the prospects of a collapse in a central, core part of their financial system too awful to contemplate.

We move on, therefore, to a (descriptive) account of, first, how such cases of potential failure have, in practice, been handled, and, second, how such operations have been financed. Data on this matter are reported in Tables 16.1 and 16.2, and on the second in Tables 16.3 and 16.4.

Table 16.1   Methods of dealing with failing banks

Methods	One method		Two methods		Total	
Rescue package (Emergency aid or capital injection)	11	*(4)**	11	*(2)*	**22**	*(6)*
Take-over by bank(s)	33	*(13)*	16	*(4)*	**49**	*(17)*
Special administration or Fund	12	*(1)*	11	*(3)*	**23**	*(4)*
Liquidation	27	*(10)*	4	*(1)*	**31**	*(11)*
Subtotal	83	*(28)*	42	*(10)*		
Total	**83**	**(28)**	**21**	**(5)**	**104**	**(33)**

* The numbers in italics within brackets represent the cases in countries in which the Central Bank combines the monetary and supervisory functions.

Table 16.2   Cases in which two methods were applied

Two methods	Rescue package		Take-over		Special administration		Liquidation	
Rescue package	–		7	*(1)*	1	*(0)*	3	*(1)*
Take-over	7	*(1)**	–		9	*(3)*	0	*(0)*
Special administration	1	*(0)*	9	*(3)*	–		1	*(0)*
Liquidation	3	*(1)*	0	*(0)*	1	*(0)*	–	
Total	**11**	**(2)**	**16**	**(4)**	**11**	**(3)**	**4**	**(1)**

* The numbers in italics within brackets represent the cases in countries in which the Central Bank combines the monetary and supervisory functions.

Table 16.3   Sources of funding for failing banks

Sources of funding	One source		Two sources		Three sources		Four sources		Total	
Central Bank	2	*(1)**	18	*(5)*	5	*(0)*	2	*(0)*	**27**	*(6)*
Deposit insurance	22	*(9)*	11	*(3)*	5	*(0)*	2	*(0)*	**40**	*(12)*
Government	18	*(3)*	5	*(0)*	3	*(0)*	2	*(0)*	**28**	*(3)*
Banks	9	*(5)*	12	*(6)*	2	*(0)*	2	*(0)*	**25**	*(11)*
No external funding	23	*(8)*	–		–		–		**23**	*(8)*
Subtotal	74	*(26)*	46	*(14)*	15	*(0)*	8	*(0)*		
Total	**74**	**(26)**	**23**	**(7)**	**5**	**(0)**	**2**	**(0)**	**104**	**(33)**

* The numbers in italics within brackets represent the cases in countries in which the Central Bank combines the monetary and supervisory functions.

Table 16.4   Cases in which two sources of funding were used

Two sources of funding	Central Bank		Deposit insurance		Government		Banks	
Central Bank	–		6	*(1)*	4	*(0)*	8	*(4)*
Deposit insurance	6	*(1)**	–		1	*(0)*	4	*(2)*
Government	4	*(0)*	1	*(0)*	–		0	*(0)*
Banks	8	*(4)*	4	*(2)*	0	*(0)*	–	
Total	**18**	*(5)*	**11**	*(3)*	**5**	*(0)*	**12**	*(6)*

* The numbers in italics within brackets represent the cases in countries in which the Central Bank combines the monetary and supervisory functions.

As already noted, in only about one third of the cases was the bank(s) in difficulties liquidated (wound-up). The most common response was to arrange for a bank to be taken over by another bank, in many cases with assistance or encouragement from the regulatory authorities. In the remaining cases, the rescue was directly handled by the regulatory authorities, either by a rescue package, or by the regulator administering the bank directly. The latter could often be described as cases of partial, or complete, nationalisation by a public sector body.

In 33 of the cases in the Appendix, the failing bank was registered in a country where the Central Bank combined the micro and macro functions of monetary control and supervision. Direct rescue packages, and partial nationalisation, were marginally less common in such countries, and arranged bank take-overs more common, but the sample is so small, and the allocation by type often so judgementally arbitrary, that such distinctions are not significant.

The second main question that we have sought to illustrate, (from the basic data in Appendix 3), is how these operations were financed. In 23 cases, about one quarter of the sample, no external financing was used. In 22 cases the deposit insurance fund took on the whole burden, and in 18 cases the Government did so. It is comparatively rare for the commercial banks to put up money in such cases just by themselves, 9 cases; they are much more likely to do so in conjunction with one of the other official bodies, 16 cases. It is very rare for a Central Bank to undertake a rescue just by itself, 2 cases.[21] It will almost always, as already noted in the Introduction, do so in conjunction with commercial banks (8 cases), or one of the public sector bodies (10 cases), or with two, or more, categories of supporting institutions (7 cases).

When we look at the sub-set of cases arising in countries where the micro and macro functions of banking regulation and monetary policy are combined, the impression is that the finance of failing banks in undertaken more through the private sector, i.e. banks, and less by the public sector. In these countries there were relatively few direct calls on the Government for the funding of rescues (3 cases), and, perhaps more surprisingly, the Central Bank itself was relatively infrequently involved (6 cases). We do, however, need to stress once again the small, and non-random, size of the sample.

The overall set of cases has indicated that support is not only given to keep the (main) banks afloat, but also to assist their large clients in some cases. In such cases (e.g. cases 5, 6 and 34 in Appendix 3), the authorities were actively involved (either with money or with strong pressure) to support these banks *and* their large industrial borrowers/depositors. Furthermore, the secondary banking crisis in the UK (case 92) showed that a Central Bank cannot always restrict its support to main banks and may feel compelled to assist secondary banks if it believes that problems at secondary banks can have serious repercussions on the major primary banks.

What lessons, if any, can we learn from this listing of recent cases of banks which have run into difficulties? First, there have been many such cases covering a wide range of (most) developed countries. Bank failures are not uncommon, nor limited to a few countries. They can be expected to occur. Second, the authorities have been reluctant to see such failures end in straightforward liquidation. In only 31 cases out of 104 were the banks liquidated and in 20 cases out of these 31 liquidations were deposit insurance payouts made. Third, a system where the Central Bank remains in charge of supervision and regulation is somewhat more likely to involve the commercial banks with financing rescues and there is less likelihood of a call upon the public (tax-payers) purse than when the regulatory function is hived off to a separate agency.

Although this latter reliance on self-financing may be seen as desirable, it is doubtful how far it will be sustainable much longer. It does, quite largely, depend on the cohesion of a well-defined group of banks who are prepared to finance a self-supporting regime under the leadership, usually, of a Central Bank. This is most easily achieved when such banks form a clear-cut cartel with a defined membership.

Indeed, where the cartel is particularly strong, as in Germany, it is possible for the member banks to finance the small number of rescues necessary in such circumstances without reference to either the Central Bank or the government. In such circumstances the supervisory and regulatory agency may be independent of both the government and the Central Bank. Whether such a system could survive in a much more competitive banking milieu is debatable.

The erosion of such cartels, under the influence of international competition and deregulation, has led to growing problems with such a system. Greater competition made commercial banks less willing to participate, and reduced the clout of the Central Bank in dragooning unwilling commercial bank 'volunteers'. Moreover, the growing fuzziness of the dividing line between banks and non-banks, the problems raised by foreign banks (and Home vs Host responsibilities), would allow for endless discussion and recrimination over the question of what share of the 'rescue' each 'volunteer' should undertake. For example, the problems that the Bank of England faced in organising the joint Central Bank/bank rescue of Johnson Matthey Bankers were so severe that it called into question the future use, and viability, of this technique.

In so far as the structure of the banking system so develops that implicit CB/bank insurance becomes problematical, then the normal way forward has been to codify and to standardise the insurance system so that each participant's obligations and rights becomes known. Such explicit insurance is usually given statutory support in an Act of Government. See, again, the details of Deposit Insurance recorded in Appendix 1b. There are manifold problems with such explicit deposit insurance. It is extraordinarily hard either to define risk in banking, or to do so in such a way as will avoid (undesirable) portfolio re-adjustments. Large branch banks will claim, with some justification, that they are inherently less risky (per pound of deposits) than small branch banks. In part because the perceived problem is one of systemic contagion, rather than independent, stochastic illness, it is not possible to identify *ex ante* the level of premium that will meet, to any objective level of probability, the potential calls on the explicit insurance fund. In general, therefore, it is necessary to have a funding back-stop to an explicit insurance fund. In some large part because such a back-stop is, by nature, open-ended, whereas the own-funds available to a Central Bank are limited, the back-stop is usually a Government guarantee, with an implied potential *ex post* call on the tax-payer.

As already noted, there is a particularly acute problem with the treatment of large banks. Whereas they are generally less risky and likely to fail, (e.g. because of greater diversification), they are more likely to be rescued, should they nevertheless run into difficulties; 'too big to fail'. They are also more likely to be multi-nationals, whose treatment will therefore involve international ramifications. The only suggested solution is to be even tougher in supervising such banks. But whether this 'solution' has implications for the question of who, which agency, should be responsible for such supervision is less clear. Such huge banks will often have, or be able to generate, considerable political clout. There is, perhaps, a case for keeping the supervision of such very large banks in the hands of an (independent) Central Bank on the grounds that it may be better able to stand up against them at times of confrontation, but this argument is thin.

So far we have examined the taxonomy of LOLR, bank 'rescue' and insurance, largely without reference to the question of whether the function of regulation and supervision *should* be undertaken by the Central Bank, or hived off to a separate agency. There are several approaches possible here. We shall concentrate on three. First, that the Central Bank should (continue to) be primarily responsible for these functions by itself. Second, that a Government financed, and appointed, separate body should do the job. Third, that there should be some division of responsibilities and functions between the Central Bank and a separate (quasi-governmental) body.

We start with the principle that, he who pays the piper, calls the tune. So long as rescue and insurance were undertaken on an implicit Central Bank/ bank basis, without government finance or involvement, then the Central Bank would normally want, as indeed the commercial banks under its wing would also want it to do, to undertake the conjunct function of regulation and supervision. But this is increasingly ceasing to be so in many countries.

When, and if, the system switches to one wherein the insurance is explicit, particularly when enacted by Statute and provided with financial backstop by the Government, then the balance of advantage shifts. If the tax-payer is seen as potentially liable, then the politician will reckon that she has the ultimate responsibility, so that the regulatory/supervisory agency should answer to the Government. While the Government may, therefore, feel impelled to take ultimate responsibility, it too is likely to delegate authority to a quasi-autonomous body (a Quango), if only to escape the onus and mud flung about when failures do occur. If so, particularly if the Central Bank wishes to maintain its independence of action in other fields, there is a much stronger case for a separation of function, with a division between the Central Bank and the agency, or agencies, charged with regulation, supervision, authorisation, closure and insurance.

It would, however, be difficult to make such a division of responsibilities complete. A problem with an explicit, (government-based), insurance scheme, is that the process of pay-out and the provision of funds is often lengthy, bureaucratic and cumbersome. In contrast, the need of banks for funding in the case of liquidity/solvency crisis is often sudden and immediate. If only because of institutional and organisational structure, the Central Bank generally remains the only source of *immediate* funding. So, it may be, in practice, hardly possible to divorce the Central Bank completely from a large role in any 'rescue' exercise, even if the ultimate responsibility and 'deep pockets' lies with the Government.

To some extent such a divorce may be possible if the Central Bank only lends against first-class collateral, or if the lending is both requested, and indemnified, by the separate regulatory agency. Nevertheless, the fact that the Central Bank remains the only practicable source of immediate funding does mean that a separate agency would need to work very closely with the Central Bank. So, whereas it *may* be possible to create a clear division of *responsibility*, there is likely to be a continuing overlap in operation and decision-making.

This latter consideration may suggest some formal division of responsibilities with a separate, quasi-governmental, body responsible for deposit insurance, conduct of business regulations and consumer protection; whereas the Central Bank would continue to supervise the clearing and payment system, be responsible for systemic stability, and undertake Lender of Last Resort operations. This, however, raises several difficult questions. First, who would be responsible for closing weak banks, (authorisation would presumably be done by the separate authority)? Closure might, in some cases, impinge *both* on systemic stability *and* deposit insurance. The Central Bank may then be in favour of keeping the troubled bank afloat with Lender of Last Resort support, in particular when collateral reduces almost completely its own risk.[22] The Deposit Insurance Agency, however, may favour an early suspension of payments (and closure) to prevent (further) losses. One answer might be to make *both* institutions responsible, and allow closure at the request of either, unless the other authority made a written plea to the Chancellor for stay of execution, but this runs up against the problem that decisions will often be required in such cases in hours, rather than days.

A second, more conceptual, problem is that the Central Bank, responsible for systemic stability, would tend to focus on the 'systemic' banks and leave the smaller banks to the separate agency, which would effectively reinforce the 'too big to fail' problem. However, the failure of banks other than the main Clearing (Settlement) banks could also cause systemic problems, so there would remain a fuzzy overlap between those banks primarily supervised by the Central Bank and those primarily under the direction of the separate authority. But this could, perhaps, be settled by diplomacy between two institutions, which would have to work very closely together. A third problem is who would take the lead, e.g. in international forums, in discussing and implementing capital adequacy requirements. The establishment of such requirements, and – just as important – the agreement of phased consequential measures when they are breached, as has been proposed in the USA, obviously impinges on both the (potentially separable) regulatory functions, of systemic stability and consumer protection.

We can, therefore, see numerous difficulties in proceeding further with this third alternative, that of dividing the supervisory functions between two separate institutions. Nevertheless, this route is looking increasingly attractive to the authorities in the UK (Quinn, 1993). In some respects it mirrors what has already been done in the USA.

16.4 CONCLUSIONS

The fact that the functions of banking regulation and supervision on the one hand, and monetary policy on the other, are separated in about half the countries reviewed, and combined in the other, suggests that there are no overwhelming arguments for either model. And that is what we find.

The main case that is usually presented for separation is on grounds of 'conflict of interest'. In its simplest form, that Lender of Last Resort assistance injects additional base money, the argument is feeble. There are, however, stronger grounds for claiming that those concerned with the 'health' of the banking system have, on occasions, sought to restrain interest rate increases desired for other macro reasons, but this may in part reflect a difference of view about how financial factors affect the economy. Such views may, in turn, depend on the particular structure of the banking system, so the question of the appropriate design of regulatory system will need to be answered against the particular financial/banking structure of each country, rather than being capable of resolution as an abstract generality.

This latter is particularly relevant in an examination of a Central Bank's role as 'guarantor' of the smooth functioning of the payment system. While it is possible to envisage the development of systems that are both efficient and safe, that remains still many years in the future. For the time being, there is likely to be an important role for the Central Bank both in organising and supporting such systems. This implies both an assumption of credit risk, and/or a need to deal with emerging liquidity risks. If so, the Central Bank is likely to want to maintain some regulatory and supervisory functions in order to limit such risks. This is, perhaps, the strongest current ground for advocating the continuing combination of such functions.

The main, historical, basis for arguing in favour of such a combination was rather the Central Bank's objective of preventing contagious systemic crises. Despite the growing chorus of academics deploring such rescues on grounds of moral hazard, there is no evidence of the authorities becoming more willing to accept failures (NB recent events in Scandinavia and Japan). But Central Banks *are* tending to retreat from their previous primary role for two related reasons. First the banking system is becoming less clearly defined, fuzzier; consequently it is less easy to persuade the members of the banking club to agree to cooperate in financing rescues. So, the second reason is that the Central Bank is less able to organise cooperation on a self-regulatory basis. There is more need to turn to the Government both for statutory measures, and for ultimate financial support. This latter means that the regulatory/supervisory function is tending to shift away from Central Bank control to an independent body more directly under political control. This is, we argue, largely the consequence of structural developments. Even so, the continuing role of the Central Bank as the only available source of immediate last resort liquidity means that, even if formally separated, the two bodies would have to work in practice very closely together.

Consequently, even though a formal separation of function may now become more common among countries than in the past, there remains a question whether that change would make much difference to the practical realities.

APPENDIX 1A: MONETARY AND SUPERVISORY AGENCIES

Country	Monetary agency	Supervisory agency	
Australia	Reserve Bank of Australia (CB)	Reserve Bank of Australia (CB)	C 1
Austria	National Bank of Austria (CB)	(Federal) Ministry of Finance (MF)	S 2
Belgium	National Bank of Belgium (CB)	Banking and Finance Commission	S 3
Brazil	Central Bank of Brazil (CB)	Central Bank of Brazil (CB)	C 4
Canada	Bank of Canada (CB)	Office of the Superintendent of Financial Institutions (MF)	S 5
Denmark	Danmarks Nationalbank (CB)	Finance Inspectorate (MI)	S 6
Finland	Bank of Finland (CB)	Bank Inspectorate (MF) Bank of Finland (CB)	S 7
France	Banque de France (CB)	Banque de France (CB) Commission Bancaire	C 8
Germany	Deutsche Bundesbank (CB)	Bundesaufsichtsamt für das Kreditwesen Deutsche Bundesbank (CB)	S 9
Greece	Bank of Greece (CB)	Bank of Greece (CB)	C
Hong Kong	Hong Kong Monetary Authority (CB?)	Hong Kong Monetary Authority (CB?)	C 10
India	Reserve Bank of India (CB)	Reserve Bank of India (CB)	C
Ireland	Central Bank of Ireland (CB)	Central Bank of Ireland (CB)	C
Italy	Banca d'Italia (CB)	Banca d'Italia (CB)	C
Japan	Bank of Japan (CB)	Ministry of Finance (MF) Bank of Japan (CB)	S 11
Luxembourg	Luxembourg Monetary Institute (CB)	Luxembourg Monetary Institute (CB)	C 12
The Netherlands	De Nederlandsche Bank (CB)	De Nederlandsche Bank (CB)	C
New Zealand	Reserve Bank of New Zealand (CB)	Reserve Bank of New Zealand (CB)	C
Norway	Norges Bank (CB)	Banking, Insurance and Securities Commission (MF)	S 13
Philippines	Central Bank of the Philippines (CB)	Central Bank of the Philippines (CB)	C
Portugal	Banco de Portugal (CB)	Banco de Portugal (CB)	C
Spain	Banco de Espana (CB)	Banco de Espana (CB)	C 14
Sweden	Sveriges Riksbank (CB)	Swedish Financial Supervisory Authority	S 15
Switzerland	Swiss National Bank (CB)	Federal Banking Commission	S 16
United Kingdom	Bank of England (CB)	Bank of England (CB)	C
United States	Federal Reserve Board (CB)	Office of the Comptroller of the Currency (MF) Federal Reserve Board (CB) State Governments Federal Deposit Insurance Corporation	S 17
Venezuela	Banco Central de Venezuela (CB)	Superintendency of Banks	S 18

Notes on Monetary and Supervisory Agencies

Those countries were selected for which data were available in OECD (1987), OECD (1992) and IBCA (various Country Reports).

C   = Combined
S   = Separated
CB = Central Bank
MF = Ministry of Finance (and Economy)
MI = Ministry of Industry

1. There is no lender of last resort of the conventional type available to Australian banks. Only the nine authorised dealers in the short-term money market have access to borrowing facilities at the Reserve Bank.
2. The Ministry of Finance is the banking regulation and supervisory authority. The role of the National Bank of Austria is similar to that of the Bundesbank (see below) in so far as the Bank does statistical work for the Ministry of Finance and gives advice on supervisory matters.
3. The Banking Commission is a legally autonomous public institution and has a twofold task: controlling the banks and controlling the issuing of public securities. A law concerning financial transactions and financial markets passed in June 1991 and provided among other things for the extension of the powers of the Banking Commission. The Banking Commission will change its name to the Banking and Finance Commission and will be responsible for recognition of companies on the stock exchange and partly for their careful monitoring.
4. The National Monetary Council, which is dominated by government officials and chaired by the Finance Minister, coordinates monetary policy and determines prudential regulations, while the Central Bank of Brazil is the executive arm for the monetary and supervisory policy.
5. The Office of the Superintendent of Financial Institutions (OSFI) was created in June 1987, and is the product of the merger of the Office of the Inspector General of Banks and the Superintendent of Insurance. OSFI is responsible for the supervision of all regulated financial institutions that are federally incorporated, that is banks, trust and loan companies, insurance companies and cooperatives. The Superintendent is an officer of the Department of Finance (like his predecessor the Inspector General).
6. The Finance Inspectorate was formed at the end of 1987 as a result of the merger of the Bank Inspectorate and the Insurance Industry Inspectorate. The Finance Inspectorate is a directorate of the Ministry of Industry. The Nationalbank is the granter of liquidity support, while the Inspectorate is responsible for the supervision of banks. The Inspectorate has no formal link with the Nationalbank, although there is in practice cooperation between the two on many issues.
7. The Bank of Finland supervises foreign exchange operations, international operations and the use of central bank credit by banks. The Bank Inspectorate is administratively subordinate to the Ministry of Finance. It is responsible for the regulation and supervision of banks, securities firms and unit trusts.
8. The Banking Commission (Commission Bancaire) is a composite body chaired by the governor of the Banque de France. It includes representatives from Trésor Public, Conseil d'État, Cour de Cassation and some selected persons. The Banking Commission supervises compliance with the prudential regulations. The inspections and on-site examinations are carried out by the Banque de France on behalf of the Banking Commission.The Committee on Bank Regulation (Comité de la Réglementation Bancaire) establishes prudential rules. The Committee on Credit Institutions (Comité des Etablissements de Crédit) is responsible for licensing new banks. In all three commissions both the Banque de France and the Ministry of Economy and Finance are represented.
9. The Bundesaufsichtsamt is entrusted with the supervision of banks. It is responsible for sovereign acts, such as licensing and issuing regulations, whereas the Bundesbank is involved in current supervision by collecting and processing bank supervisory returns.

The Banking Act provides for cooperation with the Bundesbank (communicate information, and the Aufsichtsamt has to consult the Bank on new regulations).

10. The Office of the Exchange Fund managed the foreign exchange reserves. The Office of the Banking Commissioner was responsible for supervision. On 1 April 1993 both Offices merged formally into a single body, the Hong Kong Monetary Authority.

11. The Ministry of Finance (in particular the Banking Bureau) has broad responsibility for licensing, regulating, supervising banks (authority derived from the Banking Law). The Bank of Japan has no regulatory power stemming from law. The Bank of Japan's authority is rather contractual and is generally based on an individual agreement with its client banks.

12. On supervisory matters the Institute is advised by a consultative committee in which a number of bankers participate.

13. The Banking, Insurance and Securities Commission, founded in 1986, is administratively subordinate to the Ministry of Finance. This Commission has the authority to supervise all financial institutions, whereas the Minister of Finance grants licences to set up a bank.

14. Under general directives of the Ministry of Economy and Finance, the Banco de España is responsible for the supervision of private banks, savings banks and credit cooperatives. The Official Credit Institute (Instituto de Crédito Oficial) is the intermediary between the Ministry of Economy and Finance and the official credit institutions, which provide official credit (their market share is less than 10%). The Institute is responsible for the supervision of these official credit institutions.

15. The Bank Inspection Board used to be responsible for the supervision of banks. Supervisors of banks, securities and insurance companies merged into Swedish Financial Supervisory Authority as of 1st July 1991.

16. The Federal Banking Commission is an independent federal authority.

17. The Office of the Comptroller of the Currency, an agency within the US Treasury Department, supervises national banks and federally licensed branches of foreign banks. The Federal Reserve Board and the State Governments supervise state chartered banks which are members of the Federal Reserve System. State chartered, non-member banks are supervised by the State Governments. The Federal Reserve Board has the authority to supervise all banking holding companies and their subsidiaries. In addition, the autonomous Federal Deposit Insurance Corporation has some supervisory responsibilities.

18. The Superintendency of Banks (Superintendencia de Bancos) is responsible for supervision of banks. It must inform the Ministry of Finance and the Central Bank of serious problem detected. As a 'watch dog' however, the Superintendency has no power to act on its findings; only the Ministry of Finance and the Central Bank may do so.

Sources: OECD (1987), *Prudential Supervision in Banking* (Paris).
OECD (1992), *Banks under Stress* (Paris).
IBCA, 'Country Reports of Banking Systems' (London).
Financial Times Business Information (1991), 'Banking in the EC, 1991: Structures and Sources of Finance' (London).
Several Central Banks.

APPENDIX 1B: DEPOSIT INSURANCE AGENCIES

Country	Name of scheme	Administration	Membership year established	Level of protection	Level in $ 1	Funding	Contingency funding
Australia	No scheme	–	–	–	–	–	–
Austria	Deposit Guarantee Fund	PR	Compulsory 1987	ASh 200,000	$18,000	On demand	Max. one-third of member banks' liability reserve; Government backed bonds may be issued
Belgium	Intervention Fund 2	J	Voluntary 1985	BFr 500,000	$15,400	0.02% p.a. of BFr deposits	None, insurance limited to assets in fund
Brazil	Preparing a scheme 3	–	–	–	–	–	–
Canada	Canada Deposit Insurance Corporation	PU	Compulsory 1967	C$60,000	$47,100	0.1% p.a. of protected class of deposits	Borrowing up to C$ 6 bn authorised; further borrowing subject to Parliamentary approval
Denmark	Deposit Guarantee Fund	PR	Compulsory 1987	DKr 250,000	$41,300	0.2% p.a. of non-bank deposits until	Borrowing from from banks, with possible

continued on page 364

APPENDIX 1B: CONTINUED

Country	Name of scheme	Administration		Membership year established	Level of protection	Level in $ 1	Funding	Contingency funding
Finland	Deposit Guarantee Fund of the Commercial Banks 5	Governing Board	PR	Compulsory 1969	No ceiling	No ceiling	Fund reaches its target level of DKr 3 bn	guarantee of Ministry of Industry
France	Deposit Guarantee Fund	French Banking Association	PR	Compulsory 1980	FFr 400,000	$75,200	On demand, calls up to FFr 200 mn p.a.	Extra calls up to FFr 1,000 mn can be made in regard to a five-year period
Germany	Einlagen-sicherungs-fonds	Federal German Banking Association	PR	Voluntary 6 1966	Up to 30% of bank's equity capital	Up to 30% of bank's equity capital	0.03% p.a. of total deposits	Annual levy may be doubled
Greece	Preparing a scheme	–		–	–	–	–	–
Hong Kong	No scheme 7	–		–	–	–	–	–

Between 0.01% and 0.5% p.a. of total assets

Country		Scheme			Compulsory/Voluntary	Coverage limit	$ equivalent	Premium	Notes
India	PU	Deposit Insurance and Credit Guarantee Corporation	Deposit Insurance and Credit Guarantee Corporation		Compulsory 1962	Rs 30,000	$1,000	0.04% p.a. of total deposits	Government backing through the Reserve Bank subject to Parliamentary approval
Ireland	PU	Deposit Protection Fund	Central Bank of Ireland		Compulsory 1989	80% of first I£ 5,000; 70% of next I£ 5,000; 50% of next I£ 5,000	$16,800	0.2% of total I£ deposits	Fund is recalculated annually
Italy	J	Interbank Deposit Protection Fund 8	Interbank Deposit Protection Fund Council		Voluntary 1987	100% of first L1,200mln; 75% of next L800mln	$551,500	Max. of 1% of total deposits; amount not to exceed L 2 bn	Two options: defer payment or diminish the compensation to be paid
Japan	J	Deposit Insurance Corporation 9	Deposit Insurance Corporation		Compulsory 1971	¥ 10 mln	$81,100	0.012% p.a. of domestic Yen deposits	Borrowing up to ¥500 bn from Bank of Japan subject to Ministry of Finance approval
Luxembourg	PR	Deposit Guarantee 10	Association for the Guarantee of Deposits		Voluntary 1989	LFr 500,000	$15,400	On demand, max. of 5% p.a. of own funds	—

continued on page 366

APPENDIX 1B: CONTINUED

Country	Name of scheme	Administration	Membership year established	Level of protection	Level in $ 1	Funding	Contingency funding
The Netherlands	Collective Guarantee Scheme 11	De Nederlandsche Bank	J	Compulsory 1980	NF 40,000	$22,600	On demand, max. of 5% p.a. of own funds	Government backing subject to parliamentary approval
New Zealand	No scheme	–	–	–	–	–	–
Norway	Commercial Banks' Contingency Fund 12	Commercial Banks' Contingency Fund Board	J	Compulsory 1961	No Ceiling 13	No Ceiling	0.015% p.a. of total assets until Fund reaches 2% of aggregate deposits	Guarantees issued by the member banks in proportion to their non-bank deposits; these guarantees are collaterized with cash or government bonds deposits with Norges Bank
Philippines	Permanent Insurance Fund	Philippines Deposit Insurance Corporation 14	PU	Compulsory 1963	P40,000	$1,600	0.083% p.a. of total deposits	Government backing subject to Senate approval

	Scheme	Organization	Status	Coverage (local)	Coverage ($)	Contribution	Backing
Portugal	Preparing a scheme	–	–	–	–	–	–
Spain	Deposit Guarantee Fund 15	Banco de Espana	PU	Voluntary 1977	Pts 1,500,000	$13,500	0.2% p.a. of total deposits, supplemented by a contribution from the Banco de Espana 16	Government backing through the Banco de Espana, subject to approval by Royal Decree
Sweden	Preparing a scheme 17	–	–	–	–	–	–
Switzerland	Convention XVIII 18	Swiss Bankers' Association	PR	Voluntary 1984	SFr 30,000	$20,800	On demand	Underwritten by member banks
United Kingdom	Deposit Protection Fund	Deposit Protection Board 19	J	Compulsory 1982	75% of first £20,000	$23,400	Initial contribution plus calls subject to max of 0.3% of £ deposits	Parliament may increase the maximum percentage payable; £125 mn advance facility with the Bank of England
United States	Federal Deposit Insurance Corporation	Federal Deposit Insurance Corporation 20	PU	Compulsory 21 1934	$100,000	$100,000	0.23% of total domestic deposits	Borrowing up to 3 bn from the Treasury
Venezuela	Not known	–	–	–	–	–	–

Notes on deposit insurance agencies

Those countries were selected for which details were provided on the monetary and supervisory agencies in appendix 1a.

PU Officially organised.
PR Industry arrangements.
J   Joint by authorities and participating banks.

1. Exchange rates against US $ on January 25, 1993

2. The Intervention Fund is created through a protocol signed by the Rediscount and Guarantee Institute and the Belgian Banking Association. The Institute, an intermediary of the National Bank of Belgium, has two functions: to rediscount short-term commercial bills presented to it by financial institutions, which are passed on to the National Bank, and to manage the Intervention Fund. However, the Institute needs the approval of the Intervention Fund Committee, which consists of representatives of the contributing banks, for important decisions, such as rescue operations.

3. In September, 1988, the National Monetary Council created a new type of financial institution classified as 'multiple banks', which can act in a similar way to the European universal banks. All multiple banks are to participate in a new deposit insurance scheme set up by the National Monetary Council. The scheme needs approval of Congress.

4. The agency is led by a five member board appointed by the Minister of Industry, the chairman and one member being independent individuals with economic and legal expertise, two members nominated by the insured banks and one by consumer interests. The board accepted an offer by the Nationalbank to provide secretariat services as it was thought that a permanent independent administration would not be practical.

5. The Deposit Guarantee Fund of the Commercial Banks is an independent institution owned by its members (commercial banks), and has its own governing board. In addition, there are similar guarantee funds owned by savings banks and cooperative banks.

6. Voluntary, but de facto compulsory, since a banking licence will not be issued to a bank that does not participate in a depositor protection scheme.

7. After having circulated a consultation paper on the options for a deposit protection scheme (Hong Kong, 1992), the government decided in January 1993 not to have one, but to amend legislation to give preferential treatment to small depositors in the liquidation of a bank.

8. The Interbank Deposit Protection Fund is organised as a banks' consortium under the aegis of the Italian Banking Association and the Banca d'Italia.

9. The Governor of the Deposit Insurance Corporation is the Vice-Governor of the Bank of Japan. The management also includes representatives of the private financial institutions, who are members of it.

10. It is a mutual, non-profit making association.

11. The Collective Guarantee Scheme is established in joint cooperation between the banks and the Nederlandsche Bank.

12. The Contingency Fund is an independent legal identity and its activities are administered by a board of directors comprising seven members. Five of the members are elected by the member banks, while one member is appointed by the Norges Bank and the last member is the director of the Banking, Insurance and Securities Commission.

13. The Commercial Banks' Contingency Fund has no formal obligation to cover the losses of all depositors in a failing bank; the law states that the board decides on the degree of coverage in each individual case. But in practice deposits have always been covered in full.

14. The Philippines Deposit Insurance Corporation's Board is chaired by the Central Bank Governor, with the PDIC president and the Undersecretary of Finance as members.

15. The Deposit Guarantee Fund (Fondo de Garantia de Depositos) is a branch of the Banco de Espana and is engaged in preventing bank crises and in insuring deposits. The first type of intervention includes the surveillance activity on a problem bank from the fund, take-over operations and finally the possibility of selling troubled banks. In addition, the Banking Corporation (Corporacion Bancaria) was created with the objective to acquire a majority shareholding in troubled banks, to re-establish sound management and a secure base for operations and ultimately to sell back the shareholding to the private sector. If it is clear that a bank cannot be returned to a healthy state, then it is liquidated. However, it was decided to enlarge the Deposit Guarantee Fund, which was considered to be a more satisfactory means of dealing with ailing banks.

16. From 1994 on the Banco de Espana will stop its contribution to the Deposit Guarantee Fund.

17. Sweden has been working on the introduction of a deposit protection scheme. However, this is postponed till the present banking crisis is resolved. To deal with the banking crisis, a temporary Bank Support Authority has been set up to channel government support to the troubled banking sector (see Appendix 3).

18. The so-called Convention XVIII is an agreement among the members of the Swiss Bankers' Association under which banks mutually guarantee savings deposits. The convention does not provide the depositor with a legal claim. Although it has therefore no legal status as deposit insurance, we rank the convention under deposit insurance agencies, as its purpose is to provide deposit protection.

19. The Deposit Protection Board consists of the Governor of the Bank of England as Chairman, two other ex-officio members of the Bank of England, three members of contributory institutions, together with a number of officers of the Bank of England.

20. The Corporation is run by a three member Board of Directors. Two directors are appointed by the President for six-year terms and third is the Comptroller of the Currency, an ex-officio member.

21. Compulsory for FED member and national banks.

Sources: OECD (1987), *Prudential Supervision in Banking* (Paris).
Financial Regulation Report (1991), 'Deposit Insurance in the EC – A Comparative Survey' (October), pp. 10–12.
Hong Kong (1992), Consultation Paper: Deposit Protection Scheme' (February).
The South East Asian Central Banks (SEACEN) (1991) 'Deposit Insurance Schemes: Its Nature, Role and Issues' (Kuala Lumpur),
Rita Carisano (1992), *Deposit Insurance: Theory, Policy and Evidence*, (Aldershot: Dartmouth).
Several Central Banks.

APPENDIX 2: INFLATION PERFORMANCE

Table　　　　　Average annual inflation rates

MONETARY AND SUPERVISORY FUNCTIONS COMBINED

Countries	1980–91	1980–87	
Australia	7.9[1]	(8.7)[2]	
Brazil (D)[3]	547.9	(153.4)	
France	6.7	(8.4)	
Greece	19.6	(21.0)	AVERAGE
India (D)	9.5	(9.5)	
Ireland	8.3	(10.9)	All countries:
Italy	10.6	(12.8)	48.4%　(21.5%)
Luxembourg	4.5	(5.3)	
Netherlands	2.9	(3.4)	
New Zealand	10.6	(13.3)	Industrial countries:
Philippines (D)	15.3	(16.2)	9.5%　(11.1%)
Portugal	16.8	(19.3)	
Spain	9.6	(11.4)	
United Kingdom	7.5	(7.7)	

MONETARY AND SUPERVISORY FUNCTIONS SEPARATED

Countries	1980–91	1980–87	
Austria	3.7[1]	(4.2)[2]	
Belgium	4.6	(5.6)	
Canada	6.3	(7.0)	AVERAGE
Denmark	6.2	(7.5)	
Finland	7.0	(7.7)	All countries:
Germany	2.9	(3.1)	7.1%　(6.8%)
Hong Kong (D)[3,4]	8.9	(8.7)	
Japan	2.6	(2.8)	
Norway	7.6	(9.0)	Industrial countries:
Sweden	8.3	(8.4)	5.3%　(5.9%)
Switzerland	3.7	(3.5)	
United States	5.4	(5.8)	
Venezuela (D)	25.5	(14.6)	

Source: International Financial Statistics, *Yearbook 1992* (IMF).

1. Average annual inflation rates for 1980–91.
2. Average annual inflation rates for 1980–7.
3. Developing Countries.
4. During the 1980–91 period Hong Kong had a separated regime for monetary policy and banking supervision (see Appendix 1A).

Following Heller (1991), we calculate the inflation performance of Central Banks with supervisory authority and Central Banks without such a responsibility. We measure the inflation rate by the average annual increase in consumer prices during the period 1980–91. To compare with Heller, we also provide the average annual inflation for the period 1980–7 within brackets. These results differ slightly, because we obtain the consumer prices from the International Financial Statistics of the IMF, while Heller obtains the consumer prices from the World Development Report of the World Bank and from Price Waterhouse. We take the same group of 27 countries as in appendix 1A (monetary and supervisory agencies), and distinguish between countries where the monetary and supervisory functions are combined and countries where these functions are separated. Heller has a group of 16 countries and splits them in three groups: Central Banks without supervisory authority, Central Banks that share supervisory authority, and Central Banks with supervisory authority. As developing countries with their high inflation rates confuse the analysis, we calculate separately the average annual inflation rate for industrial countries in both groups (following the two categories, industrial and developing countries, in the International Financial Statistics (IMF)). Our sample includes all industrial countries, except Iceland, and we regard the inflation performance in these countries as the relevant measure.

Our evidence is in line with Heller's and supports the thesis that *Central Banks without supervisory responsibility have a better inflation track record.* The eleven Central Banks (located in industrial countries) in our sample without such responsibility had an average inflation of 5.3 per cent for 1980–91, while the other eleven Central Banks with supervisory responsibility experienced an average inflation of 9.5 per cent. For the 1980–7 period these figures are 5.9 per cent and 11.1 per cent (Heller reports 3.3 per cent for CB's without supervisory authority, 6.5 per cent for CB's which share such authority, and 9.6 per cent for CB's with supervisory authority). The results do not change, if the developing countries are included. Although a longer time period is desirable, our sample with almost all industrial countries confirms clearly Heller's finding that Central Banks that concentrate fully on monetary policy tend to be more successful in achieving the goal of price stability than Central Banks that have (major) supervisory responsibilities.

As noted in the main text, there may be some correlation between the dependency of the Central Bank for monetary policy and its responsibility for supervision; and it may be the former, rather, than the latter that drives the relative inflation performance. Heller (1991, pp. 278–9) argues in a similar way that:

> It may well be that independent central banks are better in attaining the goal of price stability and that these independent banks also do not tend to have supervisory responsibilities. But in a way, this argument, if found to be true, would support the basic hypothesis: namely that bank supervisory responsibility is a governmental function that is unlikely to be given to a truly independent central bank. In other words, the supervisory role for a central bank does tend to be associated with significant strings in terms of greater dependence on the government.

However, we do not see a causal link between a Central Bank's dependency and its role in banking supervision other than that in those countries where the Central Banks were *dependent* on the government for monetary policy, there may have been some tendency for Central Bank officials to give more weight to other fields in which they could still take the lead, often including more micro-level relationships with financial intermediaries. Our final conclusion is therefore that a Central Bank's involvement in supervision does not necessarily weaken its stance on monetary policy; and consequently we consider a Central Bank's inflation performance and its role in supervision as two, more or less separate, issues. As we argue in the main text, the structure of a country's banking and financial system is probably more important for the conduct of monetary policy, and hence its inflation performance.

APPENDIX 3: SURVEY OF BANK FAILURE

AUSTRALIA

1 Bank of Adelaide, 1979 (IBCA pp. 28-9).

Method: Take-over by bank.
Funding: Banks.
Lead organiser: Reserve Bank of Australia (central bank and supervisor).

The collapse of the Bank of Adelaide arose out of poor property investments made by the bank's finance company subsidiary. After an outflow of call money from the Bank of Adelaide, the major trading banks (with the approval of the Reserve Bank) provided a subordinated loan facility of 50mn dollars. The major trading banks and the Reserve Bank indicated, however, that they would not support Bank of Adelaide and the Reserve Bank advised the Bank of Adelaide to seek a merger with a larger bank. The Bank of Adelaide merged with the Australia & New Zealand Banking Group Ltd.

2 State Bank of Victoria, 1990 (*FT* 29 Aug 90; *FT* 19 Oct 90; *FT* 20 Nov 91; *ECN* 01 Sep 90).

Method: Take-over by bank.
Funding: Government.[1]

The State Bank of Victoria (SBV), owned by the State government of Victoria, ran into difficulties after the crash of its Tricontinental merchant bank subsidiary and its bad debts of 2.7bn dollars were 1bn dollar more than the group's capital base. Commonwealth Bank, one of Australia's big four banks and owned by the federal government, acquired SBV for 1.6bn dollars from the State government as part of a deal which led to the sale to the private sector of up to 30 per cent of the equity of the enlarged bank in 1991. It is understood that the State government of Victoria has provided financial assistance for the bail-out of SBV.

AUSTRIA

3 Allgemeine Wirtschaftsbank, 1975 (IBCA, p. 54).

Method: Liquidation.
Funding: Banks.

It turned out after the failure that the Allgemeine Wirtschaftsbank (AWB), with a balance sheet total of approximately 690mn shillings, had been a fraudulent enter-

---

1. In this Appendix 'government' refers usually to the Central Government. However, in this case it refers to the Government of one of the States in Australia.

prise. The owner and manager of the bank granted large-scale credits to companies close to him (in the last balance sheet this item accounted for about 90 per cent of total claims outstanding). The loans and the exorbitant interest were never repaid by these companies. The balance sheet as well as the profit and loss account were falsified. In order to keep up routine business and to plug 'gaps' in the balance sheet, the AWB increasingly engaged in interbank business. The 1973 annual general audit revealed the malpractice. After the appointment of a government commissioner in 1974, the bank was liquidated in 1975. In October 1974, eleven major banks in Vienna raised 28mn shillings for savings depositors. Depositors owning less than 50,000 shillings were fully paid off and those with claims between 50,000 shillings and 500,000 received 50,000 shillings apiece, while those with claims of over 500,000 shillings received nothing. However, the banks were under no obligation to meet claims of depositors of a failing bank. The 1979 Banking Act provided for the creation of joint facilities for the protection of savings deposits.

4 ATS Bank für Teilzahlungskredite, 1977.

Method: Liquidation.
Funding: Banks.

The failure of ATS Bank für Teilzahlungskredite (with a balance sheet total of about 180mn shillings) is traceable to the over-ambitious business policy of Horst Melcher, owner and director of the bank. Gross negligence (falsification of balance sheets) led to the institution's bankruptcy. Largely responsible for the insolvency of ATS were participations in non-bank enterprises (e.g. suppliers of one-armed bandits, restaurant, travel agency, motel), in which the major borrowers and Melcher himself were personally involved. After the appointment of a government commissioner in 1976, the bank was liquidated in 1977. The ATS caused mainly banks to suffer losses (via interbank deposits). Losses in connection with interbank deposits were covered within the framework of solidarity programmes by the banking sector concerned. Small depositors received a maximum compensation of 50,000 shillings per person thanks to a relief programme organised by all sectors.

5/6 Österreichische Länderbank and Creditanstalt Bankverein, 1980s (*FT* 26 Mar 86; *FT* 09 Oct 91; *FT* 24 Mar 93; IBCA pp. 19–20).

Method: Capital injection.
Funding: Government.

The Austrian government first nationalised Österreichische Länderbank and Creditanstalt Bankverein in 1946 and refloated 40 per cent of its interest in both banks in 1956. In the 1980s the central government bailed out first Länderbank and then Creditanstalt, as they experienced losses on their main industrial debtors. Länderbank was threatened by the bankruptcy of several Austrian large borrowers. As a result of the credits to Eumig and Klimatechnik Länderbank had suffered losses to the amount of 4.2bn shillings. As of 1981, the bank had written off 1.2bn shillings from its reserves and its operating results. As regards the remaining 3bn shillings, the federal government, i.e. the co-owner, met its obligations and adopted the 1981 Guarantee Law. The Law enabled Länderbank to enter the uncollectable receivables as 'dead assets' and write them off over a period of 25 years. The federal government undertook to annually compensate the bank for the write-off and for the lost interest earnings of the dead assets. In the case of Creditanstalt the government had to save industrial stakes on account of various external effects.

Creditanstalt owned industrial interests received federal grants to the amount of about 7.1bn shillings in 1985. However, in the 1990s the central government started a process of gradually privatising both banks to prepare them for the increasingly tough European competition. In 1991 Länderbank merged with the City of Vienna's municipal Zentralsparkasse into Bank Austria. The federal government's share in Creditanstalt has been brought down from 60 per cent. As of January 1993, it comes to less than 50 per cent, though the government has still a majority of the voting power. In Austria, our classification of these two banks is disputed. Conventional wisdom in Austria has it that these two cases were *not* failures. It is said that both banks would have survived even without state intervention although in a scaled down form.

7 Bankhaus Rössler, 1992–3.

Method: Rescue-package, and afterwards take-over by bank.
Funding: Banks, and deposit insurance.

At the beginning of December 1992, when Bankhaus Rössler (balance sheet total of approximately 1.5bn shillings) was threatened with insolvency, the banking supervisory authorities prohibited the bank from operating until February 17, 1993. The factors actually triggering the close down of the bank included creditor banks' withdrawal of interbank deposits and the bankruptcy of two major debtors, in which the bank had held stakes. A policy of generous overdrafts on customer accounts also added to the bank's problems. The supervisory authorities called for the creditor banks and owners to submit a plan sketching out proposals for the future of Rössler. At the beginning of 1993, the creditors, owners, banking supervisory authorities and the Austrian National Bank agreed on a going-concern plan aiming at an out of court compromise to save the bank. Rössler Bank was taken over by Kathrein Bank without recourse to public money. No non-bank customers lost money. The rescue was provided by the owners, bank creditors and the deposit guarantee fund.

BELGIUM

8 Banque pour l'Amérique du Sud, 1976 (IBCA p. 17).

Method: Liquidation.
Funding: Deposit Insurance.

The first bank failure in Belgium, since the legal and institutional reforms affecting the banking system were implemented in 1935, did not occur until August, 1976, when Banque pour l'Amérique du Sud collapsed. This small bank, which was the Belgian subsidiary of an Argentinean family-owned group, collapsed in mysterious circumstances. The Rediscount and Guarantee Institute (which administers the Belgian deposit insurance fund) repaid all Belgian franc deposits, amounting to 45.7mn francs. The Institute was eventually able to recover this from the bank's assets.

9 La Banque Van Loo (IBCA pp. 17–8).

Method: Liquidation.
Funding: Deposit Insurance.
Lead organiser: Banking Commission (supervisor).

La Banque Van Loo, a small family-owned bank, specialised in providing finance to the Brussels livestock market. The bank was declared bankrupt after the managing partner of the bank had filed a brankruptcy petition in January 1978. This petition triggered an investigation by the Banking Commission, which revealed that the bank's accounts had been totally falsified. In a desire not to upset the smooth functioning of the livestock markets and in view of the lack of information about the true state of affairs of the bank, the Commission decided not to require immediate suspension of the bank's activities. However, with effect from 19 January 1978, the Commission, in collaboration with the Institute, set in motion a rescue operation designed to ensure the bank's customers and employees against the consequences of its being declared bankrupt. The Rediscount and Guarantee Institute reimbursed the bank's depositors who were presumed to have acted in good faith and who could show proper title. However, there was a reimbursement ceiling per person and all interest relating to 1977 was excluded, since the rates offered by the bank were deemed excessive. The Institute paid out some 400mn francs of which it expected to recover almost nothing.

10 Banque Belgo-Centrade, 1979 (IBCA pp. 18–9).

Method: Liquidation.
Funding: Deposit Insurance.
Lead organiser: Banking Commission (supervisor).

Judicial investigations into the affairs of Banque Belgo-Centrade revealed that the bank had been acting to aid some of its customers in the evasion of taxes. On discovery of this tax evasion, the Banking Commission suspended the bank's activities for one month. Afterwards the Commission, with the Commercial Court (which discovered the tax evading activities), decided that liquidation was the appropriate solution. The bank was declared bankrupt. The Rediscount and Guarantee Institute intervened on behalf of those depositors who had acted in good faith and were not involved in the scheme for the evasion of taxes. The Institute paid in full individuals who had Belgian franc deposits, up to a certain ceiling, after which repayment was only partial. The Institute had paid out some 22mn francs.

11 Banque Andes, 1980 (IBCA pp. 19–20).

Method: Take-over by bank.
Funding: Deposit Insurance.

Banque Andes was a medium-sized bank incorporated in Belgium, but had a large proportion of foreign shareholders. The bank had liquidity problems and was threatened with a run on deposits. The shareholders wished either to dispose of their interests in the bank or to put it into liquidation. In the meantime, the Rediscount and Guarantee Institute granted the bank a 200mn francs line of credit. In the event, certain assets and the deposits from the public were taken over quickly by another Belgian bank. The line of credit was never utilised and no creditor other than a shareholder suffered any loss.

12 Geoffrey's Bank, 1980 (IBCA p. 20).

Method: Take-over by bank.
Funding: Deposit Insurance.
Lead organiser: Banking Commission (supervisor).

The Banking Commission had long been concerned with the poor liquidity, the lack of proper management and control procedures and with the concentration of Geoffrey's Bank's loans in problem sectors of the economy. After the medium-sized bank began to make losses, the Banking Commission and the Rediscount and Guarantee Institute placed certain conditions on the bank with a view to remedying the situation. Groupe Bancaire Gesbanque, a medium-sized member of a foreign financial group, purchased the bank. The Institute assisted in the successful take-over by means of a loan of 5mn francs and a creditline of 10mn francs to Gesbanque.

13 Banque Copine, 1982 (IBCA p. 21).

Method: Take-over by bank.
Funding: Deposit Insurance.
Lead organiser: Banking Commission (supervisor).

The Banking Commission was concerned with the weak management of the bank as well as its financial position. After the bank's profitability and the value of its assets deteriorated, the Commission insisted on a reorganisation and appointed a special commissioner. In the meantime, adverse press comment led to a run on the bank's deposits. To counteract this, the Rediscount and Guarantee Institute opened a line of credit in the bank's favour, guaranteed by the bank's holdings of government paper. Banque Copine drew 1.4bn francs on this line. In addition, the Institute made available a subordinated loan of 125mn francs, later raised to 500mn francs, from the Intervention Fund. In December 1982 Famibanque, another bank incorporated in Belgium, took over the customer deposits and customer loans of Banque Copine, thus mitigating the effect of the closing of the latter's branches.

CANADA

14/15 Canadian Commercial Bank and Northland Bank, 1985 (IBCA p. 34).

Method: Rescue package, and afterwards liquidation.
Funding: Banks, government, deposit insurance, and central bank (liquidity support).

Canadian Commercial Bank:
Canada's first banking crisis for 62 years came in March 1985 when a rescue package was put together for Alberta-based Canadian Commercial Bank (CCB), Canada's then tenth largest bank. CCB was a regional bank and represented 0.6 per cent of the total assets held by all banks in Canada. The bank had high loss experience on loans in the real estate and energy sectors. The support group comprised the federal government (60mn dollars), the Alberta provincial government (60mn dollars), the six major chartered banks (60mn dollars between them based on each bank's size) and the Canadian Deposit Insurance Corporation (75mn dollars). The support group was also committed to purchase a package of the bank's problem loans. At that moment there were problems with the savings and loans industry in the USA and with Johnson Matthey Bankers in the UK. It was also stated that the bank's failure would have hurt the economy of West Canada. The Bank of Canada provided assurances that it would provide liquidity for CCB, if requested, as well as for any other Canadian bank.

Northland Bank:
Following the announcement of the rescue package for CCB, Northland Bank, another small Alberta-based regional bank, began to encounter problems in attracting

and retaining deposits. The Bank of Canada granted also liquidity support for Northland.

In early September 1985 the Inspector General of Banks concluded, following a review of both banks' operations, that the two banks were no longer viable, which led the Bank of Canada to announce that it had withdrawn its liquidity support for the two banks. Presumably because the authorities had encouraged depositors not to withdraw their deposits from the ailing banks, the federal government agreed to repay all uninsured depositors in CCB and Northland. This is estimated to have cost some 900mn dollars tax-payers' money. The contributions of the six major banks were not recovered. Only the Bank of Canada is likely to make recoveries, since its advances to the banks were secured on the borrowing bank's assets. These two cases are the only bank failures in the past 60 years in Canada. It should be noted that in aggregate, the combined assets of CCB and Northland Bank represented less than 1 per cent of assets held by all Canadian banks. The collapses of the CCB and Northland Bank were officially investigated by Estey (1986).

16/17 Mercantile Bank of Canada and Morguard Bank of Canada, 1985 (IBCA p. 35).

Method: Take-over by bank.
Funding: No external funding.

Since the collapse of CCB and Northland in September 1985 other small regional banks, including Mercantile and Morguard, suffered from significant deposit withdrawals for no other reason than loss of depositor confidence. It was a flight of deposits from the small banks to Canada's six largest banks. A number of small banks laid open their loan books in late 1985 for a peer review of the quality of their portfolios; they published the satisfactory conclusions of the reviews in a bid to restore confidence.

Mercantile Bank:
Mercantile Bank, a Montreal based bank, was involved in wholesale bank business. The bank began to experience trouble attracting deposits. The major six banks provided short term loans to Mercantile. There were rumours in the market that the Bank of Canada had guaranteed these loans, but they were unsubstantiated. A few weeks later, Mercantile was purchased by the Montreal based National Bank of Canada. The National Bank of Canada had advances outstanding to the Mercantile amounting to 1.6bn dollars.

Morguard Bank:
Morguard Bank was taken over by Security Pacific Bank of Canada in November 1985.

18 Continental Bank of Canada, 1985–6 (*FT* 11 Nov 86; IBCA p. 35).

Method: Rescue package, and afterwards take-over by bank.
Funding: Central bank (liquidity support), and banks.

Continental Bank, which appears to be purely the victim of the loss of depositor confidence, struggled on its own. Continental and British Bank of Columbia (see next case) were also victims of a run on deposits which followed the failure of CCB and Northland Bank. Continental Bank arranged lines of credit totalling 2.9bn dollars in October 1985 from Bank of Canada and the chartered banks to compensate for the withdrawal of wholesale deposits. The Bank of Canada provided a 1.4bn dollars term advance, and this term loan was renegotiated on three occasions and was due to expire in January 1987. The Bank of Canada reported that total liquidity advances to the Continental Bank reached a peak of 2.8bn dollars in 1986. After having been dependent for a year on these advances, Continental was taken over by Britain's Lloyds Bank in November 1986. The government is understood to have played a key role in moving Continental towards a stronger partner. Lloyds paid 200mn dollars for 90 per cent of Continental's assets and the bulk of its liabilities.

19 Bank of British Columbia, 1985–6 (*FT* 27 Nov 86; IBCA p. 35).

Method: Rescue package, and afterwards take-over by bank.
Funding: Central bank (liquidity support), and deposit insurance.

The Vancouver-based Bank of British Columbia was the subject of a balance sheet reconstruction and a change of senior management in fiscal 1984. In April 1986 the Bank of British Columbia (BBC) announced the closure of one third of its domestic branches and of its office in London and some senior management changes. In its 1986 Annual Report the Bank of Canada reported that total liquidity advances to the Bank of British Columbia reached a peak of 975mn dollars in the spring of 1986. In November 1986 BBC was finally taken over by the Hong Kong & Shanghai Banking Corporation. Hong Kong & Shanghai Bank acquired almost all the assets and liabilities of BBC for an initial amount of 63.5mn dollars (46mn dollars). To facilitate the transaction, the Canada Deposit Insurance Corporation paid 200mn dollars to the Hong Kong & Shanghai Bank. A special act of parliament was required to complete the transaction.

DENMARK

20 Kronebanken, 1985 (IBCA pp. 23–4).

Method: Rescue package, and afterwards take-over by bank.
Funding: Banks, and central bank (liquidity support).
Lead organiser: Bank Inspectorate (supervisor).

In December 1984 the Bank Inspectorate (the predecessor of the Finance Inspectorate) decided that losses in Kronebanken, Denmark's seventh largest bank, were so large that the bank would need external support to continue operations. The Big 3 banks and Danmarks Nationalbank provided pro rata a guarantee of 500mn kroner against losses incurred by Kronebanken in excess of its own funds. It emerged that the bank had suffered losses on loans and guarantees of 1.3bn kroner and had exceeded its lending limits to a single customer – Flexplan, an engineering company. These losses were about 400mn kroner in excess of equity. Possible merger deals with both Provinsbanken and Jyske Bank fell through in early 1985. Supported by the guarantee and by a commitment from the Nationalbank to cover its liquidity requirement, Kronebanken was allowed to continue business under new management. A merger was eventually agreed with Provinsbanken in June 1985 by which Kronebanken was effectively absorbed. Consequently the guarantee against losses and the liquidity support lapsed.

21 6. juli Banken, 1987 (IBCA pp. 24–5).

Method: Closure, and afterwards take-over by the bank.
Funding: Banks, and central bank (liquidity support).
Lead organiser: Finance Inspectorate (supervisor).

Set up in 1984 as one of a growing number of niche banks, specialising in high yielding deposits, 6. juli Banken had payments suspended by the Finance Inspectorate on 23 March 1987. The bank had made large losses as a result of imprudent lending to developers. At first the Nationalbank and the large banks refused to intervene, since 6. juli Banken was a specialised bank. But in the face of public and political pressure, the Danish Banking Association agreed to put forward proposals for a general deposit guarantee fund and established an ad hoc scheme to repay non-bank depositors with 6. juli Banken. The Nationalbank gave a commitment to supply liquidity support to the scheme, which only covered about 50 per cent of the total amount of deposits. After further public criticism, Sydbank took over the bankrupt 6. juli Banken on condition that it did not incur a financial loss. The Nationalbank agreed and granted substantial liquid funds to Sydbank at favourable rates of interest: up to 700mn kroner over 18 months at 5 per cent below the interbank rate. In addition, subordinated capital was injected: 100mn kroner by the two largest mortgage credit institutions, Kreditforeningen Danmark and Nykredit, which both stood to lose considerable amounts as major depositors with 6. juli Banken.; 125mn kroner by the Nationalbank; 225mn kroner by Sydbank itself. The assets were transferred to a liquidation company and the deposits directly to Sydbank.

22 C&G Banken, 1987 (IBCA p. 25).

Method: Liquidation.
Funding: Deposit insurance, and central bank (unsecured liquidity support).

Again, proper loan procedures had not been followed to the extent that C&G Banken, a small bank, had overlent to a single customer, Ranum Gruppen, a construction company which went bankrupt. Losses totalled 600mn kroner out of a balance sheet of 1.6bn kroner. After supervisory intervention a 100mn kroner (about 15mn dollars) infusion of capital was provided by the principal shareholders. Additional capital, after further deterioration, was not forthcoming. The problems became apparent at a very late date. The Nationalbank had advanced 369mn kroner (unsecured liquidity support as was the general rule at that time) on the assumption that the main shareholders would keep the bank solvent. In the week up to 28 October 1987 a close examination by the Finance Inspectorate assisted by outside experts indicated that the need to provide for bad credits was much larger than hitherto expected and that the bank was therefore deeply insolvent. After communicating this to the Nationalbank and the bank's main shareholders, all parties involved concluded that a suspension of payments was unavoidable. Denmark had coincidentally put in place in 1987 a deposit insurance scheme. By a special action of the Danish Parliament, up to 50mn kroner (about 7mn dollars) in deposits was deemed covered by the new insurance fund. The bank was declared bankrupt on 17 May 1988, and liquidation was initiated. At that time the law on deposit insurance had come into force, making it a regular case for the agency.

23 Aarhus Discontobank, 1988 (*FT* 19 Jan 88).

Method: Take-over by bank.
Funding: No external funding.

The small Aarhus Discontobank, which served the city of Aarhus and had assets of 1.3bn kroner, was acquired by Aktivbanken, the Jutland regional bank with assets of 14bn kroner (2.17bn dollars) in January 1988. The Aarhus bank had to make substantial loss provisions and was expected to report a sizeable deficit for 1987. Part of the losses had arisen in a company which had lost money on a joint venture bicycle manufacturing project in China.

24 DK Sparekassen, 1989 (*FT* 22 Dec 88; *FT* 23 Feb 89).

Method: Take-over by bank.
Funding: No external funding.
Lead organiser: Finance Inspectorate (supervisor).

DK Sparekassen, the fifth largest savings bank with assets of about 8bn (1.12bn dollars) and a regional network of 45 branches, ran into difficulties in autumn 1988. The Finance Inspectorate had told DK Sparekassen to find another bank to provide it with a sounder financial base. It was acquired by Bikuben, Denmark's second largest savings bank, in February 1989.

FINLAND[2]

* Government Guarantee Fund, 1992–3 (*FT* 15 Oct 92; Wall Street Journal 28 Jan 93).

Method: Special fund.
Funding: Government.

The government provided a 28bn markkas support package for the banking sector in 1992, with a further 20bn markkas in 1993. Because of the inadequate resources of the private deposit guarantee funds (see appendix 1b), the Finnish government created the Government Guarantee Fund on Norwegian lines with maximum liabilities totalling 20bn markkas in April 1992 (see Norway). In addition, the government decided in June 1992 to invest 8bn markkas in preference capital issued by banks to sustain the banks' lending ability and to prevent the aggravation of the emerging credit crunch. The facility was available either in August 1992 or in December 1992. By the latter date, 7.9bn markkas was used and almost all banks in the country has used the facility. After a bill to increase the borrowing limit of the Fund from 20bn markkas to 50bn markkas did not receive a required five-sixths majority in Parliament in January 1993, the government presented a budget that would allow an extra 20bn markkas in state support for Finland's troubled banks in 1993. This additional bank support (channelled directly from the budget rather than through the Government Guarantee Fund) consists of 15bn markkas for outright capital investment and 5bn markkas for guarantees. Although this implies that, in the future, the important bank support decisions will be made by the government and the funds needed will come through the general budget, the Government Guarantee Fund will do the administration of bank support, also when this support

2. See Llewellyn (1992) for an analysis of the performance of banks in Scandinavia.

is granted by the government. To remove doubts on the willingness of the parliament to support the banking system, the parliament passed a special resolution on 23 February 1993, which states that *"the state guarantees that Finnish banks are able to meet their commitments on time under all circumstances."*

25 Skopbank, 1991–3 (*FT* 04 Oct 91; *FT* 26 Mar 92; *FT* 15 Jun 92; *FT* 15 Oct 92).

Method: Capital injection, and afterwards special fund.
Funding: Central bank, and government.
Lead organiser: Bank of Finland (central bank).

The central bank was forced to step in and take direct control of Skopbank, the fourth largest commercial bank after it collapsed in September 1991 from a combination of bad loans and bad stockmarket investments. The central bank injected 2bn markkas in share capital, guaranteed its liquidity and purchased its largest problem assets with a transaction worth 9.5bn markkas. In December 1991, the Bank of Finland wrote off 1.9bn markkas worth of Skopbank loans. However, as a part of the same deal, Skopbank also wrote off 1.5bn markkas of its loans to an industrial conglomerate which had fallen in the hands of the central bank in the September operation. In March 1992 Skopbank received a further capital injection of 1.5bn markkas from the central bank. This amount was part of the 8bn markkas made available for the banking sector. In June 1992 the Bank of Finland sold its holding in Shopbank to the Government Guarantee Fund for 1.5bn markkas (349mn dollars). It was financed through a short-term credit line which the Bank of Finland extended to the Government Guarantee Fund for as long as required. As a result of its rescue operation the Bank of Finland estimated that it had lost 4.9bn markkas. In November 1992, the Government Guarantee Fund committed a further 1.5bn markkas to Skopbank, of which 1bn could be used in 1992. The future of Skopbank is under discussion and negotiations over the sale of Skopbank will continue.

26 Kansallis-Osake-Pankki, 1992–3 (*FT* 13 Aug 92; *FT* 30 Sep 92; *FT* 16 Oct 92; *FT* 22 Jan 93; *FT* 9 Feb 93).

Method: Special fund.
Funding: Government.

Kansallis-Osake-Pankki (KOP), Finland's largest commercial bank, had to accept a 1.7bn markkas (422mn dollars) capital injection from the government to strengthen its capital base and improve its capital requirement ratio by 1.5 per cent to 8.8 per cent in August 1992. The financial injection to KOP took the form of preferred capital and came from the 8bn markkas provision made by the Finnish government. KOP's chief executive officer since February 1992 is reorganising the bank. In February 1993, KOP announced a 3.7bn markkas pre-tax loss in 1992, more than double the 1.64bn markkas deficit in 1991. The huge 1992 loss is symptomatic of the crisis in Finnish banking, which has been plagued by recession and bad debts. KOP has indicated it would need a capital injection, either through a rights issue or through support from the government guarantee fund, or possibly a combination of both. The bank's international capital adequacy ratio at the end of 1992 was 9.13 per cent, but this is expected to fall towards 8 per cent during 1993 in the face of further losses.

27 Finland Savings Bank, 1992–3.

Method: Special fund.
Funding: Government.

Because of the deep problems of the Finnish savings banks (incidentally, the original owners of Skopbank), 41 local savings banks were merged in 1992 to form a nationwide savings bank, called the Finlands Savings Bank. The group of merging banks represented about half of the number and by far the largest part of the assets of the Finnish savings banks. The Government Guarantee Fund supported this merger by deciding in June 1992 to provide it 5.3bn markkas in capital funds and 1.4bn markkas in the form of guarantees to subordinated debentures. Additionally, it gave a loan of 0.5bn markkas to the Savings Banks' Guarantee Fund (see Appendix 1B), which in turn gave a corresponding grant to the Finland Savings Bank. In December 1992, the Government Guarantee Fund decided to inject a further 4.7bn markkas in fresh capital into the Finland Savings Bank.

28 Union Bank of Finland, 1992–3 (*FT* 16 Oct 92).

Method: Special fund.
Funding: Government.

After Unitas, the holding company of Union Bank of Finland, disclosed a 1.5bn markkas loss before extraordinary items for the first eight months of 1992, it sought 1.75bn markkas in preference capital from the government, the maximum possible sum allowed under the 8bn markkas capital scheme.

29 STS-Bank, 1992 (*FT* 25 Nov 92).

Method: Special fund, and take-over by bank.
Funding: Government.

STS-Bank, a former savings bank recently transformed into the country's sixth-largest commercial bank and traditionally controlled by the labour organisations, was taken over in November 1992 by Kansallis-Osake-Pankki (KOP, see above mentioned case). The take-over was organised in cooperation with the Government Guarantee Fund, which will assume responsibility for some of the problem loan portfolio of some 2.2bn markkas (430mn dollars). KOP paid 75mn markkas to take over 67 per cent of STS and would make a public offer for the remaining shares. It was also to invest a further 50mn markkas for a 10 per cent stake in the company taking over STS's problem loans, with the Government Guarantee Fund injecting 450mn markkas for the balance. However, exact amounts are not yet disclosed.

FRANCE

30 Banque Internationale pour l'Afrique Occidentale, 1988 (*FT* 06 Dec 88; IBCA p. 32).

Method: Take-over by bank.
Funding: No external funding.
Lead organiser: Commission Bancaire (supervisor).

Banque Internationale pour l'Afrique Occidentale (BIAO) was bailed out by Banque Nationale de Paris (BNP), the largest state-owned bank. BNP, which had only an indirect holding, was pressurised by the Commission Bancaire into giving substantial support in its capacity as lead shareholder. BNP took over with a direct 51 per cent stake. No outside funding was involved, but there was a capital restructuring at the order of the banking supervisors. Provisions on sovereign debt risks had to be brought up to 40 per cent, at a total cost of 600mn francs (101.5mn dollars) and wiped out the bank's entire capital and reserves.

31/32/33 BAII, UBAF and Kuwaiti French Bank, 1989–1990 (IBCA p. 32).

Method: Take-over by bank.
Funding: No external funding.
Lead organiser: Commission Bancaire (supervisor).

BAII, UBAF and Kuwaiti French Bank received the same kind of support as in the above mentioned example. Respectively, BNP, Credit Lyonnais and CIC Paris, as minor shareholders were forced by the Commission Bancaire to take over these banks. This shows that even a minority shareholding in a consortium bank can involve the large French banks being pressurised by the Commission Bancaire into giving substantial support in the capacity of 'actionnaire référence' (lead shareholder).

34 Al Saudi Bank, 1988 (IBCA pp. 32–3).

Method: Take-over by bank.
Funding: Banks.
Lead organisers: Banque de France (central bank), and Commission Bancaire (supervisor).

Al Saudi Bank, a medium-sized institution with Saudi owners, collapsed in October 1988. Al Saudi's business came mostly from the foreign market. After recycling petrodollars to third world debtors in the late 1970s, the bank was left with large numbers of poor-quality loans amounting to 2.2bn francs. It was well known in the market, a few months before its eventual collapse, that Al Saudi Bank was having problems. Nevertheless, it is understood that the Banque de France reassured banks, telling them that new or existing shareholders would inject funds. Only one of the shareholders, the 'Hariri Groups, injected 300mn francs, which was still inadequate compared with the requirements of the Commission Bancaire. A particular detail is that Thomson CSF, the state controlled electronics and defence group, had deposited 400mn francs in the troubled bank. The banking authorities tried at lengths to rescue Al Saudi. First, in May 1988, in the Banque de France froze all deposits by the French banks, including Thomson CSF. Then, in October 1988, the Banque de France called on French banks and French subsidiaries of foreign banks to grant 1.9bn francs interest free loans to Al Saudi Bank (a so-called solidarity call based on Article 52 of the Bank Law). Société de Banque Thomson, the bank of Thomson CSF, acquired Al Saudi, including its portfolio of non-performing loans, for a nominal 1 franc. This purchase gave Thomson the opportunity to recoup the fiscal deficit, thus reducing accordingly the losses incurred by other creditors. Thomson limited its loss to a fraction of its total deposits in Al Saudi Bank, 44 per cent for the 5 most important depositors and 30 per cent for the others. The remaining assets of Al Saudi went into a new bank, Banque Française de l'Orient, with fresh capital of some 600mn francs, supplied by several banks.

35 Banque de Participations et de Placements, 1989 (IBCA pp. 33–4).

Method: Closure, and afterwards take-over.
Funding: Deposit insurance.
Lead organiser: Commission Bancaire (supervisor).

The Banque de Participations et de Placements (BPP) was created in 1985 after the takeover of the former Banque Stern by the Lebanese INTRA group. An on-the-spot inspection of BPP by the Commission Bancaire revealed that BPP had falsified its loan declaration, thereby concealing the size of its loans to the INTRA group. On 20 January 1989, the Commission asked the shareholders to inject fresh capital to meet capital adequacy requirements. Because the shareholders refused to do so, the authorities withdrew BPP's license in February 1988 and appointed a liquidator for the bank. The Lebanese controlled BPP was closed down with a deficit estimated at 250mn francs. The deposit guarantee fund, administered by the French Banking Association, reimbursed depositors for 40mn of the 190mn total franc deposits. BPP was eventually taken over in September 1989 by the French Lagarde Group.

36 United Banking Corporation, 1989 (IBCA p. 34).

Method: Liquidation.
Funding: Deposit insurance.
Lead organiser: Commission Bancaire (supervisor).

United Banking Corporation (UBC), a 100 per cent Lebanese owned bank, collapsed in May 1989. With a balance sheet of 1.6bn francs, the bulk of its deposits were in foreign currency from non-residents and its interbank borrowings were limited. UBC had its license revoked after an apparent fraud added to the bank's overlending to high-risk countries and left it needing an estimated 400mn francs fresh capital injection to meet the Commission Bancaire's capital requirements. 54mn of the 121mn total francs deposits, was reimbursed to depositors through the deposit guarantee fund.

37 Lebanese Arab Bank, 1989 (IBCA pp. 34–5).

Method: Liquidation.
Funding: Deposit insurance.
Lead organiser: Commission Bancaire (supervisor).

Another Lebanese controlled bank to run into trouble in France was Lebanese Arab Bank (LAB). Some 240mn francs in loans of LAB's total balance sheet of 1.2bn francs appeared to be at risk and required provisions plus a capital injection estimated at 200mn francs. In mid–1989 the bank's license was withdrawn and the Commission Bancaire named a judicial administrator. No other French banks were among LAB's mainly non-resident creditors. Its deposits were mostly in foreign currency and therefore not covered by the deposit guarantee fund, which reimbursed 42.4mn of the 157mn total franc deposits.

GERMANY

38 Bankhaus I.D. Herstatt, 1974 (ECN 22 Sep 84).

Method: Liquidation.
Funding: Banks.
Lead organiser: Bundesbank (Central Bank).

Herstatt, one of Germany's then largest private banks, was closed down by the Bundesbank in June 1974 because of losses in the Forex market. The losses arising from foreign exchange deals were originally estimated to be 83mn pounds but later estimates put this at 200mn pounds. The Herstatt affair revealed gaps in Germany's supervisory system largely because the Bundesbank had no formal supervisory role, while the independent bank regulators were slow to spot warning signs. The Bundesbank failed to act decisively. The Bundesbank first made light of Herstatt's growing difficulties, then tried to mount a rescue, then closed the bank at 10.30am New York time. It thereby did maximum harm to its international reputation, since many foreign, in particular American, banks, engaged in forex deals on the day the bank closed, suffered losses if they were caught half way through the transaction. Only one of the two legs of forex deal was executed. Herstatt was closed by the German banking authorities 4.30pm German time, after Herstatt's counterparts had settled the European currency leg of the transactions. The losses of Herstatt's counterparts derived from the inability of the German bank to settle the dollar leg through CHIPS, the US payment system (although Herstatt's correspondent bank in New York had already input the payment orders for the settlement of the dollar leg through CHIPS (at the time still operating in next-day settlement mode), the failure of Herstatt prevented their completion). The episode caused great disruption to CHIPS. The failure of Herstatt ensured big losses for scores of depositors. Although West German banks raised a levy to pay out in full those depositors with less than 20,000dm (7,600 dollars) with Herstatt, the rest had to take what the liquidator could realise. In the end they got between 45 per cent (West German institutions) and 65 per cent (private creditors) of their claims.

39 Schröder, Münchmeyer, Hengst & Co., 1983 (*FT* 08 Nov 83).

Method: Emergency aid.
Funding: Banks.

Schröder, Münchmeyer, Hengst and Co., a seemingly prestigious private bank, over-extended itself in lending to industry, especially to the IBH building machinery group. SMH's lending to IBH and its subsidiaries was put at more than 800mn dm, compared with the bank's own capital of 110mn dm. The collateral originally put up by IBH turned out to be too little to cover the gap. By channelling part of its lending to IBH via its Luxembourg subsidiary, which was not open to scrutiny by West German authorities, SMH could expand its credit beyond limits allowed under German law. The banking community rushed in to support before the worst could happen and pledged over 600mn dm (225mn dollars) to keep SMH, a bank with assets of 2.2bn dm, afloat.

GREECE

40 Bank of Crete, 1988 (IBCA p. 12).

Method: Special administration.
Funding: Central bank.
Lead organiser: Bank of Greece (central bank and supervisor).

The Bank of Greece has not yet allowed a Greek bank to fail. The only recent case of the Bank of Greece assisting a Greek bank has been that of the Bank of Crete. This was a privately-held bank, owned by George Koskotas, who was alleged in 1988 to have diverted fraudulently 30bn drachmas of the Bank of Crete's funds over 3 years. The bank's deposits were guaranteed by the Bank of Greece and it is now run by a government appointed commissioner. There are now moves to return the bank to the private sector.

HONG KONG[3]

41 Hang Lung Bank, 1983–9.

Method: Special administration, and afterwards take-over by bank.
Funding: Government[4] (liquidity support from the Exchange Fund).

After being nursed for over a year with the help of the Standard Chartered Bank, the Hang Lung Bank was acquired by the government on 28 September 1983 through the Hang Lung Bank (Acquisition) Ordinance (Cap. 345). After the takeover, top management of the bank consisted of staff seconded from the Hongkong Bank. The bank was insolvent on acquisition. Temporary liquidity support was immediately provided through deposits by the Exchange Fund (the predecessor of the Hong Kong Monetary Authority). Funds were later injected into the bank to enable it to comply with various requirements of the Companies Ordinance and the Banking Ordinance, and to have sufficient capital to trade. Part of this was used to acquire new shares in the bank and part was directly passed to the inner reserves of the bank. The full extent of the government's assistance has not been disclosed. Hang Lung's problems were mainly local. After acquisition, the problems of the bank were sorted out gradually. The bank was eventually sold to the Dao Heng Bank Limited in 1989. As part of the deal, non-performing loans of Hang Lung were transferred to the Overseas Trust Bank Limited (OTB) which was also under government ownership.

42 Overseas Trust Bank, 1985.

Method: Special administration.
Funding: Government (Exchange Fund).

---

3. At the time of these cases Hong Kong had a separated regime for monetary policy and banking supervision (see appendix 1a).
4. Hong Kong has no fully fledged Central Bank, and hence no distinction can be made between the government and the Exchange Fund (which manages the reserves, see appendix 1a). The funds used by the Exchange Fund would be classified as Central Bank funding in other countries. However, we thought it right to treat it as government funding in the Hong Kong cases, as the Exchange Fund is part of the government.

The Overseas Trust Bank's (OTB) problems have an international dimension, involving one or two leading political figures in the Region, notably in Malaysia. The bank was acquired by the Government on 7 June 1985 through the Overseas Trust Bank (Acquisition) Ordinance (Cap. 379). This was triggered by the former management of the bank 'throwing-in the towel' while facing increasing pressure from the government to put their increasingly rotten house in order. The bank was insolvent on acquisition. As in the case of Hang Lung Bank, staff seconded from Hongkong Bank took over the top management immediately after acquisition. The Exchange Fund also injected funds into the bank in December 1985 following the provision of temporary liquidity support through deposits. 2bn HKdollars was used for the subscription of new preference shares of the bank. This is a matter of public record. Funds were also passed directly into inner reserves. The full extent of the government's assistance has so far not been disclosed. The ultimate cost of the government rescue can only be determined upon the sale of OTB. The bank is being put up for sale.

43 Hong Kong Industrial and Commercial Bank, 1985–7.

Method: Special administration, and afterwards take-over by bank.
Funding: No external funding.

Hong Kong Industrial and Commercial Bank (HICB) was the subsidiary bank of Overseas Trust Bank (OTB) which was taken over by the government together with OTB. At the end of 1987, the bank was sold to the Dah Sing Bank. The sale proceeds were absorbed into the accounts of OTB. There was no direct cash injection by the Exchange Fund into this bank.

44 Ka Wah Bank, 1985–6.

Method: Take-over by bank.
Funding: Government (Exchange Fund).

The Overseas Trust Bank (OTB) failure in 1985 led to the deterioration of the situation of a number of other local banks. The Ka Wah Bank, which had been under intensive care with the help of the Hongkong Bank at that time, was the largest of these and there was little hope of the bank surviving, with hugh non-performing loans largely arising from fraudulent acts of its then existing management. A government takeover, however, had been ruled out as the Executive Council and the Legislative Council had made it clear that they would not support another takeover after OTB. As the repercussion of a bank collapse was considered unacceptable, a 'white knight' had to be found. After half a year of negotiations, CITIC agreed to acquire the bank with certain financial support from the government. These include, inter alia, government guaranteeing, at some cost, the recoverability of the loan portfolio of the bank. The acquisition was completed in June 1986. The net cost to the Exchange Fund has yet to be established as loan recovery actions are continuing.

45 Wing On Bank, 1985–6.

Method: Take-over by bank.
Funding: Government (Exchange Fund).

The rescue of the Wing On Bank was based on a strategy similar to that of the Ka Wah Bank. Financial support from the Exchange Fund took the form of an indemnity to the bank. This indemnity in effect protected the Hang Seng Bank Ltd. which took over Wing On against downside risks. The deal was completed in June 1986, after a half a year of negotiations. As the Wing On Bank's problems were less serious, the eventual liability on the Exchange Fund will be relatively small compared to that of Ka Wah. Wing On Bank has just been sold by the Hang Seng Bank to Dah Sing Holdings which now owns Dah Sing Bank, HICB and Wing On Bank.

46 Union Bank, 1985–6.

Method: Take-over by bank.
Funding: Government (liquidity support from the Exchange Fund).

The Union Bank had been on the intensive care list since May 1985 when the Commissioner of Banking and the auditors became concerned about the security for Indonesian loans. As the situations deteriorated, the Commissioner, in exercise of his power under section 13 of the former Banking Ordinance, directed Jardine Fleming & Co. Ltd. to assume control and carry on the business of the bank with effect from 27 March 1986, and to advise the Board of the bank of any serious proposal for the participation of a new investor. Support from the Exchange Fund took the form of a credit line, on normal commercial terms, sufficient to ensure that the claims of all depositors and other creditors can be met in full on time. The possibility of running down the bank, however, had always been part of the contingency plan while attempts at finding a suitable buyer were being made. Eventually following the acquisition of a majority interest in the bank by Modern Concepts Limited, in which China Merchants Steam Navigation Company Limited has a 68 per cent interest and Search International Limited a 32 per cent interest, the management control of the bank was returned to its Board of Directors in July 1986. The line of credit from the Exchange Fund was withdrawn at the same time. No cost on the part of the Exchange Fund was involved.

47 Hong Nin Bank, 1986–7.

Method: Take-over by bank.
Funding: Government (liquidity support from the Exchange Fund).

Hong Nin Bank's problem was caused by losses arising from the concentration of loans to particular groups. This was aggravated by the creditor banks withdrawing their lines and deposits at the time when sale of the bank was being negotiated between its main shareholder and First Pacific Holdings Limited. To prevent the situation from deteriorating, the Commissioner of Banking exercised his powers in June 1986 to restrict further lending by the bank without his approval and, subsequently, assumed control of and carried on the business of the bank in September 1986, pursuant to Section 52(1) of the Banking Ordinance. Liquidity support from the Exchange Fund during the period took the form of deposits, again at commercial rates, and a line of credit at penal rates to enable the bank to meet all its obligations in full as and when they fell due. Throughout the period, liquidation of the bank had not been ruled out as an alternative to resolving the bank's problems. Exchange Fund support was gradually withdrawn *18 months* after the sale of the bank to First Pacific in March 1987 through the repayment in full of outstanding Exchange Fund deposits with the bank. No cost was therefore involved.

48 Bank of Credit and Commerce Hong Kong Ltd., 1991–2.

Method: Liquidation.
Funding: No external funding.

Following the closure of most BCCI's global operations in July 1991 (see Luxembourg for the full story), the Commissioner of Banking assumed control of and closed Bank of Credit and Commerce Hong Kong (BCCHK) and BCCI Finance (Hong Kong) Limited on 8 July 1991 pursuant to section 52(1)(C) of the Banking Ordinance to preserve the assets of the institution. Throughout the period during which the Commissioner of Banking assumed control of the bank until the bank formally came under liquidation in March 1992, it had been made clear that there was no case for using the Exchange Fund under section 3(1) of the Exchange Fund Ordinance since the failure of the bank was unlikely to affect the exchange rate stability of the territory. Liquidity support which would only be provided on commercial terms was also ruled out of the ground that it would be imprudent to do so while pledge of support from the bank's main shareholder, the Abu Dhabi government, was not forthcoming. There was therefore no involvement on the part of the Exchange Fund at all. However, liquidity support on normal commercial terms was provided to Standard Chartered Bank, Dao Heng Bank, Dao Heng Bank, and First Pacific Bank on normal commercial term to tide them over the subsequent bank runs caused by groundless rumours.

IRELAND

49 Irish Trust Bank, 1976 (IBCA p. 8).

Method: Liquidation.
Funding: Government.

An order for the winding up of Irish Trust Bank, a relatively small bank, was made by the Supreme Court on 26 March 1976. In this case the government stepped in and paid off all depositors.

50 Merchant Bank Limited, 1982 (IBCA p. 8).

Method: Liquidation.
Funding: No external funding.

Merchant Bank Limited was liquidated. An official liquidator was appointed by the High Court on 24 May 1982. Some depositors's funds were lost as the government did not intervene in light of the relatively small size of the institution and its non-retail focus. The failures of Irish Bank Trust and Merchant Bank Limited have been the only two bank failures in Ireland this century.

ITALY

51 Banca Steinhauslin SpA, 1981–2 (IBCA p. 19–20).

Method: Special administration, and afterwards take-over by bank.
Funding: Banks.
Lead organiser: Banca d'Italia (central bank and supervisor).

Banca Steinhauslin SpA (Stein) run into difficulties when one of its directors, Mr Niccolai, was arrested on charges of fraud and misappropriation of funds. Up to 40bn lire was put in high yielding savings accounts and not recorded in Stein's books (this implied an additional tax avoidance benefit for the depositors) by Mr Niccolai. In September 1981, these operations were discovered by the internal audit department of Stein and communicated to Banca d'Italia. Another private bank, Credito Romagnolo, was called in to provide the major part of the funds required to cover Stein's liquidity needs. The credit lines which were made available to Stein totalled 50bn lire, and these proved sufficient to satisfy the bank's requirements in the first few months after Mr Niccolai's imprisonment. In fact, Stein did not witness any run on deposits although these had declined since the September discovery. In November 1981, Banca d'Italia appointed 3 Special Administrators to manage Stein for the following year. Only depositors, which were found to be unaware of the illegal aspects, were reimbursed with no loss. At the end of the special administration period, Stein's operations were back to normal and with the approval of Banca d'Italia, Stein was sold to a small private bank Banco di San Gemignano e San Prospero.

52 Banco Ambrosiano SpA, 1982 (*FT* 11 June 85; *FT* 17 Nov 82; IBCA p. 20).

Method: Closure, and afterwards take-over by bank.
Funding: Banks (both private and state-owned) and central bank.
Lead organiser: Banca d'Italia (central bank and supervisor).

During the 1970s, inspired by its managing director, Mr Roberto Calvi, Banco Ambrosiano (BA) created a group of considerable size with a substantial proportion of foreign operations. A subsidiary holding company was formed in Luxembourg. After an extensive audit of the Banco Ambrosiano Group which had confirmed that operations carried out by BA's foreign companies (both banks and other businesses) were completely unsupervised, Banca d'Italia asked BA to modify the structure of its group. By June 1982, the non-banking subsidiaries (domestic and foreign) owed BA banks (domestic and foreign) about 1bn dollar, the majority of which had been raised on the international financial markets by those same banks. After the uncovering of this, BA was placed under special administration at the request of its own board of directors on 17 June 1982. Meanwhile, Mr Calvi was found dead under Blackfriars Bridge in London on 18 June 1982. A substantial run on deposits and the non-payment of large sums owed by the foreign non-banking subsidiaries caused a major liquidity crisis. Although a group of banks provided large amounts of funds under special arrangements, BA was judged bankrupt after a further assessment by the Banca d'Italia. On 6 August 1982 compulsory liquidation was proved. In order to protect depositors and creditors and under the aegis of Banca d'Italia, the original pool of banks which had provided liquidity agreed to finance a new bank, Nuovo Banco Ambrosiano (NBA). Four private (Institutio Mobiliare Italiana was one of them) and three state-owned bank shareholders endowed NBA with capital of 600bn lire. The state-private ownership split was 50–50. NBA took over the domestic Italian assets and all the liabilities of BA and it received special advances from Banca d'Italia, at 1 per cent interest rate. Banca d'Italia granted further significant advances at the official discount rate to satisfy NBA's liquidity requirements in the first months of its operations. The take-over did not include the Luxembourg holding company and other foreign subsidiaries, which caused international criticism. However, NBA reimbursed foreign banks some 1bn dollar in deposits placed with BA in Milan. In May 1984, an agreement was reached and the foreign banks who lent to the Luxembourg and foreign subsidiaries were to recover 406mn dollars, some 60 per cent of their claims. In 1989, NBA merged with Banca Cattolica del Veneto, creating Banco Ambrosiano Veneto.

53 Cassa di Risparmio di Prato, 1988–91 (IBCA p. 21).

Method: Emergency aid, and afterwards take-over by bank.
Funding: Banks, and deposit insurance.

The only major example of the Deposit Protection Fund being put in place was the case of Cassa di Risparmio di Prato. This Tuscan savings bank had concentrated on financing the textiles industry in the region. However, with the economy's downturn, the bank's problems loans accounted for over 50 per cent of the total loan book in 1988. additional liquidity was initially provided through an injection of 200bn lire from nine other Tuscan savings banks. The Deposit Protection Fund followed with additional capital injections of 800bn lire and a further 430bn lire which was due by end-December 1991. In March 1992, the Fund sold its 73 per cent stake in Cassa di Risparmio di Prato to Monte dei Paschi di Siena Banking Group. Monte dei Paschi di Siena, the biggest bank in Tuscany, wanted to strengthen its home base in Tuscany.

JAPAN

54 Sanwa Shinkin, 1991 (*ECN* 23 Mar 91; *FT* 25 July 91).

Method: Take-over by bank.
Funding: No external funding.
Lead organiser: Ministry of Finance (supervisor).

Sanwa Shinkin, a small bank with branches in desirable parts of Tokyo, was taken over by Tokai Bank, a leading commercial bank in March 1991. Sanwa Shinkin is no kin of Sanwa Bank. No outside funding was involved because of the attractiveness of Sanwa Shinkin's branch network.

55 Toho Sogo Bank, 1991 (*FT* 25 Jul 91; *FT* 29 Oct 91).

Method: Take-over by bank.
Funding: Banks, central bank, and deposit insurance.

Toho Sogo Bank, a provincial bank with estimated 30bn yen in bad loans, ran into difficulties when an important customer, a local shipbuilder, experienced financial difficulties. Iyo Bank, the 21st largest of Japan's regional banks, took over Toho Sogo Bank with an 8bn yen 5-year loan from the deposit insurance fund at an interest rate 5 per cent below government bonds interest rate (profit 2bn yen (15mn dollars)). The regional banks' association granted Iyo Bank 1bn yen (7.5mn dollars). The Bank of Japan planned to assist by maintaining a series of concessionary loans to Toho Sogo after the takeover.

56 Toyo Shinkin Bank, 1992 (*ECN* 09 May 92).

Method: Rescue package.
Funding: Banks, and deposit insurance.
Lead organiser: Ministry of Finance (supervisor).

Toyo Shinkin Bank stumbled under the combined weight of 340bn yen (2.6bn dollars) in forged certificates of deposit issued in its name, and estimated bad debts of 252bn yen. The rescue of the Osaka-based credit union was organised by the finance ministry after months of negotiation with recalcitrant creditors. The authorities have made the Industrial Bank of Japan (IBJ) bear most of the burden, even thought Toyo Shinkin is part of the Sanwa Bank Group. Sanwa refused to accept sole responsibility for the mess. IBJ was viewed by the authorities as the main bank of Nui Onoue, the Osaka-based restaurant owner to whom a Toyo Shinkin employee issued the forged CDs. IBJ was considered responsible because it released to Ms Onoue collateral, in the form of its own debentures, which she had lodged at the bank to back the 240bn yen she borrowed from the IBJ group. Ms Onoue replaced the forged Toyo Shinkin CDs as collateral and used the IBJ debentures to borrow somewhere else. IBJ has to forgive 70 per cent of its loans to Toyo Shinkin, taking a loss of some 11bn yen. Fuji Bank had to write off a similar amount. In addition, several non-bank lenders had to forgive sums that Toyo Shinkin owed it. Finally, the deposit insurance corporation lent 20bn yen at less than market interest rates to Toyo Shinkin.

These last two cases are the only instances to date in which the deposit insurance fund has been used in the rescue take-over of a troubled bank. Previous rescues have been funded entirely by the banks carrying out the acquisition, sometimes under pressure from the Finance Ministry (see first case). There has been no bank failure since the Second World War.

57 Co-operative Credit Purchasing Company, 1992–3 (*FT* 1 Sep 92; *FT* 12 Oct 92; *FT* 27 Jan 93).

Method: Special fund.
Funding: Banks, and central bank.

The government announced plans for a possible bail-out of Japan's troubled banking industry in September 1992. In January 1993, the Co-operative Credit Purchasing Company (CCPC) was formally established. This industry body is designed to help banks with an increasing burden of non-performing, property related loans, after the collapse of the asset bubble. CCPC has a staff of 20 people, and has started from 1 February 1993 to buy the rights to the collateral of non-performing loans. This will allow banks to write-off their exposure more quickly and, in theory, put a floor under falling property prices through the independent assessment of the collateral. The body is to be financed by the participating banks in the form of capital and concessional loans. However, it is understood that the Bank of Japan is likely to increase the amount commercial banks can borrow from it at cheaper rates on the understanding that the funds are pumped indirectly into the new company. As well as this indirect assistance, the banks would like tax concessions on write-offs from the Ministry of Finance.

LUXEMBOURG

58 Schröder, Münchmeyer, Hengst International S.A., 1983 (IBCA p. 16).

Method: Emergency aid.
Funding: Banks.

Schröder, Münchmeyer, Hengst International S.A. (SMH International) is the 100 per cent-owned Luxembourg subsidiary of the German investment bank, Schröder, Münchmeyer, Hengst & Co. (SMH). SMH International played a crucial part in SMH's excessive lending to the bankrupt IBH group, with a substantial portion of SMH's commitment being routed through Luxembourg. Nevertheless, when SMH failed in November 1983, the lifeboat of German banks set up by the Bundesbank to rescue SMH had no consequent legal obligation to rescue SMH International as well. Even so, the German banks concerned decided that there was a moral obligation, and SMH International was rescued in the same way as SMH. (See Germany for SMH.)

59 Bank of Credit and Commerce International, 1991 (*FT* Behind Closed Doors 1991).

Method: Liquidation.
Funding: Deposit insurance.
Lead organiser: Bank of England.

The Bank of Credit and Commerce International (BCCI) has established a holding company with a banking subsidiary in Luxembourg. However, most of its activities were channelled through branches in the Cayman Islands and London. BCCI's complex structure enabled it not only to escape consolidated supervision, but also to deliberately confuse regulators by shuffling its assets between different jurisdictions. In 1985, the Luxembourg Monetary Institute asked Price Waterhouse to review BCCI's treasury operations which ran into losses of at least 633mn dollars. Price Waterhouse put the error down to management incompetence rather than fraud. After further difficulties, regulators from eight countries decided to pool their efforts in a 'college', with the Bank of England in the lead, in 1987. After Price Waterhouse uncovered false or deceitful lending practices, the regulators approved a bail-out by Abu Dhabi, BCCI's main shareholder. US and Luxembourg gave BCCI a deadline to move its operations. The final blow came after the Bank of England commissioned Price Waterhouse to prepare a special report after 600mn dollars of unrecorded deposits were found. On 5 July 1991 the college of regulators closed down BCCI's world wide operations. Those deposits covered by the Luxembourg deposit insurance scheme have been reimbursed.

THE NETHERLANDS

60 Amsterdam American Bank, 1981 (IBCA, pp. 19–20).

Method: Liquidation.
Funding: Deposit Insurance.
Lead organiser: De Nederlandsche Bank (central bank and supervisor).

Amsterdam American Bank (AAB), a subsidiary of Mid American Credit Corporation, was a relatively small bank and involved to a large extent in trade finance operations with Latin America. AAB did not comply adequately with instructions of the De Nederlandsche Bank (DNB) to withdraw certain credit facilities to foreign borrowers, some of whom were connected with the bank's ultimate shareholders. DNB, therefore, used its powers to intervene in the interest of the creditors and appointed a secret receiver. After the Court approved the emergency regulations, on petition of the DNB, the collective guarantee scheme become operative. Claims up to the then maximum of 30,000 guilders were paid out. Depositors not eligible under the guarantee scheme lost their money. Considering the negative own resources of AAB, it was adjudicated bankrupt on 23 October 1981.

61 Tilburgsche Hypotheekbank N.V., 1981–3 (IBCA, pp. 20–1).

Method: Rescue package, and afterwards liquidation.
Funding: Banks, and deposit insurance.
Lead organiser: De Nederlandsche Bank (central bank and supervisor).

Tilburgsche Hypotheekbank (THB), a mortgage bank, had been experiencing problems since the late 1970s, due to the slump in the real estate market. In 1981 it suffered heavy loan losses, which were reported to De Nederlandsche Bank (DNB) by the bank's external auditors. Consultations between the supervisory board of the bank and DNB resulted in replacement of the management and the granting by three large mortgage banks of 18mn guilders of subordinated loans to THB to offset the loan losses incurred. After a further worsening of the solvency position, DNB tried to organise a take-over by several of the major banks. However, in view of the general bad quality of THB's loan portfolio, the banks did not cooperate and DNB asked the Court for emergency regulations. It is understood that the potential loss of depositors was over 200mn guilders. Approximately 90 depositors were covered by the collective guarantee scheme and between 2–3mn guilders was paid out. However, many depositors had claims in the form of bearer bonds which are not covered by the scheme and consequently were not compensated. Shareholders, who also lost substantial sums of money, set up a commission to investigate the collapse. The collapse of THB, which was finally made bankrupt in August 1983, caused much controversy within the Dutch banking community and internationally; criticism was directed against both DNB and THB's external auditors.

62 Westland/Utrecht Hypotheekbank N.V., 1981–2 (IBCA p. 21).

Method: Take-over by financial institution.[5]
Funding: Banks, and other financial institutions.
Lead organiser: De Nederlandsche Bank (central bank and supervisor).

Westland/Utrecht Hypotheekbank (WUH), the largest mortgage bank in the Netherlands, suffered heavy losses due to its exposure to the real estate sector at the beginning of the 1980s, and rumours about its financial position in 1981 made it difficult for it to raise money. In July 1981 De Nederlandsche Bank (DNB) organised a consortium of four commercial banks and an insurance company to buy WUH. In Autumn 1981 WUH agreed to sell mortgages worth 3bn guilders to the Algemene Burgerlijke Pensioenfonds (ABP), the large Dutch state pension fund. However, the negative trend continued. ABP provided further support in the form of 300mn guilders of subordinated, convertible loans and an insurance company, Nationale Nederlanden N.V., acquired a majority interest in WUH. Results for WUH then improved and no depositor lost any money.

63 Friesch-Groningse Hypotheekbank N.V., 1982 (IBCA p. 21).

Method: Take-over by bank.
Funding: No external funding reported.

Friesch-Groningse Hypotheekbank (FGH), the third largest mortgage bank, also ran into difficulties because of the slump in the real estate market. Various meas-

---

5. This case will be classified as a take-over by bank, since we do not have a separate entry for non-bank financial institutions.

ures of support were discussed and in 1982 the then Post Office Savings Bank (now part of the Internationale Nederlanden Group) took a 5 per cent interest in the bank and also granted subordinated, convertible loans. In the case of full conversion of these loans, the Post Office Savings Bank would be able to increase its interest in FGH to 40 per cent. No depositors with FGH lost money.

64 N.V. Slavenburg's Bank, 1981–3 (IBCA p. 21).

Method: Take-over by bank.
Funding: No external funding reported.

Heavy loan loss provisions in 1980/1981 caused a sharp decline in profits and resulted in a near collapse for Slavenburg's Bank. The bank was heavily involved in tax evasion, and several managers, among them Mr Piet Slavenburg, were arrested on charges of fraud. In 1983 Crédit Lyonnais of France took over the bank and its name was changed to Crédit Lyonnais Bank Nederland (CLBN). At the same time Crédit Lyonnais guaranteed to CLBN and De Nederlandsche Bank that CLBN's loan loss reserves would be maintained at adequate levels to cover its non-performing loans.

NEW ZEALAND

65 DFC New Zealand Limited, 1989.

Method: Liquidation.
Funding: Government.
Lead organiser: Reserve Bank of New Zealand (central bank and supervisor).

DFC New Zealand Limited and subsidiaries (DFC) was placed in statutory management by the government, acting on recommendation of the Reserve Bank of New Zealand, in October 1989. This action was based on advice from DFC's directors that DFC was unlikely to be able to meet its obligations, following substantial loan losses. Statutory management (under ultimate Reserve Bank control) enabled an assessment of DFC to be made and facilitated the implementation of a solution. This involved: transfer of the DFC swaps book; a restructuring of DFC's debt; injection of funds by DFC's shareholders and the government; and utilisation of tax losses for the benefit of DFC's creditors. The injection of funds by the government was made in the context of the government's former ownership of DFC and the fact that DFC's ownership at the time of its failure was connected to the government. DFC's major creditors will receive full recovery of principal over a period of some years, in addition to partial recovery of interest. DFC is being gradually liquidated.

NORWAY[6]

66 Andresens Bank, 1980 (IBCA p. 35).

Method: Take-over by bank.
Funding: No external funding reported.

6. See Llewellyn (1992) for an analysis of the performance of banks in Scandinavia. See Commission on the Banking Crisis (1992) for a discussion of the Norwegian banking crisis.

Andresens Bank, a major commercial bank, ran into difficulties because of the high level of its problem loans to the shipping sector. It was taken over by Christiania Bank in 1980.

67 Fiskernes Bank, 1983 (*FT* 04 Nov 83; IBCA p. 35).

Method: Take-over by bank.
Funding: No external funding.

Fiskernes Bank, previously Norway's eight largest commercial bank, which played an important role in providing credit for business and industry along Norway's north western and northern coast, was also heavily committed to the shipping sector. Heavy losses on shipping led to Fiskernes' downfall. Again it was Christiania Bank which came to the rescue and took over the bank from 1 January 1984. The deal of 196mn kroner (26.4mn dollars) was finalised in November, 1983. Christiania, with assets totalling 31.4bn kroner, compared with 3.2bn kroner for Fiskerness, was in a position to provide the fresh capital the latter needed.

68 Sørlandsbanken, 1980s (IBCA p. 35).

Method: Rescue package, and afterwards take-over by bank.
Funding: Central bank, and deposit insurance.

Sørlandsbanken, a regional bank, had problems in the late seventies when it lost money on an export finance deal in the Middle East. It also got into trouble with the Bank Inspectorate (the predecessor of the Banking, Securities and Insurance Commission, founded 1986), because it contravened the Banking Act by lending more than 50 per cent of its equity to one customer. The bank received support both from the Central Bank and from the Commercial Banks' Contingency Fund. Partly as a result of its problems a merger was arranged with Kristiansands Privatbanken in 1984 and a new bank, Agdarbanken, was consequently founded. The bank's name has subsequently been changed back to Sørlandsbanken in 1985. The position of Sørlandsbanken remained weak until it finally merged with Christiania Bank in 1990 (without government intervention).

69 Sunnmørsbanken, 1988 (*FT* 13 Jan 89; *FT* 07 Feb 89; Financial Regulation Report Oct 91 pp. 21–3).

Method: Special administration, and afterwards take-over by bank.
Funding: Deposit insurance, and central bank (liquidity support).

Sunnmørsbanken, a medium sized Norwegian commercial bank, was saved from insolvency when the Central Bank and the Commercial Bank's Contingency Fund intervened in September 1988 as lenders of last resort. Sunnmørsbanken's liquidity problems stemmed from losses on loans to the petroleum sector, shipping and shipyards, and fish-farming. Following three failed rescue attempts, the Contingency Fund absorbed Sunnmørsbanken in February 1989. Later on, the Contingency Fund contributed to the subsequent acquisition of Sunnmørsbanken by Christiania Bank without losses to creditors.

70 Norion Bank, 1989 (Financial Regulation Report Oct 91 pp. 21–3).

Method: Liquidation.
Funding: Deposit insurance.

One of the newly started commercial banks, Norion Bank, was placed under public administration and wound up without losses to non-bank depositors. Support was provided by the Commercial Banks' Contingency Fund in 1989.

71 Realkreditt, 1991 (*FT* 03 Dec 91; *FT* 06 Dec 91).

Method: Take-over by bank.
Funding: Central bank, and government.

Realkreditt, Norway's biggest mortgage company, experienced asset quality problems and weak earnings in October 1991. Realkreditt's liquidity has been secured through direct support from the central bank and the company's 13 largest bondholders who pledged to maintain their inventories of the company's bonds despite the failure of the proposed merger with Christiania Bank. Realkreditt secured a 450mn kroner loan from the central bank. After a second attempt to merge with Christiania failed, Den norske Bank (DnB) took over Realkreditt in December 1991. The complex deal was forced by the government and DnB received a 5.9bn kroner (920mn dollars) capital injection in a government backed bail-out in which DnB would also acquire Realkreditt (see also below).

* Government Bank Insurance and Investment Funds, 1991–2 (*FT* 23 Mar 92; *FT* 24 Nov 92; Financial Regulation Report Oct 91 pp. 21–3).

Method: Special fund.
Funding: Deposit insurance, central bank, and government.

The Norwegian banking system moved into a far-reaching crisis at the end of the 1980s. The banks had to concede heavy loan losses, and to make even larger provisions against probable future losses. The first heavy losses emerged in 1987, and in succeeding years they worsened dramatically. The Commercial Banks' Contingency Fund had at the end of 1990 a paid-in and available capital of approximately 4bn kroner. This amounted to more than the statutory 2 per cent of total non-bank deposits. On this basis, and because the development in several member banks, in particular the larger banks, still showed a negative trend, the Fund decided in December 1990 that 3bn kroner of its capital should be applied to support member banks with subordinated capital, i.e. preferential capital. In addition, the Commercial Banks' Contingency Fund has obtained support loans from the Norwegian Government Bank Insurance Guarantee Fund, which was established by law on 15 March 1991. The purpose of the Fund is to contribute to securing the solidity of the banking system. On application the Government Fund may grant interest-bearing support loans to the Commercial Banks' Contingency Fund and the Savings Bank Contingency Fund, the two deposit insurance funds. After the situation further deteriorated, the Government Bank Insurance Fund was allowed to provide loans and capital support directly to banks. Moreover, a Government Bank Investment Fund was set up in the autumn of 1991 to undertake investment in banking activity on a more commercial basis, and in conjunction with private investors. In connection with the establishment of these Government Funds, the Norges Bank announced that it would contribute to support confidence, amongst other things by supplying special liquidity support if this should be required. State funds of 15.5bn kroner have been allocated to both these Government Funds in 1991 and 1992. The Government Bank Insurance fund is responsible for designing the bank rescue package and overseeing the state's new bank acquisitions (i.e. crisis management), while the Government Bank Investment Fund plays an investor role.

Under the state's rescue programme the Funds have become the sole owner of Fokus and Christiania Bank and 70 per cent owner of Den norske Bank (see below). These three banks combined account for about 85 per cent of Norwegian commercial banks' aggregate total assets. Smaller banks, such as Sparebanken Nord-Norge, Sparebanken Midt-Norge, Sparebanken Rogaland, Union Bank, Sparebanken Vest, Oslobanken and Samvirkebanken, have also received support from the Norges Bank and from both Government Funds.

72 Fokus Bank, 1990–2 (*FT* 28 Jun 91; *FT* 27 Aug 91; *FT* 12 Dec 91; *FT* 15 Oct 92; *FT* 24 Nov 92).

Method: Special fund.
Funding: Deposit insurance, central bank (guarantee for liquidity support), and government.

Fokus Bank, Norway's third biggest bank, received a conditional 1.5bn kroner guarantee from the Commercial Banks' Contingency Fund in December 1990. Fokus needed this to meet new capital adequacy rules. This paper guarantee was transferred to conditional preference capital in June 1991 under stringent conditions, including a demand to write down the par value of Fokus' shares. In August 1991 Fokus received another 650mn kroner preference capital from the Government Bank Insurance Fund (despatched through the Commercial Banks' Fund). Finally, in December 1991 the Government Bank Insurance Fund took over Fokus Bank providing a new capital injection of 475mn kroner, while writing off the bank's present share capital. Further capital was obtained from the Government Fund in 1992.

73 Christiania Bank, 1991–2 (*FT* 19 Aug 91; *FT* 15 Oct 91; *FT* 23 Mar 92; *FT* 15 Oct 92; *FT* 24 Nov 92; *FT* 26 Feb 93).

Method: Special fund.
Funding: Deposit insurance, central bank (guarantee for liquidity support), and government.

Christiania Bank, Norway's second biggest bank, got also assistance from the Commercial Banks' Fund. It was the first to receive support from the Government Bank Insurance Fund in August 1991 after it announced losses in its shipping loans division. The bank received a conditional cash injection of up to 2.1bn kroner. The cash injection came from the Commercial Banks' Fund which, in turn, got an interest-bearing loan from the Government Fund. In addition, the central bank repeated its support of Christiania's liquidity. After total capital injections for 1991 totalled 7.9bn kroner, the Government Fund virtually nationalised Christiania. The Government Fund supplied Christiania Bank with further core capital of 1.9bn kroner in November 1992. Net losses at Christiania fell to 1.3bn kroner in 1992 from 9.2bn kroner a year earlier.

74 Den norske Bank, 1991–2 (*FT* 03 Dec 91; *FT* 23 Mar 92; *FT* 24 Nov 92).

Method: Special fund.
Funding: Deposit insurance, central bank (guarantee for liquidity support), and government.

In a bailout of Den norske Bank (DnB), Norway's biggest bank, the government provided 5.9bn kroner in 1991 and became majority shareholder (see also Ralkreditt). DnB was barely saved from technical insolvency by this complex capitalisation orchestrated by the state. After further capital injections into Den norske Bank by the Government Bank Insurance Fund in November 1992 (1.5bn kroner in preference capital and a guarantee of 600mn kroner), the Fund raised its shareholding from 55 per cent to 70 per cent.

PORTUGAL

* Recent bank failures have been concentrated amongst caixas economicas (special credit institutions) in offshore islands. The Caixa Economica de Funchal became a bank after it experienced difficulties and its depositors became its shareholders. The government organised a huge equity increase by state-controlled entities. In the case of Caixa Acoreana Faelense, the depositors also became shareholders (IBCA p. 20).

SPAIN

* Spanish Banking Crisis, 1978–83 (IBCA pp. 18–9).

During the five years to the beginning of 1983, 54 out of the 109 banks in existence experience financial difficulties. During this period, 3 banks were rescued directly by the Banca de Espana, 6 passed through the Banking Corporation,[7] 35 entered the Deposit Guarantee Fund and 10 were taken over by other banks. As a result, 3 banks were liquidated, 49 were taken over by other banks or banking groups and one Rumasa Group Bank is still in the hands of the Deposit Guarantee Fund. Rather than reporting all cases (see IBCA pp. 19–25), the most important cases will be discussed.

75 Banco de los Pirineos, 1981–4 (IBCA p. 22).

Method: Liquidation.
Funding: Deposit insurance.

Banco de los Pirineos was rescued and put into 'suspension of payments' in December 1981. The bank was struck off the Register of Banks and Bankers in 1984 and ultimately liquidated. The Deposit Guarantee Fund paid out up to the maximum guaranteed.

---

7. Although the Banking Corporation was created to assist banks in serious trouble, it was decided to enlarge the Deposit Guarantee Fund, which was considered to be a more satisfactory means of dealing with ailing banks.

76 Banca Catalana, 1982–3 (*FT* 09 Apr 83; *FT* 14 Oct 85; IBCA p. 23).

Method: Special administration, and afterwards take-over by bank.
Funding: Deposit insurance, and central bank.

Banca Catalana fell in November 1982. The bank was in the Deposit Guarantee Fund till November 1983, when it was sold to a banking consortium made up principally of the big eight banks and administered by Banco de Vizcaya. In April 1984, Banco de Vizcaya exercised its option to purchase fully Banca Catalana. The bank is undergoing a 10-year cleaning-up process under Banco de Vizcaya (now Bilbao Vizcaya Group). The Banca de Espana and the Deposit Guarantee Fund, and the Banking Corporation (the special bank rescue fund) are reckoned to have poured in 276bn pesetas (1.7bn dollars), and the eventual cost is estimated at around 100bn pesetas.

77 Banca Mas Sarda, 1982 (*FT* 14 Oct 85; IBCA p. 22).

Method: Take-over by bank.
Funding: No external funding.

Banca Mas Sarda, on old family bank which used to be mainly involved in wholesale banking, had to be rescued and refloated as part of the Banco de Bilbao Group (now Bilbao Vizcaya Group). Although a hole of 19bn pesetas existed, Banca Mas Sarda was taken over in May 1982 without assistance from the Deposit Guarantee Fund.

78 Banco Atlantico, 1983–4 (*FT* 14 Feb 84; *ECN* 24 Mar 84; IBCA p. 24).

Method: Special administration, and afterwards take-over by bank.
Funding: Deposit insurance.

In February 1983 the failed Rumasa group, the Spanish wine-to-hotels conglomerate, was taken over by the state. Banco Atlantico was the only one of the 20 Rumasa banks that was profitable at that time. The Deposit Guarantee Fund acted as administrator of Banco Atlantico (assets of about 270bn pesetas (1.7bn dollars) from February 1983 till March 1984, when it was sold for 5.1bn pesetas (34mn dollars) to a consortium made up of the Arab Banking Corporation (70 per cent), the state-owned Banco Exterior de Espana (25 per cent), and Banco Arabe Espanol (5 per cent).

SWEDEN[8]

79 Första Sparbanken, 1991–3 (*FT* 17 Oct 91; *FT* 03 Apr 92; *FT* 14 Sep 92).

Method: Rescue package.
Funding: Government.

Första Sparbanken, one of the large savings banks, was hit by heavy credit losses in the property and construction sectors. In October 1991 the Swedish government

8. See Llewellyn (1992) for an analysis of the performance of banks in Scandinavia. See Ministry of Finance Sweden (1993) for a discussion of the Swedish banking crisis.

guaranteed a 3.8bn kronor (609mn dollars) loan, provided by Sparbanksgruppen, to save Första from threatened insolvency. The government helped further with a new 7.3bn kronor (1.2bn dollars) rescue package in April 1992. Bankers and Finance Ministry officials had met in order to work out a way of saving Första after the bank announced its credit losses for 1991 reached 5.7bn kronor. Its troubles have been complicated by the fact that it is one of the 11 regional savings banks which planned to form a single large savings bank group this year. The aim is to stream-line the industry by creating the largest savings bank in the country with 540bn kronor in assets. The complications arose because of the emergency loan (in Octo-ber 1991) to Första from Sparbanksgruppen, the largest savings bank group, which will help to form the new banking group.

80 Nordbanken, 1992–3 (*FT* 14 Sep 92; *FT* 6 Oct 92; *FT* 5 Nov 92).

Method: Special administration (nationalisation).
Funding: Government.

Nordbanken, the second largest commercial bank, has been bailed out by the gov-ernment for 25bn kronor. Prior to the bail-out 20 per cent of the shares were listed on the stock exchange, while the remaining 80 per cent were government owned. The bank is no longer listed on the stock market as the government bought back this 20 per cent in the crisis. As a result Nordbanken became wholly-owned by the government in mid-September 1992. As the charge for bad debts was estimated at 12bn kronor and the operating revenues only 2bn kronor to 2.5bn, the bank re-ceived 10bn kronor of new capital from the government in November 1992. The government transferred 60bn kronor worth of non-performing loans to a new company called Securum, which is wholly-owned by the government and separate from Nordbanken. Securum is likely to receive further financial support from the government.

81 Gota Bank, 1992–3 (*FT* 14 Sep 92; *FT* 30 Sep 92; *FT* 26 Feb 93).

Method: Rescue package.
Funding: Government.

Gota AB, the Swedish holding company which owns Gota Bank, the fourth largest commercial bank, applied to the courts for a receiver as its capital had been ex-hausted. It suspended all payments to creditors on 16 September 1992. However, this did not affect Gota Bank which continued to operate normally after the Swed-ish government guaranteed on 9 September to meet the bank's obligations. The bankruptcy of the holding company brought substantial losses of 1.5bn kronor (275mn dollars) to its chief shareholder, Trygg-Hansa SPP, the insurance conglomerate, while many large Swedish companies and other banks risked losing about 1.5bn kronor in loans and other financial support. Gota Bank was finally nationalised in December 1992, because there seemed to be no end to its financial losses. Gota Bank's operating loss was 2.4bn kronor (306mn dollars) in 1992 compared to 1.9bn kronor in 1991 after credit losses reached 12.5bn kronor (SKr 3.7bn kronor in 1991). The loss was reported despite 4.5bn kronor in financial insurance and 6bn kronor in state guarantees in 1992. The government agreed to provide an additional 4bn kronor in guarantees to Gota in January 1993.

* Bank Support Authority, 1992–3 (*FT* 2 Nov 92; *FT* 6 Nov 92; *FT* 3 Mar 93; *ECN* 9 Jan 93).

Method: Special fund.
Funding: Government.

After Norway and Finland established special Government Fund in March 1991 and April 1992 respectively (see Norway and Finland), Sweden was the last Scandinavian country to announce plans in November 1992 for a special fund (Bank Support Authority) to back its troubled banking sector. Credit losses in the Swedish financial sector amounted to 100bn kronor (18.7bn dollars) in 1990–92, and it is expected that at least as much again will be lost in the next few years. The Swedish government promised unlimited financial assistance to its banking sector, as the tax minister said on 5 November 1992: '*All obligations will be met, regardless of the final amount.*' Sweden has publicly underwritten its financial system. A law passed in December 1992 guarantees that banks and some other credit institutions, such as mortgage banks, will meet their commitments on a timely basis. No limit is set to the amount or the length of this guarantee. The support, generally in the form of loans and guarantees, is to be administered through the Bank Support Authority. The government made clear that it had no intention to end up owning the banks which are covered by the proposals, although it has made exceptions such as Nordbanken and Gota. The government got the ownership in these cases as repayment of government support appeared to be out of the question.

Apart from the above mentioned cases, Skandinaviska Enskilda Banken (SE Banken, Sweden's largest commercial bank), Swedbank (the savings bank which was formed from 11 savings banks), and Foreningsbanken (Swedish cooperative bank) are seeking government support to strengthen their capital base.

SWITZERLAND

82/83 Weisscredit and Bankag, early 1980s (IBCA p. 37).

Method: Liquidation.
Funding: No external funding.
Lead organiser: Federal Banking Commission (supervisor).

In the cases of Weisscredit and Bankag, which were the largest of the bank failures in the 1980s, the authorities persuaded major banks to take over parts of the liquidated business. Although these cases represented the largest bank failures, they were both small banks. Under Swiss law holders of savings deposits have some preference in the event of the winding up of a bank.

84 Banque Commerciale SA, 1983 (IBCA p. 36).

Method: Liquidation.
Funding: No external funding.
Lead organiser: Federal Banking Commission (supervisor).

Banque Commerciale SA was forced to close by the Federal Banking Commission in November 1983. This forced closure was to a large extent due to the bank's discomfiture caused by an inadequate spread of risks and its disguising of this fact through the use of a Cayman Island subsidiary.

85/86/87 Banca di Partecipazioni ed Investimenti SA (Lugano), Mebco Bank SA (Geneva) and Spar and Hypothekenbank AG (Lucerne), 1988–91 (IBCA p. 37).

Method: Liquidation.
Funding: Deposit insurance.
Lead organiser: Federal Banking Commission (supervisor).

Banca di Partecipazioni ed Investimenti SA (Lugano), Mebco Bank SA (Geneva) and Spar and Hypothekenbank AG (Lucerne) have had their licences withdrawn and, as a result, gone into liquidation. Under a mutual guarantee scheme of the members of the Swiss Bankers' Association, depositors were paid up to 30,000 francs per depositor. Although this mutual guarantee scheme (which is called Convention XVIII) is no official deposit insurance scheme, we rank it under deposit insurance as it provides *de facto* deposit protection.

88 Caisse d'Épargne du Valais Société Mutuelle, 1987 (IBCA p. 37).

Method: Take-over by bank.
Funding: No external funding reported.
Lead organiser: Federal Banking Commission (supervisor).

The Federal Banking Commission encouraged Swiss Banking Corporation to take over Caisse d'Épargne du Valais Société Mutuelle in 1987. Since the bank was taken over as a whole, none of the depositors lost money.

89 Spar und Leihkasse Thun, 1991 (*FT* 07 Feb 92; *FT* 20 May 92; *ECN* 15 Feb 92).

Method: Liquidation.
Funding: Deposit insurance.
Lead organiser: Federal Banking Commission (supervisor).

In October 1991, the Federal Banking Commission forced Spar und Leihkasse Thun to close without warning, after the three major banks refused to buy it. Thun suffered from on overexposure in the mortgage credit business. The failure of the Thun Bank, a sizeable regional bank with assets of 1.1bn francs (411mn pounds) near Berne, revealed many problems in the Swiss banking system arising from liberalisation. It undermined the assumption that one of the big universal banks would always be a rescuer of last resort in such cases. Second, it showed that traditional supervision procedures were no longer adequate. Depositors were protected up to 30,000 francs for each savings depositor, the private guarantee scheme's ceiling.

In the wake of this closure many people withdrew their savings from other regional banks. Banks, therefore, unveiled a two-layer system designed to prevent any more forced closures. First, the Union of Swiss Regional Banks, which represents the smaller local banks that are in great difficulties, has formed an examining board to discover problem cases and try to solve them. Union officials have said that about a dozen on their 185 member banks will be examined. Ideally, another bank will be found to take on the problem bank or its assets. See the next two cases.

90 Bank EvK (Ersparniskasse von Konolfingen), 1992 (*FT* 05 Feb 92; *ECN* 15 Feb 92).

Method: Take-over by bank.
Funding: No external funding.
Lead organiser: Federal Banking Commission (supervisor).

In February 1992, Union Bank of Switzerland (UBS), the largest Swiss bank, took over the 2bn francs (1.4bn dollars) assets of one of the country's largest regional banks, Bank Evk (Ersparniskasse von Konolfingen). UBS found that EvK was, on the whole, a good bank without fundamental problems, but it had to make special provisions on bad loans last year and that left it with insufficient capital and reserves to comply with the Federal Banking Commission's stiff requirements. At the time of the closure of Spar und Leihkasse Thun, UBS provided a liquidity guarantee for EvK.

91 Eko Hypothekar- und Handelsbank, 1992 (*FT* 29 Oct 92).

Method: Closure, afterwards take-over by bank.
Funding: No external funding.
Lead organiser: Federal Banking Commission (supervisor).

Eko Hypothekar- und Handelsbank, another large regional bank, was closed by the Federal Banking Commission. But following approval by its shareholder, Ekobank was taken over by Credit Suisse, Switzerland's third largest bank, one week later. Ekobank's branches were reopened, but as Credit Suisse branches. The takeover occurred in the context of the earlier mentioned safety net, following the collapse of Spar und Leihkasse Thun. Ekobank, based in Olten, had assets of 1.6bn francs (1.1bn dollars) at the end of 1991, and employed about 100 people. It was owned, and its assets and liabilities were totally guaranteed, by the local community. As part of the takeover agreement, the potential liability of the community for future losses was limited to 40mn francs.

UNITED KINGDOM

92 Secondary banking crisis, 1973–5 (IBCA pp. 61–3).

Method: Emergency-aid.
Funding: Banks, and central bank.
Lead organiser: Bank of England (central bank and supervisor).

The growth in the early 1970s of the relatively unsupervised 'secondary' sector institutions was rapid. A speculative boom in property came to an abrupt end at the end of 1973, and most of the concerns which later required support had interests in property finance. The secondary banking crisis threatened to produce a series of domino collapses that could have had serious repercussion on the major primary sector banks. A lifeboat was launched to provide liquidity for these secondary banks suffering a run on deposits. The support was in the form of loans of specified maturity, subject to review. The lifeboat was coordinated by the Bank of England and included the big four clearing banks and the Scottish clearing banks. Beneficiaries of lifeboat assistance fell into two categories. In the majority of the cases, the burden of risk was born collectively by the lifeboat members. In other cases, the risk of loss was shouldered entirely by the applicant institution's clearing bank. An exposure ceiling of 2/5ths of the clearers' collective capital and reserves was agreed by the lifeboat members with the Bank of England in August 1974. In absorbing the excess over the clearing banks' limit, the Bank of England incurred significant exposure under individual arrangements, and it is thought that its final exposure was well in excess of the 10 per cent in lifeboat finance initially agreed. The lifeboat thus probably fended off the destabilising effects of secondary banking failures in the UK and on the international financial system as a whole.

93 Johnson Matthey Bankers Ltd., 1984 (IBCA pp. 63–7).

Method: Capital injection.
Funding: Central bank, banks, parent company, and others.
Lead organiser: Bank of England (central bank and supervisor).

The near collapse of Johnson Matthey Bankers (JMB), the banking, gold bullion and commodity trading subsidiary of the Johnson Matthey Group, in September 1984, was not symptomatic of deeper problems in the UK domestic banking system. After a reported reversal in its profits in July 1984, JMB appeared to have very large exposures to several commercial debtors, the two largest of which were 'loosely associated groups run by businessmen from Pakistan'. These two latter exposures were 76 per cent and 34 per cent of JMB's capital base. JMB failed to report these large exposures correctly to the Bank of England. Provisions for the two large loans would eradicate JMB's available capital. The Bank of England feared for London's position as the leading international gold bullion market, since Johnson Matthey was one of the five London gold price fixers. After the Johnson Matthey Group could not provide enough capital and potential purchasers (approached by the Bank of England) withdrew, the Bank itself had to provide support for JMB. In the solution to the crisis, the parent company sold JMB to the Bank for 1 pound, after having agreed to inject 50mn pounds into the bank. An indemnity totalling 150mn pounds was agreed to meet JMB's losses, of which the Bank itself provided 75mn pounds and, after considerable and difficult discussions, the four London clearing banks agreed to divide 35mn pounds between them, the members of the gold market 30mn pounds and the other members of the accepting houses committee 10mn pounds. All of this indemnity was subsequently recovered. Later, in 1985, the Bank sold JMB's gold bullion business to a major Australian bank, Westpac. The Bank's failure to prevent the collapse of JMB is understood to have strained its relationship with the Treasury.

94 British & Commonwealth Merchant Bank, 1990 (*FT* 02 Jun 90; *FT* 04 Jun 90; *FT* 09 Jun 90; *FT* 16 Jan 91; *FT* 26 Sep 92)

Method: Liquidation.
Funding: Deposit insurance.

Confidence in British & Commonwealth Holdings, a large financial services group, was gradually lost following the disclosure at Easter 1990 of a heavy write-down at its leasing subsidiary, Atlantic Computers. British & Commonwealth Holdings and its subsidiaries went into administration in June 1990, after the Securities and Investments Board (SIB) removed British & Commonwealth Merchant Bank (BCMB), the merchant bank subsidiary of the group, from its list of authorised banks and ordered SIB-regulated firms to remove client money. The SIB did so after it was clear that some major creditor banks refused to renew a 70mn pounds standby facility to BMCB. In the preceeding weeks the Bank of England failed to replace this facility by a new standby facility of 100mn pounds. In two meetings with the four UK clearing banks, as well as Standard Chartered, Royal Bank of Scotland, Chase Manhattan and the Hongkong and Shangai Banking Corporation, the Bank tried to persuade them to contribute 12.5mn pounds each to the 100mn pounds lifeboat. Under the deposit protection scheme, depositors were paid out 75 per cent of their deposits, up to the maximum of 15,000 pounds. After the final winding up, further payments have been made to BMCB's creditors up to a total of 78p in the pound.

Two other small banks, Chancery and Edington, went into administration in 1991. In both cases the Deposit Protection Board made the statutory payouts.

95 Bank of Credit and Commerce International, 1991 (*FT* Behind Closed Doors 1991; *FT* 23 Oct 92).

Method: Liquidation.
Funding: Deposit insurance.
Lead organiser: Bank of England (central bank and supervisor).

The Bank of Credit and Commerce International (BCCI) was closed by the Bank of England on 5 July 1991. Though a petition for winding up was presented in July 1991, the winding up order was not made before January 1992. In October 1992 the Deposit Protection Fund had paid out 50mn pounds on the insured deposits. The total liability for the Fund can go up to 85mn pounds. See Luxembourg for the full story. The collapse of BCCI led to an official investigation by Lord Justice Bingham (1992).

96 Lifeboats, 1991–93 (*FT* 26 Mar 93).

Method: Rescue package.
Funding: Central bank, and banks.
Lead Organiser: Bank of England (central bank and supervisor).

In the second half of 1991, after the closure of BCCI, the Bank of England launched financial lifeboats for a number of small and medium-sized banks. A lifeboat involves either the Bank putting funds into a troubled bank or the injection of money from commercial banks with a guarantee from the Bank. In 1993 the Bank of England disclosed that some banks were still in receipt of Bank funds. The rescue of small banks was prompted by the withdrawal of wholesale deposits. These deposits were withdrawn because small banks were thought to be particularly vulnerable to the recession, other small banks such as British & Commonwealth Merchant Bank, Chancery and Edington (see above), had already been closed and the closure of BCCI led investors to rethink where they placed their funds. The Bank initiated the lifeboats, because in mid-1991, after the closure of BCCI, it believed there was considerable nervousness in the financial markets and that the collapse of small banks could have had damaging consequences. The Bank did not disclose which banks had been rescued. It is understood that City Merchants Bank, part of the Invesco MIM Group, had received 40mn pounds from National Westminster Bank and that an indemnity had been given to NatWest by the Bank. It is also understood that the Bank played a role in organising a 200mn pounds cash lifeboat for National Home Loans, one of the largest mortgage lenders, in July 1991. The funds were provided by the eight largest UK clearing banks.

UNITED STATES

Rather than giving a detailed survey of all US banks with difficulties in the last decade, only the well-known savings and loans debacle and a few major bank failures and rescues in the last decade will be summarised.

97 Savings and loans debacle, 1980s (Heffernan 1992).

Method: Special fund (liquidation, or take-over by banks after restructuring).
Funding: Deposit insurance, and government.

The savings and loans industry suffered in the 1980s as a result of a concentration of credit risk in the real estate market and interest rate risk, the latter arising because of assets in the form of long term fixed interest loans and mortgage backed securities, valued on their books at the original purchase price. A rise in the interest rates reduced the value of these securities and also forced the savings and loans banks (S&Ls) to bear the burden of fixed interest loans in an environment of rising interest rates. The Federal Savings & Loan Insurance Corporation (FSLIC), the deposit insurance fund for savings and loans banks, was placed under the auspices of the Federal Home Loan Bank Board (FHLBB), their supervisory agent. After certificates, issued by the FSLIC to support the S&Ls' capital, appeared to be insufficient, the FHLBB introduced a programme to replace the management of the S&Ls, until the FSLIC could sell or liquidate them. However, the deteriorating condition of insolvent S&Ls strained the resources of the FSLIC, and the FSLIC was declared insolvent in early 1987, with its deficit estimated to exceed 3bn dollars. In the 1989 Reform Act, the FSLIC was dissolved and the Savings Association Insurance Fund was established under the auspices of the Federal Deposit Insurance Corporation. In addition, the Act created the Resolution Trust Company (RTC) to take over the caseload of insolvent S&Ls. The RTC received 50bn dollars additional public funding to liquidate or sell the insolvent S&Ls. The Act also disbanded the FHLBB, replacing it with the Office of Thrift Supervision under the direction of the Secretary of the Treasury.

98 Continental Illinois Bank, 1984 (ECN 26 May 84; Sprague 1986[9]).

Method: Special administration, and afterwards sale.
Funding: Deposit insurance, central bank (secured liquidity support), and banks.

Before the crisis in May 1984 started, Continental Illinois had assets of 41.4bn dollars. The Chicago bank had lent so recklessly to oil drillers in the energy boom and property speculators in the real estate boom, that it had 2.3bn dollars in nonperforming loans. In the aftermath of the Penn Square collapse in July 1982 and the LDC debt crisis, Continental experienced funding difficulties in its domestic markets. Fed funds and certificate of deposit (CD) markets began to dry up and Continental had to turn to more expensive Eurodollar deposits. In early 1984 Continental was anxious about its funding. On 8 May 1984, rumours that Continental was considering bankruptcy were spread on Reuters. Some of the foreign banks started to pull out funds, later joined by domestic banks, which resulted in a run on Continental's wholesale deposits. In the days preceding official assistance, the

---

9. See Sprague (1986) for an illuminating insider résumé of the Continental bailout, the biggest bank failure in the USA.

loss of deposits exceeded 6bn dollars. The Federal Reserve Board stepped in with liquidity assistance. In an initial package the Federal Deposit Insurance Corporation (FDIC) provided 1.5bn dollars and fifteen banks provided 0.5bn dollars as a subordinated loan to Continental. In combination with this first package the Fed announced to be prepared to meet any extraordinary liquidity requirements and the FDIC promised to protect fully all depositors and other general creditors of Continental. The Continental use of the rescue package peaked at 13.7bn dollars on 13 August 1984: 7.4bn dollars in Fed borrowings (fully secured), including 3.5bn dollars later assumed by the FDIC; 4.1bn dollars in safety net borrowings from other banks; and 2bn dollars in capital notes from the FDIC and the banks, later reduced to 1bn dollar from the FDIC. The FDIC took out billions of dollars of bad loans and appointed new managers to run the remaining 'good bank'. The FDIC refloated parts of Continental Illinois over a period of time.

99 Bank of New York computer failure, 1985 (ECN 12 Jul 86).

Method: Emergency-aid.
Funding: Central bank (secured liquidity support).

In November 1985, the Bank of New York ran up enormous net cash flow deficit when its computer broke down. Although the machine sold government securities, it could neither deliver them nor collect the money owed to the bank. The Fed made an overnight loan of 22.6bn dollars from the discount window, collateralised by 36bn dollars in securities. Although the problem was sorted out in 24 hours, the bank had to pay the interest out of its own pocket, which amounted to 5mn dollars.

100 First Republic Bank, 1988 (ECN 19 Mar 88; ECN 06 Aug 88).

Method: Special administration, and afterwards take-over by bank.
Funding: Deposit insurance.

The biggest bank in Texas, First Republic Bank, admitted defeat due to a fall in the value of its property loans, and called in the Federal Deposit Insurance Corporation (FDIC) for restructuring talks in March 1988. First Republic had only 812mn dollars of pure equity left. It earlier forecasted a loss of 450mn dollars for 1988. First Republic was formed by the takeover of the adventurous InterFirst Bank by the supposedly more conservative Republic Bank Dallas. In August 1988 North Carolina National Bank (NCNB) took over First Republic, which doubled the size of the old NCNB paid about 225mn dollars for a 20 per cent stake in (but voting control of) all the banks, except one credit card company, owned by the old First Republic holding company. The FDIC filled the negative equity hole of 1.1bn dollars. It also forgave a 1bn dollar loan and paid 960mn dollars for its non-voting 80 per cent stake. NCNB got the option to buy out FDIC at 107 per cent of the new bank's book value for the next five years. In addition, the FDIC would cover all losses caused by First Republic Bank's 5bn dollars worth of non-performing, predominantly property-backed, loans.

Two other large Texas banks, First City (1988) and MCorp (1989), ran also into difficulties and required huge amounts of federal support.

101 Freedom National Bank, 1990 (FT 8 Jan 91; ECN 12 Jan 91).

Method: Liquidation.
Funding: Deposit insurance.

Freedom National Bank, a small community bank based in Harlem (New York), failed in 1990. The FDIC decided to liquidate the bank without fully protecting large depositors. Only 50 cents in the dollar was paid out on all accounts larger than 100,000 dollars. Since this bank's customers were mainly black, subsequent rescues of other banks, where the depositors were protected from losses, led to charges of racial bias being levied against the authorities.

102 Bank of New England, 1991 (ECN 12 Jan 91; FT 02 Apr 91; FT 23 Apr 91).

Method: Capital injection, and afterwards take-over by banks.
Funding: Deposit insurance, and central bank (liquidity support).

The Bank of New England, which was once America's 15th biggest bank with assets of 32bn dollars, was America's 3rd biggest failure. The bailout of the Bank of New England by the federal authorities, in January 1991, was expected to cost at least 2.3bn dollars. Its depositors have been saved by the federal deposit insurance, while its bond- and stockholders have taken a major loss. It was argued that the authorities should have put the Bank of New England, a fifth of whose loans were not performing, out of its misery many months ago. Unlike Continental Illinois, bailed out in 1984, the FDIC has not taken over Bank of New England's problem loans. Instead, on 7 January it took control as a quasi receiver. The FDIC has provided 750mn dollars in working capital. After earlier bidders were dismissed, Bank of England was finally was finally taken over by the New York based finance group, KKR (Kohlberg, Kravis and Roberts), and the Fleet/Norstar Financial Group in April 1991. In their joint bid the two groups took over the three Bank of New England 'bridge banks' with combined assets of about 15bn dollars. The FDIC received 125mn dollars of which 100mn dollars in preferred stock and 25mn dollars in cash.

VENEZUELA

103 Banco Nacional de Descuento, 1978–84 (FT 07 May 85; IBCA p. 7–8, 45).

Method: Special administration, and afterwards liquidation.
Funding: Central bank, and government.

Banco Nacional de Descuento (BND), a commercial bank, was first rescued in 1978, then later reopened after the government bought its shares. The government acted decisively to protect all creditors against losses and placed BND's shares in Fondo de Inversiones de Venezuela (Venezuela Investment Fund), a 20-year irrevocable trust at the Central Bank, which held 99 per cent of BND's share capital. Before the intervention the Central Bank supported this bank, among other banks (see below). The Finance Ministry shut BND down in May 1984, after constantly having to make new capital injections (Bs 8bn since 1978) to cover BND's continuous losses. BND had Bs 9.5bn in assets when it was finally closed down.

104 Banco de Los Trabajadores, 1982 (IBCA p. 7–8).

Method: Special administration.
Funding: Central Bank, and government.

Banco de Los Trabajadores (BTV), a hybrid multifunctional commercial bank, was rescued in November 1982 and became 50 per cent government owned afterwards (owned also by the Venezuelan Labour Federation). Total assets at the time of intervention were Bs 26bn (6bn dollars at that time) or 20 per cent of the total commercial bank system's assets at 31 December 1982, making it the biggest banking bankruptcy in the history of Latin America.

Both these interventions (together with rescues of three smaller banks in 1982) were caused by a lack of liquidity to honour cheques in the Venezuelan cheque clearing house. By badly distributing their loan portfolio into illiquid, overvalued real estate, these banks could not stand any substantial loss of deposits. The Central Bank decided to intervene and take over the banks rather than to continue to support these losing banks as Central Bank assistance to state banks fell 42 per cent from Bs 4.1bn to Bs 2.4bn in 1983.

Sources

FT, Financial Times (1982–92).
ECN, The Economist (1982–92).
IBCA, Country Reports of Banking Systems, (London).
Several Central Banks.
Financial Regulation Report (1991), (London: *Financial Times*), (October).
FT, (1991), '*Behind Closed Doors* (BCCI: The Biggest Bank Fraud in History)' (November).
Shelagh Heffernan (1992), Lecture Notes (London: City University Business School).

NOTES

1. In the Netherlands, where the prohibition of bank-insurance mergers was lifted in January 1990, the Central Bank (responsible for banking supervision) and the Insurance Chamber signed a protocol to establish a working relationship in co-ordinating supervision of bank-insurance conglomerates. See OECD (1992, p. 79–87) for recent developments in the field of cross-sector supervision.
2. See also the Maastricht Treaty (Council and Commission of the European Communities, 1992): In Article 105, Para 6, it is explicitly stated that the (European) 'Council may, acting unanimously . . ., confer upon the European Central Bank specific tasks concerning policies relating to the prudential supervision of credit institutions and other financial institutions *with the exception of insurance undertakings*', (emphasis added).
3. The European Commission has set the minimum at 15,000 ECU in its proposal. A concession to member states, which prefer some kind of co-insurance (notably the UK and Ireland), is made in allowing member states to guarantee at least 90 per cent of deposits up to the 15,000 ECU level (EC, 1992a).
4. See, for example, Richard Dale (1992b, p. 1) in his note on 'Deposit insurance worries for regulators':

   Deposit insurance has emerged as a key regulatory issue both in the EC and the US. But whereas the EC is mainly concerned with strengthening and standardizing deposit insurance arrangements in Europe, the US is focusing its attention on the need for greater discipline in financial markets.

The major problem with deposit insurance is well known: it creates 'moral hazard' by removing depositor discipline and encouraging risk-taking by banks. Hence the ceiling typically imposed on deposit insurance coverage. Yet the paradox today is that in country after country deposit insurance ceilings have tended to be ignored in favour of total protection for depositors.

For instance, in Japan no depositor has had to claim from the deposit insurance fund since its inception more than two decades ago. In the US the authorities have routinely dealt with failing banks in a manner that safeguards all, and not merely insured, depositors. While in Europe, there has been a parallel reluctance to tolerate any major deposit losses: bank bailouts are the preferred solution, as illustrated by recent events in Scandinavia.

BCCI was an exception to the general rule, reflecting the impracticality of organizing a rescue operation. But the political fall-out from the ensuing deposit losses may have further strengthened national authorities' predisposition to avoid such collapses in the future.

5. There are a number of other somewhat minor issues relating to the twin questions of 'conflict' and 'efficiency'. For example, does the combination of functions lead to improved information and understanding in the Central Bank? Or does it lead to problems of confidentiality and 'Chinese Walls' within the Central Bank itself? Does the combined function lead to advantages, or problems, in dealing with banks? One Central Banker (Muller, 1981) has noted that the kind of relationship sought with banks on behalf of monetary policy (e.g. co-operation, gentlemen's agreement) may be very different from that holding in the relationship between supervisors and bankers, which may be much tougher. In general, the 'purity' of the overall relationships, e.g. between the Central Bank and the banks, may be obscured by the twin responsibility of the former.

6. We initially had thought that this might have been the case in Denmark. In a particular case (case 22 in Appendix 3), the Central Bank provided liquidity support to a bank in difficulties and the supervisory agency then went ahead and closed that bank without any consultation with the Central Bank. However, further research indicated that the problems were communicated to the Central Bank and all parties involved concluded that a suspension of payments was unavoidable.

7. See, for example, the Lamfalussy Report (BIS, 1990b) and the recent Padoa Schioppa Report (EC Commission, 1992b).

8. It should be noted that some important net settlement systems provide neither unwinding nor settlement finality explicitly at present.

9. Examples of net settlement systems can be found among others in the USA (CHIPS), the UK (CHAPS), Germany (EAF), France (Sagittaire) and Italy (SIPS). See BIS (1990a) and EC Commission (1992c) for the details of large value payment systems in the major developed countries.

10. As the ECU clearing and settlement is a closed circuit, net debtors will normally square their position by borrowing from net creditors. However, net creditors might be unwilling to extend lending to some net debtors, when this additional lending would exceed credit limits set on these debtors. The ECU Banking Association has therefore implemented an intermediation facility, under which the surplus of the net creditor(s) will effectively be channelled through all other

clearing banks who will each lend up to a maximum of ECU 5mn to the net debit bank(s). This arrangement can potentially cover a shortage of ECU 215mn (i.e. 5 × 43) (EC, 1992c).

11. The Committee of Governors of the EC Central Banks felt that it should be entrusted with the oversight responsibility for the private ECU clearing and settlement system, but it remains silent on the direct responsibility for the system (EC Commission, 1992b).

12. The fear of losing customer business is, for example, a market related incentive for banks to prevent payment disruptions. However, it can be questioned whether this outweighs the cost of foregone interest on banks' reserves.

13. The Federal Reserve has announced that it will charge a fee for daylight overdrafts on Fedwire from April 1994.

14. In Japan (BOJ–NET; no overdrafts), the Netherlands (Central Bank System; collateralised overdrafts) and Switzerland (SIC; no overdrafts) a major part of large value transfers is already settled on a real-time gross basis without credit exposures. The Banque de France is moving to a gross settlement system with partially collateralised daylight overdrafts (TBF). The CHAPS settlement banks have announced plans to move to a collateralised gross settlement system in the UK (Bank of England, 1992).

15. See, for example, the earlier discussed improvements in the Swiss gross settlement system, SIC, and the proposed arrangements for the French system, TBF.

16. Another source of credit exposure which originates beyond the settlement system, is two tier and correspondent bank arrangements. In tiering arrangements 'second tier' banks may have to use the services of settlement banks to exchange payment orders and to settle their positions because only the settlement banks have settlement accounts at the Central Bank. Correspondent banking is the main vehicle for international payments since in all industrial countries to date, direct access to their payment systems is subject to being located in that country (EC Commission, 1992b). It can be questioned whether these agency relations will be eliminated fully as the holding of positive settlement accounts or collateral at one or more payment systems can be expensive, especially for small and foreign banks. It is essentially the same trade-off between efficiency and risk as in net or gross settlement with daylight exposure compared with gross settlement without such exposure.

17. The credit exposure in traditional instruments, such as interbank deposits and CDs, amounts to the full principal value, while the exposure in off-balance instruments is limited to the replacement cost of the contract's cash flows, the so-called credit equivalent value.

18. The earlier discussed payment system of Switzerland, SIC, provides a good example of a privately owned and operated system with continuous settlement in reserves (i.e. Central Bank money) and no overdrafts.

19. See Summers (1991) for a different view. Apart from a role for the Central Bank in regulating and overseeing the payment system (and providing settlement across its books), with which we agree, Summers argues also for a role for the Central Bank in operating large value payment systems, because of the critical nature and 'safety net' attributes of such systems.

20. Our thanks are due to IBCA for making available its country reports and to the *Financial Times* for using *FT* Profile, a computerised database of *Financial Times* and *Economist* cuts from 1982. An initial draft was sent to a number of Central Banks, but *not* to all countries for which we provide cases of bank failures. We are very grateful to them for corrections and additional information. Any remaining errors are our responsibility.

21. Note that in Appendix 3 we classify the support coming from the Exchange Fund in Hong Kong as government funding, because we regard the Exchange Fund as part of the Government rather than as a Central Bank. Even when the 6 cases in which the Exchange Fund supported banks are excluded, the Government undertook in 12 cases a rescue by itself, and the Central Bank only in 2 cases.

22. See, for example, Schwartz (1991, pp. 109–10) for a comment on US practice. She argues that 'The lending practices of the Federal Reserve Banks have allowed hundreds of nonviable or insolvent banks since 1985 to remain open long beyond the point of viability, . . . The collateral the Federal Reserve Banks accept is usually the most liquid, high-quality assets the borrowing institutions hold. When the borrowers are finally closed, the FDIC repays the Federal Reserve Banks in cash ahead of all other creditors. With the haircut of the collateral, these are riskless loans for the Fed. Hence there is no incentive to shut the discount window'.

17 Bank Insolvency and Deposit Insurance: A Proposal (1993)*

17.1 INTRODUCTION

The experience of recent bank failures in several major countries – Johnson Matthey in the UK, Continental Illinois in the USA and Canadian Commercial Bank – has pointed up a number of intractable problems facing central banks and bank regulatory authorities. First, if really large banks are always to be prevented from failing, then either there will be inequitable treatment between large and small, with a resulting tendency towards oligopoly, or all banks must enjoy similar protection, which will exacerbate moral hazard problems. This issue is discussed in section 17.2.

Second, the growth of wholesale money markets and liability management have further erased the distinctions between illiquidity and (potential) insolvency. So, central bank lender of last resort action will generally involve a risk of loss. In the past central banks have often persuaded their major commercial banks to share the burden of some of that potential loss, via indemnities, and so on. But commercial banks have become increasingly unwilling to play this role. What alternatives exist? This forms the subject of section 17.3.

Deposit insurance may help, both to prevent bank crises and to limit the damage of any that still occur. There is a lively debate in the US literature whether such insurance should be provided by the private or public sectors, and whether it should cover all deposits, or only deposits providing transactions services, for example demand deposits. In section 17.4, I argue that such insurance needs to be provided by the public sector and comprehensively cover all deposits.

It is practically impossible to calculate banking risk *ex ante*, so deposit insurance premiums cannot be *objectively* related to risk. This leads to moral hazard problems, and thus provokes direct regulatory constraints on the assumption of risk. In my conclusion, section 17.5, I propose the adoption of a co-responsibility approach in order to mitigate some of the problems arising from 100 per cent deposit insurance coverage.

* Chapter 6 in P. Arestis (ed.), *Money and Banking: Issues for the Twenty-First Century*, (Macmillan, 1993): 75–94.

17.2 MORAL HAZARD AND THE BAGEHOT PROBLEM

On Friday, 14 March 1986 the *New York Times* carried a report of the testimony of the chairman of the Federal Deposit Insurance Corporation (FDIC) before the Senate banking committee. The paper reported:

> The chairman of the FDIC told Congress today that the agency's implied policy of not liquidating large insolvent banks would now be applied to smaller banks. 'The time has come to treat all banks alike until we have a mechanism in place to permit any bank to fail, irrespective of size,' L. William Seidman said, 'But at this point that is just not possible.'

Whether or not it ever was feasible to contemplate the failure of really large bank in any country, the difficulties faced by Continental Illinois induced the regulatory authorities in the USA both to provide full 100 per cent insurance, *ex post*, to all depositors at Con. Ill., whether or not they had been legally insured beforehand, and also to express in public their conviction that it would be necessary to prevent the failure of at least the eleven or so largest banks in the USA under all circumstances. Even if it may have been widely assumed beforehand that the authorities would not allow a really large bank to fail, there had been some uncertainty about how the authorities would respond in the event that hypothetical possibility occurred. Now it has become clear, beyond peradventure, that really large banks would be rescued, come what may, in the USA. Most observers believe that this also holds true in the UK and in most other countries.

This step, however, has put the authorities on the horns of a dilemma. If there is to be one law for the large banks, which can rely on rescue under all circumstances, and another more severe law for the small banks, which would be allowed to fail, then the implications for all (not 100 per cent insured) depositors become obvious. The safety of the large bank is greater, irrespective of the riskiness of its portfolio. Consequently, deposit funds would flow to the large banks, away from the small, unless the small were prepared to pay a premium for funds, which need not be related to the relative riskiness of their own portfolios. That would be inequitable.

On the other hand, if *all* banks are to be fully protected, with all depositors receiving *de facto* 100 per cent deposit insurance, as now appears to be the case in the USA, then widespread moral hazard problems could increase considerably. Since there is no risk of loss to depositors, a bank desiring to adopt a riskier and/or excessively expansionary strategy, would be able to obtain additional funds simply by paying a very small margin above the going market rate. Although there still remain certain checks to risk-taking (for example, the stake of the equity holder, who remains at risk; the desire to maintain the reputation and a conservative image; the visible effect of changes in the market value of the equity of banks whose shares are quoted on the stock exchange; the future job prospects and self-esteem of managers; and so on) circumstances could develop that would lead some bankers, subject to such moral hazard, consciously to adopt a *much* riskier strategy, particularly when market conditions have eroded the existing value of the equity holders' net position to a point at which they, and the management, had nothing further to lose from a risky strategy, and quite a lot to gain. Recent developments in the US, notably relating to the behaviour of a set of Savings and Loan Associations (S&Ls), show that such moral hazard risk is far from hypothetical. With their net asset position already seriously impaired, many S&Ls, insured by the Federal Savings and Loan Insurance Corporation (FSLIC), invested heavily in 'junk bonds', and consciously adopted various high-risk strategies.

In so far as the moral hazard problem of 100 per cent insurance raises the predilections of bankers for an excessively risky strategy, the authorities are likely to respond by seeking to impose additional direct constraints over risk-taking. This is likely to involve higher required capital adequacy ratios, more stringent controls over the structure of the asset portfolio, more frequent examinations, and, consequently, higher compliance costs of regulation. The result is likely to be increasing distortions in bank portfolios, as banks try to avoid and evade the effect of such additional regulations.

The advent of this problem was described and analysed in a brilliant article by Hirsch (1977). It is worth quoting at length from this work:

> There is a continuing dilemma faced by central banks anxious to prevent their support of banking stability from weakening banking competition and long-term banking efficiency. The central bank has to find a means of checking moral hazard. It can take the 'English' route of informal controls and inculcation of a club spirit among the commercial banks to play the game according to the established conventions which are seen to be in the interests of all participants. In return for the insurance premium of responsible behaviour, insurance cover is comprehensive and assured . . . The alternative strategy is for the central bank to attempt to exert its counterforce to moral hazard through a continued market discipline which makes no demands on commercial banks to depart from their individual profit orientation but confronts them with a contingent risk of failure. Insurance here is less than comprehensive and available only along with significant self insurance (e.g. of the equity and of large deposits, which are in effect 'deductibles' from the insured risk). This may be categorised as the German and to the lesser extent the American approach to the lender of last resort function. The difficulty with this approach is that it appears unlikely in practice to be applied evenly to banks of different size, because failure of big banks is generally, and surely correctly, regarded as more disruptive to the financial system than failure of small ones. Consequently, the greater the perceived risk of particular banks being

allowed to go under, the greater will be the tendency for bank depositors to seek shelter in the banks considered too large for the authorities to subject to such therapy, and the greater the tendency towards banking concentration... Thus informal controls lead to cartelisation, 'market' controls to oligopoly. Whichever strategy the central banking authorities choose, their ultimate support for banking stability tends to discourage banking competition. Neither strategy, therefore, is dominant as a means of promoting internal efficiency (pp. 251–2).

The passage of time allows us to qualify Hirsch's conclusions. First, the pressures of increasing competition, especially international, have undermined what Hirsch describes as the 'English' route. Cartelised clubs have now largely disappeared from the English financial scene. That option is quickly disappearing.

Perhaps more important, Hirsch did not appreciate that the problem of equity, of one law for the large and another for the small, would drive the authorities, explicitly now in the USA (and, many commentators feel, implicitly in the UK in the aftermath of Johnson Matthey), to a position in which a wider range of bank depositors, perhaps extending almost to *all* bank depositors, now enjoy effectively 100 per cent insurance. But, as Hirsch noted, that then:

Would itself tend to induce distortions of the kind noted in the case of public health insurance – viz, encouraging extravagance or carelessness (moral hazard) and consequential excess 'output' of banking services for the public (p. 247).

One partial answer to that, as already noted, is more stringent regulation. But that causes further distortions. Either way, the authorities seem to be caught in an increasingly uncomfortable bind. As noted earlier, the American authorities, at least, are looking for 'a mechanism... to permit any bank to fail, irrespective of size. But at this point that is just not possible.' No such mechanism, or means, to allow really large banks to fail has yet been established. In its absence, there remains a serious problem for the authorities.

17.3 ILLIQUIDITY, INSOLVENCY AND THE ROLE OF THE CENTRAL BANK

In his great work, *Lombard Street*, Bagehot (1873) sought to distinguish between situations of illiquidity, when the central bank should provide support loans, and conditions of insolvency, when the central bank should not do so. Bagehot proposed two rules to guide the Bank of England in dealing with a crisis of confidence. The first was 'That these [LOLR] loans should only be made at a very high rate of interest' (p. 97). The second was:

> That at this rate these advances should be made on all good banking securities ... No advances indeed need be made by which the Bank will ultimately lose. The amount of bad business in commercial countries is an infinitesimally small fraction of the whole business. That in a panic the bank, or banks, holding the ultimate reserve should refuse bad bills or bad securities will not make the panic really worse; the 'unsound' people are a feeble minority, and they are afraid even to look frightened for fear their unsoundness may be detected. The great majority, the majority to be protected, are the 'sound' people, the people who have good security to offer (p. 97).

Bagehot was, however, unduly optimistic when claiming that bad business represented only an infinitesimal fraction of the whole. Moreover, Bagehot described as 'good' securities those that could be readily realised and convertible in *good* times, but might be virtually unsaleable, or only saleable at a considerable loss, during a panic. Thus Bagehot was advocating advancing loans on the collateral of securities to be valued at their 'normal' market price, not at their current value. Put another way, Bagehot differentiated between 'good' and 'bad' (securities and borrowers), on the basis of whether they would return to solvency under 'normal' conditions, not whether they were necessarily solvent at current market prices. In almost any existing state one can imagine future conditions that would make portfolios either increase, or decrease, in value (relative to deposit liabilities). The problem for central banks is to decide how *probable* future recovery has to be to make it worthwhile to undertake support lending *now*. Bagehot's suggestion that this can be relatively easily done, by valuing securities at their worth in 'good' or normal times, was not a little oversimplified, and the suggestion that a line can thereby be drawn between illiquidity and insolvency was misleading, if only because no one can accurately specify what future 'normality' will entail for market prices, nor how soon it may be established. The central bank has to make a judgement about the likely probability distribution of future outcomes and assess how such distributions may in turn be affected by its own present actions.

So, the distinction between illiquidity and insolvency was fuzzier and more uncertain than Bagehot allowed, even then: it has become increasingly so now. If a financial intermediary is confidently believed to be solvent, in the sense that it will certainly be able to repay loans at a market rate of interest, then other financial intermediaries, and private lenders, will be prepared to provide funds freely to that intermediary to meet any short-term excess net withdrawals. In other words, if you are believed to be solvent, the market will lend to you freely. There is no need then to apply to a lender of last resort, particularly not at a penal rate, and also not in so far as that approach in itself could signal particular weakness to others in the marketplace.

So, with the development of well-functioning, broad, wholesale money markets and liability management, it will normally be the case that a bank which cannot adjust its liquidity position satisfactorily on such markets will be a bank whose long-term solvency is doubted by others in that market.[1] Liquidity problems, which are not resolved through ordinary market mechanisms, generally imply the risk of insolvency; though the reverse is not necessarily true. For example, a bank can face insolvency problems without the fact being widely known in the market. Thus, Johnson Matthey did not face any serious illiquidity problems during the months when it came to realise, under outside pressure from the Bank of England to examine and rectify its own position, that it had a serious solvency problem.

There have been a number of cases recently of central bank lender of last resort assistance, undertaken in the initial belief that the problem was one of temporary illiquidity. In several of these cases the central bank shortly thereafter discovered that insolvency problems lurked behind the initial surface illiquidity difficulties. A good example is to be found in the secondary, or fringe, banking crisis of 1973–4. At the beginning of the crisis, in December 1973, the problem was thought to be simply a liquidity difficulty, with the need being to recycle deposits being lost by the secondary banks. In order to undertake this recycling operation, the Bank of England sought the help of the clearing banks (where most of the deposits, withdrawn from the secondary banks, were being placed), in an operation that subsequently became familiarly known as 'the lifeboat'.

Indeed, in *principle*, such support was only to be granted if the institution was considered to be ultimately solvent and likely to remain so; that is, the objective of 'the lifeboat' was to provide *liquidity* support, not solvency support. However, the problems (for example, of the property market) which had initially led to a withdrawal of funds from the secondary banks, and a refusal of lenders to place more money with such banks, through wholesale markets, deteriorated further, and the difficulties of several of the companies receiving assistance from the 'lifeboat' took on a new aspect. What had originally been perceived as liquidity problems now turned out to be solvency problems. Moreover, it was perhaps inevitable that a few institutions judged at the outset to be possibly viable should, in the event, be proved to be insolvent, given the rapidity with which the initial investigations had to be carried out and the complexity of some of the groups which had been built up by the secondary banks.

This latter problem is worth emphasising. The central bank will frequently be asked to make a snap judgement whether or not to provide support to an institution whose position is extremely uncertain, and which cannot often be quickly ascertained with any great clarity. The central bank will be faced with an *immediate* illiquidity problem, and will simply not know at all clearly

the extent, if any, of the solvency problems that are likely to be present
also. There is a need for an immediate decision; little time to link; and
generally an incomplete and insufficient information base on which to make
the judgement. If help is not provided to meet the immediate liquidity problem, the bank involved is bound to close with possible contagion effects,
which may require larger action by the central bank later, and more disruption to the economy and the financial system in general, than if it had acted
earlier. On the other hand, if the central bank does provide support under
these conditions, it may be assuming a solvency risk of an unknown, but
potentially sizeable, magnitude. Such difficult decisions, which have to be
taken under great pressure, have faced the Bank of Canada recently, for
example in the case of the Canadian Commercial Bank (CCB) and, of course,
the Bank of England in the Johnson Matthey Banking (JMB) affair.

Central bank action to provide lender of last resort assistance does not
necessarily involve the assumption of any significant risk of loss. A central
bank can insist on only making loans against the collateral of assets whose
value may more than match such loans. However, that would raise the question of why the bank did not sell those assets, rather than go to the lender
of last resort, especially if such assistance is only supplied at penal rates,
and may represent, of itself, a semi-public signal of weakness. Consequently,
by the time that a commercial bank comes to seek the assistance of the
central bank, it may either have realised its more immediately liquid assets
and/or have appreciated that it does, indeed, have a potential solvency problem. Under such circumstances, the option of making loans to that bank
which are fully secured by excellent collateral is probably no longer available, nor sufficient to meet the needs of the bank in difficulties.

So, central bank lender of last resort action is often likely to involve
placing funds with the bank in trouble in a form which is not fully secured
by unquestioned collateral, and may, therefore, imply some considerable risk
of loss. The potential risk of loss in some cases, where a large bank is
facing a major withdrawal of funds, should the central bank seek to replace
them all, could be very large indeed. So, in such cases, partly to spread the
risks, central banks normally try to involve the commercial banks in the
conduct of such rescues. As early as 1890, the Bank of England persuaded
the major banks in the City of London to join with it in providing a line of
credit to Barings to provide funds, if necessary, to see it through the difficulties
brought about by its involvement with lending to Argentina. More recently,
both in the fringe banking crisis, as already described, and in the case of
Johnson Matthey, the Bank of England persuaded the main clearing banks
to take a part in sharing the burden of possible loss arising from the rescue
process. Again, the Bank of Canada followed the same route in the CCB
affair.

Even in the earlier fringe bank crisis, the extent of the potential loss and
involvement for the clearing banks from their membership of 'the lifeboat'

was such that they felt that a limit had to be introduced. Thus, by August 1974, the amount of support lending had reached 1.2 billion pounds, and the clearing banks came to the conclusion that they must put some limit on their financial involvement in 'the lifeboat', for fear that otherwise, in all the circumstances of the time, they might risk putting their own financial soundness in doubt. Subsequently, however, the JMB affair in the UK, and the CCB affair in Canada have demonstrated an increasing unwillingness of the major clearing banks to take a joint part in shouldering the potential burden of loss from these rescue efforts.

In bygone days, when the business of banking was limited to a restricted cartel of banks, the feeling of membership of the 'club', and concern about possible contagion and loss of reputation, should a club member fail, were such as to make it easier for the central bank to persuade other leading commercial banks to join in taking on the burden of potential loss from the rescue. In today's more competitive conditions, the banks at the centre of the system frequently see the failing banks as being a relatively imprudent competitor. Why then, they feel, should they penalise their own shareholders for the sake of such a competitor? Moreover, the very success of central banks in restricting contagious financial panics in the years from the 1930s through to more recently, may well have reduced the feeling that there was any self-interest involved in nipping a potential panic in the bud before it spread. In any case, the willingness of the main commercial banks to come to the assistance of the central bank in bearing the potential burden of loss from rescue packages for other banks has noticeably diminished recently. The UK clearing banks publicly carped at being asked to play a part in indemnifying the Bank of England against some proportion of its loss in the rescue of JMB. There is a clear warning now that the Bank of England, and other central banks, may find it increasingly hard, if not impossible, to persuade other commercial banks to assist them in future rescue packages.

This could lead to serious problem for central banks. They may not have sufficient funds of their own, given the reluctance of other commercial banks to support them, to accept the potential losses involved in a future rescue exercise. Clearly, a central bank can continue to decide at its own discretion how to cope with disasters, and problems of illiquidity and insolvency at the smaller end of the banking spectrum, but there needs to be some forethought given now to the problem of how to cope with a potentially *large* illiquidity/insolvency problem. If the Bank of England, and other central banks in a similar situation, cease to be able to rely on the help and support of the much larger funds of the major commercial banks, they could face potential problems where they simply did not have the capacity to cope with the situation themselves. Presumably, in such cases when the private financial community is not prepared to put up the funds, and the amount involved is too great for the central bank to absorb, there would be no alternative but an approach to the public sector for help. The Johnson Matthey affair revealed the difficult nature of the constitutional relationship between the Bank and the government in such cases. With the growing reluctance of the commercial banks to take on much of the burden of such rescues themselves, future rescue packages within the financial system are increasingly likely to involve a joint effort between the government and the Bank. This has not been so in the past. Unless some consideration is given now to the best way of conducting such a joint governmental/central bank rescue operation, the complications of trying to put such a delicate constitutional innovation into place in the middle of a crisis could lead to an avoidable disaster.

17.4   DEPOSIT INSURANCE

In view of the increasing unwillingness of the financial community to provide a degree of communal self-insurance in support of the central bank, the option of relying on the central bank to arrange rescue packages, and to protect the banking system from contagious failures, is now looking somewhat more problematical. Many economists, however, would say that such reliance on the central bank for systemic protection against contagious crises was both unnecessary and inferior to another alternative. This latter would be to encourage deposit insurance, preferably through the private market. The existence of (full) deposit insurance would not only serve to prevent runs, because such insurance would mean that the depositor need no longer try to withdraw his deposit in the face of perceived bad news but also such insurance would allow the community to accept the effects of banking failures with greater equanimity, because the wealth and well-being of the depositor would be, to that extent, protected.

There are, however, only a few historical examples of insurance actually being provided *privately* to banks. There are two main reasons why it has proven difficult for the *market* to provide deposit insurance. The first is that, as we shall discuss shortly, it is difficult to assess accurately the degree of risk undertaken by financial intermediaries, and thus to relate the premiums to be paid for insurance to such risk. It is virtually impossible to do so without having access to the books of the financial intermediaries concerned. Moreover, the insurance agency will want direct control over the assumption of risk by the insured intermediaries. So, the private insurance agencies would need full access to banks' internal bookkeeping, and to be able to impose certain limits on the structure of bank portfolios. But it is unlikely that banks, or other financial intermediaries, would willingly accede permission to private insurance agencies both to examine their books *and* to impose constraints on their freedom to adjust their asset portfolios. It may require state – public sector – coercion, or, at the minimum, strong support to force financial intermediaries to accept such intrusion by insurance agencies. This suggests that any private sector insurance agency in this field would need the strong backing of the public sector: indeed, the extent of public sector involvement might have to be such that the insurance agency might just as well be a public body in any case.

Thus Benston (1983) writes:

U.S. history . . . provides lessons that should be heeded. Deposit guarantee systems were established in New York (1828), Vermont (1831), Indiana (1834), Ohio (1845) and Iowa (1858). The New York and Vermont systems were state run, the others were based on mutual agreements among participating banks. They operated successfully, largely because they empowered system officials to monitor operations of the participating banks and to control excessive risk-taking. Yet a second wave of deposit guarantee plans for state banks proved less successful. With one exception (Mississippi), the plans did not include effective supervision and they failed . . . the Mississippi plan (1915), which included supervision and bank examinations, continued until 1930. Thus, effective supervision appears to be a necessary aspect of deposit insurance (pp. 8–9).

The second main problem facing a private-sector insurance agency is the nature of banking risks. The probability of a bank failure is not in the same actuarial category as the probability of death or a car smash. It depends largely on the interaction of the macroeconomic policy conjuncture with the legal and institutional structure of the banking system. Both these conditions are under the control of government, and can not be influenced favourably, or otherwise, by the actions of the private insurance agency. In general, the probability of a wave of bank failures is extremely low, but should it come the potential cost could be enormous. Chari and Jagannathan (1984) claim that, 'Since bank runs are an economy wide phenomenon, the investment risks we model are aggregate, *uninsurable* risks' (p. 5).

Diamond and Dybvig (1983) argue that:

Because a private insurance company is constrained by its reserves in the scale of unconditional guarantees which it can offer, we argue that deposit insurance probably ought to be governmental for this reason. Of course, the deposit guarantee could be made by a private organization with some authority to tax or create money to pay deposit insurance claims, although we would usually think of such an organization as being a branch of government (p. 413).

Thus:

The credible [government] promise to provide the insurance means that the promise will not need to be fulfilled. This is in contrast to privately provided deposit insurance. Because insurance companies do not have the power of taxation, they must hold reserves to make their promise credible. This illustrates a reason why the government may have a natural advantage in providing deposit insurance (p. 416).

Given the low probability, and high cost, of a bank run, the size of reserves necessary among private insurance agencies to provide a credible promise to meet all bank failures would be enormous, and therefore extremely expensive to maintain. This was exemplified recently by the inability of private insurance to provide a credible promise to meet losses in the face of runs on S&Ls in Ohio and Maryland, leading to a full-scale shift of S&Ls to the public-sector-run FSLIC. Indeed, the failure of one large S&L in Ohio was sufficient to exhaust the reserves of the private insurance agency. This practical example of the superiority of public sector over private sector insurance in the financial field may have killed the argument for private provision of insurance in this area for some time.

So, insurance should be undertaken by a *public* sector agency. But whether public or private the problems of setting premiums which accurately reflected the potentiality for loss in this field remain overwhelming. These problems have been nicely described in two papers – Horvitz (1983) and Goodman and Shaffer (1983). Thus the latter claim that:

> New and probably unforeseen (or at least underestimated) sources of risk have continued to emerge, and probably will always do so ... there is inevitably a lag between the emergence of a new source of risk and its perception, measurement, and incorporation into the premium schedule. This lag creates a theoretical incentive for banks to shift their portfolios to ever-changing forms of risky investment, a possibly riskier and certainly less stable situation than if banks merely settle permanently into a few fixed risky activities. Like the dog chasing its own tail, a risk-based premium would thus find itself always playing catchup, in the process driving its goal ever more swiftly just beyond its reach (pp. 13–14).

And Horvitz (1983, p. 274) notes, *inter alia*, that the risk of loss to an insuring agency does not depend only, or possibly even primarily, on its (limited) ability to constrain the assumption of risk by banks, but rather on the speed and firmness with which the agency may act to close down a problem bank when it starts going wrong.

Be that as it may, the practical difficulties of trying to establish risk-related premiums have generally meant that such efforts have been aborted. Instead, in most cases the premiums are related directly to the volume of insured deposits. But, as already noted, the provision of insurance via premiums unrelated to risk causes moral hazard and potential additional risk-taking. So, such provision of insurance needs to be associated with controls on the assumption of risk. Such constraints on freedom can generally only

be satisfactorily undertaken by the public sector, or an agency to which the
public sector has effectively delegated state powers. This reinforces the case
for having the combined functions of insurance, supervision and regulation
undertaken by public-sector bodies.

Even with public-sector insurance, there remains a question of the extent
of its coverage. There is a trade-off; the effectiveness of insurance in preventing runs is greater the more comprehensive such coverage; on the other
hand, moral hazard is less worrisome when there are certain depositors, and/
or other creditors of the bank, which are *not* fully insured. Thus, if large
depositors, or inter-bank deposits, are not covered, or only partially covered, by insurance, they will have every incentive to withdraw their deposits rapidly in the face of a possibility of a bank failure. Indeed, it is exactly
those classes of depositors, who have the information and incentive to check
the conditions of the banks with whom they place their money, who are
most likely to initiate a stampede of withdrawals; much more so than the
individual small depositor, who will frequently be the last to learn of the
conditions of his bank, and in any case faces considerable costs in transferring his account from the bank, with which he will have built up an informational relationship, to another, possibly some distance away.

The success of the FDIC in preventing any contagious bank failures since
its establishment in 1933 did not depend only on the insurance of deposits
under its statutory cut-off point, currently of 100,000 dollars, but also, as
Dale (1984) noted:

> Second, and just as important, there is *de facto* protection for uninsured
> deposits arising from the FDIC's favoured method of dealing with failed
> banks – the so-called 'purchase-and-assumption' transactions. Under a pur-
> chase-and-assumption transaction the FDIC replaces bad assets with cash
> while deposits and other non-subordinated liabilities are assumed by another
> bank. In such assisted mergers all depositors, insured and uninsured, are
> made whole (p. 19).

But this *de facto* 100 per cent insurance of even the formally uninsured
depositors tended to increase moral hazard, and therefore could be held responsible for the US banking system becoming increasingly risky. Consequently, the FDIC began to change this policy, beginning with the failure of
the Penn Square bank, which was a particularly bad case of excessively
risky and bad banking. Then, in March 1984, the FDIC indicated that it
would pursue a 'modified pay-out' policy which, as Dale (1984) describes:

> Would combine a pay-off of insured deposits with a cash advance to un-
> insured depositors and other general creditors based on the present value
> of anticipated collections by the receivership. Under this 'modified pay-
> off' scheme, uninsured depositors would be exposed to losses arising out

of the receivership in a way that does not happen when the FDIC organizes assisted mergers (p. 21).

It was partly this enhanced expectation of loss among potentially uninsured depositors that led to a haemorrhage of funds from Continental Illinois when it came under suspicion in May 1984. And it was the concern about the possible consequences for the banking sector, if one of the really large banks in the country was allowed to fail, that led the authorities once again to provide *de facto* 100 per cent insurance to all depositors at Continental Illinois, and thence to the problems, and dilemma, indicated by the earlier quotation from Seidman (1986).

The hope had been that the potentiality for loss, among at least *some* groups of bank creditors, would cause those creditors to maintain a watchful eye on the riskiness of individual banks, and, by so doing, signal by their own actions (to withdraw funds and/or to sell the bank's equity in the market), that not all was right in their view, and hence to place pressure on the bank's management to change its strategy. The difficulty remains how to expose bank creditors to a sufficient risk of loss, to place market pressure on banks to avoid risk, and thus to limit moral hazard, without at the same time exposing such creditors to such sizeable losses that they will be induced to withdraw their funds in a panic at the merest suspicion of potential bank failure. How does one find the middle way between moral hazard on the one hand, and contagious failures among financial institutions on the other?

One answer, proposed several times in the USA, is to force a division in banking structures. Thus, there would be one set of deposit balances, effectively transactions balances, that is, sight and small time deposits, which would be segregated and given 100 per cent deposit insurance. Against these deposits, the banks would be required to hold a strictly constrained set of safe, largely government, securities. The other creditors of the bank, primarily holding large time deposits and CDs, would be hived off into a separate financial intermediary, with no insurance, but against which the bank could hold an unconstrained asset portfolio. I doubt whether this would work. First, the constraints on the asset portfolio for the insured deposits would mean that the interest payable on such deposits would be low. Banks could, therefore, offer higher interest rates on the uninsured deposits in the other part of their business, and the provision of transaction services would tend to slip away from the constrained institutions to the unregulated institutions, in the same way as money market mutual funds were tending to attract transactions balances from regulated banks in the US. So, unless there was an ever extending fence of controls preventing transaction services being provided by competing institutions, there would be a tendency for such payments services to move from the tightly constrained, and 100 per cent insured, segment of banks.

Second, much of the adverse externality arising from contagious bank failure results not just from the fall in transactions balances, but from the loss of wealth to depositors, whether that loss occurs in demand deposits, time deposits or CDs, and, just as important, from the withdrawal of credit facilities, and subsequent calls for repayment of outstanding loans by receivers. Thus, the damage to the economic framework would continue to be serious if the system was so organised as to allow large-scale contagious failures of banks financed entirely through means other than demand deposits. I have explored this latter issue more fully in Goodhart (1987). Moreover, there is no evidence that runs are more frequently initiated by withdrawals of demand deposits. It is more often the refusal of large wholesale depositors to roll over their time deposits and CDs that precipitates the run on a bank.

17.5 A PROPOSAL

Banking crises can involve large losses to the economy. The authorities will strive to prevent them occurring, but now face three inter-related problems:

1. As described in section 17.1, large banks are now *de facto* guaranteed. If small banks receive a similar guarantee, moral hazard and excessive risk-taking is thereby encouraged. If large banks are effectively guaranteed, while small banks are allowed to go bankrupt, this is not only inequitable, but it will tend to lead towards oligopoly and concentration of financial power among a few major commercial banking institutions.
2. With increasing competition, particularly internationally, commercial banks have shown themselves increasingly disinclined to support the central bank in assuming the burden of meeting failures among their more imprudent colleagues. The situation could well occur when a central bank could not afford by itself to rescue a failing bank, and the commercial banks would look the other way. In such a case there may well be no alternative but to appeal to the government, and ultimately to the taxpayer for help. Whether or not this situation is to be deplored, it is foreseeable. It is, therefore, better to decide in advance how to deal with this, rather than to get into a possible constitutional muddle about who can do what and how, in the middle of a rapidly-breaking financial crisis.
3. If one should try to deal with the possibility of bank crises by deposit insurance, such insurance would have to be provided by the *public* sector, and be comprehensive. But in the absence of any way of assessing risk *ex ante*, such insurance will, inevitably, be mispriced, with encouragement for excessive risk-taking, leading consequently to more intervention by the authorities to place direct constraints on banks' portfolios. The option of coping with this problem by dividing banks into separate component parts, with one part fully uninsured and tightly constrained,

with the other totally uninsured *but* given complete freedom, will not, I claim, work in practice.

It is difficult to avoid having to try to find an optimal balance between deposit insurance plus external constraints on portfolio management and moral hazard on the one hand, and some potentiality for loss and consequential risk of contagious runs on the other.[2] The trick is to find the right balance.

In my view, such a better balance could take the form of co-responsibility of the insured, in the sense that the insured would not receive 100 per cent coverage, but some lesser percentage (perhaps subject to a minimum level which would be repayable in full, in order to provide complete depositor protection for widows and orphans).[3] Thus, every depositor (including inter-bank deposits) holding sterling deposits with a bank located in the UK, and supervised by the Bank of England, might be compulsorily fully insured by a Deposit Insurance Board, but the coverage of that insurance, beyond some minimum value, should be less than 100 per cent. (Currency deposits held with banks in the UK could not be fully insured, because the authorities might not be able to make good their promise to provide such foreign currencies in the case of loss; similarly, sterling deposits held with banks abroad could not be similarly insured, because the authorities would have no means of supervising and regulating them.) Because of the impossibility of assessing risk in advance, the levy to finance such an insurance scheme would have to continue to be related *pro rata* to the balance sheet size of the individual members, with the size of the levy broadly intended to keep the Insurance Board self-financing in the long run, noting that part of the losses would be absorbed by the co-responsibility of the insured. Nevertheless, because of the high cost of potential failures, the guarantee of the insurance board would have to be backed up by the promise of financial support from the taxpayer, if needs be.

The key question, however, remains the percentage of co-responsibility to be adopted. In my view, setting the ratio as high as 25 per cent, the present level under the limited existing depositor insurance schemes in the UK, would be far too high to prevent runs. Faced with such a penalty, professional investors would still withdraw their deposits at the first whiff of difficulty. Instead, it would be more sensible to provide an automatic repayment (full insurance) of *at least* 80 per cent or even perhaps 90 per cent of deposits placed with the bank, with the remaining funds at risk being paid proportionately to the revealed loss on the valuation of the asset book. For example, if a failing bank was only able to pay its creditors 60p in the pound, and there was an automatic immediate repayment of 80 per cent of the value of deposits, then I would see the depositor as receiving in return, eventually, $80 + (0.6 \times 20) = 92$p. So, in this case, the co-responsibility formula would lead depositors to pick up 8p out of the total loss of 40p involved, while leaving the Insurance Board to pick up the remaining 32p. As Horvitz (1983) notes:

'The losses of the deposit insurance system are not closely related to the riskiness of insured institutions. Losses are more a function of the timing of the closing of a failed bank or savings institution' (p. 274). Under the present system, however, the incentive for the supervisor is generally to hang on and to allow a failing institution to continue, in the hopes that some favourable development will occur, which will allow him to avoid the unpleasant final step of closing the bank. A possible advantage of the co-responsibility scheme is that it will provide certain pressures on the authorities to act more quickly and decisively. In part, of course, those pressures arise from the tendency of investors to withdraw their funds from the bank, and to sell the bank's equity, in order to avoid the remaining residual losses under a co-responsibility system. So, any co-responsibility system *does* involve some residual risk of contagious bank failures.

The objective would be to set the co-responsibility proportion low enough to prevent the widespread development of runs, and to make bank failures more feasible, both small and large, while at the same time making the risk of loss to the insured depositor high enough to encourage some market monitoring, and to limit banks' assumption of risk. The fact that this would be difficult does not obviate the need to try it.

The present methods of trying to avoid contagious bank failures, both in the UK and in the USA, are beginning to run into increasing problems. There will be no alternative but to try and reform the system. I believe that this proposal would provide the best possible reform.

NOTES

1. There are a few qualifications and exceptions. For example, as once happened in New York, a computer 'foul-up' in a money market bank led to payments, but not receipts, being booked. This rapidly resulted in a huge net deficit position, which could not be satisfactorily resolved in the market because of prudential limits on intra-day exposures. The Federal Reserve Bank of New York had to step in to resolve the situation, even though the bank with the deficit was absolutely solvent.
2. A (risk-weighted) capital adequacy requirement would support, and could even replace, deposit insurance, since the available equity would provide a safety buffer for the depositor. This route still leaves problems of trying to find the right balance, both in setting and calibrating the required ratios (too much causes disintermediation, too little involves higher risk) and in dealing with those cases where actual capital falls below the required ratio. The comparative advantages, and balance, between capital adequacy requirements and deposit insurance nevertheless would repay further study.
3. An alternative suggestion proposed by Baltensperger and Dermine (1987, Section 3.3) would be to impose an *ex post* penalty on depositors who withdraw funds from their bank once a 'run' has been deemed to start. While this is an ingenious idea, there are, I believe, likely to be some practical problems involved.

18 The Regulatory Debate in London (1988)*

Three recent widespread developments have been forcing the authorities, including governments, Central Bank, and other regulatory authorities, to review once again the aims, basis and form of regulation in financial markets.

First, the liberalisation of financial markets and the erosion of barriers, of demarcation lines, between differing financial institutions is causing the authorities to have to review the coverage, scope and organisation of their regulatory systems. This is particularly marked in the case of Britain, but changes of a similar kind are taking place in many other financial centres.

Second, this same phenomenon now transcends national boundaries. The development of a much more international financial market means that financial systems, and regulatory controls over such systems, can no longer be thought of in purely national terms. This is frequently viewed in global terms, with the phrase a one-world financial system, but the most immediately important aspect of this for us in London is regional, with the development of a single European market, including the market for financial services, being put in place by 1992.

Third, the experience of continuing, or even increasing, instability in financial markets, (as witnessed by the continuing major fluctuations and misalignments in the dollar exchange rate, and the Stock Exchange crash of October 1987), occurring at the same times as there has been a breakdown of the stability of the velocity of money, that is in the relationship between the monetary aggregates and the growth of nominal money incomes, may lead to some reconsideration of the appropriate macroeconomic role for monetary policy, and of how the regulatory system may best be able to support such a role.

Let me turn first to the effect of the erosion of demarcation lines between financial intermediaries. In particular, the traditional distinction between banks and non-banks is, it seems to me, likely to become blurred in the foreseeable future. If so, the common dividing line between those regulatory authorities who are responsible for the banking system, and those who are responsible for non-bank financial intermediaries will need some reconsid-

* LSE Financial Markets Group, *Special Paper Series*, 007 (1988).

This paper is an extension and development of an earlier paper written jointly with Professor M. King, 'Financial Stability and the Lender of Last Resort Function: A Note', LSE Financial Markets Group, *Special Paper Series*, 002. I am grateful to Professor King, both for the use of parts of this earlier paper, and for his seminal contribution to the development of various ideas on this topic. The remaining errors, however, are all mine.

eration. Again, the dividing line between those financial institutions to be supervised by Central Banks or bank regulators, and those to be subject to other, rather differently aimed, regulation is sometimes drawn at the point dividing those institutions taking deposits, denominated in nominal terms. Again, I think it quite likely that the menu of available forms of liability, may widen and extend for example to include indexed deposits, or deposits that enjoy a certain 'with-profit' addition, while at the same time transactions and payments services may also become provided on the basis of other forms of liabilities than pure nominally-denominated deposits.

The economist, Eugene Fama, has defined a bank as a financial intermediary which jointly provides transactions and payment services and portfolio management at the same time. But increasingly, certain, though sometimes limited, payments and transactions services are being provided by other, non-bank, financial intermediaries. Money Market Mutual Funds have done so in the US, as does the Merrill Lynch cash management fund. It would not be difficult for unit trusts to tack on a limited payment service to their existing functions. The development of ATMs, home banking and electronic transfers to and from a central computer, should enable any financial intermediary, indeed virtually any institution with access to the appropriate technology, to handle certain forms of transactions services in an efficient way. The more expensive segment of the payments system remains that based on paper cheque transfers. The new entrants to the payments system may, however, choose to leave that to the existing bank and building society intermediaries. Besides being left to cope with the more expensive, paper cheque, rump of the payments system, the banks may also find that their widespread system of branches, their branch network, becomes something of a white elephant in the new electronic world. Be that as it may, I believe that it is arguable that the distinction between banks and non-banks in coming decades may come to reside not so much in the particular money-like quality of their liabilities, but in the differing characteristics of the main assets in their portfolios. Thus, I believe that banks will come to be identified by their particular function of making, and of holding in their portfolios, loans which are not, and cannot be, securitised and resold on primary markets. Whereas it is possible to establish at any time a relatively objective evaluation of the market value of non-bank financial intermediaries' assets, I believe that banks will remain special by virtue of the inability of anyone to give an objective evaluation to their loan portfolio.

Let me, however, return to more immediate and practical considerations. The erosion of functional boundaries within the financial system, the desire to maintain efficiency within an increasingly competitive national and international financial system, and some feeling that there is additional safety in diversification, is making regulators increasingly unsure exactly where the regulatory boundaries should be drawn. This is, perhaps, most clearly observable in the USA. The Chairman of the Fed, Alan Greenspan, would appear to want to liberalise the US financial system by dismantling some of the artificial boundaries introduced by the Glass–Steagall Act, and allow for a further extension of the financial holding company mechanism; while on the other hand he is, at the same time, resisting what might seem to be a logical corollary of that in the shape of the Brady Commission proposal that the Central Bank be the single regulatory overlord of the wider financial system. It is difficult to assess exactly how the lessons, as perceived by most commentators, of the Crash of 1987 will affect the momentum for change. The difficulties that some of the investment houses in New York found themselves facing made a number of commentators feel happier with the required separation between such houses and the banking system, even though the investing houses, and the banks, might jointly have been somewhat safer against a variety of shocks by being more diversified. At the same time, the events of the crash showed both that the Central Bank could not stand aside from a major financial disturbance within the financial system more broadly, even if this did not occur within the banking system more narrowly, defined. Moreover, not only was the Central Bank involved, but its interventions, both to pump in liquidity and to put pressure on commercial banks to maintain and extend their credit lines to the investment houses, were crucial in the critical moments of defusing the crisis. Meanwhile, the S.E.C. was not-able for its inability to intervene in an effective way.

The more effective intervention of a Central Bank, than of any more *general* regulatory authority is, perhaps, inherent in the structure of the financial system, because many such crises have to be met by the ability to dig into relatively deep financial pockets, and the Central Bank has that ability, whereas ordinary regulatory authorities do not. So, in any really serious financial disturbance, the Central Bank not only cannot stand aside, but must become more closely involved. If that is so, does it not also follow that general, if not particular, oversight for the regulatory structure in the whole financial system should be placed with the Central Bank.

One of the concerns of Central Banks in this field is to limit both their range of responsibilities and their political exposure. I understand such sensitivity, but it still seems to me to stand in the way of a logically coherent structure. Another concern of the Fed is to restrict access to its lender of last resort support role and also to limit deposit insurance, and hence moral hazard, to a narrowly delineated range of financial institutions. But this raises a number of difficult issues. Would the problem of contagious panic, and the resulting externalities from a financial crisis, be greatly less if Goldman Sachs, or Warburgs, or Nomura went bust than if an equivalently sized bank failed. Investment houses have fewer, and in some cases no, deposits, so it can be argued that there is less risk of a multiple collapse of the system as depositors rush into currency. But the concept of the serious features of a contagious panic being represented by a rush out of bank deposits into currency is somewhat outdated. Nowadays the prospect of a bank, or even a group of a banks, failing is likely to lead depositors to shift their deposits into another part of the banking system, or even banks abroad, which are seen as stronger, rather than to withdraw their funds into currency itself. Some economists regard such a flight of deposits from one bank of the banking system to another as having no larger effect on the real economy, not involving any externalities. I believe that the analysis is incorrect. Banks normally fail because some large segments of their loan portfolios turn out to have been bad risks. The shift of deposits from such banks to others is likely to exacerbate the difficulties of those sectors, whose economic difficulties are seen as having helped to cause the fall in bank asset values, from receiving any further credit. There will tend to be a rush to perceived quality in bank asset portfolios, further withdrawing funds from the sectors now perceived as riskier. This withdrawal of credit from such riskier sectors is likely to exacerbate the initial downturn and help to generate a crisis. This latter process seems to me just as likely to occur if funds are withdrawn, en masse, from the securities market as from any other part of the financial system.

Anyhow, similar concerns, as in the USA, about the organisation, the structure, and the multiplicity of regulators with overlaps between them, is now also visible in the UK, in the context of our new regulatory framework. For example, banks, building societies, and insurance companies all have had their own parent regulators in the guise of the Bank of England, the Commissioner of Building Societies, and the Department of Trade and Industry, before the establishment of new regulatory layers arising from the Financial Services Act. Now, any of these institutions, such as a commercial bank, which now also operates in capital markets, or provides fund management or financial advice, will have to join, and abide by the rules of the relevant self-regulatory organisation, which in turn is subsidiary to the Securities and Investments Board, which in turn is again subject to the FSA. So, in addition to their own parent regulator, these financial intermediaries will now have to work to one or more other regulatory bodies in various aspects of their operations. In addition, there is now on the horizon, and getting ever closer, a larger and larger role for the European Commission in the establishment, maintenance and enforcement of European-wide regulatory requirements. From a starting point of a simple and relatively light, some would say lax, system, we have moved rapidly in the UK to a much more complex, and hence onerous, system of financial regulation.

What were the underlying purposes of this major change? It was, I think, threefold. The first criterion was the creation of an adequate framework for investor protection. The second was the promotion of greater competition in the market for financial services, in order to ensure a level playing field, as the demarcation barriers between differing financial intermediaries and their various functions came down. The third was to protect and support the role of the City of London as a major financial centre by enhancing its reputation for fair play, without being so burdensome as to enhibit its development as an internationally competitive centre. Most of the subsequent regulatory action has focused on the first of these objectives.

Here, I have to say that I have certain reservations about whether the underlying approach to investor protection, as preferred by Professor Jim Gower in his *Review of Investor Protection*, which was then incorporated into the FSA, and subsequently developed by the SIB, is in fact appropriate and the best option to choose. Let me to try to explain the nature of my reservations.

There have traditionally been two approaches to the maintenance of high quality service, and of client or investor protection in the area of professional services. And I do speak of professional services more generally, because there are a lot of similarities between the problems of insuring client welfare within all professional services, including not only financial services, but also such services as medicine, law, accounting, and so on. This is an area characterised by inherent information asymmetries between customer and client. This *has* to be so, because what the client is largely purchasing is the professional and expert knowledge of the provider of the service. It is also an area where there are high search costs, again largely because customers cannot easily discern between the relative expertise and ability of differing professionals. It is also an area where there are considerable economies of dual capacity, that is to say that it is normally cheaper to entrust the execution of the exercise to the same professional who first disagnoses what is best to do. This obviously leads to a potentiality for conflict of interest, but this is as apparent in, for example, the garage business, or medicine, or law, as it is within the financial system. Again the need for a client to obtain such professional services is usually, one hopes, infrequent, but this does have the disadvantage that quality cannot be maintained by the hope to obtain repeat purchases, whereas the potentiality for disastrous loss to the customer, if the advice is bad, negligently given or fraudulent, is considerable.

In the face of these problems of quality maintenance and investor protection in the professional services, two alternative kinds of approach have been traditionally adopted. The first of these has been that self-regulatory 'club' approach; the second has been the statutory approach based on some degree of official government intervention, even if the body to which the regulatory function is delegated is a quasi-governmental body, or quango, rather than a formal official body.

The Club approach has been, perhaps, the more commonly adopted, certainly in the UK, with central, unofficial, self-elected, bodies in medicine, law, accounting, etc., fixing entry qualifications, setting out standards of good practice, and in many cases enforcing these. In some instances, the professional 'Club' arranges insurance, or some form of recompense, for customers and clients who have been harmed by negligent members of its profession; as has been the case with the Stock Exchange, and remains the case for the Law Society and the Association of British Travel Agents. The 'Club' Approach has traditionally and historically been encouraged and utilised by the British authorities as the basis of regulation within the UK financial system. It has many advantages. It is cheap and flexible, allowing regulatory practices to be pragmatically adapted to the changing structure of the financial system.

There are, however, problems in running such 'clubs'. First the club officials are in a position of some power and this can lead to conflicts of interests and unhappiness especially when the club officials are commercial competitors with other club members. Second, members of a common profession may tend to be too lenient in enforcing discipline and standards of behaviour on their close professional colleagues, while at the same time much too restrictive with respect to entry qualifications and too supportive of oligopolistic charging, fee-levying practices. Think of the American Medical Association. One way of mitigating such problems is to arrange for, at least some of, the club officials to be independent of the commercial interests involved. I have argued in a number of places, notably in my book on *The Evolution of Central Banks* (1988), that viewing the Central Bank as the independent arbiter and non-competitive organiser of the club of commercial banks is a fruitful analogy.

Even with an independent arbiter as 'club' organiser, the club approach still has certain limitations. Self-regulation within a club only works if there is a cohesion among members with a community of interest, and a relatively light approach to regulatory formalities. The conditions that are most propitious to this are those that involve clearly defined demarcations between institutional functions, so that each member of the club is undertaking a closely similar kind of business, with single capacity and limited competition. Indeed, some measure of oligopolistic practice provides often the cement that holds many of these clubs together.

Financial innovation, competition, and those forms of de-regulation that have led to the erosion of artificial barriers between financial functions have been inimical to the continuation of the club approach to investor protection, and has forced the authorities in the UK to move towards the second approach, the statutory or state-intervention approach. This has a number of clear advantages. It is not so prone to oligopolistic abuse, though it remains far from immune from it as the literature on 'capture' indicates; it is, therefore, *potentially* more consistent with perfect competition and 'the public interest'. There are fewer enforcement problems, and less tendency to go easy on a colleague, where one might otherwise think there but for the grace of God go I. It is easier to construct a level playing field.

Nevertheless there are many problems. Whereas the 'capture' literature portrays the regulator as always being tempted to collude with the regulated, the natural incentive for a regulator is to try to ensure that nothing goes wrong during his own terms of office. The regulator in situ when, say, the regional banking system, or the local futures market collapses, will have his or her reputation branded forever, whereas the regulator who keeps a clean bill of health in terms of avoiding such collapses, but only at the cost of imposing undue, excessively costly, regulatory burdens on the system may appear to the general public – if not to the industry itself – to be doing his job properly. Thus there may be an inherent tendency towards *over-regulation* in statutorally based regulatory systems.

This concern has led some commentators in the USA to welcome the current multiplicity of regulators there, i.e. divided between Federal, State and Insurance Bodies, on the grounds that it actually does provide some competition in laxity between the regulators, by allowing potential customers to chose the laxer regulator to be supervised by, and thus offsets the incentive to over-regulate. They feel that this putative advantage overcomes the complexity, and frictions, inherent in a system of regulation through committees of different, and often rival, regulatory bodies. In the UK, however, there is little competition between differing regulatory bodies to regulate the same function: instead, a financial institution which now carries out a range of separate functions in the UK will face in each case differing, though single monopoly, regulators for each separable function.

Thus, as part of the framework for investor protection, capital adequacy requirements are to be imposed on member firms by the individual self-regulatory organisations (SROs). This means that many banking institutions undertaking securities business will be subject to two sets of regulations on capital adequacy, one imposed by the Bank of England and the other, for example, by The Securities Association (TSA). Discussions are proceeding to try to ensure that the two sets of requirements do not conflict. They provide an opportunity to consider the basis for capital adequacy requirements and the reasons for them. The Bank of England has interests which are rather different from those of the TSA. In particular, the Bank is concerned with its lender of last resort function. Should this give rise to differing criteria for capital adequacy requirements?

Anyhow, to revert to my main theme, we have moved decisively in the UK from an informal 'club' approach to regulation to a statutory based system of much greater complexity and cost. As I indicated earlier, such a statutory system has a number of real advantages over an informal club approach: it is less subject to oligopolistic inefficiency, and can maintain and enforce a more level playing field in a more ferociously competitive world. Nevertheless, besides complexity and cost, statutory systems of regulation have certain clear failings: they tend to be much more rigid, inflexible and constraining.

Consequently, before adopting any specific statutory controls, it is important to be *absolutely* clear about their necessity, and to work out in some detail the comparative costs and benefits involved. Whereas, if the regulatory system remains informal, as it was when based on the club approach, one can be much more arbitrary and relaxed in one's initial approach, since what turns out not to work, or to be excessively restrictive, can after the event be changed.

The approach that the UK authorities had applied to regulation, when operating the informal club system, was to look at the procedures and behavioural methods of the better-run institutions and markets, and to recommend that such best practice methods be applied by all. This was not a terribly intellectually demanding method, nor was it one based on any first principles, nor on much economic analysis. Indeed, that part of the Bank responsible for regulation and supervision has always been notably reluctant to take on any economists onto its staff. Whether despite this, or perhaps because of this, this system nevertheless worked pretty well within the informal club approach. Moreover, the attempt to get all to follow the best practices of the most successful could be broadly interpreted and applied, and could easily be adjusted in an ad hoc way to the particular differing circumstances and form of each individual institution and market. It was a flexible approach, a non-intellectual approach, a pragmatic approach, and one that worked fairly well.

The error as I see it, which was made initially by Gower, and has since been embodied in the SIB rulebooks, was to attempt to translate exactly this same 'best practice' approach from the informal system, where it worked, to a more formal statutory system, in which, for example, customers can sue whenever such codified best practices are not followed, for example under section 62 of the FSA.

This latter means inevitably that 'best practice', rather than being *broadly* understood has to be codified in *minute* detail, for example in those parts of the rulebook relating to relations with a whole range of differing classes of clients, treatment of clients' money, the relationship between analysts and market dealers, etc. This adds enormously to the costs and complexity of the whole exercise. The massive rulebooks that will have to be mastered, which are growing at such a rate, and are already so large, that it has become a speciality in itself; the additional computer systems that will have to be installed, and perhaps especially the severe extra costs that are now being imposed on the small financial intermediary. Besides such resource costs, I am also worried that the codification of 'best practice' as at a point of time will result in dynamic inefficiency, as I cannot see how it can do other than impede the future flexible adaption of the financial system to changing circumstances.

Frankly, I do not think that this approach, the statutory codification of 'best practice' was either necessary or desirable to meet the major aims of regulation, nor do I believe that it would pass a cost/benefit test. If the situation is such that one must turn to a statutory approach, then I believe that there are two better lines of attack. First, one could try to mimic the more informal methods, by providing a major element of discretion to the supervisory body, while at the same time giving it statutory powers to control entry, require information, and remove authorisation for due cause, as actually occurred in the 1979 and 1987 Banking Acts. Alternatively, one could seek to restrict the scope of detailed regulation much more closely to the key essential features, which I would enumerate as again involving some control over entry, i.e. to fit and proper persons, and the requirement to provide accurate and timely information, but now also including in a statutory system some measure of deposit and client money insurance, and associated with that capital adequacy requirements. These last two subjects, deposit insurance and capital adequacy, in turn raise major issues of both principle and practice, which there is not time to enter into here. But *it is* these issues, i.e. the design and form of deposit insurance schemes and capital adequacy provisions that should form the centrepiece of a regulatory system, not the present, misguided, and, I believe, almost unworkable attempt to enforce 'best practice' onto a financial system through a statutory legalistic format.

You may reply that, even though deposit insurance may protect a client from fraud or from actually losing their money as a result of negligence or fraud, it still leaves the client being capable of being ripped off. I believe that in a world of severe information asymmetry, the best way to tackle this is to try to provide appropriate information wherever possible, rather than going down the extraordinarily complex route of trying to get everyone to behave in the best possible manner, and to monitor and enforce this latter, which is hideously difficult. For example, let us take the problem of conflict of interest, as represented by dual capacity. The present means of dealing with this is to try artifically to prevent the natural internal flows of information within an institution, that would provide additional profits to it, by the installation of separating 'Chinese walls'. But, if people are really worried about being short-changed by market makers operating in a dual capacity format, then they are always free to turn to single capacity firms to carry out their orders. So long as the price at which their order is put through the market is made perfectly apparent, and is made immediately comparable with the best market price available at that same time, and so long as the client knows clearly whether he is dealing with a single or dual capacity institution, it seems to me that this is a more suitable case for caveat emptor than for major extensive state intervention.

Let me move on, however, in conclusion from the national to the international forum. Here, I would ask how the regulatory system that we have hastily, and in my view in some respects wrongheadly, constructed in the UK, is going to dovetail into the wider European system? Recent developments have highlighted the interaction between domestic regulation and the 'global' market. Many of the securities firms and banks involved have international operations, and the harmonisation of regulation has become urgent, particularly so now in view of the forthcoming unification of the European market in 1992. Let me take a couple of examples of areas where there is a need to think in international terms. First, for example, following the Crash in October 1987, many of those involved with the consideration of the reform of the regulatory system in the USA have been advocating the introduction of circuit breakers. Yet, so long as there are alternatives markets abroad on which the same securities, or synthetic versions thereof, can be traded, all that such circuit breakers will achieve will be disintermediation to these other financial markets, which may, or may not, be capable of bearing the additional load which may be suddenly flung upon them by the operation of such circuit breakers. Again, the growth of the share of certain national banking systems, indeed in particular the Japanese in the euromarket business, has often been ascribed to their relatively low capital adequacy requirements. In search of the attempt to provide a common and fair basis for supervision, the Bank of England and the Federal Reserve Bank of New York initially published proposals on capital adequacy requirements for banks in January 1987, and these have since been somewhat amended and agreed internationally in the Cooke Committee of the BIS.

This latter seems quite a major step forward in international regulatory harmonisation, and one wonders how far it can be followed up in other regulatory fields. Even so, such attempts to harmonise regulations internationally soon come up against the problem that the practical impact and burden of any such particular scheme will depend in fact on the precise accounting and fiscal, and perhaps also on the legal, systems in operation in each country. If we aim to unify markets and to harmonise regulation, to help provide a level playing field internationally, do we also have to contemplate harmonising the professional infrastructure? Do we welcome that, or do we balk at the difficulties involved?

Finally, I wonder how, for example, the SIB's detailed rule book will fit in with the wider European regulatory system? Will the UK have to ask for derogations to keep its current peculiar system of regulation from being undermined by the kind of international competition in laxity that many commentators might in this instance applaud.

19 The Costs of Regulation (1988)*

This paper addresses the question of the costs involved in establishing the new regulatory framework in the UK. One of the transitional costs involved relates to the time and effort that will have to be expended by all concerned to keep abreast of all that is taking place. That cost is clearly noticeable in the case of recent developments in financial regulation in the UK. I believe that the rule book of the Securities and Investments Board (SIB) on *The Regulation of Investment Business*[1] weighs in at 4½ lbs, and it has been revised and amended so many times in the last 12 months that the exercise of keeping one's red folder in correct order and shape has reached major proportions. Indeed, up until now I have to admit to having failed, and stacked pages of amendments to earlier redrafted Chapters to await proper filing and attention.

But this is only a light-hearted apologia for a further confession that I have done no independent empirical research on the actual costs of the new regulatory structure. Instead I shall largely rely on the recent book by David Lomax, the Group Economic Adviser of the National Westminster Bank, entitled *London Markets after the Financial Services Act*.[2] He is, like me, something of a critic of the new regulatory structure; it may be that some of his estimates are on the high side. Certainly we would welcome a careful costing assessment from the regulatory authorities themselves. It would, I expect, be a salutary exercise for them, and useful information for the rest of us.[3]

19.1 THE COSTS: KIND AND NATURE

First, however, I shall list the kind and nature of costs that I shall consider. These are of different forms, some more tangible and quantifiable than others. First, there are the direct resources costs of the regulatory system – people, equipment and buildings – which could have been used for other purposes. For an estimate of these, I shall rely directly on Lomax's research. Second, there are the charges that may fall on investment houses in order to finance the compensation fund. I shall review how far these should be treated as economic costs. Third, there is the possibility that additional resources, for example, of skilled labour, might have been attracted from abroad, or from

* Chapter 1 in A. Seldon (ed.), *Financial Regulation – or Over-Regulation?* (IEA, 1988). 7–31.

the UK, to work in relatively high value-added activities in the City, but for the discouragement imposed on those same activities by the additional burden of the regulatory system. Fourth, there is the possibility that regulation may lessen competition, raise costs and lead to static inefficiency. Fifth, there is the possibility that regulation may serve to hinder innovation in financial intermediation, thereby leading to dynamic inefficiency.

Direct Resources Costs

Let me start with the direct resources costs. In his final Chapter, 'The Financial Services Act – An Assessment', David Lomax writes:

> The direct costs of the new systems will be very great. The SROs and SIB are likely to cost about 20 million pounds a year, and the internal costs in the City institutions could easily amount to five times as much as that, giving a total annual cost of over 100 million pounds. The number of compliance officers operating in the City is likely to amount to well over a thousand. There will also be bureaucratic costs in terms of time and effort in satisfying the new requirements. Some tens of millions of pieces of paper will be floating around the City as a result of this new system. The cost is therefore very high, and indeed is substantially greater than any identified losses suffered by investors in public 'scandals' in recent years.

Of the total annual cost of 20 million pounds for running the SIB and the SROs, Lomax reckons (Chapter 3, Section 9) that the SIB alone is likely to cost about 8 million pounds.

In some part the extent of these costs has been increased by the degree of overlap and the complexity of the resulting bureaucratic structure. Let me quote again at some length from his concluding chapter:

> There is a substantial risk, in fact, that we now have massive overkill of the supervisory structure in the financial industry. Supervisory authorities with responsibilities for financial institutions include institutions operating under the Financial Services Act, the Bank of England, the Building Societies Commissioner, and the Department of Trade and Industry (for insurance). Many areas of business are now specifically the responsibility of more than one institution, operating under different legislation. For example, the Bank of England has the responsibility for the health of banks as a whole, while the FSA institutions are responsible for their investment activity.
>
> Even within the institutions of the FSA, there is substantial duplication and double reporting. Many institutions will be reporting to several SROs.

A unit trust has to report both to IMRO and to LAUTRO. Many institutions will have to provide similar information not just to SROs, but also to RIEs and the RCHs [Recognised Investment Exchanges and Recognised Clearing Houses].

This system seems clearly to be excessive for what is required, since there can be no justification from a supervisory point of view for demanding the same information twice, or for twice demanding compliance with similar rules.

The concept of lead regulator has been introduced to try to deal with this, but this seems to be a worthy effort by those in a supervisory process to make the best of what one could regard as a bad legislative structure. Efforts should certainly be made in due course to tidy up the overlap between the supervisions stemming from different legislation.

As regards the FSA system itself, one could hope for further rationalisation. Does more or less the same work have to be done by an RIE, and RCH, and/or an SRO? If need be should the regulatory rules be changed so as to allow one of these organisations to carry out a function and take responsibility on behalf of the others? Do we need to have five SROs?

Would it be the end of the world if LAUTRO and FIMBRA were to merge, possibly with IMRO as well?

There is little question in my mind that these are, indeed, real economic costs. The costs consist for the most part of the pay and rations of skilled professionals, whose abilities would certainly find alternative outlets in gainful employment, even with the present level of aggregate unemployment. If I may quote my own Foreword to Lomax's book: 'The new system will involve platoons of ombudsmen, companies of specialist lawyers, battalions of regulators, and brigades of compliance officers, form fillers up, etc.'.

Financing the Compensation Fund

The second potential category of costs is that of financing the compensation fund. This has two components, the first the management costs, which are real resource costs and should be added to the 100 million pounds per annum, plus resource costs already mentioned, and the second represents the costs of building up the compensation fund, which Lomax states (Chapter 3, section 10) may be built up to 100 million pounds a year. This latter, however, is not a resource cost: it will either be redistributed to claimants, or returned in due course to those subscribing.

There are a number of points to make, however. First, the initial hopes of the SIB to relate premium payments to some measurement of risk do not seem to have borne any fruit. The payments are, Lomax states, to be essentially related *pro-rata* to the profits of each investment business, and not to any measure of riskiness. Standard economic theory shows that this will introduce moral hazard, where the existence of insurance increases the risk of loss occurring, and thereby leads to a need for additional regulation that might otherwise have been avoided.

Second, even though those payments represent redistributions rather than resource costs, they do still involve a financial burden on intermediation. This will have to be recouped in higher charges, commissions and margins. The evidence is that the price elasticity of demand for financial services is high.[4] Consequently the increased financial burden of such costs is likely to have more influence on the volume of financial transactions undertaken here than if such elasticities had been low. Against this, the greater confidence that investors may have in the financial system, because of the customer insurance now available, could raise transactions volume. I have no way of measuring the comparative effect of these two factors on the volume of financial transactions.

Burden of Regulation and Risk of Losing Business

My third category of cost stems from the associated risk that the burden arising from regulation in Britain might divert business from this country to other countries. This, however, is one facet of the consequential costs to which all concerned seemed particularly alive from the outset. Thus in his *Review of Investor Protection*,[5] Jim Gower commented that, in deciding how far to go in introducing further regulation,

(i) it would be self-defeating to impose restrictions so severe that they cannot be complied with except at disproportionate trouble and expense, and (ii) that it would be detrimental to the national interest if controls were disproportionately strict in comparison with those of other financial centres to which the business could move.

In the subsequent formulation of the regulations much consideration was given to this issue, notably in the more relaxed regulatory treatment to be applied to such categories as professional investors and wholesale markets,[6] categories which are clearly the most internationally footloose.

So, while there has always been some potential danger that excessive regulation could lead to a transfer of business abroad, on the whole it seems that the process has actually been handled so as to limit this danger.[7] Perhaps I may again quote David Lomax's conclusion at some length:

There is a risk that the burden of regulation on City institutions, stemming both from the Bank of England and from the SIB, will make companies operate so as to minimise their supervisory costs, which could involve

certain transactions being booked, or taking place abroad. Most foreign
companies seem of the view that they can operate according to the new
legislation without wasting capital, although there may be some effort of
management time in adapting to the new situation. All the markets have a
strong incentive to maximise their trading, so they will act to prevent the
new legislation being used to stifle market growth.

Internationally competitive industries, such as in particular the Eurobond
industry, have managed to obtain changes in the rules so as to accommodate their practices. Many reputable City institutions consider that many
of the rules go well beyond what is required to give fair and proper protection to investors and clients. While being efficiently regulated, it is
very important that London regulates itself cheaply, and with minimal
implicit taxation, so that it will remain internationally competitive as a
financial centre.

Risk of Reduced Competition

My fourth category of risk involves the possibility that regulation might
lessen competition, raise costs and lead to static inefficiency. Concern about
this led to the requirements that the regulations of the SIB and SROs should
be submitted to the Office of Fair Trading for the OFT's assessment. When
this was done, the OFT expressed worries that the SIB's principle of the
need for 'polarisation' would reduce competition in the provision of advice
about, and the marketing of, life assurance and unit trusts, worries that were
overridden by the Secretary of State because of the importance attached by
the SIB to the principle of polarisation. Furthermore, the difference in the
treatment of commissions payable to independent insurance brokers as compared with company representatives is liable to shift the structure of the
insurance industry towards greater concentration. To quote Lomax again:

> A maximum commission scale has other implications. It puts a ceiling on
> the income of independent brokers and they have complained that this is
> unfair and is 'too low to ensure the maintenance of a leading independent
> intermediary market'. What is the moral or other justification for allow-
> ing higher commissions to be paid to company representatives than to
> independent brokers?

The life assurance industry has been under a process of concentration for
some time, and these new proposals will certainly not slow down that
process. Since the independent broker will now have both a legal responsibility to put his client into the best investment, and at the same time
receives equal commissions from whatever company he uses, there may
be some inevitable pressure on brokers to put customers into the most
respectable and best established companies. A broker might feel that a

strong argument would be required to override that consideration and to justify putting a client into a small or less well known company. This would make it more difficult for small companies, which cannot afford substantial direct sales forces, to make their way in the world and the same process of merger which is taking place in other industries might possibly go more quickly in the insurance business from now on.

These are issues that have already arisen. I am rather more concerned about the restrictive practices that may develop in future under the coverage and camouflage of the regulatory system. Some USA economic theorists, mostly from Chicago, of whom Stigler[8] is the best known, have argued that regulation is, even from the outset, a means whereby powerful coordinated interest groups, often, perhaps usually, the main established companies in the industry, can transfer wealth from the less well co-ordinated, usually the customers, to themselves. I do not think that that analysis is a valid description of the regulatory process in the UK, which more often represents a reaction, sometimes an over-hasty reaction, to some scandal which public opinion has put on the political agenda.

At the outset, therefore, regulation in the UK *does* have some considerable public service characteristics, though generated perhaps rather as a defensive response to a perceived public outcry than as a planned form of social engineering. The problem is that public, and political, attention soon moves on elsewhere, and the regulators and regulated are left to live in a close embrace with each other for better or for worse. Under these conditions there must be an inevitable tendency for the regulators to seek an easy cohabitation with the regulated. The regulated will 'capture' the regulators. Although the importance of the supposed distinction between self-regulation and statutory, external regulation was, I believe, absurdly exaggerated, the use of practitioners to form the main body of regulators hardly diminishes the likelihood of 'capture'.

I do not see this kind of cost as likely to be severe initially. My worry would be that it could increasingly creep forward, as practitioners took steps and established precedents, that were to the advantage of the profit margins and business positions of the existing members of that part of the industry. If you are employed by Bank X, and are appointed to serve on your SRO, you are hardly going to ignore the implications for Bank X of each issue that comes before your SRO.

Stifling Innovation

My final category of costs relates to the possibility of regulation stifling financial innovation, and causing thereby dynamic inefficiency. Let me, once more, refer to a possible example of this in the life insurance sector, identified by David Lomax, who writes that

Certainly, it will be more difficult for companies to enter the market and to increase their market share rapidly, as indeed was done by Abbey Life some 20 years ago. A fixed commission system leads to stability in the industrial structure, and will not slow down any move towards mergers and concentration in the industry.

It remains to be seen whether the commission system will have any inhibition on the development of new products, and thus on financial innovation. It is very difficult to establish a system of calculating commissions which is fair as between competing products. If this were not done accurately, then there must be a bias towards selling certain products. Even if it were done accurately at a fixed point in time, innovation will change the relative competitive balance between the different products.[9]

More generally, the compilation of the SIB's rule book on the *Regulation of Investment Business* has appeared to me to have been based on the identification of current best practices in this field, and the codification of such practices as the model for all to follow. My concern here is that technological change and innovation will alter the form of best practice over time out of recognition: codification in a rule book must surely slow that process. Imagine an equivalent team of regulators doing the same exercise as now some 15 years ago: Would we then have had as many innovatory changes in our financial system as have occurred?

Let me take a particular case. I believe that electronic developments may well drastically change the form and nature of financial markets, market makers and clearing processes over future years. Such innovation might be expedited by competition in the provision of marketing services. Yet the establishment of Recognised Investment Exchanges (RIEs), through which all transactions must be put, imposes a degree of artificial monopoly which could serve to restrict change.

Novelty is a disturbing experience for the established, including established authorities and regulators. It upsets the tidiness of life. There is some natural tendency for the innovators to be relatively new, small, often buccaneering institutions. How far does the whole process of regulation, with its authorisations, codifications of best practice, and so on, further shift the balance of advantage towards the *status quo* and away from innovation?

Having reviewed these various categories of costs, I would contend that the figure for my first category, resource costs, of over 100 million pounds per annum is large; the other potential categories of cost are not so easily quantifiable. In one case, with respect to the diversion of business abroad, some considerable care has been taken to limit such costs, but I would still be worried about the static and dynamic inefficiencies that may increasingly build up over time. Indeed, Lomax goes as far as to conclude that 'the only major threat to the future health of the financial services industry in the UK is that of excessive or inappropriate regulation'.

19.2   OBJECTIVES OF REGULATION

Against such potential costs and threats, what were the objectives that the Financial Services Act and the SIB are meant to secure? Regulation has several potential objectives. One of these is protection against the risk that some sizeable parts of the system as a whole may collapse, i.e. systemic risk. This is a risk which the Bank of England is much concerned with in its supervision of the banking system and of associated wholesale financial markets. Although some aspects of the SIB's regulations may bear on potential systemic risk, for example, in its rules for RIEs and for the clearing houses and settlement systems connected with such markets, there has been very little emphasis on systemic issues in this latter part of the regulatory framework, and I shall accordingly also put this subject on one side.

Instead, the emphasis of the Gower Report, Financial Services Act and SIB has all been on investor protection, protection against fraud, negligence, conflicts of interests, mismanagement, etc. Some of my friends who espouse liberal economic theory argue that external governmental regulation of this kind is fundamentally unnecessary, because there are various mechanisms which private market forces will naturally bring to bear, in order to mitigate the problems potentially caused to customers by bad behaviour amongst the purveyors of financial services. The protection against such bad behaviour most frequently adduced is the advantages that good reputation brings in providing continuing demand for one's product. This is, indeed, a reliable guarantor of good behaviour where conditions are such that the seller intends and wishes to be involved in many repeated contracts with each individual purchaser. This will generally be the case in wholesale financial markets, where all those involved are professional, well-informed, and generally acting for institutions with a sizeable capital base.

The essentially professional wholesale markets, notably the euro-markets, both money and bond markets, have worked well, with relatively few scandals emerging, despite absence of any official supervision. Again Lomax has noted:

In point of fact, the international bond markets have been run as far as I can see in an exemplary manner. There have been remarkably few complaints of poor behaviour, and few if any scandals have reached the press. Perhaps a cynic might argue that is because many people engaging in those markets are evading taxes, and therefore they cannot afford to go public with any complaints. But that would seem to me certainly in no sense the reason for the perceived lack of scandal. The fact is that the international bond markets have been run by some of the major international financial organisations, of substantial standing and reputation, and they have done so very well. They have put into place two very efficient clearing systems, and these markets and systems have been used by governments, international organisations, and corporates of the highest standing.

There is thus no mess to clear up. The British authorities have for practical reasons virtually no alternative but to accept the market as it stands and to give their blessing to the existing regulatory, market and clearing system structure, with perhaps some modification to fit in more formally with the FSA. But there is no reason why this acceptance of reality should lead to any inadequacy of the regulatory standards.

And this has apparently now been, to some large extent, appreciated with the announcement in May[10] that the euro-bond market was to be treated as a 'designated investment exchange', on an equal footing to other foreign market-places.

There is, however, considerably more of a problem in maintaining standards of behaviour when the contracts are between relatively small institutions (or those with little capital left to lose, however large they may be in other respects), and smaller investors. The intermediary then has not so much to risk from losing its reputation, and indeed in cases of fraudulent behaviour may be consciously aiming to take the clients' money and disappear with it. The sums of money invested by the small clients, though absolutely small in value, may well be a sizeable proportion of their total wealth, so that a single case of bad behaviour by the intermediary may spell disaster to the client. We are *not* then in a state where the expectation of repetition makes the establishment of a good reputation of key business importance.

In addition, the small investor is likely to be more inexperienced and less well informed.

Asymmetric Information and Client Risk

This problem, of asymmetric information and client risk (of disaster), is faced in many services, besides that of financial intermediary, notably medicine, law, accountancy, etc. Generally a way of raising standards has been for the purveyors to join together in clubs to set entry qualifications, and in many cases, such as the London Stock Exchange and Association of British Travel Agents, to set up compensation funds to provide (some partial) reimbursement for those harmed by bad behaviour by a club member. In addition, in a few areas rating agencies have been set up, though the public nature of information makes the remuneration of such agencies perhaps somewhat problematical.

One can see clearly enough why the authorities may want to intervene to prevent excessive restriction of trade by these private sector clubs. But, apart from using the legal, coercive powers of the state to prevent misrepresentation, for example, by claiming to have qualified as a doctor, or a stockbroker (pre-October 1986, at least) when this is not true, why should, or need, the authorities seek to require the establishment of clubs to maintain standards when the private sector will generally do so independently? In a few cases the purveyors of services may be so diffuse, or in such a new field, that private clubs for the maintenance of standards have not yet been established; it may be that some slight encouragement from the authorities might provide the spur for association. But is it necessary to impose external rules and regulations on all involved in the financial system because entry qualifications and standards of conduct have not yet been established among, shall we say, commodity futures dealers?

Admittedly, there has to be a regular close relationship between the government and privately established ruling clubs of purveyors of professional services, e.g. the BMA, auditors, etc.; and one important, and too rarely undertaken, role for government is to limit potential restraints imposed on free competition by such clubs. But is the extent of detailed official and external intervention now introduced into financial services either necessary or desirable? Consider, for example, the concern about conflicts of interest, which conflicts may become worse the greater the multiplicity of capacities and functions undertaken by financial intermediaries. If clients were really concerned about such possibilities, there should be a thriving market for single capacity, agency institutions to prosper, despite perhaps having to charge higher prices (because they could not enjoy possible economies of scope). So long as institutions did not misrepresent their position, and their modes of operation, to clients, is it really necessary to pursue the requirements of polarisation, Chinese walls, etc., which seek to put asunder those activities that economies of scale and scope were bringing together?

I must confess that I find myself truly unsure on the question of how far market forces will suffice to provide the 'correct' degree of entry control, standards of conduct, investor protection and reimbursement (when standards have slipped) in services subject to information asymmetry in general, and in financial services in particular. Should the state usually act to *limit* the various privately adopted controls (to encourage competition) or to *reinforce* them (to raise standards)?

Insurance Provision and the State

In general, I believe that the private provision of insurance (re-imbursement for losses caused by poor behaviour or mismanagement) is liable to be less than optimal if provided solely by the institutions within the financial system. The larger, well-capitalised, diversified institutions will not be willing to pay large premiums because they will argue, correctly, that they are safe anyhow (note especially the position of the clearing banks). The smaller institutions will not be willing to pay proportionately much heavier premiums because they will argue, correctly, that relative risk cannot be objectively quantified and that an (arbitrary) heavier loading of risk premiums on them is inequitable.

If so, the provision of a desirable level of depositor insurance – though how does one hope to estimate this? – probably does require some external, governmental pressure. Moreover, given the difficulty of risk assessment, experience indicates that the authorities tend to plump for *pro rata* premiums. But since, then, insurance premiums are not related to risk, this will induce moral hazard, whereby some institutions, for example, those with little capital to lose, are encouraged to undertake excessively risky policies and can attract depositors by paying only slightly higher interest rates, since owners of the institution reap most of the benefits if the risky strategy succeeds and the loss falls largely on the insurance agency if it fails.

This latter consideration implies that the authorities *do* need to go further to establish norms for capital adequacy (though how that might be done in practice is yet another hugely complicated, important and difficult issue that I shall not pursue here), and procedures for dealing with institutions with impaired capital.

Furthermore, in those instances where private clubs have not already established entry qualifications for themselves, there is, I believe, a case for the authorities insisting that there be some initial authorisation, and check whether the service is to be provided by fit and proper persons. Otherwise, with asymmetric information and inexperienced investors, the risk of being fleeced by unscrupulous purveyors, who may misrepresent their position, in falsely claiming to be covered by insurance, for instance, may be too great for comfort. When they have absconded, or otherwise lost the clients' monies, recourse to the law will not generally get the money back, and certainly not quickly.

Thus I can see the case for external measures to require a more generous depositor insurance scheme, initial authorisation scheme (from some recognised body), and capital adequacy requirements, but why go further than that?

If the main purpose of the exercise is, as I have thought, to establish better investor protection, I cannot see any reason to go further than this trilogy, of widespread, generous depositor protection scheme, buttressed by capital adequacy requirements and some (preferably simple) initial authorisation. Yet the massive rule book, codifying best practice, and the associated required battalions of regulators, compliance officers, etc. testify to a much more interventionist approach. Why was this adopted?

WHY OVER-REGULATION?

Besides a desire for better investor protection, resulting from certain minor, but well-publicised, scandals in recent years, the other main public concern apparently was whether small, inexperienced investors were being pushed into purchasing inappropriate policies by high-pressure door-to-door ('cold-calling') insurance salesmen, who themselves had a pecuniary incentive to peddle certain policies, whether appropriate in each case or not. No doubt, some measure of reform here was needed. As earlier noted, the current SIB decision *vis-à-vis* the distinctions between independent broker and company representative, and the extent of information even now to be provided on commissions, have left some critics unsatisfied. In any case this specific complaint could be met by specific reforms, and hardly provides any justification for the more extensive intervention in financial intermediation now upon us.

When I read the lengthy and detailed SIB rule book, I am not left with the impression that the establishment of rules and regulations has been kept to the *minimum* required to provide reasonable investor protection against loss and cold-calling, nor that much concern has been expended on limiting the costs of the whole exercise. Instead, the approach seems much more interventionist at heart, as if those running the SIB see their role as one of enforcing *best* practice methods of operation on all those working in the financial services sector. Sometimes I have heard it claimed that the law of agency forces the SIB to require best standards of practice throughout the sector. I have never found this argument set down at any length or in clear written form. I would like to know what the SIB saw as its basic objectives. Certainly, if the objectives were restricted to reasonable investor protection and limitation of the abuses of cold-calling by insurance brokers, it would surely have seemed possible to devise much, much cheaper ways of achieving those ends, without having to incur the sizeable costs outlined in the first part of this paper. Of course, the objective of the regulators may be wider than investor protection, but we do not know clearly what such wider objectives are, nor how weighty might the additional benefits be, and whether they more than counter-balance the various costs of regulation.

In my view the basic problems with the present legislation and its prospective execution by the SIB appeared right at the start of the exercise. The Terms of Reference given to Professor Gower asked him to consider what statutory protection might be necessary for investors, without any suggestion that he review the *costs* as well as the *benefits* of the exercise. Given those terms, and the difficulty of undertaking any realistic cost/benefit exercise in this area, about which Jim Gower was decidedly sceptical,[11] the likelihood always was that the associated costs would be given little weight in the formulation of the legislation. Moreover, the incentive for regulators, especially when they do not bear the burden of the costs themselves, is to impose such comprehensive regulations that they will not personally be likely to be held responsible for failures and failings during their own term of office. Since success for a regulator, when the costs of regulations are not taken fully into account, can be measured by the absence of newsworthy failures, the incentive will often be for over-regulation.

Now I am aware that cost-benefit analyses are notoriously difficult to undertake, and certainly cannot be undertaken in any purely objective value-free manner. What worries me is the lack of attention to costs evidenced at virtually all stages of the current exercise, for example to the relative costs of different approaches to the encouragement of good behaviour, such as tougher penalties for transgression, or more internal monitoring via compliance officers, or more public monitoring via requiring more published information.

The subject of economics concerns how to make the best of a limited and scarce volume of, consequently costly, resources. I contend that the recent regulatory exercise was not, during its formative period, subject to such economic analysis, and that it would have been better had such analysis been applied in a critical vein at a much earlier stage.

NOTES

1. London: The Securities and Investments Board (1987).
2. London: Butterworths (1987).
3. Comments made by participants at the June 1987 IEA conference, and subsequently, suggest that far from David Lomax's estimates being on the high side, they are probably too low.
4. *Cf.*, for example, the paper by Patricia Jackson and Gus O'Donnell, 'The effects of stamp duty on equity transactions and prices in the UK Stock Exchange', *Bank of England Discussion Paper*, 25 (October 1985).
5. Cmnd. 9125, HMSO, 1984, section 1.15.
6. The Bank/Treasury grey paper on 'The future regulation of the wholesale markets in sterling, foreign exchange and bullion' (December 1986).
7. I am less sanguine about this now, in September 1987, than I was in June. The regulatory process has such a built-in momentum that, even though this danger *is* appreciated, it will be difficult to limit the burden being imposed on professional, wholesale, internationally-mobile institutions and markets.
8. 'The Theory of Economic Regulation', *Bell Journal of Economics and Management Science*, 2 (1) (Spring 1971).
9. Lomax, Chapter 7.
10. *Financial Times* (18 May 1987).
11. Gower, *Review of Investor Protection*, 9125, para. 1.16 (1984).

20 Investor Protection and Unprincipled Intervention? (1987)*

20.1 WHAT IS THE JUSTIFICATION FOR REGULATION?

In recent years many economists, and lawyers, especially in the USA, have become increasingly hostile to government intervention in, and regulation of, industry. The older concept that such intervention is applied as a public-service means to correct market failure is now denounced as a travesty of the facts, and as ignoring the political process whereby regulation is introduced, and made acceptable to the regulated. This process, it is claimed, usually ends up with the general customer losing out at the expense of the bureaucracy of regulators and the established firms in the regulated industry, protected from competition by the regulations themselves. That criticism extends to financial regulation: George Benston, a US economist specialising in this branch of the discipline, has written[1] that

> with the exception of deposit insurance, most regulations [on financial services] are not useful except for those who benefit from constraints on competition.

My US free-market friends would be aghast, and astonished, that a Conservative Government, supposedly pledged to the support of markets and the abolition of quangos, could have reneged so far on their principles as to establish a major new quango to impose a multiplicity of regulations on many previously completely free, and internationally successful, markets, such as the Euro-bond market and the London International Financial Futures Exchange (LIFFE).

While I do not myself fully share in the 'liberal' denunciation of (all) government regulation, I do believe that the *prima facie* case against is strong enough to require the authorities to be required to justify the imposition of such regulations. In particular, what are the guiding, strategic principles behind them? Yet, during the whole exercise leading up to the present position, from the Gower Report, through the debates on the Financial Services Act, towards the implementation of the draft rules, regulations and orders of the Securities and Investment Board (SIB), the emphasis has always been on

* *Economic Affairs* (February/March 1987): 8–9.

practicalities and mechanisms, with little reflection on the underlying justification for, and principles of, the exercise.

20.2   ARGUMENTS FOR REGULATION

After this introduction it may come as a surprise that I do believe that there
is justification for much that the SIB is intending to do, but not for all. As
an economist, I would group the arguments for government   intervention
into three categories:

  (i)   where there is a natural monopoly, as in a pipe-line or rail-road;
 (ii)   where there are externalities, in the form of (part of) the costs of some
        exercise falling on society rather on those who undertake it;
(iii)   where there are informational asymmetries, in the sense that one party
        to a bargain has far more access to relevant information than the other.

Case (i) is not relevant to financial services. The main example of Case (ii)
in the financial market concerns the possibility that the failure of a bank, or
intermediary, may lead to a contagious panic, endangering the continued
functioning of major parts of the system. Some of my liberal colleagues
doubt the existence of such externalities, or that they are any worse in finance than in other parts of industry. In the main, however, concern with
problems which affect the working of the system as a whole has been left
the province of the Bank of England. The SIB has placed little emphasis on
this function, perhaps less than it should. Even so, some of its measures,
concerning, for example, the conduct of Recognised Investment Exchanges
(RIEs) and capital adequacy requirements[2] should help to make the whole
financial system safer.

20.3   A CASE FOR 'CAVEAT EMPTOR'

Instead, the whole thrust of the Financial Services Act and SIB, following
the earlier Gower Report,[3] has been with the protection of the individual
investor, especially the uninformed investor (Aunt Agatha), in the face of
problems of information. Many of my liberal colleagues would say that this
too was quite unnecessary. If information is felt to be insufficient, a private
market should develop for information-providing institutions, like credit-rating agencies, and 'good' firms will have an incentive to pay to be rated to
prove that they *are* good. If conflicts of interest in dual capacity firms are
perceived as a real problem, it should prove profitable to establish single-
capacity firms for the nervous to patronise. If 'cowboys' are entering the
field and harming the reputation of the rest, the latter will have an incentive

voluntarily to form 'clubs' for certification. So liberals would rely on information, due process of law and 'caveat emptor'.

In the operation of many institutions and markets their case is compelling. It is, in my view, less compelling in circumstances where not only are informational asymmetries extreme, but also the results of a single incorrect decision can be devastating. Moreover, some of the supposed private market alternatives – credit rating agencies, for example, and voluntary deposit insurance schemes – simply have not taken root here. In our complex world many crucial relationships have to be based on trust. As an individual consumer I do not have the time, or skill, to check out the risks of a new drug, and many do not have the time, or skill, to assess the riskiness of financial investments. What they want is to be assured that their trust will not be abused, in the sense that a minimum degree of qualification is required to start business, and that in the event of negligence, fraud or even simple bad luck that the poor and uninformed are not wiped out, and can obtain part of their money back more surely, cheaply and quickly than might otherwise be possible through the courts of law.

These latter objectives the SIB is moving to achieve. The three crucial elements are (i) deposit insurance, (ii) minimum qualifications as fit and proper persons, and (iii) capital adequacy. It is a pity that the SIB has not made the design of compensation/insurance schemes more the centre of its approach, but recent newspaper reports indicate that they have some imaginative ideas. Yet such insurance can cause the insured financial intermediaries to undertake even riskier activities, as the 'downside' risk falls now on the insurance agency, so 'fit and proper person' and 'capital adequacy' requirements – besides being worthwhile in themselves – would be required to counter the 'moral hazard'[4] of insurance. Accordingly, Chapters I and II of *Regulation of Investment Business* seem right in principle, even if challengeable, no doubt, on details.

20.4 'NANNY-STATE' INTERVENTION WITH A VENGEANCE

The point where I join my liberal colleagues in querying the underlying principles begins with Chapter III, on 'Conduct of Business Rules'. From this point onwards (except for Chapter VIII on 'Compensation Schemes'), the SIB goes beyond the remit of protecting investors from disaster and ensuring minimum qualifications. Instead, the objectives of the rules are to ensure that a person authorised to carry on investment business

> observes high standards of integrity and fair dealing in the conduct of investment business and *complies with best market practice* . . .[5]

Moreover, in the proposed Ombudsman draft of December 1986 (itself an exercise in bureaucratic superfluity, given the existing complaints procedure

– soon we may have one Ombudsman for every 1,000 inhabitants), the SIB notes that its 'objective in this, as in other aspects of its policy, has been to insure that standards obtain consistently across the securities industry as a whole'.[6] The Board thus appears to be embarked on a procedure of deciding what is current 'best practice', codifying it, and requiring everyone to ensure that they comply with that. This is 'nanny-state' intervention with a vengeance. Indeed, making everyone comply with 'best practice' is even more ambitious than the usual socialist demand that everyone must be, at least, 'average'. More seriously, there are no general economic arguments that I know to support the requirement that standards should be consistently applied at 'best-practice' quality. Rather the reverse is the case: people should be allowed to choose between cheaper/lower standard and more expensive/ higher standard options.

20.5 UNNECESSARY DIRIGISME

But have they the necessary information to choose? So long as the poor and uninformed are protected by insurance (compensation schemes), and misrepresentation is prevented, why not let them choose? The alternative approach that – even with insurance – everyone has to be protected by requiring only the best is notably paternalistic. It is also likely to inhibit innovation and development; codification always does. It will also be extremely expensive, not so much in the direct costs of the bureaucracy itself, but more in the heavy costs of compliance. Some of these costs have, thankfully, been assuaged by relaxing the best-practice safeguards for certain classes of investor, but even this 'relaxation' now involves a whole taxonomy of investor classification (six at the last count: ordinary, execution only, occasional customer, experienced, business and professional), so that the repeated maxim 'know your customer' takes on a new meaning.

Moreover, some of the formalities in the Customers Agreement Letters,[7] the treatment of interest payments on clients' money,[8] and the various constraints on who can say what to whom about which investment opportunities, to take only a few examples, are unnecessarily *dirigiste*.

In many cases it will hardly be possible to monitor the observance of best-practice rules. The most cautious and reputable will have to bear the compliance costs; the less so will largely ignore them. Where monitoring and compliance costs are high, as they will be here, how can one judge whether the benefits are commensurate? Has *any* attempt been made at a cost/benefit measurement by any of the authorities involved before embarking on this exercise?

Investor protection is good, but do we require the SIB to go further and intervene in more detail into the conduct of financial activities? On what *principles* is it to be justified?

NOTES

1. 'The Regulation of Financial Services' in G.J. Benston (ed.), *Financial Services: The Changing Institutions and Government Policy* (Englewood Cliffs, N.J.: Prentice-Hall, 1983).
2. As in Chapter II, 'Financial Regulation Proposals' of *The Regulation of Financial Business* (London: Securities and Investments Board, 1987).
3. Len Ross criticises the Gower Report in 'Investor Protection – Why Gowers is Wrong', *Economic Affairs*, 4 (4) (July–September 1984).
4. 'Moral hazard' is defined (in Arthur Seldon and F.G. Pennance, *Everyman's Dictionary of Economics*, London: Dent, 2nd edn., 1975) as 'the proclivity of individuals to increase the likelihood or size of a risk against which they have insured'.
5. Draft of September 1986, p. 3.61; my italics.
6. p. 1, para. 6.
7. Chapter III, Part IV.
8. Regulation 2.3, Chapter VI, for example.

21 Financial Regulation and Supervision: A Review of Three Books (1987)*

Much attention is being paid to the regulation and supervision of financial institutions and in this field there have been three important books published recently. They are:

- E.P.M. Gardener, *UK Banking Supervision; Evolution, Practice and Issues* (London: Allen & Unwin, 1986).
- E.J. Kane, *The Gathering Crisis in Federal Deposit Insurance* (Cambridge, MA: MIT Press, 1985).
- G.J. Benston, R.A. Eisenbeis, P.M. Horvitz, E.J. Kane and G.G. Kaufman *Perspectives on Safe and Sound Banking: Past, Present and Future*, (Cambridge, MA: MIT Press 1986).

In the foreword to Kane's book, Richard Schmalensee commented:

> Until quite recently this regulation (of financial services) has not received scholarly attention commensurate with its economic importance; it seemed to fall into a large crack, separating students of regulation, whose backgrounds rarely equipped them to analyse financial markets, and students of finance, who were not generally much interested in regulation and its effects.

Recent events, such as greater interest rate volatility and credit risks, have, however, put increased pressure on regulatory systems, and have led economists to reassess the operation and adequacy of such regulation, as these three books attest. The large crack is, therefore, being filled, albeit still rather too slowly; for instance, in the UK there has been virtually no analysis published yet by academic economists of the Financial Services Act.

21.1 CONTENT AND FORMAT

The book on UK banking supervision consists of four introductory chapters by the main editor, Gardener, giving a general oversight of the regulatory system in the UK. This is followed by a collection of thirteen separate articles

---

* *National Westminster Bank Quarterly Review* (August 1987: 55–64).

on particular aspects of the subject, such as Evolution and Practice (section B) and Capital Adequacy (section D). These latter articles are each self-contained papers, initially prepared and (mainly) published on another occasion. This combination of specially prepared general introduction, followed by carefully chosen relevant readings, works well.

The book on *Safe and Sound Banking* in the USA brings together five eminent US economists, who have specialised in this field, in a study commissioned by the American Bankers Association. The authors divided the work among themselves, each contributing drafts of a couple, or more, of the eleven chapters. With the possible exception of Paul Horvitz, the authors appear to share a common view-point, that is that the main weakness of the American regulatory system is the mispricing of risk inherent in the present system of setting premiums for deposit insurance by the federal deposit insurance agencies, the Federal Deposit Insurance Corporation (FDIC) and the Federal Savings & Loan Insurance Corporation (FSLIC). The remedy for this, say the authors, should be to restore greater market discipline on bankers who assume untoward risk. Consequently, despite the divided authorship, the book is coherent and clearly focused. Moreover, the joint authorship allows a wider range of related issues to be covered by specialists. On the other hand, the coverage, including the extent of detail and approach, of the various chapters is quite variable, and there is considerable repetition.

Kane's book, *The Gathering Crisis in Federal Deposit Insurance*, is by contrast much more narrowly focussed, and considerably shorter. Although it is essentially an extended essay on a single topic, that is the disadvantages, implications and possible remedies of the present method of charging for deposit insurance in the USA, many American experts in this field believe, as already noted, that this topic does represent *the* main regulatory problem there.

All of these three books can be comfortably read by students and practising bankers and regulators. Kane, in particular, has a racy style with a nice line in metaphor. None of the work in this field yet exhibits much analytical rigour, and Gardener in particular tends to rely unduly on assertion, loosely supported by a rather general appeal to the lessons of history (see pp. 34–38 and 46–49). On the whole the British contributors accept the current *status quo* of UK banking regulation. There is little criticism. It would be, perhaps, unfair to point to Johnson Matthey and the new Banking Supervision Act as evidence that there *are* grounds for such criticism, since most of the papers were written before the story broke. Even so, the tone of the British book was generally rather bland, even deferential to the wisdom of the authorities. In contrast, the Americans sharply criticise the current conduct of regulation in the USA, particularly the operating methods of the FDIC. In the process they challenge much of the conventional wisdom in this field that the British authors accept and reiterate. Consequently, I found

Safe and Sound Banking the most stimulating book of the three, even if my own belief in much of the conventional wisdom remained intact at the end. On the other hand a virtue of the British book, and a failing of the American, is that the British are cognisant of regulatory systems and approaches in other countries, whereas the Americans rarely raise their eyes beyond the US border. Since regulatory institutions and methods differ widely between countries this narrow focus in their work makes it harder to distinguish the features that are particularly American from those of more general validity.

21.2   BRITISH VIEWPOINT AND THE AMERICAN ALTERNATIVE

Let me now revert to the differences in tone and approach between the British and the American books. Besides the need for some protection for the small investor, who might find it difficult to obtain the information he needs to take sound decisions, all are agreed that systemic failure, that is the failure of the financial system, must be prevented. The British, however, see the banking system as potentially fragile in a context of sometimes irrational investors. Thus Gardener claims (p. 48):

> In the short run, even a single bank failure can have far-reaching and disproportionate consequences. The loss of wealth that may be occasioned through a bank failure is not the same as the loss of an equal amount of other kinds of wealth. Many theoretical economists fail to recognize this important operational fact. Bank failures may give rise to far-reaching negative externalities. (That is, damaging effects elsewhere.)

The failure of one bank may immediately raise questions about the solvency of all other banks. Although deposit insurance may eradicate retail deposit runs of the US Great Depression variety, the modern wholesale money markets, for example, are not similarly protected. Indeed, because they are better informed, the sensitivity of wholesale markets to rumours is almost certainly higher than in less sophisticated retail markets. In practice, however, these markets appear sometimes to exhibit markedly unstable features following a crisis and rumours. The latter may eventually become self-fulfilling and a source of more instability. Systematic irrationality appears to be the paradoxical occasional product of apparently efficient markets.

The US authors would disagree fundamentally with virtually all of that (*Safe and Sound Banking*, Chapter 2 especially). In the first place, they claim that individual, or even limited collections of, bank failures, have *not* had severe economic implications in US history. Thus (p. 74):

> The evidence from most of US history indicates that, contrary to general belief, the adverse effects of bank runs and bank failures on the community

have, for the most part, not been much greater than the effects of financial difficulties of most other business firms of comparable relative size and importance in the community, and may often be considerably less.

It is only when there is a contagious run into currency (cash) and bank reserves (deposits with the central bank) reducing the money supply with a given high-powered monetary base, that there is real systemic risk; and, of course, an alert, competent Central Bank could offset that. Thus (p. 45):

> In the absence of a loss of faith by depositors in all banks, withdrawn deposits will be transferred to another bank, either directly by check or indirectly by a redeposit of currency . . . Under these conditions, the bank run is not contagious. To the extent that any economic harm – including financial instability – is suffered from a liquidity problem, it arises from losses to shareholders and the reshuffling of a constant amount of deposits among depositors and banks.

Again (p. 47),

> But as long as deposits are redeposited at some banks and are not withdrawn from all banks, the contagiousness is limited and contained to the troubled bank, and is not transmitted system wide.

The question then is straightforward. Let us assume that the Central Bank can and does keep the money stock on a steady course (and that there is deposit insurance to protect the small depositor); does it matter then if some, or even a sizeable proportion of, banks fail, and if so, why? Unlike the US authors, I believe that it does matter, primarily because it may disrupt key *credit* relationships. Bank failures normally arise from an impairment in perceived asset values (with US economists often ascribing this latter to incorrect official policies). Bank borrowing is still largely based on personal customer relationships, *not* a market investment, with imperfections and asymmetries of information being of key importance. If a bank, or banks, fail because the credit risk of a set of customers is perceived as having worsened, the access to credit of those customers, and those like them, will be generally impaired. Thus, even if the money stock remains unchanged, a series of bank failures may have a major impact on the composition of banks' asset portfolios. Kaufman, the principal author of Chapter 2, is aware of the likelihood of a 'flight to quality' under such circumstances (see pp. 47–9, and also note 7, p. 79), but tends to dismiss these effects as of secondary importance. This would be our main point of difference; certainly more research is necessary into the effects of crises on bank asset portfolios and on the ability of certain types of customers to obtain credit.

21.3   FALL IN ASSET VALUES

The US authors also tend to assume that the falls in asset values that are the proximate cause of banking problems, such as energy lending in the case of Penn Square and Continential Illinois banks, relate to (once-and-for-all) changes in external conditions. Since the losses are given, they argue that these should be immediately incorporated into market accounting, instead of being disguised and partially borne by an insurance agency and taxpayer. To use their language, 'the hit has been made and stockholders, and, in the case of economic insolvency, uninsured depositors should take their haircut' (sic!). Only one escape clause is allowed (see Chapters 2 and 8 in *Safe and Sound Banking*). Kaufman accepts that forced ('fire-sale') realisation of assets may drive prices below some 'equilibrium' market value (p. 46).

> Thus, if sufficiently severe, bank runs may transform solvent banks into insolvent banks. Whether banks whose FSVA < MVD [value of deposits greater than fire sale value of assets] but EMVA > MVD ['equilibrium' value of assets greater than value of deposits] should be declared insolvent by the regulators is a difficult question, the answer to which may be dictated by public policy.

In my view, this dichotomy between a given 'equilibrium' market value and 'fire-sale' values is dangerously oversimplified. All market values are conditional on the authorities' own policy response: there is no such thing as a policy-free, unconditional equilibrium value.

Furthermore, the personal customer relationship involved in much, probably still most, bank borrowing makes market valuation problematical. Kane suggests (Chapter 8, p. 223):

> Where comparable secondary markets for nontraded assets have not yet developed, regulators could facilitate the use of market-value accounting by arranging periodic auctions of instruments selected to produce data suitable for appraising other categories of assets and liabilities.

First, I doubt whether the specific information required to value heterogeneous loans could allow for securitisation of much of the loan book by this route. Second, if I am wrong and the whole, or bulk, of banks' loan books can, in future, be securitised, I do not believe that the combination of a fixed value deposit base supporting a variable market value asset book would prove a long-term viable form of intermediation. Banks would transform themselves into mutual collective investment funds with their liabilities varying in value in line with their asset values.

21.4   WHY HAVE DEPOSIT INSURANCE?

If a competently operated Central Bank can prevent any adverse systemic consequences of bank failures by keeping the money stock on track, why do the Americans feel the need for the FDIC as well? Primarily this was because the US Federal Reserve (Fed.) failed to operate competently in the Great Depression, and US economists remain suspicious about the future wisdom of official discretion. Moreover, there remains the function of individual depositor protection, though the present limit of 100 per cent protection up to 100,000 dollars seems excessive for that purpose, especially since that limit can be greatly extended (and abused) through deposit brokers. There is, however, a third reason, which the US authors, oddly enough, hardly discuss. This is that, in the absence of such insurance, large, diversified banks are *de facto* safer than small unit banks. The present FDIC system acts as a support and subsidy for the US unitary bank system, without which it might become unviable. It is not necessarily unreasonable to provide conscious support for smaller institutions. Thus Revell, (*UK Banking Supervision*, Chapter 10, p. 173) notes:

> Big may be beautiful and big banks may be safer, but the innovations usually come from the smaller institutions, . . . A jungle in which only the most powerful can survive is not what I understand by a competitive banking system.

There is little discussion in the US books about the role of the FDIC/FSLIC in sustaining their particular fragmented banking structure. Instead, there is continuous harping on the failure of the insurance agencies to relate their premium charges to any measure of risk, and the consequent incentives that such mispricing can provide to excessive risk-taking. There *is* undoubtedly a problem here. When the capital of an insured intermediary is eroded, (as happened with members of the Savings and Loan Associations (S & Ls) in the early 1980s when they were caught between long-term fixed interest mortgages and short-term deposits in a milieu of sharply rising interest rates), the limitation on down-side risk, provided by such insurance, as compared with up-side profit possibilities, must tempt managers and stock-holders to adopt a riskier strategy. At the same time the availability of insured (brokered) deposits provides them with the funds to pursue this strategy at a minimal margin over the going market rate of interest for deposits.

Even so, both the extent of concern with this particular facet of institutional influence on risk-bearing activity and the confidence exhibited in the adoption of risk-related premiums as a remedy, seem to me to be exaggerated. As a starter, no one seems to ask how much risk would be socially optimal for banks to undertake anyhow. For the US authors the answer is relatively simple; it is the amount of risk that the market would require in the absence of imperfections. Thus (*Safe and Sound Banking*, Chapter 1, p. 4):

Excessive risk-taking is defined as risks that a bank would not take were it not for the presence of underpriced deposit insurance or uninformed investors whom the banker need not compensate for the possibility of failure.

21.5 CONTROLS ON RISK-TAKING

There are, however, a whole host of other institutional and sociological factors influencing risk-taking, such as limited liability. Indeed, the discussion in Chapter 7 on 'Alternative Sources of Market Discipline' in *Safe and Sound Banking*, considers double liability for stockholders and the potentially valuable role of subordinated debtholders. If, for example, the bankruptcy costs on senior bank management were dramatically raised (public beheading?), risk aversion would doubtless increase. It is possible to influence risk aversion by a range of institutional devices. Why just concentrate on deposit insurance?

Moreover, as Kane recognises in his book (p. 82), even in the absence of explicit risk-related premiums, it remains possible for the insurance agencies to impose implicit costs on riskier intermediaries, for example, by greater agency interference in their business. The problem then, he suggests, is not so much that insurance agencies have no way of seeking to deter excessively risky behaviour, but rather that public-sector bureaucracies are too slow to identify such risks, and are constrained by the politicians from reacting. Thus, Kane writes (pp. 140–1):

Deposit insurance bureaucrats have had great difficulty recognising and regulating emerging forms of risk in timely fashion. The problem is that government bureaucracies are inherently slower than their clients in adapting to changes in opportunities for risk-taking and are constrained in their adaptation by restrictions imposed by elected politicians.

Incidentally, the contrast between the confidence of these US economists in investors' ability to use limited information to arrive at equilibrium underlying market values and their doubts about the ability of voters similarly to respond with a rational use of available information is remarkable. Thus Kane (pp. 162–3) deplores a situation in which:

The policy of routinely bailing out financially devastated institutions imposes enormous unaccounted expense and unrecognised liabilities onto the deposit insurance agencies and through them onto taxpayers.

Why is it so much easier to fool the voter than the investor?

21.6 PRIVATISATION OF DEPOSIT INSURANCE

A couple of years ago at this juncture one would have confidently expected US free-market economists to advocate transferring (all) deposit insurance to private sector insurance companies. At least this particular issue has been (temporarily) closed by the sorry experience of the S & Ls in Ohio and Maryland, whose non-Federal insurance proved insufficient. The US authors reluctantly accept that private insurance would not have the credibility to act as the core central deposit insurance agency but they still advocate encouraging some supplementary insurance functions for the private sector (*Safe and Sound Banking*, pp. 304–8). Even in this more limited role, questions remain under what circumstances the private insurance company would have the necessary rights:

- To require particular forms of prudential behaviour,
- To inspect intermediaries to ensure that such behaviour was being adopted;
- To withdraw insurance; and
- To require the closure of the insured intermediaries.

All of these functions have been seen as being properly in the official domain, but presumably the US authors would dispute that.

21.7 RISK RELATED PREMIUMS AND REGULATION

Finally the confidence of some of these authors that risk-related premiums could be successfully introduced, and thereby solve the main US regulatory problem, seems to me to be wishful thinking.

There are, at least, three serious problems involved:

- It is extremely difficult for anyone, even if not suffering from the handicap of being a bureaucrat, to assess *ex ante* banking risks;
- The extent of loss to the insurer depends not only on the risks assumed by the bank, but also on the agency's speed of reaction to developing bank losses, and in particular on the insurer's ability to close the institution;
- If the outcome of a bank's examination would have a significant effect on its (relative) cost structure, the whole process of examination and supervision would lose its cooperative features and become (even more) confrontational.

These problems are nicely discussed by Horvitz in Chapter 16 of *UK Banking Supervision*. Possibly in part because of the third problem, the recent proposals by the insurance agencies in the USA 'for risk-related premiums involve relatively small differentials. . . . It is not at all clear that differentials of this magnitude will have a significant effect in inhibiting risk-taking by a management so inclined. Yet it is also not clear that there is an actuarially sound basis for an *ex ante* differential larger than those numbers' (p. 279).

At present, the authorities that can close banks in the USA are those that provide their original charters, *not* the insuring agencies. Kane would transfer the right to close banks to the insuring agencies, and indeed would require them to do so when the calculated market value of net worth goes below some low, but positive value, such as 1 or 2 per cent of assets (Kane, Chapter 6, pp. 151–5, and *Safe and Sound Banking*, p. 309). That may be alright when the impairment in a failing bank's asset values is due to individual problems, such as fraud, but what happens when a whole class of banks faces falling asset values due to (an unforeseen) change in market conditions, as happened in the early 1980s with interest rate movements and weaknesses in real estate, farming and energy loans? Relying no doubt on the belief that no serious problem *can* arise as long as the aggregate money stock remains unaffected, Kane would stick to his guns. Thus (p. 162):

> Even the Federal Reserve's capacity for bailing out insolvent institutions needs to be constrained. Except in the event of a *bona fide* crisis – as defined by the condition that a given percentage (say, at least 5 percent) of aggregate deposit institution assets has been involved in *de jure* failures within the last twelve or eighteen months – the Fed should not be allowed to lend funds to an institution whose net worth is negative in market value.

In my view the US financial system would have been much more fragile and dangerous if those precepts had been followed. Even so, the authorities do face real problems in reacting to events that reduce capital adequacy in segments of the financial system below some appropriate level, and they need to review the nature of the incentives that they can apply to management to rebuild their capital.

21.8 TAILPIECE

Finally, while the publishers can be pleased with the general standards of presentation and proof-reading, I did enjoy the misprint in *Safe and Sound Banking* (p. 209) which referred to 'Bank Holiday Companies' (sic)!

Bibliography

Adonis, A. and Tyrie, A. (1990) Subsidiarity, as History and Policy', Pamphlet, Institute of Economic Affairs: London, IEA (December).

Aftalion, F. (1983) 'The political economy of French monetary policy', In *The Political Economy of Monetary Policy: National and International Aspects*, D. Hodgman) (ed.) (Boston: Federal Reserve Bank of Boston) 7–25, and 'Discussion' of above by Robert Raymond: 26–33.

Aghion, P. and Bolton, P. (1990) 'Government Domestic Debt and the Risk of Default: A Political-economic Model of the Strategic Role of Debt', in *Public Debt Management: Theory and History*, R. Dornbusch and M. Draghi (eds.) (Cambridge UK: Cambridge University Press): 315–44.

Aghion, P., Hart, O. and Moore, J. (1992) 'The Economics of Bankruptcy Reform', *Journal of Law, Economics and Organisation*, 8: 523–46.

Aharony, J. and Swary, I. (1983) 'Contagion Effects of Bank Failures: Evidence from Capital Markets', *Journal of Business*, 56(3): 305–22.

Akhtar, M.A. (1983) 'Financial innovations and their implications for monetary policy: an international perspective', *Bank for International Settlements Economic Papers*, (9).

Akhtar, M.A. and Harris, E.S. (1987) 'Monetary policy influence on the economy: an empirical analysis', *Federal Reserve Bank of New York Quarterly Review* (Winter): 19–32.

Alchian, A.A. and Klein, B. (1973) 'On a correct measure of inflation', *Journal of Money, Credit and Banking*, 5(1), Pt 1 (February 1973): 183–91.

Alesina, A. (1989) 'Politics and Business Cycles in Industrial Democracies', *Economic Policy* (8): (April).

Alesina, A. and Grilli, V. (1991) 'The European Central Bank: Reshaping Monetary Politics in Europe', CEPR Discussion Paper (563).

Alesina, A. and Roubini, N. (1990) 'Political cycles in OECD economies', National Bureau of Economic Research, Working Paper 3478 (October).

Alogoskoufis, G. and Portes, R. (1991) 'International Costs and Benefits from EMU', *European Economy*, Special Issue (1): 231–45.

American Enterprise Institute Conference (1985) 'Monetary Policy in a Changing Financial Environment', 8 February, with papers by Bennett McCallum, Vance Roley, Gerald Dwyer Jr. and J. Merrick and A. Saunders, *Journal of Money, Credit and Banking*, 17(4), Pt 2 (November).

American Enterprise Institute Conference (1982) 'Current Issues in the Conduct of US Monetary Policy', 4–5 February 1982, with papers by W. Poole, R. Bryant, W. Fellner, W. Arnett, B. Friedman, S. Black, J. Pierce, R. Anderson and J. Rasche, and P. Tinsley *et al.*, reproduced in *Journal of Money, Credit and Banking*, 14(2), Pt 2 (November).

Andersen, P.S. (1985) 'The stability of money demand functions: an alternative approach', *BIS Economic Papers* (14).

Anderson, R. and Enzler, J.J. (1987) 'Toward realistic policy design: policy reaction functions that rely on economic forecasts', Chapter 10 in *Macroeconomics and Finance*, R. Dornbusch, S. Fischer and J. Bossons (eds): 291–330 (MIT Press: Cambridge, Mass).

Arestis, P. (ed.) (1993) *Money and Banking: Issues for the Twenty-First Century*

467

(London: Macmillan).

Argy, V. (1988) 'Money growth targeting – the international experience', Centre for Studies in Money, Banking and Finance, Macquarie University, Working Paper No. 8806A (August).

Armendariz, B. and Williamson, J. (1993) 'The G-7's Joint-and-Several Blunder', *Essays in International Finance* (181): (Princeton Department of Economics, April).

Artis, M.J. (1968) 'The Monopolies Commission Report', *Bankers' Magazine*, 206(1494) (September): 128–135: also see Section IV, 'Efficiency', (ed.) M.J. Artis, in H.G. Johnson (ed.), *Readings in British Monetary Economics* (Oxford: Clarendon Press, 1972).

Artis, M.J. (1984) 'Monetary control in the United Kingdom', *Economic Review*, 2(2) (November): 19–23.

Artis, M.J. (1991) 'One Market, One Money: An Evaluation of the Potential Benefits and Costs of Forming an Economic and Monetary Union', *Open Economics Review*, 2: 315–21.

Artis, M.J. and Lewis, M.K. (1976) 'The demand for money in the United Kingdom, 1963–73', *Manchester School*, 44(2): 147–81.

Artis, M.J. and Lewis, M.K. (1984) 'How unstable is the demand for money in the United Kingdom?' *Economica*, 51: 473–6.

Artus, P. (1987) 'La politique monetaire en France dans un contexte d'innovation financière de dereglementation et de plus grande mobilité des capitaux', Banque de France, Direction Generale des Étu les, Working Paper 87–36/2 (March).

Association for the Monetary Union of Europe (1992) 'Questions and Answers about Monetary Union in Europe', 26 rue de la Pépinière, Paris pamphlet.

Atkeson, A. and Bayoumi, T. (1993) 'Private capital markets and adjustment in a currency union: evidence from the United States', Chapter 3 in *Policy issues in the operation of currency unions*, eds. P. Masson and M.P. Taylor (Cambridge: Cambridge University Press).

Atkinson, P. and Chouraqui, J.-C. (1987) 'Implications of financial innovation and exchange rate variability on the conduct of monetary policy', *Journal of Foreign Exchange and International Finance*, 1(1): 64–84.

Attanasio, O.P. and Padoa-Schioppa, F. (1991) 'Regional Inequalities, Migration and Mismatch in Italy, 1960–86), in *Mismatch and Labor Mobility*, ed. F. Padoa Schioppa (Cambridge: Cambridge University Press): 237–321.

Avery, R.B. *et al.* (1987) 'Changes in the use of transaction accounts and cash from 1984 to 1986', *Federal Reserve Bulletin*, 73: 179–96.

Axilrod, S.H. (1985) 'US monetary policy in recent years: an overview', *Federal Reserve Bulletin*, 71(1): 14–24.

Axilrod, S.H. and Lindsey, D.E. (1981) 'Federal Reserve System implementation of monetary policy: analytical foundations of the new approach', *American Economic Review*, 71(2): 246–52.

Baba, Y., Hendry, D.F. and Starr, R.M. (1987) 'U.S. money demand, 1960–1984', Nuffield College Oxford, Discussion Paper, (27).

Bagehot, W. (1873) *Lombard Street* (London: Kegan, Paul & Co.).

Balbach, A.B. (1981) 'How controllable is money growth', *Federal Reserve Bank of St Louis Review*, 63 (April): 3–12.

Baldwin, R.E. (1991) 'On the microeconomics of the European monetary union', in *The Economics of EMU, European Economy*, Special Edition (1):21–35.

Baltensperger, E. and Dermine, J. (1987) 'Banking Deregulation in Europe', *Economic Policy* (April): 64–109.

Bank of Canada (1991) 'The implementation of monetary policy in a system with zero reserve requirements, *Discussion paper* 3 (revised) (September) (Toronto: Bank of Canada).

Bank of England (1980) 'Methods of monetary control', *Bank of England Quarterly Bulletin*, 20(4) (December): 428–9.

Bank of England (1982) 'The role of the Bank of England in the money market', *Bank of England Quarterly Bulletin*, 22(1) (March): 86–94.

Bank of England (1982a) 'The supplementary special deposits scheme', *Bank of England Quarterly Bulletin*, 22(1): 74–85.

Bank of England (1982b) 'Composition of monetary and liquidity aggregates, and associated statistics', *Bank of England Quarterly Bulletin*, 22(4): 530–7.

Bank of England (1984) 'Some aspects of UK monetary policy', a lecture given by the Governor at the University of Kent, reproduced in the *Bank of England Quarterly Bulletin*, 24(4) (December): 474–81.

Bank of England (1984a) 'Funding the public sector borrowing requirement: 1952–83', *Bank of England Quarterly Bulletin*, 24(4): 482–92.

Bank of England (1984b) *The Development and Operation of Monetary Policy, 1960–1983* (Oxford: Clarendon Press).

Bank of England (1987) 'Measures of broad money', *Bank of England Quarterly Bulletin*, 27(2): 212–9.

Bank of England (1988) 'Bank of England operations in the sterling money market', *Bank of England Quarterly Bulletin*, 28(3): 391–409.

Bank of England (1991) 'Is there a "Credit Crunch?"', *Bank of England Quarterly Bulletin*, 31(2) (May): 256–9.

Bank of England (1992) 'Developments in Wholesale Payments Systems', *Bank of England Quarterly Bulletin* (November): 449–57.

Bank of England and H.M. Treasury (1986), 'The future regulation of the wholesale markets in sterling, foreign exchange and bullion', Consultation, 'gray', paper, December.

Bank for International Settlements (BIS) (1983) *Fifty-third Annual Report*. Basle, 68–78.

Bank for International Settlements (BIS) (1986) *Recent Innovations in International Banking*. Report of a Committee of Central Bankers, chaired by Samuel Cross, Basle: BIS.

Bank for International Settlements (1990a) 'Large-Value Funds Transfer Systems in the Group of Ten Countries' (the 'Pink Book'), Basle (May).

Bank for International Settlements (1990b) 'Report of the Committee on Interbank Netting Schemes of the Central Banks of the Group of Ten Countries (the Lamfalussy Report)', Basle (November).

Bank for International Settlements (1992) 'Recent Developments in International Interbank Relations (the Promisel Report)', Basle (October).

Bank of Japan, Research and Statistics Department (1985) 'Characteristics of interest rate fluctuations amidst deregulation and internationalization of financing', special paper no. 126, (October).

Bank of Japan, Research and Statistics Department (1988a) *Quarterly Economic Outlook*, Special Paper, (163) (Spring).

Bank of Japan, Research and Statistics Department (1988b) 'On the recent behaviour of the money supply' (in Japanese), *Monthly Review*.

Bank of Japan, Research and Statistics Department (1988c) *Annual Review of Monetary and Economic Developments in Fiscal 1987*, (June).

Bank of Japan (eds.) (1995) *Financial Stability in a Changing Environment* (London: Macmillan).

Banque de France, Direction Generale des Etudes (1987) 'L'evolution des instruments de la politique monetaire en France et la nouveau dispositif de controle monetaire', Note No. 87. 24/2 (March).

Barbato, M. (1987) 'The evolution of monetary policy and its impact on banks',

Review of Economic Conditions in Italy, (2): 165–208.

Barnett, W.A. (1982) 'The optimal level of monetary aggregation', *Journal of Money, Credit and Banking*, 14(4), part 2: 687–710.

Barnett, W.A., Offenbacher, E.K. and Spindt, P.A. (1984) 'The new Divisia monetary aggregates', *Journal of Political Economy*, 92(6): 1049–85.

Baron, D. (1982) 'A Model of the Demand for Investment Banking and Advising and Distribution Services for New Issues', *Journal of Finance*, 37(4): 955–76.

Barre, R. *et al.* (1969) 'Commission Memorandum to the Council on the Coordination of Economic Policies and Monetary Cooperation within the Community', *Bulletin of the European Communities*, Supplement 3 March.

Barro, R.J. (1977) 'Unanticipated money growth and unemployment in the United States', *American Economic Review*, 67(2): 101–15.

Barro, R.J. (1978) 'Unanticipated money, output and the price level in the United States', *Journal of Political Economy*, 86(4): 549–80.

Barro, R.J. (1986) 'Recent developments in the theory of rules versus discretion', *Economic Journal*, 96 (Supplement): 23–37.

Barro, R.J. (1989) 'Interest-rate targeting', *Journal of Monetary Economics* 23(1): 3–30.

Barro, R.J. and Gordon, D.B. (1983a) 'Rules, discretion and reputation in a model of monetary policy', *Journal of Monetary Economics*, 12(1): 101–21.

Barro, R.J. and Gordon, D.B. (1983b) 'A positive theory of monetary policy in a natural rate mode', *Journal of Political Economy*, 91(4): 589–610.

Bayoumi, T. and Eichengreen, B. (1992) 'Shocking Aspects of European Monetary Unification', NBER Working Paper (3949) (January).

Bayoumi, T. and Masson P.R. (1991) 'Fiscal Flows in the United States and Canada: Lessons for Monetary Union in Europe', International Monetary Fund (November).

Bayoumi, T. and Rose, A.K. (1993) 'Domestic Savings and Intra-national Capital Flows', *European Economic Review*, 37(6) (August): 1197–202.

Beach, W.E. (1935) *British International Gold Movements and Banking Policy, 1881–1913* (Cambridge, Mass: Harvard University Press).

Bean, C. (1987) 'The impact of North Sea oil', Chapter 3. In *The Performance of the British Economy*, R. Dornbusch and R. Layard (ed.) (Oxford: Clarendon Press).

Bean, C. (1992) 'Economic and Monetary Union in Europe', *Journal of Economic Perspectives*, 6(4) (Fall): 31–52.

Bean, C., Cohen, D., Giavazzi, F., Giovannini, A., Vives, X. and Wyplosz, C. (1992) 'European Monetary Union under Attack', manifesto published in major European newspapers.

Beckerman, W. (1985) 'How the battle against inflation was really won', *Lloyds Bank Review*, January, 1–12.

Begg, D. et al. (1991) *Monitoring European Integration: The Making of Monetary Union* (London: Centre for Economic Policy Research).

Begg, D., Fischer, S. and Dornbusch, R. (1991) *Economics*, 3rd edition (McGraw-Hill International, Maidenhead, UK).

Begg, D. and Portes, R. (1992) 'Enterprise Debt and Economic Transformation: Financial Restructuring of the State Sector in Central and Eastern Europe', CEPR Discussion Paper (695).

Benston, G.J. (1983) 'Deposit Insurance and Bank Failures' *Economic Review*, Federal Reserve Bank of Atlanta (March): 4–17.

Benston, G.J., (1990) 'U.S. Banking in an Increasingly Integrated and Competitive World Economy', *Journal of Financial Services Research*, 4 (December): 311–39.

Benston, G.J. (1992) 'International Harmonization of Banking Regulations and Cooperation Among National Regulators: An Assessment', in Fingleton, John and D. Schoenmaker (eds) *The Internationalisation of Capital Markets and the*

Regulatory Response (London: Graham and Trotman), revised version (June 1993).

Benston, G.J. (1993) 'Universal Banking: An Analysis of Disadvantages and Advantages', Emory Business School, draft (July).

Benston, G.J. (ed.) (1983) *Financial Services: The Changing Institutions and Government Policy* (Englewood Cliffs, N.J.: Prentice-Hall).

Benston, G.J., Brumbaugh, R.D. Jr., Guttentag, J.M., Herring, R.J., Kaufman, G.G. and Litan R.E. and Scott, K.E. (1989) *Blueprint for restructuring America's financial institutions: Report of a task force* (The Brookings Institute, Washington, DC).

Benston, G.J., Eisenbeis, R.A., Horvitz, P.M., Kane, E.J. and G.G. Kaufman (1986) *Perspectives on Safe and Sound Banking: Past, Present and Future* (Cambridge, MA: MIT Press).

Benston, G.J. and Kaufman, G.G. (1988) *Risk and Solvency Regulation of Depository Institutions: Past Policies and Current Options* (New York: New York University Graduate School of Business Administration, Salomon Center Monograph Series in Finance and Economics, Monograph).

Berlin, I. (1958) *The Two Concepts of Liberty* (Oxford: Clarendon Press).

Bernanke, B.S. (1983) 'Non-monetary Effects of the Financial Crisis in the Propagation of the Great Depression', *American Economic Review*, 73(3): 257–76.

Bernanke, B.S. and Gertler, M. (ed.) (1987) 'Banking and macroeconomic equilibrium', In *New Approaches to Monetary Economics*, W.A. Barnett and K. Singleton (ed) (New York: Cambridge University Press).

Bernanke, B.S. and Lown, C.S. (1991) 'The Credit Crunch', *Brookings Papers on Economic Activity*, 2: 205–48.

Bhide, A. (1993) 'The hidden costs of stock market liquidity', *Journal of Financial Economics*, 34(1) (August): 31–52.

Bingham Report (1992) *Inquiry into the Supervision of The Bank of Credit and Commerce International*, London: House of Commons, October.

Bini-Smaghi, L., Padoa-Schioppa T. and Papadia, F. (1993) 'The Policy History of the Maastricht Treaty: The Transition to the Final Stage of EMU', Banca d'Italia, mimeo (February).

Bini-Smaghi, L. and Vori, S. (1992) 'Rating the EC as an Optimal Currency Area: Is it Worse than the US?'. Chapter 6 in *Finance and the International Economy*: 6 of the Amex Bank Review Awards, ed. R O'Brien (Oxford University Press).

Binyon, M. (1990) 'The European System of Central Banks'. *The Times*, 3 (December): 25.

Bisignano, J. (1991) 'Corporate Control and Financial Information' Chapter 8 in *Finance and the International Economy*: 5, The Amex Bank Review Prize Essays, ed. R. O'Brien (Oxford University Press): 106–21.

Bisignano, J. (1992) 'Banking Competition, Regulation and the Philosophy of Financial Development: A Search for First Principles', in: *The Internationalisation of Capital Markets and the Regulatory Response*, J.A. Fingleton and D. Schoenmaker (ed) (London: Graham & Trotman): 69–102.

Black, F. (1970) 'Banking and interest rates in a world without money: The effects of uncontrolled banking', *Journal of Bank Research*, Reprinted in: Fischer Black, *Business Cycles and Equilibrium* (Basil Blackwell, New York).

Black, F. (1987) 'A gold standard with double feedback and near zero reserves', in: Fischer Black, *Business Cycles and Equilibrium* (Basil Blackwell, New York) 115–120.

Black, J., de Meza, D. and Jeffreys, D. (1992) 'House Prices, the Supply of Collateral and the Enterprise Economy', University of Exeter Department of Economics, Working Paper.

Black, S.W. (1982) 'The effects of alternative monetary control procedures on exchange rates and output', *Journal of Money, Credit and Banking*, 14(4), part 2: 746–60.

Blanchard, O. and Katz, L. (1992) 'Regional Evolutions', *Brookings Papers on Economic Activity*, 1: 1–61.

Blinder, A.S. (1987) 'Credit rationing and effective supply failures', *Economic Journal*, 97(386): 327–52.

Blommestein, H.J. (1993) 'Financial Sector Reforms and Monetary Policy in Central and Eastern Europe', in *The New Europe: Evolving Economic and Financial Systems in East and West*, eds. D.E. Fair and J. Raymond (Amsterdam: Kluwer Academic Publishers).

Blommestein, H.J., and Spencer, M.G. (1993) 'The Role of Financial Institutions in the Transformation to a Market Economy', Paper presented at IMF and World Bank Conference on 'Building Sound Finance in Emerging Market Economies', Washington (June).

Bloomfield, A.I. (1959) *Monetary Policy under the International Gold Standard, 1880–1914* (monograph, Federal Reserve Bank of New York).

Blundell-Wignall, A., Lowe, P. and Tarditi, A. (1992) 'Inflation, Indicators and Monetary Policy', in A. Blundell-Wignall (ed.), *Inflation, Disinflation and Monetary Policy* (Sydney: Reserve Bank of Australia): 249–98.

Blundell-Wignall, A. and Thorp, S. (1987) 'Money demand, own interest rates and deregulation', Reserve Bank of Australia Research Discussion Paper (8703) (May).

Board of Governors of the Federal Reserve System (1988) 'Monetary policy report to Congress pursuant to the full employment and balanced growth [Humphrey-Hawkins] Act of 1978', Federal Reserve Board Press Release (13 July).

Bofinger, P. and Gros, D. (1991) 'A Multilateral Payments Union of the Republics of the Soviet Union', Centre for European Policy Studies, mimeo, Brussels (November).

Bomhoff, E.J. (1983) *Monetary Uncertainty* (Amsterdam: North Holland).

Bomhoff, E.J. (1985) 'Monetary targeting in West Germany, Holland and Switzerland', *Contemporary Policy Issues*, II (Fall): 85–98.

Boone, P. (1993) 'Russia's Balance of Payments Prospects', Chapter 12 in *Changing the Economic System in Russia*, eds. A. Aslund and R. Layard (London: Pinter Publishers Ltd): 210–29.

Bordes, C. and Strauss-Kahn, M.-O. (1988) 'Dispositifs de controle monetaire en France et chocs sur la vitesse dans un environment en mutation', *Economies et Societés* (1): 105–54.

Borts, G.H. (1991) 'The financial crisis in the US and the need for banking reform', *Economic Journal of Hokkaido University* 20, 29–37.

Bouey, G.K. (1982a) 'Monetary policy – finding a place to stand', Paper presented at the Per Jacobbson Lecture, 5 September, (mimeo) (Bank of Canada).

Bouey, G.K. (1982b) 'Recovering from inflation', Notes for Remarks to the Canadian Club, Toronto, Ontario, 29 November, reprinted in the *Bank of Canada Review*, December.

Boughton, J.M. (1993) 'The economics of the CFA franc zone', Chapter 4 in *Policy issues in the operation of currency unions*, eds. P. Masson and M.P. Taylor (Cambridge University Press).

Boulton, L. (1993) 'Time for west to help Russia's transformation', *Financial Times*, 1 March 1993.

Boyd, J.H. and Gertler, M. (1993) 'U.S. Commercial Banking: Trends, Cycles, and Policy', Paper Presented at CEPR/ESF Conference on 'Financial Regulation', Toulouse, June; also intended for *NBER Macroeconomics Annual*.

Brayton, F., Farr, T. and Porter, R. (1983) 'Alternative money demand specifications and recent growth in M1', Processed, Board of Governors of the Federal Reserve System (May).

Brittan, S. (1980) 'A coherent budget at last', *Financial Times*, (27 March): 24.

Broaddus, A. and Goodfriend, M. (1984) 'Base drift and the longer run growth of M1: experience from a decade of monetary targeting', *Federal Reserve Bank of Richmond Economic Review*, 70(6): 3–14.

Brock, W.A. and Mirman, L.J. (1972) 'Optimal economic growth and uncertainty: the discounted cases', *Journal of Economic Theory*, 4: 479–513.

Broder, E.-G. (1992) 'EMU – Acceleration or collapse? Honorary President's opening address', The European Finance Convention and Ecu Week, Special Issue, ed. C. Cassuto: 9–13.

Bruni, F. (ed) (1993) *Prudential Regulation, Supervision and Monetary Policy* (Centro di Economia Monetaria e Finanziaria Paolo Baffi, Università Commerciale Luigi Bocconi).

Brunner, K. and Meltzer, A.H. (1972a) 'Money, debt, and economic activity', *Journal of Political Economy*, 80(5): 951–77.

Brunner, K. and Meltzer, A.H. (1972b) 'A monetarist framework for aggregative analysis', *Proceedings of the First Konstanzer Seminar, Kredit und Kapital*, Beideft 1, Berlin.

Brunner, K. and Meltzer, A.H. (1983) 'Strategies and tactics for monetary control', in *Money, Monetary Policy, and Financial Institutions*, K. Brunner and A.H. Meltzer (eds), Carnegie-Rochester Conference Series on Public Policy, 19, (Amsterdam: North Holland).

Brunner, K. and Meltzer, A.H. (1988) 'Money and credit in the monetary transmission process', *American Economic Review*, 78(2): 446–51.

Bruno, M. and Sachs, J. (1985) *Economics of Worldwide Stagflation* (Oxford: Blackwell).

Bryant, R.C. (1982) 'Federal Reserve control of the money stock', *Journal of Money, Credit and Banking*, 14(4), part 2: 597–625.

Budd, A. and Holly, S. (1986) 'Does broad money matter?', *The London Business School Economic Outlook*, 10(9): 16–22.

Buiter, W.H. (1992) 'Should we worry about the fiscal numerology of Maastricht', CEPR Discussion Paper Series (668) (June): 221–44.

Buiter, W.H. (1985) 'A guide to public sector debt and deficits', *Economic Policy*, 1 (November): 14–79.

Buiter, W.H. and Armstrong, C.A. (1978) 'A didactic note on the transaction demand for money and behavior towards risk', *Journal of Money, Credit and Banking*, 10 (November): 529–38.

Buiter, W.H. and Kletzer, K.M. (1991) 'Fiscal implications of a common currency', Chapter 8 in *European Financial Integration*, eds. A. Giovannini and C. Mayer (Cambridge University Press: Cambridge, UK).

Buiter, W.H. and Miller, M.H. (1982) 'Real exchange-rate overshooting and the output cost of bringing down inflation', *European Economic Review*, 18(1–2): 85–123.

Buiter, W.H. and Miller, M.H. (1983) 'Changing the rules – economic consequences of the Thatcher regime', *Brookings Papers on Economic Activity*, (2): 305–79.

Burdekin, R.C.K. (1986) 'Cross-country evidence on the relationship between central banks and governments', Federal Reserve Bank of Dallas Research Paper (8603).

Burger, A.E., Kalish L. III, Babb C.T. (1971) 'Money stock control and its implications for monetary policy', *Federal Reserve Bank of St Louis Review*, 33: 6–22.

Cable, J. (1985) 'Capital Market Information and Industrial Performance: The Role of West German Banks', *Economic Journal*, 95 (March): 118–132.

Callaghan, J. (1976) 'Speech to Labour Party Conference', 28 September, as reported in *The Times* (29 September) 1.

Calvo, G.A. (1978). 'On the time consistency of optimal policy in a monetary economy', *Econometrica*, 46 (November): 1411–28.

Cameron, R. (1967) *Banking in the Early Stages of Industrialization* (Oxford University Press: New York).

Capie, F.H. and Webber, A. (1985) *A monetary history of the United Kingdom, 1870–1982* (London: George Allen and Unwin).

Capie, F.H. and Wood, G.E. (1986) 'The long run behaviour of velocity in the UK', Centre for Banking and International Finance, Centre for the Study of Monetary History, The City University, Discussion Paper (23) (May).

Capie, F.H. and Wood, G.E. (ed.) (1990) *Unregulated Banking: Chaos or Order* (London: Macmillan).

Carey, G. (1993) Interview, *Financial Times* (15 February).

Carlson, K. (1989) 'Do Price Indexes Tell Us About Inflation? A Review of the Issues,' *Federal Reserve Bank of St. Louis Review* (November/December).

Carraro, C. (1989) 'The tastes of European central bankers', in M. de Cecco and A. Giovannini (eds) *A European Central Bank* (Cambridge: Cambridge University Press): 162–89.

Carr, J. and Darby, M. (1981) 'The role of money supply shocks in the short-run demand for money', *Journal of Monetary Economics*, 8 (September): 183–200.

Cecco, M. de (ed.) (1987) *Changing Money: Financial Innovation in Developed Countries* (Oxford: Basil Blackwell).

Centre for European Policy Studies (CEPS) (1994) 'European Payment Systems and EMU', (Brussels) *CEPS Working Party Report*, 11 April).

Chari, V.V. and Jagannathan, R. (1984) 'Banking Panics, Information and Rational Expectations Equilibrium', Northwestern University Center for Mathematical Studies in Economics and Management Science, *Discussion Paper* (618) (July).

Chouraqui, J.-C., Driscoll, M. and Strauss-Kahn, M.-O. (1988) 'The effects of monetary policy on the real sector: an overview of empirical evidence for selected OECD economies', *OECD Working Papers* (51) (April).

Chowdhury, G., Green, C.J. and Miles, D.K. (1986) 'An empirical model of company short-term financial decisions: evidence from company accounts data', *Bank of England Discussion Paper* (26).

Chowdhury, G., Green, G. and Miles, D.K. (1989) 'Company Bank Borrowing and Liquid Lending', *National Westminster Bank Review*: 45–52.

Chown, J. and Wood, G. (1992/93) 'Russia's Currency – How the West can Help', *Central Banking*, (3) (Winter): 39–46.

Claassen, E.M. (1984) 'Monetary Integration and Monetary Stability: The Economic Criteria of the Monetary Constitution', Chapter I.3 in *Currency Competition and Monetary Union*, ed. P. Salin (Martinus Nijhoff: The Hague).

Clay, Sir Henry (1957) *Lord Norman* (London: Macmillan).

Clifford Chance (1992) 'Legal Aspects of the ECU as a Single Currency for Europe', processed, 19 October, 200 Aldersgate Street, London.

Clinton, K. and Chouraqui, J.-C. (1987) 'Monetary policy in the second half of the 1980s: how much room for manoeuvre?' OECD Department of Economics and Statistics, Working Papers (39) (February).

Coase, R. (1937) 'The nature of the firm', *Economica*, New Series, 4, reprinted in *Readings in Price Theory*, eds. G.J. Stigler and K.E. Boulding (Homewood, Ill.: Richard D. Irwin Inc., 1952).

Cohen, B.J. (1993a) 'Beyond EMU: The Problem of Sustainability', *Economics and Politics*, 5(2) (July): 187–203.

Cohen, B.J. (1993b) 'The Triad and the Unholy Trinity: Lessons for the Pacific Region' in *Pacific Economic Relations in the 1990's: Conflict or Cooperation,* eds. R.A. Higgott, R. Leaver and J. Ravenhill (Sdyney: Allen and Unwin): 133–58.

Cohen, D. and Wyplosz C. (1989) 'The European Monetary Union: An agnostic Evaluation', in *Macroeconomic Policies in an Interdependent World* eds. R. Bryant et al. (International Monetary Fund: Washington).

Collins, S. and Rodrik, D. (1991) 'Eastern Europe and the Soviet Union in the World Economy', Institute for International Economics, Policy Analyses, Washington (32) (May).

Commission on the Banking Crisis (1992) *Report by the Commission on the Banking Crisis*, Norwegian Official Reports NOR 1992: 30E, Oslo.

Commission of the European Communities (1977) *Report of the Study Group on the Role of Public Finance in European Integration* [MacDougall Report], Brussels, Commission of the European Communities.

Commission of the European Communities (1990) 'One Market, One Money: An Evaluation of the Potential Benefits and Costs of Forming an Economic and Monetary Union', *European Economy* (44) (October).

Commission of the European Communities (1992) 'Proposal for a Council Directive on Deposit Guarantee Schemes', COM(92) 188 final – SYN 415, Brussels (June).

Commission of the European Communities (1992a) 'Easier Cross-Border Payment, Breaking down the Barriers', Commission Working Document (March).

Commission of the European Communities (1992b) Directorate-General Financial Institutions and Company Law, 'Report of the Payment Systems Users Liaison Group to Sir Leon Brittan', 14 February.

Commission of the European Communities (1992c) Directorate-General Financial Institutions and Company Law, 'Report of the Payment Systems Technical Development Group to Sir Leon Brittan', 20 February.

Commission of the European Communities (1993) Directorate-General for Economic and Financial Affairs, 'Stable Money-Sound Finances', *European Economy* (53).

Commission of the European Communities (1993) 'Proposal for a Council Directive to Reinforce Prudential Supervision', COM(93) 363 final – SYN 468, Brussels (July).

Committee of Central Bank Governors Report (1990) *Draft Statute of the European System of Central Banks and the European Central Bank.* Committee of Governors of the Central Banks of the Member States, November. Brussels: European Commission (mimeograph).

Committee of Governors of the Central Banks of the Member States of the European Economic Community (1992) 'Issues of Common Concern to EC Central Banks in the Field of Payments', Report of the Ad Hoc Working Group on EC Payment Systems [the Padoa-Schioppa Group], September.

Committee of Governors of the Central Banks of the Member States of the European Economic Community (1993) *Annual Report 1992*, Basle (April).

Committee of London and Scottish Bankers, 1988 *Annual Abstract of Statistics* (LSB, London).

Committee for the Study of Economic and Monetary Union [Delors Report] (1989) *Report on Economic and Monetary Union in the European Community*, Luxembourg, Office for Official Publications of the European Communities.

Congdon, T. (1988) *The Debt Threat* (Oxford: Basil Blackwell).

Conseil National du Credit (1986) *Rapport Annuel* (Paris: Banque de France).

Conseil National du Credit (1987) *Rapport Annuel*, Edition provisoire (Paris: Banque de France).

Cosimano, T.F. and Jansen D.W. (1987) 'The relation between money growth variability and the variability of money about target', *Economic Letters*, 25: 355–8.

Council of the European Communities (1970) *Report to the Council and the Commission on the realisation by stages of Economic and Monetary Union in the Community* [Werner Report], Supplement to Bulletin II-1970 of the European Communities, Luxembourg, Office for Official Publications of the European Communities.

Council of the European Communities (1992) *Treaty on European Union* (commonly known as the Maastricht Treaty), Office for Official Publications of the European Communities, Luxembourg, signed on 7 February.

Council of the European Communities and Commission of the European Communities (1992) *Treaty on European Union* [Maastricht Treaty], Luxembourg, Office for Official Publications of the European Communities, including the Protocol on the Statute of the European System of Central Bank and of the European Central Bank, 148–71.

Courchene, T.J. (1992) 'Reflections on Canadian Federation: Are there Implications for European Economic and Monetary Union?', Paper presented at Conference on 'Public Finance and the Future of Europe', LSE, 21 (September) (mimeo).

Cover, J.P. and Keeler, J.P. (1987) 'Estimating money demand in log-first-difference form', *Southern Economic Journal*, 53(3): 751–67.

Cressy, R. (1993) 'Loan commitments and business starts: An empirical investigation on UK data', SME Centre, Warwick Business School, preliminary draft (February).

Crow, J.W. (1988) 'The work of Canadian monetary policy', paper presented at the Eric S. Hanson Lecture, University of Alberta (18 January) (mimeo) (Bank of Canada).

Cukierman, A. (1992) *Central Bank Strategy, Credibility and Independence: Theory and Evidence* (Cambridge, Mass.: MIT Press).

Cukierman, A., Edwards, S. and Tabellini, G. 1992 'Seigniorage and political instability', *The American Economic Review* 82(3): 537–555.

Cukierman, A., Webb, S.B. and Neyapti, B. (1992) 'Measuring the Independence of Central Banks and its Effects on Policy Outcomes', *The World Bank Economic Review*, 6: 353–98.

Currie, D. (1992) 'European Monetary Union: Institutional Structure and Economic Performance', *Economic Journal*, 102(411) (March): 248–64.

Cuthbertson, K. (1988a) 'The demand for M1: a forward-looking buffer stock model', *Oxford Economic Papers*, 40: 110–81.

Cuthbertson, K. (1988b) 'The encompassing implications of feedforward versus feedback mechanisms: a comment', mimeo, Newcastle University (July).

Cuthberston, K. (1993) 'Monetary Control: Theory, Empirics and Practicalities', in *Money and Banking: Issues for the Twenty-First Century*, ed. P. Arestis (London: Macmillan).

Cuthbertson, K. and Taylor, M.P. (1987) 'Buffer-stock money: an appraisal', Chapter 5. In *The Operation and Regulation of Financial Markets*, C. Goodhart, D. Currie and D. Llewellyn (eds.) (London: Macmillan).

Dale, R. (1984) 'Continental Illinois: the Lessons for Deposit Insurance', *The Banker* (July): 19–22.

Dale, R. (1992a) 'Basle after BCCI', in *Financial Regulation Report* (Financial Times Business Information: London, June): 1.

Dale, R. (1992b) 'Deposit Insurance Worries for Regulators', *Financial Regulation Report* (October): 1–2.

Dale, R. (1993) 'Do we need supervisors', in *Financial Regulation Report* (Financial Times Business Information: London, June): 1–2.

Darby, M. *et al.* (1987) 'Recent behavior of the velocity of money', *Contemporary Policy Issues*, 5 (January): 1–32.

Davidson, J.E.H. (1984) 'Money Disequilibrium: An Approach to Modelling Monetary Phenomena in the UK', London School of Economics (mimeo).

Davidson, J.E.H. (1987) 'Disequilibrium money: some further results with a monetary model of the UK', Chapter 6. In *The Operation and Regulation of Financial Markets*. C. Goodhart, D. Currie and D. Llewellyn (ed.), (London: Macmillan).

Davidson, J.E.H. and Ireland, J. (1987)'Buffer stock models of the monetary sector', *National Institute Economic Review* (121) (August): 67–71.

Davis, E.P. (1992) *Debt, Financial Fragility and Systematic Risk* (Oxford University Press).

Davis, R. (1990) 'Introduction to the issues of intermediate targets and indicators'. *FRBNY Quarterly Review* (Summer): 71–83.

De Grauwe, P. and Heens, H. (1993) 'Real Exchange Rate Variability in Monetary Unions', *Recherches Economiques de Louvain*, No. 1–2, Special Issue, 105–17.

De Grauwe, P. and Vanhaverbeke, W. (1993) 'Is Europe an optimum currency area?: Evidence from regional data', Chapter 5 in *Policy Issues in the Operation of Currency Unions*, eds. P. Masson and M.P. Taylor (Cambridge University Press).

de Largentaye, B.R. (1992) 'In the light of the disquieting experience of September and October 1992, can the ECU zone still be said to hold some lessons for the countries of the former Soviet Union?', *The European Finance Convention and Ecu week*, special issue, ed C. Cassuto, 122–24.

Delors Report (1989) *Report on Economic and Monetary Union in the European Community*. Committee for the Study of Economic and Monetary Union. Luxembourg: Office for Official Publications of the European Communities, (June).

De Nardis, S. and Micossi, S. (1991) 'Disinflation and re-inflation in Italy and the implications for transition to Monetary Union', *Banca Nazionale del Lavoro Quarterly Review* (177) (June): 165–96.

Deutsche Bundesbank (1980) 'Control of the Money Supply in the Federal Republic of Germany', Memorandum (14), to the Treasury and Civil Service Committee of the House of Commons on *Monetary Policy* 11, Minutes of Evidence: 290–7 (24 February): 163–11.

Deutsche Bundesbank (1985) 'The longer-term trend and control of the money stock', *Monthly Report*, 37(1) (January): 13–26.

Deutsche Bundesbank (1987) *The Deutsche Bundesbank: its monetary policy instruments and functions*. Special Series (7).

Deutsche Bundesbank (1988) 'Methodological notes on the monetary target variable "M3"', *Monthly Report* 40(3): 18–21.

De Vecchis, P. (1990) 'Moneta e carta valori. Profili generale e divitto privato', *Enciclopedia Giuridica Treccani*.

Dewald W.G. and Lai T.-H. (1987) 'Factors affecting monetary growth: ARIMA forecasts of monetary base and multiplier', *Kredit und Kapital*, 20(3): 303–16.

Dewatripont, M. and Tirole, J. (1993) 'The Prudential Regulation of Banks'. Paper presented at the CEPR/ESF Conference on 'Financial Regulation', Toulouse (June).

Diamond, D.W. (1984) 'Financial Intermediation and Delegated Monitoring', *Review of Economic Studies*, 51(3): 393–414.

Diamond, D.W. (1991) 'Monitoring and Reputation: The choice between bank loans and directly placed debt', *Journal of Political Economy*, 99(4) (August): 689–721.

Diamond, D.W. and Dybvig, P.H. (1983) 'Bank Runs, Deposit Insurance, and Liquidity', *Journal of Political Economy*, 91(3): 401–19.

Dickens, R.R. (1987) 'International comparison of asset market volatility: a further application of the ARCH model', *Bank of England Technical Paper* (15) (February).

Directorate-General for Economic and Financial Affairs, Commission of the European

Communities (1990) 'One market, one money; an evaluation of the potential benefits and costs of forming an economic and monetary union'. *European Economy*, 44 (October).

Dornbusch, R. (1988) 'The European Monetary System, the Dollar and the Yen', Chapter One in *The European Monetary System*, eds. F. Giavazzi, S. Micossi and M. Miller (Cambridge University Press).

Dornbusch, R. (1990) 'Two-track EMU, now!' in *Britain and EMU* (London: Centre for Economic Performance in association with the Financial Markets Group, London School of Economics): 103–12.

Dotsey, M. (1986) 'Japanese monetary policy: a comparative analysis', *Bank of Japan Monetary and Economic Studies*, 4(2): 105–27.

Dotsey, M. (1987) 'The Australian money market and the operations of the Reserve Bank of Australia: a comparative analysis', *Federal Reserve Bank of Richmond Economic Review* (September/October): 19–31.

Dotsey, M. (1988) 'The demand for currency in the United States', *Journal of Money, Credit and Banking*, 20(1): 22–40.

Dow, C. and Saville I. (1988) *A Critique of Monetary Policy* (Oxford: Clarendon Press).

Dowd, K. (1989) *The State and the Monetary System* (Hemel Hempstead: Philip Allan and New York: St Martin's Press).

Dowd, K. (1992) The mechanics of indirect convertibility, Research paper 92/9 (The centre for research in economic development and international trade (CREDIT), Department of Economics, University of Nottingham, Nottingham).

Dowd, K. (1994) 'Competitive banking, bankers' clubs and bank regulation', *Journal of Money, Credit and Banking*, 26(2):289–308.

Dowd, K. and Lewis, M.K. (1992) *Current Issues in Financial and Monetary Economics* (London: Macmillan).

Doyle, M.F. (1989) 'Regional Policy and European Economic Integration', in Committee for the Study of Economic and Monetary Union, *Report on Economic and Monetary Union in the European Community*, Collection of Papers, Luxembourg: Office for Official Publications of the EC: 69–80.

Drayson, S.J. (1985) 'The housing finance market: recent growth in perspective', *Bank of England Quarterly Bulletin*, 25(1): 80–91.

Drèze, J. and Bean C. (1990) 'European Unemployment: Lessons from a Multicountry Econometric Study', *Scandinavian Journal of Economics*, 92(2): 135–165.

Driffill, J. (1988) 'Macroeconomic policy games with incomplete information', *European Economic Review*, 32: 533–41.

Duck, N.W. and Sheppard, D.K. (1978) 'A proposal for the control of the UK money supply', *Economic Journal*, 88(349): 1–17.

Dudler, H.-J. (1980a) 'Money-market management, supply of bank reserves and control of central-bank money stock', in *The Monetary Base Approach to Monetary Control*, BIS, Basle (September).

Dudler, H.-J. (1980b) Evidence to Treasury and Civil Service Committee on *Monetary Policy*, 11, Minutes of Evidence (10 November): 297–307.

Dudler, H.-J. (1984) *Geldpolitik und ihre Theoretischen Grundlagen* (Frankfurt am Main: Fritz Knapp Verlag).

Dudler, H.-J. (1986) 'Geldmengenpolitik und Finanzinnovationen', *Kredit und Kapital*, Heft 4: 472–95.

Dudler, H.-J. (1987) 'Financial innovation in Germany', Chapter 7 in *Changing Money*, de Cecco (ed.) (Oxford: Basil Blackwell).

Dutkowsky, D.H. and Foote, W.G. (1988) 'The demand for money: a rational expectations approach', *Review of Economics and Statistics* 70(1): 83–92.

Dutton, J. (1984) 'The Bank of England and the Rules of the Game under the

International Gold Standard: New Evidence', Chapter 3 in *A Retrospective on the Classical Gold Standard*, M.D. Bordo and A.J. Schwartz (eds) (University of Chicago Press: Chicago).

Dwyer, G.P. Jr. (1985) 'Federal Deficits, Interest Rates and Monetary Policy', *Journal of Money, Credit and Banking*, 17(4), part 2: 655–81.

Easton, W.W. (1985) 'The importance of interest rates in five macroeconomic models', *Bank of England Discussion Papers* (24) (October).

Edison, H.J., Miller, M.H. and Williamson, J. (1987) 'On evaluating and extending the target zone proposal', *Journal of Policy Modelling*, 9(1): 199–224.

Eichengreen, B. (1990) 'Costs and Benefits of European Monetary Unification', CEPR Working Paper (453) (September).

Eichengreen, B. (1991) 'Is Europe an Optimum Currency Area?', in Borner, S. and Grubel, H. (eds.), *The European Community after 1992: Perspectives from the Outside* (London: Macmillan): 138–61.

Eichengreen, B. (1992a) '*Golden Fetters: The Gold Standard and the Great Depression, 1919–1939* (New York, Oxford University Press).

Eichengreen, B. (1992b) 'Should the Maastricht Treaty be Saved?', *Princeton Studies in International Finance* (74), December.

Eichengreen, B. (1993) 'Labor markets and European monetary integration', Chapter 6 in *Policy issues in the operation of currency unions*, P. Masson and M.P. Taylor (eds) (Cambridge University Press).

Engle, R.F. and Granger, C.W.J. (1987) 'Cointegration and error correction: representation, estimation and testing', *Econometrica* 55(2): 251–76.

Enzler, J.J. and Johnson, L. (1981) 'Cycles resulting from money stock targeting', in *New Monetary Control Procedures*, Federal Reserve Staff Study, 1, Board of Governors of the Federal Reserve System: (Washington, DC)

Estey, W.Z. (1986) *Report of the Inquiry into the Collapse of the CCB and Northland Bank*, Ottawa (Canada): Ministry of Supply and Services (August).

Evans, P. (1981) 'Why have interest rates been so volatile?', *Federal Reserve Bank of San Francisco Economic Review* (Summer): 7–20.

Evans, P. (1984) 'The effects on output of money growth and interest rate volatility in the United States', *Journal of Political Economy* 92(2): 204–20.

Fair, D.E. (1986) *Shifting Frontiers in Financial Markets* (Dordrecht, Netherlands: Martinus Nijhoff)

Fama, E. (1980) 'Banking in the theory of finance', *Journal of Monetary Economics*, 6(1): 39–57.

Fama, E. (1983) 'Financial intermediation and price level control', *Journal of Monetary Economics* 12(1): 7–28.

Fay, S. (1987) *Portrait of an Old Lady* (Harmondsworth: Viking).

Federal Reserve Bank of New York (1990) *Intermediate Targets and Indicators for Monetary Policy: A Critical Survey* (New York: FRBNY).

Federal Reserve Bank of New York (1993) Colloquium on 'The Role of the Credit Crunch in the Recent Recession' (12 February).

Federal Reserve Staff Studies (1981) *New Monetary Control Procedures*, 2 vols (Washington: Board of Governors of the Federal Reserve System).

Feldstein, M. (1988) 'Rethinking international economic coordination', *Oxford Economic Papers*, 40(2): 205–19.

Feldstein, M. (1992) 'The case against EMU', *The Economist*, 13 June.

Fetter, F.W. (1965) *Development of British Monetary Orthodoxy* (Cambridge, Mass.: Harvard University Press).

Fforde, J.S. (1983) 'Setting monetary objectives', in *Central Bank Views on Monetary Targetting*. P. Meek (ed.) Federal Reserve Bank of New York, 1983; also reprinted in (Bank of England) *The Development and Operation of Monetary Policy*.

(Oxford: Clarendon Press).

Filc, W., Hubl, L. and Pohl, R. (eds.), (1988)   *Herausforderungen der Wirtschafts-politik* (Berlin: Duncker and Humblot).

Fildes, C. (1993)   'Scenes of Financial Horror Need a Happy Ending', *The Daily Telegraph* (15) February.

Financial Secretary of H.M. Treasury, *Financial Statement and Budget Report*. Otherwise known as FSBR or Budget Redbook which accompanies present UK Budgets. London: HMSO (annually).

Fingleton, J. and Schoenmaker, D. (1992)   eds. *The Internationalisation of Capital Markets and the Regulatory Response* (London: Graham and Trotman).

Fischer, S. (1982)   'Seigniorage and the Case for a National Money', *Journal of Political Economy*, 90(21) (April): 295–313.

Fischer, S. (1988)   'Recent developments in macroeconomics', *Economic Journal*, 98(391): 294–339.

Fisher, I. (1906)   *Nature of Capital and Income* (New York: The Macmillan Company).

Fisher, I. (1911)   *The Purchasing Power of Money* (New York: The Macmillan Company).

Fisher, I. (1926)   *The purchasing power of money*, 2nd edn (Macmillan, New York).

Fisher, I. (1932)   *Booms and Depressions* (New York: Adelphi).

Flux, A.W. (1911)   'The Swedish Banking System', from *Banking in Sweden and Switzerland*, National Monetary Commission, vol. XVII (Government Printing Office: Washington).

Folkerts-Landau, D. (1990)   *Systemic Financial Risk in Payment Systems* (Washington, D.C.: International Monetary Fund, June).

Folkerts-Landau, D. and Garber, P.M. (1992)   'The ECB: A Bank or A Monetary Policy Rule', in: *Establishing a Central Bank: Issues in Europe and Lessons from the US*, M.B. Canzoneri, V. Grilli and P.R. Masson (eds.) (Cambridge: Cambridge University Press): 86–110.

Folkerts-Landau, D., Garber, P.M. and Weisbrod S.R. (1991)   'Supervision and Regulation of Financial Markets in the New Financial Environment', in *Financial Regulation and Monetary Arrangements after 1992*, C. Wihlborg, M. Fratianni and T.D. Willett (eds.) (Amsterdam: Elsevier): 43–57.

Folkerts-Landau, D., Garber, P. and Lane, T. (1993)   'Payment System Reform in Formerly Centrally-Planned Economics' Paper presented at IMF and World Bank Conference on 'Building Sound Finance in Emerging Market Economies', Washington (June).

Foot, M.D.K.W., Goodhart, C.A.E. and Hotson, A.C. (1979)   'Monetary Base Control', *Bank of England Quarterly Bulletin*, 19(2): 149–59, June, reproduced in Chapter 6 in *Development and Operation of Monetary Policy, 1960–1983*, ed. Bank of England (Oxford: Clarendon Press, 1984).

Foot, M.D.K.W. (1981)   'Monetary targets: their nature and record in the major economies', in *Monetary Targets*, B. Griffiths and G.E. Wood (eds.) (London: Macmillan).

Forte, F. (1977)   'Principles for the assignment of public economic functions in a setting of multi-layer government', in 'Report of the Study Group on the Role of Public Finance in European Integration', Vol. II, Office for Official Publications of the EC (Luxembourg).

Francke, H.-H. and Hudson, M. (1984)   *Banking and Finance in West Germany* (New York: St Martin's Press).

Fraser, P. and MacDonald R. (1993)   'European excess stock returns and capital market integration: an empirical perspective', Chapter 7 in *Policy Issues in the Operation of Currency Unions*, P. Masson and M.P. Taylor (eds.) (Cambridge University Press).

Fratianni, M. and Hagen von J. (1990) 'Public Choice Aspects of European Monetary Unification', *Cato Journal*, 10(2) (Fall): 389–411.

Fratianni, M., Hagen von J. and Waller, C. (1992) 'The Maastricht Way to EMU', Princeton Essays in International Finance (187): (June).

Freedman, C. (1983) 'Financial innovation in Canada: causes and consequences', *American Economic Review*, 73(2): 101–6.

Frenkel, J.A. and Goldstein, M. (1988) 'Exchange rate volatility and misalignment: evaluating some proposals for reform', paper presented at Federal Reserve Bank of Kansas City Conference on Financial Market Volatility', 17–9 August.

Frenkel, W.G. (1992) 'Reforming the Banking Industry in the CIS' *Journal of International Banking Law*, 7, Issue 9 (September): 365–72.

Freris, A. (1991) 'The exchange fund and monetary policy', Ch. 1 in Y.C. Jao, (ed.), *Monetary management in Hong Kong: The changing role of the exchange fund*, (Chartered Institute of Bankers, Hong Kong Centre).

Frey, B. and Schneider F. (1981) 'Central bank behavior: a positive empirical analysis', *Journal of Monetary Economics*, 7: 291–316.

Friedman, B.M. (1980a) 'Debt and economic activity in the United States', In *The Changing Roles of Debt and Equity in Financing U.S. Capital Formation*. (ed.) B.M. Friedman (Chicago: University of Chicago Press) 91–110.

Friedman, B.M. (1980b) 'Postwar changes in the American financial markets', In *The American Economy in Transition*, M. Feldstein (ed.) (Chicago: University of Chicago Press): 9–78.

Friedman, B.M. (1982) 'Federal Reserve policy, interest rate volatility, and the U.S. capital raising mechanism', *Journal of Money, Credit and Banking*. 14(4), part 2: 721–45.

Friedman, B.M. (1988a) 'Monetary policy without quantity variables', *American Economic Review Proceedings*, 78(2): 440–5.

Friedman, B.M. (1988b) 'Targets and instruments of monetary policy', National Bureau of Economic Research Working Paper, (2668) (July).

Friedman, M. (1956) 'The quantity theory of money – a restatement', In *Studies in the Quantity Theory of Money* M. Friedman (ed.) (Chicago: University of Chicago Press).

Friedman, M. (1959) *A program for monetary stability* (Fordham University Press, New York).

Friedman, M. (1968) 'The Role of Monetary Policy', *American Economic Review*, 58(1) (March).

Friedman, M. (1970) 'A theoretical framework for monetary analysis', *Journal of Political Economy*, 78 (March/April): 193–228.

Friedman, M. (1971) 'A monetary theory of nominal income', *Journal of Political Economy*, 79 (March/April): 323–37.

Friedman, M. (1980) Memorandum to Treasury and Civil Service Committee on *Monetary Policy*, Session 1980–81, H.C. (1979–80) 720, Memorandum 9 (London: HMSO).

Friedman, M. (1982) 'Monetary theory: policy and practice', *Journal of Money, Credit and Banking*, 14(1): 98–118.

Friedman, M. (1984a) 'Monetary policy of the 1980s', Chapter 2. In *To Promote Prosperity*, J. Moore (ed.) (Stanford: Hoover Institute Press).

Friedman, M. (1984b) 'Lessons from the 1979–82 monetary policy experiment', *American Economic Review*, 74(2): 397–400.

Friedman, M. and Meiselman, D.I. (1964) 'The Relative Stability of Monetary Velocity and the Investment Multiplier in the United States, 1897–1958', Research Study (2) in *Stabilization Policies: Commission on Money and Credit* (Englewood Cliffs, NJ: Prentice-Hall).

Friedman, M. and Schwartz, A.J. (1963) *A Monetary History of the United States 1867–1960* (Princeton, Princeton University Press).

Friedman, M. and Schwartz, A.J. (1969) 'Money and Business Cycles', in *The Optimum Quantity of Money and Other Essays* (New York: Macmillan & Co Ltd): 189–235.

Friedman, M. and Schwartz, A.J. (1982) *Monetary Trends in the United States and the United Kingdom.* (Chicago: University of Chicago Press).

Fries, S.M. and Lane, T.D. (1993) 'Transforming the Financial Structure in Emerging Market Economies', Paper presented at the IMF and World Bank Conference on 'Building Sound Finance in Emerging Market Economies', Washington (June).

Fry, M.J. (1988) *Money, Interest, and Banking in Economic Development* (Baltimore: Johns Hopkins University Press).

Fuhrer, J. and Moore, G. (1992) 'Monetary policy rules and the indicator properties of asset prices', *Journal of Monetary Economics* 29(2): 303–36.

Fukui, T. (1986) 'Recent developments of the short-term money market in Japan and changes in monetary control techniques and procedures by the Bank of Japan', Bank of Japan, Research and Statistics Department, Special Paper, (130) (January).

Galbraith, J.A. and Rymes, T.K. (1992) 'Desired bank reserves in the absence of legal reserve requirements', Draft paper prepared for presentation at the CEA 1992 meetings, May.

Gale, D. (1982) *Money: In Equilibrium* (Cambridge: Cambridge University Press).

Gale, D. (1983) *Money: In Disequilibrium* (Cambridge: Cambridge University Press).

Gale, D. and Hellwig, M. (1985) 'Incentive-compatible debt contracts: the one-period problem', *The Review of Economic Studies*, 52(4): 647–64.

Gardener, E.P.M. (1986) *UK Banking Supervision; Evolution, Practice and Issues* (London: Allen & Unwin).

Gardener, E.P.M. (1991) 'International Bank Regulation and Capital Adequacy: Perspectives, Developments and Issues', in: *Banking Regulation and Supervision in the 1990s*, J.J. Norton (ed.) (London: Lloyd's of London Press): 97–120.

Geisler, K.-D. (1986) 'Sur "Kausalitat". von Geldmenge und Sozialprodukt', *Kredit und Kapital*, Heft 3, 325–39.

Germany, J.D. and Morton, J.E. (1985) 'Financial innovation and deregulation in foreign industrial countries', *Federal Reserve Bulletin*, 71(10): 743–53.

Gerschenkron, A. (1962) *Economic Backwardness in Historical Perspective* (Cambridge, Mass.: Harvard University Press.).

Gertler, M. (1988) 'Financial structure and aggregate economic activity: an overview', NBER Working Paper, (2559) (April), subsequently published in the *Journal of Money, Credit and Banking*, 20(3), part 2: (August): 559–89.

Gertler, M. and Hubbard, G.R. (1988) 'Financial factors and business fluctuations', paper presented at Federal Reserve Bank of Kansas City Conference on Financial Volatility, Jackson Hole, Wyoming, 17–9 August.

Getty, G. (1991) 'Equity dollars', Manuscript, Dec.

Getty, G. (1992) 'A world without banks', Draft manuscript, April.

Giavazzi, F. (1989) 'The Exchange Rate Question in Europe', in *Macroeconomic Policies in an Interdependent World*, eds R. Bryant et al. (International Monetary Fund: Washington).

Giavazzi, F. and Giovannini, A. (1989) *Limiting Exchange Rate Flexibility* (Cambridge, MA: MIT Press).

Giavazzi, F., Micossi S. and Miller M. (1988) *The European Monetary System* (Cambridge University Press).

Giersch, H., et al. (1992) 'Manifesto against EMU', *Frankfurter Algemeine Zeitung* 11 June.

Giovannini, A. (1991) 'The Currency Reform as the Last Stage of Economic and

Monetary Union: Some Policy Questions', CEPR Discussion Paper (591) (October).

Giovannini, A. (1992) 'Central Banking in a Monetary Union: Reflections on the Proposed Statute of the European Central Bank', *CEPR Occasional Papers* (9).

Giovannini, A. (1992a) 'Central Banking in a Monetary Union: Reflections on the Proposed Statute of the European Central Bank', paper prepared for Carnegie-Rochester Conference, 24–25 April.

Giovannini, A. (1992b) 'Desirable EMU', *The Economist*, 11–17 July, 6.

Giovannini, A. (1993) 'Comments on Goodhart and Bryant', Discussants' comments prepared for the Conference on 'The International Monetary System: What we know and need to know', Princeton University, mimeo, 16 April.

Glasner, D. (1989) *Free Banking and Monetary Reform* (Cambridge: Cambridge University Press).

Goldfeld, S.M. (1973) 'The demand for money revisited', *Brookings Papers on Economic Activity*, (13): 577–638.

Goldfeld, S.M. (1976) 'The case of the missing money', *Brookings Papers on Economic Activity*, (3): 683–730.

Goodfriend, M. (1983) 'Discount window borrowing, monetary policy, and the post-6 October 1979. Federal Reserve operating procedure', *Journal of Monetary Economics*, 12: 343–56.

Goodfriend, M. (1985) 'Reinterpreting money demand regressions', in *Understanding Monetary Regimes*, K. Brunner and A.H. Meltzer (eds.) Carnegie-Rochester Conference Series on Public Policy, 22 (Amsterdam: North-Holland).

Goodfriend, M. and King, R.G. (1988) 'Financial deregulation, monetary policy, and central banking', *Federal Reserve Bank of Richmond Economic Review*, 74(3) (May/June): 3–22.

Goodhart, C.A.E. (1969) *The New York Money Market and the Finance of Trade, 1900–1913* (Cambridge, Mass: Harvard University Press).

Goodhart, C.A.E. (1972) *The Business of Banking, 1891–1914* (London: Weidenfeld and Nicolson).

Goodhart, C.A.E. (1984) *Monetary Theory and Practice*. (London: Macmillan).

Goodhart, C.A.E. (1984) 'Disequilibrium Money – A Note', Chapter 10, 254–276, in *Monetary Theory and Practice* (Macmillan: London).

Goodhart, C.A.E. (1985) *The Evolution of Central Banks* (LSE, STICERD monograph), subsequently published under the same title by MIT Press, Cambridge, Mass., 1988.

Goodhart, C.A.E. (1986) How can non-interest-bearing assets co-exist with safe interest bearing assets?, *British Review of Economic Issues* 8(19) (Autumn): 1–12.

Goodhart, C.A.E. (1987) 'Why do Banks Need a Central Bank?', *Oxford Economic Papers* 39, 75–89. (Chapter 1 in this volume.)

Goodhart, C.A.E. (1988) *The Evolution of Central Banks* (Cambridge, MA:, MIT Press).

Goodhart, C.A.E. (1989) 'The Conduct of Monetary Policy'. *Economic Journal*, 99(396) (June): 293–346. Chapter 6 in this volume.

Goodhart, C.A.E. (1990) 'Are Central Banks Necessary?' in *Unregulated Banking: Chaos or Order?* in F. Capie and G.E. Wood (eds) (London, Macmillan).

Goodhart, C.A.E. (1992a) 'Can We Improve the Structure of Financial Systems?', Schumpeter Lecture at the European Economic Association, 7th Annual Congress, 30 August (*European Economic Review*, 37(2/3) (April 1993): 269–91; Chapter 2 in this volume).

Goodhart, C.A.E. (ed.) (1992b) *EMU and ESCB after Maastricht* (Financial Markets Group, LSE: London).

Goodhart, C.A.E. (1992) 'The ESCB after Maastricht', Chapter 1.8 in *EMU and ESCB after Maastricht*, ed. C. Goodhart (Financial Markets Group, LSE: London).

Goodhart, C.A.E. (1993) 'The External Dimension of EMU' *Recherches Economique de Louvain*, 59(1–2), Special Issue, 65–80, also Chapter 3.2 in *EMU and ESCB after Maastricht*, ed. C. Goodhart (London: LSE, Financial Markets Group, 1992).

Goodhart, C.A.E. (1994), 'Central Bank Independence', *Journal of International and Comparative Economics* 3: 1–12. Chapter 4 in this volume.

Goodhart, C.A.E. and Crockett. A.D. (1970) 'The importance of money', *Bank of England Quarterly Bulletin*, 10(2): 159–98: reprinted in *Monetary Theory and Practice* (Macmillan: London, 1984): 21–66.

Goodhart, C.A.E. and Schoenmaker, D. (1993) 'Institutional separation between supervisory and monetary agencies', Financial Markets Group, LSE, Special Paper (52) (April).

Goodhart, C.A.E. and Smith, S. (1993) 'Stabilisation', in 'The Economics of Community Public Finance: Reports and Studies', *European Economy* (5): 417–55.

Goodman, L.S. and Shaffer, S. (1983) 'The Economics of Deposit Insurance: A Critical Evaluation of Proposed Reforms', *Federal Reserve Bank of New York Research Paper (8308)* (August).

Gordon, R.J. (1984) 'The short run demand for money: a reconsideration', *Journal of Money, Credit and Banking*, 16, part 1: 403–34.

Gorton, G. and Kahn J. (1993) 'The design of bank loan contracts, collateral, and renegotiation', paper presented at CEPR/ESF Conference on 'Financial Regulation', Toulouse (June).

Gower, J. (1984) *Review of Investor Protection*, (London: Her Majesty's Stationary Office, Cmnd 9125).

Granger, C., W.J. (1981) 'Some properties of time series data and their use in econometric model specification', *Journal of Econometrics*, 16(1).

Greenfield, R.L. and Yeager, L.B. (1983) 'A *laissez-faire* approach to monetary stability', *Journal of Money, Credit and Banking*, 15(3) (August).

Greenfield, R.L. and Yeager, L.B. (1986) 'Money and credit confused: an appraisal of economic doctrine and Federal Reserve procedure', *Southern Economic Journal*, 53(2): 364–73.

Greenfield, R.L. and Yeager, L.B. (1989) 'Can monetary disequilibrium be eliminated?' *Cato Journal*, 9, Fall, 405–21.

Greenspan, A. (1988) 'Statement before the US Senate Committee on Banking, Housing and Urban Affairs', Press Release, Federal Reserve Board, (13 July).

Greenwald, B.C. and Stiglitz, J.E. (1988) 'Imperfect information, finance constraints, and business fluctuations' and 'Money, imperfect information, and economic fluctuations', Chapters 7 and 8 in *Finance Constraints, Expectations, and Macroeconomics*, M. Kohn and S.-C. Tsiang (eds.) (Oxford: Clarendon Press).

Greider, W. (1988) *Secrets of the Temple.* (New York: Simon and Schuster).

Grice, J., Bennett, A. and Cumming, N. (1981) 'The demand for £M3 and other aggregates in the United Kingdom', *Treasury Working Paper* (20) (August).

Grice, J., Bennett, A. and Cumming, N. (1984) 'Wealth and the demand for £M3 in the United Kingdom, 1963–1978', *Manchester School*, 52(3): 239–71.

Griffiths, M. (1992) 'Monetary union in Europe: Lessons from the nineteenth century – an assessment of the Latin Monetary Union', unpublished.

Griffiths, B. and Wood, G.E. (1981) 'Introduction' in *Monetary Targets*, same eds (London: Macmillan).

Grilli, V. (1988) 'Exchange rates and seignorage', Unpublished manuscript.

Grilli, V. (1989) 'Seigniorage in Europe', Chapter 3 in *A European Central Bank? Perspectives on Monetary Unification after Ten Years of the EMS*, eds. M. de Cecco and A. Giovannini (Cambridge University Press).

Grilli, V., Masciandaro, D. and Tabellini G. (1991) 'Political and Monetary Institutions and Public Financial Policies in the Industrial Countries', *Economic*

Policy, 13: 341–92.

Grossman, S. and Hart, O. (1982) 'Corporate Financial Structure and Managerial Incentives' in *The Economics of Information and Uncertainty*, ed. J.J. McCall (University of Chicago Press).

Gros, D. (1991) 'A Soviet Payments Union?', Centre for European Policy Studies, mimeo, Brussels (October).

Gros, D. (1993) 'Costs and benefits of economic and monetary union: application to the former Soviet Union', Chapter 2 in *Policy Issues in the Operation of Currency Unions*, P. Masson and M.P. Taylor (eds) (Cambridge University Press).

Gros, D. and Thygesen, N. (1992) *European Monetary Integration: From the European Monetary System to European Monetary Union* (London: Longmans).

Group of Thirty (1989) 'Clearance and Settlement Systems in the World's Securities Markets' (New York & London) March.

Guttentag, J.M. and Herring, R. (1983) 'The Lender-of-Last-Resort Function in an International Context', *Princeton Studies in International Finance* (151).

Guttentag, J. and Herring, R. (1987) 'Emergency Liquidity Assistance for International Banks', in: *Threats to International Financial Stability*, R. Portes and A.K. Swoboda (eds.) (Cambridge: Cambridge University Press): 150–86.

Gwilliam, D.R. (1992) 'The auditor and the law: some economic and moral issues', Chapter 11 in *Accounting and the Law*, eds. M. Bromwich and A. Hopwood (Prentice-Hall and ICAEW): 191–204.

Hacche, G. (1974) 'The demand for money in the United Kingdom: experience since 1971'. *Bank of England Quarterly Bulletin*, 14(3): 284–305.

Hafer, R.W. (1985) 'Comment on "Money Demand Predictability"', *Journal of Money, Credit, and Banking*, 17(4), part 2: 642–6.

Hafer, R.W. and Hein, S.E. (1984) 'Financial innovations and the interest elasticity of money demand: some historical evidence', *Journal of Money, Credit and Banking*, 16(2): 247–52.

Hafer, R.W. and Kool, C.J.M. (1983) 'Forecasting the money multiplier: implications for money stock control and economic activity', *Federal Reserve Bank of St Louis Review* (October): 22–33.

Hall, R.E. (1982) 'A Review of Monetary Trends in the United States and the United Kingdom from the Perspective of New Developments in Monetary Economics', *Journal of Economic Literature*, 20 (December): 1552–56.

Hall, R.E. (1983) 'Optimal fiduciary monetary system', *Journal of Monetary Economics* 12(1): 33–50.

Hall, R.E. (1986) 'Optimal monetary institutions and policy', in C.D. Campbell and W.R. Dougan, eds., *Alternative monetary regimes*, Ch. 6 (The Johns Hopkins University Press, Baltimore, MD).

Hall, S. and Henry, B. (1987) 'Wage models', *National Institute Economic Review* (119) (February).

Hall, S. and Wilcox, J. (1988) 'The long run determination of the UK monetary aggregates', Bank of England (mimeo) (April).

Hamada, K. and Hayashi, F. (1985) 'Monetary policy in postwar Japan', in *Monetary Policy in Our Times* A. Ando, H. Eguchi, R. Farmer and Y. Suzuki (eds.) (Cambridge, Mass.: MIT Press).

Hamada, K. (1974) 'Alternative Exchange Rate Systems and the Interdependence of Monetary Policies', in R.Z. Aliber (ed.) *National Monetary Policies and the International Financial System* (Chicago: University of Chicago Press).

Hamburger, M.J. (1983) 'Recent velocity behavior, the demand for money and monetary policy', Conference on Monetary Targetting and Velocity (Federal Reserve Bank of San Francisco).

Hamilton, J. (1987) 'Monetary factors in the Great Depression', *Journal of Monetary*

Economics, 19(2): 145–70.

Hanke, S.H. and Schuler, K. (1990), 'Keynes and currency reform: some lessons for Eastern Europe', *Journal of Economic Growth*, 4(2): 10–16.

Hanke, S.H. and Schuler, K. (1991) 'Currency Boards for Eastern Europe', *The Heritage Lectures*, 355 (Washington: The Heritage Foundation).

Hanke, S.H., Jonung L. and Schuler, K. (1993) *Russian currency and finance: A currency board approach to its reform* (London and New York: Routledge).

Hansson, A.H. (1993) 'The Trouble with the Ruble: Monetary Reform in the Former Soviet Union', Chapter 10 in *Changing the Economic System in Russia*, A. Åslund and R. Layard (eds.) (London: Pinter Publishers Ltd): 163–82.

Harris, A. (1992) 'A New Twist to Ease the Slump', *Financial Times*, Monday (20 July): 17.

Hart, O. (1993) 'Theories of Optimal Capital Structure: A Managerial Discretion Perspective', in *The Deal Decade: What Takeovers and Leveraged Buyouts Mean for Corporate Governance*, ed. Margaret Blair (The Brookings Institute): 15–53.

Hart, O. and Moore, J. (1993) 'Debt and Seniority: An Analysis of the Role of Hard Claims in Constraining Management', LSE, Working Paper (May).

Havrilesky, T. (1988) 'Monetary policy signalling from the administration to the Federal Reserve', *Journal of Money, Credit and Banking*, 20(1): 83–101.

Havrylyshyn, O. and Williamson, J. (1991) 'From Soviet disUnion to Eastern Economic Community', Institute for International Economics, *Policy Analyses in International Economics* (35) (October).

Hay, M. and Peacock, A. (1992) presenters of *Social Policies in the Transition to a Market Economy*, Report of a Mission to the Russian Federation organized by the United Nations: January 1992 (The David Hume Institute and the United Nations).

Hayek, F.A. (1976) *Denationalisation of money*, Hobart special paper, no. 70 (London: Institute of Economic Affairs).

Hayek, F.A. (1984) The future unit of value, in: P. Salin, ed., *Currency competition and monetary union*, Ch. 1 (Martinus Nijhoff, The Hague: Netherlands).

Healy, N.M. (1987) 'The UK 1979–82 "Monetarist Experiment": why economists will still disagree', *Banca Nazionale del Lavoro Quarterly Review* (163) (December): 471–99.

Heller, H.R. (1988) 'Implementing Monetary Policy', *Federal Reserve Bulletin*, 74(7): 419–29.

Heller, H.R. (1991) 'Prudential Supervision and Monetary Policy', in J.A. Frenkel and M. Goldstein (eds.), *International Financial Policy: Essays in Honor of Jacques J. Polak* (Washington, DC: IMF): 269–81.

Hendry, D.F. (1979) 'Predictive failure and econometric modelling in macroeconomics: the transactions demand for money', Chapter 9 in *Economic Modelling* P. Ormerod (ed.) (London: Heinemann).

Hendry, D.F. (1985) 'Monetary economic myth and econometric reality', *Oxford Review of Economic Policy*, 1(1): 72–84.

Hendry, D.F. (1988) 'The encompassing implications of feedback versus feedforward mechanisms in econometrics', *Oxford Economic Papers*, 40: 132–49.

Hendry, D.F. and Ericsson, N.R. (1983) 'Assertion without empirical basis: an econometric appraisal of "Monetary Trends in . . . the United Kingdom" by Milton Friedman and Anna Schwartz', Bank of England Panel of Academic Consultants, Panel Paper, (22) (October).

Hendry, D.F. and Neale, A.J. (1988) 'Interpreting long-run equilibrium solutions in conventional macro models: a comment', *Economic Journal*, 98(392): 808–17.

Hester, D.D. (1981) 'Innovations and monetary control', *Brookings Papers on Economic Activity*, (1): 141–89.

Hirsch, F. (1977) 'The Bagehot Problem', *Manchester School* (September): 241–57.

Hodgman, D.R. (1983) *The Political Economy of Monetary Policy: National and International Aspects.* Federal Reserve Bank of Boston.

Hoffman, J. and Keating, G. (1990) *The European System of Central Banks* (London: Credit Suisse First Boston, Economics Booklet).

Hogan, L.I. (1986) 'A comparison of alternative exchange rate forecasting models', *Economic Record*, 62(177): 215–23.

Holden, K., Peel, D. and Thompson, J. (1985) *Expectations: Theory and Evidence*, (London: Macmillan).

Holmans, A. (1990) 'House Prices: Changes through time at the National and Sub-National Level', UK Government Economic Service Working Paper (110).

Holtfrerich, C.-L. (1988) 'The monetary unification process in nineteenth-century Germany, relevance and lessons for Europe today', Chapter 8 in *A European Central Bank*, M. de Cecco and A. Giovannini (eds) (Cambridge University Press).

Holtfrerich, C.-L. (1992) 'Did Monetary Unification Precede or Follow Political Unification of German in the Nineteenth Century?' paper presented at the European Economic Association Conference, Dublin (August).

Holtham, G., Keating, G. and Spencer, P. (1988) 'Developments in the demand for liquid assets in Germany and the UK', paper presented at the Conference on Monetary Aggregates and Financial Sector Behavior in Interdependent Economies, Board or Governors of the Federal Reserve System (Washington, DC) 26–7 (May).

Hoover, K. and Sheffrin, S. (eds) (1995) *Monetarism and the Methodology of Economics* (Cheltenham, Glos: Edward Elgar).

Horn, G.A. and Zwiener, R. (1992) 'Wage Regimes in a United Europe: A Simulation Study on QUEST', Chapter 4 in *Macroeconomic Policy Coordination in Europe*, R. Barrell and J. Whitley (eds) (London: Sage Publications): 83–101.

Horvitz, P. (1983) 'The Case Against Risk-Related Deposit Insurance Premiums', *Housing Finance Review* (July). Reprinted as Chapter 16 in E.P.M. Gardener (ed.) *UK Banking Supervision: Evolution, Practice and Issues* (London: George Allen & Unwin, 1986).

Hoshi, T., Kashyap, A. and Scharfstein, D. (1990) 'Bank monitoring and investment: Evidence from the changing structure of Japanese corporate banking relationship' in *Asymmetric Information, Corporate Finance and Investment*, ed. R. Glenn Hubbard (University of Chicago Press).

Hoskins, W.L. (1985) 'Foreign experiences with monetary targeting: a practitioner's perspective', *Contemporary Policy Issues*, 111: 71–83.

House of Commons (1985) *Building Societies Bill*, (HMSO: London).

Howe, G. (1979) 'Budget Statement', *Hansard*, 968, (London: HMSO): 241–4.

Howe, G. (1981) 'The fight against inflation', The Third Mais Lecture, City University Business School pamphlet (May).

Hughes-Hallett, A. and Vines, D. (1993) 'On the Possible Costs of European Monetary Union', *Manchester School Journal*, 61 (March): 35–64.

Humphrey, T.M. (1975) 'The Classical Concept of the Lender of Last Resort', *Federal Reserve Bank of Richmond Economic Review*, 61 (January/February): 2–9.

Humphrey, T.M. and Keleher, R.E. (1984) 'The Lender of Last Resort: A Historical Perspective', *Cato Journal*, 4(1) (Spring/Summer): 275–318.

Ickes, B.W. and Ryterman, R. (1992) 'The Interenterprise Arrears Crisis in Russia', *Post-Soviet Affairs*, 8(4): 331–61.

Ickes, B.W. and Ryterman, R. (1993) 'Roadblock to Economic Reform: Inter-Enterprise Debt and the Transition to Markets', Paper presented at IMF and World Bank Conference on 'Building Sound Finance in Emerging Market Economies', Washington (June).

Ireland, J. and Wren-Lewis, S. (1988) 'Buffer stock money and the company sector', paper presented at the Money Study Group Conference, Oxford (23 September).

Isard, P. and Rojas-Suarez, L. (1986) 'Velocity of money and the practice of monetary targeting: experience, theory, and the policy debate', Chapter 3 in *Staff Studies for the World Economic Outlook*, International Monetary Fund: Washington, D.C. (July): 73–112.

Italianer, A. and Vanheukelen, M. (1992) 'Proposals for Community Stabilisation Mechanisms: Some Historical Applications', Paper presented at Conference on 'Public Finance and the Future of Europe', LSE (21 September) (mimeo).

Jackman, R., Layard, R. and Nickell, S. (1991) *Unemployment: Macroeconomic performance and the labour market* (Oxford University Press).

Jackson, P. and O'Donnell, G. (1985) 'The effects of stamp duty on equity transactions and prices in the UK Stock Exchange,' Bank of England Discussion Paper, 25, October.

Jaffee, D.M. and Russell, T. (1976) 'Imperfect information and credit rationing', *Quarterly Journal of Economics*, 90(4): 651–66.

Jao, Y.C. (1984) 'A libertarian approach to monetary theory and policy', *Hong Kong Economic Papers* no. 15.

Jensen, M.C. and Meckling, W. (1976) 'Theory of the Firm: Managerial Behaviour, Agency Costs and Capital Structure', *Journal of Financial Economics*, 3: 305–60.

Johannes, J.M. and Rasche, R.H. (1979) 'Predicting the money multiplier', *Journal of Monetary Economics*, 5: 301–25.

Johannes, J.M. and Rasche, R.H. (1981) 'Can the reserves approach to monetary control really work?', *Journal of Money, Credit and Banking*, 13 (August): 298–313.

Johnson, K.H. (1983) 'Foreign experience with targets for monetary growth', *Federal Reserve Bulletin*, 69 (October): 745–54.

Johnson, H.G. (1968) 'Problems of Efficiency in Monetary Management', *Journal of Political Economy*, 76(5) (September/October): 971–90; reprinted in *Readings in British Monetary Economics*, (ed.) H.G. Johnson (Oxford: Clarendon Press, 1972): 285–308.

Johnson, S., Kroll, H. and Horton, M. (1993) 'New banks in the Former Soviet Union: How do they Operate?', Chapter 11 in *Changing the Economic System in Russia*, eds. A. Aslund and R. Layard (London: Pinter Publishers Ltd): 183–209.

Johnston, R.A. (1985) 'Monetary policy – the changing environment', T.A. Coghlan Memorial Lecture, University of NSW (May), reprinted in *Reserve Bank of Australia Bulletin* (June).

Johnston, R.B. (1983) *The Economics of the Euro-Market* (London: Macmillan).

Johnston, R.B. (1984) 'The demand for non interest bearing money in the United Kingdom', *Treasury Working Paper*, (28).

Johnston, R.B. (1985) 'The demand for liquidity aggregates by the UK personal sector', *Treasury Working Paper*, (36).

Jonson, P.D., Moses, E.R. and Wymer, C.R. (1977) 'The RBA 76 model of the Australian economy', In *Conference in Applied Economic Research*, Reserve Bank of Australia (December).

Jonson, P.D. and Rankin, R.W. (1986) 'On some recent developments in monetary economics', *Economic Record*, 62(179): 257–67.

Jonung, L. (1985) 'The economics of private money: The experience of private notes in Sweden, 1831–1902', Nationalekonomiska Institutionen, Draft, Sept.

Judd, J.P. and Motly, B. (1984) 'The "Great Velocity Decline" of 1982–83: a comparative analysis of M1 and M2', *Federal Reserve Bank of San Francisco Economic Review*,(Summer): 56–74.

Judd, J.P. and Scadding, J.L. (1982) 'The search for a stable money demand function: a survey of the post-1973 literature', *Journal of Economic Literature*, 20 (September): 993–1023.

Judd, J.P. and Scadding, J.L. (1982) 'Liability management, bank loans, and deposit "market" disequilibrium', *San Francisco Federal Reserve Bank Review* (Summer): 21–44.

Kaldor, N. (1983) 'Keynesian Economics after Fifty Years', Paper delivered at the Keynes Centenary Conference in Cambridge, June 1983, and printed in *Keynes and the Modern World*, eds J. Trevithick and G.N.D. Worswick (Cambridge University Press,) also Chapter 2 in *Further Essays on Economic Theory and Policy by Kaldor*, eds F. Targetti and A.P. Thirlwall (London: Gerald Duckworth & Co Ltd, 1989).

Kaldor, N. (1982) *The Scourge of Monetarism*, (Oxford: Oxford University Press).

Kane, E.J. (1985) *The Gathering Crisis in Federal Deposit Insurance* (Cambridge MA: MIT Press).

Kane, E.J. (1992) 'Corporate capital and government guarantees', *Journal of Financial Services Research* 5(4): 357–68.

Kareken, J.H. (1981) 'Bank regulation and the effectiveness of open market operations', *Brookings papers on Economic Activity* no. 2.

Kareken, J. and Wallace, N. (1981) 'On the Indeterminacy of Equilibrium Exchange Rates', *Quarterly Journal of Economics*, 96 (May): 207–22.

Kaufman, G.G. (1992) 'Capital in banking: Past, present and future', *Journal of Financial Services Research* 5(4): 385–402.

Keating, P. (1985) 'Statement by the Treasurer, The Hon. Paul Keating, M.P', Press Release, Canberra (January), reprinted in *Reserve Bank of Australia Bulletin* (February): 507–9.

Kenen, P.B. (1969) 'The Theory of Optimum Currency Areas: An Eclectic View', in *Monetary Problems in the International Economy*, R. Mundell and A. Swoboda (eds) (University of Chicago Press).

Kenen, P.B. (1992) 'EMU after Maastricht', Chapter 1 in *EMU and ESCB after Maastricht*, ed. C. Goodhart (London: LSE, Financial Markets Group), also Group of 30 (Washington).

Kenen, P.B. (1993a) 'The EMS and EMU: Lessons from September', *International Economy*, forthcoming.

Kenen, P.B. (1993b) 'EMU, Exchange Rates and the International Monetary System', *Recherches Economiques de Louvain* (1–2), Special Issue: 257–81.

Kenen, P.B. (ed) (1995) *Understanding Interdependence: The Macroeconomics of the Open Economy* (Princeton, NJ: Princeton University Press).

Keohane, R.O. (1984) *After hegemony: Cooperation and discord in the world political economy* (Princeton University Press).

Keynes, J.M. (1936) *The General Theory of Employment Interest and Money*, reprinted 1973 for the Royal Economic Society (London: Macmillan).

Key, S.J. (1992) 'Deposit-Protection Schemes: Issues for an E.C. Directive', CEPS Research Report (11), Brussels (December).

Key, S.J. and Scott, H.S. (1991) 'International Trade in Banking Services. A Conceptual Framework', Group of Thirty Occasional Papers (35) (Washington D.C.).

Kindleberger, C.P. (1984) *A Financial History of Western Europe* (London: Allen & Unwin).

Kindleberger, C.P. (1989) *Manias, Panics and Crashes*, 2nd Edition (London: Macmillan).

King, M.A. (1993) 'Debt Deflation: Theory and Evidence', Presidential address to the European Economic Association, Helsinki (August).

King, R.G. and Plosser, C.I. (1984) 'Money, credit and prices in a real business cycle', *American Economic Review*, 74 (June): 363–80.

King, S.R. (1986) 'Monetary transmission: through bank loans and bank liabilities?'

Journal of Money, Credit and Banking, 18(3): 290–303.

Klein, B. (1974) 'The competitive supply of money', *Journal of Money, Credit and Banking* 6(4).

Kloten, N. (1987) 'The control of monetary aggregates in West Germany under changing conditions: the impact of innovations, the internationalisation of financial markets and the EMS', paper presented at the Second Surrey Monetary Conference on Financial Innovation, Deregulation and the Control of Monetary Aggregates, University of Surrey, Guildford, 8–10 April.

Kneeshaw, J.T. and van den Bergh, P. (1989) 'Changes in central bank money market operating procedures in the 1980s', BIS Economic Papers no. 23, Jan.

Knoester, A. (1979) 'Theoretical Principles of the Buffer Mechanism, Monetary Quasi-Equilibrium and its Spillover Effects', Institute for Economic Research, Discussion Paper Series (7908/G/M), Erasmus University, Rotterdam.

Knoester, A., Kolodziejak, A. and Muijzers, G. (1990) 'Economic Policy and European Integration', Research Memorandum 9001, Department of Applied Economics, Nijmegen, Netherlands, reprinted as Chapter 12 in *Exchange Rate Regimes and Currency Unions*, eds E. Baltensperger and H.-W. Sinn (London: Macmillan 1992): 248–84.

Knoester, A. and van Sinderen, J. (1982) 'Economic policy and unemployment', In *Unemployment: a Dutch Perspective*, A. Maddison and B.S. Wilpstra (eds.) The Hague.

Kohli, U. and Rich, G. (1986) 'Monetary Control: The Swiss Experience', *Cato Journal*, 5(3) (Winter).

Kohn, M. (1988) 'The finance constraint theory of money: a progress report', Dartmouth College Working Paper (August).

Kohn, M. and Tsiang, S.-C. (1988) *Financial Constraints, Expectations, and Macroeconomics* (Oxford: Clarendon Press).

Kopecky, K.J. (1984) 'Monetary control under reverse lag and contemporaneous reserve accounting: a comparison' and 'A reply', by R.D. Laurent, *Journal of Money, Credit and Banking*, 16(1): 81–92.

Kornai, J. (1980) *Economics of Shortage* (Amsterdam: North-Holland).

Krugman, P. (1992) 'Lessons of Massachusetts for EMU', in *A Single Currency for Europe: Monetary and Real Impacts* (London: CEPR publications), also presented at Conference on the transition to EMU, Estoril, 11–18 Jan. 1992.

Krugman, P. (1993) 'What do we need to know about the International Monetary System,' *Essays in International Finance*, 190 (Princeton, NJ: Princeton University Press) (July); also in P. Kenen (ed.) (1995) *Understanding Interdependence*; *The Macroeconomics of the Open Economy* (Princeton, NJ: Princeton University Press).

Kydland, F.E., and Prescott, E.C. (1977) 'Rules rather than discretion: the inconsistency of optimal plans', *Journal of Political Economy*, 85 (June): 473–91.

Kydland, F.E., and Prescott, E.C. (1982) 'Time to build and aggregate fluctuations', *Econometrica*, 50 (November): 1345–70.

Laidler, D.E.W. (1983a) *Monetarist Perspectives* (Oxford: Philip Allan).

Laidler, D.E.W. (1983b) 'The buffer stock notion in monetary economics', *Economic Journal, Supplement*, 94: 17–34.

Laidler, D.E.W. (1985) 'Comment on "Money Demand Predictability"', *Journal of Money, Credit and Banking*, 17(4), part 2: 647–53.

Laidler, D.E.W. (1985) 'Monetary policy in an open economy', *Economic Review*, 2(4): 23–8.

Laidler, D.E.W. (1986) 'What do we really know about monetary policy?', *Australian Economic Papers*, 25(46): 1–16.

Laidler, D.E.W. (1988a) 'Taking money seriously', University of Western Ontario Department of Economics Research Report (9904).

Laidler, D.E.W. (1988b) 'Monetarism, microfoundations and the theory of monetary policy', Working Paper, Centre for the Study of International Economic Relations, Working Paper (8807c). Paper presented at a Conference on Monetary Policy at the Free University of Berlin, 31 August–2 Sept.

Laidler, D.E.W. and Bentley, B. (1983) 'A small macro-model of the post-war United States 1953–72', *Manchester School*, 51 (December): 317–40.

Laidler, D.E.W. and Parkin, M.J. (1970) 'The demand for money in the United Kingdom, 1956–1967: some preliminary estimates', *Manchester School*, 38(3): 187–208.

Lamfalussy, A. (1981) '"Rules vs. Discretion": an essay on monetary policy in an inflationary environment', BIS Economic Papers (3).

Lane, T.D. (1984) 'Instrument instability and short-term monetary control', *Journal of Monetary Economics* 14: 209–24.

Laney, L.O. (1985) 'An international comparison of experiences with monetary targeting: a reaction function approach', *Contemporary Policy Issues*, Vol. III (Fall): 99–112.

Laurent, R.D. (1979) 'Reserve requirements: are they lagged in the wrong direction?' *Journal of Money, Credit and Banking*, Vol. II (August): 301–10.

Lawson, N. (1980) 'Britain's policy and Britain's place in the international financial community', Speech at the Financial Times 1980 Euromarket Conference, 21 January, H.M. Treasury Press Release.

Lawson, N. (1981) 'Thatcherism in practice: a progress report', Speech to the Zurich Society of Economics, 14 January, H.M. Treasury Press Release.

Lawson, N. (1982) 'Financial discipline restored', Conservative Political Centre Pamphlet. (May).

Lawson, N. (1983) 'Mansion House Speech', H.M. Treasury Press Release, October.

Lawson, N. (1984) 'The British Experiment', The Fifth Mais Lecture, City University Business School pamphlet (June).

Lawson, N. (1985) 'Mansion House Speech', H.M. Treasury Press release, 17 Oct.

Lawson, N. (1986) 'Monetary policy', Lombard Association Speech, H.M. Treasury Press Release, 16 April.

Lawson, N. (1988) 'The State of the Market', Speech to the Institute of Economic Affairs, H.M. Treasury Press Release, 21 July.

Layard, R. and Nickell, S. (1986) 'Unemployment in Britain', *Economica*, 33, supplement: 121–70.

Layard, R., Nickell, S. and Jackman, R. (1991) *Unemployment, Macroeconomic Performance and the Labour Market* (Oxford: Oxford University Press).

Lehment, H. and Scheide, J. (1992) 'Die europäische Wirtschafts – und Währungsunion: Probleme des Übergangs', *Die Weltwirtschaft* (1) (March): 50–67.

Leigh-Pemberton, R. (1986) 'Financial change and broad money', Loughborough University Banking Centre Lecture in Finance, *Bank of England Quarterly Bulletin*, 26(4): 499–507.

Leigh-Pemberton, R. (1987) 'The instruments of monetary policy', Seventh Mais Lecture at the City University Business School, 13 May *Bank of England Quarterly Bulletin*, 27(3): 365–70.

Leigh-Pemberton, R. (1990) The United Kingdom's proposals for economic and monetary union, *Bank of England Quarterly Bulletin*, 30(3): 374–7.

Leijonhufvud, A. (1977) 'Costs and Consequences of Inflation', Chapter 9 in *The Microeconomic Foundations of Macroeconomics* (London: Macmillan): 265–312.

Leijonhufvud, A. (1992) 'High Inflations and Contemporary Monetary Theory', *Economic Notes* by Monte dei Paschi di Siena, 21(2): 211–24.

Leland, H.E. and Pyle, D.H. (1977) 'Information Asymmetries, Financial Structure and Financial Intermediaries', *Journal of Finance*, 32(2): 371–87.

Levitt, M. ed, (1992a) 'How to prepare companies for European Monetary Union', *De Pecunia*, Report of the Association for Monetary Union of Europe, Special Issue (June): 1–72.

Levitt, M. (1992b) 'EMU – the next steps', *The European Finance Convention and Ecu Week*, Special Issue, C. Cassuto (ed.): 27–33.

Lewis, M.K. and Davis, K.T. (1987) *Domestic International Banking*, Oxford: Philip Allan.

Lindsey, D.E. (1986) 'The monetary regime of the Federal Reserve System', Chapter 5. In *Alternative Monetary Regimes*. (ed. C.D. Campbell and W.R. Dougan) (Baltimore: Johns Hopkins University Press).

Lindsey, D.E., Farr, H.T., Gillum, G.P. Kopecky, K.I. and Porter, R.D. (1984) 'Shortrun monetary control', *Journal of Monetary Economics*, 3: 87–111.

Lindsey, D.E. and Spindt, P. (1986) 'An evaluation of monetary indices', Federal Reserve Board, Division of Research and Statistics, Special Studies Paper (195).

Litan, R. (1987) *What Should Banks Do?*, Brookings Institution, Washington, DC.

Llewellyn, D.T. (1985) 'The difficult concept of money', *Economic Review*, 2(3) (January): 17–21.

Llewellyn, D.T. (1992) 'The Performance of Banks in the UK and Scandinavia: A Case Study in Competition and De-Regulation', *Sveriges Riksbank Quarterly Review*.

Lomax, D. (1987) *London Markets after the Financial Services Act* (London: Butterworths).

Long, J.B., Jr. and Plosser, C.I. (1983) 'Real business cycles', *Journal of Political Economy*, 91 (February): 39–69.

Long, M.F. and Talley, S.H. (1993) 'Strengthening the Russian Banking System: The International Standard Banks Program', Paper presented at IMF and World Bank Conference on 'Building Sound Finance in Emerging Market Economies', Washington (June).

Longworth, D. and Muller, P. (1991) 'Implementation of monetary policy in Canada with same day settlement: Issues and alternatives', Working paper, 1991–3 (Bank of Canada, Toronto).

Lubrano, M., Pierse, R.G. and Richard, J.F. (1986) 'Stability of a UK money demand equation: a Bayesian approach to testing exogeneity', *Review of Economic Studies*, 53: 603–34.

Lucas, R.E., Jr. (1972) 'Expectations and the neutrality of money', *Journal of Economic Theory*, 4 (April): 103–24.

Lucas, R.E., Jr. (1976) 'Econometric policy evaluation: a critique', In *The Phillips Curve and Labor Markets* (ed. K. Brunner and A.H. Meltzer). Carnegie-Rochester Conference Series on Public Policy, 1 (Amsterdam: North-Holland): 19–46.

Maastricht Treaty (1992) *Treaty on European Union*, Council of the European Communities (Office for Official Publications of the European Communities, Luxembourg) (7 February).

MacDougall, Sir Donald *et al.* (1977) *Report of the Study Group on the role of public finance in European Integration*, Office for official publications of the EC, Luxembourg.

Macfarlane, I.J. (1984) 'Methods of monetary control in Australia', paper presented at the New Zealand Association of Economists Annual Conference, Massey University (August).

Malo de Molina, J.L. (1992) 'The Peripheral Countries in the face of European Monetary Union', *The European Finance Convention and Ecu Week*, Special Issue, ed. C. Cassuto: 21–26.

Mankiw, N.G. (1988) 'Recent developments in macroeconomics: a very quick refresher course'. *Journal of Money, Credit and Banking*, 20(3), part 2: 436–39.

Martin, L.L. (1993) 'International and Domestic Institutions in the EMU Process', *Economics and Politics*, 5(2) (July): 125–44.

Mascaro, A. and Meltzer, A.H. (1983) 'Long-and short-term interest rates in a risky world', *Journal of Monetary Economics*, 12 (November): 485–518.

Masera, R.S. (1992) 'Single market, exchange rates and monetary unification', Osservatorio e Centro di Studi Monetari, Quaderni di Ricerca (25), LUISS Rome (December).

Masson, P.R. and Taylor, M.P. (1993) 'Currency unions: a survey of the issues', Chapter 1 in *Policy Issues in the Operation of Currency Unions*, P. Masson and M.P. Taylor (eds.) (Cambridge University Press).

Matthews, R.C.O. (1954) *A Study in Trade Cycle History* (Cambridge University Press).

Maude, F. (1990) Europe's choice: unity or division. In *Economic and Monetary Union*, proceedings of the seminar on this topic at Hambros Bank Ltd, 11 October 1990 (London: British Invisibles Exports Council).

Mayer, C. (1988) 'New Issues in Corporate Finance', *European Economic Review*, 32(5) (June): 1167–89.

Mayer, C. (1990) 'Financial Systems, Corporate Finance, and Economic Development' in *Asymmetric Information, Corporate Finance, and Investment*, ed. R. Glenn Hubbard, NBER (University of Chicago Press).

Mayer, T (1987) 'The debate about monetarist policy recommendations', *Kredit and Kapital*, 20: 281–302.

Mayer, T (1988) 'Monetarism in a world without "money"', University of California, Davis, Research Program in Applied Macroeconomics and Macro Policy, Working Paper (56).

Mazzaferro, F. (1992) 'Unity through Diversity: Bank notes and coins in the European Monetary Union', San Paolo Bank, Research and Strategies Unit, (mimeo).

McCallum, B.T. (1981) 'Price level determinacy with an interest policy rule and rational expectations', *Journal of Monetary Economics* 8(3): 319–329.

McCallum, B.T. (1985) 'Bank Deregulation, Accounting Systems of Exchange, and the Unit of Account: A Critical Review', *Carnegie–Rochester Conference Series on Public Policy*, 23.

McCallum, B.T. (1985) 'On consequences and criticisms of monetary targeting', *Journal of Money, Credit and Banking* 17(4), part 2: 570–97.

McCallum, B.T. (1986) 'Some issues concerning interest rate pegging, price level determinacy, and the real bills doctrine', *Journal of Monetary Economics* 17(1): 135–60.

McCallum, B.T. (1987) 'The case for rules in the conduct of monetary policy: a concrete example', *Weltwirtschaftliches Archiv*, Bd. 123: 415–28.

McCallum, B.T. (1988) 'Postwar developments in business cycle theory: a moderately classical perspective', *Journal of Money, Credit and Banking*, 20(3), part 2: 459–71.

McCulloch, J.H. (1986) 'Beyond the historical gold standard', In *Alternative Monetary Regimes*, C.D. Campbell and W.R. Dougan (eds.) (Baltimore: Johns Hopkins University Press: 73–81).

McKinnon, R.I. (1963) 'Optimum Currency Areas', *American Economic Review*, 53 (September): 717–25.

McKinnon. R.I. (1973) *Money and Capital in Economic Development* (Washington, D.C.: Brookings Institute).

McKinnon, R.I. (1984) *An International Standard for Monetary Stabilisation* (Washington: Institute for International Economics).

McKinnon, R.I. (1991a) 'Financial Control in the Transition from Classical Socialism to a Market Economy', *Journal of Economic Perspectives*, 5(4) (Fall): 167–122.

McKinnon, R.I. (1991b) *The Order of Economic Liberalization: Financial Control in the Transition to a Market Economy* (Baltimore: Johns Hopkins University Press).

McKinnon, R.I. (1992) 'Taxation, Money and Credit in a Liberalizing Socialist Economy', in *The Emergence of Market Economies in Eastern Europe*, eds. C. Clague and G.C. Rausser (Oxford: Basil Blackwell): 109–28.

McKinnon, R.I. (1993) 'Financial Growth and Macroeconomic Stability in China, 1978–92: Implications for Russia and Eastern Europe'. Paper presented at the Conference on 'Transition of the Communist Countries in Pacific Asia', San Francisco (May).

McKinnon, R.I. and Ohno, K. (1988) 'Purchasing Power Parity as a Monetary Standard', paper presented at a Conference on the Future of the International Monetary System (Toronto: York University).

Meek, P. (ed.) (1983) *Central Bank Views on Monetary Targeting*. Federal Reserve Bank of New York.

Meen, G.P. (1985) 'An econometric analysis of mortgage rationing', U.K. Government Economic Service Working Paper, 79.

Melitz, J. (1988) 'Monetary Discipline and Cooperation in the European Monetary System: A Synthesis', Chapter 3 in *The European Monetary System*, eds, F. Giavazzi, S. Micossi, and M. Miller (Cambridge University Press): 51–79.

Melitz, J. (1991a) 'Brussels on a Single Money', *Open Economics Review*, 2: 323–36; also CEPR Discussion Paper (556) (July).

Melitz, J. (1991b) 'A suggested reformulation of the theory of optimal currency areas', CEPR Discussion Paper (590) (October).

Melitz, J. (1993) 'A Multilateral Approach to the Theory of Optimal Currency Areas', INSEE Working Paper (9305) (February).

Melitz, J. (1993) 'Reflections on the Emergence of a Single Market for Bank Reserves in a European Monetary Union', CEPR Discussion Paper (818) London, Center for Economic Policy Research, July.

Melitz, J. and Vori, S. (1992) 'National Insurance against Unevenly Distributed Shocks in a European Monetary Union', paper presented at Conference on 'Public Finance and the Future of Europe', LSE, (21 September) (mimeo).

Mengle, D.L., Humphrey, D.B. and Summers, B.J. (1987 'Intraday Credit: Risk, Value, and Pricing', *Federal Reserve Bank of Richmond Economic Review* (January/February): 3–14.

Micossi, S. and Tullio, G. (1991) 'Fiscal imbalances, economic distortions, and the long run performance of the Italian economy', paper prepared for the International Workshop on 'Global Macroeconomic Perspectives', Rome 29–30 May.

Milbourne, R. (1987) 'Re-examining the buffer-stock model of money', *Economic Journal, Conference Supplement*, 97: 130–42.

Miles, D.K. and Wilcox, J.B. (1988) 'The transmission mechanism', Bank of England mimeo.

Miller, M.H. and Sprenkle, C.M. (1980) 'The precautionary demand for narrow and broad money', *Economica*, 47(188): 407–22.

Miller, S.M. (1988) 'Long-run and short-run money demands: an application of co-integration and error-correction modelling', (June) (mimeo).

Mills, T.C. (1982) 'The Information Content of the UK Monetary Aggregates', Bank of England, mimeo, presented at the AUTE Conference (University of Surrey) April, see the 1983 Conference Supplement of the *Economic Journal*, 142.

Mills, T.C. (1983a) 'Composite monetary indicators for the United Kingdom: construction and empirical analyses', *Bank of England Discussion Papers, Technical Series*, 3.

Mills, T.C. (1983b) 'The information content of the UK monetary components and aggregates', *Bulletin of Economic Research*, 35(1): 25–46.

Ministry of Finance Sweden (1993) *Measures for Strengthening the financial system*, The Swedish Government Bill 1992/93:135, Stockholm.

Minsky, H.P. (1977) 'A Theory of Systematic Fragility' in *Financial Crisis: Institution and Markets in a Fragile Environment*, E.I. Altman and A.W. Sametz (eds.) (New York: Wiley International).

Minsky, H.P. (1982) 'The Financial Instability Hypothesis: Capitalistic Processes and the Behaviour of the Economy', in *Financial Crises: Theory, History and Policy*, C.P. Kindleberger and J.-P. Laffargue (eds.) (Cambridge University Press): 13–29.

Monticelli, C. and Viñals, J. (1993) 'European Monetary Policy in Stage 3: What are the issues', in *The Monetary Future of Europe*, eds. de la Dehesa *et al.* (London: Centre for Economic Policy Research, Chapter 11; and CEPR Occasional Paper (12) March 1993.

Moore, B.J. (1988a). 'The endogenous money supply', *Journal of Post Keynesian Economics*, 10(3): 372–85.

Moore, B.J. (1988b) *Horizontalists and Verticalists: The Macroeconomics of Credit Money* (Cambridge: Cambridge University Press).

Moore, B.J. (1989) 'A simple model of bank intermediation', *Journal of Post Keynesian Economics*, 12(1), (Fall): 10–28.

Moore, B.J. and Threadgold, A. (1985) 'Corporate bank borrowing in the UK, 1965–1981', *Economica*, 52 (February): 65–78.

Moore, G.R., Porter, R.D. and Small, D.H. (1988) 'Modeling the disaggregated demands for M2 and M1 in the 1980's: the US experience', Paper presented on 26 May to the Federal Reserve Board Conference on Monetary Aggregates and Financial Sector Behavior in Interdependent Economies.

Moran, M. (1984) *The Politics of Banking* (London: Macmillan).

Morishima, M.(1993) 'Banking and Industry in Japan', LSE Financial Markets Group, Special Paper (51) (January).

Mourmouras, A. and Russell, S. (1992) 'Bank regulation as an antidote to price level instability: A 'real bills' model that yields 'quantity theory' prescriptions', *Journal of Monetary Economics* 29(1): 125–50.

Muller, H.J. (1981) 'Macro- en Microtoezicht (Monetary Policy and Banking Supervison)', in: *Zoeklicht op Beleid (Focus on Policy)*, E. den Dunnen, M.M.G. Fase and A. Szász (eds) (Leiden: Stenfert Kroese): 173–87.

Mullineaux, A. (ed.) (1992) *European Banking* (Oxford: Blackwell).

Mundell, R.A. (1961) 'A Theory of Optimum Currency Areas', *American Economic Review*, 51 (September): 657–65.

Muscatelli, V.A. (1988) 'Alternative models of buffer stock money: an empirical investigation', *Scottish Journal of Political Economy*, 35(1) 1–21.

Nakajima, Z. and Taguchi, H. (1993) 'Towards a more stable financial framework: Long-term alternatives – An overview of recent bank disruption worldwide', Bank of Japan, Institute for Monetary and Economic Studies, preliminary draft (July).

National Board for Prices and Incomes (NBPI) Report No. 34, *Bank Charges*, Cmnd. 3292 (HMSO: London, 1967).

Neumann, J.M. (1992) 'In die Ära der Euro-Mark', *Frankfurter Allgemeine Zeitung* (97) (25 December).

Newlyn, W.T. and Rowan, D.C. (1954) *Money and Banking in British Colonial Africa: A Study of the Monetary and Banking Systems of Eight British African Territories* (Oxford: Clarendon Press).

Niehans, J. (1981) 'The appreciation of sterling causes, effects, policies', Money Study Group Discussion Paper, (February) (mimeo).

Nobay, R.A. (1992) 'The Political Economy of European Monetary Union', Liverpool Research Papers in Economics and Finance (93–01) (December), also in the *Greek Economic Review*, December 1991.

Oates, W.E. (1972) *Fiscal Federalism* (New York: Harcourt Brace Jovanovich).

OECD (1992) *Banks under stress* (Paris).

OECD, Ad Hoc Group of Monetary Experts (1991) 'A "Credit Crunch"? The Recent Slowdown in Bank Lending and its Implications for Monetary Policy', Economics and Statistics Department draft (9 December).

Padilla, A.J. and Pagano, M. (1993) 'Sharing Default Information as a Borrower Discipline Device', Paper presented at CEPR/ESF Conference on 'Financial Regulation', Toulouse (June).

Padoan, P.C. and Pericoli, M. (1992) 'Single Market, EMU and Widening. Responses to Three Institutional Shocks in the European Community', Department of Economics, University of Trento, Discussion Paper (8) (December).

Panić, M. (1992) *European Monetary Union: Lessons from the Classical Gold Standard* (London: Macmillan).

Pavel, C. (1986) 'Securitization', *Federal Reserve Bank of Chicago Economic Perspectives*, 10(4): 16–31.

Pecchioli, R.M. (1987) *Prudential Supervision in Banking* (Paris: OECD).

Pepper, G. (1977) 'The Mechanism for the Control of the Money Supply – Further Thoughts', *W. Greenwell Monetary Bulletin* (February).

Pepper, G. (1979) 'A Monetary Base for the UK – A Practical Proposal', W. Greenwell Monetary Bulletin (July).

Pepper, G. (1980) 'Monetary Base Control', *W. Greenwell Monetary Bulletin* (April).

Pepper, G. (1990) *Money, Credit and Inflation*, Institute for Economic Affairs, Research Monograph (44) (London: IEA, April).

Perotti, E.C., (1992) 'Conditionality of Directed State Credits in Russia: A Tool for Decentralization and Restructuring', mimeo, Boston University (December).

Persson, T. (1988) 'Credibility of macroeconomic policy: an introduction and a broad survey', *European Economic Review*, 32: 519–32.

Persson, T. and Tabellini, G. (1992) 'The Politics of 1992: Fiscal Policy and European Integration', *Review of Economic Studies*, 59(4) (201) (October): 689–702.

Persson, T. and Tabellini, G. (1992a) 'Federal Fiscal Constitutions. Part 1: Risk Sharing and Moral Hazard', CEPR Discussion Paper (728) (October).

Petersen, M.A. and Rajan, R.G. (1992a) 'The Effect of Credit Market Competition on Firm-Creditor Relationships', University of Chicago, Graduate School of Business, Unpublished.

Petersen, M.A. and Rajan, R.G. (1992b) 'The Benefits of Firm-Creditor Relationships: Evidence from small business data', University of Chicago Graduate School of Business, Unpublished (September).

Phelps, E.S. (1968) 'Money wage dynamics and labor market equilibrium', *Journal of Political Economy*, 76 (August): 678–711.

Phelps, E.S. (1972) *Inflation Policy and Unemployment Theory: The Cost–Benefit Approach to Monetary Planning* (London: Macmillan).

Pippenger, J. (1984) 'Bank of England Operations, 1893–1913', in *A Retrospective on the Classical Gold Standard, 1821–1931*, M.D. Bordo and A.J. Schwartz (eds) (Chicago: University of Chicago Press).

Pisani-Ferry, J., Italianer, A. and Lescure, R. (1993) 'Stabilisation Properties of Fiscal Arrangements: A Simulation Analysis', in 'The Economics of Community Public Finance: Reports and Studies', *European Economy* (5): 511–38.

Pissarides, C. and McMaster, I. (1990) 'Regional Migration, Wages and Unemployment: Empirical Evidence and Implications for Policy', *Oxford Economic Papers*, 42: 812–31.

Pollak, R. (1975) 'The Intertemporal Cost-of-Living Index', *Annals of Economic and Social Measurement*, 4(1).

Pollock, A.J. (1991) 'Collateralised money: An idea whose time has come again', Mimeo., Private circulation.

Pöhl, K.O. (1990) 'Prospects of European Monetary Union', in *Britain and EMU* (London: Centre for Economic Performance in association with the Financial Markets Group, London School of Economics): 3–14.

Poloz, S.S. (1990) 'Real Exchange Rate Adjustment between Regions in a Common Currency Area', in *Choosing an Exchange Rate Regime. The Challenge of Smaller Industrial Countries*, eds, V. Argy and P. De Grauwe (International Monetary Fund): 374–77.

Poole, W. (1982) 'Federal Reserve operating procedures: a survey and evaluation of the historical record since October 1979.' *Journal of Money, Credit and Banking*, 14, (4), part 2: 576–96.

Porter, M.E. (1991) 'Capital Choices: Changing the Way America Invests in Industry', *Journal of Applied Corporate Finance*, 5: 4–16.

Porter, R.D. and Bayer A. (1983) 'A monetary perspective on underground economic activity in the United States', *Federal Reserve Bulletin*, 70: 177–89.

Power, M. and Freedman J., (1991) 'Law and Accounting: Transition and Transformation', *Modern Law Review*, 54 (November): 777–83.

Pozdena, R.J. (1987) 'Commerce and Banking: The German Case', *FRSF Weekly Letter*, Federal Reserve Bank of San Francisco 18 December.

Prud'homme, R. (1993) 'The potential role of the EC budget in the reduction of spatial disparities in a European Economic and Monetary Union', in 'The Economics of Community Public Finance: Reports and Studies', *European Economy* (5): 317–51.

Qian, Y. and Xu, C. (1993) 'Why China's Economic Reforms Differ: The M-Form Hierarchy and Entry/Expansion of the Non-State Sector', Revised Version, March, forthcoming *The Economics of Transition*.

Quinn, B. (1993) 'The Bank of England's Role in Prudential Supervision', Speech given at a Westminster and City Programmes Conference on 'Re-examining City Regulation' (London) (24 March).

Radecki, L. (1982) 'Short-run monetary control: an analysis of some possible dangers', *Federal Reserve Bank of New York Quarterly Review*, 7 (Spring): 1–10.

Radecki, L. and Wenninger, J. (1985) 'Recent instability in M1's velocity', *Federal Reserve Bank of New York Quarterly Review* (Autumn): 16–22.

Rajan, R.G. (1992) 'Insiders and Outsiders: The choice between informed and arm's length debt', *Journal of Finance*, 47(4) (September): 1367–400.

Rasche, R.H. (1985) 'Interest rate volatility and alternative monetary control procedures', *Federal Reserve Bank of San Francisco, Economic Review*, (Summer): 46–63.

Rasche, R.H. (1988) 'Demand functions for U.S. money and credit measures', Paper presented at the Conference on 'Monetary Aggregates and Financial Sector Behavior in Interdependent Economies', mimeo. Federal Reserve Board, Washington, DC (May): 26–27.

Rasche, R.H. and Johannes, J.M. (1987) *Controlling the Growth of Monetary Aggregates* (Kluwer Academic Publishers).

Rasche, R.H. and Meltzer, A.H. (1982) 'For the Affirmative', and P.D. Sternlight and S.H. Axilrod, 'For the Negative' in the Journal of Money, Credit and Banking Debate on 30 April', 'Is the Federal Reserve's Monetary Control Misdirected', reproduced in *Journal of Money, Credit and Banking*, 14(1) (February): 119–47.

Reserve Bank of Australia (1985) 'The Reserve Bank's domestic market operations', mimeo, Sydney (May).

Reserve Bank of New Zealand (1986) *Financial Policy Reform* (Wellington, New Zealand: RBNZ).

Reserve Bank of New Zealand (1987a) 'A layman's guide to monetary policy in the New Zealand context', *Reserve Bank Bulletin*, 50 (June): 104–10.

Reserve Bank of New Zealand (1987b) 'Post-election briefing paper to the Minister of Finance', Special Paper, Wellington (August).

Reserve Bank of New Zealand (1993) 'Proposed revisions to banking supervision arrangements', in *Financial Regulation Report* (London: Financial Times Business Information, June): 2–10.

Richards, O.P. (1990) 'The Case for an Evolutionary Stage 2', Samuel Montagu, London (31 July) (mimeo).

Richardson, G. (1978) 'Reflections on the conduct of monetary policy', *Bank of England Quarterly Bulletin*, 18(1): 51–8.

Rich, G. and Beguelin, J.-P. (1985) 'Swiss Monetary Policy in the 1970s and 1980s', *Monetary Policy and Monetary Regimes*, Graduate School of Management, University of Rochester Center Symposia Series, CS17.

Rich, G. and Schiltknecht, K. (1980) 'Targetting the Monetary Base – The Swiss Approach', in *The Monetary Base Approach to Monetary Control*, ed. BIS, Basle (September).

Roley, V.V. (1985) 'Money demand predictability', *Journal of Money, Credit and Banking* 17(4), part 2: 615–41.

Roley, V.V. (1986) 'Market perceptions of U.S. monetary policy since 1982', *Federal Reserve Bank of Kansas City Economic Review* (May): 27–40.

Rosenblum, H. and Storin, S. (1983 'Interest rate volatility in historical perspective', *Federal Reserve Bank of Chicago Economic Review*, 7 (January, February): 10–9.

Ross, L. (1984) 'Investor Protection – Why Gower is Wrong', *Economic Affairs* 4(4) (July–September, 1984).

Roth, H.I. (1986) 'Leading indicators of inflation', *Federal Reserve Bank of Kansas City Economic Review* (November): 3–20.

Rymes, T.K. (1989) 'The theory and measurement of the nominal output of banks, sectoral rates of savings and wealth in the national accounts', Chapter 7 in: R.E. Lipsey and H.S. Tice (eds), *The Measurement of Saving, Investment and Wealth* (University of Chicago Press for the NBER, Chicago).

Sachs, J. and Lipton, D. (1992) 'Russia: Towards a Market-Based Monetary System', *Central Banking*, 3(1) (Summer): 29–53.

Sachs, J. and Lipton, D. (1993) 'Remaining Steps to a Market-Based Monetary System in Russia', Chapter 9 in *Changing the Economic System in Russia*, eds A. Åslund and R. Layard (London: Pinter Publishers Ltd): 127–62.

Sala-i-Martin, X. and Sachs, J. (1990) 'Federal Fiscal Policy and Optimum Currency Areas', Harvard, mimeo, since republished as Chapter 7 in *Establishing a Central Bank: Issues in Europe and Lessons from the US* (eds) M.B. Canzoneri, V. Grilli and P.R. Masson (Cambridge University Press: 1992).

Salin, P. (ed.) (1984) *Currency Competition and Monetary Union* (Martinus Nijhoff: The Hague).

Sargent, T.J. (1986) *Rational Expectations and Inflation* (New York: Harper & Row).

Sargent, T.J. (1987) *Dynamic Macroeconomic Theory* (Cambridge, Mass.: Harvard University Press).

Sargent, T.J. and Wallace, N. (1975) '"Rational" expectations, the optimal monetary instrument, and the optimal money supply rule', *Journal of Political Economy*, 83(2): 241–54.

Sargent, T.J. and Wallace, N. (1982) 'The Real-Bills Doctrine Versus the Quantity Theory: A Reconsideration', *Journal of Political Economy*, 90 (December):

1212–36.

Sargent, T.J. and Wallace, N. (1983) 'A Model of Commodity Money', Federal Reserve Bank of Minneapolis, Research Department Staff Report, 85.

Sargent, T.J. and Wallace, N. (1985) 'Interest on reserves', *Journal of Monetary Economics* 15(3).

Savage, D. (1984) 'Monetary targets – a short history', *Economic Review*, 2(1) (September): 3–7.

Sayers, R.S. (1936)) *Bank of England Operations, (1890–1914)* (London: P.S. King & Son Ltd).

Schlesinger, H. (1984) 'Zehn Jahre Geldpolitik mit einem Geldmengenziel', In *Offentliche Finanzen und Monetare Okonomie*. (ed. W. Gebauer) (Frankfurt am Main: Fritz Knapp Verlag): 123–47

Schlesinger, H. (1988) 'Kontinuitat in den Zielen. Wandel in der Methoden', *Herausforderungen der Wirtschaftspolitik*. (eds. W. File, L. Hubl and R. Pohl), Berlin: Duncker & Humblot: 197–210.

Schnadt, N. (1994) *The Domestic Money Markets of the UK, France, Germany and the US*, Subject Report, no. VII, Paper 1, City Research in Project, London Business School, January.

Schnadt, N. and Whittaker, J. (1993) 'Inflation-proof currency?, The feasibility of variable commodity standards', *Journal of Money, Credit and Banking*, 25(2): 214–221.

Schneider, F. (1993) 'The federal and fiscal structures of representative and direct democracies as a model for a European federal union', in 'The Economics of Community Public Finance: Reports and Studies', *European Economy* (5): 191–212.

Schoenmaker, D. (1993) 'Home Country Deposit Insurance?', Chapter 7 in: *Contemporary Issues in Money and Banking*, P. Arestis (ed.) (London: Macmillan Press, Second Edition).

Schwartz, A.J. (1991) 'The Misuse of the Fed's Discount Window', Shadow Open Market Committee, Policy Statement and Position Papers (29–30 September): 109–11.

Scott, D.H. (1993) 'Revising Financial Sector Policy in Transitional Socialist Economies', Paper presented at the IMF and World Bank Conference on 'Building Sound Finance in Emerging Market Economies', Washington (June).

Scott, H.S. (1990) 'A payment system role for a European System of Central Banks'. In *For a Common Currency, the European Currency, an Optional Currency* (Committee for the Monetary Union of Europe): 77–106.

Scott, H.S. (1992) 'Supervision of international banking post-BCCI', *Georgia State University Law Review*, 8(3) (June): 487–510.

Securities and Investments Board (1987) *The Regulation of Financial Business* (London: Securities and Investments Board).

Seidman, W.L. (1986) 'Testimony to Senate Banking Committee' reported in the *New York Times* (14 March) D.1.

Seldon, A. (ed.) (1988) *Financial Regulation-Or Over-Regulation* (London: Institute of Economic Affairs).

Seldon, A. and Pennance, F.G. (1975) *Everyman's Dictionary of Economics* (London: Dent, 2nd edn).

Selgin, G.A. (1988) *The theory of free banking: Money supply under competitive note issue* (Rowman and Littlefield, Totowa, NJ).

Selgin, G.A. and White, L.H. (1987) 'The evolution of a free banking system', *Economic Inquiry* 25, 439–457.

Sentana, E. Shah M. and Wadhwani, S. (1992) 'Has the EMS reduced the cost of capital?' Discussion Paper (134) LSE Financial Markets Group, (March).

Shadow Financial Regulatory Committee (1989) Messrs Aspinwall, Benston *et al*, 'An Outline of a Program for Deposit Insurance and Regulatory Reform', Statement no. 41, (13 February) (mimeo), reprinted in *Journal of Financial Services Research* (1992), 6 (Supplement): S78-S82.

Sharpe, S. (1990) 'Asymmetric information, bank lending and implicit contracts: A stylized model of customer relationships, *Journal of Finance*, 45(4) (September): 1069–087.

Shaw, E.S. (1973) *Financial Deepening in Economic Development* (New York: Oxford University Press).

Shibuya, H. (1992) 'Dynamic Equilibrium Price Index: Asset Price and Inflation', *Bank of Japan Monetary and Economic Studies*, 10(1) (February): 95–109.

Shigehara, K. (1990) 'Shisankakaku No Hendo To Infureshon' (Asset Price Movement and Inflation)', *Kinyu Kenkyu*, 9(2) (July).

Shiller, R.J. (1989) *Market Volatility* (Cambridge Mass.: MIT Press).

Shimizu, Y. (1992) 'Problems in the Japanese Financial System in the Early 1990s' *Hitotsubashi Journal of Commerce and Management*, 27 (November): 29–49.

Simonson, D.G. and Hempel, G.H. (1993) 'Banking lessons from the past: The 1938 regulatory agreement interpreted', *Journal of Financial Services Research*, 7(3) (September): 249–68.

Simpson, T.D. (1984) 'Changes in the financial system: implications for monetary policy', *Brookings Papers on Economic Activity* (1): 249–65.

Sims. C.A. (1972) 'Money, income and causality', *American Economic Review*, 62(4): 540–52.

Skorov, G. (1992) 'From Economic Reform to Hyperinflation', *Central Banking*, 3(3) (Winter 1992–93): 28–38.

Smith, D. (1978) 'The demand for alternative monies in the UK, 1924-77', *National Westminster Bank Quarterly Review*, November 1978: 35–49.

Smith, D. (1980) 'The monetary conundrum', *London Business School Economic Outlook*, 5(2): 1–2.

Snyder, C. (1928) 'The measure of the general price level', *Review of Economic Statistics* (February): 46–52.

Solomon, A.M. (1981) 'Financial innovation and monetary policy', paper presented before the joint luncheon of the American Economic and American Finance Associations, (28 December) (mimeo) (Federal Reserve Bank of New York).

Solomon, A.M. (1984) 'Some problems and prospects for monetary policy in 1985', Remarks before the Money Marketers of New York University, (20 November), (mimeo). (Federal Reserve Bank of New York).

Spahn, B. (1992) 'The Case for EMU; A European View', Johann Wolfgang Goethe Universitat Frankfurt, Fachlereich Wirtschaftsvissenschaften, August Arbeitspaper (29).

Spencer, G. and Garey, D. (1988) 'Financial policy reform: the New Zealand experience', Reserve Bank of New Zealand Discussion Paper (G88) 1 (April).

Spindt, P.A. and Tarhan, V. (1987) 'The Federal Reserve's new operating procedures: a post mortem', *Journal of Monetary Economics* 19: 107–23.

Sprague, I.H. (1986) *Bailout* (New York: Basic Books).

Sprague, O.M.W. (1910) *History of Crises under the National Banking System*, National Monetary Commission (sixty-first Congress, second Session, Senate Document (538), Washington, DC: Government Printing Office).

Sprenkle, C.M. and Miller, M.H. (1980) 'The Precautionary Demand for Narrow and Broad Money', *Economica*, 47 (November): 407–421.

Stanhope, N. (1993) 'Proposed Directive for Co-ordination of Deposit Guarantee Schemes', in: *Financial Regulation Report* (London: Financial Times Business Information, June): 14.

Steinherr, A. (1992) 'The role of the ECU on the way of EMU', *The European Finance Convention and Ecu Week*, Special Issue, ed. (C. Cassuto): 54–60.

Steinherr, A. and Huveneers, C. (1990) 'Universal Banks: The Prototype of Successful Banks in the Integrated European Market? A view inspired by German experience', Research Report (2), CEPS Financial Markets Unit, Centre for European Policy Studies, Brussels.

Sternlight, P.D. and Axilrod, S.H. (1982) 'Is the Federal Reserve's monetary control policy misdirected?' arguing for the negative in the JMCB Debate, 30 April 1981, reprinted in the *Journal of Money, Credit and Banking* 14(1): 119–47.

Stevens, G., Thorp, S. and Anderson, J. (1987) 'The Australian demand function for money: another look at stability', Reserve Bank of Australia Research Discussion Paper (8701).

Stigler, G.J. (1971) 'The Theory of Economic Regulation', *Bell Journal of Economics and Management Science*, 2(1), Spring.

Stigler, G.J. (1981) in U.S. Congress Joint Economic Committee, *Government Price Statistics*, two Parts (Washington D.C.).

Stiglitz, J.E. and Weiss, A.M. (1981) 'Credit Rationing in Markets with Imperfect Information', *American Economic Review*, 71(3): 393–410.

Stiglitz, J.E. and Weiss, A.M. (1983) 'Incentive Effects of Terminations: Applications to the Credit and Labor Markets', *American Economic Review*, 73(5): 912–27.

Summers, B.J. (1991) 'Clearing and Payment Systems: The Central Bank's Role', in *The Evolving Role of Central Banks* (Washington: IMF): 30–45.

Summers, L.H. (1986) 'Do we really know that financial markets are efficient?' in *Recent Developments in Corporate Finance,* ed. J. Edwards *et al.* (Cambridge: Cambridge University Press).

Summers, L.H. (1988) 'Comment' on B.T. McCallum', *Journal of Money, Credit and Banking*, 20(3), part 2: 472–6.

Summers, L.H. (1992) Comment on Stanley Fischer, 'Stabilization and Economic Reform in Russia', *Brookings Paper on Economic Actively*, 1: 77–126.

Suzuki, Y. (1986) *Money, Finance and Macroeconomic Performance in Contemporary Japan.* (New Haven: Yale University Press).

Suzuki, Y. (1988) Monetary policy in Japan-price stability and stable growth under the floating exchange rate regime', paper presented at the PACE/FMG Conference on Japanese Financial Growth in London (October).

Suzuki, Y. Kuroda, A. and Shirankawa, H. (1988) 'Monetary control mechanism in Japan', Paper presented at the Conference on Monetary Aggregates and Financial Sector Behavior in Interdependent Economies, at the Federal Reserve Board, Washington, DC (May).

Tamura, T. (1987) 'Monetary control in Japan', Paper presented at the Second Surrey Monetary Conference on Financial Innovation, Deregulation and the Control of Monetary Aggregates, University of Surrey, Guildford, 8 April 10.

Taylor, M.P. (1987) 'Financial innovation, inflation and the stability of the demand for broad money in the United Kingdom', *Bulletin of Economic Research* 39(3): 225–33.

Tett, G. (1993) 'Reform of E. European Banks "a priority"', *Financial Times*, 3 August.

Thatcher, M. (1988) Parliamentary answers Question Time on 10 March, as reported in *The Times*, 11 March 1988: 2.

The Economist, 1992, 'The end of inflation?', Leader in *The Economist* (22–28Feb.): 11–12.

The Economist (1993) 'Can Europe put EMU together again', *The Economist*, 8–14 (May).

Thomas J.J. (1988) 'The politics of the black economy', *Work, Employment and Society*, 2 (June): 169–90.

Thompson, E.A. (1981) 'Free banking under a labor standard', Prepared for the US gold commission. Manuscript (Economics Department, UCLA, Los Angeles, CA).

Thompson, E.A. (1986) 'A perfect monetary system', Paper presented at the Liberty Fund/Manhattan Institute Conference on Competitive Monetary Regimes, New York.

Thornton, H. (1802) *An Enquiry into the Nature and Effects of the Paper Credit of Great Britain* (London: Hatchard).

Thygesen, N. (1988) 'Decentralisation and accountability within the central bank; any lessons from the U.S. experience?' in P. de Grauwe and T. Peeters (eds.) *The Ecu and European Monetary Integration* (London: Macmillan): 91–114.

Thygesen, N. (1989) 'A European central banking system – some analytical and operational considerations'. In *Collection of Papers Submitted to the Committee for the Study of Economic and Monetary Union*, the Delors Committee Report (Luxembourg: Office for Official Publications of the European Communities): 157–75.

Thygesen, N. (1990) *Monetary Management in a Monetary Union* (University of Copenhagen) (mimeo).

Timberlake, R.H., Jr. (1978) *The Origins of Central Banking in the United States* (Cambridge, Mass.: Harvard University Press).

Timberlake, R.H., Jr. (1984) 'The Central Banking Role of Clearinghouse Associations', *Journal of Money, Credit, and Banking*, 16(1) (February): 1–15.

Tinsley, P.A., Farr, H.T., Fries, G., Garrett, B. and Muehlen, P.V.Z. (1982) 'Policy robustness: specification and simulation of a monthly money market model', *Journal of Money, Credit and Banking*, 14(4), part 2: 829–56.

Tobin, J. (1958) 'Liquidity Preference as Behavior Towards Risk', *Review of Economic Studies*, 25(67): 65–86.

Tobin, J. (1963) 'Commercial banks as creators of 'money'. Chapter 22 In *Banking and Monetary Studies*. (ed. D. Carson) (Homewood, Illinois: Richard Irwin Inc.)

Tobin, J. (1983) 'Monetary policy: rules, targets and shocks', *Journal of Money, Credit and Banking*, 15(4) 506–18.

Tobin, J. (1985) 'Financial Innovation and Deregulation in Perspective', *Bank of Japan Monetary and Economic Studies*, 3(2).

Treasury and Civil Service Committee (1981) *Monetary Policy: Report* London: HMSO.

Treasury, Her Majesty's (1984) *Building Societies: A New Framework*, Cmnd. 9316 (HMSO: London, July).

Treasury, Her Majesty's *Financial Statement and Budget Report* (FSBR Redbook), various years.

Treasury, HM (1989) *An Evolutionary Approach to EMU* (London: HMSO).

Treasury, H.M. and Bank of England (1980) *Monetary Control* (London, HMSO), Cmmd 7858.

Trehan, B. (1988) 'The practice of monetary targeting: a case study of the West German experience', *Federal Reserve Bank of San Francisco, Economic Review*, 30–4.

Tresch, R. (1981) *Public Finance: A Normative Theory* (Business Publications: Plano, Texas).

Triffin, R. (1960). *Gold and the Dollar Crisis*, New Haven, Conn: Yale University Press.

Ueda, K. (1988). 'Financial deregulation and the demand for money in Japan', Paper presented at the Conference on Monetary Aggregates and Financial Sector

Behavior in Interdependent Economics, at the Federal Reserve Board, Washington D.C., 26–27 May.

Vaciago, G. (1985) 'Financial innovation and monetary policy: Italy *versus* the United States', *Banca Nazionale del Lavoro Quarterly Review* (155): 309–26.

van der Ploeg, F. (1991) 'Macroeconomic Policy Coordination Issues during the Various Phases of Economic and Monetary Integration in Europe' in *The Economics of EMU, European Economy*, Special Edition 1, Brussels: European Communities: 136–64.

Van Rompuy, P., Abraham F. and Heremans, D. (1991) 'Economic Federalism and the EMU', in *The Economics of EMU, European Economy*, Special Edition 1, Brussels: European Communities: 109–35.

Vaubel, R. (1984) 'The Government's Money Monopoly: Externalities or Natural Monopoly', *Kyklos*, 37(1): 27–58.

Vital, C. (1990) 'Swiss Interbank Clearing: Further Experience with a Queuing Mechanism to Control Payment System Risk', Paper Presented at the Conference 'Electronic Bankinig im Auslandszahlungsverkehr' (München: Institute for International Research) (18–19 April).

Vittas, D. (1992) 'Thrift Regulation in the United Kingdom and the United States, A Historical Perspective' (Washington: World Bank) (September).

Vives, X. (1991) 'Banking competition and European integration', in: A. Giovannini and C. Mayer (eds), *European financial integration* (Cambridge University Press, Cambridge, UK).

Volcker, P.A. (1978) 'The role of monetary targets in an age of inflation', *Journal of Monetary Economics*, 4: 349–39.

von Hagen, J. (1988) 'Alternative operating regimes for money stock control in West Germany: an empirical evaluation', *Weltwirtschaftsliches Archiv.* 124(1): 89–107.

von Hagen, J. (1992) 'Fiscal Arrangements in a Monetary Union – Evidence from the US' in *Fiscal Policy, Taxes and the Financial System in an Increasingly Integrated Europe*, D. Fair and C. de Boissieux (eds.) (Deventer: Kluwer).

von Hagen, J. (1993) 'Monetary union and fiscal union: a perspective from fiscal federalism', Chapter 10 in *Policy issues in the operation of currency unions*, P. Masson and M.P. Taylor (eds) (Cambridge University Press).

Waigel, T. (1992) 'Kein "Esperanto Geld" – EZB sollte nach Deutschland', *Handelsblatt* (24 March).

Wallace, N. (1983) 'A Legal Restrictions Theory of the Demand for "Money" and the Role of Monetary Policy', *Federal Reserve Bank of Minneapolis Quarterly Review* (Winter): 1–7.

Wallace, N. (1988) 'A suggestion for oversimplifying the theory of money'. *The Economic Journal* 98, Conference Supplement, 25–36.

Wallich, H.C. (1984a) 'Recent techniques of monetary policy', *Federal Reserve Bank of Kansas City Economic Review*, (May): 21–30.

Wallich, H.C. (1984b) 'A broad view of deregulation', Remarks at the Conference on Pacific Basin Financial Reform organised by the Federal Reserve Bank of San Francisco, (2 Dec.) (mimeo).

Walsh, B. (1993) 'The Irish Pound and the ERM: Lessons from the September Crisis and its Aftermath', paper prepared for the Academic Working Group of the Association for the Monetary Union of Europe, London (April/May).

Walsh, C. (1992) 'Fiscal Federalism: An Overview of Issues and a Discussion of their Relevance to the European Community', paper presented at Conference on 'Public Finance and the Future of Europe', LSE (21 September) (mimeo).

Walsh, C.E. (1982) 'The Federal Reserve's operating procedures and interest rate fluctuations', *Federal Reserve Bank of Kansas City Economic Review*, 8–18.

Walsh, C.E. (1984) 'Interest rate volatility and monetary policy', *Journal of Money, Credit and Banking*, 16(2): 133–50.

Walters, A. (1986) *Britain's Economic Renaissance* (New York: Oxford University Press).

Walters, A. and Hanke, S. (1992) 'Currency Boards' in J. Eatwell, M. Milgate, P. Newman (eds.), *The New Palgrave Dictionary of Money and Finance* (London and Basingstoke, The Macmillan Press Ltd): 558–61.

Wang, R.W. (1980) 'The FOMC in 1979: introducing reserve targetting', *Federal Reserve Bank of St. Louis Review*, 62(3): 2–25.

Weitzman, M.L. and Xu, C. (1993) 'Chinese Township Village Enterprises as Vaguely Defined Cooperatives', Unpublished, Revised draft (April).

Wenninger, J. (1986) 'Responsiveness of interest rate spreads and deposit flows to changes in market rates', *Federal Reserve Bank of New York Quarterly Review* (Autumn): 1–10.

Wenninger, J. (1988) 'Money demand: some long-run properties', *Federal Reserve Bank of New York Quarterly Review* (Spring): 23–40.

Wenninger, J. and Radecki, L.J. (1986) 'Financial transactions and the demand for M1. '*Federal Reserve Bank of New York Quarterly Review* (Summer): 24–9.

Werner, P. *et al.*(1970) *Report to the Council and the Commission on the realisation by stages of Economic and Monetary Union in the Community* – Werner Report – (Supplement to Bulletin II – 1970 of the European Communities, Brussels).

White, L.H. (1984a) 'Competitive payments system and the unit of account', *The American Economic Review* 74(4): 699–712.

White, L.H. (1984b) *Free Banking in Britain, Theory, Experience and Debate, 1800–1845* (Cambridge University Press).

White, L.H. (1987) 'Accounting for non-interest-bearing currency: A critique of the legal restrictions theory of money', *Journal of Money, Credit and Banking* 19(4): 448–456.

White, L.H. (1989) 'What kinds of monetary institutions would a free market deliver?', *Cato Journal*, 9(2): 367–391.

White, W.R. (1976) 'The demand for money in Canada and the control of monetary aggregates', Bank of Canada, mimeo.

Williamson, J. (1992a) *The Economic Consequences of Soviet Disintegration* (Washington: Institute for International Economics).

Williamson, J. (1992b) 'Trade and Payments after Soviet Disintegration', Institute for International Economics, *Policy Analyses in International Economics* (37) (June).

Williamson, J. (1983) *The Exchange Rate System* (Washington: Institute for International Economics) (revised).

Williamson, S.D. (1987) 'Financial intermediation, business failures, and real business cycles. *Journal of Political Economy*, 95(6): 1196–216.

Willms, M. (1983) 'The monetary decision process in the Federal Republic of Germany', in *The Political Economy of Monetary Policy: National and International Aspects*. (ed. D.R. Hodgman). Federal Reserve Bank of Boston, 34–48, also the 'Discussion' by H.-J. Dudler, 59–64.

Wojnilower, A.M. (1980) 'The central role of credit crunches in recent financial history', *Brookings Papers on Economic Activity* (2): 277–339.

Wolf, H.C. (1992) 'Economic Disintegration: Are there Cures? Chapter 4 in *Finance and the International Economy*: 6 of the Amex Bank Review Awards, ed. R. O'Brien (Oxford University Press).

Woodford, M. (1988) 'Expectations, finance and aggregate instability', Chapter 12. In *Finance Constraints, Expectations, and Macroeconomics*. (ed. M. Kohn and S-C Tsiang) Oxford: Clarendon Press, 230–61.

Wood, G.E. (1990) 'One money for Europe?', *Journal of Monetary Economics*, 25(2) (March): 313–322.

Wooley, J. (1984) *Monetary Politics: The Federal Reserve and the Politics of Monetary Policy* (New York: Cambridge University Press).

Woolf, E. (1993) 'A return to rational concepts', *Accountancy* (April): 119–20.

Yam, J. (1991) 'The development of monetary policy in Hong Kong', Chapter 3 in Y.C. Jao (ed.) *Monetary management in Hong Kong: The changing role of the exchange fund* (Chartered Institute of Bankers, Hong Kong Centre).

Yeager, L.B. (1983) 'Stable money and free-market currencies', *Cato Journal*, 3, Spring, 305–326.

Yoshino, N. (1993) 'Changing Behavior of Private Banks and Corporations in Japan,' paper presented at Bank of Japan Conference on 'Financial Fragility', (28/29 October).

Yusuf, S. (1993) 'China's Collective and Private Enterprises: Growth and its Financing', Paper presented at IMF and World Bank Conference on 'Building Sound Finance in Emerging Market Economies', Washington (June).

Name Index

All personal names are included. Corporate names are included where they are the originators of documents.

Subject Index